Revolutionizing Innovation

Revolutionizing Innovation

Users, Communities, and Open Innovation

Dietmar Harhoff and Karim R. Lakhani, editors

The MIT Press
Cambridge, Massachusetts
London, England

MIT Press books may be purchased at special quantity discounts for business or sales promotional use. For information, please email special_sales@mitpress.mit.edu

This book was set in Sabon LT Std by Toppan Best-set Premedia Limited. Printed and bound in the United States of America.

Library of Congress Cataloging-in-Publication Data

Revolutionizing innovation : users, communities, and open innovation / edited by Dietmar Harhoff and Karim R. Lakhani.
    pages   cm
  Includes bibliographical references and index.
  ISBN 978-0-262-02977-3 (hard cover : alk. paper)   1. Technological innovations–Economic aspects.   2. Diffusion of innovations   3. Research, Industrial.   4. New products.   5. Technology–Social aspects.   I. Harhoff, Dietmar, editor.   II. Lakhani, Karim R., editor.
  HC79.T4R496 2016
  338'.064—dc23
                                                                          2015030653

10 9 8 7 6 5 4 3

Dedicated to Eric von Hippel
Scholar, Professor, Colleague, Mentor, Doktorvater, and Friend

Contents

Preface

This book came about as a "Festschrift"—a celebration of an academic colleague's achievements—for Massachusetts Institute of Technology Professor Eric Arthur von Hippel on the occasion of his 70th birthday. Over the past fifteen years, von Hippel has collaborated with a global community of scholars to lay the foundations for a new paradigm in innovation research. In this new framework, users, communities, and openness are the dominant forces driving innovation. They complement and/or replace the often closed and proprietary innovation processes traditionally studied by academic scholars.

What initially started as an informal "workshop" of not more than 10 current and former doctoral students and co-authors of Eric von Hippel sitting around a conference table at the MIT Sloan School of Management discussing new emerging trends in user innovation is now a global society of scholars more than 200 strong. These researchers are actively developing theory and marshaling evidence on the salience of user and community-based approaches to innovation for firms, economies and societies.

Contributors to this volume include many close colleagues of Eric von Hippel. All of them contributed new and original chapters to what we hope is a standard reference for scholarship on the salient aspects of user and community innovation. Authors included in this volume are among the major research contributors who are advancing theory, empirical studies, policy, and practice in this new innovation paradigm. The work represented here takes a uniquely multi-disciplinary view with contributions from economics, history of science and technology, government statistics, law, management, and policy.

We would like to thank all the past participants and organizers of the annual OUI conference—The International Open and User Innovation Workshop—for enriching our understanding of this new paradigm. We are indebted to the contributors to this volume for supporting a project that took far longer to complete than initially planned. We are very grateful to Myriam Rion (Max Planck Institute for Innovation and Competition, Munich) and Whitney Jacks (Harvard Business School) for superbly helping to coordinate the construction of this volume. John Covell, our editor at MIT Press, consistently and unwearyingly nursed the formation of this book. Two anonymous reviewers of the volume provided very helpful advice and feedback that improved the final draft. Finally we would like to thank our families for all their love and patience while we juggled multiple projects, priorities, and papers in the midst of editing and completing this book.

Munich and Boston, August 2015
Dietmar Harhoff and Karim R. Lakhani, editors

Contributors

Efe Aksuyek
ETH Zurich

Yochai Benkler
Harvard Law School

Stefan Perkmann Berger
Vienna University of Economics and Business

James Bessen
Boston University School of Law

Jörn H. Block
Universität Trier

Helena Canhão
Lisbon Medical School, University of Lisbon

Jeroen P.J. de Jong
Utrecht School of Economics

Emmanuelle Fauchart
Université de Strasbourg

Dominique Foray
Ecole Polytechnique Fédérale de Lausanne

Nikolaus Franke
Vienna University of Economics and Business

Johann Füller
Universität Innsbruck

Helena Garriga
ETH Zurich

Fred Gault
Tshwane University of Technology, Pretoria

Fredrik Hacklin
ETH Zurich

Dietmar Harhoff
Max Planck Institute for Innovation and Competition, Munich

Joachim Henkel
Technische Universität München

Cornelius Herstatt
Technische Universität Hamburg-Harburg

Christoph Hienerth
WHU—Otto Beisheim School of Management, Koblenz

Venkat Kuppuswamy
Kenan-Flagler Business School, University of North Carolina

Karim R. Lakhani
Harvard Business School

Christopher Lettl
Vienna University of Economics and Business

Christian Lüthje
Technische Universität Hamburg-Harburg

Ethan Mollick
Wharton School, University of Pennsylvania

Hidehiko Nishikawa
Hosei University, Tokyo

Alessandro Nuvolari
Sant'Anna School of Advanced Studies, Pisa

Susumu Ogawa
Kobe University

Pedro Oliveira
Católica-Lisbon School of Business and Economics

Frank Piller
RWTH Aachen University

Christina Raasch
Technische Universität München

Susanne Roiser
University of Applied Sciences Wiener Neustadt, Vienna

Fabrizio Salvador
IE Business School, Madrid

Pamela Samuelson
University of California, Berkeley, School of Law

Tim Schweisfurth
Technische Universität München

Sonali K. Shah
University of Illinois at Urbana-Champaign

Annika Stiegler
Technische Universität München

Christoph Stockstrom
Technische Universität Hamburg-Harburg

Katherine J. Strandburg
New York University School of Law

Stefan Thomke
Harvard Business School

Andrew W. Torrance
University of Kansas School of Law

Mary Tripsas
Carroll School of Management, Boston College

Georg von Krogh
ETH Zurich

1

Revolutionizing Innovation: Fundamentals and New Perspectives

Dietmar Harhoff and Karim R. Lakhani

In the early 20th century Joseph A. Schumpeter proposed a theory of innovation over several works that put at its core the profit-seeking incentives of either large manufacturing firms with market power or start-up entrepreneurial firms as the drivers of technical change. This view of the incentives of the formal economic organization to innovate has become the dominant scientific paradigm for economists, management scholars, business people, and policy makers. It forms the core intellectual foundation of innovation and entrepreneurial studies as taught in many business schools and economics departments today, strongly influences normative perspectives held by graduates and practitioners, and shapes the scholarly research agenda.

Beginning in the late 1970s and continuing to this day, Eric von Hippel and his colleagues—many of them contributors to this volume—developed a very different view of innovation, arguing that *users* are as important as or more important than producers as sources of innovation in modern societies. Initially von Hippel was a lone voice, but over time, many have been persuaded by his arguments and those of colleagues and co-authors.

Von Hippel's academic work on user innovation began with a 1976 *Research Policy* article titled "The Dominant Role of Users in the Scientific Instrument Innovation Process." In this empirical article he provided the first quantitative evidence flatly contradicting the prevailing Schumpeterian view that innovations are developed by firms (entrepreneurial or incumbents). His initial study documented the sources of over 100 of the most scientifically and commercially important innovations in four types of scientific instruments over several decades. His central finding was that 77 percent had been fully developed by scientists who had a direct use-need for the particular functionality rather than by scientific instrument companies who had somehow figured out the market need and then innovated. This startling finding initially stirred next to no interest among academics or practitioners. It was viewed as an oddity—a case of "scientists being scientists." However, von Hippel regarded it as initial evidence for a phenomenon that would likely prove to be very widespread and both economically and socially very important.

Over succeeding years, von Hippel and an increasing cadre of international colleagues devoted their energies to further empirical explorations of the sources and drivers of innovation in additional fields, as well as to the development of theory to explore and explain more deeply the economic underpinnings of innovation by users. Today major structural components of a new user innovation paradigm have been clarified and made explicit by this collective effort that combines theory development and a large and rapidly growing body of empirical evidence from a range of contexts. The result is a rich and inviting platform for research policy and practice that an increasing number and range of academics, policy makers, and practitioners are beginning to exploit and further develop.

Important theoretical understandings and related research topics in this new field of user innovation include the following: Understanding that *sticky information* can strongly affect the locus of innovation; understanding of how user innovators profit from developing their innovations and why they are often willing to reveal their designs to both peer users and firms without charge; modeling of the conditions under which innovation development is economically viable for users, and an appreciation that the range of innovation opportunities viable for users is increasing over time; modeling of the conditions under which user innovations become commercial products; understanding of the role that "lead users" play and of the pathways user innovations traverse to commercialization; and, finally, modeling of strategies that producers can take as they increasingly face both perils and opportunities from freely available user innovations that complement and/or compete with their own commercial offerings.

Important empirical topics centrally associated with the new user innovation paradigm include measurement of the scale and scope of user innovation activities, both within general populations and within specific communities of practice. If something has not been measured, in practical terms it does not exist—and the long-time exclusive focus on measurement of producer innovation in effect rendered user innovation invisible. The community of user innovation scholars is now rectifying this lacuna by major surveys of nationally representative samples of citizens in multiple countries and via surveys of firms engaged in user innovation. Additionally the definition of innovation in the Oslo Manual—used to coordinate the collection of innovation-related data across governmental entities—is being changed to include user and non-user developments diffused for free via peer-to-peer channels rather than by markets.

An increasingly important complement to the user innovation perspective has been the rise of community models for innovation that harness the efforts of thousands of innovators in collectively producing goods and in essence democratizing the innovation process. The first clear exemplar of this approach has been the rise of the free/open source software movement. Not many scholars or practitioners anticipated that fully functional user communities could self-organize and create software products that could replace and often compete against commercial offerings. Even more surprising has been the response from private organizations in embracing free/open source practices and their subsequent investment of private effort in the creation of a public good. The community-innovation perspective has become mainstream and is now implemented in all sorts of organizations in the public, nonprofit and private sectors. Related is the extraordinary rise of crowdsourcing firms that are creating two-sided platforms by aggregating thousands of globally distributed problem solvers to partake in solving problems for industry, academe, government, and nonprofits.

Innovation policy topics drawn forward by the new user innovation paradigm centrally include a reassessment of the role of intellectual property in a world where both user and producer innovation exists. User innovation, for reasons now being understood and mapped, can often—perhaps always—flourish without government intellectual property rights monopolies. This discovery casts into question societies' need for allocating temporary monopoly rights to producers, which lies at the heart of many economic models of innovation. A second major new topic is the need for novel policies to reduce or eliminate market failure associated with diffusion in the user innovation paradigm. Users, who do not share in the benefits that others gain from adopting their innovations, will regard those benefits as an externality, and so underinvest in diffusion from the viewpoint of overall social welfare.

Finally, with respect to practice, novel methods have been and are being developed to accommodate the role of users in innovation. Major examples are toolkits for user innovation that enable users to innovate more effectively, lead user search methods that enable producers to more effectively discover user innovations of potential market value, and finally crowdfunding platforms that allow users to directly access funding to further develop and scale their innovations.

This volume is organized in the following six parts consisting of 25 new and original contributions from cutting-edge scholars from around the world:

I   Fundamentals of User Innovation
II   The Community Perspective
III Legal Aspects of User and Community Innovation
IV   User Innovators in New Roles
V   User Interactions with Firms
VI   From Theory to Practice: Experiments, Toolkits, and Crowdfunding
     for Innovation

The work showcased here covers diverse fields like economics, history of science and technology, government statistics, law, management, and policy. The empirical contexts range from developing international and national statistics to industrial and consumer products, to software and algorithms, and to financial services. Below we briefly describe each of the chapters in the volume and highlight the key contributions they make to scholarship.

I Fundamentals of User Innovation

2 Context, Capabilities and Incentives—The Core and the Periphery of User Innovation

In chapter 2, Dietmar Harhoff describes the early development of the user innovation paradigm and points to the "core" elements of the perspective developed by Eric von Hippel and other scholars. He argues that the *core* theory proposed a simple, yet elegant solution to the fundamental *sticky information* problem. Users in sticky information environments would not transfer need information, but complete prototypes to manufacturers who would then imitate and refine the solutions created by users. He proposes to go beyond this core view and consider other user contributions to innovation as well. He refers to these as the *periphery* of user innovation and claims that the economic impact of periphery contributions could be quite large. For example, if firms find ways to draw external users and customers into the innovation process, then the measurement of contributions made to the economy by innovative users would have to be reframed. He suggests that users may very well contribute their technical solution concepts (but not full prototypes) to manufacturers, thus escaping the sticky information problem and saving the cost of having to come up with an invention and a prototype independently. He employs large-scale data from a recent inventor survey which was undertaken in Europe, Japan, and the United States. The data have the advantage of distinguishing explicitly between users and customers as an external source of knowledge relevant for a particular invention process and patent.

As Harhoff shows, users (and customers) are the most important sources of knowledge for inventors across all major technologies. Moreover the inventors indicate in the survey which types of collaboration (either formal or informal) they have undertaken—again, across major technologies, users and customers are particularly prominent as collaborators of the inventors. Results from a descriptive multivariate analysis suggest that high importance of user-origin information and collaboration between inventors and users are associated with above-average patent value and with particularly high rates of commercialization. These results are intriguing as they come from data covering inventions made in more than 20 countries and in a broad set of technologies. They suggest that the measurement of economic effects due to innovative users may have to apply a broader approach than has been used so far.

Harhoff's contribution is to show that the knowledge users possess is extremely relevant for a broad range of commercial inventive activity and necessitates an updating of our managerial guidelines on how to incorporate users into the innovation process. In addition, this chapter highlights the need for policy makers to update their innovation measurement tools and related policies for encouraging innovation.

3   Cost Advantages in Innovation—A Comparison of Users and Manufacturers

A substantial body of research has now persuasively established that users innovate for a range of private, intrinsic and pro-social motives. In chapter 3, Christian Lüthje and Christoph Stockstrom address the cost advantages that users may have in the innovation process that enable them to exceed manufacturer capabilities. Indeed they provocatively argue that users may be more efficient in deriving innovations than manufacturers. They use detailed case studies of users innovating in the medical market, namely physicians, to justify their assertions and framework.

The Lüthje and Stockstrom perspective on the efficiency of user innovation is based on three distinct advantages that users have in the course of developing their solutions: (1) opportunity and need identification, (2) first solution development, and (3) testing and refining initial solutions. The first advantage is driven by the fact that users are serving a market of one, namely themselves. They do not need to invest in learning about the issues and problems faced by anyone else; rather, as the literature has shown, they use their own local needs and solution knowledge to understand both the problem and the required solution. Comparatively, firms need to invest significant resources to identify idiosyncratic customer needs and then conduct the assessment that the (identified) needs are generalizable and serve a potentially large market. Second, users with deep problem domain knowledge will be more able to derive solutions from other domains that contain applicable knowledge components while firms will be hamstrung by matching problem knowledge with the specific solution base they have developed within the organization. Finding and implementing "out-of-the-box" solutions will be a lot easier for users instead of firms. Finally, users will have more freedom and ability to test their solutions and iterate on an improved product as compared to manufacturers because they have direct and unhindered access to the use environment. This chapter hence contributes to our understanding of the sources of economic efficiency in the innovation process when considering the role of users and manufacturers.

4   The Empirical Scope of User Innovation

A critique of the user innovation literature is that the empirical foundations are based on case studies that may be selecting product classes or users that have propensity to innovate. Hence the findings of the literature may not be broadly applicable in the economy and society. In chapter 4, Jeroen P. J. de Jong assembles and reviews emerging research that shows the broad scale of innovation by both individual citizens and user-firms, their practices to protect intellectual property, and their ability to diffuse their innovations.

Utilizing data from large-scale innovation surveys at the industry and national level, de Jong reports that 15 to 20 percent of all firms are user innovators, while in samples of consumers this range is 4 to 6 percent. He finds that in consumer populations very few innovators apply for intellectual property protection—instead they share their work for free. In businesses the application of formal intellectual property rights is more substantial, but still rarely exceeds 50 percent. Finally, de Jong investigates to what extent and how user innovations diffuse to other economic actors. Part of their innovations appears to be useful to others; that is, depending on the sample, 5 to 25 percent is adopted by other users or by commercial producers for further development and commercial sale. This chapter thus provides a substantial empirical foundation for researchers and practitioners to understand the vast scale and scope of user innovation activity and the practices used by both individual users and firm-users to protect their innovations and to encourage diffusion.

5   User Innovation and Official Statistics

The discovery of the widespread presence of user innovation activity by both individual consumers and firms and its salience to a range of innovation outcomes and entrepreneurial ventures (see chapter 14) has resulted in various national statistics offices formally incorporating specific questions and measures on user innovation in national surveys and industrial census efforts. Fred Gault, in chapter 5, traces the history of the efforts to both incorporate general innovation measures and more specifically user innovation metrics in official national statistics.

Gault outlines the important impact of von Hippel's two books in spurring official statistics organizations in United States, Canada, and Europe to adopt user innovation measures to augment the typical manufacturer-centric perspectives taken in surveys of firms. For example, national survey work in Canada has shown that 40 percent of manufacturing firms engage in user innovation activities in substantial ways: split between 20 percent purchasing technologies with the explicit intention to modify and adapt for their own idiosyncratic purposes and the other 20 percent investing in resources to develop *de novo* technologies to implement in their own production operations. He further presents the various ways in which European, Asian and African surveys indicate the generality of user innovation among firms and heterogeneity in diffusion outcomes. The contribution of this chapter is to show how user innovation concepts are now firmly anchored in national statistical agencies and that the provision of representative population-based samples can inform innovation policy at the national and transnational levels.

II The Community Perspective

6 Managing Communities and Contests to Innovate with Crowds

An emerging theme and perspective in innovation scholarship is that secular trends in declining communication costs, modular technologies and digitization are all enabling the democratization of the innovation process. This means that more external actors, outside the traditional firm, innovate and can do so with distant others through information technologies. The emergence of communities for user-based innovation has been documented quite extensively over the last decade. During the same time period external actors have also been harnessed to participate through online contests. In chapter 6, Karim R. Lakhani provides a historical and current perspective on the use of communities and contests to organize external innovation.

Lakhani first discusses the types of innovation problems that are well-suited to each of the institutions and then posits the important role of individual self-selection into these institutions as the basis for differentiation from the traditional firm focused approach to innovation. Self-selection yields a match between the task and the worker's innate knowledge, skills and abilities and also solves the worker incentive problem as individuals are self-motivated to exert effort instead of relying on managerial fiat or employment contracts to guarantee work. He then shows the comparative advantages of communities versus contests by highlighting the incentives versus knowledge reuse trade-off faced in most innovation settings and the differences in the search process engendered by varying disclosure policies. Lakhani concludes by discussing the emergence of hybrid organizations that are able to straddle both the closed and democratized institutions of driving innovation and gives example of large firms that are able to do both.

7 Knowledge Sharing among Inventors: Some Historical Perspectives

A central tenant within the research on user and open innovation has been that participants freely reveal their knowledge to other actors and often collectively share in creating important inventions. While modern examples of user and open source software communities vividly illustrate voluntary knowledge disclosures and the underlying incentive mechanisms that enable them, there are many historical precedents for such behaviors. In chapter 7, James Bessen and Alessandro Nuvolari provide extensive historical examples of the salience of both cooperating and competing innovators engaging in knowledge disclosures yielding significant performance gains.

Contrary to the expectations of most economic historians and scholars of technical change, Bessen and Nuvolari show that knowledge sharing among innovators in the past was not extremely rare and that key technologies at the heart of European and American industrialization, such as high-pressure steam engines, iron and steel production techniques, steamboats, textile machinery, airplanes, etc., were at times, and in certain places, developed through processes of collective invention. They further argue that patents were not universally important to innovation and in some cases may have hindered the advancement of the technical frontier, as in the case of aviation. Hence the core principles underlying a community-based innovation system have historical roots, suggesting that the relationship between institutions governing innovation and incentives is rich and subtle, and, depending on the context, does not appear to conform to expectations about the role of intellectual property in driving innovation.

8 Private-Collective Innovation: The Effects of the Number of Participants and Social Factors

A long standing literature in economics and organizational research has tried to theorize the drivers of cooperation in a range of institutional settings. In the case of open and user innovation, the joint work of von

Hippel and von Krogh established the circumstances under which private actors exert effort in the creation and sustenance of public goods. The basic model presented by them argues that own-use, learning and peer recognition benefits are typically only available to those that contribute, and that these factors outweigh any potential benefit from free-riding. In chapter 8, Georg von Krogh, Helena Garriga, Efe Aksuyek, and Fredrik Hacklin further extend this perspective by considering how the number of participants and social factors may be important to set the stage during the initiation phases of communities.

The authors use Gächter and colleagues' experimental work on knowledge sharing or concealing in two-person games and current advances in behavioral economics to create a simulation study to understand their application to a community setting. The authors find that an individual's decision to share or conceal knowledge depends on not only personal social preferences but also the number of innovators in the group and the expected decisions that prompt participation. They also find that participation can be characterized to some extent and triggered by the number of participants. Individuals participating in open and user communities not only weigh the expected gains or losses that will result from their participation but also predict how the members of the social ecosystem will interact to produce individual utility functions. The contribution of this work is to consider the dynamics of the community as a whole and the importance of conditional cooperation within emerging open innovation communities.

9   On the Democratization of Innovation through Communal Organizations

What are the factors that may predict if user and open innovation communities will constitute a long-term and persistent locus of innovation? In chapter 9, Emmanuelle Fauchart and Dominique Foray create an economic framework to understand how communities, as vertical integrations of users into the production of goods and services, can be sustainable economic organizations and competitors to firms.

The authors reflect on the fact that past experiments in other forms of member-driven cooperative organizations have not been able to achieve long-term viability and that open and user innovation communities may be particularly susceptible to the potential inefficiencies in community organizations and to market failures (that the initially created impetus for forming a community may eventually vanish). In the chapter, the authors derive three propositions that may adjudicate long-term survival of innovation communities. In particular, communities seem to emerge and persist in markets where there are very low capital investment requirements, there are relatively low opportunity costs of member-contributors, goods produced are primarily information-centric, participation occurs virtually, and task coordination occurs via modularity.

10 When von Hippel Innovation Met the Networked Environment: Recognizing Decentralized Innovation

In chapter 10, Yochai Benkler explicates the factors that have led the 21st century to be increasingly dominated by decentralized forms of innovation and the institutional changes needed to assure their continued success. Benkler posits that the explosion in various models for user innovation in this century can be primarily explained by two main facts. First, between Eric von Hippel's initial insights on the salience of the user innovator in 1976 (the publication of his first article) and present day (2014) a major shift is that many production goods we care about can in fact be 'finished' and 'distributed' using widespread capital equipment already placed in service, and thus the barriers to moving a user innovation from the user's 'garage' to the world at large are lower. Second, the drastic reduction in communication and search costs now means that the ability of users to cooperate with each other about what they are doing, and share the results of their experiments, has increased dramatically, resulting in user communities developing their knowledge incrementally and collaboratively with relatively low cost as compared to a firm-based actor.

Benkler then argues that supporting this type of widespread experimentation and innovation requires a very different institutional infrastructure than the one currently in place in many societies. He argues that this new world of decentralized innovation needs research exemptions, low cost recombinatorial access, and freedom to operate instead of strong patents or expansive copyright laws, and a focus on corporate appropriation. Benkler's contribution is to provide a framework for future scholars and practitioners to understand the significant changes in society needed to fulfill the promise of decentralized innovation.

III Legal Aspects of User and Community Innovation

11 Freedom to Tinker

The basic first step in user and open innovation typically starts off with an individual tinkering with an available technology and/or product for their own use needs or to satisfy their intellectual curiosity. In chapter 11, Pamela Samuelson addresses how in the United States, patent, trade secret and trademark laws provide considerable freedom to tinker while copyright law may hinder tinkering, adversely impacting software innovation by users.

Samuelson's analysis of United States law shows that the *first-sale* rule for most products means that owners, namely users, are within their full rights to modify as they will, once they legally acquire the asset that is being modified. Similar strictures in trade secret law allow for the owner to reverse engineer technologies and to modify them for their own use. Trademark law also does not prevent a user from acquiring trademarked goods and services or from modifying them and reselling them as their own under a different trademark. Samuelson then devotes the remainder of the chapter to the various ways in which copyright works and how the legal code governing subsequent use and modification creates significant encumbrances for user and open innovators. She also offers various suggestions that can be implemented by courts to enable software innovators to continue to improve and push the technical frontier without getting into legal entanglements.

12 Intellectual Property at the Boundary

In chapter 12, Katherine J. Strandburg examines the legal and intellectual property consequences of user innovation communities becoming more prevalent. In particular, Strandburg argues that an implicit assumption in most patent doctrine is that inventors are *atomistic*, that is, a single individual or entity (a firm or university) retains the monopoly rights conferred by the patent, and that innovation occurring in communities poses significant challenges to current perspectives on the impact of patents on innovation.

Strandburg shows that an innovation community's decision to forgo formal intellectual property regimes calls into question three key assumptions that dominate current legal scholarship: (1) creative work requires large up-front investments, (2) free-riding will prevent a sufficient return on those investments, and (3) legally defined property rights are the only or best way to allocate returns on investments in creative work. Strandburg then creates a framework for how communities need to negotiate when they interact with parties outside of the community with the caveat that the typical tools of boundary negotiation between individuals and firms may not be available due to the lack of workable means of conducting transactions and/or very high costs to the community. The chapter closes with a call for certain areas of research to accommodate the very specific requirements of communities interacting with other stakeholders.

13   Will Innovation Thrive without Patents? A Natural Experiment in Biotechnology

Do innovators require patent protections as a major incentive to innovate? It is taken for granted within the economic and legal literatures that patents and the subsequent monopoly rights they confer are important instruments for motivating innovators. In chapter 13, Andrew W. Torrance examines the potential incentive and legal impact of the recent passage of the America Invents Act in 2011 and a specific provision that bans patenting human organisms.

The chapter provides a broad overview of the U.S. patent system and the significant change made to patent law by the America Invents Act. It then shows how the US courts have been very reluctant toward patenting any material related to human beings. The specific exceptions to human organism patenting are then discussed with the perspective that this new law creates a rare opportunity to observe a natural experiment in which innovation may operate unconstrained by patents, and that the results of this experiment may provide a model for future reform of the patent system to the benefit of innovation, especially open and user innovation.

IV   User Innovators in New Roles

14   When Do User Innovators Start Firms? A Theory of User Entrepreneurship

The extant literature on user-based innovation has convincingly shown that users have both access to sticky local knowledge and motivation that helps them develop functionally novel innovations. In chapter 14, Sonali

K. Shah and Mary Tripsas expand the scope of the impact of user innovation in the economy by considering the role of these innovators in creating new economic enterprises. In particular, the important contribution of this chapter is the authors' development of a theoretical framework that predicts the circumstances under which a user innovator may enter a product market as compared to manufacturers. Ongoing empirical work by Shah and colleagues and others has demonstrated that a significant portion of entrepreneurial start-ups have roots in user innovation with some industries reporting between 29 percent (medical devices) to 87 percent (juvenile products) of new firms having users as founders. Significantly, 46 percent of all innovative US start-ups that survive beyond the crucial first five years have users as founders.

The Shah and Tripsas model of user entrepreneurship is based on the differences between users' and manufacturers' assessment of the potential financial returns to entering the product market and their profit thresholds. Informational asymmetries are at the core of the user innovation model and they also apply to user entrepreneurship. Simply put, users have access to more information earlier and this enables them to identify opportunities ahead of incumbent manufacturers. In addition entrepreneurial start-ups typically have lower profit thresholds than incumbents, allowing them to enter into markets well ahead of the resolution of uncertainty about the profit potential in a new segment. Shah and Tripsas extend their analysis by explicating the circumstances under which a particular product concept may be more or less amenable to user entrepreneurship. These circumstances include open product design (sharing of design information in the user community), modularity (task partitioning and focus on only the salient tasks for innovation), industry life cycle (earlier is more favorable for users), and the regulatory burden (harder for users to meet intensive regulatory hurdles).

15   Users as Service Innovators: Evidence across Healthcare and Financial Services

In chapter 15, Pedro Oliveira and Helena Canhão provide evidence of the critical role played by users in the development of services. They show that despite services representing more than 80 percent of US employment and 76 percent of gross value added, the study of the user origins of service innovation remains relatively understudied and underinvestigated. Partially this is due to the fact that services are intangible and often involve simultaneous production and consumption. However, as has been shown previously, a careful tracing of the sources of innovation—in this case financial services and health care delivery—indicates the importance of users in generating the key underlying service innovations.

The basic mechanism underlying user-based service innovation development is the same as in the traditional view of user innovation in products, namely users experience (service) needs ahead of producers and some of them have the ability and incentives to create a corresponding set of service-based innovations to satisfy those needs. Oliveira and Canhão provide extensive documentation of these effects in two sectors (financial services and health care) that have extensive producer participation (banks and hospitals). The banking data show that key innovations in the past and in modern times have been led by users. Similarly, in a variety of chronic disease settings, patients develop the majority of therapies and devices that help bring relief to themselves. The chapter provides the fundamental empirical evidence to show the existence of a set of economic activities done by users that have previously been thought to be the exclusive provenance of producers, with significant implications for service developers.

16   Technique Innovation

New product and service innovations often bring with them new ways of accomplishing a particular task. Similarly, attempts to do new tasks or old tasks in new ways can drive the search for better solutions. In both situations the underlying innovation is one of *technique*, a skillful activity that is essential to the use of the new product or service innovation. In chapter 20, Christoph Hienerth provides a comprehensive overview and research framework to analyze technique innovation by using two illustrative mini cases (Impressionist paintings and anesthetic treatments) and a major case of developing techniques in rodeo kayaking.

Borne out of his studies with colleagues in user innovation, Hienerth also noticed that users were spending substantial time and effort improving and innovating on techniques. Indeed one can argue the bulk of user time is spent on learning and improving techniques instead of creating new products and services exclusively. Hienerth further speculates that focusing on technique innovation allows scholars to look at more general trends of industry evolution and design spaces. The emergence of new techniques may signal the start of a new round of competition among firms and the resultant entry and exit of firms. Technique innovation with existing artifacts can be a signal of open design spaces. Once the techniques as well as the artifacts start to change, that can be an indication that new design spaces are emerging and that existing solutions and designs will likely be displaced. Hienerth's major contribution of the technique innovation concept creates lots of opportunities for scholars to closely examine use and technology simultaneously, as well as the potential for interaction among them.

17   The Power of Community Brands—How User-Generated Brands Emerge

Johann Füller, in chapter 17, provides evidence of the role of users in creating brands. Historically, marketing and communication activity by firms has been targeted at users to encourage consumption and to build differentiation through the promotion of various product or company specific branding efforts. The marketing and brand creation effort, both the creative aspects of the messaging and the more mundane parts of promotion, were handled by firm employees. However, the rise of community-based products and services has subsequently given users the opportunity to engage in marketing efforts and to be responsible for generating brand ideas and messaging.

Füller uses the case examples of community brands like *Apache* web server software and the online community of outdoor enthusiasts *Outdoorseiten.net* to explicate the role of users in brand creation. He shows that community brand creation occurs as a means for the group to self-identify and enhance pro-social motives. Community brands are, however, used to serve the same function as firm-based brands, namely to signal quality and attract new customers and reinforce the message of belonging for existing customers. He also shows that through the distribution of the branding activities among their members, communities are able to build strong brands at practically no cost. Like user innovations, community brands may become a real alternative to the company-generated brands paradigm.

V   User Interactions with Firms

18   Selling to Competitors? Competitive Implications of User–Manufacturer Integration

Joachim Henkel, Annika Bock, and Jörn H. Block, in chapter 18, examine the strategic challenges faced by incumbent firms as they realize that the user innovations they have developed may be sufficiently important to justify expanding into a new line of business that serves other (potentially competing) users. Given the broad prevalence of user innovation in the economy and in contrast to the exploration of user entrepreneurship (chapter 14), where end-users establish new firms to commercialize their innovations, Henkel et al. contribute to the literature by focusing attention on the opportunities and dilemmas faced by executives of firms that happen to have created innovations that initially served their own internal needs. The basic motivation for their analysis is quite straightforward: Employees inside of firms find that their suppliers cannot satisfy their advanced needs and thus invest in user innovation efforts. These user innovations solve their own internal problems and enable the firm to achieve gains in delivering their products or services. The firms then face a basic choice—should these innovations be made available to other users who are also competitors? This basic research question is of direct relevance to both practitioners and academics studying user innovation.

The authors first provide qualitative evidence and intuition of this strategic dilemma by detailing how two firms in very different industries (loose tea packaging and infrastructure construction) handled the situation. In the case of the tea company, the firm decided to make the technology available to only nondirect competitors, while the construction company decided to sell the new user innovations to all users, including competitors. The authors then create a game-theoretic model to examine the strategic choices faced by such user-innovator firms. The model and subsequent analysis provide guidance on the choices faced by executives with a counterintuitive consideration that firms may be better off enabling their (even most direct) competitors with the user innovation because, in the long run, the knowledge about these innovations will spillover. Then other manufacturers will enter with competing products and thus the focal firm will lose the revenue potential of commercializing the innovation. The authors' chapter provides direct guidance to managers and provides an important marker for future scholars as to the strategic interactions that user innovation may unleash.

19   When Passion Meets Profession: How Embedded Lead Users Contribute to Corporate Innovation

Cornelius Herstatt, Tim Schweisfurth, and Christina Raasch, in chapter 19, examine how lead users who are employees of the firm can be beneficial to a firm's innovation process and outcomes. While the extant literature on user innovation has shown that internal lead users can make significant process-based innovations (Henkel et al.'s previous chapter examines the strategic implication of those innovations becoming separate product lines), the sources of product innovation have shown to be primarily external users. Herstatt, Schweisfurth, and Raasch consider the possibility that firms may be diverse enough to have employees that have the same level of lead user characteristics as external users, and "embedded lead users" (ELUs) may provide distinct informational advantages to the internal innovation process.

The authors conduct a qualitative, inductive study of ELUs in 23 firms in three distinct industries (sports products, leisure products, and healthcare/medical devices) to derive their insights. Their findings suggest that ELUs are present in many firms and they contribute novel ideas and solutions that are substantially different from external lead users and the efforts of internal R&D staff. Their ability to boundary span user communities, end user markets and firms enables informational advantages that help in creating unique insights for new product and service innovations. In addition ELUs exhibit hybrid motivations (pecuniary and nonpecuniary) that boost effort and the informational advantages they have in their unique positions. The identification of ELUs by the authors provides rich ground for further research into quantifying and measuring the importance of these individuals. Their presence and engagement in the innovation process may enable many firms to create products that will include lead user considerations and may indeed indicate that a greater share of innovations can be attributed to users who are simply embedded in the firm.

20   Exploring Why and to What Extent Lead Users Share Knowledge with Producer Firms

Why would external lead users reveal important and strategic knowledge to firms in the first place? This important question is addressed by Christopher Lettl, Stefan Perkmann Berger, and Susanne Roiser in chapter 20. One of the practical consequences of the findings about the importance of lead users in the innovation process has been the systematic incorporation of the concept within the structures of traditional firms through the joint development of the *lead user method* with various leading organizations including 3M, HILTI, Johnson & Johnson, and Nortel. This approach gets the firm's R&D unit to work systematically and collaboratively with lead users in both target and analogous markets to derive breakthrough new product and service concepts that will benefit most directly the sponsoring organization. Lettl, Berger, and Roiser investigate the motivations and process underlying the willingness of these lead users to freely reveal knowledge to firms when the underlying intellectual property that is ultimately generated through those interactions is typically owned by the sponsoring organization and the users may themselves not have any practical and direct use for the products created.

The authors use an inductive and qualitative approach by interviewing 19 participants in lead user workshops in five industrial contexts including consumer goods, food processing, aircraft construction, manufacturing, and telecommunication. They find that lead users have a very sophisticated sense of the trade-offs for their "free" participation in the innovation workshops. In particular, they anticipate primarily personal private benefits for their participation ranging from future income potential as a consultant to reputational burnishing and credibility. They report as additional benefits enjoying the puzzle and problem solving aspects of the work, enjoying the social process of interacting with other users, and having an impact on the firm's direction. Lead users also have an expectation that the product concepts they are involved in developing will ultimately see the light of day in the marketplace. The authors, importantly, also find that lead users in the workshops engage in selective revealing instead of freely revealing and disclosing all their knowledge. This kind of selective revealing is related to the degree of initial openness by the sponsoring organizers and the other participants, and the potential for future private gains from the knowledge and information held by the participants. This chapter is important in that it most directly considers the systematic set of incentives that the literature and practitioners need to consider as lead user research gets further acceptance within the mainstream of innovation management and as firms try to systematically work with users over the entire innovation process.

21   Crowdsourcing at MUJI

A natural next step in integrating user feedback within the innovation process is to enable crowds of users to participate in both idea generation and idea selection tasks for a firm. In chapter 21, Susumu Ogawa and Hidehiko Nishikawa provide a detailed case history of Japan's leading design retailer's, Ryohin Keikaku (commonly referred to as MUJI), lessons from utilizing their users perspectives, ideas and commitment as the only input into the innovation process. Since 2000, MUJI has been running various trials to build their capabilities to effectively harness their crowd of users. The range of products designed by their customers was quite diverse, from the MUJI car (a custom designed Nissan urban vehicle) to light fixtures and sofas. Ogawa and Nishikawa use the MUJI example to illustrate the important lessons available to firm managers when utilizing crowd input and provide illustrative evidence for performance comparisons between crowd-generated designs and internal efforts.

MUJI was crowdsourcing before the term appeared in the common press and vernacular. Executives at the firm had realized that crowds could be used to both generate ideas and select among the vast variety of options generated. The firm initially chose a market-based approach to select among the ideas generated by their customers. Indeed it is one of the earliest forms of *crowdfunding* innovative activity. Those that were interested in the user suggested products had to pre-commit buying intent by providing advance payment for the products. If the pre-orders reached a certain threshold, then the company would commit to producing the product, otherwise the design would simply go into the archive. This selection/funding model yielded very good results and many of the products created and brought to market far exceeded the expectations (by a factor of 10). While MUJI is no longer using crowdfunding to confirm the viability of user generated ideas, it has found that a simple voting heuristic from its users can essentially create very similar demand signals. Ogawa and Nishikawa also report that matched comparisons between user-generated and selected products and internally developed products show that user innovation tends to produce products with higher novelty, originality and increased sales. The case study provides a very illuminating portrayal of a firm that has, in some segments, figured out how to harness the diversity of knowledge in its user base by enabling both generation and selection of ideas.

VI   From Theory to Practice: Experiments, Toolkits, and Crowdfunding for Innovation

22   The Innovators' Tools

Stefan Thomke's contribution in chapter 22 introduces the general concept of tools for innovation and their salience for open and user innovation models. Thomke first provides a grounding in the relative importance of tools for the underlying historical and modern advances in scientific and technological development. He then shows how modern information-intensive tools (simulation, design confirmation, etc.) aide in innovation development by both reducing the cost of experimentation for users and increasing opportunities for iterative problem-solving and learning by highlighting their usage in industries like automotive and pharmaceuticals.

Tools also enable the shift of the locus of innovation and product development from its traditional concentration among manufacturers to users. Thomke shows how toolkits enable the unbundling of need information from solution information during the innovation-related problem solving effort. Traditionally, manufacturers have invested considerable resources to understand user needs and then to provide their specialized capabilities to solve their problems. This process in a range of industries is inefficient with many iterations between users and manufacturers—as each side tries to discover the exact problem at hand and the appropriate solution approach. Toolkits in a range of industries from foods to semiconductors have effectively enabled users with a specialized user-centric design language and capability to "experiment" so that they can fully understand their own needs and requirements in a low-cost manner. Once users have finalized their designs, the toolkit effectively translates that information to the manufacturing site so that it enables cost-effective production. Thomke also discusses that the unbundling of need information and solution information poses distinct business model challenges as traditional firms are not geared toward becoming builders of toolkits and low-cost information enabled production. Thomke closes the chapter by discussing important research questions that remain to be addressed as more and more firms enable their own customers to innovate by offering toolkits that are coupled with two-sided markets and/or general innovation platforms (e.g., Apple App Store and various 3D printing marketplaces).

23 Design Toolkits, Organizational Capabilities, and Firm Performance

In chapter 23, Frank Piller and Fabrizio Salvador extend the notion of user innovation toolkits to consider not just users that have specialized skills and knowledge to develop semiconductors or software but any general user that may be interested in customizing products and services for their own use in tandem with offerings from manufacturers, namely mass customization. Piller and Salvador contribute to our understanding of how innovation is further democratized through mass customization by developing a theoretical model underlying the capabilities needed by manufacturers to enable the manufacturer-customer co-creation process and by empirically verifying their constructs through a database on 120 firms that offer various mass customization toolkits.

Piller and Salvador show that effective mass customization requires firms to invest in three distinct capabilities: (1) *solution space definition* wherein the firm concentrates customization activity by customers on which user needs diverge, (2) *robust process design* that enables firms to easily reuse and recombine existing organizational and supply chain resources, and (3) *choice navigation* to assist customers with reducing the combinatorial explosion of choices when many elements are available for customization simultaneously. Their empirical analysis reveals that managerial practice and firm strategy severely lag behind academic research in understanding how the capabilities may be developed and put into action. In particular, business models for many firms need to change to accommodate the full range of customer value creation potential that could be unleashed if mass customization were available more broadly.

24   The Value of Toolkits for User Innovation and Design

In chapter 24, Nikolaus Franke demonstrates how laboratory experimental evidence can be marshaled to derive causal evidence of the salience of toolkits for innovation. In particular, Franke's research program is focused on understanding the value created by the self-design task of user innovation toolkits and the generality of the findings to a diverse set of products and individuals. Franke's research establishes an excellent benchmark for how innovation theories can be tested with insights that are both practically relevant and scholarly salient.

Franke's chapter shows that user innovators express a significantly higher willingness to pay for products that they design themselves as opposed to the best-selling professionally designed products. The findings from the work done by him and his colleagues are stable and unambiguous. For a range of products and services, under ideal experimental conditions that take into account various selection effects and nonrandomized participation, Franke shows that user innovation toolkits increase the willingness to pay (using both hypothetical and actual cash outlays) by an average of 89 percent with a range between 19 and 208 percent. Franke also shows that the price premium of self-design by users via toolkits is driven by the self-satisfaction achieved through the design process and the ability to achieve a "perfect" product that fits precisely the needs of the user. This chapter serves to confirm the value of the theories generated by the broad-based academic community on user and open innovation and also creates a benchmark for excellence in research design by demonstrating how causal inference for innovation tasks can be derived through combining laboratory experiments with real-world applications.

25   Crowdfunding: Evidence on the Democratization of Start-up Funding

Ethan Mollick and Venkat Kuppuswamy close this volume with a fascinating overview of how crowdfunding is democratizing access to financial capital for innovative ideas and projects. While there have been historical examples of projects being funded by numerous contributors (e.g., the financing of the Statue of Liberty in New York), it has only been in this century where web-enabled platforms have sprung up to allow innovators to request financing for their ideas from multitudes of people in the world at very low thresholds (even as low as $1). Just as users, communities and contests democratize access to the crucial problem-solving part of the innovation process, crowdfunding is enabling users and user-entrepreneurs to circumvent traditional channels and bottlenecks in the financing of innovation.

Mollick and Kuppuswamy present data from a unique analysis and survey of design, technology, and video games projects that attempted to raise money using the largest crowdfunding site, Kickstarter, before mid-2012. The results they found are quite fascinating. Their sample includes 272 projects that ultimately raised an average of $111,469 (s.d. = $641,026) from 355,135 individuals. Of the funded projects more than 90 percent remained ongoing commercial concerns with 90 percent reporting revenues of at least $100,000 and on average employing 2.2 individuals. Beyond the descriptive statistics on funding and success patterns, Mollick and Kuppuswamy contribute to the literature by discussing how the process of crowdfunding enables user-entrepreneurs to determine market demand (so that they may make career choices), changes the economics of user-driven production by providing seed capital for making bigger investments in research and development and production, and finally creates a quality signal for traditional venture capital firms about the founding team and the market. All in all, their study points to significant research and practitioner impact of this rapidly rising practice of financing innovation.

Taken as a whole, the chapters in this volume provide a comprehensive view of the emerging paradigm of user and open innovation. Indeed, as one steps back and surveys the entire volume, it does appear that the innovation process itself is being revolutionized, transitioning from a manufacturer-centric model to one dominated by users and communities and predicated on openness. If in the last century Eric von Hippel was primarily a lone voice in academia advocating for the existence of this new paradigm, in this new century a large group of scholars from around the world, in a range of disciplines, have now joined him in providing empirical evidence and a theoretical foundation for this new paradigm. This volume serves to curate the underlying scholarship and provide direction for new research that can add to the scholarly foundation of this new innovation paradigm.

I
Fundamentals of User Innovation

2

Context, Capabilities, and Incentives—The Core and the Periphery of User Innovation

Dietmar Harhoff

User innovation is by now an established framework, playing an increasingly important role in innovation research and management. In the years of its conception, the theory and empirical results underpinning user innovation were initially met with surprise and, in some cases, rejection. This reaction may be understandable given that the concept of user innovation ran counter to a long-preferred model in which innovation originated largely from manufacturing firms. This view has by now given way to a more differentiated paradigm in which users play a central role.

User innovation provides an elegant, yet simple solution to the *sticky information* problem described by Eric von Hippel. Need information may be well known to the user but be costly to transfer to manufacturers. The solution to the problem is that the user becomes an innovator and then transfers a working prototype to a manufacturing entity. In the course of the many case studies that have been undertaken to demonstrate that users are indeed a major source of innovation, user innovation has typically been recorded only if the user did provide the first working prototype. This definition served the purpose of clarity and its use contributed to avoiding spurious empirical results. But at the same time, by delineating user innovation in this conservative manner, the extent of user contributions to the overall innovation process could have been underestimated. Innovations that come about as a consequence of user involvement, but in which users for some reason are not visible as the builders of prototypes, will be referred to as the "periphery" of user innovation in this chapter. I suggest that the *periphery* is economically important and present some data supporting this view.

The chapter first explores the *core* and *periphery* of user innovation conceptually. The data come from a recent large-scale survey of inventors to show, first, that users and customers provide highly important information for invention processes. Second, users and customers are the preferred partners for formal and informal collaboration in invention processes. Moreover a descriptive multivariate analysis suggests that high importance of user-origin information and collaboration between inventors and users are associated with above-average patent value and with particularly high rates of commercialization of inventions. Hence, even in a context that most classical user innovation studies have avoided—invention processes with subsequent patenting, mostly in manufacturing firms—external users make a strong contribution to innovation. The implications of these results are discussed in the final section of the chapter.

The Core Concept—Early Perspectives of User Innovation

Prior to Eric von Hippel's seminal contributions, a number of studies had already provided evidence that innovation in equipment and processes was often undertaken by the firms employing the respective machinery and production processes. Enos (1962) had identified innovations in oil refining and found that almost all of the innovations came from oil refiners. Freeman (1968) showed that particularly successful chemical production processes were typically developed by process users. Pavitt (1984) developed an important taxonomy of innovation in which in-house innovation activity was a dominant mode of innovation. Von Hippel (1976, 1988) then showed that this form of innovation was not limited to firms, but that individual users were a dominant source of innovation in a range of fields, such as scientific instruments. Moreover he provided a coherent model in which need information, solution capabilities and incentives interacted such as to make users in many contexts the most likely originators of innovation. In many cases, the innovation originates with *lead users* (Urban and von Hippel 1988; Morrison et al. 2000; Franke et al. 2006) who are at the leading edge in particular fields and can expect considerable benefits from developing innovations to solve problems in their immediate context of use.

What makes the user innovation, at least in in many contexts, superior to innovation by manufacturers? The view that emerged in a series of studies in the user literature is that users have better insights into the context in which the innovation will be used. Information on the user's needs and the context of use are hard to replicate since the respective information is *sticky* (von Hippel 1994). Solution-based information or solution capabilities may be easier to muster than the sticky information describing the context of use. Taken together with strong incentives for innovation (in particular those experienced by *lead users*) and additional advantages either due to low cost (see Hienerth et al. 2011; and also Lüthje, chapter 3 in this volume) or particular capabilities for innovation, a situation emerges in which users rather than manufacturers become the parties initiating innovations. Indeed users were shown to make seminal contribution to innovation in studies such as those by Herstatt and von Hippel (1992), Morrison et al. (2000), Franke and von Hippel (2003), Lüthje (2003), among others. While early studies had focused on industrial processes and equipment, subsequent research also demonstrated that consumer products were not exempt from the user innovation phenomenon (Shah 2000; Lüthje 2004; Tietz et al. 2005). Quite to the contrary, users were shown to form communities where members freely reveal their innovations and thus support a cumulative and *democratized* process of invention and improvement. This is the focus of the chapters in part II of this volume.

Extensions to the Early Perspective

In the early contributions to the user innovation literature, the activities of user innovators had been described quite narrowly. It was expected that user innovators would reveal their solutions freely and fully, that they would not integrate vertically into manufacturing or commercialization of the innovative solution, and that they would not try to obtain patent protection for their innovations. There is an interesting paradox here: while the classical view of user innovation solves the public good problem of generating an innovative solution, the user who is only interested in solving his or her own problem is not a particularly likely candidate for tackling the equally fundamental diffusion problem. To arrive at wide diffusion of the innovation, early models assumed that other (non-innovative) manufacturers would observe users carefully and then imitate and commercialize the innovation. The innovation provided by the manufacturer would often refine the functional breakthroughs of the user and provide further improvements in design, safety, and other dimensions (Riggs and von Hippel 1994).

Shah (2004) and Shah and Tripsas (2007) were among the first to study user entrepreneurship, namely situations where users innovated and then formed startups to commercialize their innovation themselves. The notion that user innovators may themselves become providers of an innovative product (at least in its prototypical incarnation) is firmly established by now. User innovation is—in this sense—a source of entrepreneurial opportunity and thus again valuable for an economy. Baldwin et al. (2006) take note of this extension and describe a longitudinal model of innovation that provides a particularly interesting extension of the initial concepts. They study hybrid agents such as user-manufacturers who provide a bridge between the very simple early prototypes the user innovator has built and the later production of refined versions of the product by a capital-intensive manufacturer. In other work, the notion of full free revealing of innovation-related information which may be the preferred option in some circumstances (Harhoff et al. 2003) gave way to a more nuanced view in which revealing may be selective (Henkel 2006). While these and other extensions relax the initial sharp delineation of user innovation somewhat, I argue below that there are more types of hybrid activities in which users can make a valuable contribution, and I study these contributions using data representing economic activity in a broad range of technologies and industries. In this regard, the *periphery* that I explore is also related to the contributions in parts IV and V of this volume where scholars study user innovation in new roles and the interaction between users and firms.

The Periphery—User Contributions to Innovation

Much of the literature has focused on the described *core* and has thus been able to demonstrate very cleanly that user innovation exists and that it has considerable impact. The extensions just described then relaxed some of the narrow definitions and views. However, this *user innovation core* is still largely based on case studies of particular industries or communities. Given that even an extensive collection of cases can never measure the economic impact of a phenomenon at large, this constituted (until recently) a weakness of the literature. After all, case studies are often being selected to demonstrate a phenomenon, not to measure its effect. Moreover, by today's standards, some of the early definitions of user innovation appear rather strict, even if they were necessary to delineate the user innovation phenomenon clearly from other forms of innovation.

To escape an overly narrow focus on clean cases of user innovation we have to ask to what extent users contribute to innovation processes where they ultimately do not build the prototype or first installation. Users may engage in activities such as providing solution-related information to a manufacturer in order to support the refinement of user innovations. But they may also provide knowledge which allows the manufacturer to actually come up with the first prototype—based on user contributions. I attempt to explore the importance of such user contributions in an empirical exploration using inventor survey data.

An Empirical Exploration of User Contributions to Patented Inventions

In the following analysis I employ data collected in a survey of inventors. The PatVal2 survey was undertaken as part of a project sponsored by the European Commission. Within this project, a team of investigators collected primary data with a self-administered survey of inventors for 20 European countries (Austria, Belgium, Switzerland, Czech Republic, Germany, Denmark, Spain, Finland, France, United Kingdom, Greece, Hungary, Ireland, Italy, Luxembourg, the Netherlands, Norway, Poland, Sweden, and Slovenia), Israel, the United States, and Japan. Since the questionnaire differed in some regards for the United States, only the data for Europe and Japan will be used in this chapter. Details on sampling, survey approach and questionnaire construction are presented in Gambardella et al. (2014). The dataset used here contains information on patent applications filed at the European Patent Office with priority dates from 2003 to 2005. The survey took place between November 2009 and February 2010 in Europe. In Japan, the full-scale survey was started in October 2010 and closed at the end of July 2011. As can be expected, more than 80 percent of the patent filings covered in the dataset stem from large organizations which are privately held. Descriptive statistics for the overall data are again provided in Gambardella et al. (2014). I use a dataset with 12,762 observations in most tables, since missing information on some items reduces the size of the sample.

These data come with a number of advantages. First, the data allow me to distinguish between knowledge contributions from users and from customers to the invention process of another party. In many discussions and in surveys, the terms are treated as synonyms. In the case of consumer goods purchased by consumers directly for their own use, the end user and the customer are indeed the same. In the case of supply chains, where aircraft producer firms can be, for example, buying landing gear to incorporate in a plane for an end user, customer and user are clearly not the same. The same applies to the case of firms or families: For example, in the case of a mother buying a product for her child, or an engineer specifying a process machine that an operator in the production department will actually use, customer and end user are not the same. Conceptually the distinction is likely to matter for the following reason: *Sticky information* about use need and context of use are unlikely to be fully transferred to an intermediary *customer*—hence, when end user input is important, user information should turn out to be more valuable than customer information. Ultimately, it is an empirical question if the distinction matters in the analysis of survey data. As we will see below, the distinction is actually important.

Second, the data include information on collaboration (formal and informal) between the inventing party and users or customers. This information is important in order to see if highly organized forms of knowledge transfer are more effective than arm's-length relationships. Third, the database is international in scope and representative for the population of patents in Europe. Thus it goes far beyond a case study of a particular community or industry. This is welcome in order to see effects of user involvement at large—but it also comes with disadvantages which I discuss below. Finally, the dataset contains information on the value of the respective patent and on its commercialization. The latter variable is of particular interest if we are interested in the diffusion of innovation without which any welfare gain from innovation would be rather limited.

Importance of External Information and Collaboration Partners

In the survey, inventors were asked for the importance of external parties as sources of knowledge for the invention process. In table 2.1, these assessments are tabulated by main technological field.

Table 2.1
Importance of external parties as sources of knowledge by main technological area

Technological area	Universities	PROs	Customers	Source of knowledge Users	Suppliers	Competitors	Consulting	N
Electrical engineering	21.6%	11.7%	31.8%	31.8%	16.3%	23.7%	5.8%	2,979
Instruments	27.2%	14.9%	37.6%	42.4%	19.4%	25.5%	7.5%	1,884
Chemistry	32.5%	17.7%	30.1%	32.7%	17.4%	24.6%	7.9%	3,020
Mechanical engineering	13.6%	7.3%	39.7%	43.9%	27.4%	25.9%	6.3%	4,016
Other fields	13.6%	8.9%	42.6%	51.3%	28.7%	28.3%	8.2%	863
Total	21.9%	12.0%	35.5%	38.7%	21.3%	25.2%	6.9%	12,762

Note: Cells contain the percentage of respondents in the respective technological area indicating that the respective external party was an important or very important source of knowledge.

Consider first the statistics for the overall importance of the different sources of knowledge. Clearly, the two most relevant sources are customers and users. Interestingly, while the two variables have very similar univariate distributions—their bivariate correlation far from being perfect (ρ = 0.68)—inventors apparently distinguish between the two sources. 38.7 percent of inventors state that users are important or very important as sources of knowledge for the invention process, 35.5 percent deem customers to be important in this regard. Competitors (25.2 percent), universities (21.9 percent), and suppliers (21.3 percent) constitute sources of somewhat lesser importance. Public research organizations (PROs, 12.0 percent) and consulting organizations (6.9 percent) are even less relevant on average. Taken together, these results are striking: The invention process is usually taken to be technology-oriented. But the data in table 2.1 show that the demand side is deemed to be the most important source of knowledge. This assessment is made by those individuals who are best-positioned to provide it—the inventors themselves.

The importance of different types of knowledge for the invention process should differ across technological areas. This expectation is born out in the data as table 2.1 shows. Across five main technologies, users are the most important source of information for invention processes. Universities are highly relevant for inventions in chemistry (32.5 percent) and instruments (27.2 percent), but even in chemistry customers (30.1 percent) and users (32.7 percent) are highly important. Users have particularly high relevance in mechanical engineering (43.9 percent), instruments (42.4 percent) and in the residual group of technologies (other fields—51.3 percent).

Externally provided information may become so important that the organizations pursuing inventions for the purpose of patenting will collaborate with players representing the most relevant sources of information. Collaboration may occur either formally, that is, on a contractual basis, or informally. Patterns of collaboration are explored in table 2.2 which lists the percentage of responding inventors who indicate that the invention process involved a formal or an informal collaboration with a particular type of collaborator.

Cases in which inventors did not know about the collaboration status are conservatively allocated to *no collaboration,* which is the residual group. Unfortunately, for the collaboration variable no distinction was

Table 2.2
Incidence of formal and informal collaboration by type of collaborator and main technological area

Main technological area	Type of collaborator					
	Universities	PROs and other public organizations	Customers and/or product users	Suppliers	Competitors	N
Electrical engineering	6.5%|4.3%	4.4%|2.6%	10.8%|12.2%	9.1%|7.9%	1.9%|1.9%	2,979
Instruments	8.2%|6.1%	8.3%|8.2%	11.9%|16.5%	12.8%|10.3%	0.6%|1.8%	1,884
Chemistry	8.9%|5.2%	8.6%|4.6%	11.0%|12.5%	10.5%|9.5%	1.3%|1.4%	3,020
Mechanical engineering	6.3%|6.6%	3.4%|2.1%	14.3%|18.7%	14.3%|15.0%	1.1%|1.9%	4,016
Other fields	8.5%|7.5%	4.3%|3.0%	11.5%|25.3%	14.6%|15.3%	1.2%|2.3%	863
Total	7.4%|5.7%	5.6%|3.8%	12.2%|15.9%	12.0%|11.4%	1.3%|1.8%	12,762

Note: Cells contain the percentage of respondents indicating that there was collaboration between the own organization and the respective source. Formal collaboration is indicated by the figure to the left, informal collaboration by the figure to the right of the separator.

made in the survey between customers and users; hence I use the pooled responses. Across all main technological areas, a clear result emerges: Collaboration is a relatively frequent event, and users and customers are the most popular collaboration partners in invention processes. In more than 25 percent of all invention processes, some form of collaboration occurred. Giuri et al. (2007) have shown that data on co-application of patents seriously underestimates the incidence of collaboration in invention. The results in table 2.2 support this view (see also Gambardella et al. 2014 for a more detailed analysis regarding the extent of collaboration). The collaboration patterns revealed in table 2.2 add to the impression that even in the technology-oriented process of inventing, users and customers make important contributions. These collaborations are unlikely to be identified in user innovation studies which impose—for good reasons—relatively conservative criteria and delineations when seeking to identify user innovations.

User Contributions to Patent Value and Commercialization

Table 2.3 summarizes econometric evidence from a multivariate analysis in which I present regression results for two dependent variables: the value of the patented invention and the incidence of commercialization.

The dependent variable *value* is constructed from a subjective, ordinal response of the inventor to the following question: In comparison with other patents in your industry or technological field, how would you rate the economic value of this patent? Response categories were *top 10%*; *top 25%, but not top 10%*; *top 50%, but not top 25%*; and *bottom 50*. The incidence of commercialization is taken from the binary response to the question: Have the applicant(s) or affiliated parties ever used this patented invention commercially, i.e., in a product, service or in a manufacturing process? As independent variables, we first use the measures for importance of knowledge from universities, PROs, customers, users, suppliers, competitors and consulting firms. These are coded as zero for responses indicating no use or very low importance of the respective source, 1 for cases of intermediate importance, and 2 for responses indicating high or very high importance. Technically the use of two dummy variables would be correct, but the econometric results are actually not affected by the coding used here. The set of regressors is then augmented by variables describing collaboration patters—a dummy variable was coded for formal or informal collaboration with the types of organizations listed in table 2.3 already. As controls, I include dummy variables for the technological field (34 groups), priority years (2 group variables) and inventor country (21 groups). The coefficients of these control variables are not shown in table 2.3.

The value variable is analyzed using an ordered probit estimator. A positive regression coefficient would indicate an increase of patent value. Columns 1 and 2 contain the respective results. The first model shows that patents that rely heavily on information coming from universities or PROs tend to be economically more valuable in the assessment of the inventors. This confirms earlier results of Gambardella et al. (2008) who used the PatVal1 data. Similarly the use of information from consultants and from users is associated with an above-average value of patented inventions. Although the sample contains 11,260 observations for which we have responses in all variables, the significance levels are modest in most cases, pointing to the fact that patent value is usually a noisy variable. In model 2, I allow formal and informal collaboration with external actors to have separate effects. The most interesting result is the positive effect emanating from informal collaboration with users or customers. The effect of user-based information is barely diminished by the inclusion of the collaboration variables. Clearly, there are concerns of endogeneity and other problems—we cannot take these simple results as causal evidence. But the results are suggestive—user involvement occurs in cases where the final patent appears to be more valuable than in cases where no contributions are made by users.

In columns 3 and 4, first results from a probit analysis of the commercialization variable are shown. I tabulate marginal effects and their standard errors in the two columns. In column 3, the collaboration variables are again excluded, in column 4 they are added to the probit regression. Since they turn out to be statistically highly significant, I turn to the results of column 4. High importance of knowledge from customers and users is associated with a strong and significant increase in commercialization rates—the likelihood of commercialization increases by 3.83 percent (s.e. 0.74 percent) if customer-provided information becomes more important. In the case of user-based information, the increase is 3.40 percent (s.e. 0.72 percent). In the case of formal collaboration with users or customers,

Table 2.3
Multivariate results for patent value (ordered probit) and commercialization (probit)

Variables	(1)	(2)	(3)	(4)
	Patent value		Commercialization (0/1)	
Universities	0.0416**	0.0387*	-0.0464**	-0.0466**
	[0.0159]	[0.0159]	[0.00699]	[0.00702]
PROs	0.0429*	0.0355+	-0.0235**	-0.0204*
	[0.0190]	[0.0193]	[0.00847]	[0.00861]
Customers	0.00908	0.00609	0.0486**	0.0383**
	[0.0167]	[0.0172]	[0.00723]	[0.00744]
Users	0.0373*	0.0335*	0.0370**	0.0340**
	[0.0166]	[0.0167]	[0.00714]	[0.00718]
Suppliers	-0.0129	-0.0310+	0.0331**	0.0191**
	[0.0148]	[0.0161]	[0.00644]	[0.00704]
Competitors	0.0126	0.0145	-0.0140*	-0.00861
	[0.0143]	[0.0144]	[0.00625]	[0.00632]
Consulting	0.0603**	0.0481*	-0.00718	-0.00800
	[0.0197]	[0.0201]	[0.00872]	[0.00890]

Table 2.3 (continued)

	Formal	Informal	Formal	Informal
Collaboration with users or customers	-0.0101	0.0694*	0.0684**	0.0726**
	[0.0343]	[0.0313]	[0.0152]	[0.0139]
Collaboration with suppliers	0.0562	0.0774*	0.0653**	0.0301+
	[0.0356]	[0.0356]	[0.0158]	[0.0159]
Collaboration with competitors	0.110	0.123	0.0239	-0.0645+
	[0.0933]	[0.0798]	[0.0420]	[0.0337]
Collaboration with universities	0.0205	0.00924	-0.0266	0.00417
	[0.0417]	[0.0465]	[0.0183]	[0.0205]
Collaboration with government research and other public research org.	0.129**	0.0610	-0.0251	-0.0218
	[0.0472]	[0.0559]	[0.0212]	[0.0247]
Observations	11,260		12,762	
log-likelihood	-14,808	-14,790	-8,215	-8,177
chi2	490.2	526.5	1041	1117
dof	63	73	63	73

Note: Standard errors in brackets. ** $p < 0.01$, * $p < 0.05$. All regressions include 34 dummies for technological areas ($p < 0.001$), 2 dummies for priority years (n.s.) and 21 dummies for country of invention ($p < 0.001$).

commercialization is 6.84 percent (s.e. 1.52 percent) more likely, informal collaboration comes with an increase of 7.26 percent (s.e. 1.39 percent). Only formal collaboration with suppliers appears to be similarly relevant (6.53 percent, s.e. 1.58 percent). Suppliers are also important as a source of knowledge, regardless of collaboration. Commercialization rates are substantially lower when knowledge from universities or PROs is important. The latter result is not surprising—inventions made in the immediate proximity of academic research may take a long time to reach the market and may have to undergo various refinements before being brought out commercially.

The results have been tested in various robustness checks. Variables describing the size of the applicant, the type of organization, and other contextual data describing the locus of invention have in some cases significant coefficients, but these variables do not change the statistical result in a major way. Applying population weights to the statistics presented here does not change the results, either. To summarize, the overall results show that taking information from users and/or customers into account in the invention process goes along with higher patent value and an increase in the likelihood of commercialization. Moreover collaboration—either formal or informal—with customers or product users also has a positive association with value and commercialization.

Conclusions

I started this chapter by pointing to the insightful contributions that had come from a user innovation perspective which employed—for the purpose of clarity and for avoiding spurious results—rather strict definitions regarding the contributions of users to innovation. A second wave of studies extended these results and studied the emergence of user communities, user-entrepreneurs, user-manufacturers, and user-purchasers. This extended view treated user innovation in the strict sense as the starting point and center of the overall evolution of innovation ecosystems. From *pure* user innovation some entrepreneurial behavior emerged that then supported the diffusion process. I used the term *user innovation core* to characterize the contributions in the spirit of these two approaches.

The point of this chapter is to show that there may be other forms of user contributions to innovation that go unmeasured and unappreciated if one focuses exclusively on the user innovation core. In this potentially large area—which I called the *periphery of user innovation*—users may make important contributions but never assume the role of the pure user innovator, nor venture into entrepreneurial or manufacturing functions after having been the pure user innovator initially. In the periphery cases of user innovation, users and customers may simply be formal or informal partners of manufacturers in the development of innovations or improvements to innovations. Users may not provide the first prototype, but they can contribute demand-side and technical information, either in random interactions or informal or formal collaboration with inventors who then turn their information into inventions some of which may be patented. Or they may simply not become visible as innovators since they arrive at their novel solutions in the context of their households (see von Hippel et al. 2012, and the contributions in part IV of this volume).

The data used in this chapter were drawn from a context that user innovation studies typically avoid—invention processes that involve patenting. But even in this context, it can be shown that users and customers are the most frequently sought external sources of knowledge and that they are the most prominent collaboration partners. I used data on the inventions' value and incidence of commercialization to show that user knowledge and user collaboration are associated with above average patent value and with a strong increase in the likelihood of commercialization. The evidence presented here suggests that user contributions are highly relevant in the economy at large, not just in particular niches. The data also have some unique advantages in terms of their validity—responses from inventors at the patent level are probably better suited than answers from managers to identify sources of information and collaboration patterns.

A number of caveats apply and should be taken into account. Patents do not cover the full range of innovations that are being generated in an economy. But they cover a large share—studies usually indicate that about one half of inventions are patented. Moreover I have used responses from a survey, and clearly, the analysis cannot establish causal relationships. More elaborate analyses are needed to pursue the scope and importance of the *periphery of user innovation* further. But it seems clear at this point that the overall impact of the user innovation *periphery* may be large and worth pursuing in future research.

References

Baldwin, C., E. von Hippel, and C. Hienerth. 2006. How user innovations become commercial products: A theoretical investigation and case study. *Research Policy* 35 (9): 1291–1313.

Bogers, M., A. Afuah, and B. Bastian. 2010. Users as innovators: A review, critique, and future research directions. *Journal of Management* 36 (4): 857–75.

Enos, J. L. 1962. *Petroleum Progress and Profits: A History of Process Innovation*. Cambridge: MIT Press.

Franke, N., and E. von Hippel. 2003. Satisfying heterogeneous user needs via innovation toolkits: The case of Apache Security software. *Research Policy* 32 (7): 1199–1215.

Franke, N., E. von Hippel, and M. Schreier. 2006. Finding commercially attractive user innovations: An exploration and test of 'lead user' theory. *Journal of Product Innovation Management* 23 (4): 301–15.

Freeman, C. 1968. Chemical process plant: Innovation and the world market. *National Institute Economic Review* 45 (1): 29–57.

Gambardella, A., D. Harhoff, and B. Verspagen. 2008. The value of European patents. *European Management Review* 5 (2): 69–84.

Gambardella, A., P. Giuri, D. Harhoff, K. Hoisl, M. Mariani, S. Nagaoka, and S. Torrisi. 2014. Invention processes and economic uses of patents: Evidence from the PatVal2 Survey. Unpublished manuscript. Milano.

Giuri, P., M. Mariani, S. Brusoni, G. Crespi, D. Francoz, A. Gambardella, W. Garcia-Fontes, 2007. Inventors and invention processes: Results from the PatVal-EU Survey. *Research Policy* 36 (8): 1107–27.

Harhoff, D., J. Henkel, and E. von Hippel. 2003. Profiting from voluntary information spillovers: How users benefit by freely revealing their innovations. *Research Policy* 32 (10): 1753–69.

Henkel, J. 2006. Selective revealing in open innovation processes: The case of embedded Linux. *Research Policy* 35 (7): 953–69.

Herstatt, C., and E. von Hippel. 1992. From experience: Developing new product concepts via the lead user method: A case study in a "low-tech" field. *Journal of Product Innovation Management* 9 (3): 213–21.

Hienerth, C., E. von Hippel, and M. Berg Jensen. 2011. Innovation as consumption: Analysis of consumers' innovation efficiency. Working paper 4926–11. Sloan School of Management, MIT. Available at SSRN: http://ssrn.com/abstract =1916319.

Hüner, A. K. 2013. *Der Wissenstransfer in User-Innovationsprozessen: Empirische Studien in der Medizintechnik*. Wiesbaden: Springer Gabler.

Lüthje, C. 2003. Customers as co-inventors: An empirical analysis of the antecedents of customer-driven innovations in the field of medical equipment. In *Proceedings of the 32nd Annual Conference of the European Marketing Academy (EMAC)*. Published on CD-Rom. Glasgow: EMAC.

Lüthje, C. 2004. Characteristics of innovating users in a consumer goods field: An empirical study of sport-related product consumers. *Technovation* 24 (9): 683–95.

Lüthje, C., and C. Herstatt. 2004. The lead user method: An outline of empirical findings and issues for future research. *R & D Management* 34 (5): 553–68.

Lüthje, C., C. Herstatt, and E. von Hippel. 2005. User-innovators and "local" information: The case of mountain biking. *Research Policy* 34 (6): 951–65.

Morrison, P. D., J. H. Roberts, and E. von Hippel. 2000. Determinants of user innovation and innovation sharing in a local market. *Management Science* 46 (12): 1513–27.

Pavitt, K. 1984. Sectoral patterns of technical change: Towards a taxonomy and a theory. *Research Policy* 13 (6): 343–73.

Polanyi, M. 1983. *The Tacit Dimension.* Gloucester, MA: Smith.

Riggs, W., and E. von Hippel. 1994. Incentives to innovate and the sources of innovation: The case of scientific instruments. *Research Policy* 23 (4): 459–69.

Shah, S. 2000. Sources and patterns of innovation in a consumer products field: Innovations in sporting equipment. Working paper 4105. Sloan School of Management, MIT.

Shah, S. K. 2003. Community-based innovation and product development: Findings from open source software and consumer sporting goods. Unpublished PhD thesis. Sloan School of Management, MIT.

Shah, S. K. 2004. From innovation to firm and industry formation in the windsurfing, skateboarding and snowboarding industries. Working paper 05–0107. University of Illinois Urbana-Champaign.

Shah, S. K., and M. Tripsas. 2007. The accidental entrepreneur: The emergent and collective process of user entrepreneurship. *Strategic Entrepreneurship Journal* 1 (1–2): 123–40.

Tietz, R., P. D. Morrison, C. Lüthje, and C. Herstatt. 2005. The process of user-innovation: A case study in a consumer goods setting. *International Journal of Product Development* 2 (4): 321–38.

Urban, G. L., and E. von Hippel. 1988. Lead user analyses for the development of new industrial products. *Management Science* 34 (5): 569–82.

von Hippel, E. 1976. The dominant role of users in the scientific instrument innovation process. *Research Policy* 5 (3): 212–39.

von Hippel, E. 1986. Lead users: A source of novel product concepts. *Management Science* 32 (7): 791–805.

von Hippel, E. 1988. *The Sources of Innovation.* New York: Oxford University Press.

von Hippel, E. 1994. "Sticky Information" and the locus of problem solving: Implications for innovation. *Management Science* 40 (4): 429–39.

von Hippel, E. 1998. Economics of product development by users: The impact of "sticky" local information. *Management Science* 44 (5): 629–44.

von Hippel, E. 2001. User toolkits for innovation. *Journal of Product Innovation Management* 18 (4): 247–57.

von Hippel, E. 2005. *Democratizing Innovation*. Cambridge: MIT Press.

von Hippel, E., J. P. J. de Jong, and S. Flowers. 2012. Comparing business and household sector innovation in consumer products: Findings from a representative survey in the UK. *Management Science* 58 (9): 1669–81.

3

Cost Advantages in Innovation—A Comparison of Users and Manufacturers

Christian Lüthje and Christoph Stockstrom

Eric von Hippel initiated a paradigm shift. By showing the prevalence of user-driven innovations in several industries, his research in the early 1980s fundamentally questioned the dominating understanding of that time, characterized by the idea of manufacturer-centric innovation systems. Growing empirical evidence on users developing technology, software, physical products and services underlined that important innovative activities took place beyond the scope of manufacturer-centric innovation research, which failed to answer questions such as: Why should users innovate at all? Or, how is it possible that users produce outcomes that are at least as substantial and widely adopted as those developed by institutions specifically devoted to commercial innovation? Eric von Hippel's work refocused the attention on users as a more natural source of innovation than manufacturers.

The first question indicates that, according to traditional models, users should not have a clear incentive to innovate, at least not unless they change their functional role and start to sell their developments in markets. Market theories, innovation models, and marketing approaches have long focused on profits linked to the commercial exploitation of innovations by selling them (e.g., see von Hippel 2005; Harhoff et al. 2003; Riggs and von Hippel 1994) and consequently led to an underestimation of private benefits stemming from other forms of exploitation. Undoubtedly, one merit of the work on user innovations initiated by Eric von Hippel has been to broaden the understanding of potential incentives driving users to innovate.

The first studies on this matter revealed that industrial users innovate because they want solutions that better meet their needs. Investigating individual end users and consumers as well as user communities, subsequent studies identified a number of further benefits. Users not only value the activity of innovating but also freely share innovation-related information with others to achieve social benefits, such as increasing one's status within a community of peers or developing feelings of affiliation to a group (Baldwin et al. 2006; Franke and Shah 2003; Füller 2006; Füller et al. 2007; Harhoff et al. 2003; von Krogh and von Hippel 2006). Consequently users will often realize a higher benefit from innovating than manufacturers, simply because their possibilities of profiting go far beyond the financial rewards stemming from commercial exploitation. Thus users frequently have a benefit-related advantage relative to manufacturers.

However, aside from the aforementioned benefit-related advantages, innovating users also enjoy cost-related advantages. These cost-related distinctions help answer the second question raised above, namely why users develop beneficial innovations, often without having invested in dedicated resources for innovation. We argue that several factors acting on innovating users allow them to operate in low-cost zones of innovation. We propose that users, relative to manufactures, should have a stronger inclination to exploit existing assets and to build upon solution and need-related knowledge they already possess.

It is important to note that the argumentation and anecdotal evidence presented in this chapter does exclusively apply to the development of innovation prototypes for own use rather than to cost advantages of users in large scale production or distribution of innovations. These latter kinds of advantages on the side of the users are not very realistic—at least not outside the areas of software and automatized Internet-based services. Cost advantages in production and distribution are also less relevant for explaining users' innovation activities as users tend not to innovate to benefit from commercial exploitation.

After discussing the general incentive conditions for low-cost innovation by users, we turn to a detailed discussion of cost-related advantages of users and structure this discussion along the main stages of a typical innovation process: (1) opportunity and need identification, (2) solution development, and (3) testing and refinement. We will summarize the empirical evidence supporting the notion that it is both rational and perfectly possible for users to successfully exploit existing tangible resources, skills, and knowledge in all three stages. The discussion will also draw on several examples of innovating users, particularly taken from the medical field, to illustrate why and how users succeed in developing beneficial innovations at comparatively low cost. While most of our examples draw on individual user inventors and some of our arguments primarily apply to them, we argue that they hold for user firms as well, albeit sometimes to a lesser extent. In the last section we discuss conclusions that can be derived from the existence of significant cost-related advantages of innovating users.

Incentive Conditions for Low-Cost Innovation

For inventors, one major avenue to efficient solutions is to heavily rely on existing knowledge, skills, and tangible assets, meaning resources that are already in their possession or easily accessible rather than acquiring new resources for innovation (Martin and Mitchell 1998; Stuart and Podolny 1996; Helfat 1994). Of course, manufactures as well as users have a clear incentive to keep the cost of innovating low by exploiting the resources they already control. Applying existing and local assets for developing solutions fits the general economic incentive of minimizing innovation-related costs (Rosenkopf and Nerkar 2001) while achieving a desired level of benefit. For instance, manufacturers constantly seek to expand and to leverage their expertise, intellectual property or production facilities in which they have invested in the past (von Hippel 2005). In the long run, however, there are limitations to renewing and leveraging existing resources for developing innovations. Strategic considerations may therefore lead manufacturers to invest into new capabilities and resources they anticipate to be superior in the future to the ones they currently possess (Barney 1991; Wernerfelt 1984). After all, strategic investments in new innovation-related resources will increase the likelihood of developing new products and services performing well in the market place. This is the basis for generating future revenue streams and for securing competitive advantages.

In contrast to this, users very often do not profit monetarily by selling or licensing innovations to others.[1] Instead, users tend to innovate because they expect to directly profit from their innovations by using, consuming, and applying them in their individual use context (von Hippel 1988). The rather insignificant role of profit expectations from sales is partly due to the fact that financial benefits from the diffusion of an innovation often entail intellectual property issues. Securing, enforcing, and/or licensing intellectual property are costly to attempt, with very uncertain outcomes (von Hippel 2005; Harhoff et al. 2003). Shah (2000) has reported on the frequency and effectiveness of patenting for user innovations in sports. She finds few attempts to patent and almost no success in licensing and obtaining royalties. Similar results were obtained in user innovation studies conducted in the field of medical equipment (Lüthje 2003). In addition, when trying to get better solutions for in-house use, innovating users are hardly influenced by competitive considerations. At least for individual end users and consumers, innovation activities are frequently not channeled by the aim of obtaining use-related advantages over other users. This focus on satisficing solutions leads them to typically innovate by leveraging existing resources and creates comparatively little incentive to strategically invest in new capabilities and resources to outperform other users in the present or maintain competitiveness in the future.

In sum, the focus on benefits other than from selling the innovation should prompt all types of innovating users (individuals and firms) to intensively screen their existing resources with regard to their applicability for developing new solutions. The strong incentive to build upon existing resources and the freedom to disregard strategic investments can, in turn, constitute a relative advantage of users over manufacturers. Users may achieve a higher level of innovation efficiency than manufacturers by consequently drawing on their knowledge and creatively exploiting their idiosyncratic capabilities and assets rather than investing in the acquisition, combination and exploitation of new resources. This contribution is related to a recent study by Hienerth et al. (2011) which is the first to provide quantitative support for the relative efficiency of user innovators. They find users of whitewater kayaking equipment to be significantly more efficient than producer firms in developing equipment and infrastructural innovations. The following discussion may help explain why users are comparatively more efficient at developing innovations.

In the remaining sections of this chapter, we aim at illustrating the entire spectrum of causes enabling users to innovate at lower costs than producers. We will enrich the discussion with quantitative and anecdotal evidence of user innovation in different fields. We particularly report

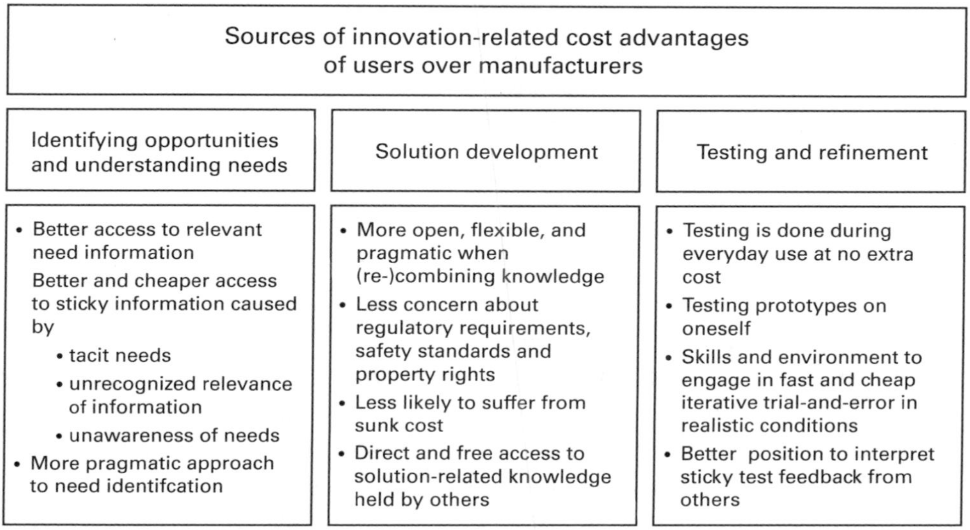

Sources of innovation-related cost advantages of users over manufacturers		
Identifying opportunities and understanding needs	**Solution development**	**Testing and refinement**

• Better access to relevant need information
Better and cheaper access to sticky information caused by
  • tacit needs
  • unrecognized relevance of information
  • unawareness of needs
• More pragmatic approach to need identifcation
	• More open, flexible, and pragmatic when (re-)combining knowledge
	• Less concern about regulatory requirements, safety standards and property rights
	• Less likely to suffer from sunk cost
	• Direct and free access to solution-related knowledge held by others
		• Testing is done during everyday use at no extra cost
		• Testing prototypes on oneself
		• Skills and environment to engage in fast and cheap iterative trial-and-error in realistic conditions
		• Better position to interpret sticky test feedback from others

Figure 3.1

Sources of innovation-related cost advantages of users over manufacturers

examples from the medical field that we collected through interviews with innovating physicians. The discussion centers on cost-related advantages that users realize in the course of the following innovation activities: (1) advantages in the course of opportunity and need identification, (2) advantages in the process of developing the first solution and (3) advantages in testing and refining initial solutions. For a summary, see figure 3.1.

Three Innovative Activities

Identifying Opportunities and Understanding Needs

To recognize innovation opportunities, innovators have to develop an understanding about unmet user needs. For most innovating users, it makes perfect sense to only utilize their local knowledge about user needs. As mentioned above, users innovate because they expect to benefit from using. Users should therefore find it rational to ignore general needs of the marketplace in favor of developing innovations that are precisely tailored at their own specific needs. Note that this does not necessarily imply that a given innovation will represent a viable solution for the innovating user only. If a user's preferences, by chance, reflect the needs of a larger user group, her innovation may also satisfy a more general demand. Nevertheless, the innovation activities are primarily guided by the users' deep understanding of their own needs.

Researchers find support for the extensive use of local need information, for instance by showing that having urgent needs correlates with the innovation activity level of users (Franke and Shah 2003; Morrison et al. 2000). In a survey conducted with surgeons, the innovators in the sample realized more problems and limitations when working in the operation room than their non-innovating counterparts (Lüthje 2003). Similar results were obtained for innovating users in outdoor sports. The innovation-related rewards were strongly related to the users' personal needs (Hienerth et al. 2011; Lüthje 2004). In another study conducted with mountain biking enthusiasts, only 17 percent of the innovating users reported having considered needs of other users which they personally did not encounter. They almost exclusively developed prototypes for the specific kind of mountain biking they personally performed (Lüthje et al. 2005).

The incentives for acquiring need-related information are different for manufacturing firms. They have to generate new products and services that meet the needs of the entire marketplace or a profitable market segment. Innovators that wish to develop generally useful innovations will quickly realize the necessity to go beyond the need information they already possess. This is why manufacturers often conduct studies to collect information about emergent and future customer needs from a broad range of users. As soon as manufacturers engage in market research activities, the cost of opportunity recognition significantly increases. This is particularly true if they do not dispose of direct or free access to existing need-related information of users. This is, for instance, often the case regarding information gathering in user communities on the Internet. Many user communities are *terra prohibita* for manufacturers as the communities are formed as deliberate counter movements to closed and manufacturer-governed innovation (Dahlander and Magnusson 2005). Accessing those communities is either impossible or would require long-term investments in order to develop a trustful and continuous relationship. Other communities and user platforms governed by intermediaries usually charge for providing access to need-related information. Consider the example of the online community Sermo—a social network dedicated to medical problems and exclusively open to physicians. Pharmaceutical firms and manufactures of medical equipment are charged with up to 1 million USD for getting access to a broad set of discussions and surveys (Pettypiece 2007).

High costs of opportunity recognition may not only be induced by poor access to need-related information. Relative disadvantages may also be determined by the attributes of the need-related information itself. Manufacturers need to invest more than users whenever the development of innovations requires a high amount of "sticky" information about user needs and attributes of the use context (von Hippel 2005). The stickiness of a given unit of information is defined as the incremental expenditure required to transfer that unit of information from its point of origin to the information seeking party in a usable form (von Hippel 1998, 1994). Information stickiness can be caused by the tacit nature of the information (Nelson 1982). User needs are often tacit because they are deeply rooted in the personal experience of individuals and can hardly be encoded in explicit terms (Polanyi 1983). Tacit user needs are prevalent in all product or service areas in which a significant part of the user benefit originates from sensual perceptions such as viewing, hearing, or tasting. Also desired tactile properties of a hand tool (e.g., a medical instrument) or the kinesthetic sensations produced by a piece of sport equipment (e.g., the "pop force" needed for jumping with a kite board) are difficult to specify precisely—even if the users have a clear idea of what they want in their mind (see examples in Lüthje et al. 2005; Shah 2000).

Other use-specific information may not be tacit in itself. Rather, users may not be aware that a given piece of information is important for solution development (von Hippel 2005: 68). Put differently, stickiness may be caused by a lack of awareness regarding the relevance of a given piece of information. If manufacturers miss directly asking for hidden information—which is very likely considering the information asymmetry between users and manufactures—it won't be considered. von Hippel and Tyre (1995) provide several illustrative examples of new production machinery that failed to perform well after their introduction into the factories. In all cases the root cause for the failure was that the developers lacked important information. This information could have been easily transferred to the machine developers. Unfortunately, the personnel in the user firm missed the relevance of this specific information, mainly because of the huge amount of information which potentially could have been important to know by the developers.

Need information may also be sticky if users are not fully aware of (all) their needs. A lack of awareness is likely in newly emerging and latent needs. Users often need to encounter a new use problem or a new use experience repeatedly and in different use conditions before they can derive a clear need for innovation. In the survey of mountain bikers already cited, the innovating users were asked to indicate how they recognized the need which was solved by their idea. Most mountain bikers reported that they became aware of the need only after frequent, repeated experiences and not following just a single incident (Lüthje et al. 2005).

Stickiness of information represents a challenge for both manufacturers and innovating users. But users have to invest less than manufacturers to react to this challenge. First, users have the possibility of developing a better understanding of their tacit and emerging needs at no incremental cost, as they encounter their needs during activities that they engage in anyway. In addition users often just forgo a deep analysis of their tacit needs and the use context. They react more pragmatically by engaging in experimental problem solving via repeated cycles of trial and error. As we will discuss more extensively in a later section, users are in a position to carry out valid experiments quickly and at low cost (von Hippel 2005).

Manufacturers seem to have fewer options allowing them to stay in a low-cost corridor of opportunity identification and need recognition. They can accept the clear advantages of users and can decide to move the locus of problem solving from the manufacturer to the user. This would relieve the manufacturers from gathering sticky need information. Most appropriate, manufacturers should work with the aid of user innovation toolkits in order to support the translation of user needs into appropriate and viable solution concepts (Franke et al. 2010; von Hippel 2005). However, to provide a useful toolkit, manufacturers need to sufficiently understand the relevant solution space. All other potential measures aiming at uncovering and transferring need-related information are associated with heavy spending. Manufacturers may employ techniques such as empathic design studies (Leonard and Rayport 1997) or lead user projects (Lüthje and Herstatt 2004; von Hippel 1986). These methods are specifically designed to uncover tacit or latent needs and to develop a deep understanding of hidden yet relevant attributes of the use context. However, they require considerable effort on behalf of the producers, both in terms of financial investment and methodological training of personnel (Olson and Bakke 2001).

Solution Development

Low-cost innovation continues to be an important aim during problem solving and prototype development. Innovators of all types should have a strong inclination to employ their existing tangible assets and to (re-)use existing intangible resources. Innovators should start to search for solutions close to the competences and knowledge they already possess (Martin and Mitchell 1998; Stuart and Podolny 1996). The rationale of relying on existing resources can be understood by considering that identifying, matching, and applying new knowledge from external sources is often associated with high cost (Rosenkopf and Nerkar 2001). A solution element outside the existing body of knowledge is often embedded in a context the problem solver is not familiar with. Following the concept of absorptive capacity, this is likely to complicate all steps involved in the use of external solution-related knowledge (Cohen and Levinthal 1990).

There is broad empirical support for this tendency. For example, studies joining biographical data of inventors with the nature of their patents indicate that inventors usually recombine solution components that are salient and available to them (Fleming et al. 2007). More specifically, also user innovators have been found to rely on existing tangible and intangible resources. Slaughter (1993) studied the history of innovation of panels used in the construction of houses. She found that the users of the panels tended to innovate very efficiently. Instead of compiling new assets and acquiring external knowledge, they immediately started developing solutions by using skills, materials, and equipment available at the construction site (von Hippel 2005). Similar patterns were found in the user innovation cases analyzed by Shah (2000) and Tietz et al. (2005) in sports. In their survey of mountain bike enthusiasts, Lüthje et al. (2005) found that only 15.6 percent of the sampled innovating users reported having acquired new knowledge for developing their invention. The vast majority of users indicated that they already possessed the solution-related knowledge that they applied. This knowledge was either linked to their job expertise or was acquired through other hobbies. Lüthje et al. (2010) studied a large set of user patents in the field of medical equipment and compared them with patents assigned to independent non-user inventors with a technological background. Their findings show that user inventors applied significantly deeper and broader existing technological knowledge located within the medical field and within the domain of medical technology. Independent non-user inventors, in contrast, drew more heavily on broad and deep knowledge from technology areas outside the field of medical technology. Thus both inventor groups particularly accessed knowledge that was local to them.

Relying on existing stocks of solution-related knowledge does not necessarily imply being trapped in a limited search in the close environment of the focal inventive problem. The likelihood of tapping into new solutions is linked to the heterogeneity and conceptual distance of the knowledge domains covered by the experiences of the users. The following example taken from the field of dental surgery provides a good illustration for the transfer of prior knowledge across rather distant domains: Dr. S., a dentist specializing in oral surgery and implantology, is very active in developing solutions for tooth implants for patients who had to have some of their natural teeth removed. He realized that the luxation, as performed in existing extraction procedures, damaged the surrounding tissue of the tooth. This makes it difficult to implant replacements after the extraction. Pondering a solution to this problem, Dr. S. recognized an analogous problem in car repairs. He detected a structural similarity with the problem of removing bearings from an axle using a special puller. The existing solutions in car repair were local to him as Dr. S. is a passionate hobby mechanic working on cars. Drawing on the knowledge gained through his hobby, he devised an extraction system that allowed for longitudinal extraction of tooth roots. Similar to pullers used in car repairs, the object to be removed is attached to a screw. Spacers are used to apply counter pressure and the object is longitudinally extracted by applying traction to it by tightening the screw. This procedure leaves the surrounding hard and soft tissue intact.

While drawing on available resources is rational for all inventors, we propose that users have a striking advantage regarding the use of existing solution-related knowledge: They should be more open, flexible, and pragmatic when it comes to combining elements from their knowledge base in a new way in order to develop original solutions at low cost. Especially individual users usually do not hesitate to transfer knowledge from areas outside the target field as soon as they realize that it could help solve the target problem. They readily transfer knowledge from hobbies, former jobs, and fields of private interest and apply general-purpose items even if the outcome represents an unconventional and rather pragmatic solution lying outside the typical solution space of manufacturers.

The higher flexibility of users in using existing solution-related information from other domains can be explained by the fact that they typically do not need to account for the commercial potential of a solution. They neither have to consider negative implications of a new solution for a product brand or a firm image nor do they have to bother about the serviceability and the reparability of their solutions to the same extent as if they wanted to sell their innovation. In addition innovating end users are often unconcerned about regulatory requirements, safety standards, and sometimes even ignore property rights (von Hippel 2005). Another important reason explaining why users might face relatively lower transfer barriers is that they do not realize sunk costs. Unlike manufacturers, users have rarely invested in specialized assets that would become obsolete by the advent of a new solution. In sum, users not aiming at commercializing their inventions have to account for a lower number of restrictions and negative side effects than manufacturers. This constitutes a clear advantage of users regarding the creative re-use of general assets and the flexible transfer of prior knowledge across domains.

The following example from the medical field illustrates this nicely (Kane et al. 2009; McGuire 2008): A physician in the ER of a hospital had to solve a puzzling clinical situation. He needed to remove an angled serrated saw blade from a patient's hand and wondered how this could be done without damaging the surrounding tissue. Turning to an online community of doctors he was active in, the physician received a pragmatic solution within a short period of time. Another ER doctor suggested a method involving a drinking straw. The straw was to be slit along its side and placed underneath the serration of the blade, a solution likened to a sheath or a shoehorn. This allowed the physician to pull the blade out without damaging the finger.

This example also highlights another clear advantage of users in the process of solution development: Users often have direct and free access to solution-related knowledge held by others. Users are increasingly embedded in (virtual) user networks and engaged in (online) user communities (Füller et al. 2007; Baldwin et al. 2006; Lüthje et al. 2005; Franke and Shah 2003). Many of these networks are not exclusively dedicated to one single, narrowly defined knowledge domain but are rather interdisciplinary in nature. They comprise members from diverse (sub-) disciplines within a wider field of interest. One example of an interdisciplinary community in the medical field is the social networking site Sermo.com. The community is open to physicians and has 115,000 members from 68 medical specialties. Ozmosis, radRounds, and SpineConnect are other prominent examples of communities in the medical field. In communities with a broad scope, users are likely to interchange information about solutions from different medical fields, thereby becoming familiar with solutions existing in other areas of application. The following example depicts the value of user networks that cut across the borders of neighboring use fields and application areas: Dr. R. specializes in foot surgery. Through long experience in replacing and fixing torn tendons, Dr. R.realized that the methods and tools available in the market were unsatisfactory, as the process of positioning the tendon was cumbersome and there was a high risk of damaging it during the surgery. Dr. R. developed a method and a guiding device that allowed for significant reductions in surgery time as well as better protection of the tendon. The new method was partly based on solution elements formerly not applied in the target field but well-established in other areas of medical treatment. Some of these solution principles were transferred by the inventor himself. Other important solution elements were suggested by colleagues working in the field of orthopedics. Studying a sample of 196 user innovations in medical technology, Hüner et al. (2011) found support for the importance of these professional networks: 33 percent of the surveyed users stated that they received important knowledge for their innovation from colleagues working in other medical fields. To conclude, by engaging in broadly oriented user communities, users will be exposed to solutions and practices from other application areas which will help them identify new solutions and evaluate their transfer potential to the inventive problem at hand (Kalogerakis et al. 2010).

The rationale of manufactures for engaging in online user communities (e.g., see Bonaccorsi and Rossi 2003) may provoke conflicts in their interaction with users (Dahlander and Magnusson 2005), thereby making it difficult for producers to access these rich sources of solution information. Manufacturers and users would need to establish trust and agree on interaction norms and issues of ownership (O'Mahony 2003; Ridings et al. 2002). It seems, however, that manufacturers are intensifying their efforts for establishing fruitful cooperation models with users and user communities (e.g., see Jeppesen and Frederiksen 2006). In addition manufacturers are increasingly getting access to external knowledge through open innovation platforms (Pisano and Verganti 2008). On these platforms, manufacturers have the possibility of inviting external contributors, such as product and service users, to develop concepts and prototypes for specific, predefined innovation tasks (Bogers et al. 2010; Verona et al. 2006).

Testing and Refining Solutions

After developing a first prototype, users and manufacturers typically enter into a phase of testing and refining in order to improve the reliability, functionality, and usability of their innovations (Ozer 1999). Lower testing costs of users relative to manufacturers could originate from advantages regarding running the tests and/or advantages linked with the analysis of test results.

The first user advantage might be realized when running the test experiments, namely when operating prototypes in appropriate test environments to learn about their performance. The users' test beds usually are their everyday use environments in which they carry out their use activities anyway. Users therefore have "a low-cost laboratory for testing and comparing different solutions" (von Hippel 2005: 75). In extreme cases, the users themselves may "be the lab," meaning that they can test an innovative concept on themselves without the need for any test environment at all. Again, this is illustrated by an example from the medical field. Dr. Mu., a trained dentist, jaw and facial surgeon, as well as anesthetist, developed a method of applying sedatives via a Band-Aid. The method allowed for a pain-free and economical administration of sedatives, thereby avoiding the negative impact of general anesthesia on the cardiovascular system of patients. One challenge was to clarify if sedatives could be administered transdermally at all and if the resulting anesthetic effect would last long enough for surgical procedures. Dr. Mu. resorted to blind-testing the Band-Aid alongside a placebo on his wife (a trained operating room nurse and dentist) and himself. In doing so, he could establish the viability of the concept without incurring any monetary expenses and without having to recruit test subjects.

The important role of free-test laboratories can be appreciated in examples demonstrating that users have to run several repeated experiments until they reach an appropriate solution. Consider the example of a mountain biker who developed a foam ring around the pedal axle near the crank to add friction so that the pedals are prevented from free-spinning when taking the feet off during jumps (Lüthje et al. 2005). This user reported that he had to test several alternative concepts and then iteratively refined the solution approach chosen. After all, the user-innovator needed to determine the best type of foam to use, how much material to use, where to place it exactly etc. A very similar example that depicts the high need for iterative and repeated testing is the aforementioned development of a tooth extraction device. The necessary force to be applied for tooth root extraction from the human jaw decreases the more the tooth is luxated before extraction. As both, extensive luxation and extreme traction force would harm the surrounding gum tissue, the inventor had to find an appropriate compromise between the two attributes. He needed several tests until he was able to find a balance that was efficient and minimized the damage to the gum. As the optimal ratio was strongly depending on the state of the tooth to be extracted and the properties of the surrounding tissue, the frequent and diverse exposure of treatment cases allowed the user to considerably speed up the complex field test process.

All these anecdotes highlight that users do not have to create a test environment; it already exists in the context of ordinary product use practice. Users therefore face low variable costs of experimentation. This enables users to engage in an iterative trial-and-error process and incremental learning by doing (von Hippel and Katz 2002; von Hippel 2001; von Hippel and Tyre 1995). If the costs of experimentation are low, the amount of information learned in each trial and error cycle can be rather small, and still the experiment is efficient. Consequently users can make only slight variations in just small parts of their prototypes in order to better understand the causality between the variations of the model design and its performance during the test. Such a procedure reduces the problem-solving complexity and may lead to more sophisticated user-generated solutions. While users may be at a disadvantage when it comes to testing large numbers of prototypes, they are clearly in a better position than manufacturers whenever prototypes have to be tested in many different use situations or under different environmental conditions. We interpret the possibility of engaging in iterative and incremental learning in various conditions as a significant advantage of users when compared to other innovator groups who have to bear higher variable costs in the course of test trials.

Aside from running trials at low costs, users may have an advantage in analyzing and interpreting the test results. The outcomes generated through usage tests have properties of sticky information if test users find it difficult to articulate feedback on their test experiences. Test users might feel that something is wrong about the prototype but are unable to point out what it is and how it should be modified. This is illustrated by the example of Dr. Mo., a surgeon specializing in oral, jaw, and facial surgery, who developed a system for bone segment navigation for the precise positioning of bone segments during surgical procedures. The system was extensively tested by himself and colleagues working in the same medical department. During testing, his colleagues stated that they had difficulties grasping the visual display of the bones making it difficult to reduce the distance between the current position of a bone segment and its desired position. Unfortunately, they were not able to specifically articulate what element of the visualization was actually causing this problem. It was only through his own use experience that Dr. Mo. was able to interpret the answers of his colleagues. He reprogrammed parts of the software to provide two additional forms of data display.

Manufacturer laboratories for testing prototypes have undergone considerable changes supported by developments in information technology. Methods such as rapid prototyping and simulations have substantially lowered the variable cost of experimentation, allowing manufacturers to greatly improve the efficiency of testing large numbers of different prototypes (Thomke et al. 1998). This potentially puts them at an advantage over users when the number of prototypes is very large. However, both methods typically require considerable up-front investments in equipment, software and know-how. What is more, the outcomes of the tests will only be as accurate as the information on which the simulation and the prototype are based. Therefore, there is still a need to properly understand the use environment with all the factors potentially influencing the appropriateness of the innovation to be developed. As indicated earlier, information on complex use contexts is often sticky as it is hard to assess its relevance in advance. In addition it seems hard to believe that manufactures should be able to develop a leading-edge skill level needed (e.g., sport skills, surgery expertise) to engage in sophisticated learning-by-doing and realistic field tests (Shah 2000). Manufacturers may therefore be forced to integrate users to recreate realistic test environments. This strategy, however, entails considerable costs. For example, several manufacturers of medical devices have recently built and equipped own hybrid operating rooms on their premises, allowing them to obtain customer feedback on modern operating room technology (Medica 2010, Maquet 2006). The cost for setting up such modern facilities is estimated to amount to 2 to 3 million USD (Koll 2010).

Conclusions

It is increasingly evident that users frequently modify and develop products and services, although they rarely pursue benefits from selling their inventions. This initially puzzling observation is partly explained by considering additional private benefits, other than selling, that users reap from innovating. By drawing on existing empirical studies and anecdotal evidence from the medical field, we argued that another explanation for the high level of user innovation activities is rooted in the innovation-related relative cost advantages over manufacturers that users often enjoy. They have the incentive as well as the possibility to innovate in low-cost innovation niches during all the phases of an innovation process. In contrast to this, the need to meet regulatory requirements and to strategically invest in new resources and capabilities to maintain future competitiveness may put manufacturers in a less favorable cost position than users.

It is reasonable to assume that a significant part of all existing user innovations would have never been developed by producers, as users often breed solutions only meeting the needs of very few. And this is positive. As argued in this chapter, users are particularly efficient when they work on problems deeply rooted in their specific use context and when they develop innovations closely linked to their idiosyncratic needs. If manufacturers decided to develop all these specific innovations, it would very likely be welfare reducing. In most cases, the marginal costs of the idiosyncratic innovation would probably exceed the marginal benefit. Manufacturers instead develop innovations which appeal to a broader set of potential customers and meet high standards in terms of reliability, serviceability, and conformity with regulatory requirements. And rational users will rarely decide to replicate or substitute innovation activities requiring considerable investments in knowledge production or equipment to develop and to generate a desired innovation. Even if users can definitely contribute valuable input to those innovations as well, they will rarely have cost advantages for *entirely* generating new products and services of this type. To sum up, the relative cost advantages of users and manufacturers lead to a welfare enhancing division of labor through which innovations tend to be generated by the most efficient innovator.

It is sometimes argued that dispersed user innovation may still show inefficiencies because it involves redundant innovation effort. Many users may work in parallel on very similar problems without knowing about the related activities of other users. The risk of redundant efforts cannot be dismissed. There are, however, arguments that parallel effort is not necessarily equivalent to redundant or useless work. First, challenging innovation problems may require more than one user (team) in order to be solved. The mere number of problem solvers engaged in parallel efforts will increase the probability of finding an appropriate solution to a focal innovation task. Given that users tend to freely reveal their innovations—very often at low costs on the Internet—the best solution may have good chances of subsequently diffusing in the user population and "winning" the unintended competition. Second, although different users may work on problems that appear to be very similar, not all involved users may need exactly the same solution. There is often not one best solution fitting the needs of all users in all relevant use conditions.

To conclude, innovating users exploiting their distinctive cost advantages can be interpreted as a virtue for the efficiency of innovation systems as they complement producer innovation by providing solutions to idiosyncratic needs at low cost. A recent research conducted in whitewater kayaking is the first study to provide quantitative data on a direct comparison of the efficiency of consumer and producer innovation (Hienerth et al. 2011). The clear indication of significant advantages on the users' side suggests that more research is needed to measure the relative efficiency of user innovation activities. The Hienerth et al. (2011) study also highlights that it is promising to further investigate under which conditions or for which types of innovation users may constitute a particularly efficient source of innovation.

Note

1. Admittedly, researchers have also documented several examples of users commercializing their own innovations. Capturing economic benefit beyond that derived from the own use is therefore not impossible. However, most activities toward commercialization of user innovations happen in a process that Shah and Tripsas (2007) coined as "accidental entrepreneurship." Their findings clearly show that the entrepreneurial intent of users tends to come *after* solution development and that users were typically not aware that "'just' a useful idea could be a commercial opportunity" (Shah and Tripsas 2007: 130).

References

Baldwin, C., E. von Hippel, and C. Hienerth. 2006. How user innovations become commercial products: A theoretical investigation and case study. *Research Policy* 35 (9): 1291–1313.

Barney, J. 1991. Firm resources and sustained competitive advantage. *Journal of Management* 17 (1): 99–120.

Bogers, M., A. Afuah, and B. Bastian. 2010. Users as innovators: A review, critique, and future research directions. *Journal of Management* 36 (4): 857–75.

Bonaccorsi, A., and C. Rossi. 2003. Why open source software can succeed. *Research Policy* 32 (7): 1243–58.

Cohen, W. M., and D. A. Levinthal. 1990. Absorptive capacity: A new perspective on learning and innovation. *Administrative Science Quarterly* 35 (1): 128–52.

Dahlander, L., and M. G. Magnusson. 2005. Relationships between open source software companies and communities: Observations from Nordic firms. *Research Policy* 34 (4): 481–93.

Fleming, L., S. Mingo, and D. Chen. 2007. Collaborative brokerage, generative creativity, and creative success. *Administrative Science Quarterly* 52 (3): 443–75.

Franke, N., M. Schreier, and U. Kaiser. 2010. The "I designed it myself" effect in mass customization. *Management Science* 56 (1): 125–40.

Franke, N., and S. Shah. 2003. How communities support innovative activities: An exploration of assistance and sharing among end-users. *Research Policy* 32 (1): 157–78.

Füller, J. 2006. Why consumers engage in virtual new product developments initiated by producers. *Advances in Consumer Research. Association for Consumer Research (U. S.)* 33 (1): 639–46.

Füller, J., G. Jawecki, and H. Mühlbacher. 2007. Innovation creation by online basketball communities. *Journal of Business Research* 60 (1): 60–71.

Harhoff, D., J. Henkel, and E. von Hippel. 2003. Profiting from voluntary information spillovers: How users benefit by freely revealing their innovations. *Research Policy* 32 (10): 1753–69.

Helfat, C. E. 1994. Evolutionary trajectories in petroleum firm R&D. *Management Science* 40 (12): 1720–47.

Hienerth, C., E. von Hippel, and M. Berg Jensen. 2011. Innovation as consumption: Analysis of consumers' innovation efficiency. Working paper 4926–11. Sloan School of Management, MIT. Available at SSRN: http://ssrn.com/abstract =1916319.

Hüner, A., C. Stockstrom, and C. Lüthje. 2011. An empirical analysis of user innovation in the medical devices industry. In *IPDMC. 18th International Product Development Management Conference.* Delft.

Jeppesen, L.B., and L. Frederiksen, L. 2006. Why do users contribute to firm-hosted user communities? The case of computer-controlled music instruments. *Organization Science* 17 (1): 45–63.

Kalogerakis, K., C. Lüthje, and C. Herstatt. 2010. Developing innovations based on analogies: Experience from design and engineering consultants. *Journal of Product Innovation Management* 27 (3): 418–36.

Kane, G.C., R.G. Fichman, J. Gallaugher, and J. Glaser, J. 2009. Community Relations 2.0. *Harvard Business Review* 87 (11): 45–50.

Koll, S. 2010. *Der OP der Zukunft. www.industrieanzeiger.de.*

Leonard, D., and J. F. Rayport. 1997. Spark innovation through empathic design. *Harvard Business Review* 75 (6): 102–13.

Lüthje, C. 2003. Customers as co-inventors: An empirical analysis of the antecedents of customer-driven innovations in the field of medical equipment. In *Proceedings of the 32nd EMAC Conference.* Glasgow.

Lüthje, C. 2004. Characteristics of innovating users in a consumer goods field: An empirical study of sport-related product consumers. *Technovation* 24 (9): 683–95.

Lüthje, C., and C. Herstatt. 2004. The lead user method: An outline of empirical findings and issues for future research. *R&D Management* 34 (5): 553–68.

Lüthje, C., C. Herstatt, and E. von Hippel. 2005. User-innovators and "local" information: The case of mountain biking. *Research Policy* 34 (6): 951–65.

Lüthje, C., A. Hüner, and C. Stockstrom. 2010. Knowledge base and technological impact of user innovations: Empirical evidence from the medical devices industry. In *IPDMC. 17th International Product Development Management Conference,* Murcia.

Maquet. 2006. MAQUET Surgical Academy. *Healthcare Purchasing News* 30 (4): 10.

Martin, X., and W. Mitchell. 1998. The influence of local search and performance heuristics on new design introduction in a new product market. *Research Policy* 26 (7/8): 753–71.

McGuire, S. 2008. The cutting edge. *Medical Marketing and Media* 43 (1): 55–56.

Medica. 2010. MAQUET eröffnet Hybrid-Operationssaal in der Surgical Academy. *Medica.de*: 13.09.2010.

Morrison, P. D., J. H. Roberts, and E. von Hippel. 2000. Determinants of user innovation and innovation sharing in a local market. *Management Science* 46 (12): 1513–27.

Nelson, R. R. 1982. The role of knowledge in R&D efficiency. *Quarterly Journal of Economics* 97 (3): 453–70.

O'Mahony, S. 2003. Guarding the commons: How community managed software projects protect their work. *Research Policy* 32 (7): 1179–98.

Olson, E. L., and G. Bakke. 2001. Implementing the lead user method in a high technology firm: A longitudinal study of intentions versus actions. *Journal of Product Innovation Management* 18 (6): 388–95.

Ozer, M. 1999. A survey of new product evaluation models. *Journal of Product Innovation Management* 16 (1): 77–94.

Pettypiece, S. 2007. Pfizer to assess doctors' opinions using Sermo networking site. *Bloomberg.com*: October 15, 2007.

Pisano, G. P., and R. Verganti. 2008. Which kind of collaboration is right for you? *Harvard Business Review* 86 (12): 78–86.

Polanyi, M. 1983. *The Tacit Dimension*. Gloucester, MA: Smith.

Ridings, C. M., D. Gefen, and B. Arinze. 2002. Some antecedents and effects of trust in virtual communities. *Journal of Strategic Information Systems* 11 (3/4): 271–95.

Riggs, W., and E. von Hippel. 1994. Incentives to innovate and the sources of innovation: The case of scientific instruments. *Research Policy* 23 (4): 459–469.

Rosenkopf, L., and A. Nerkar. 2001. Beyond local search: Boundary-spanning, exploration, and impact in the optical disk industry. *Strategic Management Journal* 22 (4): 287–306.

Shah, S. 2000. Sources and patterns of innovation in a consumer products field: Innovations in sporting equipment. Working paper 4105. Sloan School of Management, MIT.

Shah, S. K., and M. Tripsas. 2007. The accidental entrepreneur: the emergent and collective process of user entrepreneurship. *Strategic Entrepreneurship Journal* 1 (1–2): 123–140.

Slaughter, S. 1993. Innovation and Learning during Implementation: A Comparison of User and Manufacturer Innovations. *Research Policy* 22 (1): 81–95.

Stuart, T. E., and J. M. Podolny. 1996. Local search and the evolution of technological capabilities. *Strategic Management Journal* 17 (S1): 21–38.

Thomke, S., E. von Hippel, and R. Franke. 1998. Modes of experimentation: An innovation process and competitive variable. *Research Policy* 27 (3): 315–32.

Tietz, R., P. D. Morrison, C. Lüthje, and C. Herstatt. 2005. The process of user-innovation: A case study in a consumer goods setting. *International Journal of Product Development* 2 (4): 321–38.

Verona, G., E. Prandelli, and M. Sawhney. 2006. Innovation and virtual environments: Towards virtual knowledge brokers. *Organization Studies* 27 (6): 765–88.

von Hippel, Eric. 1986. Lead users: A source of novel product concepts. *Management Science* 32 (7): 791–805.

von Hippel, Eric. 1988. *The Sources of Innovation*. New York: Oxford University Press.

von Hippel, Eric. 1994. "Sticky information" and the locus of problem solving: Implications for innovation. *Management Science* 40 (4): 429–39.

von Hippel, Eric. 1998. Economics of product development by users: The impact of "sticky" local information. *Management Science* 44 (5): 629–44.

von Hippel, Eric, and M. J. Tyre. 1995. How learning by doing is done: Problem identification in novel process equipment. *Research Policy* 24 (1): 1–12.

von Hippel, E. 2001. User toolkits for innovation. *Journal of Product Innovation Management* 18 (4): 247–57.

von Hippel, E. 2005. *Democratizing Innovation*. Cambridge: MIT Press.

von Hippel, E., and R. Katz. 2002. Shifting innovation to users via toolkits. *Management Science* 48 (7): 821–33.

von Krogh, G., and E. von Hippel. 2006. The promise of research on open source software. *Management Science* 52 (7): 975–83.

Wernerfelt, B. 1984. A resource-based view of the firm. *Strategic Management Journal* 5 (2): 171–80.

4

The Empirical Scope of User Innovation

Jeroen P. J. de Jong

User innovation refers to innovations developed by end users rather than by producers. User-innovators can be either firms or individual consumers. They are distinguished from producer-innovators by the fact that they expect to benefit from their innovation efforts by using a product or a service. All others, lumped together under the term *producers*, only benefit from innovation by selling their output, by licensing or product commercialization (von Hippel 2005). Any firm or individual can be a producer or user-innovator in specific situations. For example, Sony is a manufacturer of electronic equipment, but it is also a user of machine tools. With respect to the innovations that it develops for its electronic products, Sony is considered a producer-innovator, but if we would investigate innovations in its machinery or production processes, the company may qualify as a user-innovator. Likewise, an individual inventor developing a new transport device for manually disabled people would be a producer-innovator, but if he would develop the device primarily for personal use (being manually impaired), he would be a user-innovator.

Empirical user innovation studies have concluded that the most significant innovations in many fields were originally developed by users. It has also been shown that substantial shares of users engage in innovation, that their innovations are generally unconstrained by intellectual property, and that their innovations serve a general interest, namely diffuse to other economic actors, which increases social welfare (von Hippel 2005). Although these results are compelling, empirical evidence has usually been collected for very specific cases. von Hippel's earlier work demonstrating the significance of users as a source of functionally novel innovations was concerned with scientific instruments, automated clinical chemistry analyzers and pultrusion processes (e.g., see von Hippel 1976).

Likewise, when summarizing empirical evidence on the share of user-innovators, von Hippel (2005) cited studies of printed circuit CAD software, pipe hanger hardware, library information systems, surgical equipment, outdoor consumer products, and mountain biking equipment. A general criticism is that this work does not generalize to larger populations. As von Hippel (2005: 20) observed:

[E]ach of the studies looked at innovation rates affecting a particular product type among users who care a great deal about that product type . . . university surgeons care a great deal about having just-right surgical equipment, just as serious mountain bikers care a great deal about having just-right equipment for their sport. As the intensity of interest goes down, it is likely that rates of user innovation drop too.

A hostile critic might conclude that given the specific samples, user innovation is actually rather marginal. This is one of the reasons that researchers recently started to explore the incidence and diffusion of user innovation in broad samples, including businesses and individual end consumers. In this chapter, I review and discuss this emerging literature.

Thus this chapter takes stock of recent empirical work on the incidence and diffusion of user innovations. First, I summarize empirical evidence on the share of user-innovators in broad samples of firms and consumers. A general finding is that 15 to 20 percent of all firms are user-innovators, while in samples of consumers this range is 4 to 6 percent. For samples of firms, I will also discuss to what extent user innovation overlaps with process innovation, as this alternative innovation indicator is already present in the official statistics. Second, findings regarding the protection of user innovations with intellectual property rights are discussed. In consumer populations very few innovators apply for these—they rather share their work for free or don't bother about diffusion at all. In businesses the application of intellectual property rights is more substantial, but rarely exceeds 50 percent. Third, I review to what extent and how user innovations diffuse to other economic actors. Part of their innovations appears to be useful to others; that is, depending on the sample, 5 to 25 percent is adopted by other users or by commercial producers for further development and commercial sale. In summary, recent empirical evidence indicates that user innovation is widely present and suggests that it is economically meaningful. I end with some concluding remarks regarding the implications of recent empirical findings for measurement and policy.

Incidence of User Innovation

In Over the past few years a new line of research has emerged in which user innovation has been measured in broad samples of firms and individual end consumers.

In the case of innovating firms a legitimate question is to what extent user innovation resembles with process innovation. Why do we need separate indicators? Innovating user firms modify existing techniques, equipment or software for in-house use, or create those entirely from scratch for internal purposes (von Hippel 2005). Conceptually, user innovation can be expected to overlap with traditional process innovation indicators. More specifically, user innovation should be a subset of process innovation. The Oslo Manual, which guides statistical offices in collecting and interpreting innovation data with CIS surveys, defines process innovation as "the implementation of a new or significantly improved production or delivery method. This includes significant changes in techniques, equipment and/or software" (OECD/Eurostat 2005: para 163). However, the manual sets a low threshold for what qualifies as an innovation: "[T]he minimum requirement . . . is that the . . . process . . . must be new or significantly improved to the firm. This includes . . . processes and methods . . . that have been adopted from other firms or organizations" (para. 148). Accordingly, to qualify as a process innovator, it is sufficient to adopt a piece of technique, equipment or software, while user innovation excludes adoption, and requires some kind of development effort and functional novelty.

I argue that it is important to distinguish user innovation from broader process innovation indicators. Past studies have shown that user innovations are marked by functional novelty (e.g., Riggs and von Hippel 1994), provide an important feedstock for commercial producers' new product development efforts (Lilien et al. 2002; de Jong and von Hippel 2009), can lead to new venture creation and the emergence of new industries (Shah and Tripsas 2007), are more likely to be commercially attractive and serve the needs of other users (Franke and von Hippel 2003), and enhance social welfare (Henkel and von Hippel 2005). In contrast, when process innovations are adoptions, these benefits would barely or not apply.

For individual end consumers, the situation is different. User innovation by consumers is not at all recorded in official surveys, and until recently it could be considered dark matter—unmeasured, and so impossible to include in economic or policymaking analyses. Table 4.1 lists the survey studies that researchers have done to identify user-innovators in broad samples of firms and consumers.

Samples of Firms

An early study identifying user innovation in a sample of firms was done by Arundel and Sonntag (1999). Back in 1998, as part of their survey of Advanced Manufacturing Technologies, Statistics Canada sampled manufacturing plants with at least 10 employees. Among other questions, data were collected on the adoption, modification and development of specific technologies. From their findings it can be inferred that 41.0 percent of the Canadian manufacturing plants went beyond the adoption of technologies "off-the-shelf," but modified existing technologies to better fit their internal needs, or developed their own technologies from scratch for application in their operations.[1] In 2007 the AMT survey was updated by Schaan and Uhrbach (2009). From their findings it can be estimated that 39.8 percent of the Canadian manufacturing plants with >20 employees and >$250K revenues were user-innovators—close to Arundel and Sonntag's original finding.

Another project to measure user innovation was done in the Netherlands, drawing on computer-assisted telephone interviewing. In 2007, de Jong and von Hippel (2009) piloted questions in a panel of high-tech SMEs. They utilized two indicators of the presence of user innovation: (1) had the firm developed new process equipment or software for its own use; (2) had the firm modified existing process equipment or software for its own use within the past three years. Next respondents were asked to select their most recent innovation and report what it was about (open-ended question). After cleaning the data for falsely identified cases, 54.0 percent of the sample appeared to be user-innovators.

This survey method gave rise to a second type of user innovation indicators in which respondents are first asked whether they innovated in software or physical products, and if they created their innovation from

Table 4.1
Share of user-innovators in broad samples of firms and consumers

Source	Country	Year	Sample	Estimate
Firm surveys				
Arundel and Sonntag (1999)	Canada	1998	3,702 manufacturing plants with >10 employees	41.0%
Schaan and Uhrbach (2009)	Canada	2007	6,478 manufacturing plants with >20 employees and $250K revenues	39.8%
De Jong and von Hippel (2009)	Netherlands	2007	498 high-tech SMEs with <100 employees	54.0%
De Jong and von Hippel (2008)	Netherlands	2008	2,416 small firms with <100 employees	21.0%
Flowers et al. (2010)	United Kingdom	2009	1,004 SMEs with 10–250 employees	15.3%
Kim and Kim (2011)	South Korea	2009	3,081 manufacturers with >10 employees	17.7%
Consumer surveys				
von Hippel et al. (2012)	United Kingdom	2009	1,173 individual end consumers ≥18 years	6.1%
De Jong (2011)	Netherlands	2010	533 consumers ≥18 years	6.2%
Ogawa and Pongtalanert (2011)	USA	2010	1,992 consumers ≥18 years	5.2%
Ogawa and Pongtalanert (2011)	Japan	2011	2,000 consumers ≥18 years	3.7%
Kuusisto et al. (2013)	Finland	2012	993 consumers of 18–65 years	5.4%
de Jong (2013)	Canada	2013	2,021 consumers ≥18 years	5.6%

Note: Reported frequencies are population estimates, with the exception of de Jong and von Hippel (2009) and Ogawa and Pongtalanert (2011).

scratch or by modifying an existing product. Survey scripts would follow up with open-ended questions to obtain a detailed description of what the firms have done, and why. These descriptions were then screened to eliminate "false positives"—reported examples that are in fact not innovations. Finally, additional false positives were eliminated via additional questions, namely if respondents know of equivalent products already available on the market, and if they developed their innovations for customers (which would make the example a product innovation). De Jong and von Hippel's (2008) study of 2,416 small- and medium-sized enterprises was a next application of this method. In this sample (covering all commercial industries including agriculture, manufacturing, construction, retail, trade, financial services, business services, personal services, and hotels and restaurants) 21.0 percent of all Dutch SMEs was estimated to be a user-innovator.

In the United Kingdom, Flowers and colleagues (2010) applied the same method to document user innovation by SMEs with 10 to 250 employees. They found that in the past three years, 15.3 percent of the businesses developed or modified hardware or software for their own process-related needs, without similar offerings being available on the market. This was the equivalent of 30,500 companies. Even more interesting is that Flowers et al. followed up on respondents' most recent innovations to record their time and money expenditures. They found that for every user innovation, companies spent on average 107 person-days and £44,500 in out-of-pocket costs. When evaluated at the average salary for UK workers, this represented an annual spending on user innovation of £1.7 billion. It was also estimated that the annual R&D-spending by similar firms was £2.6 billion, indicating that investments in user innovation are not marginal.

An alternative method was applied by Kim and Kim (2011) in a sample of manufacturing firms with more than 10 employees in South Korea. Their study represents a third type of survey method which first uses the national Community Innovation Survey (CIS) to identify potential user-innovators. The CIS identifies process innovators, and also if process innovations were developed in-house (OECD/Eurostat 2005). These process innovators can be contacted for a follow-up survey to see if they are truly user-innovators, and to collect data on their innovation processes.

Applying this method Kim and Kim found that 17.7 percent had engaged in user innovation in the past three years.

The aforementioned surveys share some common findings. First and foremost, the frequency of user innovation in firm surveys is substantial, even in broad samples of small firms. Second, user innovation appears to be contingent on firm size, industry types and technical capabilities. Larger organizations are more process-intensive, which calls for in-house innovation, and indeed studies report that the frequency of user innovation increases with size (e.g., de Jong and von Hippel 2008; Flowers et al. 2010). For industry types, generally manufacturers are more process intensive and likely to innovate for their own process-related needs (e.g., de Jong and von Hippel 2009). For technical capability, it has been found that high-tech firms are more likely to innovate (e.g., de Jong and von Hippel 2009). In general, these explanations are well in line with the broader literature on firms' process innovation (e.g., Cohen and Klepper 1996; Levin et al. 1987).

A third finding is that, although user innovation is conceptually a subset of process innovation, this does not show up in empirical analyses. De Jong and von Hippel (2008) found that 10 percent of the firms in their sample were user-innovators, but had responded negatively to the CIS process innovation indicator. They concluded that "user innovation apparently measures . . . innovation that remains hidden" (de Jong and von Hippel 2008: 16–17). In more recent surveys similar findings were obtained (Schaan and Uhrbach 2009; Flowers et al. 2010). These results stress the importance of collecting separate indicators for user innovation, and also to initiate follow-up studies on the ability of official surveys to capture all (process) innovation activities by firms.

Samples of Consumers

More recently researchers have started to explore user innovation in samples of individual end consumers. Consumers may innovate in their leisure time by creating and/or modifying everyday items for their own benefit.

The first survey to empirically estimate the frequency of user innovation in a broad sample of consumers was done by von Hippel et al. (2012). While collecting data from 1,173 UK consumers aged 18 and over, their methodology was inspired by the UK survey of SMEs mentioned in table

4.1. The survey was done by computer-assisted telephone interviewing. It started by asking consumers whether they had created and/or modified software in the past three years, then ditto for the creation and/or modification of hardware. For each of these options open-ended questions were asked to exclude false positives (e.g., "I bought a piece of Ikea furniture and put it together myself.") Additional false positives were eliminated via analysis of responses to two screening questions. If respondents knew of equivalent products already available on the market, or if they had developed the innovation as part of their jobs, their claimed innovations were excluded. In effect, the survey was designed to identify only innovations with some kind of functional novelty that consumers had developed in their leisure time.

von Hippel and colleagues (2012) estimated that 6.1 percent of the UK consumer population had engaged in user innovation in the past three years. This is the equivalent of 2.9 million individuals aged 18 and over. Additionally the researchers had asked respondents to identify their most recent innovation example and to report how much time and money they had spent on it. Innovating consumers on average spent 7.1 days and £1,098 out-of-pocket costs per year. At the macro level and when evaluating person-days at average UK workforce salaries, total annual spending by consumers on innovation was estimated to £3.2 billion. In comparison, estimated annual R&D expenditures by companies on consumer products were £2.2 billion. Although R&D does not represent all producers' innovation expenditures, these findings suggest that user innovation cannot be neglected.

Other consumer surveys have come to similar conclusions. De Jong (2011) organized a survey of Dutch consumers aged 18 and over. In applying a slightly different survey method (providing more specific cues to improve recall, but still including open-ended and other screening questions to filter out false positives), I found that 6.2 percent of the Dutch consumer population had engaged in user innovation in the past three years. Subsequently Ogawa and Pongtalanert (2011) organized replication studies in the United States and Japan, and found user innovation frequencies of 5.2 and 3.7 percent, respectively. They also included time and money questions in their surveys, and estimated that in both countries consumers are spending billions of dollars on innovation. Moreover in recent studies in Finland (Kuusisto et al. 2013) and Canada (de Jong

2013), a more or less standardized methodology emerged to adequately measure user innovation in broad samples of consumers. The method first offers a list of specific cues, including computer software, household fixtures and furnishing, tools and equipment, and more. For each the respondent indicates if she/he has created an innovation in the past three years to satisfy his/her personal needs, then a list of questions is asked to eliminate false positives (for details, see Kuusisto et al. 2013). Applying this method, the share of innovating consumers were 5.4 percent in Finland and 5.6 percent in Canada, respectively.

Consumer surveys show that in absolute numbers, many consumers develop or modify products for personal use, and spend considerable time and money on it. It has also been found that user innovation frequency varies with gender, education attainment, and technical training. Males are generally more likely to be innovating consumers, and the same applies to those with higher education and technical training (von Hippel et al. 2011). Obviously, education and training reflect personal capability for innovation: Highly educated engineers are most likely capable of developing fixes for their personal problems.

Openness of User Innovation

Beyond the frequency of user innovation, a key question is to what extent user innovations spread (are meaningful to others and of economic value). In this regard surveys have explored if users protect their innovation-related knowledge with intellectual property rights. In the traditional, linear model of innovation, it is assumed that innovations originate from producers and are supplied to consumers via goods that are for sale, so that eventually economic growth and social welfare are enhanced. A potential problem, however, is that private investments in innovation may end up being too low due to knowledge spillovers and the ability of other economic agents to "free-ride" on others' investments (Arrow 1962). As a consequence policy makers offer intellectual property rights (IPRs) so that producer-innovators can secure temporary monopolies to benefit from their efforts (Levin et al. 1987). This creates a situation that we here label as *closed innovation*, namely innovating actors who are potentially restricting further application of their innovation-related knowledge via IPRs.

Compared to innovating producers, user-innovators are generally less concerned with IPRs. They innovate primarily for personal need or in-house use benefits, and do not need to conquer a market to recoup their innovation investments. Moreover user innovation does not automatically imply the presence of a big market of other users facing sufficiently similar needs. Producers generally employ product development strategies to meet the needs of homogeneous market segments. This strategy of "few sizes fit all" leaves many user firms and end consumers dissatisfied with commercial products on offer so that they are triggered to innovate for themselves (von Hippel 2005), but then user needs can be pretty diverse so that applying for IPRs is less useful.

We define *open innovation* as innovation without intellectual property. It might be preferable from a social welfare perspective, as the application of IPRs does not seem to result in net economic value in many fields (Bessen and Meurer 2008). To explore the openness of user innovation, most of the surveys discussed above asked respondents if they had protected their innovations with IPRs—including patents, copyrights, trademarks, and the application of confidentiality agreements. Results for both firm and consumer samples are shown in table 4.2.

In their survey of high-tech SMEs, de Jong and von Hippel (2009) identified 364 user innovation cases for which they asked respondents (business owners or managers) if they had protected their innovation-related knowledge with IPRs. This applied to only 12.5 percent of the cases. In contradiction, other firm surveys reported higher percentages. Schaan and Uhrbach (2009), in a subsequent study of manufacturing plants that had reported to be technology modifiers or technology creators, found that 53.3 percent of their sample protected their knowledge with IPRs. This percentage, however, also included "secrecy" as a protection method. Flowers et al. (2010), analyzing 200 user innovation cases, found that 35.5 percent was protected, and Kim and Kim (2011) found 43.8 percent for South Korean manufacturing firms. In general, the odds of protection seem to increase with firm size, a finding that is further discussed below.

A direct investigation of openness was presented by de Jong (2010). Drawing on a database of high-tech small firms in the Netherlands who had previously developed user innovations, I organized a new survey in which respondents were asked to identify and report on their most recent

Table 4.2

Protection of user innovations with IPRs by firms and consumers

Source	Country	Year	Sample	Protection with IPRs
Firm surveys				
De Jong and von Hippel (2009)	Netherlands	2007	364 user innovations developed by high-tech SMEs with <100 employees	12.5%
Schaan and Uhrbach (2009)	Canada	2008	1,277 user innovations developed by manufacturing plants with > 20 employees and $250K revenues	53.3%
Flowers et al. (2010)	United Kingdom	2009	200 user innovations developed by SMEs with 10–250 employees	35.5%
Kim and Kim (2011)	South Korea	2009	370 user innovations developed by manufacturers with >10 employees	43.8%
De Jong (2010)	Netherlands	2010	81 user innovations developed by high-tech SMEs (<100 employees)	13.6%
Consumer surveys				
von Hippel et al. (2012)	United Kingdom	2009	104 user innovations developed by consumers ≥18 years	1.9%
Ogawa and Pongtalanert (2011)	United States	2010	114 user innovations developed by consumers ≥18 years	8.8%
Ogawa and Pongtalanert (2011)	Japan	2011	83 user innovations developed by consumers ≥18 years	0.0%
Kuusisto et al. (2013)	Finland	2012	176 user innovations developed by consumers of 18–65 years	4.7%
De Jong (2013)	Canada	2013	539 user innovations developed by consumers ≥18 years	2.8%

producer and user innovations. I analyzed only those 81 respondents who had recently engaged in both types of innovations, so that a direct comparison was possible. A first finding was that while high-tech firms were inclined to protect the intellectual property of their new products (60.3 percent), the same firms did not bother about protecting their user innovations (only 13.6 percent protected). Next, in a binary logistic regression model, I controlled for some of the usual determinants of the propensity to protect, including time and money expenditures and innovation collaboration. After adding these controls the distinction between producer and user innovations was still significant at $p < 0.001$. Moreover I found that high-tech small firms were more willing to share their user innovations than their product innovations. Drawing on a multiple-item scale measuring firms' willingness to freely reveal (e.g., "We are willing to share this innovation for free") the average score for product innovations was 1.2, while for user innovations it was 2.3 (minimum = 1.0, maximum = 5.0). These results suggest that user innovation is indeed more open than producer innovation.

In samples of consumers the incidence of protection has been found to be much lower. von Hippel et al. (2012) reported that only two out of 104 consumer innovations were patented. Similar findings were obtained for user innovations by American and Japanese consumers (Ogawa and Pongtalanert 2011), and more recently in Finland (Kuusisto et al. 2013) and Canada (de Jong 2013).

Some tentative conclusions can be drawn based on these surveys. First, user innovation seems more open than producer innovation. This seems most true for consumers, but also for high-tech small firms who are competing with differentiated products rather than unique production processes. A disclaimer, however, is that many of these firms will still not be inclined to freely share their knowledge. Rather than IPRs, they may prefer secrecy as a more effective protection method to exclude rivals from imitation—a similar preference has been documented for the broader category of process innovation (Levin et al. 1987). For larger organizations, findings certainly differ from consumers. In the Canadian, British, and South Korean samples quite a few firms were eager to protect their knowledge. We speculate that especially large manufacturers are more likely to operate in oligopolistic markets where competitive advantage revolves around unique production processes, and then it makes sense to exclude rivals from copying innovative processes.

Diffusion of User Innovation

Finally, the recent surveys have shown that some user innovations spread to others. Past work has documented that user innovations can be valuable to other users. Users and producers generally know different things and accordingly employ different types of knowledge in the innovation process. Users tend to develop innovations that are functionally novel, as they are most aware of where and how commercially available products fail to meet their specific needs. In contrast, producers tend to develop innovations that are improvements on well-known needs, but in which they can apply their superior engineering and design skills to increase robustness, sustainability and technical quality (Riggs and von Hippel 1994).

From a social point of view, it is important that innovations diffuse across society. When innovations are developed by producers, the pathway to diffusion is well known, as producers have a strong incentive to sell what they have developed to all interested consumers and/or firms. Besides, their knowledge will involuntarily spill over to other innovating actors as a consequence of labor mobility, site visits of external actors, and more. Ideally, user innovations should diffuse too, or multiple users with similar needs would need to invest in similar innovations. This would lead to considerable duplication and be inefficient from a social welfare point of view.

In general, three mechanisms have been identified for the diffusion of user innovations. First, users may reveal their innovations to others for inspection, copying and adoption without charge. Second, users may start a new business to introduce a commercial version of their innovation to the market. Third, commercial producers may adopt users' innovations to further improve and sell them as commercial products. Survey evidence for these mechanisms is discussed next.

Free Revealing

Users are less likely to apply for IPRs than producers, but some go even further by actively revealing their innovations for free, so that their innovation-related knowledge becomes a public good. They may do so hoping that commercial producers will adopt and improve their innovations so that more robust and reliable solutions become available. Alternatively, free revealing can be driven by expected recognition of peers and reputation gains, communal norms of reciprocity (i.e., benefit from other users' contributions like in open source software) and the desire to set informal standards (Harhoff et al. 2003).

After early studies demonstrated that users freely share their innovations in specific industries, for example, in medical equipment, open source software, semiconductor process equipment, and mine pumping engines (von Hippel 2005), recent studies find similar results for broad samples. Seven of the previously discussed surveys asked if innovators had revealed the details of their innovations to others for free; see table 4.3.

These empirical findings suggest that many of the innovations developed by users are of interest to the innovator only, or alternatively, the user does not bother about revealing her innovation for any reason (e.g., not considered of general interest, too much time needed to reveal its design on the Internet). However, the table also shows that some innovations are apparently of a more general interest (and diffuse to others; see later). In samples of firms about 10 percent of the user innovations are freely revealed. Beyond this, there is a subset of user firms (not listed in table 4.3) revealing selectively, for example, to close social ties, and/or for nonmonetary compensations like discounts on future orders and other favors. For example, in a sample of innovating high-tech small firms selective revealing was practiced by 13 percent (de Jong and von Hippel 2009).

In consumer samples the share of freely revealed innovations is higher: in the 10 to 30 percent range. This reflects that innovating consumers generally have no direct commercial interests, and do not bother to bargain for compensation or any favors. In fact, many innovating consumers tend to be excited if other people show interest in their solutions and adopt those for personal use (von Hippel et al. 2012). Apparently, recognition by others constitutes a benefit to these innovators.

However, it must be noted that the overall economic impact of user innovation hinges to a large extent on the value that others also gain from adopting those innovations. While 10 to 30 percent of the users reveal their innovations to others, 70 to 90 percent do not—implying that other firms/individuals who may benefit from the same innovation, would need to develop it by themselves again. Kuusisto et al. (2013) argued and found initial evidence that the diffusion of user-developed innovations will be

Table 4.3
Free revealing by firms and consumers, and adoption by other actors (firms or consumers)

Source	Country	Year	Sample	Free revealing	Adoption
Firm surveys					
De Jong and von Hippel (2009)	Netherlands	2007	364 user innovations developed by high-tech SMEs with <100 employees	12.0%	24.7%[b]
Schaan and Uhrbach (2009)	Canada	2007	1,277 user innovations developed by manufacturing plants with >20 employees and $250K revenues	10.9%	26.3%[b]; 25.3%[c]
Flowers et al. (2010)	United Kingdom	2009	200 user innovations developed by SMEs with 10–250 employees	12.5%	19.5%
Kim and Kim (2011)	South Korea	2009	370 user innovations developed by manufacturers with >10 employees	9.5%[a]	3.2%
Consumer surveys					
von Hippel et al. (2012)	United Kingdom	2009	104 user innovations developed by consumers ≥18 years	28.9%	17.1%
Ogawa and Pongtalanert (2011)	USA	2010	114 user innovations developed by consumers ≥18 years	18.4%	6.1%
Ogawa and Pongtalanert (2011)	Japan	2011	83 user innovations developed by consumers ≥18 years	10.8%	5.0%
Kuusisto et al. (2013)	Finland	2012	176 consumer innovations developed by consumers of 18–65 years	26.7%	18.8%
De Jong (2013)	Canada	2013	539 consumer innovations developed by consumers ≥18 years	33.6%	21.2%

a. This percentage reflects companies' willingness to freely reveal.
b. Adoption by commercial producers only.
c. Adoption by other users only.

Table 4.4

Entrepreneurship indicators for user-innovators and broad consumer population

GEM indicator	User-innovators ($N = 33$)	Dutch consumers aged 18–64 ($N = 2,133$)
Entrepreneurial intentions	15.2%	7.4%
Nascent entrepreneurship	9.1%	3.1%
Startup entrepreneurship	3.0%	4.1%
Established entrepreneurship	3.0%	8.0%

Source: De Jong (2011: 56)

negatively affected by a novel type of market failure: Value that others may gain from a user-developed product is an externality from the viewpoint of innovating users, who therefore do not invest effort in supporting diffusion to the extent that would be socially optimal.

New Venture Creation

If users have developed an innovation that other people like, they generally receive requests to build them a copy. Users then sometimes decide to start their own business to commercialize their innovations, and accordingly become producers—despite that they were initially driven by personal need. Examples of entirely new industries which emerged via such a process are juvenile products, rodeo kayaking equipment, and dishwasher machines (Shah and Tripsas 2007).

Systematic empirical studies demonstrating the relationship between user innovation and new venture creation have yet to be undertaken. A first attempt was reported by de Jong (2011). After an extensive screening procedure, I obtained a sample of 33 Dutch consumers who had developed a user innovation in the past three years. Next I analyzed how these innovators performed on various indicators adopted from the Global Entrepreneurship Monitor (GEM) (Hartog et al. 2010). Table 4.4 offers descriptive statistics for user-innovators and all Dutch consumers aged 18 to 64.

I found that user-innovators were more likely to have entrepreneurial intentions and to engage in nascent entrepreneurship. Thus 15.2 percent expected to start a new business within the next three years, and 9.1 percent was actively involved in the process of business creation but had not yet received any income. Within the broad consumer population these percentages were 7.4 and 3.1, respectively. Next I found that user-innovators were less likely to be established entrepreneurs, that is, being an owner/manager of a registered business with salaries or wages being generated for more than 42 months already. Although the sample size is very modest, table 4.4 gives a first hint that user innovation and entrepreneurship are correlated—but obviously these findings do not prove causality. It may be that innovating consumers are more likely to recognize opportunities to build a business and then do so. Alternatively, user innovation and early-stage entrepreneurship may reflect people's general proactivity to take charge and pick up challenges and opportunities in life. More research is needed to explore how these concepts are related.

Adoption by Commercial Producers
The third diffusion mechanism is that commercial producers can take up users' innovations, develop them further, and then introduce them to the market for sale. In an emerging industry user-innovators tend to be most active in the early stages when a homogeneous market need has yet to be identified. Producers typically enter later when sufficient numbers of users can be identified with homogeneous needs (von Hippel et al. 2011).

Survey results regarding frequency of adoption are shown in the right-hand column of table 4.3. Note that most studies did not distinguish between adoption by producers and other users but asked for adoption in a broad sense. In the samples of Dutch high-tech SMEs and Canadian manufacturing plants adoption by commercial producers was around 25 percent of all reported innovations. Moreover Schaan and Uhrbach (2009) found that another 25.3 percent was adopted by other users. For consumers these general adoption rates are lower, namely 5 to 20 percent, but across the globe this would still represent a large number of innovations which are apparently useful to others. The only "outlier" is the South Korean sample in which few manufacturers reported that other business had picked up their inventions. Kim and Kim (2011) argued that this may be due to cultural reasons and the presence of hierarchically organized industry structures (*chaebols*).

In summary, although most user innovations seem of interest to the innovator alone, it is generally found that 5 to 25 percent are useful to other agents and get adopted either in part or as a whole. Adoption of user innovations is definitely also done by commercial producers.

Concluding Remarks

Discussed in this chapter is evidence collected in broad surveys of firms and consumers in multiple countries. User innovation proved to be present in large parts of the economy and practiced by many businesses and individual consumers. Substantial money and time investments were involved, and this is currently at best partially recorded in official statistics (firms) or still invisible (consumers). Moreover user innovation was found to be more open (unconstrained by intellectual property) than traditional producer-innovation. Finally, user innovations diffuse, they appear to some extent to be useful to other economic actors.

In the near future user innovation is likely to become even more important, empowered by the Internet specific types of user innovation, including open source projects and other distributed forms of innovation. Moreover easy-to-use design tools such as CAD software and 3D printers are becoming more widely available. As the average world education level is improving, an increasing share of world citizens will be able to innovate for themselves (Baldwin and von Hippel 2011). It is therefore of considerable importance to start exploring the implications of user innovation for current innovation metrics and policies, respectively.

To those involved in innovation metrics, we recommend further work to more explicitly capture user innovation. Until the actual levels of user innovation and expenditures are made clear, it will be difficult to get governments to take the policymaking needs of user-innovators serious. In this regard, current measurement practices are among the major reasons that policy makers still favor the sequence of R&D and subsequent commercialization. Moreover, as far as I know, there are no official surveys that attempt to measure user innovation by consumers. The challenge is to start piloting questions in the social surveys that statistical offices implement throughout the world.

For policy makers, the implications of the emerging user innovation phenomenon are yet to be explored in detail. Since user innovations are functionally novel contribute to the emergence of new industries, provide useful feedstock of innovation for producers, and contribute to social welfare, it is important to study how and what hampers user innovation, and how policy makers can intervene. Although too early for specific recommendations, I offer for consideration two design principles. First, it is important that policy should target users rather than the traditional producer based on (assumed) market failures. Second, as user innovation is not confined to businesses, policies should also be applicable to individual innovators viduals. Of course, this would be a giant step from an incumbent policy point of view, as it could potentially wipe out incumbent producers (Baldwin and von Hippel 2011). The next few years will likely bring to fruition some interesting new practices and policy insights due to work that is currently in progress.

Note

1. More specifically, Arundel and Sonntag (1999) found that 76 percent of their respondents were adopting at least one advanced manufacturing technology. Within this group, 53.9 percent did so by modifying existing technologies or by creating them from scratch.

References

Arrow, K. J. 1962. Economic welfare and the allocation of resources for invention. In *The Rate and Direction of Inventive Activity: Economic and Social Factors*, ed. R. R. Nelson, 609–25. Princeton: Princeton University Press.

Arundel, A., and V. Sonntag. 1999. Patterns of advanced manufacturing technology (AMT) use in Canadian manufacturing: 1998 AMT survey results. Research Paper 88F0017MIE, No. 12. Science, Innovation and Electronic Information Division, Statistics Canada, Ottawa.

Baldwin, C. Y., and E. von Hippel. 2011. Modeling a paradigm shift: From producer innovation to user and open collaborative innovation. *Organization Science* 22 (6): 1399–1417.

Bessen, J., and M. Meurer. 2008. *Patent Failure: How Judges, Bureaucrats, and Lawyers Put Innovators at Risk*. Princeton: Princeton University Press.

Cohen, W. M., and S. Klepper. 1996. A reprise of size and R&D. *Economic Journal* 106 (437): 925–51.

De Jong, J. P. J., and E. von Hippel. 2008. *User Innovation in SMEs: Incidence and Transfer to Producers. Scales Research Reports, H200814*. Zoetermeer: EIM Business and Policy Research.

De Jong, J. P. J., and E. von Hippel. 2009. Transfers of user process innovations to producers: A study of Dutch high tech firms. *Research Policy* 38 (7): 1181–91.

De Jong, J. P. J. 2010. The openness of user and producer innovation: A study of Dutch high-tech small firms. Paper presented at the User and Open Innovation workshop, Cambridge, MA, August 2–4.

De Jong, J. P. J. 2011. *Uitvinders in Nederland* (Inventors in the Netherlands). EIM Research Report A201105. Zoetermeer: EIM Business and Policy Research.

De Jong, J. P. J. 2013. User innovation by Canadian consumers: Analysis of a sample of 2,021 respondents. Unpublished manuscript. Commissioned by Industry Canada.

Flowers, S., E. von Hippel, J. de Jong, and T. Sinozic. 2010. *Measuring User Innovation in the UK: The Importance of Product Creation by Users.* London: NESTA.

Franke, N., and E. von Hippel. 2003. Satisfying heterogeneous user needs via innovation toolkits: The case of Apache Security software. *Research Policy* 32 (7): 1199–1215.

Godin, B. 2006. The linear model of innovation: The historical construction of an analytical framework. *Science, Technology and Human Values* 31 (6): 639–67.

Harhoff, D., J. Henkel, and E. von Hippel. 2003. Profiting from voluntary information spillovers: How users benefit by freely revealing their innovations. *Research Policy* 32 (10): 1753–69.

Hartog, C., J. Hessels, A. van Stel, and J. P. J. de Jong. 2010. *Global Entrepreneurship Monitor 2009 the Netherlands: Entrepreneurship on the Rise.* EIM Research Report A201011. Zoetermeer: EIM Business and Policy Research.

Henkel, J., and E. von Hippel. 2005. Welfare implications of user innovation. *Journal of Technology Transfer* 30 (1/2): 73–87.

Kim, Y., and H. Kim. 2011. User innovation in Korean manufacturing industries: Incidence and protection. Working paper 2011–1. KAIST Business School. Available at SSRN: http://ssrn.com/abstract=1763015.

Kuusisto, J., J. P. J. de Jong, F. Gault, C. Raasch, and E. von Hippel. 2013. *Consumer Innovation in Finland: Incidence, Diffusion and Policy Implications. Proceedings of the University of Vaasa, Reports 189.* Vaasa: University of Vaasa.

Levin, R. C., A. K. Klevorick, R. R. Nelson, and S. G. Winter. 1987. Appropriating the returns from industrial R&D. *Brookings Papers on Economic Activity* (3): 783–820.

Lilien, G. L., P. D. Morrison, K. Searls, M. Sonnack, and E. von Hippel. 2002. Performance assessment of the lead user idea-generation process for new product development. *Management Science* 48 (8): 1042–59.

OECD/Eurostat. 2005. *Oslo Manual: Guidelines for Collecting and Interpreting Innovation Data.* Paris: OECD.

Ogawa, S., and K. Pongtanalert. 2011. *Visualizing invisible innovation content: Evidence from global consumer innovation surveys. Working paper.* Kobe University. Available at SSRN; http://ssrn.com/abstract=1876186.

Riggs, W., and E. von Hippel. 1994. The impact of scientific and commercial values on the sources of scientific instrument innovation. *Research Policy* 23 (4): 459–70.

Schaan, S., and M. Uhrbach. 2009. Measuring user innovation in Canadian manufacturing 2007. Working paper 88F0006X, No. 3. Statistics Canada, Ottawa.

Shah, S. K., and M. Tripsas. 2007. The accidental entrepreneur: The emergent and collective process of user entrepreneurship. *Strategic Entrepreneurship Journal* 1 (1/2): 123–40.

von Hippel, E. 1976. The dominant role of users in the scientific instrument innovation process. *Research Policy* 5 (3): 212–39.

von Hippel, E. 2005. *Democratizing Innovation*. Cambridge: MIT Press.

von Hippel, E., J. P. J. de Jong, and S. Flowers. 2012. Comparing business and household sector innovation in consumer products: Findings from a representative study in the UK. *Management Science* 58 (9): 1669-81.

von Hippel, E., S. Ogawa, and J. P. J. de Jong. 2011. The age of the consumer-innovator. *MIT Sloan Management Review* 53 (1): 27–35.

5

User Innovation and Official Statistics

Fred Gault

This chapter looks at the gradual appearance of official statistics on user innovation, a progression that is still at an early stage but well enough along to see the potential for official statistics to support public policy debate leading to possible policy intervention and increased welfare as a result. The early work was stimulated by the appearance of *The Sources of Innovation* by Eric von Hippel (1988) and spurred along by the appearance in 2005 of *Democratizing Innovation* (von Hippel 2005).

The example, on which the chapter is based, is the introduction of official statistics on user innovation in business. Consumers, as user innovators, are then examined and this requires changes to the tools used to produce business statistics; a modified definition of innovation, and the need for social surveys, as opposed to business surveys, to collect the information.

Some Definitions

As this is a chapter on innovation, user innovation, and official statistics, the three concepts are defined before turning to the policy motivation for this work.

Innovation, for statistical purposes, is defined in the Oslo Manual as the implementation of a new or significantly improved product (good or service), or process, a new marketing method, or a new organizational method in business practices, workplace organization or external relations (OECD/Eurostat 2005, para. 146). *Implementation* in the definition connects innovation to the market and this is a key point for the discussion that follows.

User innovation in firms occurs when they introduce a new or significantly improved transformation or delivery process, marketing method, or organizational method including business practices, workplace organization, or their external relations, to benefit the firm. Recall that firms do not normally sell processes, they sell products. Of course, the firm may decide to establish a new business line to sell a process it has developed, but that process then becomes a product of the firm.

User innovation can also occur when individuals as consumers change a good or a service to improve the benefit they derive from it or develop a new good or service for the same reason.

Official statistics are those produced by the statistical system of a country and can come from the statistical office, the central bank, research institutes, regulators, or other organizations that form part of the system. Examples of official statistics are gross domestic product (GDP), employment figures, balance of payments, and merchandise trade. They are important as they are an input to policy and policy influences the lives of people.

Policy Motivations

In the 1980s there was a preoccupation in the policy community with the use and planned use of advanced manufacturing technologies, and the concern was that some industries or regions were not adopting these key technologies at a sufficient rate to make the industry or region competitive. This interest was driven, in part, by the recession of 1981–82 and was focused on economic recovery.

The US Bureau of the Census, over several years, under the leadership of Gaylord Worden, developed and tested a survey instrument that allowed a plant manager to walk through the production area and tick off the use and planned use of production technologies, including communication technologies, and those related to managing supply and delivery. A pilot version of this survey was run by Statistics Canada for the year 1987 and for 1988, there was a survey done by the US Bureau of the Census and by Statistics Canada for 1989 with common questions on the use and planned use of technologies.

Between these two surveys appeared the book, *Sources of Innovation*, by Eric von Hippel (1988) which stressed the role of the user in innovation. A member of the team at Statistics Canada had reviewed the book (Ducharme 1989) and a question was added to the 1989 survey to ask if any of the firms that had adopted any of the technologies in the list had modified them. A third of the population had modified the technologies that had been adopted and in subsequent surveys the question expanded to cover adoption by acquiring and modifying the technologies, and adoption by developing the technologies that the firms needed but could not find on the market. This was also the appearance of the first official statistics on user innovation (Statistics Canada 1989, 1991).

In the 1998 survey, 26 percent of firms adopting the technologies in the survey list modified them and 28 percent of firms adopted by developing the technologies as they were not available. These results raised questions about where user innovation fitted into innovation and technology use policies of the time. They made visible the role of user innovation in the innovation process and distinguished it from just buying and using technology that was new to the firm. In the latter situation the firm was still classified as a process innovator, but its means of innovating differed considerably from that of firms that were user innovators.

At the same time as evidence was accumulating that firms, as users, changed their production technologies, there was a worldwide debate on innovation fueled in part by the 1990–91 recession. Experimental surveys had been done in the 1980s in the Nordic countries, in Canada, Germany, and the United States and there was a move to codify the knowledge gained so that it could be used to guide the collection of official statistics. This gave rise to the first edition of the Oslo Manual in 1992. Draft versions of the manual guided the first European Community Innovation Survey (CIS) for the year 1992.

The first edition of the Oslo Manual contained a reference to user innovation in connection with technology adoption. The reference reappeared in the second edition but vanished from the third as the view at the time was that the manual should focus on innovation and not on technology use and planned use. Meanwhile, the book, *Democratizing Innovation,* by Eric von Hippel appeared in 2005 with much case study evidence for user innovation. This inspired a collaboration with Statistics Canada to probe user innovation in manufacturing and to gain more insight into how it was funded and how the knowledge gained was shared or protected. It also resulted in follow-up and analysis of existing questions in CIS-like surveys on user innovation in process technology in Korea and Mozambique.

Democratizing Innovation contained many examples of consumers, or
end users, changing their goods or services for their own benefit and this
raised questions about the welfare gains of transferring the knowledge
gained from this kind of activity (Henkel and von Hippel 2004, Baldwin
and von Hippel 2010). This had implications for social policy on the culture of innovation and entrepreneurship.

There were two social policy issues inherent in this work, the enhancement of welfare arising from sharing the knowledge gained from changing goods and services for personal benefit and the building of a culture
of innovation in which everyone could participate, not just businesses.

Use and Planned Use of Technology

The interest in the 1980s in surveys of the use of technologies, including
manufacturing technology, information and communication technologies
(ICTs) and later biotechnologies was driven by competitiveness and the
need to know how countries were performing by region, over time and in
comparison with other countries. This is what motivated the work at the
US Bureau of the Census (US Department of Commerce 1989) which led
to the 1988 survey of use and planned use of advanced manufacturing
technologies. Statistics Canada had piloted a survey based on the US
Bureau of the Census questionnaire in 1987 (Statistics Canada 1987) and
repeated the survey for 1989 (Statistics Canada 1989). This led to two
outcomes.

The first was a collaboration between Robert Tinari of the US Bureau
of the Census and Statistics Canada to produce Canada–US comparisons
of the findings of the survey. This dealt with the five industries covered in
the US survey and Canada lagged behind the United States in each one. As
a result surveys of use and planned use of technologies were supported
and carried out for the following two decades as part of the production
of official statistics for Canada and were done before either country considered doing an official survey of innovation (Ducharme and Gault
1992).

The second outcome, triggered by the publication of Eric von Hippel's
book, *The Sources of Innovation* (von Hippel 1988), was the addition to
the Canadian questionnaire of a question about the modification of the
technologies that had been adopted by the firms using them. This was the

"official" signal of the presence of user innovation in manufacturing firms. Of the firms that had adopted the technologies, a third reported that they had modified the technologies to improve them, a classic case of user innovation. Not probed in this survey was how users adopted the technologies.

Technologies can be adopted and used in three ways. The first is the acquisition (purchase, rental, or leasing) of off-the-shelf technologies, which are then used as delivered. If the technology is new to the firm, this, in an innovation survey governed by the Oslo Manual (OECD/Eurostat 2005), is counted as process innovation but it is not user innovation. The second is the acquisition of available technologies, which are then modified to work better for the purposes of the firm. This is user innovation. The third results from the recognition that no technology is available to solve the process problem of the firm and the firm adopts the needed technology by developing it. This is also user innovation as it is the user firm solving the problem for its own benefit.

Subsequent surveys in Canada asked about the three methods of adoption. The 1998 Survey of Advanced Manufacturing Technologies examined the use and planned use of 26 advanced manufacturing technologies (AMTs) in establishments (plants) with at least 10 employees. A key finding (Arundel and Sonntag 2001) was that for the 76 percent of firms that adopted at least one of the technologies, 46 percent of establishments bought off-the-shelf *only*, while 26 percent modified the equipment that they purchased, and 28 percent adopted by developing the technology in the absence of market supply. To keep the respondent burden to a minimum, the survey did not ask how the modification was made or the details of the development.

These were not case study results but population estimates based on a statistical sample of the manufacturing sector. That 46 percent of establishments had bought off-the-shelf technologies *only* is important as firms that adopted a technology by developing it could also adopt by purchasing a technology and modifying it or by buying off-the-shelf technologies. Firms that adopted by purchasing and modifying a technology could also buy technologies off-the-shelf. Had the statistics been presented for all establishments that bought off-the-shelf, the number would have been very large and misleading. What matters is adoption by modification, or by development, as that is where the user innovation occurs.

In 2007, Statistics Canada conducted another survey of the use and planned use of advanced manufacturing technology and asked about adoption by in-house modification or development (Statistics Canada 2008a). While the lists of technologies vary between the 1998 survey and that of 2007, the propensity of plants in manufacturing to use or plan to use at least one of the technologies in the list has increased from 76 percent in 1998 to 92 percent in 2007. The propensity to modify or develop at least one of the technologies for the same two surveys was 26 and 28 percent in 1998 (Arundel and Sonntag 2001) and 21 and 22 percent in 2007 (Schaan and Uhrbach 2009). While this appears to be a declining trend, when adjusted for the increased propensity to adopt at least one advanced manufacturing technology between 1998 and 2007, the fraction of plants adopting or planning to adopt by modification or development has remained more or less the same: About 20 percent of manufacturing plants in Canada are adopting advanced technologies by purchasing and modifying them, and a comparable proportion are adopting by developing the technology needed in the absence of a suitable product available on the market. These figures are additive as the population of plants using at least one of the technologies in the survey were divided into three unique classes; those buying off-the-shelf only, those buying and modifying, and those developing their technology. The evidence of user innovation as a result is about 40 percent of the population.

With the publication of the results of the 2007 survey, the concept of user innovation was firmly established in official statistics. The time was right to ask the user innovators about how and why they did it and what they did with the knowledge that they created. These questions had been developed in case study work (von Hippel 2005) and were being introduced to surveys (de Jong and von Hippel 2009). This led to a follow-up survey to the 2007 survey of advanced technology (Statistics Canada 2008b, Schaan and Uhrbach 2009), with the active collaboration of Eric von Hippel (Gault and von Hippel 2009).

One of the findings was that user innovators had a propensity to share, or to freely reveal (Harhoff et al. 2003), the knowledge that resulted from user innovation, at least in Canada and the Netherlands. This was not surprising as the result had been well established in earlier case studies (von Hippel 2005). What was surprising was that a study of user innovation in Korea showed a low propensity to share such knowledge (Kim and Kim 2011), a result also found by Zita and Lopes (2011) in Mozambique. The fact that sharing happens in industrialized countries, but not in a newly industrialized country, or in a developing country, raises questions. It may be that the firms in Mozambique saw a competitive advantage in their user innovation they were reluctant to share, while the Korean firms may have been constrained by the *chaebols* of which they were a part. These are topics for future work.

To be clear, the question raised is about the difference in the propensity to share knowledge resulting from user innovation in countries at different stages of development and with different cultures, not the occurrence of user innovation in these countries for which there is an extensive literature. In this literature the term *user innovation* is not always used but it is nonetheless the subject. Examples are the work of Jorge Katz (1987) in Latin America, Sanjaya Lall (1987) in India, and Linsu Kim (1997) and Enos and Park (1988) in Korea. Much of the focus of this work was on the accumulation of the capabilities to innovate (Bell et al. 1982, Bell 2006). The next step is to build upon this work and the work of Eric von Hippel to advance the understanding of user innovation by both firms and consumers in developing countries.

Manuals and User Innovation

One of the uses of official statistics is international comparability and to achieve this, there have to be agreed standards for the measurement and the interpretation of the results. For the last fifty years the expert group that provides these standards has been based at the OECD, and it is the Working Party of National Experts on Science and Technology Indicators (NESTI). The best-known NESTI product is the Frascati Manual, which guides the collection and interpretation of statistics on research and development (OECD 2002).

In the case of innovation, there were many experimental surveys conducted in the 1980s and discussed at NESTI, and toward the end of the decade a decision was made to codify the tacit knowledge on measuring innovation by writing a manual. Because of the early support of the Nordic Fund for Industrial Development, and Nordic delegations to NESTI, this became the Oslo Manual (OECD 1992), which was used as it was developed to guide the first of the European Union Community Innovation Surveys (CIS) for reference year 1992.

At this time it was not clear how to deal with user innovation or the measurement of technology use. However, the manual, in its discussion of "Diffusion of Innovation" (OECD 1992: 45) did deal with the use and planned use of technologies, linking them in a prescient way to the use of management practices more than a decade in advance of the change in the definition of innovation in the third edition of the Oslo Manual. In paragraph 185, user innovation is defined:

185 Use and planned use of technologies can be linked to other questions related to innovation. Questions on whether the technology was modified to improve productivity or ease of use give insight into the propensity to innovate on the factory floor.

The same statement appears in the second edition of the manual (OECD/Eurostat 1997: 77) as paragraph 259. The drafters of the Oslo Manual of the time were very aware of the importance of user innovation in firms that had been introduced to official statistics through the work of Eric von Hippel and the technology use surveys of the US Bureau of the Census and Statistics Canada.

The third edition of the Oslo Manual (OECD/Eurostat 2005) was a radical change from the previous two editions. The definition was expanded from just technological product and process innovation to include organizational change and use of business practices and to include the development of existing markets or the finding of new ones. Also the word "technological" was dropped. So was reference to the use and planned use of technologies and any hint of user innovation.

To place this in context, the period from 1997 to 2005 at the OECD was one of looking at technology development and use as separate activities from innovation. The Working Party on Indicators for the Information Society (WPIIS) was established in 1997; there was work on biotechnology leading to a framework for statistical development and the start of work on nanotechnology and on emerging technologies. In addition there was significant work on the business practice of knowledge management (OECD 2003). Much of this work was not integrated with the work on innovation in NESTI, with the possible exception of the outcomes from the knowledge management work that appeared in parts of the third edition of the Oslo Manual. It was therefore an opportune time for another book, *Democratizing Innovation*, by Eric von Hippel (2005), which renewed interest in the role of the user as part of the innovation process. Before that, some discussion of how the Oslo Manual was implemented is offered in order to show that user innovation did not disappear completely from official statistics in this period.

Implementing the Oslo Manual: Innovation Surveys

A manual, such as the Oslo Manual, can provide the guidelines for the collection and interpretation of data, but for the data to be collected there has to be a questionnaire administered as part of a survey. If the core questions are common, and are understood in the same way in different languages and cultures (a major caveat), the responses to the core questions can be used to support international and interregional comparisons. In the case of innovation measurement, the most widely used questionnaire was that of the Community Innovation Survey (CIS) of the European Union. It began as a pilot in 1993 for the reference year 1992 (CIS.1) and has continued ever since.

While there are many observations that can be made about CIS and its evolution over time, the one focus here is on the possibility of detecting user innovation in firms through a review of the question that follows the determination that the firm was engaged in process innovation. The most recent version of CIS, CIS 2010, asks the following questions.

Who developed these process innovations?

1. Your enterprise itself
2. Your enterprise together with other enterprises or institutions
3. Your enterprise by adapting or modifying processes originally developed by other enterprises or institutions
4. Other enterprises or institutions

Options 1, 2, and 4 appear in all previous CIS questionnaires, after CIS.1, and are discussed in Gault (2010, 2012). Option 3 is new to CIS 2010 and probes the possibility that the firm engaged in process innovation by modifying processes developed elsewhere, one of the two categories of user innovators identified in the technology use and planned use surveys. Option 1 asks if the firm developed the process innovation itself, the other category of user innovation already identified. Option 2 deals with collaboration and what is not answered is who controls the collaboration. If the innovating firm involves another organization to achieve its objective, this is also user innovation. However, if the other organization is collaborating in order to transfer its technology to the firm, it is not user innovation. The fourth option is likely to be capital investment in which purchases are made from other organizations. So long as the purchased technology is new to the firm, it counts as process innovation (OECD/Eurostat 2005).

To establish the extent to which user innovation is occurring in firms responding to categories 1 to 3, a follow-up survey is required such as the one conducted in Canada (Schaan and Uhrbach 2009) and in the Korea (Kim and Kim 2011). A small study in Mozambique did find that all respondents to category 1 were user innovators, but much more evidence is needed. If a strong link can be established, then respondents to category 1 provide an under bound on the percentage of user innovators in the population covered by the CIS. This is an important topic for future research as an indication of how much user innovation is present in categories 1 to 3 would mean that the presence of user innovation and its magnitude could be inferred from standard CIS results.

Bringing Consumer Innovation into Official Statistics

In 2006, a decade after the first OECD Blue Sky Forum in Paris, 250 people from 25 countries gathered in Ottawa to consider the future of OECD work on indicators of science, technology, and innovation (OECD 2007). One of the 250 was Eric von Hippel who gave a paper in which he made the following point (von Hippel 2007: 134).

Products, services and processes developed by users become more valuable to society if they are somehow diffused to others that can also benefit from them. If user innovations are not diffused, multiple users with similar needs have to invest to (re)develop similar innovations, which, as was noted earlier, is a poor use of resources from the social welfare standpoint.

The point of enhancing welfare has been discussed by Henkel and von Hippel (2004), further developed in Baldwin and von Hippel (2010), and applied in Finland (Ministry of Employment and the Economy 2010).

The diffusion of new or significantly improved products or processes is indeed important from the social welfare perspective and all of the diffusion mechanisms open to the firm can result in changes detected by a CIS-like survey. A new process resulting from user innovation can be transferred to the producer so that the product improves and, ideally, the producer would say, in response to a CIS questionnaire, that the product innovation was the work of another organization. The process could be seen as a new product line and the firm could either produce it or spin off a new firm to produce and sell it. Both cases would appear in a CIS-like survey. The firm could give the knowledge away to a peer group (firms doing the same sort of things) or to a community of practice (firms actively trying to solve such problems) and that would show up as process innovation in all of the firms that adopted it. The case with the least increase in welfare is that the firm does nothing with the knowledge other than benefit from it. In that case the firm will still be recorded as a process innovator. As far as official statistics are concerned, there is no problem. All activity is captured, but this is not the case for consumers that change the goods or services that they use.

Consumers do change goods or services (von Hippel 2005), but where are they in official statistics? Proceeding as in the last paragraph, the consumer could take the prototype back to the producer and ask that it be produced. If it is, the innovation would appear in a business survey like CIS. The consumer could start a firm, and again this and the innovation is captured in CIS-like surveys. The consumer could share the knowledge with a peer group or a community of practice and here there is a problem as the Oslo Manual requires that the new or significantly improved product be "implemented" which in paragraph 150 of the Oslo Manual translates into "introduced on the market." In the case of sharing the knowledge needed to produce the new or significantly improved product, there is no market and therefore there is no innovation.

This led to an animated discussion in the course of a Finnish project on consumer innovation and a modest proposal for a modification to Oslo resulted (Gault 2012). The proposal was to replace "introduced on the market" in paragraph 150 of the manual by "made available to potential users." This refers to a product, not to a process, and for firms little changes. The way in which their products are made available to potential users is through the market. However, the change does provide the firm with the additional option of sharing knowledge with "potential users."

An example is the development of a software product shared with members of a community that freely reveal their work.

For consumers, there is a change as those that share the knowledge of how to improve their good or service with a peer group or community of practice, the potential users, can now be classified as innovators. Those that do not share the knowledge with potential users and keep the benefit for themselves are not innovators. To find out whether the knowledge is shared, and how, requires a social survey of individuals or the addition of questions to existing social surveys.

Should the change to paragraph 150 be adopted in a future revision of the Oslo Manual, the stage is set for bringing consumer innovation into the domain of official statistics, leading to estimates of the magnitude of the activity, or indicators of consumer innovation, which could support a public policy debate around an innovation culture or a sharing society and ways of encouraging such activity. Should this happen, Eric von Hippel will have ensured the place of consumer innovation in official statistics.

As it takes years to revise a manual, and in the spirit of user innovation, there is no reason why the revised definition cannot be used in the interim to gain experience of its value in collecting and interpreting data on user innovation. The underlying assumption is that manuals are like technologies (Gault 2011), and there is no reason why users should not adopt the manual by modifying it for their own benefit. There is also a case of user adoption by developing a new manual to meet the needs of the users, the Bogotá Manual (RICYT/OEC/CYTED 2001), but, as with manufacturing technologies, the most common case is that of adopting the manual as it is produced.

Work in progress in Finland will use social surveys to find the percentage of people who change goods or services for their own benefit. This builds upon similar surveys conducted in Portugal (Oliveira and von Hippel 2011) and the United Kingdom (Flowers et al. 2010), and on the many case studies that demonstrate that users change products. The next step is to ask those users that change their products what they did with the prototype or the knowledge needed to produce it. They either transferred the knowledge or they did not. If the knowledge was not transferred, they are not user innovators. If the knowledge is transferred, there are three questions to establish to where it was transferred.

Did you:

1. Provide a prototype, or detailed description, of your new or improved product to a producer?
2. Start a business to sell your new or improved product?
3. Share the knowledge of how to make the new or improved product with potential users?

Positive responses to options 1 and 2 would provide useful information about the role of consumer innovation in the innovation activities of firms. A positive response to 3 would provide a magnitude of the extent to which users share knowledge with other users, a practice well established in the open source software community. Of course, these categories are not exclusive.

What about the Public Sector?

The work of Eric von Hippel has inspired work on user innovation in firms and by consumers but can it also have influence on official statistics on innovation activities in the public sector (Morrison et al. 2000), and especially user innovation?

Starting with the Oslo Manual, public sector organizations can do all of the innovation activities found in the manual such as R&D, capital expenditure, knowledge acquisition, training, design .... However the resulting product is not "introduced on the market" but it is "made available to potential users." The same change that includes consumers that share the knowledge of their new or improved product with potential users can also include public sector innovation.

Work in public sector innovation is reviewed in Gault (2012), and there is considerable activity in this area in Denmark (Bloch 2010a, b; Bugge et al. 2011) and the United Kingdom (Clark et al. 2008; Harris and Albury 2009; LSE Public Policy Group 2008; Mulgan 2007). The OECD is also examining public sector innovation as part of the NESTI agenda.

In principle, the change to the Oslo Manual, proposed to accommodate consumers that share the knowledge of how to produce their new or improved product with potential users, can also be used to accommodate public sector organizations that change or develop products (goods or services). This is an important contribution as it makes possible an Oslo family of manuals dealing with innovation in business, in the public sector and by individual consumers, leading to innovation indicators that can be compared across countries and over time. However the story does not end there.

So far, this chapter has considered the consumer as the user of goods or services produced by the business sector. There is no reason not to extend this thinking to the use of public sector products by consumers. As in the business case, the consumer can bring the knowledge back to the producer in the hope of a better product (if the tax form is reorganized, as suggested, it is easier to fill in, takes less time, delivers the same information, but results in fewer errors), start a firm to sell the knowledge (a software package that makes it easier and less burdensome to fill in and submit a tax form), or share the knowledge with potential users. The consumer can also use the knowledge for personal benefit and not share it, but then it is not a user innovation.

Summary

This chapter has reviewed the place of user innovation in official statistics, including surveys of the use and planned use of technologies and the analysis of and follow-up to innovation surveys. The policy relevance of consumer innovation has led to a suggestion for a small revision to the Oslo Manual that could have significant impact on the future of official statistics for consumer innovators, based on social surveys, and for public sector innovators.

An extensive community of researchers over the years have worked on case studies related to all aspects of user innovation, and this work will continue to inform the development and interpretation of the results of business and social surveys that should give rise to official statistics on user innovation, and then to policy debate, policy intervention, revision, and learning.

Note

The author acknowledges helpful comments from Jeroen de Jong, Dietmar Harhoff, Joachim Henkel, and Erika Rost.

References

Arundel, Anthony, and Viki Sonntag. 2001. *Patterns of advanced manufacturing technology (AMT) use in Canadian manufacturing: 1998 AMT Survey Results 88F0017MIE, no. 12*. Statistics Canada, Ottawa.

Baldwin, Carliss, and Eric von Hippel. 2010. Modeling a paradigm shift: From producer innovation to user and open collaborative innovation. Finance working paper 10–038, Harvard Business School; Working paper 4764–09, Sloan School of Management, MIT.

Bell, Martin. 2006. Time and technological learning in industrialising countries: How long does it take? How fast is it moving (if at all)? *International Journal of Technology Management* 36 (1–3): 25–39.

Bell, Martin. D. Scott-Kemmis, and W. Satyarakwit. 1982. Limited learning in infant industry: A case study. In *The Economics of New Technology in Developing Countries*, ed. F. Stewart and J. James, 138–56. London: Frances Pinter.

Bloch, Carter. 2010a. *Measuring pubic innovation in the Nordic countries. Final report*. Danish Centre for Studies in Research and Research Policy, Aarhus.

Bloch, Carter. 2010b. *Towards a conceptual framework for measuring public sector innovation. Module 1: Conceptual framework*. Danish Centre for Studies in Research and Research Policy, Aarhus.

Bugge, Markus M., Peter S. Mortensen, and Carter Bloch. 2011. *Measuring public innovation in Nordic countries. Report on the Nordic pilot studies: Analysis of methodology and results*. Danish Centre for Studies in Research and Research Policy, Aarhus.

Clark, John, Barbara Good, and Paul Simmonds. 2008. Innovation in the public and third sectors. Innovation index. Working paper. NESTA, LONDON.

De Jong, Jeroen P.J., and Eric von Hippel. 2009. Transfers of user process innovations to process equipment producers: A study of Dutch high-tech firms. *Research Policy* 38 (7): 1181–91.

Ducharme, Louis Marc. 1989. Book reviews: The functional source of innovation. *R&D Management* 19 (4): 349–50.

Ducharme, Louis Marc, and Fred D. Gault. 1992. Surveys of manufacturing technology. *Science and Public Policy* 19 (6): 393–99.

Enos, J., and W. H. Park. 1988. *The Adaption and Diffusion of Imported Technology: The Case of Korea*. London: Croom Helm.

Flowers, Stephen, Eric von Hippel, Jeroen de Jong, and Tanja Sinozic. 2010. *Measuring user innovation in the UK: The importance of product creation by users. Project report*. NESTA, London.

Gault, Fred, and Eric von Hippel. 2009. The prevalence of user innovation and free innovation transfers: Implications for statistical indicators and innovation policy. Working paper 4722–09. Sloan School of Management, MIT.

Gault, Fred. 2010. *Innovation Strategies for a Global Economy, Development, Implementation, Measurement and Management*. Cheltenham, UK: Edward Elgar.

Gault, Fred. 2011. Social impacts of the development of science, technology and innovation indicators. Working paper 2011–008. UNU-MERIT, Maastricht.

Gault, Fred. 2012. User Innovation and the Market. Working paper 2011–009. UNU-MERIT, Maastricht.

Harhoff, Dietmar, Joachim Henkel, and Eric von Hippel. 2003. Profiting from voluntary information spillovers: How users benefit by freely revealing their innovations. *Research Policy* 32 (10): 1753–69.

Harris, Michael, and David Albury. 2009. Why radical innovation is needed to reinvent public services for the recession and beyond: The Innovation Imperative. Lab discussion paper. NESTA, London.

Henkel, Joachim, and Eric von Hippel. 2004. Welfare implications of user innovation. *Journal of Technology Transfer* 30 (1/2): 73–87.

Katz, Jorge. 1987. *Technology Generation in Latin American Manufacturing Industries*. London: Macmillan.

Kim, Linsu. 1997. *Imitation to Innovation. The Dynamics of Korea's Technological Learning*. Boston: Harvard Business School Press.

Kim, Youngbae, and Hyunho Kim. 2011. User innovation in Korean manufacturing firms: Incidence and protection. Working paper KCB-WP-2011–01. KAIST Business School, Seoul.

Lall, Sanjaya. 1987. *Learning to Industrialise: The Acquisition of Technological Capability by India*. London: Macmillan.

LSE Public Policy Group. 2008. Innovation in government organizations, public sector agencies and public service NGOs. Innovation Index working paper. NESTA, London.

Ministry of Employment and the Economy. 2010. *Demand and User-Driven Innovation Policy*. Helsinki: Ministry of Employment and the Economy.

Morrison, Pamela D., John H. Roberts, and Eric von Hippel. 2000. Determinants of user innovation sharing in a local market. *Management Science* 46 (12): 1513–27.

Mulgan, Geoff. 2007. *Ready or Not? Taking Innovation in the Public Sector Seriously. Provocation 03, April 2007*. London: NESTA.

OECD. 1992. *OECD Proposed Guidelines for Collecting and Interpreting Technological Innovation Data. Oslo Manual. OCDE/GD (92) 26*. Paris: OECD.

OECD. 2002. *Frascati Manual: Proposed Standard Practice for Surveys on Research and Development*. Paris: OECD.

OECD. 2003. *Measuring Knowledge Management in the Business Sector: First Steps*. Paris: OECD.

OECD. 2007. *Science, Technology and Innovation Indicators in a Changing World: Responding to Policy Needs*. Paris: OECD.

OECD/Eurostat. 1997. *Proposed Guidelines for Collecting and Interpreting Technological Innovation Data, Oslo Manual*. Paris: OECD.

OECD/Eurostat. 2005. *Oslo Manual, Guidelines for Collecting and Interpreting Innovation Data*. Paris: OECD.

Oliveira, Pedro, and Eric von Hippel. 2011. Users as service innovators: The case of banking services. *Research Policy* 40 (6): 806–18.

RICYT/OEC/CYTED. 2001. *Standardization of Indicators of Technological Innovation in Latin American and Caribbean Countries: Bogotá Manual*. Buenos Aires: RICYT.

Schaan, Susan, and Mark Uhrbach. 2009. Measuring user innovation in Canadian manufacturing, 2007. Working paper 88F0006X, no. 3. Statistics Canada, Ottawa.

Statistics Canada. 1987. *Survey of Manufacturing Technology—June 1987. The Daily, October 15, 1987*. Ottawa: Statistics Canada.

Statistics Canada. 1989. *Survey of Manufacturing Technology—The Characteristics of the Plants. Science Statistics, 13 (10)*. Ottawa: Statistics Canada.

Statistics Canada. 1991. *Indicators of Science and Technology 1989: Survey of Manufacturing Technology—1989. Catalogue 88–002, 1 (4)*. Ottawa: Statistics Canada.

Statistics Canada. 2008a. *Survey of Advanced Technology 2007. The Daily, June 26, 2008*. Ottawa: Statistics Canada.

Statistics Canada. 2008b. *Follow-up to the Survey of Advanced Technology 2007. The Daily, October 27, 2008*. Ottawa: Statistics Canada.

US Department of Commerce. 1989. *Manufacturing Technology 1988. Current Industrial Reports*. Washington, DC: US Department of Commerce.

von Hippel, Eric. 1988. *The Sources of Innovation*. New York: Oxford University Press.

von Hippel, Eric. 2005. *Democratizing Innovation*. Cambridge: MIT Press.

von Hippel, Eric. 2007. Democratizing innovation: The evolving phenomenon of user innovation. In *Science, Technology and Innovation Indicators in a Changing World: Responding to Policy Needs*, ed. OECD, 125–38. Paris: OECD.

Zita, Júlia E.B., and Avelino H. Lopes. 2011. User Innovation in the Business Enterprise Sector of Maputo Province in Mozambique. Working paper 2011–062. UNU-MERIT, Maastricht.

II
The Community Perspective

6

Managing Communities and Contests to Innovate with Crowds

Karim R. Lakhani

"Crowdsourcing"[1] innovation has become a popular trend in industry, government, and academe[2], but how much do we really know about how to best manage the crowd? My research laboratory recently organized an innovation field experiment in computational biology, with colleagues from Harvard Medical School (Lakhani et al. 2013a), to work on answering this question. Over the course of two weeks, more than 122 solvers from 89 countries created more than 650 solutions to our challenging algorithmic problem. Our analysis showed that thirty of these solutions exceeded benchmarks from Harvard and from the US National Institutes of Health, with the best advancing the state of the art by over a factor of 1,000 (Lakhani et al. 2013a). But the field experiment not only solved an important problem in the life sciences, it also yielded insights on the underlying mechanisms and boundary conditions for managing communities and contests (Boudreau and Lakhani 2015). As such, it was part of a series of field experimental studies (e.g., in partnership with Harvard Medical School, US National Aeronautics and Space Administration, and TopCoder) I have conducted to understand how to manage crowds to drive innovation.

The objectives of the Harvard Medical School experiment included developing an appropriate counterfactual performance benchmark to compare communities and contests with each other and to internally generated solutions. The impressive results achieved were not unusual. Over the past two decades, with the advent of Internet-based communications and the ongoing digitization of knowledge-intensive tasks, many high profile examples have emerged to demonstrate the viability of deploying crowds for solving innovation problems. The two most common approaches involve creating and managing a community or designing and executing a contest (Boudreau and Lakhani 2013; King and Lakhani 2013).

Community-based software development through open source software has become an important part of the global software industry with thousands of projects and participants ranging from individual developers to nonprofit foundations, entrepreneurial startups and well-established industry giants (Feller et al. 2005; Lerner and Schankerman 2010). Similarly innovation contests have been shown to be effective in solving grand challenges like developing the technology for civilian space travel, creating the 100 miles-per-gallon vehicles (Murray et al. 2012), and aiding science-based firms with internal research and development problems (Jeppesen and Lakhani 2010). These crowd-based institutions are shaping democratized innovation (von Hippel 2005) as many unaffiliated actors contribute to the creation of new technology, products, and services without the usual firm–employee contractual relationships.

This chapter discusses a framework for managing crowds, through both communities and contests. It reviews historical and contemporary examples and highlights the fact that while communities and contests are deeply rooted in history, they are now getting revived as complementary approaches to manage innovation. I first discuss the essential features of communities and contests as institutions for innovation. In particular, I consider the types of problems and the nature of the search process in both settings. I then examine the important role of individual self-selection into these institutions as the basis for differentiation from the traditional firm focused approach to innovation. Self-selection yields both a match between the task and the worker and also solves the worker incentive problem as individuals are self-motivated. I then discuss the trade-offs in selecting either a community or a contest-based model for innovation. I conclude by discussing the emergence of hybrid organizations that are able to manage both communities and contests in the midst of running a for-profit organization.

Innovation Communities

The term "community" has captured the theoretical and empirical imagination of management and sociological scholars for more than 50 years (O'Mahony and Lakhani 2011; West and Lakhani 2008). While there is a proliferation of definitions and models in the literature, in the case of innovation, it is useful to consider communities as groups of individuals, affiliated through a common technology or use condition, who connect with each other (regardless of the medium: online and/or face-to-face), and willingly and freely share with each other their problems and solutions to the various use conditions of that technology. In many cases, especially in information goods like software, the community will not only enable sharing but often will take responsibility for a collective output in the form of a working solution (Boudreau and Lakhani 2013).

Communities as drivers of technological innovation have a long standing historical track record (Nuvolari 2004; Osterloh and Rota 2007). Allen (1983) was one of the first to show the presence of a "collective invention" process that involved lots of actors sharing knowledge to increase the performance of blast furnace technology for iron-making in the second half of the 19th century. This community of engineers and entrepreneurs in England's Cleveland district set in motion practices of knowledge sharing, resulting in dramatic improvements in furnace height (from 50 to 80 feet) and operating temperature (from 600 to 1,400 Fahrenheit), that significantly reduced fuel consumption in, and increased the profitability of, iron production. The sharing practices put in place were mutually beneficial as engineers had significant job mobility and any one improvement on its own was not patentable. In addition entrepreneurs were willing to disclose performance data because they could benchmark against one another and importantly make better use of their shared assets in iron ore deposits—which served as the scarce complementary asset. Similar examples of collective invention have been observed in the development of Cornish pumping engines, Bessemer steel, and large-scale silk production (Nuvolari 2004). Osterloh and Rota (2007) also report on more modern examples of communities of innovation like the very famous Homebrew computer club at Stanford University, giving rise to, among others, Apple, and the flat panel display industry.

By far community-based innovation has had the largest impact in the software development industry. Originally software came for free with computer hardware and users tended to be university researchers and commercial research and development units that viewed software as a research tool to be developed and improved by all users (Campbell-Kelly 2003). Indeed, when IBM entered the computer market, it distributed its software code with minimal restrictions and encouraged collective modification and improvement by users; with its user group referred to as SHARE (not an acronym) (Campbell-Kelly 2003).

While the commercial and private software industry took off in the early 1960s, when entrepreneurs began to realize that software could be sold independent of hardware and less sophisticated users would want to pay for the convenience of not having to tinker with the code, the underlying ethic of sharing code remained quite strong among software developers. Thus Unix emerged in the 1970s as a Bell Laboratories research project that transformed into a fully user-developed operating system that was freely shared and modified (Salus 1994). In the 1980s, the Free Software Foundation (FSF) was founded by Richard Stallman with the express intent to create software as a public good. The FSF created intellectual property licenses that ensured that software that became a public good could not be privatized, and provided developers with easy license terms to ensure the survival of community-based software development. In the 1990s, the rise of the Internet enabled users and developers the world over to find one another and, using simple tools, to collaborate on the creation of community software—an effort that became known as the open source software movement (Raymond 1999). Today hundreds of thousands of software developers engage daily in thousands of distinct innovation communities creating software that is freely available and easily shared. This open source movement has moved beyond voluntary participation and has enlisted many firms to sponsor employees to participate in these communities. Open source software now is a well-established means of innovation within the global software industry (Lerner and Schankerman 2010).[3]

The community model for innovation does create a theoretical tension in the literature on innovation. The traditional prevailing sense is that technology development is enhanced when society grants individuals and firms limited monopoly rights in return for investments in generating innovations (Demsetz 1964). Individuals and firms make investments in innovation with the hopes of achieving private gain while taking into account some risk of knowledge spillover due to their participating in the marketplace. At the same time society favors incentives for private creation over the social loss incurred in creating knowledge monopolies (von Hippel and von Krogh 2003).

An alternative model, historically dominant in the sciences, envisages innovation effort outcomes as nonrival, nonexcludable public goods whereby knowledge is contributed to a common pool to be reused by others (Dasgupta and David 1994). At the heart of this collective-action innovation model is the dilemma of free-riding. Because in a collective-action system all outputs are public goods, it would be rational for participants to neither invest nor publicly disclose their contributions and wait for others to contribute. Society fosters innovation in collective systems by providing financial grants, subsidies, and other incentives to encourage individuals and organizations to embrace public disclosure of the effort they exert and unconditional reuse of the fruits of their labor.

Hence community efforts face a dilemma: Why would actors make private investments and then willingly give away and share the results of their efforts? Community projects can be understood as a hybrid private-collective innovation model where participants gain private benefits for public disclosure (von Hippel and von Krogh 2003). Core to this model are free-revealing actions by innovators to other members in their community subsequent to their private investment, in essence private investment in public goods, a puzzle that can be solved by recognizing that contributions to communities are not "pure public goods–they have significant private elements even after the contribution has been freely revealed" (von Hippel and von Krogh 2003, 216). The von Hippel–von Krogh model's explanation for the prevalence of communities is first based on questioning the private investment model's assumption that free revealing of innovations developed with private investment and effort constitutes a loss for the innovator(s). They show that free revealing could instead earn innovators a net benefit in terms of suggested improvements from others as well as adoption and diffusion of the original contribution. Work by von Hippel and von Krogh (2003) also challenges the assumption of the collective action model that benefits derived from freely revealed contributions are spread homogeneously, among free riders as well as innovators, positing that innovators enjoy access to highly prized selective benefits that free riders cannot obtain. The core of the private-collective innovation model is thus the accrual of such selective private benefits to the individuals who expend, at relatively low cost, effort to create nonrival, nonexcludable public goods.

Communities democratize innovation by focusing on aggregating the input of various diverse contributors on commonly shared problems. The advantage and modus operandi of community is that individual members do not need to solve all the problems that a particular set of technologies poses. Instead, members resolve their own local and micro problems and then share the outputs of their efforts with others. The scale and scope of the collaborative effort in open source communities is now quite large. For example, since 2008 the Linux operating system, which has now become ubiquitous through Google's Android system and its broad based use in enterprises and devices, has had 8,000 individuals from 800 companies contribute more than 15 million lines of code. All of these contributors simply work on issues they deem interesting (or their firms decide as being important) and then submit code back to the community for approval—with the core Linux team aggregating all these diverse inputs into a new operating system kernel approximately every 3 months.

A challenge faced by communities is the inherent need for coordination and integration across the various individuals' differentiated and shared efforts. Given that traditional employment relationships are missing[4] and that individuals are widely distributed geographically, the primary means of integration in communities is the design structure of the technological artifact itself. Baldwin and Clark (2006) have shown that architecture can replace managerial coordination and that overall system performance is based on most individuals working serially on their specific modules with a small coordination layer at the center of the community that accepts and/or rejects the various submissions made by individuals (von Krogh et al. 2003). Hence communities serve to tackle those innovation problems where individuals focus on specializing on their specific areas and where there is value to aggregating the collective work of individuals across the entire problem space.

Innovation Contests

Like communities, innovation contests have had a historically significant role in driving technological innovation. Famous historical examples abound, including the design of the dome at the famous cathedral in Florence Italy (King 2000), finding the longitude at sea (Andrewes 1996), the invention of food canning (Barbier 1994), and the systematic use of prizes to spur innovation in agriculture (Brunt et al. 2012) and aviation (KEI 2008). In more modern times, contests have been deployed in a range of settings from spurring innovation in commercial space travel (the Ansari X-Prize) to the development of vastly improved software algorithms for movie recommendations (the Netflix Prize). In addition since the early 2000s several two-sided platform based firms have emerged that offer contest services and a crowd of solvers on demand. Firms like InnoCentive (for scientific problem solving), TopCoder (for algorithms and software construction), and Kaggle (for data analytics) have amassed hundreds of thousands of individuals who are willing and able to compete and attempt to create solutions to innovation problems that originate from commercial, government and nonprofit organizations.

The logic of the contest model for innovation is quite simple and straightforward. A contest sponsor faces a problem that needs resolution. The sponsor, having made the decision that a contest is an appropriate institution for resolution, will then exert effort to both define the problem and develop criteria for evaluating the solution so that external solvers will be able to both comprehend the problem and determine for themselves the solution approaches that will be most suitable. The sponsor also sets the prize amount for a successful solution and a timeline by when solutions are due. The problem is then broadcast (today mostly through the above-mentioned platforms) to potential solvers, and they self-select into exerting effort and creating a solution. Upon passing of the deadline the (multiple independent) submitted solutions are evaluated and ranked according to the pre-established solution criteria, and the top-ranked participants are paid according to their performance. (Moldvanu and Sela 2001 provide insights on the optimal number of prizes to be offered in a contest.) Hence contests set in motion a pay-for-performance incentive scheme where participants only get benefits if they meet a certain criteria for performance (either based on a preexisting threshold or rank order of performance).

In contrast, the typical model for innovation problem solving inside the firm requires formal and informal contracting and human resources' attention so that employees are exerting the appropriate effort. Typically a manager inside the firm will define the innovation problem that needs to be resolved. The manager will then either scour for internal personnel to solve the problem or post a job listing for the position. In addition the manager also has to offer incentives and a basic work contract for the person who is selected to work on the problem. The manager will then invest in monitoring the effort of the employee to make sure that the work promised is being accomplished for the salary being provided and that there is positive progress toward problem resolution. Inevitably, the employee(s) will suffer from setbacks during the problem-solving process and the manager will be responsible for a whole host of human resource-type motivational encouragement to help the individual through the process. If, during the problem-solving process, the employee and/or manager discover that the original problem as defined does not meet the skills and abilities of the solving employee, then the problem to be solved is further refined and/or modified. Ultimately the employee and manager will develop a solution criteria that fits both the problem at hand the solution approach available to the internal solver, and the manager will hope that an effective solution is forthcoming, in essence "praying for performance."

Grossly simplified, the scenarios above caricature the differences between a contest model and an internal organizational model for innovation-related problem solving. The contest model appears to work best when the innovation problem can benefit from multiple, independent solution approaches. There is, however, a tension between the desire of the contest sponsor to have many individuals compete to solve the problem and an individual competitor's willingness to exert effort if lots of others are competing. Indeed economists studying innovation contests in particular have been concerned about the optimal number of participants, pointing to both social welfare concerns and lowered incentives; the underlying logic points to the fact that the odds of any one person winning drop as more people enter—thus decreasing effort exerted by any one competitor and also increasing overall social waste (Che and Gale 2003).

Empirical work on this issue by me and my colleagues (Boudreau et al. 2011) has shown that the nature of the innovation problem at hand mediates the relationship between increasing entry and performance. Using data from the TopCoder platforms, we show that simpler problems, those that require solutions from just one knowledge domain, have worse outcomes when the number of competing solvers increases—with the

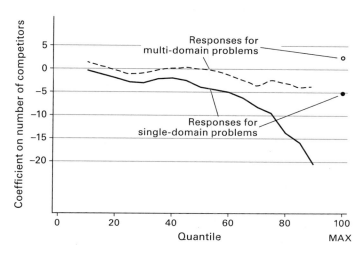

Figure 6.1

Change in response due to added competitors for single- and multidomain problems. Each point measures the relationship between performance and *No. Competitors* at the respective quantile, controlling for a fixed effect for the particular problem being solved and controlling for the distribution of skills and individuals within a given room. The solid black line relates to single-domain problems; the dashed black line relates to multidomain problems. The response of maximum score is shown at the 100 percent position (precisely the maximum), with the single domain problems shown as the solid black dot and multidomain problems shown as the white dot. (Source: Boudreau et al. 2011)

maximally best solution not improving much either, while problems that have more uncertain solution outcomes (i.e., straddling multiple knowledge domains) have a much shallower decreasing performance response with increasing competition and an unambiguously positive maximal response. Figure 6.1 from Boudreau et al. (2011) demonstrates these effects. Thus the study shows that contest designers should increase entry and participation when solutions to problems require integration of knowledge from multiple domains and conversely limit entry in cases where solutions will arrive from single knowledge domains.

The experiment discussed at the beginning of this chapter shows how contests can be managed to harness diversity and large numbers of solvers to create unique solutions to prototypical academic medicine problems involving computational biology and large data structures. In most computationally intensive fields, organizations face the challenge of both finding the right workers and identifying the appropriate approaches to solve the problems encountered. Many organizations find that they cannot effectively recruit the right talent, and often there is a mismatch between internal problem-solving resources and the current problems that need resolution (Boudreau and Lakhani 2013).

To help alleviate this bottleneck, my research laboratory worked with the Harvard Medical School's (HMS) clinical and translational science center (Harvard Catalyst) and the online contest platform TopCoder to investigate if a contest could solve an extremely challenging big-data genomics problem in immunology (Lakhani et al. 2013a). Over the course of two weeks, more than 122 solvers from 89 countries created more than 650 solutions to the problem for a total prize purse of only 6,000 USD. The analysis showed that thirty solutions exceeded by far the NIH and internal Harvard benchmarks, and the best of them advanced the state of the art by a factor of 1,000 (figure 6.2 shows the effect graphically). This was achieved via the contestants implementing 89 novel computational approaches to solve the problem. In examining the solutions, HMS researchers were simply taken aback by the sheer diversity of novel approaches used to attack the problem and the fact that none of the solvers had any background in biomedicine.

Note that contests are well suited to when innovation problems can be broken apart, isolated, and modularized so that multiple diverse solution approaches can be attempted. Unlike communities, which take responsibility for a collective output and integrate solutions across the entire spectrum of participants and tasks, contests work on singular problems with the task of integration left to the contest sponsor.[5] Contests involve wide experimentation on a singular problem, whereas communities involve joint problem solving, knowledge sharing, and accumulation over multiple problems.

Self-selection and Motives in Communities and Contests

A major difference between how firms manage innovation and the process followed by communities and contests is the means by which individuals are initiated into the problem solving effort. Inside most firms managers responsible for innovation select both the problems that need to be solved and the personnel that are assigned to the task (Nickerson

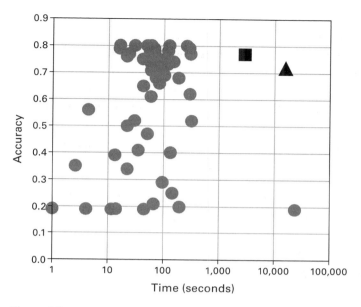

Figure 6.2

Accuracy score versus speed of contest-commissioned immunoglobulin sequence annotation code The circle represents contest entry; the square is Harvard code, and the triangle is NIH MegaBlast code. (Source: Lakhani et al. 2013a)

and Zenger 2004). Managers retain these decision rights to ensure that the fit between the objectives of the firm and the personnel hired to perform the tasks is maximized and that the essential work of innovation gets accomplished within the constraints of budget and time. Firm employees get hired on the basis of their credentials and accomplishments in the past and then are assigned to exert effort and engage in problem solving for the innovation tasks at hand.

However, core to the innovation process is the encouragement of risky, uncertain search for solutions and repeated trial-and-error experimentation and it is often very difficult to write appropriate contracts that ensure acceptable employee performance. Furthermore it is often difficult to find the appropriate observables and measures on which contracts can be written when the essential task to be accomplished is creative, nonroutine, and subtle in nature, with long gestational periods and uncertain outcomes (Holmstrom 1989; Aghion and Tirole 1994). Finally, complicating the management of creative problem solvers is the important role of intrinsic motivations in driving effort and innovative performance. Studies of innovation workers have shown both a taste for pecuniary benefits and for intrinsic motives (Sauermann and Cohen 2010). Thus managers responsible for innovation have to not just ensure that the workers have the appropriate capability and knowledge to solve the innovation problem at hand, they also need to ensure that the multidimensional motives of the workers are taken under consideration.

In contrast, a central feature of both communities and contests is the ability of the participants to decide which task they are going to work on and the level of effort they are going to exert. Neither of the approaches has an intervening agent that is mediating between the task and the problem solver. This then mitigates both the information asymmetry concerns that exist in the typical principal–agent setup of a manager and an employee—namely, is the worker appropriately skilled enough to do the task, and is the manager determining the appropriate basket of incentives to offer to the worker.

Participation Dynamics in Communities

Research in the community-based model has shown that participants joining open source software projects do so because they have self-determined that they have the relevant set of skills and interest to meaningfully contribute to the collective effort (O'Mahony and Lakhani 2011). A study I conducted involving the analysis of the joining and contribution patterns of all 356 community members over a one-year product development cycle of the nascent Freenet software project revealed that participants who became core developers (i.e., could modify the source code repository of the project) followed a specific set of actions, or a "joining script," to gain acceptance within the community (von Krogh et al. 2003). This joining script involved demonstrating technical knowledge by directly submitting source code changes and ongoing participation in the technical development of the software. Successful participants chose their own tasks and brought specific areas of expertise to the parts of the project that they found interesting and challenging. As the project evolved and the general nature of the problems to be solved became apparent to the community members, specific sets of knowledge, skills, and techniques already held by the community members were brought to the table and contributed to the collective.

Interestingly, providing credentials of previous experience or just signaling public interest in the project were not successful joining strategies.
Neither was asking for guidance as to where someone could potentially
contribute. One of the founding developers of Freenet indicated the elements needed by a community member to become a core developer (von
Krogh et al. 2003: 1229):

There are probably three kinds of people. One is, "I started working with it. I saw
these problems. I fixed them. Here they are." That person gets in. There is the
person who says, "I am a JAVA engineer from Dallas, Texas. I've been working for
five years, and I really would like to help. Give me something to do." That person
tends not to do anything. They tend to volunteer some expertise that doesn't get
exploited yet. . . . The third type of person is the visionary, who says, "I think
Freenet is great, but it needs permanent storage, announcements, and broadcast-
ing." They tend to start fighting with the core architects, if they're lucky, who are
actually making the decisions not to do that. Usually, they fight with lower-down
people on the totem pole who are given the party line. They tend to never get in.

Hence the decentralized nature of open source projects favors individuals who can self-select themselves into appropriate tasks and resolve
technical problems without overt task allocation mechanisms implemented by community leadership.

Motivation in Communities

Since members determine the tasks they are going to complete in a community, the motivation to complete the task also reflects their own priorities and beliefs. Survey-based research on the motives of participants in
open source communities points to the presence of intrinsic and extrinsic
motivations (Hertel et al. 2003; Lakhani and von Hippel 2003; Lakhani
and Wolf 2005; Roberts et al. 2006; Stewart and Gosain 2006). Intrinsic
motives consist of enjoyment, the stimulation associated with intellectual
challenge, and satisfaction derived from completing a task at hand (Amabile 1996; Csikszentmihalyi 1990; Ryan and Deci 2000), and developers
report relatively high levels of such motives (Hertel et al. 2003; Lakhani
and von Hippel 2003; Lakhani and Wolf 2005; Roberts et al. 2006).
Community participants report that both direct and indirect extrinsic
motives for accomplishing a task (i.e., for the sake of outcome) that are
produced post task accomplishment are also drivers of participation.
Direct extrinsic benefits include salary and pecuniary rewards derived
from participation as well as the potential for meeting a user need

(Lakhani and Wolf 2005; Roberts et al. 2006), while indirect extrinsic motives include career and peer signaling, learning by doing, and improving skills through peer review (Lakhani and Wolf 2005; Lerner and Tirole 2002; Roberts et al. 2006).

Scholars studying community participation have also attempted to directly link the elemental motives to various measures of output and performance. Analysis of intrinsic motives and effort show mixed findings. Neither Hertel et al.'s (2003) study of hours spent by Linux kernel developers on a project nor Roberts et al.'s (2006) study of contributors' source code contributions to the Apache project surfaced a significant positive relationship between intrinsic motivation and effort. Meanwhile Lakhani and Wolf's (2005) study of much lower profile open source projects found that a sense of personal creativity, derived from involvement in project activities, is a significant predictor of time invested. On the extrinsic front, being paid to participate naturally increases the number of hours a developer spends on a community project and the number of source code contributions made to a project (Lakhani and Wolf 2005; Roberts et al. 2006). Similarly concerns for both community and career signals drove effort by participants in well-established and nascent open source communities (Hertel et al. 2003; Lakhani and Wolf 2005; Roberts et al. 2006). In contrast to firms, motives in communities are quite a bit more diverse and like tasks are self-directed and fulfilled.

Participation Dynamics in Contests

Participation in innovation contests also follows a logic of self-selection. While the tasks to be solved are created by the organization sponsoring the contest, participation is voluntary and is determined by individuals making a calculation if the effort exerted will result in an expected payoff. Jeppesen and Lakhani's (2010) analysis of innovation contests shows the working of contests where unconventional individuals can participate and enable superior outcomes. This study casts innovation contests in terms of a search process where the problem information is broadcast to a broad base of external competitive solvers (broadcast search), who then self-select to work on problems they find interesting. The paper investigates the determinants of successful problem solvers from a population of over 12,000 scientists attempting to solve 166 internally intractable corporate science problems on the InnoCentive scientific problem solving platform. Our econometric analysis shows that technical marginality (having increasing distance between a problem field and a solver's own expertise) was a positive and significant predictor of success. In addition we found that social marginality (not connected to scientific community), in this case being a woman scientist—sociological evidence points to women being in the outer circle of the natural sciences (Zuckerman 1991; Ding et al. 2006)—positively and significantly impacted the likelihood of creating a winning solution. Under traditional circumstances, "marginal" individuals may not be invited to solve such problems. However, contests enable individuals with specialized knowledge to self-select and exert effort based on their own private information to create unexpected solutions. Thus seemingly disadvantaged structural positions (i.e., being marginal) can be turned positive with self-selection.

Boudreau and Lakhani (2012) present a direct test of the importance of self-selection in determining effort and performance in innovation contests by conducting a field experiment. Core to this work is the notion that self-selection in the economy enables efficient allocation of talent and resources to important problems. A nascent literature in the economics of innovation and science has started to note that innovation workers have certain institutional preferences, which drives their choices and effort (Stern 2004; Sauermann and Cohen 2010). This finding is also broadly consistent with theorizing by labor economists that differential incentive schemes sort and select worker effort and performance primarily on the basis of skills (Lazear 2000).

Boudreau and Lakhani (2012) worked with NASA's Space Life Sciences Directorate to secure a real computational engineering problem from the space program (the challenge involved developing an algorithm to create the optimal medical kit for various types of mission scenarios) and implemented its resolution as a contest on the TopCoder software development platform with a 25,000 USD prize purse and objective machine-generated assessment of software quality and performance. The TopCoder platform aggregates demand for software development from relatively large corporate clients and then matches it with programming supply from a pool of over 450,000 (at the time of the contest) registered software developers from around the world. These developers compete in contests to solve the software challenges put on the platform. Over 1,000 software developers participated in the experiment over a 10-day period.

The field experiment was designed to independently assess the impact of self-selection into a preferred work regime (i.e., working in a team or competing autonomously) while controlling for skills and incentives to solve a "real" innovation problem.

The experiment was novel in the sense that instead of randomly assigning individuals to teams or autonomous competition treatments, Boudreau and Lakhani (2012) sought to elicit preferences from a subset of their subjects as to their choice of work treatments. We implemented this "selection experiment" by rank-ordering all subjects based on their prior TopCoder skill rating and then creating matched pairs of individuals based on their skill. We then randomly solicited the treatment preference from one person in the matched pair and assigned that same choice to the other person in the pair. Hence we created skill-controlled treatment and control conditions. We also randomized incentives in a way that some individuals were competing for cash prizes while others for fame and recognition.

The findings from our experiment show that self-selection into the appropriate institution has major consequences for the effort exerted by the individuals. In the contest regime we show that controlling for skill and incentives, the ability to self-select roughly doubles the effort expended. Effort was measured in terms of the number of software submissions (from about 1.5 to 3 submissions) and the number hours invested (from about 7 to 14 hours). This effect of self-selection into the competition regime was of the same magnitude as the provision of cash incentives.

Taken together these studies indicate that self-selection in contests draws on a broader and wider set of individuals. These are individuals who seem to have both knowledge advantages in solving problems and a willingness to exert more effort when given the opportunity.

Motivations in Contests

Contests, with the rewards inherently limited to the number of prizes pre-allocated, do raise the question of the motives of solvers if in the final analysis most participants are simply going to lose anyway. When considering motives to participate in an innovation contest, the first and most obvious one on the menu is the monetary reward. Contests typically provide a cash prize to winners, and many participants indicate that this is indeed a major driver for exerting effort. Beyond pecuniary motives, work by Lakhani, Garvin, and Lonstein (2012) also indicates the presence of both extrinsic and intrinsic motives. Contestants report that participation and performance in contests allow them to gain reputation and fame within the community and to translate their performance into credible career signals in the broader labor market. From an intrinsic perspective, individuals indicate that participation in contests improves their own learning. For example, one prominent member of the TopCoder community and an engineer at Google wrote on his personal resume page:

I regularly participate in and organize a number of programming competitions. As a result, I am familiar with a vast number of algorithmic problems from all areas of computer science. Among the thousands of people who participate in these competitions, I am consistently ranked in the top 50 worldwide. Frankly, I believe that these competitions have taught me more about computer science and programming than all of the university courses.[6]

In addition many members find the competition format itself motivating and fun. For a segment of the population, competing and winning and getting a relative performance evaluation is energizing in itself and leads to effort exertion.

All in all, the consensus in a range of studies about communities and contests as institutions for democratized innovation points to the importance of self-selection and diverse motivations as drivers for participation, effort exertion, and finally performance.

Comparative Advantages of Communities versus Contests

Managers seeking to deploy crowds to solve their innovation problems are often confronted with the question of choosing between a community and a contest. The literature so far has not provided theoretical guidance or empirical evidence regarding the comparative advantages of using communities instead of contests. A primary challenge in implementing a rigorous comparative study is that communities and contests have so far been deployed in settings that have institutional specific details (e.g., types of problems solved, the incentives and motives of participants, self-selection of participants, and knowledge disclosure policies) that make it difficult to implement an econometric study using naturally occurring field data. However, regardless of the empirical difficulties, it is important for both the literature and practitioners to understand the relative advantages and disadvantages of such innovation approaches.

The earlier mentioned Harvard Medical School computational biology challenge (Lakhani et al. 2013a) provided an opportunity to conduct such a comparative study in a fully controlled field experimental setting in which treatment allocation could be randomly assigned and causal inferences drawn (Boudreau and Lakhani 2015). The study conceptualized the essential difference between communities and contests (and other related institutions for innovation) as one of knowledge disclosure policies while keeping constant the innovation problem, the pool of participants (skill levels), incentives, and the technological infrastructure. In contests, knowledge disclosure about viable solution approaches only occurs at the end of the contest when participants are awarded prizes and the nature and details of their (winning) final solution approach is made public. In communities, knowledge disclosure among participants occurs throughout the innovative problem-solving process, and hence both the form and timing of the disclosures are of an intermediate nature (as opposed to final). The study theorized that the choice between intermediate and final disclosure creates a first-order incentives versus reuse trade-off. While participants in intermediate disclosure systems (i.e., communities) benefit from the knowledge of others, their own private incentives to invest in costly innovative effort will decline due to loss of appropriation opportunities. At the same time the nature of the in innovative search process should be transformed due to the knowledge disclosure policies by shaping the level of independence of search and experimentation by innovators across different solution approaches (Boudreau and Lakhani 2015).

Analysis of the study data showed that the incentives versus reuse trade-off was strongly present in the intermediate disclosure (community) treatment. The community treatment had fewer participants, and they exerted less effort (hours worked and number of submissions made), explored fewer novel paths, and exited the experiment earlier as compared to those working in the final disclosure (contest treatment). The vast majority of participants did access the solutions from others (throughout the experiment), and this resulted in higher average and maximal performance as compared to the individuals working in contests. In contrast, due to the fact that the participants in the contest treatment were not aware of the solution approaches being developed by their competitors, there was more exploration and experimentation and diverse technological paths explored in the final disclosure treatment. Moreover this experimentation was mostly in the lower tail of the performance outcomes possible for this problem. The better performance of the community treatment can be attributed to the knowledge spillovers accumulated through intermediate disclosure and the participants discovering and converging on higher potential technological paths.

While performance in the community treatment was higher in the case of this particular problem, it is the combination of the incentive effect and search patterns that is most generalizable for comparative purposes and managerial action (Boudreau and Lakhani 2015). The community treatment resulted in lower participation and effort and led to group convergence on technological paths that appeared most promising, indicating that having a stock of knowledge or template about promising technological trajectories for a certain problem is an essential driver of performance. This corresponds well with field examples showing open source communities thriving in areas where a technological advance is well understood and disclosed to the community for further development (e.g., the Linux operating system relied on the prior work done on Unix, the Firefox web browser relied on Netscape Navigator and the Hadoop distributed data processing engine needed Google and Yahoo!'s contributions). Nevertheless, the contest treatment with its high incentives and diverse exploration and experimentation may be suited for situations where there is fundamental uncertainty about the most appropriate technological paths to pursue (Boudreau et al. 2011). Indeed, from a managerial perspective, a staged process that first enables diverse exploration by independent innovators in a contest setting, followed by community-based development, may be a model to pursue for the most effective innovative performance.[7]

Conclusion

The promise of crowdsourcing innovation is that many more actors, outside of the focal organization with an innovation challenge, can participate in the innovation process as opposed to the traditional process of internal hiring and effort exertion. Communities and contests offer two types of institutions to achieve these objectives. In practice, most economic organizations will utilize some sort of hybrid structure that will involve both open crowd-based and traditional organizations (Lakhani and Panetta 2007).

In the realm of communities, Apple presents an interesting model (Lakhani et al. 2013b). Contrary to press accounts about Apple being a closed innovation firm, the firm's embrace of democratized innovation through open source communities is grounded in economic logic. In the 1990s the firm had significant technical failure with a range of attempts to develop new operating systems. When Steve Jobs returned to Apple, the firm realized that its prowess and advantage laid in industrial design and software interface and not necessarily the inner core working of the operating system. Hence OS X (and now also iOS), the flagship operating systems, were developed through tight integration with open source communities. Apple, unlike Microsoft, made its revenues through hardware sales and not operating system software, and thus the linkage with collaborative communities made logical sense as Apple made its profits from complementary assets related to hardware and services. Today Apple participates in over 200 open source communities, and the firm has found that effective interaction with communities requires the presence of complementary assets that can be combined with the contributions from free and open communities. Apple's participation is not just about using the output of these communities. Rather, Apple contributes code back to these communities and also utilizes the collective output.

On the other end of the spectrum of the software industry, SAP, the global enterprise resource-planning giant, discovered that its customers wanted to collaborate and interact with each other, and the firm saw significant advantage in hosting those interactions through specialized online platforms (Iansiti and Lakhani 2009; Lakhani et al. 2014). Once enabled, SAP executives noted that its community network was addressing a range of issues, including customer support, new product development, and business process extensions. In 2012 the SAP community network stood at over 2.5 million members. On a monthly basis the community receives 1.2 million visitors and more than 3,000 discussion posts per day are made on the community site. Technical support questions get answered in less than 20 minutes from other community members with more than 85 percent of them deemed "answered" by the poster. Not only does this technical support function of the community lower SAP's costs, it also tends to be much higher quality as users in the field that have encountered the same problem before can provide direct expert advice on a resolution in place of a specialist backroom operator. SAP also uses the community to develop feature requirements for new product releases with more than 40 percent of new features being developed jointly by community members in various industrial and functional verticals. The community also engages in a range of continuing education related to technologies and products in the SAP portfolio. The social give and take of the community builds strong affiliation with both SAP and other community members; many report that they use their community activity to enhance their own learning and find new job prospects within the SAP ecosystem. In this case the SAP software becomes the core complementary asset that the firm can exploit while continuing to invest in its communities.

Innovation contest platforms are another example of hybrid organizations that have emerged to manage crowds (covering areas as diverse as data science, graphic design, advertisement, software development, and scientific problem solving). These platforms seek to aggregate both demand and supply for contests and contestants (ranging in size from tens of thousands to hundreds of thousands of members). Most organizations may not be able to sustain a large set of external problem solvers to work on their challenges. There may simply not be enough volume of problems to sustain a "custom crowd" for each organization. Hence platforms provide an aggregation and matching mechanism between organizations seeking solutions through contests and participants looking for problems to solve via contests. Interestingly, after a contest is finished, the platforms also invest in significant social activities to provide their solvers with a sense of identity and a means to learn and share knowledge about potential problem-solving approaches. Thus these platforms integrate both a contest and community function within their operations.

Contests and communities represent viable means of managing crowd-based innovation. While there are many instances when these institutions serve as substitutes to internal innovation, the current trend is toward complementary usage alongside with internal efforts. The academic and managerial challenge ahead is to layout the frameworks that enable both traditional and crowd-based institutions for innovation to be utilized in a way that maximizes problem-solving effectiveness for organizations and individuals seeking innovative outcomes.

Notes

I am very thankful to the following colleagues for being close thought partners, collaborators and coauthors: Carliss Baldwin, Kevin Boudreau, Paul Carlile, Eva Guinan, Ina Ganguli, Patrick Gaule, Ned Gulley, Connie Helfat, Marco Iansiti, Lars Bo Jeppesen, Andrew King, Nicola Lacetera, Hila Lifschitz-Assaf, Michael Menietti, Michael Tushman, Eric von Hippel, and Georg von Krogh. The Crowd Innovation Lab and the NASA Tournament Lab at the Harvard Institute for Quantitative Social Science provide the platform for much of the recent work involving field experiments. NASA colleagues Jason Crusan and Jeff Davis helped transform the ideas into experiments and proof-of-concepts in real organizations. Harvard Medical School's Dean for Clinical and Translational Research Lee Nadler is now providing the framework to bring these ideas into the academic medical center setting. The support of TopCoder and its previous and current executives (Jack Hughes, Rob Hughes, Ira Heffan, Narinder Singh, Mike Morris, and Andy Lamora) has been essential to a range of the online field experiments I have conducted.

1. The term *crowdsourcing* was coined by Jeff Howe in a 2006 article (Howe 2006) in *Wired* magazine where he discussed the emergence of platforms (markets, contests and communities) that aggregated labor for multiple task types. He referenced my study of the InnoCentive contest platform (Jeppesen and Lakhani 2010) in that article.

2. Diener and Piller (2013) estimate an annual market size of 2.3 billion euros for crowdsourcing hosting services.

3. Wikipedia, the online encyclopedia, is another example of a community-produced collective output. However, I do not include it in this discussion as it does not involve the creation of a functional technological artifact.

4. The vast majority of open source communities does not have "employees" that are contracted to work on the project and instead rely on individual volunteers or employees of firms that have an interest in the project. The communities do not have decision or resource allocation rights over the activities of the participants. In some larger open source projects (e.g., Mozilla and Linux) the supporting nonprofit foundation has hired employees to work on projects. These employees work hand in hand with community members to achieve project goals.

5. It is possible to make the integration task into a contest as well. As long as the components being integrated are modular and pre-defined. Indeed TopCoder also makes revenue from offering a complete solution that includes integration via contests.

6. Resume page for Igor Naverinouk, Engineer at Google: http://shygypsy.com/resume.html..

7. The Netflix Prize contest was designed in stages where winners of each stage disclosed the algorithms for reuse by others.

References

Aghion, Philippe, and Jean Tirole. 1994. The management of innovation. *Quarterly Journal of Economics* 109 (4): 1185–1209.

Allen, R. C. 1983. Collective invention. *Journal of Economic Behavior and Organization* 4 (1): 1–24.

Amabile, Teresa M. 1996. *Creativity in Context*. Boulder, CO: Westview Press.

Andrewes, William J.H. 1996. Even Newton could be Wwrong: The story of Harrison's first three sea clocks. In *The Quest for Longitude. Proceedings of the Longitude Symposium,* Harvard University, Cambridge, November 4–6, 1993, ed. William J. H. Andrewes, 189–234. Cambridge: Collection of Historical Scientific Instruments, Harvard University.

Baldwin, Carliss Y., and Kim B. Clark. 2006. The Architecture of participation: Does code architecture mitigate free riding in the open source development model? *Management Science* 52 (7): 1116–27.

Barbier, Jean-Paul. 1994. *Nicolas Appert: Inventeur et Humaniste*. Paris: Royer.

Boudreau, Kevin J., Nicola Lacetera, and Karim R. Lakhani. 2011. Incentives and problem uncertainty in innovation contests: An empirical analysis. *Management Science* 57 (5): 843–63.

Boudreau, Kevin J., and Karim R. Lakhani. 2012. The confederacy of heterogeneous software organizations and heterogeneous developers: Field experimental evidence on sorting and worker effort. In *The Rate and Direction of Inventive Activity Revisited*, ed. Josh Lerner and Scott Stern, 483–502. Chicago: University of Chicago Press.

Boudreau, Kevin J., and Karim R. Lakhani. 2013. Using the crowd as an innovation partner. *Harvard Business Review* 91 (4): 61–69.

Boudreau, Kevin J., and Karim R. Lakhani. 2015. "Open" disclosure of innovations, incentives and follow-on reuse: Theory on processes of cumulative innovation and a field experiment in computational biology. *Research Policy* 44 (1): 4–19.

Brunt, Liam, Josh Lerner, and Tom Nicholas. 2012. Inducement prizes and innovation. *Journal of Industrial Economics* 60 (4): 657–96.

Campbell-Kelly, Martin. 2003. *From Airline Reservations to Sonic the Hedgehog: A History of the Software Industry*. Cambridge: MIT Press.

Che, Yeon-Koo, and Ian Gale. 2003. Optimal design of research contests. *American Economic Review* 93 (3): 646–71.

Csikszentmihalyi, Mihaly. 1990. *Flow: The Psychology of Optimal Experience*. New York: Harper and Row.

Dasgupta, Partha, and Paul A. David. 1994. Toward a new economics of science. *Research Policy* 23 (5): 487–521.

Demsetz, Harold. 1964. The welfare and empirical implications of monopolistic competition. *Economic Journal* 74 (295): 623–41.

Diener, Kathleen, and Frank T. Piller. 2013. *The Market for Open Innovation.* Raleigh, NC: Lulu Publishing.

Ding, Waverly W., Fiona Murray, and Toby E. Stuart. 2006. Gender differences in patenting in the academic life sciences. *Science* 313 (5787): 665–67.

Feller, Joe, Brian Fitzgerald, Scott Hissam, and Karim R. Lakhani, eds. 2005. *Perspectives on Free and Open Source Software.* Cambridge: MIT Press.

Hertel, Guido, Sven Niedner, and Stefanie Herrmann. 2003. Motivation of software developers in open source projects: An Internet-based survey of contributors to the Linux kernel. *Research Policy* 32 (7): 1159–77.

Holmstrom, Bengt. 1989. Agency costs and innovation. *Journal of Economic Behavior and Organization* 12 (3): 305–27.

Howe, Jeff. 2006. The rise of crowdsourcing. *Wired Magazine* 14 (6): 176–83.

Iansiti, Marco, and Karim R. Lakhani. 2009. SAP AG: Orchestrating the ecosystem. In *Harvard Business School Case 609–069.* Boston: Harvard Business School Press.

Jeppesen, Lars Bo, and Karim R. Lakhani. 2010. Marginality and problem-solving effectiveness in broadcast search. *Organization Science* 21 (5): 1016–33.

KEI. 2008. Selected innovation prizes and reward programs. Research note 2008:1. Knowledge Ecology International, Washington, DC.

King, Ross. 2000. *Brunelleschi's Dome: How a Renaissance Genius Reinvented Architecture.* New York: Walker.

King, Andrew, and Karim R. Lakhani. 2013. Using open innovation to identify the best ideas. *Sloan Management Review* 55 (1): 41–48.

Lakhani, Karim R., Kevin J. Boudreau, Po-Ru Loh, Lars Backstrom, Carliss Baldwin, Eric Lonstein, Mike Lydon, Alan MacCormack, Ramy A. Arnaout, and Eva C. Guinan. 2013a. Prize-based contests can provide solutions to computational biology problems. *Nature Biotechnology* 31 (2): 108–11.

Lakhani, Karim R., David A. Garvin, and Eric Lonstein. 2012. TopCoder (A): Developing software through crowdsourcing. In *Harvard Business School Case 610–032, May 2012. (Revised from original January 2010 version.).* Boston: Harvard Business School Press.

Lakhani, Karim R., Hila Lifshitz-Assaf, and Michael Tushman. 2013b. Open innovation and organizational boundaries: Task decomposition, knowledge distribution and the locus of innovation. In *Handbook of Economic Organization: Integrating Economic and Organization Theory*, ed. Anna Grandori, 355–82. Northampton, MA: Edward Elgar.

Lakhani, Karim R., Marco Iansiti, and Noah Fisher. 2014. SAP 2014: Reaching for the cloud. In *Harvard Business School Case 614–052.* Boston: Harvard Business School Press.

Lakhani, Karim R., and Jill A. Panetta. 2007. The principles of distributed innovation. *Innovations: Technology, Governance, Globalization* 2 (3): 97–112.

Lakhani, Karim R., and Eric von Hippel. 2003. How open source software works: "Free" user-to-user assistance. *Research Policy* 32 (6): 923–43.

Lakhani, Karim R., and Robert Wolf. 2005. Why hackers do what they do: Understanding motivation and effort in free/open source software projects. In *Perspectives on Free and Open Source Software*, ed. Joe Feller, Brian Fitzgerald, Scott Hissam, and Karim R. Lakhani, 3–22. Cambridge: MIT Press.

Lazear, Edward P. 2000. Performance pay and productivity. *American Economic Review* 90 (5): 1346–62.

Lerner, Josh, and Mark Schankerman. 2010. *The Comingled Code: Open Source and Economic Development*. Cambridge: MIT Press.

Lerner, Josh, and Jean Tirole. 2002. Some simple economics of Open Source. *Journal of Industrial Economics* 50 (2): 197–234.

Moldovanu, Benny, and Aner Sela. 2001. The optimal allocation of prizes in contests. *American Economic Review* 91 (3): 542–58.

Murray, Fiona, Scott Stern, Georgina Campbell, and Alan MacCormack. 2012. Grand innovation prizes: A theoretical, normative, and empirical evaluation. *Research Policy* 41 (10): 1779–92.

National Research Council. 2007. *Innovation Inducement Prizes at the National Science Foundation*. Washington, DC: The National Academies Press.

Nickerson, Jack A., and Todd R. Zenger. 2004. A knowledge-based theory of the firm: The problem solving perspective. *Organization Science* 15 (6): 617–32.

Nuvolari, Alessandro. 2004. Collective invention during the British Industrial Revolution: The case of the Cornish pumping engine. *Cambridge Journal of Economics* 28 (3): 347–63.

O'Mahony, Siobhan, and Karim R. Lakhani. 2011. Organizations in the shadow of communities. In *Communities and Organizations*, ed. Christopher Marquis, Michael Lounsbury, and Royston Greenwood, 3–36. Research in the Sociology of Organizations 33. Bingley, UK: Emerald Group.

Osterloh, Margit, and Sandra Rota. 2007. Open source software development: Just another case of collective invention? *Research Policy* 36 (2): 157–71.

Raymond, Eric S. 1999. *The Cathedral and the Bazaar: Musings on Linux and Open Source by an Accidental Revolutionary*. Sebastopol, CA: O'Reilly Media.

Roberts, Jeffery A., Ill-Horn Hann, and Sandra A. Slaughter. 2006. Understanding the motivations, participation, and performance of open source software developers: A longitudinal study of the Apache projects. *Management Science* 52 (7): 984–99.

Ryan, Richard M., and Edward L. Deci. 2000. Intrinsic and extrinsic motivations: Classic definitions and new directions. *Contemporary Educational Psychology* 25 (1): 54–67.

Salus, Peter H. 1994. *A Quarter Century of Unix*. New York: Addison Wesley.

Sauermann, Henry, and Wesley M. Cohen. 2010. What makes them tick? Employee motives and firm innovation. *Management Science* 56 (12): 2134–53.

Stern, Scott. 2004. Do scientists pay to be scientists? *Management Science* 50 (6): 835–53.

Stewart, Katherine J., and Sanjay Gosain. 2006. The impact of ideology on effectiveness in open source software development teams. *Management Information Systems Quarterly* 30 (2): 291–314.

von Hippel, Eric. 2005. *Democratizing Innovation*. Cambridge: MIT Press.

von Hippel, Eric, and Georg von Krogh. 2003. Open source software and the private-collective innovation model: Issues for organization science. *Organization Science* 14 (12): 209–23.

von Krogh, Georg, Sebastian Spaeth, and Karim R. Lakhani. 2003. Community, joining, and specialization in open source software innovation: A case study. *Research Policy* 32 (7): 1217–41.

West, Joel, and Karim R. Lakhani. 2008. Getting clear about communities in open innovation. *Industry and Innovation* 15 (2): 223–31.

Zuckerman, Harriet. 1991. The careers of men and women scientists: A review of current research. In *The Outer Circle: Women in the Scientific Community*, ed. Harriet Zuckerman, Jonathan R. Cole, and John T. Bruer, 27–56. New Haven: Yale University Press.

7

Knowledge Sharing among Inventors: Some Historical Perspectives

James Bessen and Alessandro Nuvolari

During the 1980s innovation scholars became increasingly aware of the importance of knowledge sharing as a fundamental *source* of innovations. In one of the early studies of the phenomenon based on a large number of case studies of Irish, Spanish, and Mexican firms, Allen et al. (1983) noted that, rather surprisingly, knowledge sharing of innovations was taking place regularly even among "apparent competitors." Subsequently Eric von Hippel documented the existence of widespread and systematic knowledge sharing activities among competitors in a detailed case study of the US steel mini-mill industry, noting that plant managers routinely shared proprietary know-how with competing firms (von Hippel 1987; see also Schrader 1991). This was important because it not only diffused new techniques, but it also facilitated further cumulative improvements.

Yet von Hippel also recognized that this phenomenon might have deep historical roots, citing the historical study of Robert Allen (Allen 1983). Allen, writing about the pig iron industry of Cleveland (UK) in 1850 to 1870, observed an instance of "free exchange of information about new techniques and plant designs among firms in an industry" (Allen 1983: 2). This exchange of knowledge facilitated innovations that built cumulatively on previous advances. Allen called this behavior *collective invention*.

Nevertheless, it is still widely believed that knowledge sharing is mainly a modern development, perhaps related to the drastic reduction of costs for exchanging information brought about by advances in information and communication technologies. For example, Henry Chesbrough (2003: 24) describes today's *open innovation* as a sharp break from the paradigm of the early twentieth century when R&D labs were largely self-sufficient, only occasionally receiving outside visitors, and when researchers would only occasionally venture out to visit universities or scientific expositions. Similarly, popular history books and museums often highlight the *heroic inventor* with little attention to cooperation between innovators in the past.

Interestingly, economic historian Joel Mokyr (2009) has recently pointed to the *industrial enlightenment* as a critical precondition for the emergence and consolidation of the industrial revolution in the late eighteenth century. Mokyr's concept of industrial enlightenment refers to a knowledge revolution that progressively gained momentum during the eighteenth century. Two key-features of this knowledge revolution were (1) a drastic reduction in the costs of accessing extant bodies of knowledge (thanks to the expanding publication of scientific and technical books and journals) and (2) a concerted attempt to create a *public sphere* for the fruitful interaction between scientific researchers and practitioners confronted with technical problems. Clearly, Mokyr's *industrial enlightenment* emphasizes the historical significance of knowledge sharing activities and, in particular, the establishment of formal and informal exchanges of information between *natural philosophers* and *manufacturers*. At the same time, however, Mokyr remains skeptical about the significance of knowledge sharing among inventors competing in the same industry, delivering this stark assessment:

There are three reasonably well-documented cases of successful collective invention: the case documented by Allen (1983) of the Cleveland (UK) iron industry between 1850 and 1875, the case documented by MacLeod (1988: 112–13, 188) of the English clock and instrument makers; and the case documented by Nuvolari (2004) of the Cornish steam-engine makers after 1800. Examples of such cases are not many, and they required rather special circumstances that were not common, and collective invention in its more extreme form, to judge from its short lifespan, was vulnerable and ephemeral. (Mokyr 2008: 81)

In contrast, there is growing evidence of recent knowledge sharing that goes well beyond the steel mini-mills and open source software. Since the seminal papers by Allen (1983) and von Hippel (1987), knowledge sharing activities by competing firms have rapidly developed into one of the major themes of the innovation studies literature (see Penin 2007 and Powell and Giannella 2010 for useful surveys). Within this broad literature, an important stream of research has focused, in particular, on knowledge sharing by users (Harhoff et al. 2003; von Hippel 2005; Shah 2005).

If the nineteenth century saw little knowledge sharing, then it would be important to understand why innovation today seems so fundamentally different. Of course, the conventional assessment of nineteenth century knowledge sharing might not be accurate. Perhaps knowledge sharing occurred more frequently and was more important than is generally recognized. Indeed we are aware of numerous examples where the conventional assessment seems misleading. For example, textbooks, popular history books, and museums typically attribute the rapid growth in the productivity of US wheat production to the invention of mechanical threshers, reapers, and the like, by individual inventors such as Cyrus McCormick. However, recent scholars have found that this revolution in productivity would not have been possible without extensive biological innovation based on the sharing of knowledge and of seed varieties by farmers (Olmstead and Rhode 2008: ch. 2).

In this chapter we take a second look at the historical evidence concerning knowledge sharing activities by competing agents during the eighteenth and nineteenth centuries. As we will show, from the historical records it is clear that knowledge sharing and free revealing among inventors were important sources of innovation. Although the evidence is not sufficient to judge whether it occurred more frequently than today, knowledge sharing was common in the past, and especially in the development of some critical technologies. Furthermore there was for a long time tension between the depth and scope of open knowledge-sharing activities and the operation of patent systems.

Indeed Henkel and von Hippel (2005) argue that important welfare gains stemmed from user innovation that was openly shared without claims to intellectual property rights. On this basis von Hippel (2005) argues for a more comprehensive assessment of the welfare effects of intellectual property rights policies. The historical evidence on knowledge sharing thus raises the possibility that patent systems may not be the only factor driving innovation. In fact a careful reassessment of the historical role of knowledge sharing might provide a first step toward understanding the relative importance of patents and of knowledge sharing institutions in different markets, for different types of technologies, and at different phases of the technology life cycle.

Knowledge Sharing among Inventors: Some Historical Evidence

Allen (1983: 21) was first to speculate that "under the conditions prevailing during the nineteenth century, [collective invention] was probably the most important source of inventions." Allen's conjecture rests on the idea that before the establishment of corporate R&D laboratories, in many industries inventive activities were carried out as a by-product of investment processes without resorting to patent protection. If so, we should expect that, during the nineteenth century, a significant number of inventions were not covered by patents.

Detailed quantitative assessments of the amount of inventive activity undertaken outside the coverage of patent protection remain inherently speculative. The appeal of patents for economists and economic historians largely stems from the opportunity to study systematically the full universe of patented inventions. By contrast, any sensible catalog of the inventions that remained unpatented is likely to be fraught with omissions and related biases, or restricted in long-term comparisons. Moser's (2005, 2012) research probably provides the best quantitative snapshot of the volume of inventive activity undertaken outside the patent system in the mid-nineteenth century. Moser examined how many of the inventions put on display at the Crystal Palace exhibition of 1851 were patented. Only 11.1 percent of the 6,377 British inventions were patented.

One might be tempted to ascribe this remarkably low patent propensity to the high costs and cumbersome administrative procedures of the English patent system during the first half of the nineteenth century. However, Moser's findings are similar for the United States, where the patent system was characterized by a smooth application process and low patent fees: only 15.3 percent of 550 US exhibits were patented. Clearly, Moser's findings show that appropriating inventions by means of patents was not a major concern for many nineteenth century inventors. But can we also assume that the low level of patent propensity estimated by Moser was coupled by knowledge sharing among inventors as it assumed in the collective invention model? The answer is that we do not know yet. Much research on this issue still needs to be done. However, since the publication of Allen's paper, economic historians and historians of technology have been able to identify several other examples of knowledge sharing activities among inventors coupled with limited or no use of patent protection.

Knowledge Sharing among Inventors in the Early Modern Period

Before the Industrial Revolution, technical change was mostly the result of the accumulation of incremental innovations and improvements. Accordingly, before the eighteenth century, episodes of major innovations credited to specific individual inventors were rare—the case of Gutenberg and the printing press appears to be the most significant exception. Epstein (1998: 699) compares technological innovation in the early modern period to the invention and transmission of jokes. Jokes typically have no recognizable author and they are simply passed on by word of mouth. Interestingly, a certain degree of awareness of the *collective* nature of innovation was reflected in the common habit of using the names of localities as eponyms for specific innovations. For example, the use of eponyms such as *Bolognese* silk-throwing machine and *Dutch* loom suggest an appreciation that these inventions were the product of a community of inventors rather than a single individual.[1] Another revealing example of this awareness is Denis Diderot's conceptualization of invention. Diderot, noting that inventions emerged from adaptations and recombinations of already existing techniques by communities of artisans and technicians, had no particular qualms in asserting (in the eighteenth century) that individual inventors should be denied exclusive rights on innovations (Hilaire-Perez 2002).

This awareness of the collective nature of innovation processes and of the possible benefits arising from knowledge sharing is also revealed by guild regulations concerning the transmission of technological knowledge. Today the resilience of guild systems after 1500 is frequently seen as an institutional obstacle to the development of new technologies (Mokyr 1990: 191, 258–60). Several scholars have recently challenged this view, especially Epstein who argues that in a world of largely tacit technological knowledge, some features of the guild system, such as apprenticeship regulations, were an effective mean of transmitting and consolidating technical skills. Epstein contends that the overall contribution of the guild system to technological progress in early modern Europe was positive. Indeed the traditionally negative judgment of craft guilds appears to be based on a number of documented instances when guilds opposed introducing specific inventions. Epstein invites us to be extremely careful in drawing generalizations from these cases (Epstein 1998, see also the essays collected in Epstein and Prak 2008). It appears that guild regulations and practices, by emphasizing the *collective ownership* of skills and technical know-how, actively promoted the sharing of technical knowledge in a period when its transmission by other means such as printed texts was inherently limited (Epstein 2004). Since guild inventions took the form of incremental improvements and refinements to current processes and products, they tended to be much less visible in the historical records (Epstein 1998: 696).

An important maritime invention to emerge from the knowledge-sharing activities taking place within the guild system is the *fluyt*. The fluyt was a sailing ship developed in the Netherlands in the 1500s. This ship became the favorite cargo carrier employed by the Dutch East India Company during the seventeenth century. In his detailed historical study of the Dutch shipcarpenters' guilds, Unger (1978: 80) found evidence of regular knowledge-sharing activities regarding technological matters during work on the design of the fluyt occurring at several business and social meetings that guild members were required to attend.

Collective ownership of *trade* knowledge could result in opposition to the issuing of patents. Between 1688 and 1718, the London Clockmakers Company lobbied intensively for the repeal of specific patents related to their trades. Yet around this time a number of important innovations in clock and instrument making, such as improved versions of the thermometer and of the barometer, were successfully introduced (MacLeod 1988: 112–13; Turner 2008). Perez (Perez 2008; Foray and Hilaire-Perez 2006) has studied the knowledge-sharing practices among inventors in the highly successful Lyon silk industry. In Lyon, the manufacture of silk was organized by the powerful silk guild of the *Grande Fabrique*. Perez describes the knowledge-sharing practices of the Lyonnaise guild system as *open technique* institutions, thus drawing a parallel to Allen's notion of *collective invention* Interestingly, the *open technique* innovation system of Lyon was able to outcompete London in the production of silk. In London, in contrast, the organization of inventive activities was based on the widespread use of secrecy and patents (Cotterau 1997: 139–43).

Karel Davids (2008: 394–400) argues that free exchange of technical knowledge among inventors was a common practice among millwrights in the Netherlands during the seventeenth and eighteenth centuries. Zankstreet millwrights in the Netherlands normally refrained from applying for patents (Davids 2008: 408). Hence, according to Davids, the

Zankstreet district represented another clear-cut case of *collective invention*. Again, this is a case of an organization of inventive activities that would yield high rates of technical progress. The Zaankstreet became one of the cutting-edge industrial districts in Europe and was the first place where wind power was adopted on a massive scale during the seventeenth century.

Knowledge Sharing among Inventors during the Industrial Revolution
Knowledge sharing among inventors was further critical to the Industrial Revolution. The best-documented case of collective invention during the early nineteenth century is the development of the high-pressure steam engine in Cornwall. (Nuvolari 2004; Nuvolari and Verspagen 2007). In the Cornish mining district steam engines were used to pump water out of copper and tin mines. Since coal in Cornwall was relatively expensive, the Cornish mining district became an early adopter of Boulton and Watt engines because they represented the best practice of the time in terms of fuel efficiency. Significantly Watt patented his design for an engine with a separate steam condenser with a very broad specification. After Boulton and Watt's penetration in the Cornish market, several engineers attempted to make improvements but were frustrated by Boulton and Watt's tight enforcement of Watt's patent (Nuvolari and Verspagen 2007). The outcome was a period of stagnation in fuel efficiency.

In the wake of this disappointing experience, after Watt's patent expired in 1800, most Cornish steam engineers preferred not to patent their inventions. Accordingly, the share of Cornish patents in steam engineering for the period 1813 to 1852 fell to under one percent of the national total (Nuvolari 2004: 358). In fact in 1811 Cornish mining engineers and entrepreneurs launched a monthly publication, called *Lean's Engine Reporter*, that provided reports on steam engine performance, technical details, and operating procedures being developed in the county. The explicit intention was twofold. First, the publication would permit the rapid identification and diffusion of best-practice techniques. Second, it would create a climate of competition and emulation in the Cornish engineering community with favorable effects on the rate of technical progress. Joel Lean, a highly respected "mine captain" was entrusted with the compilation of the reports and the publication of *Lean's Engine Reporter*. It is right after the first issues of *Lean's Engine Reporter* that Cornwall attained world technological leadership in steam engineering with the introduction of a particularly successful high-pressure condensing engine that would become universally known as the *Cornish* engine (Barton 1969).[2] It can be shown that the systematic comparison of technical features, operational procedures, and performance of the engines allowed engineers to identify the best design configurations, for example, in terms of cylinder size, for attaining economies of fuel (Nuvolari and Verspagen 2009).

Although not as organized as in Cornwall, a similar ethos seems to have pervaded the nascent civil engineering profession, which was responsible for many of the innovations in transport. Very little of the problem-solving activity that underpinned the engineering of bridges, tunnels, cuttings, and embankments, for example, in the provision of roads, canals, and railways is evident in patent records. Rather, civil engineers tended to share and publish their solutions, with a view to enhancing their professional reputations (MacLeod 1988: 104–105).

In a more recent contribution, Allen (2009) suggests that the organization of inventive activities by means of collective invention was characteristic as well of other technologies developed during the Industrial Revolution. The first case he mentions is the development of coal-burning houses in London in the seventeenth century. Since most of the innovations in this field were unpatentable, builders copied and adapted innovations from each other (Allen 2009: 92–93). The second case he mentions is the adoption of clover, sainfoin, and turnips in crop rotations by open field farmers (Allen 2009: 68–74).

Furthermore, some important inventions that originally were developed by individual inventors, such as James Hargreaves' spinning jenny, were improved and refined by means of collective invention processes. For example, the original spinning jenny had 12 spindles, but very soon 24 spindles models were developed for use in cottages and models of 80 up to 120 spindles for use in workshops. According to Allen (2009b: 906), "[t]hese improvements in the jenny were accomplished without patents and were affected by collective invention."

Were these examples of knowledge-sharing activities a response to the very imperfect English patent system of the time? To obtain an English patent, an inventor had to pay expensive fees and endure unwieldy administrative procedures. Perhaps if the English patent system were more like its American counterpart—with low fees and simple procedures—more

English inventors would have chosen to appropriate returns using patents. This might have led to less knowledge sharing, though perhaps higher levels of private investment in the search for innovations. This interpretation would be consistent with the assessment of the US patent system put forward by Khan and Sokoloff (1998). According to Khan and Sokoloff (1998), the highly accessible US patent system was a key driver of technical change in the nineteenth-century American economy.

Still, it would be wrong to assume that collective invention was just a British phenomenon. For example, in his account of the development of the high-pressure engine for the western steamboats in the United States during the early nineteenth century, Hunter (1949: 121–80) emphasized the significance of various flows of incremental innovations. Moreover, with regard to the present discussion, Hunter makes a particularly intriguing observation:

Though the men who developed the machinery of the western steamboat possessed much ingenuity and inventive skill, the record shows that they had little awareness of or use for the patent system. Of more than six hundred patents relating to steam engines issued in this country down to 1847 only some forty were taken out in the names of men living in towns and cities of the western rivers. Few even of this small number had any practical significance. In view of the marked western preference for steam over water power and the extensive development of steam-engine manufacturing in the West, these are surprising figures. How is this meager showing to be explained and interpreted? Does it reflect a distaste for patents as a species of monopoly uncongenial to the democratic ways of the West, an attitude sharpened by the attempts of Fulton and Evans to collect royalties from steamboatmen? Or were western mechanics so accustomed to think in terms of mere utility that they failed to grasp the exploitative possibilities of the products of their ingenuity? Or did mechanical innovation in this field proceed by such small increments as to present few points which could readily be seized upon by a potential patentee? Perhaps each of these suggestions—and especially the last—holds a measure of the truth. At all events the fact remains that, so far as can be determined, no significant part of the engine, propelling mechanism, or boilers during the period of the steamboat's development to maturity was claimed and patented as a distinctive and original development. (pp. 175–76).

In Hunter's view, the litigation over patents taken by Robert Fulton and Oliver Evans may account for the negative attitude of western mechanics toward patents (pp. 10, 124–26). Hunter was able to document the emergence among western steamboatmen and mechanics of a number of rules of thumb in steamboat design and operating practices that were continuously refined and improved by means of information exchanges (pp. 176–80). The steady accumulation of many small changes and alterations to the design of the steamers produced improvements in carrying capacity, increases of speed, reduction of cargo collection times, and so on, leading to a rate of productivity growth without parallel in the transport technology of the period (Mak and Walton 1972).

In the United States, knowledge sharing was further important in the development of the critical cotton textile industry, one of the harbingers of industrialization. In 1814 Francis Cabot Lowell built the first commercially successful power loom in North America with the help of mechanic Paul Moody. Lowell patented this loom and his company sold patent rights and also manufactured patent looms. But Lowell's company made most of its money from producing its own cloth with this technology, and they discontinued patent licensing and sales after a few years (Gibb 1950).[3] In 1817 William Gilmour built the second commercially successful power loom in the United States with the assistance of David Wilkinson.[4] The design of this loom was more or less freely shared: Wilkinson paid ten dollars for Gilmour's drawings. Gilmour, Wilkinson, and mechanics trained by Wilkinson engaged in the business of building looms under contract to prospective cotton manufacturers (Bagnall 1893). The rapid diffusion of the power loom owes much to the "liberal" policy of Gilmour and his sponsor, Daniel Lyman. Gilmour's design proved to be superior to Lowell's, replacing it even at the mills of Lowell's company (Gibb 1950). While patent protection was important for some weaving inventions during the Industrial Revolution, such as the loom temple, other key inventions, such as the weft fork, were not patented in the United States.

Knowledge-sharing practices indeed permeated other historic nineteenth-century American industries. McGaw's (1987) study of papermaking in Berkshire, Massachusetts, during the nineteenth century documents that paper manufacturers engaged in extensive information exchanges concerning machinery to purchase and their possible adaptation to specific production tasks. In her interpretation, this knowledge sharing was key to the industrial success of the region. Similarly Wallace (1978: 211–39) found evidence of continuous free exchanges of information on the solution of technical problems among fellow mechanics and machine makers.[5]

Knowledge Sharing among Inventors during the Late Nineteenth Century

Evidence of knowledge sharing does not end with the Industrial Revolution. As mentioned above, Allen (1983) documented the importance of knowledge sharing for the British iron industry in the Cleveland district. Thanks to free exchange of information about new techniques and plant designs, "fruitful lines of technical advance were identified and pursued" (p. 2) leading to a high and sustained "rate of invention" in the industry. In 1854 Cleveland was producing 275 thousand tons of iron (about 9 percent of British production). Less than twenty years later, in 1873, Cleveland's production had increased to 2 million tons, or 30 percent of British production (Allen 1981: 37). This increase in output was driven by a sustained stream of inventions that revolutionized blast furnace practice in the Cleveland iron district. Remarkably, throughout the period 1850 to 1870, Cleveland engineers claimed very few patents (Allen 1983: 2). By and large this stream of inventions was the outcome of systematic knowledge sharing among engineers and designers of blast furnaces, as described by Allen. In the engineering literature of the 1860s and 1870s, the blast furnaces of Cleveland were recognized as the world leading technology (Allen 1981). One particularly intriguing contemporary assessment of the Cleveland iron district that was not noted by Allen in his original study was made by Eugène Schneider, the managing director of the famous Le Creusot ironworks in France. Schneider (1871: 133) observed the advantages of the Cleveland iron industry's organizational setup as favoring knowledge sharing rather than individual appropriation and protection:

Certain localities have had very restrictive habits in their industries; that is to say, habits of secrecy. In those localities, everyone hides what he is doing, or takes out a patent. The localities in which this spirit prevails very seldom advance with great speed. They remain almost always at a very low industrial level. The localities, on the other hand, which have a very liberal spirit in matters of invention and in matters of patents, advance very rapidly. The entire locality profits greatly by it, and everyone gets his share of the advantage . . . [O]ne of the most remarkable facts in the world is the immense progress which has been made by the locality of Middelsboro' . . .; 15 years ago, there was scarcely anything done there in the iron manufacture. At the present day it is the first district of the world for that manufacture, and I have found there is a most liberal spirit, everybody telling his neighbour, everybody telling any stranger who has had the honour of being admitted to those great manufacturers "This is what we do," "This is what succeeds with us," "This our invention." I have told you the result.

Other economic historians have pointed to other episodes of knowledge sharing among inventors in the late nineteenth century. Kyriazidou and Pesendorfer (1999) suggest that collective invention also was a characteristic of the Viennese bentwood furniture industry in the 1850s. The industry was highly successful, establishing Viennese chairs as a fashion item throughout the world. Also in manufacturing processes, in general, Viennese firms pioneered large-scale production methods and interchangeable parts. According to Kyriaziodou and Pesendorfer, Viennese furniture firms engaged in continuous exchanges of information both on new production techniques and new product designs: "firms were quick to copy the new products of their rivals, and even offered them under the same name in their catalogues. As a result, their chairs, which constituted the bulk of industry production, came to be known simply as 'Viennese chairs'" (Kyriazidou and Pesendorfer 1999: 144). These knowledge exchanges reduced the cost of experimentation at the level of individual firms. Firms did take patents, but they did not enforce them against their compatriots but rather against foreign firms (Kyrazidou and Pesendorfer 1999: 158). According to Kyriazidou and Pesendrofer, the main factor accounting for this pattern of information exchanges was that the continuous innovation in manufacturing and product design fueled rapid growth of industry output, limiting the emergence of possible competitive tensions.

Meyer (2003) documents extensive knowledge sharing in US Bessemer steel production. Henry Bessemer patented his process in 1856, but extensive litigation with other inventors delayed the implementation of the method until the creation of a patent pool in the United States in 1866. However, Bessemer's process did not work well at first and required substantial improvements. These were developed largely by engineering consultants such as Alexander Holley. Meyer documents how knowledge was shared through technical publications, by job mobility among engineers and by sharing patents and technical know-how among pool members. As a result the cost of Bessemer steel rail fell from $100 per ton in 1870 to $60 per ton in 1880.

These knowledge-sharing activities were not limited to manufacturing. In a recent paper Moser and Rhode (2012) describe the existence of widespread knowledge sharing in the community of American hobbyist rose breeders in the early 1900s. These knowledge exchanges were organized in the context of the American Rose Society and led to the creation of large number of new rose varieties. Plant varieties were not protected by US patents until 1930, for asexual propagation, and not until 1970 for sexually propagated varieties. Similarly in the United States highly dynamic biological innovation occurred in nineteenth- and early twentieth-century agriculture in wheat, cotton, tobacco, alfalfa, and corn, and also livestock, as documented by Olmstead and Rhode (2008). Individual farmers developed many of the improvements, and they freely shared their varieties and knowledge with others. With some crops, such as cotton, farmers organized into cooperatives to coordinate on the best local varieties. In later years, government assisted by gathering and diffusing knowledge of best practices. Although all this biological innovation is excluded from many accounts of nineteenth century innovation, it had very large benefits for social welfare.

Yet another interesting example of systematic knowledge sharing in the agricultural sector is the case of the Danish "control societies" formed by Danish farmers during the 1890s described by Faber (1931). This organizational arrangement for knowledge sharing bears a close resemblance with the Cornish case of *Lean's Engine Reporter*. Membership of the "control society" required farmers to pay a fee. In exchange for this fee, members of the society would receive regular visits from a "control assistant" monitoring both the quantity and quality of the milk produced by each cow and the food she was fed. The data gathered in this way were then published in regular reports.[6] As a result the breeding of cows underwent major improvements, leading to a rapid increase of milk production (liters of milk per cow) and a higher quality of milk (fat content of milk).

Knowledge sharing among inventors was a practice as well in developing countries that were trying to close their technology gaps and catch up with the world technological frontier. According to Saxonhouse (1974) and Otsuka et al. (1988), this was exactly what occurred in the Japanese cotton spinning industry. In Saxonhouse's view, this industry represented "the first completely successful instance of Asian assimilation of western manufacturing techniques" (Saxonhouse 1974: 150). Over the period 1880 to 1900, the Japanese cotton industry was capable of successfully adopting ring spinning frames coupled with a number of other technical and organizational improvements. The exchange of information took place within the institutional framework of the All Japanese Cotton Spinners Association (*Boren*), and in particular of its monthly bulletin called *Boren Geppo*. The journal published detailed production and costs data at the plant level. These data permitted systematic comparison across plants and in this way they enhanced the rapid diffusion of best practices. The journal also published systematic reports on innovations developed both in Japan and abroad (Saxonhouse 1974: 160).

Knowledge sharing was also a critical ingredient for the invention of the airplane. As Meyer (2013) shows, throughout the period 1880 to 1910, a vibrant international community of inventors and scientists openly reported and discussed merits and limitations of different designs of flying machines in various book-length publications and journals. Overall, few inventions for heavier-than-air flight were patented during this phase and the main line of progress consisted of inventions that were freely shared. This situation changed drastically when Wilbur and Orville Wright took their master patent for lateral control in 1906. The success of the Wrights' experiments marked a sharp turn in the history of the airplane. Lured by the prospect of commercial success, many inventors and entrepreneurs entered in this field. In contrast with the behavior of their predecessors, these inventors aggressively patented and asserted their patent rights. The case of the invention of the airplane shows a stark shift from knowledge sharing to a proprietary regime.

Why Share Knowledge?

Both von Hippel (1987) and Allen (1983) argue that the knowledge sharing activities they document are fully consistent with rational individual economic behavior. Allen suggests two possible reasons for the disclosure of information in the Cleveland iron district. First, disclosure of information about a successful blast furnace design would have enhanced the reputations of the designing engineers and of the managers of the firm. This increase in reputation might well have offset any possible reduction in profits brought about by the information disclosure. In particular, reputational concerns might have been important for the engineers, since blast furnaces were typically designed by consulting engineers who moved from firm to firm (Allen 1983: 17). Hence the diffusion of information on the design and performance of different blast furnaces allowed the best engineers to signal their talents and improve their career prospects. The second reason proposed by Allen is that the disclosure of information could increase the value of some of the assets owned by the revealing party. In the case of Cleveland, blast furnace firms typically also owned ore mines. Any improvement in the average performance of the blast furnaces was reflected in an increase of the value of the iron ore deposit, possibly making the free revealing of technical information also profitable from the point of view of the individual firm.[7]

von Hippel's (1987) interpretation of knowledge-sharing activities is more general in scope. He focuses on the *competitive value* of the unit of knowledge that is revealed. When the competitive advantage offered by the unit of knowledge in question is limited, information disclosure will not result in a dangerous competitive backlash for the revealing unit. Furthermore, if the behavior is reciprocated, this is likely to result in a generalized welfare gain for all firms participating in the knowledge exchange (von Hippel 1987: 299). Vice versa, when the unit of knowledge in question offers an important competitive advantage vis-à-vis industry rivals, we should clearly expect firms to refrain from disclosing critical product information.

von Hippel's rationale turns the focus of investigation toward understanding what market and technology conditions generate the *soft* rivalry that gives rise to knowledge sharing as well as what conditions give rise to aggressive rivalry and patenting. Bessen (2011) provides a partial answer, suggesting that under some common conditions, as technology matures the nature of firm rivalry, firms' willingness to share knowledge and their use of patents correspondingly change. In particular, knowledge sharing is more likely to occur during the early phases of the technology's life cycle or where local innovation has little effect on worldwide prices—factors that appear consistent with many of the examples discussed here.

Thus individually rational economic agents might well have good reason to share knowledge just as they might have good reason to patent. These choices, however, depend greatly on the specific circumstances, and clearly, very simple theoretical models of patenting may not reflect the richness of actual innovative behavior.

Conclusion

These many instances of knowledge sharing among inventors suggest a reappraisal of the history of innovation. It is quite evident that knowledge sharing among innovators in the past was not rare nor a marginal activity. Although we have not established the full extent of collective invention, it is clear that key technologies at the heart of industrialization, such as the high-pressure steam engines, iron and steel production techniques, the steamboat, and textile mills were at times and places developed through collective effort.

While outstanding individuals also made important contributions to these technologies, some histories tend to focus exclusively on the *heroic inventor*, but this is a history that is misleading and incomplete. The story of Cyrus McCormick and his mechanical reaper might be a more compelling narrative than the stories of farmers, often nameless, who painstakingly developed and shared new varieties of wheat that could be cultivated on the Great Plains. Yet their innovations and knowledge sharing were no less important.

The examples discussed in this chapter should make clear that patents are not universally important to innovation. Indeed many technologies were developed outside the purview of the patent system. In some industries, such as aviation, aggressive patenting put an end to a period of extensive knowledge sharing. In other industries, knowledge sharing and patents coexisted, as among the Bessemer engineers or the early mechanics who would freely share patented inventions with other mechanics but not with manufacturers (Wallace 1978). In still other industries patents were likely crucial to encouraging innovation. The relationship of innovation, patents, and knowledge sharing is a subtle and complex one. Optimal policy needs to apply to the full range of market conditions, technological maturity, and the like, in order to encourage knowledge sharing as well as proprietary incentives. An unbalanced policy may, on one hand, provide strong patent incentives to incrementally improve mature technologies, but it may, on the other hand, inhibit the development of early stage technologies, undermining the emergence and consolidation of important technological trajectories.

This brief overview of knowledge sharing suggests a continuity between innovation in the nineteenth century and today's highly innovative open source software community. The user innovation communities identified by von Hippel and his associates (von Hippel 2005; Shah 2005) appear to have much in common with early generations of innovators in the way they shared knowledge. Thus the history of knowledge sharing may be a particularly good source for understanding the institutions and incentives that help shape innovation in general.

Notes

We would like to thank Bob Allen, Christine MacLeod, Peter Meyer, Petra Moser, Kevin O'Rourke, Maarten Prak, Stefan Thomke, and Eric von Hippel for helpful comments and discussions. Alessandro Nuvolari gratefully acknowledges the Jemolo Fellowship Scheme and the hospitality of Nuffield College, Oxford while writing this chapter.

1. The convention of using the names of individual inventors as eponyms for specific technologies is probably to be traced back to the second half of the eighteenth century and is a manifestation of the cultural shift leading to the "glorification" of the heroic inventor as a national benefactor described by MacLeod (2007). MacLeod (2007) describes the British case, but analogous shifts in the public perception of inventors took place in all Western countries during the nineteenth century.

2. Notably, even though specific inventions introduced in Cornwall can be ascribed to individual inventors (e.g., the tubular boiler to Richard Trevithick, the compound engine design and the double beat valve to Arthur Woolf), the high pressure condensing engine would become known as the *Cornish* engine, giving credit to the whole community of engineers.

3. By some rough estimates, profits from patent licenses and profits on equipment manufactured and sold by the Boston Manufacturing Company comprised only 6 percent of profits from 1817 to 1823 when these activities were discontinued (calculations available from the authors).

4. Both of these loom designs were based significantly on English designs. Lowell visited English mills and Gilmour had been a mechanic at one. However, both inventors took over a year to get their models working and they had to develop complementary inventions as well.

5. In the US case, knowledge sharing activities taking place in networks of mechanics and machine makers are also described by Thomson (2009). A particular interesting case described by Thomson is the knowledge sharing activities instigated by the US government in the production of firearms during the 1820s and 1830s (Thomson 2009: 54–59).

6. The first control society in Denmark was the *Control Society of Vejen and District* created in 1895 (Faber 1931: 113). Following this highly successful example, starting in the late 1890s, "control societies" were established across the entire country.

7. Allen (1983: 4) further argues that increases in furnace height or blast temperature, being relatively minor variations of existing practices, would not have been patentable. Hence the choice for an inventor in Cleveland might have between secrecy and making the information publicly available (Allen 1983: 6). In fact there is an interesting difference between collective invention in Cleveland and in Cornish steam engines. In Cornwall, while variations is steam pressure and in cylinder sizes might have not been patentable, other, clearly patentable inventions such as the double-beat valve or the Cornish water-gauge (an instrument allowing a prompt monitoring of the level of water in the boiler), were not patented but freely shared (Nuvolari 2004: 359; Pole 1844: 109).

References

Allen, R. C. 1981. Entrepreneurship and technical progress in the northeast coast pig iron industry: 1850–1913. *Research in Economic History* 6:35–71.

Allen, R. C. 1983. Collective invention. *Journal of Economic Behavior and Organization* 4 (1): 1–24.

Allen, R. C. 2009. *The British Industrial Revolution in Global Perspective*. Cambridge, UK: Cambridge University Press.

Allen, R. C. 2009b. The Industrial Revolution in miniature: The spinning jenny in Britain, France and India. *Journal of Economic History* 69 (4): 901–27.

Allen, T. J., D. B. Hyman, and D. L. Pinckney. 1983. Transferring technology to the small manufacturing firms: A study of technology transfer in three countries. *Research Policy* 12 (4): 199–211.

Bagnall, W. R. 1893. *The Textile Industries of the United States: Including Sketches and Notices of Cotton, Woolen, Silk, and Linen Manufacturers in the Colonial Period*. vol. 1. Cambridge: Riverside Press.

Barton, D. B. 1969. *The Cornish Beam Engine*. Truro: Barton.

Bessen, J. 2011. From knowledge to ideas: The two faces of innovation. Working paper 10–35. Boston University School of Law. *http://ssrn.com/abstract=1698802*.

Chesbrough, H. 2003. *Open Innovation: The New Imperative for Creating and Profiting from Technology*. Boston: Harvard Business School Press.

Cotterau, A. 1997. The fate of collective manufactures in the industrial world: The silk industries of Lyons and London,1800–1850. In *Worlds of Possibilities: Flexibility and Mass Production in Western Industrialization*, ed. C. Sabel and J. Zeitlin. Cambridge, UK: Cambridge University Press.

Davids, K. 2008. *The Rise and Decline of Dutch Technological Leadership. Technology, Economy and Culture in the Netherlands, 1350–1800*. vol. I and II. Leiden: Brill.

Epstein, S. 1998. Craft guilds, apprenticeship and technical change in preindustrial Europe. *Journal of Economic History* 58 (3): 684–713.

Epstein, S. 2004. Property rights to technical knowledge in premodern Europe, 1300–1800. *American Economic Review* 94 (2): 382–87.

Epstein, S., and M. Prak. 2008. *Guilds, Innovation and the European Economy, 1400–1800*. Cambridge, UK: Cambridge University Press.

Faber, H. 1931. *Co-operation in Danish Agriculture*. London: Longmans.

Foray, D., and L. Hilaire-Perez. 2006. The economics of open technology: Collective organisation and individual claims in the "Fabrique Lyonnaise" during the old regime. In *New Frontiers in the Economics of Innovation and New Technology*, ed. C. Antonelli, , 239–54. Aldershot: Edward Elgar.

Gibb, G. S. 1950. *The Saco-Lowell Shops*. Cambridge: Harvard University Press.

Harhoff, D., J. Henkel, and E. von Hippel. 2003. Profiting from voluntary information spillovers: How users benefit by freely revealing their innovations. *Research Policy* 32 (10): 1753–69.

Henkel, J., and E. von Hippel. 2004. Welfare implications of user innovation. *Journal of Technology Transfer* 30 (1–2): 73–87.

Hilaire-Perez, L. 2002. Diderot's views on artists' and inventors' rights: invention, imitation and reputation. *British Journal for the History of Science* 35 (2): 129–50.

Hunter, L. C. 1949. *Steamboats on the Western Rivers. An Economic and Technological History*. Cambridge: Harvard University Press.

Khan, B. Z., and K. L. Sokoloff. 1998. Patent institutions, industrial organization and early technological change: Britain and the United States, 1790–1850. In *Technological Revolutions in Europe*, ed. M. Berg and K. Bruland. Cheltenham, UK: Edward Elgar.

Kyriazidou, E., and M. Pesendorfer. 1999. Viennese chairs: A case study for modern industrialization. *Journal of Economic History* 59 (1): 143–65.

MacLeod, C. 1988. *Inventing the Industrial Revolution. The English Patent System, 1660–1800*. Cambridge, UK: Cambridge University Press.

MacLeod, C. 2007. *Heroes of Invention: Technology, Liberalism and British Identity, 1750–1914*. Cambridge, UK: Cambridge University Press.

Mak, J., and G. M. Walton. 1972. Steamboats and the great productivity surge in river transportation. *Journal of Economic History* 32 (3): 619–40.

McGaw, J. A. 1987. *Most Wonderful Machine: Mechanization and Social Change in Berkshire Paper Making, 1801–1885*. Princeton: Princeton University Press.

Meyer, P. 2003. Episodes of collective invention. Working paper 368. US Bureau of Labor Statistics.

Meyer, P. 2013. Open sources in the invention of the airplane. *Revue Economique* 63 (1): 115–32.

Mokyr, J. 1990. *The Lever of Riches. Technological Creativity and Economic Progress*. Oxford: Oxford University Press.

Mokyr, J. 2008. The institutional origins of the Industrial Revolution. In *Institutions and Economic Performance*, ed. E. Helpman. Cambridge: Harvard University Press.

Mokyr, J. 2009. *The Enlightened Economy. An Economic History of Britain, 1700–1850*. New Haven: Yale University Press.

Moser, P. 2005. How do patent laws influence innovation? Evidence from nineteenth century World's Fairs. *American Economic Review* 95 (4): 1214–36.

Moser, P. 2012. Innovation without patents: Evidence from World's fairs. *Journal of Law and Economics* 55 (1): 43–74.

Moser, P., and P. Rhode. 2012. Did plant patents create the American rose? In *The Rate and Direction of Inventive Activity Revisited*, ed. J. Lerner and S. Stern. Chicago: University of Chicago Press.

Nuvolari, A. 2004. Collective invention during the British Industrial Revolution: The case of the Cornish pumping engine. *Cambridge Journal of Economics* 28 (3): 347–63.

Nuvolari, A., and B. Verspagen. 2007. *Lean's Engine Reporter* and the development of the Cornish engine: A reappraisal. *Transactions of the Newcomen Society* 77 (2): 167–89.

Nuvolari, A., and B. Verspagen. 2009. Technical choice, innovation and British steam engineering, 1800–1850. *Economic History Review* 62 (3): 685–710.

Olmstead, A. L., and P. W. Rhode. 2008. *Creating Abundance: Biological Innovation and American Agricultural Development*. New York: Cambridge University Press.

Otsuka, K., G. Ranis, and G. Saxonhouse. 1988. *Comparative Technical Choice in Development: The Indian and Japanese Cotton Textile Industries*. New York: St. Martin's Press.

Pole, W. 1844. *A Treatise on the Cornish Pumping Engine*. London: Weale.

Penin, J. 2007. Open knowledge disclosure: An overview of the evidence and motivations. *Journal of Economic Surveys* 21 (2): 326–48.

Perez, L. 2008. Inventing in a world of guilds: Silk fabrics in eighteenth-century Lyon. In *Guilds, Innovation and the European Economy, 1400–1800*, ed. S. Epstein and M. Prak, 232–63. Cambridge, UK: Cambridge University Press.

Powell, W., and E. Giannella. 2010. Collective invention and inventor networks. In *Handbook of Economics of Innovation*. vol. I. ed. B. Hall and N. Rosenberg, 575–605. Amsterdam: Elsevier.

Saxonhouse, G. 1974. A tale of Japanese technological diffusion during the Meiji period. *Journal of Economic History* 34 (1): 149–65.

Schneider, E. 1871. "Evidence." In *Select Committee on Law and Practice of Grants of Letters Patent for Invention*, P.P., 1871, 368 (X).

Schrader, S. 1991. Informal technology transfer between firms: Cooperation through information trading. *Research Policy* 20 (2): 153–70.

Shah, S. K. 2005. Open beyond software. In *Open Sources 2*, ed. D. Cooper, C. Di Bona, and M. Stone. Sebastopol: O' Reilly.

Thomson, R. 2009. *Structures of Change in the Mechanical Age. Technological Innovation in the United States, 1790–1865*. Baltimore: Johns Hopkins University Press.

Turner, A. 2008. "Not to hurt of trade": Guilds and innovation in horology and precision instrument making. In *Guilds, Innovation and the European Economy, 1400–1800*, ed. S. Epstein and M. Prak, 264–287. Cambridge, UK: Cambridge University Press.

Unger, R. W. 1978. *Dutch Shipbuilding before 1800*. Assen: Van Gorcum.

von Hippel, E. 1987. Cooperation between rivals: Informal know-how trading. *Research Policy* 16 (6): 291–302.

von Hippel, E. 2005. *Democratizing Innovation*. Cambridge: MIT Press.

Wallace, A. F. 1978. *Rockdale: The Growth of an America Village in the Early Industrial Revolution*. New York: Knopf.

8

Private-Collective Innovation: The Effects of the Number of Participants and Social Factors

Georg von Krogh, Helena Garriga, Efe Aksuyek, and Fredrik Hacklin

Cooperation among economic actors ranging from governments and firms to groups and individuals has been investigated from multiple perspectives, including using transaction-cost theory (Hill 1990), collective action (Olson 1968), game theory (Camerer et al. 2004; Fehr and Schmidt 1999; Gächter et al. 2010), and theories of economic organization (Combs and Ketchen 1999, Mowery et al. 1998). Recently, in organization theory, a debate has evolved around knowledge sharing in innovations of public goods, such as open source software (von Krogh et al. 2003), biopharmaceutical therapies (Hughes and Wareham 2010; Jefferson 2006), and entertainment products (West and Gallagher 2006). Eric von Hippel and Georg von Krogh's (2003) model of private-collective innovation (PCI) explains that public goods innovation takes place through the cooperation of multiple actors who expend private resources. In essence, the PCI model formalizes a compound of the private investment and collective action model of innovation. As von Hippel and von Krogh (2003) illustrate, on the basis of the open source software movement, participants in such projects use their own resources to privately invest in creating a novel contribution. In contrast to a private investment model, where these inventors, in principle, could claim proprietary rights, they instead do the opposite: They chose to freely reveal it as a public good. The model shows such ex ante counterintuitive behavior to occur in situations where the benefits contributors to public goods accrue, such as learning and peer recognition, outweigh the benefits of other participants' free-riding on the innovation outcome. Innovations resulting from the increasingly popular private–public model of collaboration have an output characterized as public goods. Thereby, this model often occupies a middle ground between producer-centered and user-centered innovation, as the case of open source software development projects illustrates, in which both firms and volunteer individuals collaborate (Baldwin and von Hippel 2011).

The PCI model analyzes several aspects of innovation, ranging from the nature of the innovation outcome—via individuals' motivations to contribute—to the process of innovation. To promote and support private-collective innovation (von Hippel 1988), it is important to identify factors that enable knowledge sharing through cooperation among innovators (e.g., users, firms, governments, and universities). The factors include aversion to inequity and reciprocity and the innovators' interdependencies (Gächter et al. 2010; Stuermer et al. 2009). The original paper on private-collective innovation offered insights into the importance of these factors (von Hippel and von Krogh 2003), but more work is needed to explore them in further detail. The PCI model suggests that the benefits of free-riding dissolve over time because process-related rewards exceed the costs of PCI (von Hippel 2005, von Hippel and von Krogh 2003, von Krogh and Spaeth 2007). The model predicts that once the balance between public goods (benefits) and private benefits has been established after some time, the benefits available to innovators will prove to outweigh the benefits available to free riders (von Hippel and von Krogh 2003). However, this outcome is not obvious during the initiation phase of PCI, before the innovation process has been set in motion. We expect that free-riding will particularly affect the initiation of private-collective innovation, as Ostrom (1990, 1998) notes it affects other collective action projects. Thus it is critical to explain the conditions under which PCI will initiate, flourish and materialize.

In this chapter, drawing on behavioral game theory, we contribute to the existing theory of PCI to shed light on some of its micro-level antecedents. In particular, we explain the role that the number of collaborators plays in determining the success of an innovation project. Specifically, we investigate knowledge sharing among individual innovators during the initiation phase of PCI. In so doing, we draw upon the experimental work of Gächter et al. (2010), where individual players (or innovators) can choose between concealing and sharing knowledge in a two-person game (or a collaborative environment). Given the particular difficulty in observing and identifying free riders in PCI, we build on a simulation study to explore how current behavioral game theories may shed light on the complex forces that influence the levels of cooperation among individual innovators in initiating PCI.[1]

The chapter is structured as follows. The next section briefly introduces the private-collective innovation model and discusses knowledge sharing from the perspective of behavioral game theory. Subsequently we present and discuss inequality-aversion from the perspective of behavioral game theory and use it as a basis for modeling the initiation of PCI. The second-to-last section briefly describes the simulation study and presents its results. The final section discusses the implications of our findings for future work on PCI.

Conditions for Private-Collective Innovation

In its foundation, the PCI model combines a private investment model of innovation, which assumes that innovators expend private resources on creating innovation-relevant knowledge, with a collective-action model of innovation, which assumes that under conditions of market failure, innovators will collaborate to produce a public good (von Hippel and von Krogh 2003, 2006). Generally, public goods innovations are characterized by nonrivalry and the nonexclusivity of benefits, both of which pose problems of collective action (Monge et al. 1998). Ostrom (1990) argued that individuals' contributions to a public good are affected by environmental and social factors, such as competition among participants. She acknowledged the existence of several types of players whose cooperative behaviors differ. Perhaps most players are "conditional cooperators" or "rational egoists" (Ostrom 1990). Conditional cooperators initiate a cooperative action and expect others to reciprocate. Free riders often disappoint these initial contributors to the public good (Ostrom 1998), and even the prospect of the free riders' failure to contribute may deter others from contributing. This can severely affect individuals' decisions to embark on collective action projects (Ostrom 1990, 1998), thereby rendering the initiation phase particularly volatile.

Community-Forming and Initiation of PCI

One might think that to explain user-related innovations, such as open source software, it would suffice to postulate a link between a user's individual motivational structures and her actions or innovations (von Krogh et al. 2012). However, the PCI model assumes the presence of a *community* of innovators, where some established social norms of cooperation induce innovators to contribute. In the initiation of PCI, a community has yet to be established; therefore community-based social norms—as well as other process-related rewards associated with PCI—are absent. In this context Gächter et al. (2010) traced the initiation of PCI to the first decision to share or conceal knowledge in a two-person game between a leader and a follower who innovate to solve similar problems. Drawing on previous work in behavioral game theory and PCI (Fehr and Schmidt 1999; Fischbacher et al. 2001; von Hippel and von Krogh 2003), the study considered costs and benefits of knowledge sharing or concealing. The results indicate that when individuals face opportunity costs of sharing their knowledge with others, they turn away from the social optimum of mutual sharing and decide to conceal knowledge instead. Studying the initiation of PCI is indeed difficult because most projects we can observe have already been initiated. Understanding the initial choices and incentives facing innovators calls for an experimental approach like the one demonstrated in Garriga et al. (2012). The study also reinvigorated an "old" idea that because innovators might pursue different interests, the sharing of knowledge among them is "fragile."

The study was the first to explore unobservable concealment of knowledge in a collaborative environment, and it could be complemented by future work. Field work based on interviews with open source software developers has shown that individuals' different social preferences (Spaeth et al. 2010; Stuermer et al. 2009; von Hippel and von Krogh 2003) may impact to a varying degree their willingness to share knowledge to initiate PCI (Gächter et al. 2010; Garriga et al. 2012). For instance, in virtual environments (e.g., Twitter, an FAQ repository of an open source software project, and discussion forums) where relationships among participants may be ephemeral, collaborative behavior can differ strongly. Individuals' aversions to incurring disadvantages (Fehr and Schmidt 1999) could affect the "fragility of knowledge sharing" (Gächter et al. 2010) and represent a constraint to PCI initiation, as actors do not want to give away knowledge if they do not expect some reciprocity. Moreover the experiment detailed in Gächter et al. focused on a limited collaboration setting of two individuals, while in a real collaborative setting, such as an open source software project, hundreds of individuals simultaneously innovate to develop a public good (Garriga et al. 2011; Stuermer et al. 2009). Yet the number of participants in PCI may also affect the inception of a knowledge-sharing environment, which is in line with Shah's previous work on the motivations of open source software developers (2006). Therefore we have still a relatively poor understanding on the initiation of PCI when *multiple* participants are involved. Against this background, the purpose of this study is to address the following question: *How does having a group of individuals with different social preferences affect the conditions for the knowledge sharing that initiates PCI?*

Initial Conditions for Knowledge Sharing

Knowledge sharing consists of "activities of transferring or disseminating knowledge from one person, group or organization to another" (Lee 2001: 324). Because individuals and organizations may either benefit or lose from sharing their knowledge under various conditions (Argote and Ingram 2000) and free riders draw upon the knowledge of others without sharing anything in return, knowledge sharing is fragile and contingent on the interests of the innovators involved in the process (Gächter et al. 2010). Thus knowledge sharing between participants is rare in overly competitive situations (Nahapiet and Ghoshal 1998; Tsai 2002). Fehr and Schmidt lamented that "[a]lmost all economic models assume that all people are exclusively pursuing their material self-interest and do not care about 'social' goals per se" (Fehr and Schmidt 1999: 817). However, despite a tendency in mainstream economics to ignore social preferences, several scholars have recently highlighted their roles in reciprocity and fairness for the success of cooperation among individuals (Dufwenberg and Kirchsteiger 2004; Fehr and Schmidt 1999, Kahneman et al. 1986; Rabin 1993).

The knowledge-sharing game allows us to investigate knowledge sharing in a one-to-one setting, where two individuals decide to share or conceal knowledge based on their expectations of certain payoffs. The study observed declining contributions when the payoffs for concealing knowledge increased. However, it has also been suggested that sharing behaviors change when more actors are involved in a public good (Oliver et al. 1985; von Hippel and von Krogh 2003), which means that free-riding may decrease as the group of innovators increases in size.

Initial conditions for knowledge sharing need to be fulfilled for a PCI environment to emerge. Previous work on the initial conditions can be complemented by further exploration of two factors: First, the free rider problem calls for a differentiated understanding of the impact of social preferences on a group of individuals' willingness to actively participate in a knowledge-sharing environment. Second, the effect of group size on knowledge sharing should be explored. In the next section, we briefly develop a simple model to account for the influence of group size on the initiation of PCI.

Modeling Knowledge Sharing in Private-Collective Innovation

Perhaps game theory is not the primary theory of choice for most innovation scholars, but it has proved useful to explore certain aspects of game theory, such as incentives, in relation to the initiation of PCI. Game theory is commonly used in studies of social decision making (Camerer 2003; Dufwenberg and Kirchsteiger 2004; Fehr and Schmidt 1999; Rabin, 1993), and it seeks to find the strategies that a group of decision makers will decide on as the individuals try to maximize their own payoffs. The Nash equilibrium refers to a set of strategies from which none of the individual players can unilaterally deviate to increase individual payoffs, as the choices of each player affect the payoffs of others (Gintis 2009).

Behavioral game theory tries to predict how players actually behave in strategic situations using intuitive utility functions. However, using utility functions to explain participants' preferences has been commonly criticized because utility functions can always be modified and altered, allowing them to explain almost anything (Camerer 2003). Nevertheless, the goal of utility functions in game theory is not to explain every possible finding but rather to explain a phenomenon that is supported by some psychological intuition and to make predictions (Camerer et al. 2004). In previous work, utility functions indicated that players only cared about maximizing their own payoffs. By contrast, more recent approaches have shifted focus from payoffs-only utilities to utilities with social considerations (Camerer 2003; Dufwenberg and Kirchsteiger 2004; Fehr and Schmidt 1999; Rabin 1993). As far as PCI is concerned, the phenomenon cannot be fully explained without these social considerations or preferences, as is clear when one studies resulting public goods like open source software projects (Garriga et al. 2011; Stuermer et al. 2009).

The study by Gächter et al. (2010) used one approach—the inequality-aversion theory suggested by Fehr and Schmidt (Fehr and Schmidt 1999; Fischbacher et al. 2001)—to explain individuals' behavior with regard to knowledge sharing. Inequality-aversion theory proposes that individuals are willing to reduce their own payoffs to increase the degree of equality. Because we are building on the setting of a game to explore conditions for PCI, we will in the following model present our experiment using inequality-aversion theory (Fehr and Schmidt 1999). We will then venture a foundation for understanding the impact of the number of participants on initiation of PCI based on our experiment.

According to Fehr and Schmidt (1999), the most common circumstance in cooperative environments is for players *not* to cooperate unless there are advantages for doing so. To conceptualize potential advantages, inequality-aversion theory considers players' payoffs and the differences between them. Another aspect of inequality-aversion theory concerns "envy and guilt" (Camerer 2003), as players will care about how much more or less they benefit compared to other players. Moreover scholars have argued that inequality aversion is a crucial motivation for players to engage in collaboration (Fowler et al. 2005), which renders the theory relevant for modeling collective settings like those of PCI.

Fehr and Schmidt's utility function models inequality aversion behavior, with α and β as measures of aversion to disadvantageous and advantageous inequities and π_i as the payoff. Consider the following equation:

$$U_i\left(\varphi_i, \varphi_j\right) = \pi_i - \alpha_i \cdot \max\left[\pi_j - \pi_i, 0\right] - \beta_i \cdot \max\left[\pi_i - \pi_j, 0\right] \tag{1}$$

In the case of PCI, inequality-aversion theory bases choices on utility functions that are dependent on the particular situations of player i and player j, with φ_i as the decision of player i to conceal or share knowledge and φ_j as the decision of player j to conceal or share knowledge, as stated in equation (1). The utility that each player attains depends on the choices φ_i and φ_j (of player i and player j, respectively), their payoffs π_i and π_j, and on the aversion coefficients α, which is the aversion against disadvantageous inequality, and β, which is aversion against advantageous inequality. The aversion coefficients are likely to vary among participants (Revelt and Train 1998). As is evident, utility functions based on Fehr and

Schmidt's work (1999) involve three parts. In the case of player i, the first part is π_i; the second part is $\alpha_i \cdot \max[\pi_j - \pi_i, 0]$; and the third part is $\beta_i \cdot \max[\pi_i - \pi_j, 0]$. In examining the utility function, we can see that inequality aversion does not capture other social aspects such as reciprocity or punishment, which are critical in PCI environments (Shah 2006). Therefore we expect the inequality aversion model in Fehr and Schmidt (1999) to only partially explain the knowledge-sharing game in PCI, which means there is a need for other theories and models to complement Fehr and Schmidt's work (Garriga et al. 2012). In this chapter we build on the introduced model for inequality aversion (equation 1) (Fehr and Schmidt 1999) and proceed in the following section to present a simulation of a knowledge-sharing environment in which PCI can be initiated.

Simulating a Knowledge-Sharing Environment of PCI

Gächter et al. (2010) created a knowledge-sharing game in which players or innovators shared or concealed knowledge in couples' interactions—that is, player j chose whether to share or conceal knowledge depending on what player i had decided.[2] We aim to represent the initiation of PCI in a collaborative setting based on this knowledge-sharing game. A representation of the decision process in the game is provided in figure 8.1, where the decisions of player j depend on previous decisions made by player i. The two possible decisions are always the same—to share or conceal information—and the payoffs for each participant will depend on the choices of both players as follows:

$$\pi_i\left(\varphi_i, \varphi_j\right) = b + \varphi_i \cdot v_i + \varphi_j \cdot (1 - \varphi_i) \cdot a_i. \tag{2}$$

The payoff functions in the experiment have a pre-fixed value for base payoff ($b = 10$), a value for sharing knowledge ($v_i = 20$) and an exclusivity gain for concealing knowledge a_i ($a_i = \{0, 10, 20, 30\}$) (Gächter et al. 2010), yielding a simplified payoff function (see equation 3). If the players care about only the monetary payoffs and exclusivity payoff of $a_i > 0$, then the game has one Nash equilibrium in pure strategies: (Conceal, Conceal) with an equal split. In games for which $a_i = 0$, there is not a single Nash equilibrium.

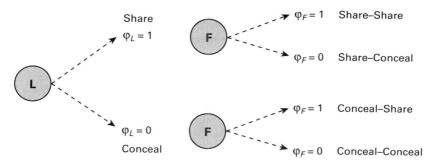

Figure 8.1

Knowledge sharing in a PCI environment

$$\pi_i\left(\varphi_i, \varphi_j\right) = b + \varphi_i \cdot v_i. \tag{3}$$

Extending the Game

The knowledge-sharing game focuses on the interaction of two players, one being the leader and the other the follower. This type of two-player game represents a "worst-case" scenario for the initiation of PCI because it severely limits the players' abilities to act according to a variety of social considerations and preferences. Therefore the two-player sets a type of "upper bound" for the fragility of knowledge sharing. In real-life settings such as an open source software development project, several followers may act at the request of a leader. When Linus Torvalds called for help with developing his prodigy operating system for his IBM 386 processor machine, later known as Linux, he did not address only one developer but rather appealed to a broad audience of potential software developers. Expanding the existing knowledge-sharing game is significant because it will allow for a setting of one leader and several followers (see figure 8.2), where the number of individuals who share knowledge varies depending on the number of individuals participating in PCI.

In the case of PCI, adding additional followers changes the outcome of the game. As von Hippel and von Krogh (2003) hypothesized, a follower's ability to acquire an exclusivity gain is ruined once he shares his knowledge with another follower (2003). Given that the leader has already decided to share, once a follower decides to do so, knowledge is "set free," diminishing the exclusivity gains of other players. Thus the likelihood of

Initialization of PCI
(one-to-one)*

Initialization of PCI
(one-to-many actors)

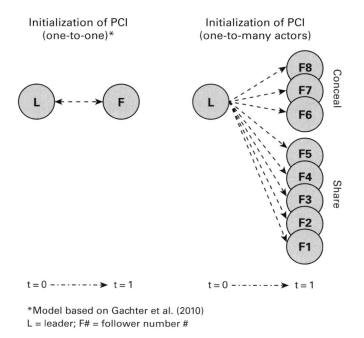

t = 0 ┈┈┈┈➤ t = 1   t = 0 ┈┈┈┈➤ t = 1

*Model based on Gachter et al. (2010)
L = leader; F# = follower number #

Figure 8.2

Modeling PCI using inequality-aversion theory (varying exclusivity payoffs)

mutual sharing in a group of several players is expected to be high because only one follower is sufficient to satisfy the mutual sharing condition. On the contrary, if none of the followers share knowledge, the mutual sharing condition is not satisfied, and each follower receives a proportional exclusivity gain.

Notes on the Simulation

In the knowledge-sharing game, players make their decisions based on potential exclusivity gains and on social considerations (Gächter et al. 2010). One of the most common and straightforward theories that takes social considerations into account is the inequality aversion theory (Fehr and Schmidt 1999). According to this theory, players dislike inequitable outcomes and are concerned with differences in the payoffs that players receive. Hence, for the simulations, we based our model of utility function on the inequality aversion theory. Within a reasonable value of disadvantageous inequality aversion of $0 \leq \alpha \leq 1$ and advantageous inequality aversion of $0 \leq \beta$ (Fehr and Schmidt 1999), player i will decide on whether to share or conceal information regardless of his gain a_j, and player j will also discard his gain a_i when computing his optimal choice.

We simulated an extension of the knowledge-sharing game in a "one-to-many" setting.[3] The simple simulation procedure included the following steps: We generated players with the utility function proposed by Fehr and Schmidt (1999) and iterated each round 100,000 times. The social parameters were estimated using the results in the Gächter et al. (2010) study as opposed to other suggested distributions.[4] We decided to use a power law distribution because it was a good fit for the experimental results. We also cross-checked our results with the discrete distribution suggested by Fehr and Schmidt, and we presented the results using a power law as it has been used previously to describe other social phenomena (Maillart et al. 2008). Next, each generated leader was randomly assigned to a certain number of followers. After this assignment, the players made decisions to share or conceal information based on the maximization of their utility functions. In cases of equal utility for sharing or concealing, the players simply tossed a coin. We simulated this procedure for sixteen different combinations of the exclusivity gains as previously mentioned, with $a_i = \{0, 10, 20, 30\}$ and $a_j = \{0, 10, 20, 30\}$.

Results

We are interested in studying the effect that the number of followers has on the outcome of the knowledge-sharing game. Figure 8.3 summarizes the results of knowledge sharing in the simulation based on the exclusivity gains of both leaders and followers. The four plots in the figure indicate the percentage of mutual sharing on the horizontal axis, and the number of followers on the vertical axis, given the leader's fixed exclusivity gain, which is shown above each graph. Each of the four curves in a plot depicts the knowledge sharing that results in a different exclusivity gain for the followers.

Our results indicate that mutual sharing decreases as leaders' and followers' exclusivity gains increase, which is consistent with Gächter et al.'s

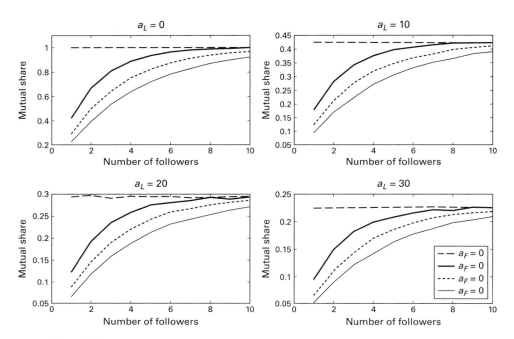

Figure 8.3

Percent of mutual sharing that is dependent on the number of followers

findings (2010). Leaders and followers tend to share less when they can gain more from concealing knowledge.

We also studied the effect that the number of followers has on sharing behaviors. Our results show that as the number of followers increases, the marginal increase in knowledge sharing decreases. Thus adding a follower to a small group makes a significant impact on the mutual sharing, while larger groups need larger inflows of new followers to gain significantly in terms of mutual sharing.

Finally, in all four plots, mutual knowledge sharing converges at a certain rate as the number of followers increases. As previously mentioned, the sharing rate is also affected by the leader's and followers' exclusivity gains. However, in all cases, a larger number of followers resulted in an increased rate of mutual sharing. Our results suggest that mutual knowledge sharing can be significantly improved for small groups of followers in particular, but adding followers to improve knowledge sharing is still a factor to consider in other groups.

Discussion and Conclusions

This study shed light on the initiation of PCI by explaining how the number of innovators affects the initial contributions and knowledge sharing that sets PCI in motion. Seeking a differentiated view, we studied the rates of knowledge sharing in more complex participation environments. We claim that an individual's decision to share or conceal knowledge depends on not only personal social preferences but also the number of innovators in the group and the expected decisions that prompt participation. Our findings indicate that participation can be characterized to some extent and triggered by the number of participants. It is fundamental to the success of PCI not only to understand how individuals weigh the expected gains or losses that will result from their participation but also to predict how the members of the social ecosystem will interact to produce individual utility functions.

In real life it may not remain true across different games that innovators' utility will be reflected in the choices they make. Innovators in our study may have been subject to various types of biases, which typically limit the general applicability of the results of a simulation such as ours. Moreover the behavior of players in simple games under controlled circumstances may also be different from players' behavior in the complex, rich, temporally extended social relationships that people enter in daily life (Gintis 2009). Simulated players who hold semi-flexible utility functions and make socially dependent decisions provide results that can inform researchers of possible connections among variables in complex phenomena. Thus we do not attempt to explain every change in behavior in a PCI initiation but rather to outline some important parameters worthy of consideration in future theory building and research.

Many private-collective innovations suffer from under-contribution and free-riding; open source software initiatives represent classic examples (Garriga et al. 2011; Stuermer et al. 2009). Often mechanisms of motivation are crucial to keep the few vital contributing members active, and using these mechanisms requires considering the potential number of additional innovators associated with a certain technology, product, or process. An important insight from our simulation is that if members feel that they will not gain an exclusivity payoff from concealing knowledge, then they will be more encouraged to share.

Our findings have implications for managers who are concerned about their own organization's ability to learn. A practical example would be firms trying to incentivize employees to document their own work-related knowledge, as is often the goal of knowledge management initiatives in an organization. The "documentation cost" may be relatively low for the employee herself, and her documenting her experience benefits the firm. The more employees document what is relevant to their jobs, the more the firm benefits. The shared knowledge can be critical for overcoming future challenges and changes that firms may face. To incentivize this sharing behavior, it seems reasonable that managers should attempt to motivate a sufficiently large pool of participants. A practical example of a technology that to some extent helps employees share their knowledge is IBM's "Innovation Jam," which is a platform for conducting mass brainstorming online (Bjelland and Wood 2008). As indicated by our results, to successfully spark sharing behavior, managers need to make sure that individuals start to receive documents from fellow employees right away. The larger the pool of users grows, the more retrieval traffic will be needed to keep the sharing behavior alive because as the number of employees making use of the documented knowledge (e.g., common sales processes across two product groups) becomes sufficiently high, exclusivity gains and free-riding benefits decrease.

These insights into knowledge management and motivations are very useful, specifically in settings with knowledge scarcity. However, future research should focus on how to motivate sharing "*the required type of knowledge*" in environments with an abundance of information. As Haas and Hansen (2001) note, more knowledge might not always lead to a more efficient organization. Thus researchers should focus not only on knowledge sharing but also on efficiency.

Finally, it is also important to realize that participants in collective endeavors such as PCI do not form homogeneous groups, and some individuals will act counter to mutual knowledge sharing, behaving mostly as free riders. By contrast, other players will have high social preferences toward sharing and will always forsake material gain in favor of social gains that follow from sharing knowledge, such as reputation. These phenomena could be captured in long-tail distributions of different social preferences in a group of followers. Future research should focus on how PCI projects or firms attract people who react to social incentives, such as reciprocity, and use it to their advantage in the creation of collective goods. We can see firms' attempts to create environments of reciprocity in "Apps" platforms in the Android Market, where contributors have higher flexibility in the design of their contributions in comparison with other platforms, such as Apple's "App Store." Hence, our research supports the argument that profit maximization is not the only factor in knowledge-sharing behavior among innovators (Harhoff et al. 2003). We need further avenues for studying social behavior in PCI, including more theoretical perspectives and broader methodological approaches. These future studies will reveal new mechanisms that encourage innovators to contribute to PCI. However, we should not forget that improving environments for PCI is not only about including individuals who respond to social factors but also about identifying the actions that will influence an individual's behavior.

Notes

This research was funded in part by the Swiss National Foundation Grant 100014_125513.

1. In this chapter we build on an earlier simulation study in which we explored the role of the social preferences in PCI (Garriga et al. 2011).

2. In Gächter et al. (2010), player j is named as the follower (F) and player i as the leader (L). For the sake of simplicity, we use the same notations for player i and player j throughout our chapter.

3. In the one-to-many setting of the knowledge-sharing game, we create one leader, player i, and several followers acting as player j.

4. According to Fehr and Schmidt (1999), α can be discretely distributed: 30 percent of the population has $\alpha = 0$; 30 percent has $\alpha = 0.5$; 30 percent has $\alpha = 1$; and 10 percent has $\alpha = 4$.

References

Argote, L., and P. Ingram. 2000. Knowledge transfer: A basis for competitive advantage in firms. *Organizational Behavior and Human Decision Processes* 82 (1): 150–69.

Baldwin, C. Y., and E. von Hippel. 2011. Modeling a paradigm shift: From producer innovation to user and open collaborative innovation. *Organization Science* 22 (6): 1399–1417.

Bjelland, O. M., and R. C. Wood. 2008. An inside view of IBM's "innovation jam." *Sloan Management Review* 50 (1): 32–40.

Camerer, C. 2003. *Behavioral Game Theory: Experiments in Strategic Interaction.* New York: Russell Sage Foundation.

Camerer, C., G. Loewenstein, and M. Rabin. 2004. *Advances in Behavioral Economics.* Princeton: Princeton University Press.

Combs, J. G., and D. J. Ketchen. 1999. Explaining interfirm cooperation and performance: Toward a reconciliation of predictions from the resource-based view and organizational economics. *Strategic Management Journal* 20 (9): 867–88.

Dufwenberg, M., and G. Kirchsteiger. 2004. A theory of sequential reciprocity. *Games and Economic Behavior* 47 (2): 268–98.

Fehr, E., and K. M. Schmidt. 1999. A theory of fairness, competition, and cooperation. *Quarterly Journal of Economics* 114 (3): 817–68.

Fischbacher, U., S. Gächter, and E. Fehr. 2001. Are people conditionally cooperative? Evidence from a public goods experiment. *Economics Letters* 71 (3): 397–404.

Fowler, J. H., T. Johnson, and O. Smirnov. 2005. Human behavior: Egalitarian motive and altruistic punishment. *Nature* 433 (7021): E1.

Gächter, S., G. von Krogh, and S. Haefliger. 2010. Initiating private-collective innovation: The fragility of knowledge sharing. *Research Policy* 39 (7): 893–906.

Garriga, H., E. Aksuyek, G. von Krogh, and F. Hacklin. 2012. Social preferences in private-collective innovation. *Technology Analysis and Strategic Management* 24 (2): 113–27.

Garriga, H., G. von Krogh, and S. Spaeth. 2011. Lecture notes in computer science. Social Computing, Behavioral-Cultural Modeling and Prediction. *In Open Source Software Development: Communities and Firms Impact on Public Good*, vol. 6589, 69–77.

Gintis, H. 2009. *The Bounds of Reason: Game Theory and the Unification of the Behavioral Sciences.* Princeton: Princeton University Press.

Haas, M. R., and M. T. Hansen. 2001. Competing for attention in knowledge markets: Electronic document dissemination in a management consulting company. *Administrative Science Quarterly* 46 (1): 1–28.

Harhoff, D., J. Henkel, and E. von Hippel. 2003. Profiting from voluntary information spillovers: How users benefit by freely revealing their innovations. *Research Policy* 32 (10): 1753–69.

Hill, C. W. L. 1990. Cooperation, opportunism, and the invisible hand: Implications for transaction cost theory. *Academy of Management Review* 15 (3): 500–13.

Hughes, B., and J. Wareham. 2010. Knowledge arbitrage in global pharma: A synthetic view of absorptive capacity and open innovation. *R&D Management* 40 (3): 324–43.

Jefferson, R. 2006. Science as social enterprise: The CAMBIA BiOS initiative. *Innovations: Technology, Governance, Globalization* 1 (4): 13–44.

Kahneman, D., J. L. Knetsch, and R. Thaler. 1986. Fairness as a constraint on profit seeking: Entitlements in the market. *American Economic Review* 76 (4): 728–41.

Lee, J. N. 2001. The impact of knowledge sharing, organizational capability and partnership quality on IS outsourcing success. *Information & Management* 38 (5): 323–35.

Maillart, T., D. Sornette, S. Spaeth, and G. von Krogh. 2008. Empirical tests of Zipf's law mechanism in open source Linux distribution. *Physical Review Letters* 101 (21): 218701.

Monge, P. R., J. Fulk, M. E. Kalman, A. J. Flanagin, C. Parnassa, and S. Rumsey. 1998. Production of collective action in alliance-based interorganizational communication and information systems. *Organization Science* 9 (3): 411–33.

Mowery, D. C., J. E. Oxley, and B. S. Silverman. 1998. Technological overlap and interfirm cooperation: Implications for the resource-based view of the firm. *Research Policy* 27 (5): 507–23.

Nahapiet, J., and S. Ghoshal. 1998. Social capital, intellectual capital, and the organizational advantage. *Academy of Management Review* 23 (2): 242–66.

Oliver, P. E., G. Marwell, and R. Teixeira. 1985. A theory of the critical mass. I. Interdependence, group heterogeneity, and the production of collective action. *American Journal of Sociology* 91 (3): 522–56.

Olson, M. 1968. *The Logic of Collective Action*. New York: Schocken.

Ostrom, E. 1990. *Governing the Commons: The Evolution of Institutions for Collective Action*. Cambridge, UK: Cambridge University Press.

Ostrom, E. 1998. A behavioral approach to the rational choice theory of collective action. *American Political Science Review* 92 (1): 1–22.

Rabin, M. 1993. Incorporating fairness into game-theory and economics. *American Economic Review* 83 (5): 1281–1302.

Revelt, D., and K. Train. 1998. Mixed logit with repeated choices: Households' choices of appliance efficiency level. *Review of Economics and Statistics* 80 (4): 647–57.

Shah, S. 2006. Motivation, governance, and the viability of hybrid forms in open source software development. *Management Science* 52 (7): 1000–14.

Spaeth, S., M. Stuermer, and G. von Krogh. 2010. Enabling Knowledge creation through outsiders: Towards a push model of open innovation. *International Journal of Technology Management* 52 (3–4): 411–31.

Stuermer, M., S. Spaeth, and G. von Krogh. 2009. Extending private-collective innovation: A case study. *R&D Management* 39 (2): 170–91.

Tsai, W. 2002. Social structure of coopetition within a multiunit organization: Coordination, competition, and intraorganizational knowledge sharing. *Organization Science* 13 (2): 179–90.

von Hippel, E. 1988. *The Sources of Innovation*. New York: Oxford University Press.

von Hippel, E. 2005. *Democratizing Innovation.* Cambridge: MIT Press.

von Hippel, E., and G. von Krogh. 2003. Open source software and the "private-collective" innovation model: Issues for organization science. *Organization Science* 14 (2): 209–23.

von Hippel, E., and G. von Krogh. 2006. Free revealing and the private-collective model for innovation incentives. *R&D Management* 36 (3): 295–306.

von Krogh, G., S. Haefliger, S. Spaeth, and M. Wallin. 2012. Carrots and rainbows: Motivation and social practice in open source software development. *Management Information Systems Quarterly* 36 (2): 649–76.

von Krogh, G., and S. Spaeth. 2007. The open source software phenomenon: Characteristics that promote research. *Journal of Strategic Information Systems* 16 (3): 236–53.

von Krogh, G., S. Spaeth, and K. Lakhani. 2003. Community, joining, and specialization in open source software innovation: A case study. *Research Policy* 32 (7): 1217–41.

West, J., and S. Gallagher. 2006. Challenges of open innovation: The paradox of firm investment in open-source software. *R&D Management* 36 (3): 319–31.

9

On the Democratization of Innovation through Communal Organizations

Emmanuelle Fauchart and Dominique Foray

Innovation democratizes if the consumers/users of the goods become themselves innovators. Eric von Hippel has suggested that the main explanation for why users may become innovators is that it is too costly for them to transfer the useful information to innovate to the manufacturers, and thus, when they have the required capabilities, it may be more rational for them to undertake innovation rather than to outsource it to manufacturers (von Hippel 1994). Yet, if this market failure may explain why users do innovate, it is not a sufficient explanation for explaining why users may form communities to undertake this innovation. User communities are found in different settings, such as sport, but are probably the most structured and visible in software production, where they have flourished. These communities are typically very informal structures composed of individuals who contribute collectively to the production of an innovation and then use it for free. A literature has started to develop that emphasizes the respective advantages of user communities, single users, and manufacturers in innovation (e.g., Baldwin and von Hippel 2011; Baldwin et al. 2006). To date this literature has largely focused on the production issues favoring one or the other locus of innovation.

In this chapter we question the ability of these user communities to constitute a persistent locus of innovation. In our approach to this question, we adopt an economic perspective and propose to look at user communities as institutional forms—"communal organizations"—constituting a vertical integration of users into the production of the goods that they use or consume. Based on this framework, we make propositions regarding the ability of user communities to constitute a persistent organizational form in the economy by questioning both the market failures driving users to vertically integrate and the potential organizational issues that such an integrated form may have to face. In our analysis we rely both on the institutional approach to organizations and on the literature on cooperatives, which has a history of studying the vertical integration of consumers into distribution or production cooperative forms.

An Economic Perspective on User Communities

We propose that communal organizations are institutional forms that have at least two remarkable features. First, user-producers are the residual claimants of the communal organization. Second, vertical integration of users into the production stage is the economic essence of a communal organization.

Users as Residual Claimants

As it is the case for cooperative undertakings in general, the first important aspect of a communal organization (CO) is to be "user owned, user controlled, and user benefited" (Cook and Chaddad 2004). In fact "the basic characteristic that distinguishes cooperatives [and communal organizations] from other businesses is that they are owned, controlled by, and intended to benefit the people they serve–the members–rather than outside investors" (Sexton and Iskow 1988). Thus the goal of a CO is to maximize value for its members rather than for external investors, in contrast to an 'investor-owned firm' (IOF).

The implication is that, in a CO, the user-members are the *residual claimants* of the organization. As owners of the CO, they have the rights on the residual income generated by the activity of the organization. They also have the residual control rights on the activity of the organization, meaning that ultimately they make the important decisions regarding the activity undertaken by the organization. These cooperative or communal principles critically distinguish a CO from an IOF. First, principal–agent hierarchical relationships are replaced by *democratic decision-making*, as ownership and control is not separated in a CO. Indeed a critical feature of COs is that user-members are not working for external investors that would impose orders upon them. They decide for themselves what the product they collaboratively make will look like and how it will be made. The important consequence is that COs should typically economize on agency costs but should instead incur mutual monitoring costs.

Second, the benefits associated with being a member of a CO are typically *mutualized*. Indeed the utility gained from being a member of a CO is not in the form of an ex ante fixed wage but in the form of the valuable collective good produced by the efforts of the CO members and consumed ex post. For instance, they get to use software that is perfectly adapted to their particular needs. Thus the good produced by the CO is the motivation for being a member and is the compensation for contributing efforts. The important consequence is that COs should typically not be concerned with the problems arising from the fact that members of the organization may pursue different goals and have unaligned interests (e.g., shirking) but should instead be concerned with the problems that may arise from the mutualization of benefits (e.g., free-riding).

Vertical Integration of Users in the Production Stage

The additional concept needed to set cooperatives [and communal organizations] apart from other organizations and to understand their role in the economy is vertical integration. . . . The action of joint vertical integration is the economic essence of a cooperative." (Sexton and Iskow 1988: 3)

The formation of communal organizations by user-innovators actually echoes the long tradition of cooperative formation by consumers. User-governed COs however represent a stronger and rarest form of consumer vertical integration as in this case the users integrate further backward and embark in producing innovations. Considering that the formation of COs is about the vertical integration of users into the production stage provides an angle through which to think of the motivations of users for forming COs as well as at the economic functions of COs. Vertical integration can arise for different reasons but the one reason that has prevailed in the past to explain consumer cooperative formation is the existence of market failures. Historically consumers have been found to integrate backward into retailing or distribution, mainly to oppose the market power of distributors (von Weizsäcker 2001). The formation of COs yet seems to respond to several market failures. First, the existence of market or monopoly power seems also to be an important motivation for integrating. Indeed factual evidence from the Linux community case supports the idea that the perceived opportunism and "holdup" of manufacturers toward their clients acts as a driver for the vertical integration of users. Yet, when it comes to innovation, at least a second market failure seems to operate as an impetus to vertical integration by users: It is too costly for manufacturers to respond perfectly to the needs of all the consumers/users, and therefore the market fails to supply all the users with the products they need. This cost results from the difficulty or impossibility of users to transfer at reasonable cost the critical information enabling manufacturers to adequately understand their needs and design a solution (e.g., von Hippel 1994). Yet, while this may explain why users are motivated to innovate, this is not a sufficient reason for the formation of communities. The innovation process needs to be complex enough to entail the collaboration of multiple users.

That CO formation is about the backward vertical integration of consumers/users also provides an angle through which to think of the efficiency or potential success or failure of COs. Indeed transaction costs economics teaches us that vertical integration is an economically rational decision if the transaction costs involved in using the market for a given activity are so high that it is possible to economize by doing this activity internally (Williamson 1981). This means that a CO makes sense for its members if they believe that they can economize on transaction costs by doing themselves the activity that they seek to integrate or, said reversely, if they believe that they can perform so well in organizing the activity themselves that they expect to be better off making it than being part in a market transaction. This indicates that COs should be found in markets where transaction costs are high for consumer-users and/or users have an advantage with regard to the cost of organizing the concerned activity (e.g., users are holders of knowledge inputs that are of value to the concerned activity) and possess unique resources for undertaking that activity in very competitive conditions (e.g., see Barney 1991 for a resource-based view of the firm). In addition, for vertical integration to be a rational decision for CO members, it is necessary that the value generated for them be high enough to justify investment in the CO rather than in alternatives usages. In other words, CO formation will be more likely if the benefit gained by the members represents a higher return than what they could get by allocating their time or resources to other occupations.

Thus, in summary, for CO formation to likely attract members it is necessary that (1) the CO form be an efficient form able to compete with or complement in a unique way alternative forms in the market and that (2) the CO provides its members with a rate of return on their investment (in time, money, etc.) at least as high as it would be in alternatives usages; meaning for instance provides them with benefits that they could only get at a higher cost in alternative settings. As an illustration, users often report to learn, to having fun, or to getting social status from their being members of innovative communities, and this belonging to a user community is oftentimes a unique or cost-effective way of getting these benefits.

Communal Organization: A Transient or Persistent Form?

There seems to be a consensus in the literature that cooperative undertakings tend to be transient rather than persistent forms in the life of industries (Cook 1995; Royer 1999). When asked recently to discuss the challenges and opportunities for a specific form of cooperative undertakings (agriculture cooperatives), two prominent researchers in this field emphasized the issues that were, according to them, challenging the survival of the cooperative form (Cook and Chaddad 2004). Fulton suggested that external forces, such as technological evolution and member individualism, would increasingly emerge as obstacles for cooperatives. In contrast, Cook suggested that it was forces internal to the coops, such as the consequences of poorly defined property rights, which would challenge coops in the future. As communal organizations share important aspects with cooperatives but also have some unique features (in particular, they further integrate the value chain and are aimed at innovation rather than at distribution), we will now examine the external and internal forces that might as well affect the ability of communal organizations to be persistent organizational forms in the life of markets.

Market Failures May Vanish

First, market failures may not be persistent; they may eventually reduce drastically or be less stringent. That is what happened to consumer cooperatives:

But even in that time [late 19th century] monopoly power and power of cartels were constrained. Local or regional monopolies or cartels in distribution lead to join efforts of the other market side by the formation of cooperatives. Consumer cooperatives became a successful movement which succeeded to keep this distribution cartels and monopolies in check. Agricultural cooperatives were successful in breaking the power of middlemen. After WWII increased mobility of consumers forced competition onto the distribution systems. Consumer cooperatives lost their function as a countervailing force against non-competing suppliers. They transformed into firms practically indistinguishable from other retailers—unless they went under altogether. (von Weizsäcker 2001)

Based on this historical observation it is legitimate to question the persistence of the market failures that are giving rise to the formation of COs in markets.

A first market failure, as mentioned earlier, is the exercise of market power by manufacturers and thus their driving consumers/users to suffer non-competitive pricing. The alleviation of this market failure can result from either a rapid adaptation of incumbent firms' behaviors or a change altogether of market structure. For instance, an incumbent monopoly may quickly set the limit price rather than maintaining its monopoly price in order to cope with a CO entry in its market. As a result a CO entrant can only transform into a durable competitor if it possesses cost advantages that enables it to compete with the limit price of the incumbent firms. As argued earlier, possessing such advantage will oftentimes require distinctive capabilities or unique resources (Barney 1991). In the markets where COs seem to persist (e.g., software), these for instance come in the form of free skills from highly qualified software engineers or passionate programmers, or from low infrastructure cost based on the usage of virtual platforms. Also incumbent firms may imitate a CO by adopting a new business model. For instance, they may decide to make profit on complementary services rather than on the product on which the CO competes. As an illustration, an incumbent software company may decide to give its software for free while making money on installation and training services or on fine tuning the software to the specific needs of the client.

The second market failure that can explain the formation of user governed COs and the undertaking of innovation by users is the failure of traditional manufacturers (non-user manufacturers) to respond perfectly to users' preferences. This failure is in part due to the cost of codifying knowledge into transferable information in a cost-effective way. How this cost will evolve in the future should have the main influence on the persistence of this market failure. Information and communication technologies have already diminished the cost of codification, but to which extent it will be reduced remains an open question. It seems, however, that manufacturers are deploying means of capturing more information from their consumers, for instance, relying more often and extensively on online communication with their user base. Toolkits may, to an extent, also be seen as another response to the problem of consumers' heterogeneous preferences, as they allow consumers to fine-tune a product to their particular needs.

Specific Inefficiencies of Community Principles

While at the start of this chapter we suggested that COs may have both advantages and drawbacks as compared to other types of firms, the literature has tended to insist on the fact that cooperative undertakings may entail specific inefficiencies. According to Royer (1999: 54),

[M]uch of the work has focused on describing problems inherent in the cooperative organizational form that creates disadvantages for cooperative [undertakings] and their members (e.g., Vitaliano 1983; Caves and Petersen 1986; Porter and Scully 1987; Staatz 1987; Cook 1995) . . . with the perception that there may be fundamental features intrinsic to the cooperative organizational form that restrict cooperatives from being able to compete effectively and that ultimately threaten their long term survival.

Cooperative undertakings in general, and COs in particular, would thus have problems stemming from the structure of property rights inherent to that type of organization (e.g., Jensen and Meckling 1979; Grossman and Hart 1986; Hart and Moore 1990; Cook 1995). A CO being "user owned, user controlled, and user benefited," the rights to the residual claims are typically limited to the CO members and limited in time to the duration of the membership. The utility from being a CO member stems from the opportunity to benefit from the "collective good" that is produced by the CO, not from the returns on the possible initial investment that the member must make in order to adhere—in some cases this initial investment may even be null. In other words, the residual claims to the value created by the CO are usually distributed in the form of patronage dividends, lower consumer goods prices, or free software. Members' shares are typically not transferable and, in traditional coops, a leaving member gives back his share without possibility to retain any residual claims.

This, a neo-institutionalism approach argues, may create important handicaps for CO to compete against IOFs (Porter and Scully 1987; Royer 1999; Staatz 1987; Cook and Iliopoulos 2000). First, it creates a *horizon problem* if the benefits that a member receives from his invest-ment in the CO is limited to the time horizon over which he expects to patronize the cooperative. The issue, as we understand it, is that there is a risk that members underinvest in assets with long-term payoffs. Accord-ing to Porter and Scully (1987), this explains why cooperative undertak-ings are less likely than other firms to undertake long-term investments, particularly in intangible assets. Second, the structure of property rights also creates a *portfolio problem* for CO members due to the fact that equity shares in the CO generally cannot be freely purchased or sold. CO members are thus impeded to diversify their portfolios, in contrast to IOF investors who can decide to sell their shares whenever they want to. In addition equity is usually returned at book value regardless of the value of the CO business and thus members usually do not receive a return on their investment reflecting the value that has been added to it, unless of course if the CO is dissolved or sold. This reinforces the tendency not to invest in new assets. Finally, in cases where members delegate tasks to a team of professional managers, the inability to use equity ownership or purchase options to compensate or motivate managers puts coops at dis-advantage when it comes to attracting and retaining good managers and when it comes to control them (Harte 1997). Also the absence of an equity market may deprive members of a means for monitoring the CO's value and evaluating management's performance (Royer 1999).

In addition to these problems, the democratic control and the mutual-ization of benefits inherent in COs may raise other problems.

First, the user controlled feature of a CO may give rise to important influence costs. Influence costs are those costs associated with activities in which members or groups engage in an attempt to influence the deci-sions that affect the benefits generated by the activity. Influence costs include both the direct costs of influence activities and the cost of poor decisions caused by influence activities. The literature hypothesizes that they are higher in a CO especially when members have heterogeneous interests (Staatz 1987). COs may also give rise to important mutual monitoring costs. Obviously mutual monitoring will cost more when the user-members are highly heterogeneous and, in particular, pursue differ-ent goals. Also mutual monitoring might be significant if frequent and complex communication among the members is required to perform the activity. Furthermore mutual monitoring may also be increased if the competencies of the user-members are very diverse or heterogeneous in quality as either ex ante coordination costs or ex post control costs will be incurred by the CO. In addition an important potential drawback of the democratic control of a CO is that making decisions will cost more than in an IOF and will furthermore tend to increase with the size of the CO.

Second, the mutualization of benefits potentially raises a free rider problem as CO members may be tempted to limit their patronage or investment knowing that they will anyway receive the same benefits as the other members, independently of their initial investment in the CO and seniority. This problem may be mitigated, however, if contributing to the CO activity provides selective benefits non accessible to lower or non-contributors. On the contrary, this problem may be enhanced if nonmembers are able to benefit from the CO activity as well.

Based on this discussion, we can make the following proposition:

Proposition 1 COs are more likely to survive in markets where (1) market imperfections are persistent due to the difficulty of incumbent firms to adjust to the CO entry, and thus transaction costs remain high; and (2) the specific inefficiencies associated with cooperative undertakings are minimized by governance choices and the characteristics of the members' population, and thus organizational costs are contained.

These elements make clear why, for instance, software is a market in which COs tend to persist and even to flourish: (1) free software is so disturbing to the business model of software firms that they cannot adjust immediately; (2) the organization costs of software COs are greatly contained by the apparent homogeneity of the user-members regarding their interests and skills, the use of virtual platforms that reduce considerably the need for capital investment, the low cost of communication and coordination between members allowed by the modern communication technologies, the continuous access to the product (by COs leaving members), the existence of selective benefits for active members, and the limited need for coordination in the production of the innovation. Overall, and despite reverse forces (free-riding, etc.), software COs are able to contain organizational costs. If software is definitely a "communal market," could that case also be applied to the automobile market? In such a case, it seems that organizational issues in table 9.1 would instead be represented in the

Table 9.1
Ability of COs to persist in markets

Issues	Enhanced if	Minimized if
Market imperfections	Persistent—incumbents cannot quickly adjust	Not persistent—incumbents can quickly adjust
Organizational inefficiencies	*Minimized if:*	*Enhanced if:*
Horizon problem	Access to benefits remain accessible to leaving members No or very low investments in assets needed to perform the activity	Access to benefits strictly limited to active members—contributors Large investment in assets needed to perform the activity
Portfolio problem	No capital investment made at entry	Large capital investment needed at entry
Control problem	Members have homogeneous interests Perfect information on members' skills Selection of members at entry	Members have heterogeneous interests Imperfect information on members' skills Free entry of new members
Free-rider problem	Access to benefits limited to members Selective benefits for active members	Access to benefits not limited to members No selective benefits for active members

"enhanced if" column. Table 9.1 summarizes the factors likely to favor or disadvantage COs in their ability to persist in markets.

Unique Benefits of Community Principles
Despite the potential inefficiencies emphasized earlier, cooperative undertakings may provide their members with unique benefits that they cannot get elsewhere or can get only at a higher cost elsewhere. For instance, farmer coops have increased the lobbying power of farmers. Also we know that software programmers who are active in OSS projects do get benefits in the form of an increased visibility, fun, or use of a product perfectly suited to their own needs. Some authors go as far as arguing that these benefits that come on top of the direct benefits accruing from the CO activity are critical for the survival of cooperative undertakings,

meaning that fighting market failures may not be sufficient to sustain a CO in the long run (e.g., Fulton 1999). For Staatz (1987: 88), "[i]n their internal organization, farmer cooperative firms may offer certain efficiencies over IOFs that help offset cooperative firms' possibly higher decision costs. . . . Farmers do not form or join cooperatives simply to reduce transaction costs; an additional motivation may be to try to redistribute rights in the farmers' favor." Thus it is important to focus not only on optimizing within a given set of property rights but also on the ability of novel designs to change the distribution of rights in favor of those controlling the organization or association. It is further necessary to look at the conditions under which cooperatives may provide benefits to their members that are simply unavailable or more costly elsewhere.

The existence of these unique benefits may affect the sustainability of a cooperative undertaking by driving the members to reevaluate the worthiness of participating in such a project. In other words, if enough individuals have a preference for reaping these unique benefits, a CO may survive even if it is at (a slight) disadvantage with an IOF in terms of cost. Inspired by the *Hotelling model of product differentiation* (with extreme locations) and by Fulton (1999), we propose the simple representation depicted in figure 9.1 (we adapt the terms to make it suited for COs). The horizontal axis represents the preference of a potential user population for the unique benefits offered by a CO. Individuals on the left-hand side (near 1) have a high preference for these benefits while those located on the right-hand side (near 0) have a negative preference for those benefits, meaning that they prefer other types of benefits specific to IOFs. The individual located in Θ is indifferent between reaping or not reaping such benefits from the CO or from an IOF. On the vertical axis are the prices at which the product is offered by the CO (p_{CO}) and by an IOF (p_1). The figure puts the CO price at a slight disadvantage (as a large disadvantage would make the coop unworthy) and shows the market share of the CO in case the preferences of the individuals for either kind of specific benefits is strong (the slope λ is steep). What is captured by this figure gives rise to the following proposition:

Proposition 2 The strength of the preference for the specific benefits that a CO can offer to its members determines the ability of a coop to survive under different price conditions. A price disadvantage can only be

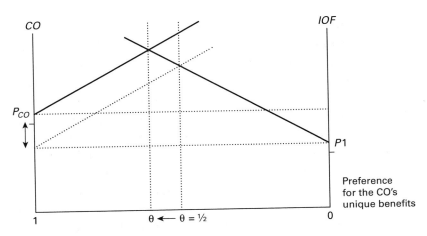

Figure 9.1

Market share of a CO versus an IOF

sustained if the CO offers additional benefits that are highly valued by its members and that they could not get at a competitive cost elsewhere.

Possible Developmental Trajectories for Communal Organizations

The Life-Cycle Theory

The notion that traditional cooperative undertakings have specific ineffi-ciencies finds support in the movement of transition of many cooperatives to a new legal form, the New Generation Coop (NGC). The NGC repre-sents an important evolution with regard to the property rights structure of cooperatives and again supports the idea that traditional coops contain important drawbacks due to their property right structure (Royer 1999). Among the important evolutions is the fact that equity shares and the associated rights can now be traded. Also capital contributions now tend to be linked to product delivery rights. The NGC model though is not without drawbacks since up front capital contributions tied to delivery rights might create financial barriers to membership.

Also Cook and Chaddad (2004) interpret the rise of the NGC form as suggesting that offensive cooperative structures are becoming more com-mon. Offensive structures have the primary objective to add value to the assets of the cooperative members (with contrast to defensive structures that seek to defend the value of their members' assets). As a result they typically need to invest capital while forming the cooperative and "as they invest in organization specific assets—including intangible assets—their ownership structure is realigned" (Cook and Chaddad 2004: 1251). Thus, as cooperatives become more vertically integrated and enter further stages in the value chain, they evolve the coop form toward the NGC form in order to realign ownership rights with use, control, and investment incentives, and benefit distribution. The rise of the NGC form thus testifies of the existence of a "user benefit–investor benefit tension" (Cook and Chaddad 2004: 1253). In other words, if benefits are mutualized while members' contributions are heterogeneous, this might be sustainable if high contributors have low opportunity costs (contribution is in time rather than in money and the opportunity cost of their time is low, for instance they contribute in their leisure time) and get high specific benefits. In other cases (high opportunity cost of members' contributions, insufficient specific benefits) heterogeneous contributions might not be compatible with mutualized benefits.

The transition to the NGC form is also predicted by the life cycle approaches of cooperative undertakings. Several authors hypothesize that although cooperative undertakings may initially serve some economic purpose in a market, they will eventually be forced to exit or reorganize (Royer 1999). In Cook's model (1995), the cooperative is formed in stage 1 to countervail opportunism and holdup by the incumbent firms. Then, if it succeeds to remedy the negative economic effects stemming from market failure, it will survive in stage 2. Yet, in reaction to the cooperative presence in the market, former competitors adjust their behavior and their price fall. At this stage, the short-run costs of using a cooperative rather than the market become more scrutinized by members. These costs, seldom recognized in the fervor of "combating a monopolist/ monopsonist" now become important. They are generated by a vaguely defined "user versus investor" set of property rights. These vaguely defined property rights lead to conflicts over residual claims and decision control—especially as cooperative undertakings become increasingly complex in their organizational structure. In stage 4, cooperative members become increasingly aware of these problems and discuss the possible options. The cooperative concludes that its options consist of: exit; continue; or transition. In stage 5, the members choose from among those options. In the same vein, in Harte's life cycle model, cooperatives are initially useful instruments for correcting or mitigating market failures. However, as market performance improves and incumbent firms adjust, the need for cooperatives diminishes. The progression of the life cycle will depend on the dynamics of the particular market. Cooperatives would be expected to persist indefinitely only in the case of chronic market failure.

Fulton (1999) hypothesizes that cooperative undertakings can only survive long if they create value for their members that they could not find elsewhere and if, thus, either they are created from the outset as an offensive form or if they eventually transit to such a form. For Fulton (1999: 431),

[A]s member commitment declines [due to the fact that the primary objective of correcting a market failure from which the member suffers has been reached or is no longer an issue], the cooperative undertakings has three basic options. The first option is to shut down or to sell to another company. The second option is to adopt a strategy of being the low cost player in the industry. The third option is to find some other dimension or characteristic to differentiate itself along. One way to differentiate is to move into a new product area where there is little or no competition from IOFs.

For instance, in the case of sugar beets, NGCs replaced the IOFs (Harris et al. 1996). Yet, creating differentiated products is a very costly business that cooperative undertakings have not traditionally undertaken (Rogers and Marion 1990; Fulton 1999) and "even if cooperatives had a structure that would allow their members to participate directly and meaningfully in the earnings from value-added enterprises, their relatively small size and their reliance on retained earnings and debt to finance growth could mean insufficient resources to play this game" (Fulton 1999).

When Is Each Trajectory Likely to Dominate?

From the previous discussion we arrive at the following proposition:

Proposition 3 The developmental trajectories followed by COs will depend on the balance between the degree to which they are at organizational costs disadvantage and the degree to which market failures persist, moderated by the extent to which they provide unique benefits to their active members.

Thus the CO form could simply disappear if it is too much at cost disadvantage with IOFs and does not provide any unique benefits to its members. It could also survive as a "hobby" firm. Then it could flourish

Table 9.2
Possible developmental trajectories followed by COs

	Market failures persist	Market failures disappear
CO at disadvantage with organizational costs	Evolution of CO form to NG CO/ Transition to IOF mode	CO disappear or persist as a "hobby" form / CO disappear
CO at parity or advantage with organizational costs	COs flourish	COs persist & coexist with IOFs
	CO provides unique benefits / CO does not provide unique benefits	CO provides unique benefits / CO does not provide unique benefits

if its advantages are overwhelming both in terms of organizational costs and unique benefits delivered to members. Also it could survive as such and coexist with IOFs. Finally, it could flourish if its cost and benefit advantages are high and market failures persist. Table 9.2 summarizes the various trajectories that COs might follow depending on the value taken by the variables affecting their ability to compete with IOFs.

Which scenario is more likely to arise is the next question. In the case of traditional consumer cooperatives, market failures have reduced greatly, due to both the adjustment of incumbent firms' behaviors and multiple evolutions that have driven to more competition in markets, whereas simultaneously the typical defensive form of cooperative undertakings was not developing distinctive advantages for its members. As the COs that we observe today represent further integration in the value chain than traditional cooperatives for which historical lessons have been drawn as well as they represent more offensive forms of cooperative undertakings, the question arises of which scenario is more likely to take place. Yet, are incumbent firms able to adjust to COs entry? Then, are COs at advantage, parity, or disadvantage with IOFs when it comes to organizational costs? The COs we know much about are in software, online gaming, online encyclopedia, and so on. In these cases COs seem to have overcome most of the costs associated with cooperative undertakings by their being opened, thus allowing leaving members to continue beneficiating from the CO good; having very low entry cost (no capital required) thus alleviating the potential discrepancy between investment and benefit; attracting members with very low opportunity cost (typically contributing during their free time); using online production platforms, thus minimizing communication and coordination costs among active members, and last but not least producing innovations that require very little coordination between the contributors. Yet, how many markets allow these features to be set up in COs? Can COs exist and persist in markets where high upfront capital investments are necessary, like in the automobile industry? How would a CO manage the tension between potentially heterogeneous investments and the mutualization of benefits in such an industry?

Finally, the free-rider problem engendered by the fact that COs tend to be opened to consumption by non- or former members seems to be compensated by the fact that active members get selective benefits (e.g., being able to move the development of software in the desired direction; see Harhoff et al. 2003). These benefits seem also to be quite unique, allowing members to get value that they cannot easily get elsewhere, such as having fun, learning, signaling one's competencies to others, showing one's abilities, helping others, and so on. Yet again, the question arises of whether these benefits could be gained in other markets or whether, on the contrary, they are very specific to those markets where COs have already started to settle down.

Conclusion

In this chapter we suggested that since COs are cooperative undertakings (Rey and Tirole 2007), the future of user communities and the potential for a democratization of innovation could be enhanced by lessons learned from the existing literature on cooperatives. While the formation of consumer cooperatives has been motivated by the existence of market failures in final goods markets, many consumer coops have eventually exited or changed their legal and organizational forms due to issues related to their structure of property rights. This structure, it has been argued, generates costs that are generally lower in investor-owned firms (IOFs) and can be overwhelming in cooperative undertakings.

Based on this literature, we have sought to identify variables susceptible to affect the likelihood and future of COs. We have suggested that the persistence of market failures, the ability of COs to limit potential organizational costs disadvantages and to provide their members with unique benefits were the key elements of the survival, persistence, and possible flourishing of COs in markets. Yet, whether there are numerous markets where these conditions can hold is a key question when it comes to the democratization of innovation through communal organizations. For instance, it seems that until now COs have been created and seem to persist in markets where many of the specific coop costs evoked can be contained due to very low or inexistent capital investment, the very low opportunity costs of member-contributors, the intangible nature of the good produced, the ability to rely fully on virtual communication, and the high modularity of the innovative goods produced. Can cooperative principles survive if, for instance, high upfront capital investment is needed for producing innovation, if more or physical coordination is required, and if members need to hire qualified personnel because they lack the competencies?

Finally, as COs represent more offensive forms of cooperative undertakings than traditional consumer cooperatives, they have at the outset the advantage of being constituted to create differentiated products or innovations thus having more chance of survival that pure defensive forms created primarily to cope with market failures. This may also mean that they may run into bigger problems as they strive to produce complex innovations requiring high financial investments.

References

Baldwin, Carliss, and Eric von Hippel. 2011. Modeling a paradigm shift: From producer innovation to user and open collaborative innovation. *Organization Science* 22 (6): 1399–1417.

Baldwin, Carliss, Christoph Hienerth, and Eric von Hippel. 2006. How user innovations become commercial products: A theoretical investigation and case study. *Research Policy* 35 (9): 1291–1313.

Barney, Jay. 1991. Firm resources and sustained competitive advantage. *Journal of Management* 17 (1): 99–120.

Caves, Richard, and Bruce Petersen. 1986. Cooperatives' shares in farm industries: Organizational and policy factors. *Agribusiness* 2 (1): 1–19.

Cook, Michael, and Fabio Chaddad. 2004. Redesigning cooperative boundaries: The emergence of new models. *American Journal of Agricultural Economics* 86 (5): 1249–53.

Cook, Michael, and Constantine Iliopoulos. 2000. Ill-defined property rights in collective action: The case of US agricultural cooperatives. In *Institutions, Contracts and Organizations: Perspectives from New Institutional Economics*, ed. Claude Ménard. 335–48. Cheltemham, UK: Edward Elgar.

Cook, Michael. 1995. The future of US agricultural cooperatives: A neo-institutional approach. *American Journal of Agricultural Economics* 77 (5): 1153–59.

Fulton, Murray. 1999. Cooperatives and member commitment. *Finnish Journal of Business Economics* 48 (4): 418–37.

Grossman, Sanford, and Oliver Hart. 1986. The costs and benefits of ownership: A theory of vertical and lateral integration. *Journal of Political Economy* 94 (4): 691–719.

Harhoff, Dietmar, Joachim Henkel, and Eric von Hippel. 2003. Profiting from voluntary information spillovers: How users benefit by freely revealing their innovations. *Research Policy* 32 (10): 1753–69.

Harris, Andrea, Brenda Stefanson, and Murray Fulton. 1996. New generation cooperatives and cooperative theory. *Journal of Cooperatives* 11: 15–28.

Hart, Oliver, and John Moore. 1990. Property rights and the nature of the firm. *Journal of Political Economy* 98: 1119–58.

Harte, Laurence N. 1997. Creeping privatisation of Irish co-operatives: A transaction cost explanation. In *Strategies and Structures in the Agro-Food Industries*, ed. Jerker Nilsson and Gert van Dijk, 31–53. Assen: Van Gorcum.

Jensen, Michael, and William Meckling. 1979. Rights and production functions: An application to labor-managed firms and codetermination. *Journal of Business* 52 (4): 469–506.

Porter, Philipp, and Gerald Scully. 1987. Economic efficiency in cooperatives. *Journal of Law and Economics* 30 (2): 489–512.

Rey, Patrick, and Jean Tirole. 2007. Financing and access in cooperatives. *International Journal of Industrial Organization* 25 (5): 1061–88.

Rogers, Richard T., and Bruce W. Marion. 1990. Food manufacturing activities of the largest agricultural cooperatives: Market power and strategic behavior implications. *Journal of Agricultural Cooperatives* 5: 59–73.

Royer, Jeffrey S. 1999. Cooperative organizational strategies: A neo-institutional digest. *Journal of Cooperatives* 14: 44–67.

Sexton, Richard, and Julie Iskow. 1988. *Factors critical to the success or failure of emerging agricultural cooperatives. Report for the US Ministry of Agriculture. Giannini Foundation Information Series 88–3.* University of California.

Staatz, John M. 1987. Farmers' incentives to take collective action via cooperatives: A transaction cost approach. In *Cooperative Theory: New Approaches*, ed. Jeffrey Royer. ACS Service Report 18. 87–107. Washington, DC: US Department of Agriculture.

Vitaliano, Peter. 1983. Cooperative enterprise: An alternative conceptual basis for analyzing a complex institution. *American Journal of Agricultural Economics* 65 (5): 1078–83.

von Hippel, Eric. 1994. Sticky information and the locus of problem solving: Implications for innovation. *Management Science* 40 (4): 429–39.

Von Weizsäcker, Christian. 2001. Conference communication.

Williamson, Oliver. 1981. The modern corporation: Origins, evolution, attributes. *Journal of Economic Literature* 19 (4): 1537–68.

10

When von Hippel Innovation Met the Networked Environment: Recognizing Decentralized Innovation

Yochai Benkler

Eric von Hippel's unique contribution to the study of innovation has been his discovery of the critical role that users play in the innovation process. His insights preceded the emergence of the thoroughly networked economy and society. They were anchored in the experience of scientific instruments, and were later extended to materials' innovations, like pultrusion and tractor shovels. His core insight was that innovation depends critically on detailed domain- and context-specific knowledge of use cases: on the shape of needs and challenges to be overcome, and on ubiquitous experimentation to meet these needs and overcome these challenges. These drivers—context specificity of needs and challenges, highly diverse and distributed insights into the context, and the need for ubiquitous experimentation in context that underlay von Hippel's claims—are persistent and stable; they existed prior to the networked society and will continue in it. But because innovators in these physical, complex mechanical areas were rarely, if ever, able to implement their invention in a widespread, usable form, and because communication among them was less fluid, their critical contributions to the innovation process were easily ignored. They did not fit the predominant model of an inventor personified by Edison: the dedicated, commercial innovator, who expends capital on experimentation, finds the perfect solution, and then patents and sells it. (That isn't really the full story of Edison either, but it is the story we tell ourselves.)

Almost a quarter of a century after von Hippel's first article on user innovation in scientific instruments, Microsoft leaked an internal document defining Linux as a real threat to Microsoft's dominance. Setting aside how convenient it was for the firm to have a "real threat" as it faced the prospect of antitrust litigation and the threat of being broken up like AT&T had been, the Halloween Memo, as that leaked document was called, marked a turning point in the public, or at least business world, perception of the plausibility and feasibility of decentralized user innovation. If decentralized users relying on a nonproprietary model could succeed in challenging Windows where IBM's OS2 had failed only four years earlier, something very special was happening.

Two critical facts changed between 1976 and 1998 (much less 2011) to make user innovation even more central to innovation. First, many production goods we care about can in fact be "finished" and "distributed" using widespread capital equipment already placed in service for filling a wide range of use needs—computers, cameras, recording devices, and the like. The barriers to moving a user innovation from the user's "garage" to the world at large are lower. Second, the ability of users to cooperate and communicate with each other about what they are doing and the results of their experiments has also changed dramatically. So the ability of user communities to develop their knowledge incrementally and collaboratively, rather than each one having to reinvent the special-purpose wheel in his or her own basement, has been all but eliminated. That combination—the capacity to build on the user innovation of others, and the capacity to "make and distribute" first prototypes—in many of the end products that are so important in the information society (software, news, images, videos, etc.) has taken user innovation and made it part of the common experience of the networked information society at large.

As we look forward into the near and intermediate future, the dynamics of user innovation will continue to play a central role, and will be more recognized as playing such a role than they have been since the industrialization of R&D. Supporting this type of widespread experimentation and innovation requires a very different institutional system than the one required by the imagined industrial model, which generalized the economics of small-molecule pharmaceuticals and star-system Hollywood movies and sound recordings. Instead of clear, strong patents, we need robust research exemptions. Instead of expansive copyright, we need robust defenses for transformative, creative reuse of materials. Freedom to operate is more important than power to appropriate.

Necessity and Passion Are the Mothers of Invention; Specific Knowledge and Ubiquitous Contextual Experimentation Its Fathers; Profit, Its Governess?

Eric von Hippel has achieved what none but a handful of academics can ever hope to achieve—he has developed a distinct, coherent, and uniquely recognizable contribution to a fundamental question in understanding human affairs. Invention and innovation are at the very heart of material welfare over time. We have known for over half a century that innovation, not efficiency or optimization, is the primary driver of growth and development. In one major tradition, following Schumpeter, it is done by large organizations that use innovation to capture markets and monopolize them, often best so when driven by smaller organizations nipping at their heels. Another major tradition avoids the organizational structure and focuses on incentives to innovate and the relative role of property and public funding in making markets in innovation function as well as they can. These are anchored in Arrow's public goods analysis, and its defense of public investments, on the one hand, and Demsetz's property-based critique, on the other hand. This latter tradition has been particularly powerful in debates over intellectual property law. The former has had a larger role in innovation economics generally, and has produced some of the most productive insights on the relationship between science and technology and the dynamics of innovation markets.

von Hippel succeeded in shining a light on a major source of innovation that falls squarely in neither of these major streams of work. Its primary distinction from the neo-Schumpeterian strand is that its focus is not on innovation within firms operating in different market structures, but on individuals and groups of *users* of innovations outside of the firms usually thought to be the engines of innovation. Its primary distinction from the latter line of literature is that its focus is not on institutionally dependent incentives to innovation, and the benefits and costs of stronger or weaker intellectual property rights; motivation is largely given by use-need, the critical task is documenting actual practices and understanding that innovation flows from need and contextually relevant experience.

In user innovation von Hippel identified a domain of invention that is absolutely critical in the overall system of innovation but was simply invisible to the main modes of analysis. As early as his 1976 paper on scientific instruments (von Hippel 1976), and followed by dozens of other case studies and two major books, von Hippel was able to identify a different class of inventors than anyone else had looked at, and a different driver of ability to invent well and creatively than did these other approaches. This class of inventors was *users*. Users are those individuals or firms that would ultimately need the invention once it got created. These users are those considered, under the other approaches, as the *customers* of a finished good, and at most brought in to "listen to the customer" sessions after invention and innovation, for refinement, but never seen as an important source of invention. The dynamic of invention, in turn, was focused neither on incentives nor on market structure and ability to bring capital to bear, but on localized, context-specific knowledge and opportunity to experiment, refine, and iterate over and over again with no direct calculation of likely market costs.

For user-innovators, the motivational drivers were necessity or passion. In some cases, like irrigation systems for farmers, or medical devices for physicians, necessity drives invention. In other cases, like extreme sports, it is passion. These drivers are not particularly sensitive to cost, they are not particularly directed at developing something with a clear timeline to market, and they do not constrain the practitioners from sharing their innovations with others, allowing networks of users to learn from each other and improve continuously on each other's work. Neither necessity for final use nor passion is particularly well described by the standard economic analysis of intellectual property. Appropriation through exclusion, capturing either monopoly profits or licensing, is not the driver and has little positive to contribute to motivating the innovation process. If anything, it is a hindrance where others' innovations are needed to be improved and mixed with a given generation's innovation practices. Similarly the dynamics of firms in more-or-less concentrated markets or of the relations between public research and private firm-based innovation are not instructive. These are the motivations of the invisible inventors, after all.

Necessity and passion may motivate, but they are not the source of comparative advantage of user-innovators over firms that aim to sell innovations to ultimate users. Two distinct characteristics of user innovation are what give it the advantage: localized, contextual knowledge of needs and uses, and a high degree of practical experimentation. First, a critical advantage von Hippel identified that these user-innovators have over the normal subjects of innovation studies is hyper-localized and contextual knowledge. It turns out that human practices and needs are much more heterogeneous and quirky than firms can readily research, identify, and specify as research targets. The real world is too diverse, too complex, for firms to explore comprehensively. What user-innovators do in the first stage of von Hippel's innovation is to act as a distributed sensor network for human needs. The needs are theirs. Often these needs are tacitly experienced long before they can be explicitly described and communicated to a third-party that could play the role that the standard models assign to the classic innovator firm. As a result users have opportunities to try and solve their problems and needs long before firms even know that the needs exist. Furthermore the uses and practices, and conditions in real world implementation, are highly diverse. Understanding user circumstances presents a classic knowledge diffusion problem, but in the inverse direction to how knowledge diffusion is normally thought of. The knowledge is tacit, or implicit, it is hard to codify completely and transmit to the would-be innovative firms. But its location is not in the hands of innovator firms, with difficulty of diffusion being from them to downstream innovators and users. It is in the hands of those who will benefit from the innovations, and knowledge of their needs has difficulty making its way "upstream." (Although the use of "upstream-downstream" metaphor breaks down once we see users as sources, as well as end-points of innovation. It becomes more a cyclical flow system than an upstream-downstream system.)

The second productive element of user innovation is ubiquitous experimentation. Because users are working in their own environments, using their own tools and systems, they construct early working models, adjust, try again, and iterate incrementally until something works. Moreover, because many users work in parallel, each on their own version of a solution, many experiments can fail cheaply (in the sense of failing locally, with few secondary effects beyond the experimenter, although obviously experiments at the individual level can be very costly—think mountain bikes or skateboards). This system of widespread, parallel, low-cost problem-solving experimentation has more in common with evolutionary dynamics than with planned R&D based on market research that projects likely consumer demand.

In von Hippel's story, the companies enter at the stage where the invention is largely done; they professionalize, standardize, package and offer an orderly framework for the distribution of the inventions. In this, they play a critical role in transforming the invention into a consumer good or a standardized system users can adopt and buy. But they are not the main source of invention for the broad range of practices that von Hippel and many others following him have documented.

von Hippel Innovation Meets the Networked Environment

von Hippel suggested that innovation is constrained by the cost of invention or experimentation, on the one hand, and the cost of communication among user-innovators, on the other hand. The cheaper something is to construct, modify, extend, and experiment with tools and machines that users need and develop, the more the user-innovators can do it, and the more innovation their collaboration can provide. The more these parties can communicate with each other, the more they can share results from their experiments, build on each other's work, and innovate more rapidly. The digitally networked environment dramatically shifted both dimensions in the "right" direction. First, most powerfully in software, but also in other areas where computer-assisted design could speed and decrease the cost of innovation even in material objects, the physical cost of constructing inventions, implementing them, testing and experimenting, and iterating became substantially cheaper. Second, and more important, the networked environment allowed users to connect with each other, share observations about needs, share results from experiments, and, ultimately, share solutions. Nowhere was this clearer than in free and open source software development. Had von Hippel not written his early work two decades earlier, we could almost have thought that he invented his theory to explain free software. In his case, however, the owl of Minerva took flight before the break of dawn.

The classic Eric Raymond self-ethnography of open source software development (Raymond 2000), scratching a developer's itch, exactly matches the user-innovator's need-based invention. The practice of bug reporting matches the role of users in identifying the wide and diverse set of needs and contextual potential failures that need solving. "All bugs are shallow" replicates the idea that with enough users experimenting, someone, somewhere, solves the problem, and from there the problem is systematization and diffusion. Indeed it was primarily in the context of observing the digitally networked environment that von Hippel began to focus on the collaborative, user-*community* aspects of user innovation, rather than primarily about the peculiar informational advantages that individual users had with regard to their needs.

Not surprisingly, commons-based innovation and creative practices, and peer production in the networked environment in particular, matched von Hippel's work perfectly. Practices that were hard to observe when done by farmers, surgeons, and building contractors, for example, became easier to observe and gained much wider cultural recognition. The critical transformation then, between 1976 when von Hippel first explored user innovation, and the first decade of the 21st century, combines (1) the fact that many production goods we care about can actually be "finished" and "distributed" using widespread capital equipment—such as computers, cameras, and recording devices. The barriers to the move of user innovation from the user's garage to the world at large are lower. No less important, (2) it has become much easier for users to cooperate and communicate with each other about what they are doing, to exchange innovations and incremental improvements, and brainstorm ideas and solutions. User communities have vastly increased the rate of incremental iteration in knowledge development and have reduced the waste involved in disparate individual experimenters reinventing the same aspects of the wheel. That capacity to build on the innovation of others and to "make and distribute" many of the end products that are critical in the information society (software, news, images, videos, etc.) has taken user innovation and made it part of the common experience of the networked information society at large.

Freedom to Operate Becomes More Important Than Power to Appropriate for Innovation

The critical implication of the role of user invention in driving the innovation process is that freedom to operate becomes more important than the power to appropriate. By "freedom to operate," I mean the legal privilege to act under technological conditions that make action in a given domain practically feasible, a privilege that does not imply the right to use law to force someone else to act or abstain from action. By "power to appropriate," I mean legal mechanisms designed to harness the power of law to prevent or require actions by others necessary to facilitate the appropriation of the added value of one's activity. This basic division plays itself out in law, in particular in questions of intellectual property law; it plays itself out in standards processes and the emphasis on open standards; and it plays itself out in control over networks, platforms and applications, as the more one needs to be a major player to deploy, the less one gets in user innovation.

I do not intend to outline here a complete set of proposals. But the proposals I set out below are intended to put some flesh on what it means to embrace the shift from securing power to appropriate to assuring the freedom to operate.

Patents

A Broad Experimental Use Exception

The United States has long had an experimental use exception. And, for a long time, commentators saw that courts would interpret this exemption narrowly. In 2002, in *Madey v. Duke*, the Court of Appeals for the Federal Circuit confirmed this fear, and defined the experimental use exemption so narrowly as to effectively render it meaningless.[1] In an ironic twist, when faced with a safe harbor for trial uses by pharmaceuticals for products that may require Federal Drug Administration approval, the Supreme Court found a broader exemption.[2] None of this resolution is set in statutory stone. The language of the statute is sufficiently flexible to make the experimental use exemption cover substantially more than its current interpretation allows. All it requires is judicial revision of the prevailing interpretation. As the *Bilski* decision suggests, in the context of business method and potentially software patents, the Federal Circuit may be ready to revise its interpretation of patent law in favor of freedom to operate at the expense of its earlier singular emphasis on power to appropriate.[3]

A broad experimental use exception is the most obvious and necessary reinterpretation of patent law that falls straight out of a recognition of the role and dynamics of user innovation. Once we shift our gaze from firms that sell patented products as the sources of invention, and see the broader set of end users as co-creators of the innovation, several things become clear. First, a large number of parties who are *prima facie* violating patents (when they innovate on existing patented technology; or are innovating near existing patents) are a critical part of the innovation ecology. These are not free riders or second-movers into a market proven at another's hazard. These are users trying to figure out how to serve a need they have that present technologies, as presently used, do not solve. When they experiment with existing, patent-burdened technologies, they are operating at the cutting edge of experimentation that will result in the next generation of innovation. For these user experimenters, however, any kind of royalty, or risk of owing a royalty on their experimental use will create practically insurmountable entry barriers. Even if firms are committed to licensing their innovations on *reasonable and nondiscriminatory* (RAND) terms, any reasonable rate that might be worth the transactions costs of licensing from the perspective of a firm will be overly burdensome in settings where inventors are end users. While some end users may be companies that can afford RAND licensing fees, the innovative dynamics most significantly facilitated by the Internet are precisely those where each individual participant in a network of user-inventors will almost certainly be unwilling or unable to pay licensing fees, even where those are set at rates that medium-size firms can readily pay. As a consequence we will see either inventors shy away from tinkering and learning new ways of doing things, which will have exactly the opposite effect of the intent of the patent system, or we will see inventors flagrantly violating patent rights, and likely resulting in a few high-profile cases dampening user innovation after the fact.

Noncommercial User-to-User Exchange as Part of an Expanded Experimental Use Exemption

A more dramatic departure from current law, but a necessary complement to it, would be to expand the experimental use exemption to noncommercial exchanges of follow-on user innovations otherwise covered by a valid patent. The basis for such an extended exemption is obvious once one recognizes the cooperative, community dimension of the von Hippel innovation. As users exchange information about modifications and inventive solutions, they may also begin to exchange instances of the innovation. As they exchange instances, they learn about each other's modifications and incorporate them into their own design. This knowledge flow is an integral part of what makes user innovation move so rapidly and include so much contextually relevant knowledge. To enable this exchange of knowledge, the experimental use exemption should be extended to cover noncommercial exchange of articles embodying this innovation, and the term "noncommercial" should be read broadly to include even exchanges in which recipients pay the cost of production and distribution. The trick here would be to identify a line over which noncommercial exchange effectively displaces a substantial portion of the market for a patented item, rather than constituting an exchange between participants in an innovation community. While distinguishing commercial from noncommercial, and market-displacing from innovation enhancing exchanges is not trivial, it requires line-drawing that is not unusual in common-law adjudication. It is well within the competence of courts to distinguish between a community of hobbyists-innovators engaged in a process of development, and an informal marketplace from some members of that core innovator community to passive end users, which displaces the patent owner's market to non-innovating end users.

Compulsory Licenses to Follow-on Innovators That Rely on Inventions Developed under the Expanded Experimental Use Exemption

Both a broadening of the experimental use exemption and the inclusion of noncommercial exchange can be achieved by judicial interpretation. A more fundamental expansion would require statutory change, and would address the risk that a user invention will fail to be adopted by the original patent holder. This may be because the original patent holder has a very different view of how it would like its product used; it may be because the original patent holder is no longer practicing in the market; or it may be because the original patent holder has made its own innovations, which are, in turn, patented, and would like to avoid competition with its own improved product. In all these cases, there is a risk either that the patent owner will not license production of the innovative product that came out of the user innovation process, or will only be willing to license at an exorbitant price that reflects its bottleneck control over deployment.

In user innovation, the users absorb most of the risks that traditional patent theory assumed were borne by the patent holder. Part of the rationale for the temporary monopoly power held by the patentee is that it compensates the patentee for all the failed experiments, all the false starts. And yet, with user innovation, the high-risk portions of exploration and experimentation are undertaken and absorbed by the users themselves. By the time more organized firms come along, there is a reasonably well-defined product, and a reasonably well-defined market for the product. What is left is product engineering, refinement, and marketing; none of which have the kind of high-risk profile traditionally associated with the justifications of patents.

To the extent that a field is typified by user innovation, it is a field in which accepting a property-like rule to cover follow-on innovation over-compensates patent holders. Instead, what would be appropriate for such a field is a liability rule, on the model proposed by Reichman (2000) and others for innovation fields in which incremental innovation is widespread. Users who innovated could go to any manufacturer to actually produce the follow-on product, and that producer would then owe the original patent owner a set damage judgment—in effect, would receive a compulsory license for practicing the follow-on innovation. Specifically, however, the rate at which the compulsory license should be set should not reflect a hypothetical license, since holdup is the precise concern, and the absorption of the risk by the user community is a major justification. Instead, the rate should be backed out of an ex post evaluation of the relative contribution of the original patented invention to the value of the infringing product, along the lines of the caution regarding issuing an injunction reflected in the Supreme Court's holding in *eBay v. MercExchange*. The idea is that damages should be assessed proportionate to the contribution of the distinct patent violated to the overall value of the innovation into which it is integrated expressed in several of the draft patent reforms proposed in the past few years. While this idea of apportioned damages was not made part of the America Invents Act in 2011, it nonetheless is an important technique for managing remuneration flows for an innovation process reconceived as one based on much more incremental and informal innovation than the traditional, property-rule-based model of patent remedies.

User Practice as Prior Art—Presumption in the Presence of a Vibrant User Innovation Community

A distinct but significant reform may not require legal statutory change, given the expansion in the definition of "prior art" by the America Invents Act, but merely a change of practice—this time, at the Patents and Trademarks Office, or a change in interpretation by courts. Given the extensive evidence regarding the prevalence of user innovation, it is important that the PTO in examinations, and courts in reviewing, consider prior art to include user community practices in the mix of sources. Because these will not be filed as patents, they will often be outside the scope of materials available to a patent examiner. Because they may not be in scientific or industry journals, they may be harder to find in normal indexed-library searches. However, as more user communities develop online dimensions, at least some of the practices are susceptible to search, and in cases of later litigation, evidence of oral traditions in user communities should be sought. This will be of particular importance in cases where a later commercial developer of a user-innovated product obtains a patent for its refined finished product, potentially restricting the freedom to tinker of the very same user community that gave rise to the invention in the first place.

A more robust version of this reform would create a presumption of prior art in any field in which there is shown to be widespread user innovation already taking place at the time of the claimed invention. This presumption could be overcome by the patent applicant or holder, by itself conducting an extensive review of user practices and showing that its innovation indeed was sufficiently novel and nonobvious relative to that widespread user practice. The primary reason for such a heightened level of review is that where a vibrant user innovation community is functioning, the likelihood that an outsider will have enough insight into the needs and context to produce a genuine innovation, or the likelihood that an insider turned patent-claimant in fact did not learn critical aspects of their innovation from someone else in a vibrant community, are very low. Since an outsider is unlikely to have sufficient contextual insight to improve on the community practices, and an insider is unlikely to have arrived at the innovation ex nihilo, the prior probability assessment of pre-existing community innovation should be reflected in the level of proof required for claimed patents in innovations in which there is a vibrant user innovator community at the time of creation.

Delenda est Carthago

The quintessential user innovation community today is software, and in this case the remedy is simple. Software patents *simpliciter* should be abolished. There is simply no continuing justification for their continued enforcement and recognition. On this too many words have been spilled by many others, and I will not repeat them here.

Copyright: Innovation and Cultural Creativity on the Net

While von Hippel's original work emphasized physical products, where patent is the relevant intellectual property barrier to innovation, much of the dynamic of user innovation occurs online. An important part of this is in free and open source software. But there are strong analogies in other, non-innovation practices of creative culture or news reporting that, while not strictly speaking *innovation*, share a similar structure to von Hippel innovation and its relationship to patent law. Remix culture has spawned much debate and many reform proposals.

Copyright law provides various doctrines with which to create substantial freedom to operate for user innovators. One example that has been enormously important was the more-or-less categorical acceptance by courts of the position that copying a computer program for purposes of reverse engineering did not violate copyright, mostly by protecting it under the fair use doctrine. The case of reverse engineering is a classic instance of efforts to leverage earlier innovation to constrain later innovation: It is the classic image of freedom to operate trumping power to appropriate. Beginning in 1988,[4] and then throughout the 1990s, circuit courts throughout the country largely protected the privilege of software developers to act in ways that formally violate copyright, say, by making an unauthorized copy or derivative work, as long as this was done as part of the process of reverse engineering: that is, figuring out how the software works so as to make use of its functionality, usually in order to create software that interoperates with the software that is being reversed engineered.[5]

This widely adopted rule came under pressure after the passage of the *Digital Millennium Copyright Act* of 1998 (DMCA) and the introduction of an increasing number of *End User Licensing Agreements* (EULAs) that prohibited reverse engineering. The DMCA's core provision constrained circumventing technological protection measures. The "anti-circumvention" provisions responded to a concern by copyright owners. They hoped to maintain, and indeed refine, their control over digitized information goods by wrapping them with encryption, so that they could avoid unauthorized copying but also enforce price discrimination—for example, by making sure that a digital music file sold in the United States for $15 could not then be resold in Europe, where it is available for 15€; or to sell one-time viewings, or three-time viewings, etc., at different pricing. The fear to which the anti-circumvention provisions responded was that other software developers would be able to build devices that would get around—circumvent—the encryption. The DMCA made both the act of circumventing a copy-protection design, and the act of making or distributing the tools to do so, civil and potentially criminal offenses. Within a short period, these provisions began to be used by companies to prevent competitors from entering their markets. The two most important cases were the *Chamberlain* case and the *Lexmark* case. In *Chamberlain*, a garage door company tried to exclude a competitor from selling a competing universal garage door opener by claiming that the competitor's garage door opener only worked by getting around its own control software.[6] In *Lexmark*, the printer company Lexmark International tried to use the DMCA to prevent competitors from making toner cartridges that could work with its own printers. It did so by including a microchip and piece of software with the cartridges, without which a competing cartridge would not be run by the printer. Another company, Static Control Components, created a compatible, unauthorized microchip that could be installed in the cartridges by other companies, which, in turn, could compete in the market for replacement toner for Lexmark printers. To do so, Static Control had to both make use of a Lexmark's Toner Loading Program, in ways that included copying it, and to circumvent the protection measure provided by the chip.[7]

The *Lexmark* decision provides a model for what a court concerned with freedom to operate should do. The first was to define narrowly the boundaries of copyright. Rather than relying on fair use, which involves substantial litigation risk, the court analyzed the program copied for its character as functional, within the classic idea/expression and merger framework. That is, copyright law specifically excludes from its coverage the idea embodied in an expression from coverage; anyone is free to express the same idea in different words. By framing its decision in terms of this basic principle of copyright law, the Sixth Circuit decision created a broad categorical freedom to operate for access controls of the kind at stake, instead of subjecting each future effort to achieve interoperability to the vagaries of fair use. Note that fair use is a four-factor doctrine, is relatively uncertain, and presents a relatively high litigation risk for defendants. Second, the court construed the DMCA's provision narrowly to avoid the facts of the case, and emphasized the importance of the core function of Static Control's program—enabling interoperability. The *Chamberlain* case before it already held that there could be no DMCA violation if there was not a copyright violation underlying the circumvention. That is, circumventing a device that does not protect against copyright violations is not a violation of the DMCA. Together, these two components anchor an important part of the broader approach: assuring that where a later innovator uses the functions, ideas, or facts embedded in a copyrighted work, even when doing so technically requires using the work itself, that act is not itself infringing. From the perspective of protecting user innovators, this freedom to operate on existing materials, free of the concern that acts necessary to learning and working with the existing state of innovation is not a copyright or DMCA violation is critical.

By contrast, the Eighth and Ninth Circuits in decisions concerning Blizzard Entertainment created a real threat to user innovation by following a path opposite to that taken by the *Chamberlain* and *Lexmark* courts. In *Blizzard v. BnetD*, Blizzard, a major computer games company, used a code to limit play of its online, multiplayer game to players who used servers that it owns and controls. BnetD was an open source project that permitted the owners of copies of Blizzard games to direct their instances of the program to play on different servers, not owned by Blizzard. The developers of BnetD were Blizzard game players who were looking to improve their user experience by building a server that was free of the constraints imposed by Blizzard on its servers. Blizzard argued that enabling its players to use their games over other systems' servers violated the terms of its end user license agreement (EULA), which, among other things, prohibited reverse engineering. While the court agreed that reverse engineering was "necessary" in order for the BnetD software to be developed, it nonetheless sided with Blizzard, holding that enforcing a prohibition on doing something that was privileged under federal copyright law was not preempted by that law. To so hold, the court would have to assume that the freedom of software developers to reverse engineer under federal copyright law was not itself a core component of federal policy, and it did so explicitly rejecting the applicability of the reverse engineering cases, going back to *Vault*, which did in fact hold that federal law preempted terms of service or a EULA that prohibited reverse engineering. The court in *Blizzard* effectively made a choice: it assured that Blizzard was able to control use of its game software by having a secure, controlled playing environment, at the expense of undermining the freedom to operate for new innovators and entrants, in particular user innovators, necessary to allow them to create new systems that interoperated with the existing systems.

In a more recent decision related to Blizzard's World of Warcraft, *MDY Indus. v. Blizzard Entertainment*, MDY had created a bot, Glider, that game players could buy and deploy to play the game for them, gain "experience" so as to advance in the game without requiring the player who bought the bot to spend hours actually playing WoW. Blizzard, in turn, created a program, Warden, that sought out players who were running the bot and booted them off the game, arguing that playing through bots instead of in person violated the terms of service, and disrupted the other players' user experience. MDY developed a version of Glider that evaded detection by Warden, and it was this feature that Blizzard charged was a violation of the DMCA. The Ninth Circuit help in favor of Blizzard, most critically by refusing to adopt the approach taken in *Chamberlain,* and finding that it was possible to violate the DMCA's anti-circumvention provision even if the device being circumvented was protecting access to the work, but not preventing a use that was itself a violation of copyright. The court essentially created a free-floating prohibition on circumvention of access control mechanisms entirely independent of whether those controls were being used to protect copyrighted materials or uses or not.[8]

The two lines of cases present fundamentally opposed pathways regarding the degree to which courts are willing to limit the freedom to operate around materials that are themselves copyrighted, or that are encrypted or include an encrypted software component. Courts and judges that recognize the value of user innovation should be concerned with preserving substantial freedom to operate around a core of protection. Specifically, *Lexmark* and *Chamberlain,* together with the reverse engineering cases (prior to the *Blizzard* cases) stand for the benefits of using two major doctrinal levers more powerfully in defense of freedom to operate for follow-on innovators and creators in general, and user innovators in particular.

- *Idea/fact versus expression doctrine*   In particular, *Lexmark* used the fact that the copying was used to achieve interoperability to anchor its holding that however initially "creative" the Lexmark code was, once it is used to protect access, then using it, and its unique features, becomes a fact about interoperability. That is to say, the function merges with the expression based on the fact that using what might otherwise have been protected elements becomes necessary to interoperate with the earlier work.

- *Preemption of licenses that constrain follow-on uses*   Courts should treat elements of copyright law that preserve freedom to operate for follow-on uses as pre-empting the field, and preempt licenses that constrain innovative follow-on uses.

- *Limitation of DMCA anti-circumvention liability*   The circumvention of control would protect against acts that themselves violate copyright, as the *Chamberlain* court did.

- *Extension of DMCA exemptions through the Librarian of Congress*   Over the past several years, the librarian of Congress has adopted several exemptions from anti-circumvention liability, such as for certain fair uses of DVD content, or for smartphone jailbreaking to install a program not authorized by the operating system or App store owner. This basic approach should be generalized to "jailbreaking" any system that prevents its user from installing and running on it legitimate software and modifications. Jailbreaking of this sort is precisely the point at which the two worldviews of innovation come into most direct conflict. The controlled-systems approach posits a system that runs smoothly and perfectly as designed by its vendor. The open, user-centric innovation system sees an ever learning system. If von Hippel innovation is to continue to be an important factor in innovation in digital devices and systems, as it has been in the past two decades, user-innovators must have access to the devices in use. In a business environment rich in controlled, proprietary devices, where even general purpose PCs are gravitating, through the extension of both iOS and Windows 8, to a controlled platform model, these kinds of exemption to allow users to tweak their devices, implement their tweaks, and share and iterate, is absolutely critical to the future of innovation.

- *Capping liability* Copyright law has a particularly nasty provision from the perspective of end users—the availability of statuary damages. User innovators who are not market actors can afford to deal with an injunction to stop doing what they are doing. The greater risk is the availability of very large statutory damages provisions that could ruin user innovators. Judges have a great deal of discretion in setting statutory damages, from as little as $750 to $150,000 per violation, depending on whether they find the infringement willful or not, and as the court otherwise "considers just." Courts should be mindful of the enormous value of user innovation, and should minimize statutory damages available against a user innovators'.

Conclusion

Thirty-five years ago, half a lifetime, literally, Eric von Hippel innovated. He shone a light on a kind of innovation that was simply invisible to the literature on innovation and intellectual property before him. While it took him decades to make this phenomenon visible, today, as the networked information economy has lowered the cost of user innovation and made innovation by communities of practice around the globe faster and more effective, the phenomenon that he described is becoming an ever more important part of our innovation ecology. Because it was invisible for so long, all our systems—in particular, law but also organizational practices and habits of mind—had been built to ignore it. Over the past decade and a half, the networked environment has made the phenomenon more visible, and increased its relative role in the innovation system as a whole. Patent law and copyright law must be adapted to this newly significant and newly recognized role of von Hippel's user innovation.

Notes

1. *Madey v. Duke*, 307 F.3d 1351 (Fed. Cir. 2002).

2. Merck KGaA v. Integra Lifesciences I, Ltd., 545 US 193 (2005).

3. In *Bilski v. Kappos*, 130 S. Ct. 3218, 561 US__, 177 L. Ed. 2D 792 (2010) the Supreme Court overturned the Federal Circuit's drastic reduction in its openness to business method and software patents. The Court did not dispute the need for a contraction of software and business method patent scope; indeed, a strong concurring opinion by Justice Stevens would have completely eliminated, categorically, business methods patents, but thought that the machine or transformation test that the Federal Circuit had adopted was too mechanical. While the Court did not replace the new standard the Federal Circuit proposed with a new one, it was clear from the opinions of both the Court of Appeals and the Supreme Court that a narrowing was warranted, and the precise debate revolves around how rigid and how radical the narrowing ought to be. We will likely find the answer out over the coming several years.

4. *Vault Corp. v. Quaid Software Ltd.*, 847 F.2d 255, 270 (5th Cir. 1988).

5. For a review of the cases and problems associated with its extension to software patents see Cohen and Lemley (2001).

6. 381 F.3d 1178 (Fed. Cir. 2004) (applying what it described as Seventh Circuit law).

7. Lexmark International, Inc. v. Static Control, 387 F.3d 522 (6th Cir. 2004).

8. *MDY Indus. LLC v. Blizzard Entertainment, Inc. and Vivendi, Inc.*, CA 9 December 2010. Available at http://docs.justia.com/cases/federal/appellate-courts/ca9/09-15932/920101214/.

References

Cohen, Julie E., and Mark Lemley. 2001. Patent scope and innovation in the software industry. *California Law Review* 89 (1): 1–57.

Raymond, Eric. 2000. The cathedral and the bazaar. http://www.catb.org/~esr/writings/homesteading/cathedral-bazaar/.

Reichman, Jerome H. 2000. Of green tulips and legal kudzu: Repackaging rights in subpatentable innovation. *Vanderbilt Law Review* 53 (6): 1743–98.

von Hippel, Eric. 1976. The dominant role of users in the scientific instrument Innovation Process. *Research Policy* 5 (3): 212–39.

III

Legal Aspects of User and Community Innovation

11

Freedom to Tinker

Pamela Samuelson

Tinkering with technologies and other human-made artifacts is as old as these artifacts themselves. People tinker for a variety of reasons: to have fun or be playful, to understand how things work, to become more actualized, to repair or make improvements to the artifacts, to adapt them to new purposes, and occasionally, to be destructive.[1]

Eric von Hippel has conducted an important set of empirical studies that document the frequency with which user tinkering has resulted in the creation of a wide range of innovative technologies (e.g., von Hippel 2005).[2] This tinkering generally occurs without much (if any) thought being given to possible restrictions that intellectual property (IP) rules might impose on the activities of tinkerers. Nor do tinkering user-innovators typically seek IP protection for their innovations. As von Hippel has shown, most user-innovators are eager to freely share their innovations with others (2005: 77–91).

This chapter discusses some doctrinal flexibilities in IP laws that allow tinkering to flourish in many contexts. Patent, trade secret, and trademark laws generally allow user-innovators considerable freedom to tinker. Although copyright law permits a modest degree of tinkering with existing products, it restricts freedom to tinker more than other IP laws. Of particular concern to user-innovators are limits that copyright law places on user rights to modify computer programs because software is so frequently embedded in a wide range of technologies these days. Because user innovations generally "promote the progress of science and useful arts," IP rules should be applied, or as necessary adapted, to permit user innovations that achieve this constitutional goal.[3]

IP Rules That Allow Tinkering with Your Own Property

The most significant IP rule that facilitates the freedom of user-innovators to tinker with artifacts they own is known in the United States as the "first sale" limit on IP rights.[4] This rule allows those who have purchased products in the marketplace considerable freedom to use, modify, and resell those products as they wish, even if the products are protected in whole or in part by IP rights.[5] That is, IP owners have the right to control the first sale of products embodying the innovation in the market, but subsequent resales or uses of those products will generally be free from the IP owners' control. An alternative, more internationally accepted way to express the same concept is that the first authorized sale of a product embodying an IP-protected innovation "exhausts" the right of the IP owner to control further distribution of that product (e.g., see Van Houweling 2011: 1064).[6]

Despite the exhaustion rule, user modifications to patented products have occasionally been challenged. The lawsuits have generally involved plaintiffs who claim that the defendants engaged in unauthorized reconstructions of their patented inventions, and defendants who claim that they were only repairing products they owned.[7] Patentees are entitled to control the manufacture and sale of products embodying their inventions, but not post-sale uses of the products. Reconstruction usurps the right to control making the invention. Because repairs typically are more limited in character, they do not run afoul of patent rights.

One exemplary mid-19th-century case, *Wilson v. Simpson*, involved a patentee who challenged a user's replacement of cutting knives for a machine that was covered by a patent.[8] The knives tended to become dull or to break every 60 to 90 days, although the patented machine in which they were used generally lasted several years. The US Supreme Court ruled Wilson's replacement of knives was a repair that did not infringe Simpson's patent.

More than a century later the Supreme Court considered the lawfulness of modifications to patented machines in *Wilbur-Ellis Co. v. Kuther*.[9] Wilbur-Ellis had refurbished and made substantial modifications to patented fish-canning machines, including the resizing of several parts. The Court observed that "in adapting the old machines to a related use [Wilbur-Ellis was] doing more than repair in the customary sense; but what they did was akin to repair for it bore on the useful capacity of the old combination, on which the royalty had been paid."[10] Hence Wilbur-Ellis' modifications to the machine did not infringe Kuther's patent.

The *Wilson* and *Wilbur-Ellis* cases are only two of a long line of precedents that have treated modifications of patented products, whether to extend the life of products embodying patented inventions or to adapt the products to new uses, as permissible repairs.[11] Thus patent law promotes freedom to tinker substantially through the exhaustion doctrine.

Trade secrecy law also provides users with considerable freedom to tinker with products they own. It is quite common for people or firms to buy products, disassemble them, study their components, and test them in various ways to figure out how they work and of what they are made. This kind of activity, widely referred to as *reverse engineering*,[12] has been defined as "the process of extracting know-how or knowledge from a human-made artifact" (Samuelson and Scotchmer 2002: 1577). Trade secrecy law regards reverse engineering as a lawful way to acquire know-how that the product's manufacturer may claim as a trade secret.[13]

There are several reasons why trade secrecy law allows reverse-engineers to tinker with existing products. From an economic standpoint, reverse engineering generally promotes competition and ongoing innovation while posing little risk of eroding lead-time advantages for producers who claim know-how embedded in their products as trade secrets (Samuelson and Scotchmer 2002: 1582–90). This is because it generally takes considerable time, money, and energy for second-comers, including user-innovators, to reverse-engineer products to extract trade secrets from them (1586–87).[14] Reverse-engineers often perceive opportunities to innovate on top of the first-comers' products, and when they do, this is likely to promote social welfare (1588–89). Although trade secrecy law does not have an exhaustion of rights doctrine as such, it has long considered reverse engineering to be a fair way to acquire secrets, perhaps in part because one who purchases products embodying secrets obtains property rights in those products that allows them to discover the secrets through use or disassembly of the products.[15] By permitting users to reverse-engineer products, trade secrecy law also provides incentives for innovators to seek patents if they wish to obtain exclusive rights to exploit their inventions.[16]

This is not to say that reverse engineering is always permissible as a matter of trade secrecy law. If someone breaches a contractual agreement which requires him not to engage in reverse engineering or uses improper means (e.g., burglary or deceit) to get access to products to reverse-engineer the secret, this may give rise to liability for trade secret misappropriation.[17] But, in general, freedom to tinker is strongly protected by trade secrecy law.

Trademark law, like trade secrecy law, protects IP owners against certain forms of unfair competition. User-innovators do not have to worry about trademark law as an impediment to their freedom to tinker because this law does not regulate what people do with products they purchase, but only acts in the marketplace that would cause confusion about who made the products. A user-innovator who alters another firm's product and tries to resell it as though it emanated from the original manufacturer might well infringe the latter's trademark rights.[18] But it is lawful for a user-innovator to modify another firm's product and resell modified versions so long as he makes clear that the product now being offered in the marketplace, although originally made by X, has been modified by Y.[19]

Until quite recently, freedom-to-tinker issues rarely arose in copyright contexts, at least in the United States.[20] One reason is because copyright law has traditionally not extended protection to technologies (e.g., see Samuelson 2007: 1928–42), and most user innovations studied by von Hippel and others have involved tinkering with technologies.[21] A second is that copyright law, like patent law, has an exhaustion doctrine. US courts have historically found tinkering with one's own copy of a copyrighted work to be unproblematic. Thus repainting and reselling a hobby horse originally created by another artist was protected by this rule,[22] as was making bedsheets out of copyrighted fabric.[23] A third is because copyright law has a fair use doctrine that may shield user-innovators who tinker with purchased products, as it did an artist who dressed Barbie dolls in sado-masochistic outfits over Mattel's objection.[24]

In many countries outside the United States, tinkering with a purchased copy of a copyrighted work may be challenged as a violation of an author's moral right of integrity. This right protects the noneconomic interests of authors in the continued existence of their works in unmodified form as a way to safeguard the authors' reputations and honor.[25]

A Canadian case, *Snow v. The Eaton Centre Ltd.*, illustrates the integrity right as a limit on a purchaser's right to tinker with its copy of a protected work.[26] Snow, a sculptor, successfully sued Eaton for violating his integrity right when during the winter holiday season Eaton put red ribbons around the necks of Snow's sculpted geese that were on display in front of Eaton's store.

The United States has long resisted adoption of moral rights, in part because of its more utilitarian approach to copyright law.[27] Its distaste for moral rights was among the reasons the United States was reluctant to join the Berne Convention for the Protection of Literary and Artistic Works, which requires member nations to protect authorial integrity rights.[28] The United States has arguably undercomplied with this Berne requirement by enacting the Visual Artists Rights Act (VARA) in 1990. VARA grants authors of only a narrowly defined category of works of visual art the right "to prevent any intentional distortion, mutilation, or other modification of the work which would be prejudicial to his or her honor or reputation."[29] This VARA right is subject to fair use (e.g., putting a mustache on a painting to make fun of the portrait) and other limitations.[30] Very little litigation has thus far challenged tinkering with, or other modifications to, visual art as a violation of this right,[31] but tinkering with visual art in the United States is now riskier than it was before VARA.

Freedom to Tinker under Siege?

In addition to VARA, four other fairly recent copyright-related developments have made tinkering with copies of copyrighted works more legally uncertain than in the past. For one thing, copyright now protects an important form of technology, namely, computer programs. Although this law permits some tinkering with software, there are significant limits on the extent to which this technology can lawfully be modified. Second, digital tools have made it much easier than ever before to tinker with copies of copyrighted works. In digital form, movies and sound recordings can be remixed and mashed up to create user-generated content for posting on sites such as YouTube. Some lawsuits have challenged the legality of digital manipulation tools and works altered through their use on copyright grounds. Third, copyright owners have been using contractual and technical restrictions to augment copyright limits on user modifications to their copies of protected works. Fourth, tinkering with technical protection measures (TPMs) used by copyright owners to protect their works from unauthorized access or copying has become risky as a result of Congress' adoption in 1998 of rules prohibiting acts of circumvention of these TPMs, as well as making tools for circumvention, as part of the Digital Millennium Copyright Act (DMCA).[32] Each of these developments is discussed below.

Tinkering with Computer Programs

In 1980 the US Congress decided that computer programs should be among the original works of authorship fixed in a tangible medium of expression for which copyright protection was available.[33] Although some nations toyed with the idea of using a different form of protection for software,[34] copyright for computer programs became an international norm in 1994.[35] This protection extends not just to human-readable source code expressions of program instructions, but also to machine-executable forms of programs.[36]

Freedom to tinker with software has been affirmed to some extent through court rulings that have allowed second-comers to reverse-engineer another firm's program as long as this is done for a legitimate purpose, such as gaining access to information necessary to develop a second program that will interoperate with the first program.[37]

Freedom to tinker with software is also permitted to some degree by a statutory provision allowing owners of copies of computer programs to modify their copies for certain purposes.[38] Congress recognized that consumers might sometimes need to be able to adapt their programs for legitimate reasons, such as to fix bugs, integrate that software into an existing computer system, create new fields for inputting data into a computer database, and the like.[39] While these kinds of software modifications are permissible, firms are forbidden to buy another firm's proprietary software, customize it for additional uses or translate it into a different programming language, and then sell modified versions in the commercial marketplace. Such adaptations would run afoul of the exclusive right to control the making of derivative works.[40] In an era of cloud computing and the rise of software-as-a-service, user tinkering with software has moreover become less possible, even for technically sophisticated persons, insofar as the software resides on remote servers to which users have only limited access (e.g., see Samuelson 2011: 1778–79).

Tinkering through Add-on and Filtering Programs

It is, of course, possible to modify the functionality of another firm's program without tinkering directly with its code, as add-on programs typically do. Add-ons might, for instance, offer a complementary feature to an existing program (e.g., a spell-checking program that runs in conjunction with another firm's word processing program) or alter the first program's functionality in other ways (e.g., see Black and Page 1993).

The first add-on program to be challenged on copyright grounds was the Game Genie, which was designed to allow customers of Nintendo videogames to make a small number of temporary changes to the play of these games (e.g., to extend the life of a favorite character). Nintendo argued that the Game Genie directly infringed derivative work rights in its games because the software modified the play of Nintendo games. It further argued that the Game Genie contributorily infringed Nintendo's derivative work rights because it provided consumers with a tool designed to enable them to make unauthorized modifications to Nintendo games. The Ninth Circuit Court of Appeals rebuffed both claims in *Lewis Galoob Toys, Inc. v. Nintendo of Am., Inc.*[41]

The Ninth Circuit noted that the Game Genie made no changes to the Nintendo code; it merely substituted its own signals for some that the Nintendo games would have supplied, under the direction of game users. This caused the court to question whether a derivative work had been created. Because the Game Genie allowed consumers to make only a small number of changes to the play of the Nintendo games, the court thought it enabled only fair uses. Also significant was the fact that the Game Genie did not undercut the market for Nintendo games because the only people likely to purchase the Game Genie were those consumers who already owned Nintendo games. The Game Genie had no utility except in conjunction with the games. The *Galoob* decision thus upheld freedom to tinker by means of add-on program development.

In reliance on *Galoob*, a company called ClearPlay developed a filtering program designed to enable owners of copies of DVD movies to make these movies more "family-friendly" (e.g., enabling families to bypass objectionable scenes of sex and/or violence).[42] During the pendency of this lawsuit, Congress passed an amendment to copyright law to affirm the lawfulness of this type of program.[43]

More direct tinkering with DVD movies was, however, held unlawful in *Clean Flicks of Colo. v. Soderbergh*.[44] After purchasing copies of DVD movies, Clean Flicks edited the movies to omit sex, violence, and objectionable language and then sold DVDs containing the modified movies. When copyright owners sued for infringement, Clean Flicks raised the first sale rule as a defense, for it had purchased as many DVDs of the movies as it had altered. The court decided, however, that uploading DVD movie contents into a database, from which the movies were edited and then reinstalled on DVD disks, was an infringement of the movie copyrights.

Contractual Restrictions on Tinkering

Because it is so cheap and easy to copy and modify digital forms of copyrighted works, many copyright owners who do not wish for users to tinker with their works have decided to supplement the legal protection that copyright law provides with mass-market license provisions that forbid licensees from reverse-engineering or modifying their copies of protected works and with TPMs that restrict what purchasers can do with their copies of copyrighted works (e.g., see Cohen 1998).

The enforceability of mass market license restrictions on reverse engineering and other forms of tinkering, which obviously interfere with freedom to tinker with purchased copies of copyrighted works, has not been definitively resolved. One appellate court refused to enforce such restrictions in *Vault Corp. v. Quaid Software Ltd.*[45] Vault sold copy-protection software, PROLOK, intended for commercial distribution to software developers who would use it as a TPM to stop consumers from making unauthorized copies of the developers' products. Quaid developed a computer program called Ramkey that enabled consumers to bypass the PROLOK copy-prevention feature. Quaid reverse-engineered PROLOK to find out how the TPM worked. Vault asserted that this reverse engineering, which involved copying of PROLOK code, infringed copyright and also violated terms of the shrinkwrap license that accompanied PROLOK, which forbade reverse engineering as well as modification of program code. The court ruled that Quaid had not infringed copyright and that to the extent that the license prohibited acts such as reverse engineering, modifications, and backup copying, the license was unenforceable because it interfered with rights that consumers had under copyright law. Other courts have, however, been more willing to enforce anti-reverse engineering clauses, at least when the reverse-engineer also infringed the other firm's copyright by copying expression from its program.[46]

The more general question about the enforceability of mass-market license restrictions on rights of users as to purchased copies of computer programs was addressed in a recent appellate court decision, *Vernor v. Autodesk, Inc.*[47] The court ruled that neither Vernor nor the architectural firm from which he bought copies of Autodesk software were actually "owners" of copies of the Autodesk programs. They were instead only licensees who were bound by restrictive terms in the mass-market licenses through which Autodesk distributed its computer programs. Because of this, Autodesk's right to control distribution of copies had not been exhausted.[48] This ruling meant that Autodesk could sue Vernor for copyright infringement because his sales on eBay of copies of Autodesk programs infringed its exclusive right to control distribution of copies of its software. Although the case did not involve the enforceability of restrictions on tinkering with Autodesk code, the court's willingness to enforce Autodesk's license restriction on resales suggests that it might also be willing to enforce anti-tinkering provisions.[49]

Of course, the *Vernor* decision will not stop purchasers of licensed software from tinkering with it insofar as their tinkering cannot be detected by the software's developer. If someone modifies Autodesk software and uses the modified version only in his firm, Autodesk is unlikely to know about any breach of an anti-modification clause. Even if Autodesk did know about the modifications, however, it might not take steps to control use of the modified software as long as the tinkering firm wasn't being public about it or trying to resell modified versions. However, a user-innovator who wanted to share with others what he learned by tinkering with a digital work might be at risk if his actions were inconsistent with mass-market license restrictions.[50]

Technical Limitations on Tinkering and the DMCA Anti-circumvention Rules

Licensing is not the only way for a firm to prevent users from tinkering with copyrighted digital content. A more secure way to achieve this result is through the use of TPMs to control what users can and cannot do with this content. Ordinary users will often have neither the technical expertise nor the inclination to spend time trying to bypass TPMs. More technically proficient persons, including would-be infringers, may well have both the skill and motivation to tinker with and circumvent TPM controls.

Congress enacted the DMCA anti-circumvention rules to provide legal protection for TPMs to deter technically proficient users from bypassing them.[51] One rule outlaws bypassing TPMs that copyright owners are using to control access to their works.[52] A second outlaws the making or offering to the public of any technology primarily designed to circumvent TPMs used by copyright owners to protect their works.[53] Under the DMCA rules, for instance, Quaid's distribution of Ramkey to bypass Vault's PROLOK TPM, discussed above, would now be illegal.

The first significant case to interpret the anti-circumvention rules was *Universal City Studios, Inc. v. Reimerdes.*[54] Reimerdes was one of several computer hackers who posted a program known as DeCSS on their websites. DeCSS was developed by a Norwegian programmer to bypass the Content Scramble System (CSS), a TPM that is ubiquitously installed on DVD movie disks as well as in DVD players. Universal, among others, had been using CSS in order to make it technically difficult for users to make unauthorized uses of its DVD movies, such as copying them onto computer hard drives. Universal sued three of these hackers for violating the DMCA rules, claiming that CSS was an effective access control that Universal was using to protect its movies, that DeCSS was designed for the sole purpose of bypassing CSS, and that by posting DeCSS on their websites, these hackers had offered an illicit circumvention tool to the public. This, Universal asserted, violated the DMCA. The hackers defended against the lawsuit mainly by challenging its constitutionality.[55]

The trial judge agreed with Universal that posting this program on the Internet violated the anti-circumvention rules. Eric Corley, the only defendant who went to trial in this case, argued that owners of copies of DVD movies should be able to decrypt CSS because their purchases of these movies entitled them to exercise first sale rights over their copies. DeCSS, in Corley's view, was a tool that allowed this lawful decryption. Judge Kaplan characterized this argument as "a corruption of the first sale doctrine."[56] Corley also argued that the DMCA rules were overbroad because they would prohibit too many fair uses. Judge Kaplan rejected this too, claiming that Congress had considered and rejected proposals to allow circumvention for fair use purposes.[57] As Judge Kaplan interpreted the

DMCA, it was immaterial whether any copyright infringement had ever occurred as a result of a violation of the anti-circumvention rules. The DMCA, in his view, had "fundamentally altered the landscape" of copyright.[58]

Because Judge Kaplan characterized CSS as an access control,[59] it follows that he would regard any user who bypassed CSS as a violator of the act-of-circumvention provision of the DMCA, even if the user was intending to make fair use of the movie's contents. Consider, for instance, "Brokeback to the Future," a user-generated video which took clips from "Brokeback Mountain" and "Back to the Future" to suggest that two characters (Doc and Marty) from the latter movie sexually longed for each other.[60] The user who generated this content almost certainly did so by using DeCSS or a similar program to tinker with CSS so that he/she could create this video. Although a very strict interpretation of the anti-circumvention rules and of copyright's derivative work right might suggest this video is unlawful, most commentators on user-generated content (UGC) have argued that videos such as this should be lawful (e.g., Lee 2008; Van Houweling 2005). The availability of "Brokeback to the Future" and many thousands of similar noncommercial UGC videos that include clips from movies, TV shows, and sound recordings on sites such as You-Tube are examples of what may well be fair use tinkering with TPMs, notwithstanding Judge Kaplan's restrictive interpretation of the DMCA.

The *Reimerdes* decision initially had a chilling effect on the activities of computer security researchers who wanted to study how and how well TPMs worked. In 2000, computer scientist Edward Felten and some of his colleagues and students decided to take up a recording industry challenge to try to break certain TPMs the industry was considering adopting for music. Rather than accept the $10,000 prize for successfully breaking the TPMs, Felten et al. decided to write a paper about what they had learned from the exercise. When representatives of the recording industry learned about this, they threatened to sue Felten, his colleagues, his university, members of the program committee for the conference at which the paper was scheduled for presentation, and those committee members' home institutions.

The industry's claim was that Felten's paper was an illegal circumvention tool because it provided so much detail—a virtual recipe—for bypassing these TPMs. If published, any technically proficient would-be infringer could use information from this paper to cause massive infringements of copyrights. The interpretation of the DMCA rules in the *Reimerdes* decision made this claim seem plausible (e.g., see Samuelson 2001).

Because of these threats, Felten and his colleagues withdrew the paper from that conference. However, they later asked a federal court to declare that publishing this paper would not violate the anti-circumvention rules. To moot this lawsuit, the recording industry withdrew its objection to the paper. The paper was then presented and published by its authors (Craver et al. 2001). Still, the threat of litigation against Felten and his colleagues cast a chill on research in this field for some time.[61]

Freedom to tinker with TPMs and TPM-protected digital content got a boost, however, from a subsequent appellate court ruling in *Chamberlain Group, Inc. v. Skylink Technologies, Inc.*[62] Chamberlain sued Skylink for violating the DMCA because its replacement garage door opener (GDO) bypassed an authentication code that Chamberlain asserted was an access control to the program on its GDO devices. The appellate court found Chamberlain's arguments to be wholly unpersuasive. It construed the anti-circumvention rules far more narrowly than *Reimerdes*. Without proof of a nexus between the tool being challenged and some copyright infringement resulting from its use, this court said there could be no violation of the DMCA rules.[63] The court gave credence to the interests of consumers in being able to purchase a GDO of their choice and to do with it as they wished; they were, after all, the owners of the GDOs. The court perceived the DMCA to have been carefully drafted to balance the interests of copyright owners and the public, and even to leave room for lawfully circumventing a TPM for fair use and other legitimate purposes.[64]

Concluding Thoughts

Chamberlain was an important precedent presaging greater freedom for those who tinker with TPMs and TPM-protected digital content as long as this tinkering was not intended to facilitate copyright infringement. It is, however, too early to conclude that *Chamberlain* has entirely vanquished *Reimerdes*.[65]

Chamberlain shows that existing IP rules can be interpreted to provide appropriate levels of protection to IP owners without undermining opportunities for ongoing innovation by users and others.[66] Freedom to tinker has been substantially protected under patent, trademark, and trade secrecy law. Because tinkering is relatively new in the copyright context, there are fewer precedents interpreting copyright law to accommodate user innovation.

Going forward, it would help if courts recognized a broad exhaustion of rights principle in copyright law when users modify their copies of copyrighted content for personal and other noninfringing purposes (e.g., see Perzanowski and Schultz 2012). User-innovator tinkering with products could also be protected by following *Chamberlain*'s lead by recognizing the legitimacy of fair use circumventions. More generally, it would greatly facilitate user innovation if courts construed the derivative work right narrowly and the fair use limit on this exclusive right broadly when users are tinkering with their own copies of copyrighted works and developing improvements.[67] Particularly important, though, may be decisions refusing to enforce license restrictions that would undermine user tinkering and follow-on innovation.[68] Eric von Hippel's work has brought user-innovators and their tinkering to the attention of the IP field. Now it is up to IP professionals and the courts to adapt IP rules so that they are flexibly interpreted in a way that promotes the ongoing progress of science and useful arts.

Notes

The concept of "freedom to tinker" has been given considerable currency by Professor Edward Felten who maintains a freedom-to-tinker.com blog. However, this concept matches well the model of user innovation about which Eric von Hippel has written so eloquently.

1. User motivations for tinkering with technologies are discussed at some length in Fisher (2010).

2. Among the conferences where user-innovators have a chance to demonstrate and share their innovations with others is Maker Faire. See http://makerfaire.com/.

3. US Const., art. I, §8, cl. 8.

4. See, for example, *Adams v. Burke*, 84 US 453 (1873) (affirming judicially created first sale limit on patent rights); *Bobbs-Merrill Co. v. Straus*, 210 US 339 (1908) (affirming the right of a purchaser to resell books without permission of the copyright owner). The first sale rule has been codified in copyright law at 17 USC §109(a).

5. Patent law also fosters the development of innovative modifications to existing products by allowing follow-on creators, such as user-innovators, to patent their inventions. This right to innovate on top of existing patents has, however, important limits. If it is necessary to incorporate an underlying invention to make products embodying the follow-on invention, the follow-on innovator will need a license from the other patentee. In general, this situation leads to good outcomes because when the follow-on innovator patents her invention, she will often be in a good bargaining position to negotiate for a cross-license that will enable her, as well as the original patentee, to make such products. The nonpatenting user-innovators that interest von Hippel do not benefit from the right to patent follow-on innovations.

6. Nations vary in the scope they give to the exhaustion right. In the European Union, the exhaustion of IP rights applies throughout the Union, but not beyond EU borders. Some countries have international exhaustion of rights rules. US law is somewhat unsettled about whether exhaustion applies to products lawfully made outside the United States. Compare, for example, *Kirtsaeng v. John Wiley & Sons, Inc.*, 133 S. Ct. 1351 (2012) (copyright) with *Jazz Photo Corp. v. Int'l Trade Comm'n*, 264 F.3d 1094 (Fed. Cir. 2001) (patent).

7. See, for example, *Aro Mfg. Co. v. Convertible Top Replacement Co.*, 365 US 336 (1961) (distinguishing between lawful repairs and unlawful reconstructions).

8. 50 US (9 How.) 109 (1850).

9. 377 US 422 (1964).

10. Id. at 425.

11. See, for example, *Bottom Line Mgmt., Inc. v. Pan Man, Inc.*, 228 F.3d 1352 (Fed. Cir. 2000) (reapplication of nonstick coating was lawful repair of cooking pans); *Hewlett-Packard Co. v. Repeat-O-Type Stencil Mfg. Corp.*, 123 F.3d 1445 (Fed. Cir. 1997) (modification of unused printer cartridges was akin to repair); *Sage Prods., Inc. v. Devon Indus., Inc.*, 45 F.3d 1575 (Fed. Cir. 1995) (replacing inner container for medical waste product was lawful repair).

12. See, for example, James Pooley, *Trade Secret Law* §5.02 (1997) (discussing reverse engineering as a generally lawful way to acquire trade secret know-how that may be embodied in another firm's product).

13. See, for example, *Kewanee Oil Co. v. Bicron Corp.*, 416 US 470, 476 (1974).

14. Some products are obviously easier to reverse-engineer than others.

15. Uniform Trade Secrets Act, § 1, cmt. 2, 14 ULA 437, 438 (1990).

16. *Kewanee*, 416 US at 489–90. If it was unlawful to reverse-engineer unpatented products, this would give the trade secret owner stronger rights over the innovation than a patent would confer and without the obligation that patent law requires to disclose the secret to get exclusive rights in the innovation.

17. See, for example, *Restatement (Third) of Unfair Competition*, §43 (1995).

18. See, for example, *Bulova Watch Co. v. Allerton Co.*, 328 F.2d 20 (7th Cir. 1964) (affirming trademark infringement ruling because of likelihood of confusion about source of altered products).

19. See, for example, *Prestonettes, Inc. v. Coty*, 264 US 359 (1924) (reversing trademark infringement decree based on sale of altered products where second producer accurately informed consumers about its alteration of the original product).

20. Freedom to tinker with copies of copyrighted products is limited by moral rights of authors to protect the integrity of their works, even after being sold in the marketplace. See infra notes 26–31 and accompanying text for a discussion of moral rights as a limit on freedom to tinker.

21. See, for example, von Hippel (2005: 20) (identifying eight categories of technology fields in which user innovation has been common).

22. See *Blazon v. DeLuxe Game Corp.*, 268 F. Supp. 416 (SDNY 1965).

23. See *Precious Moments, Inc. v. La Infantil, Inc.*, 971 F. Supp. 66 (DPR 1997). But see *Mirage Editions, Inc. v. Albuquerque A.R.T. Co.*, 856 F.2d 1341 (9th Cir. 1988) (purchaser of art book held to infringe copyright by reselling pictures from the book pasted onto ceramic tiles).

24. See *Mattel, Inc. v. Pitt*, 229 F. Supp. 2d 315 (SDNY 2002).

25. See Kwall (2010) (explaining the rationale for moral rights).

26. (1982), 70 CPR (2d) 105 (Can. Ont. HCJ).

27. See, for example, Adler (2009).

28. Berne Convention for the Protection of Literary and Artistic Works, art. 6bis, Sept. 9, 1886, *as revised* July 24, 1971 *and as amended* Sept. 28, 1979, 102 Stat. 2853, 1161 UNTS 3 (entered into force in the United States Mar. 1, 1989).

29. 17 USC §106A(a)(3) (2012). The term *work of visual art* is narrowly defined. Id., §101.

30. 17 USC §106A(a) (2012). The integrity right is also not violated where the modification is "the result of the passage of time or the inherent nature of the materials" or is "the result of conservation, or of the public presentation, including lighting and placement." Id., §106A(c).

31. See, for example, *Chapman Kelley v. Chicago Park District*, 635 F.3d 290 (7th Cir. 2011) (rejecting an integrity right claim based on Chicago's modifications to a garden planted by a conceptual artist).

32. Pub. L. No. 105-304, § 103, 112 Stat. 2860, 2863-76 (1998) (codified at 17 USC §§1201-1205).

33. Act of Dec. 12, 1980, Pub. L. No. 96–517, 94 Stat. 3015 (codified at 17 USC §§101, 117). See, for example, Samuelson (2011) (discussing why the case for extending copyright protection to software in the 1970s was fairly weak).

34. See, for example, Karjala (1984, 61–70) (describing Japanese proposal for sui generis protection of software that would have narrowed the scope of protection and shortened the duration of rights as compared with copyright).

35. Agreement on Trade-Related Aspects of Intellectual Property Rights, art. 10(1), April 15, 1994, 1869 UNTS 299, 33 ILM 1197 (1994).

36. Id.

37. See, for example, *Sega Enterp. Ltd. v. Accolade, Inc.*, 977 F.2d 1510 (9th Cir. 1992) (fair use to disassemble object code to extract interface information).

38. 17 USC §117(a). See, for example, Samuelson (1988, 188-93), discussing Section 117.

39. See, for example, *Krause v. Titleserv, Inc.*, 402 F.3d 119 (2d Cir. 2005) (permitting such software modifications).

40. 17 USC §106(2) (2012). The term *derivative work* is defined as "a work based upon one or more preexisting works, such as a translation, musical arrangement, dramatization, fictionalization, motion picture version, sound recording, art reproduction, abridgement, condensation, or any other form in which a work may be recast, transformed or adapted." Id., §101.

41. 964 F.2d 965 (9th Cir. 1992).

42. ClearPlay asked the court for a declaratory judgment that its filtering program did not infringe copyrights. See *Huntsman v. Soderbergh*, No. 02-M-1662 (D. Colo., filed Aug. 29, 2002).

43. Family Movie Act of 2005, Pub. L. No. 109-9, Title II, 119 Stat. 218, 223 (2005) (codified at 17 USC §110(11) (2012)).

44. 433 F. Supp. 2d 1236 (D. Colo. 2006).

45. 847 F.2d 255 (5th Cir. 1988).

46. See, for example, *Bowers v. Baystate Technologies*, 320 F.3d 1317 (Fed. Cir. 2003).

47. 621 F.3d 1102 (9th Cir. 2010).

48. 17 USC §§109(a), 117(a) (2012) (permitting owners of copies to redistribute those copies).

49. But see Perzanowski and Schultz (2011) (arguing that the common law exhaustion of rights doctrine should be a broader scope than the statutory first sale rule).

50. *MDY Industries, Inc. v. Blizzard Entertainment, Inc.*, 629 F.3d 928 (9th Cir. 2010) (enforcing contractual restriction on use of bots to play a videogame).

51. For a discussion of the legislative history of these provisions and some conundrums about their scope, see, for example, Samuelson (1999).

52. 17 USC §1201(a)(1)(A) (2012).

53. 17 USC §1201(a)(2), (b)(1) (2012).

54. 111 F. Supp. 2d 294 (SDNY 2000), aff'd sub nom., *Universal City Studios, Inc. v. Corley,* 273 F.3d 429 (2d Cir. 2001).

55. The hackers claimed that they had a First Amendment right to express themselves by publishing the DeCSS program. They also claimed that the anticircumvention rules were unconstitutionally overbroad because they inhibited too many lawful uses of copyrighted content. Although both the trial and appellate courts regarded software as a form of expression that the First Amendment protects, the courts soundly rejected the constitutional claims. *Corley,* 273 F.3d at 446-58.

56. *Reimerdes*, 111 F. Supp. 2d at 317, n.137.

57. Id. at 319, 337–38.

58. Id. at 323.

59. Id. at 317. For a discussion of why CSS and other widely deployed TPMs should not be considered access controls within the meaning of the DMCA, see Reese (2003).

60. See "Brokeback to the Future," YouTube video, 2:13, posted by Gillian Smith, Feb. 1, 2006, http://www.youtube.com/watch?v=8uwuLxrv8jY.

61. For a discussion of other types of research tinkering with TPMs that under *Reimerdes* might be unlawful, see Samuelson (2001). A National Academy of Sciences study committee published a report pointing to some "significant flaws" in the DMCA anti-circumvention rules for the field of computer security research (Computer Science and Telecommunications Board 2000, 311-21).

62. 381 F.3d 1178 (Fed. Cir. 2004).

63. Id. at 1204.

64. Id. at 1196–97.

65. See, for example, *MDY Indus. v. Blizzard Entm't, Inc.*, 629 F.3d 928 (9th Cir. 2010) (rejecting the nexus to infringement requirement set forth in *Chamberlain*).

66. See, for example, Fisher (2010, 1474–76) (offering eight suggestions for adapting IP laws to promote socially beneficial user innovation).

67. See, for example, Samuelson (2013).

68. See, for example, Lemley (1999) (suggesting possible doctrinal avenues to achieving this end).

References

Adler, Amy M. 2009. Against moral rights. *California Law Review* 97 (1): 263–300.

Black, Edward G., and Michael H. Page. 1993. Add-on infringements: When computer add-ons and peripherals should (and should not) be considered infringing derivative works under *Lewis Galoob Toys, Inc. v. Nintendo of Am., Inc.*, and other recent decisions. *Hastings Communications and Entertainment Law Journal* 15 (3): 615–52.

Cohen, Julie E. 1998. *Lochner* in cyberspace: The new economic orthodoxy of "rights management." *Michigan Law Review* 97 (2): 462–563.

Computer Science and Telecommunications Board (CSTB), National Research Council. 2000. *The Digital Dilemma: Intellectual Property in the Information Age*. Washington, DC: National Academy Press.

Craver, Scott A., John P. McGregor, Min Wu, Bede Liu, Adam Stubblefield, Ben Swartzlander, Dan S. Wallach, Drew Dean, and Edward W. Felten. 2001. Reading between the lines: Lessons from the SDMI challenge. In *Proceedings of the 10th USENIX Security Symposium*. ftp://ftp.cs.princeton.edu/reports/2002/657.pdf.

Fisher, William W., III. 2010. The implications for law of user innovation. *Minnesota Law Review* 94 (5): 1417–77.

Karjala, Dennis S. 1984. Lessons from the computer software protection debate in Japan. *Arizona State Law Journal* 1984 (1): 53–82.

Kwall, Roberta Rosenthal. 2010. *The Soul of Creativity: Forging a Moral Rights Law for the United States*. Stanford, CA: Stanford University Press.

Lee, Edward. 2008. Warming up to user-generated content. *University of Illinois Law Review* 2008 (5): 1459–1548.

Lemley, Mark A. 1999. Beyond preemption: The law and policy of intellectual property licensing. *California Law Review* 87 (1): 111–72.

Perzanowski, Aaron, and Jason Schultz. 2011. Digital exhaustion. *UCLA Law Review* 58 (4): 889–946.

Perzanowski, Aaron, and Jason Schultz. 2012. Copyright exhaustion and the personal use dilemma. *Minnesota Law Review* 96 (6): 2067–2143.

Reese, R. Anthony. 2003. Will merging access controls and rights controls undermine the structure of anticircumvention law? *Berkeley Technology Law Journal* 18 (2): 619–65.

Samuelson, Pamela. 1988. Modifying copyrighted software: Adjusting copyright doctrine to accommodate a technology. *Jurimetrics Journal* 28 (Winter): 179–221.

Samuelson, Pamela. 1999. Intellectual property and the digital economy: Why the anti-circumvention regulations need to be revised. *Berkeley Technology Law Journal* 14 (2): 519–66.

Samuelson, Pamela. 2001. Anti-circumvention rules: Threat to science. *Science* 293 (5537): 2028–31.

Samuelson, Pamela, and Suzanne Scotchmer. 2002. The law and economics of reverse engineering. *Yale Law Journal* 111 (7): 1575–1663.

Samuelson, Pamela. 2007. Why copyright law excludes systems and processes from the scope of its protection. *Texas Law Review* 85 (7): 1921–78.

Samuelson, Pamela. 2011. The uneasy case for software copyrights revisited. *George Washington Law Review* 79 (6): 1746–82.

Samuelson, Pamela. 2013. The quest for a sound conception of copyright's derivative work right. *Georgetown Law Journal* 101 (6): 1505–64.

Van Houweling, Molly Shaffer. 2005. Distributive values in copyright. *Texas Law Review* 83 (6): 1535–79.

Van Houweling, Molly Shaffer. 2011. Touching and concerning copyright: Real property reasoning in *MDY Industries, Inc. v. Blizzard Entertainment, Inc. Santa Clara Law Review* 51 (4): 1063–85.

von Hippel, Eric. 2005. *Democratizing Innovation*. Cambridge: MIT Press.

12

Intellectual Property at the Boundary

Katherine J. Strandburg

There is today no doubt that significant creative work—both commercial and noncommercial—is organized neither by market transactions using legally defined intellectual property nor by top-down task management within firms, but by privately ordered governance regimes.[1] For example, researchers studying user innovation have observed that user innovator communities often share information about their innovations freely with one another, while eschewing reliance on patent protection (e.g., see von Hippel 2005). These innovation governance regimes are quite different from the atomistic markets and hierarchically organized firms implicitly assumed by standard intellectual property theory. They generally rely on some combination of informal norms (often collectively enforced by reputational rewards and sanctions), more formalized governance mechanisms, and reciprocity (what von Hippel has called *know-how trading*; see von Hippel 1987).

In some contexts where such privately ordered innovation governance is observed, formal intellectual property is unavailable either as a matter of law or as a practical matter because of its expense or the time needed to acquire it. Many creative groups, however, apparently including many user innovator communities, actively discourage reliance on formal intellectual property even when it is available. For example, physicians form a user innovator community for medical procedures and methods, and they have maintained ethical strictures against patenting such innovations for over 150 years, despite the fact that such methods are potentially patentable (at least in the United States) and that physicians currently have no such strictures against patenting drugs and medical devices (Strandburg 2014).

This chapter is most interested in groups that eschew legally enforced intellectual property despite its availability, relying on private innovation governance regimes instead. As I explain in the first section, there are general reasons to expect that such alternative regimes can be more effective than formal intellectual property at encouraging innovation within some creative groups. The chapter's main focus is on the boundaries where these alternative innovation regimes butt up against the intellectual property-based market. What occurs in these boundary zones is critical to the stability of the privately ordered innovation governance regimes, to the transfer of socially valuable innovations between creative groups and outsiders, and to the potential for collaboration across these boundaries. But, except in the case of university technology transfer, the boundaries between privately ordered innovation regimes and the intellectual property-based market have yet to receive much attention from researchers. Only recently, for example, has user innovation research begun to focus on user entrepreneurship (Agarwal and Shah 2014) or on the diffusion of user innovation (see, e.g., Kuusisto et al. 2013). This chapter maps out some of the issues that arise at the points where alternative innovation governance regimes meet intellectual property-based markets. The chapter concludes with suggestions for further study of the way in which these boundary interactions affect the overall innovation environment.

Opting Out of Legally Defined Intellectual Property

The simple, oft-repeated, justification for intellectual property—that a potential award of exclusive rights to ward off free-riding competitors is necessary to provide ex ante incentives for creative work[2]–is problematic, and increasingly so, for a variety of reasons. Intellectual property is premised on at least three assumptions:

1. Creative work requires relatively large up-front investments.
2. Free-riding by competitors will prevent a sufficient return on those investments.
3. Legally defined intellectual property rights are the only or best way to solve the free-rider problem and ensure sufficient returns on investments in creative work.

All of these are contestable assumptions, particularly in situations involving creativity within ongoing communities or groups.

First Assumption: Creative Work Requires Relatively Large Up-front Investments

Designing innovative goods and services potentially may require significant investments in (1) the human capital necessary for the work, (2) tools for performing creative work (e.g., laboratories, paintbrushes and computers), (3) organizing cooperative creative work, (4) codifying information in useable embodiments, (5) producing and testing embodiments, and (6) disseminating the creative output. The necessary investments vary widely depending on the particular project at hand. Moreover, as studies of user innovation have highlighted, innovation sometimes occurs at least in part as a byproduct of some other activity, such as use, and may not require significant specialized investment. Within a creative group, such as a user innovator community, disseminating creative output may be cheap because group members constitute a readily accessible, interested, and knowledgeable audience.

Moreover, in what is by now becoming an old story, many of these costs are decreasing, some radically, as a result of digital technology (e.g., see Benkler 2006). These decreases are most apparent for digital goods, but the costs of fabricating some kinds of tangible goods are also in rapid decline due to technologies such as 3D printing. One can, of course, overstate the importance of this trend. For some creative work, such as scientific research, the decreasing costs of digital technology may be outweighed by increasing costs as the problems become more complex. Nonetheless, the assumption that innovation necessarily entails significant investment has never been true across the board and its range of validity appears to be decreasing.

Second Assumption: Free-Riding Will Prevent a Sufficient Return on Investment in Creative Work

In the standard justification for IP, free-riding occurs when competitors can cheaply copy a creative good and offer it for sale at a price that is too low to permit the creator to recoup her upfront investments. Anticipating this problem, potential creators may not invest or may invest only if they can profit from their creative output by using it in secret. Intellectual property solves this problem by giving creators legal rights to constrain the use of their creative output, thus keeping prices up above competitive levels. Note that the first and second assumptions are intertwined: The lower the investment needed for creative work, the less likely it is that free-riding will interfere with its recoupment. When creative costs are sufficiently low, first-mover advantage,[3] which provides a natural period of market exclusivity, may be sufficient to allow creators to recoup their upfront costs. (The same technological advances that lower the costs of producing creative work may also decrease first-mover advantages by lowering the costs of copying, however.)

The assumption that free-riding will deter creative activity can be false even when creative investments are not especially low as long as creators receive rewards that are not dissipated when others copy and use their creative output. Some rewards for creative activity are simply not rivalrous. For example, one of the rewards of writing music or creating a work of art is enjoying its beauty. The creator's enjoyment of the beauty of a creative work is not merely nonrivalrous; it may even be increased by others' enjoyment of the work. Similarly the use value of a user innovation may be undecreased, or even augmented, by others' use.

Moreover some rewards are not free-rideable even though they are rivalrous. For example, the intrinsic satisfaction of being first to make a particular discovery is rivalrous to some degree, but it also is inextricably bound to the first discoverer and thus is not free-rideable. Reputational rewards for creative work often are rivalrous to the extent they determine status or career opportunities, but as long as reputation is accurately tied to creative accomplishment, others' use of the creative output does not decrease (and may even amplify) reputational rewards.

Where creative output can be kept secret while it is deployed commercially, intellectual property's exclusive rights are aimed at encouraging disclosure in the face of potential free-riding. Intellectual property is not always needed to encourage disclosure, however, particularly for members of a creative group. The benefits of disclosure may include reputational rewards, access to others' innovations, opportunities for collaboration, and opportunities to improve one's creative output with the assistance of the group (Harhoff et al. 2003; see also Strandburg 2008). In some cases it may be difficult or impossible to participate in the activities of a given creative group while hiding one's creative output. If group participation is valuable enough, its benefits may offset the benefits of secrecy, encouraging free revealing.

In sum, there are many situations in which the potential for free-riding will not deter the creation, disclosure, and dissemination of creative output. This is especially likely to be the case when creative groups can employ private governance mechanisms to offer rewards, such as reputation, that are not free-rideable.

Third Assumption: Legally Defined Property Rights Are the Only or Best Way to Allocate Returns on Investment in Creative Work

Legally defined intellectual property may not be the best or only way to allocate rewards for creative work. For example, a great deal of creative work takes place within commercial firms. While these firms engage in IP-based market transactions with outsiders, they use other mechanisms—salaries, bonuses, promotions, and so forth—to allocate rewards for creative effort among their employees. They do not use legally defined intellectual property for this purpose, presumably because the transaction costs of doing so would be too high.[4] The academic research system also allocates rewards for creative activity according to publication and peer-review-based mechanisms quite apart from legally defined intellectual property. In these contexts, legally defined intellectual property rights come into play only (if at all) at the boundary of the creative group.

These examples are not special. Studies of non–IP-based innovation regimes demonstrate that many creative groups allocate rewards and credit for creative activity without resorting to (and often deliberately eschewing) legally defined IP. Why might a group opt for such an alternative regime? To begin with, intellectual property is a costly mechanism for managing creative output because it constrains the use of nonrivalrous creations, imposing deadweight social loss. Many alternative innovation governance regimes rely on rewards, such as reputation, that do not constrain the use of creative output. The intellectual property system also has high transaction costs because, among other things, of the difficulty in defining and communicating the boundaries and ownership of the rights (e.g., see Dorfman and Jacob 2011; Bessen and Meurer 2008). Alternative systems may avoid some of those costs. Moreover intellectual property is necessarily awarded and defined according to somewhat generic rules. Members of a creative group may have specialized knowledge about the relative value of various creative contributions that is not reflected in one-size-fits-all doctrine or appreciated by government officials and judges. Thus community-defined awards may more accurately promote progress.

Because of these inherent problems with legally defined intellectual property rights, it is not surprising that creative groups often adopt alternative institutional mechanisms to govern the flow of creative inputs and outputs within the group and to solve any free-rider issues that arise.

Of course, the desirability of an alternative innovation governance regime depends on its costs as well as its benefits. To employ an alternative to legally defined intellectual property, a group must have some workable means of defining and enforcing the alternative regime. There are numerous paths by which groups accomplish this. Some groups, such as high-end French chefs (Fauchart and von Hippel 2008) or extreme sports enthusiasts (Franke and Shah 2003), are small and cohesive enough that informal norms alone are sufficient for effective innovation governance. Other groups, such as Debian developers (Coleman 2013), academic scientists (Strandburg 2009, 2010 and references therein), and physicians (Strandburg 2014) have more systematized governance regimes involving mechanisms for screening newcomers and inculcating the group's norms, as well as enforcement mechanisms based on the group's control of reputation and various other benefits of group membership. Still others, such as Wikipedia, adopt formalized governance and dispute resolution regimes (Mehra and Hoffman 2009). While collective action problems and transaction costs in principle could prevent such regimes from emerging, in practice they emerge with considerable regularity and serve to facilitate innovation in lieu of legally defined intellectual property.

Intellectual Property's Place at the Boundary

Our growing understanding of how and why creative groups opt out of the intellectual property system by adopting alternative innovation governance regimes raises a set of issues that researchers have barely begun to explore. What happens when such a group (or its members) needs or desires to transact with outsiders? Creative groups must negotiate boundaries if they (1) make use of preexisting creative work by an outsider, whether intentionally or inadvertently, (2) seek to be compensated when outsiders use their creative output or to control how outsiders make use of it, or (3) desire to engage outsiders in collaborative creative work, such as, for example, by collaborating with manufacturers to disseminate embodiments of the group's creative output. Boundary issues also arise when a group's internal incentives are not aligned with social value (e.g., when it would be socially valuable to invest in disclosing or disseminating the creative work to outsiders but the creative group lacks interest in doing so).

Intellectual property is one possible "coinage" for negotiating the boundary between a creative group with a privately ordered innovation governance regime and outsiders. It often is used to facilitate transactions at the boundaries between commercial firms, for example. Using legally defined intellectual property to negotiate such boundaries may not always be feasible or desirable, however. For one thing, depending on the legal doctrines defining the intellectual property system, members of creative groups may be unable to acquire intellectual property to use in transactions with outsiders. Even if they can acquire intellectual property, there may be incompatibilities between the legally defined intellectual property regime and the group's information governance regime. In some instances, using intellectual property as a boundary-spanning mechanism may even threaten to undermine the group's innovation governance regime.

In what follows I briefly analyze several possible transaction scenarios as an initial step toward further research on these boundary issues.

Employing Outsiders' Creative Work

While some creative groups are self-sufficient, in that all their creative inputs are created within the group, many creative groups necessarily rely to some extent on the creative work of outsiders as inputs to their own creative activities. Indeed some groups, such as writers of fan fiction and mash-up artists, routinely employ and build upon the creative work of outsiders. Those outsider inputs may be subject to intellectual property rights. Even if a creative group does not knowingly build on the work of outsiders, outsiders may claim that the group's output infringes its intellectual property.

The extent to which a creative group must deal with the IP rights of outsiders depends not only on specifics of the group's creative activity, but also on the particulars of IP doctrine. For example, copyright infringement depends on copying so that creators can, at least in principle, avoid infringement by not incorporating protected aspects of other's work into their creations. Patent infringement does not depend on copying, however, and inadvertent infringement of others' IP is a possibility even for independent inventors. Copyright's fair use doctrine facilitates some kinds of creative activities, while patent law recognizes only very narrow exceptions to infringement liability.

Overall, it will be difficult for many creative groups to avoid using at least some inputs that are subject to outsiders' intellectual property rights. Transacting for information resources often is fraught with difficulties and bargaining costs may be high. Valuing intellectual property is notoriously difficult for a variety of reasons, including the difficulties in defining boundaries discussed above.

Creative groups that deploy alternative innovation governance regimes may have particular difficulties engaging in such transactions. Obviously, if a group has rejected legally defined intellectual property as a modus operandi, it will not be able to engage in cross-licensing as a mechanism to barter for access to outsider creative input. If the group makes its creative output publicly available, it may have nothing left to trade even if the outside entity makes liberal use of the group's output. Of course, it may always be possible to pay money to license outsider intellectual property, but a group that relies primarily on nonmonetary within-group exchanges may not be well organized to engage in monetary exchanges with outsiders.

Inadvertent infringement can be even more problematic because it can lead to holdup problems when the infringed IP is embedded in creative output in a way that makes the costs of redesigning around it much higher than the costs of avoiding it in the first place would have been (e.g., see Henkel and Reitzig 2010; Lemley and Shapiro 2007). Even sophisticated commercial entities in some technologies (notoriously, software) sometimes find themselves infringing inadvertently because of the vague boundaries and insufficient notice that plague the intellectual property system.

Some types of creative groups are especially likely to infringe inadvertently. If many members are making relatively small contributions, each member might have little incentive to guard against infringement. The costs of educating each member about how to avoid infringement would also be quite large. Wikipedia, for example, appears to devote considerable resources to educating its members about copyright issues and providing procedures for dealing with copyright problems.[5] Where, for example, as in open source software, the group aggregates the contributions of many contributors into a single, collective output, guarding against inadvertent patent infringement may be virtually impossible. Even in the unlikely event that individual contributors were willing and able to ensure that their own contributions were noninfringing, the collective whole might still infringe. And even if there were a central body with the expertise to assess freedom to operate, the cumulative and changing nature of the innovation process would soon render any such assessment out of date.

Commercial firms in arenas where inadvertent infringement is a hazard usually respond by building up arsenals of patents that can be asserted against competitors who might sue them for infringement. Lacking intellectual property of their own, creative groups will find it difficult to adopt this strategy. For this reason, for example, corporate users of the Linux open source operating system have created a nonprofit organization to accumulate an arsenal of patents that could be used in a counterclaim against a patent plaintiff.[6] However, this strategy is of limited effectiveness against nonpracticing entities that are not subject to threats of counter-suit.

Some creative groups may have advantages in dealing with inadvertent infringement, however. Their collaborative practices may make them nimble in redesigning around intellectual property problems, once they are identified. (An intellectual property violation may be seen as a kind of "bug" to which Linus's law "given enough eyeballs, all bugs are shallow" applies; Raymond 2000.) Moreover some creative groups make unattractive targets for holdup litigation, precisely because they do not traffic in the coinage of money and intellectual property and may not have "deep pockets." The realistic danger to a creative group's project from inadvertent infringement of outsider intellectual property thus depends greatly upon the group's type of creative activity, its innovation governance regime, how difficult it is to redesign around the outsider intellectual property, and the identities (and depths of pockets) of its members.

Outsider Use of a Creative Group's Output

Though a creative group's private governance regime can handle *internal* rewards for creative contributions and punish norm violations, it cannot control appropriation by outsiders. Of course, if the group intends to share its output freely with outsiders, this is not an issue. However, some creative groups may seek to control or profit from outsider use. If so, the potential for appropriation by outsiders might threaten the group's anticipated rewards enough to depress its creative output, just as free-riding is expected to do for the canonical commercially motivated individual or firm.

Obviously, if a creative group seeks to sell embodiments of its creative output for a profit, then sales by a free-riding outsider reduce the available profits. Even if a creative group seeks nonpecuniary rewards, such as reputational enhancement, appropriation of the group's output by an outsider may diminish those rewards. Motivations for creative work may also be undermined if an outsider's appropriation of the group's creative output is perceived as unfair or inconsistent with the group's goals and norms. For example, even those who are altruistically motivated may be unwilling to invest in creative work if someone else will use their output to rake in profits.[7]

Consider user innovator communities, for example. Suppose a manufacturer builds on a user innovator community's work to produce a product that community members would like to purchase. The manufacturer will charge a price that reflects the marginal cost of producing the product plus the value of any intellectual property it obtains on the product. If the intellectual property system awards the manufacturer rights that are overly broad by community standards in comparison to the community's contributions, the manufacturer's prices will seem unfairly high. If this happens repeatedly, the perception of unfairness might depress the group's willingness to engage in creative activity within the community's innovation governance system. More directly, the need to pay an inappropriately high price for products built upon the group's creative output will place a tax on the group's ability to produce additional creative output.

In sum, there are a variety of ways in which appropriation of a group's creative output by outsiders can decrease the rewards available to creative groups. Just like individuals or firms concerned with free riders, creative groups could, in principle, employ various means of deterring or preventing outsider free-riding. Only some of these means, such as intellectual property and secrecy, give the group fine-grained control over what outsiders can do with the group's creative output, which may be essential to some groups' achieving their goals. It is no accident that open source software relies on copyright to control what outsiders can do with the software (e.g., consider the various flavors of open source or Creative Commons licenses).[8] Open source licensing is not a panacea for all creative groups, however. Its effectiveness depends on the fact that copyright is acquired automatically, without any need to apply for it, and that creators of unauthorized modifications ("derivative works") do not acquire copyrights of their own. Because patent law does not have those features, patent equivalents to the *copyleft* license have yet to be devised (e.g., see Schultz and Urban 2012). Moreover, there is no reason to expect that the particular features of open source licenses will meet the needs of all creative groups.

Collaborating with Outsiders

At times, members of creative groups may need or wish to collaborate with outsiders who possess some particular expertise or resources not available within the group. The goal of such a collaboration might be to produce and disseminate embodiments of the group's creative output or to work jointly on a creative project. Outsider assistance is not always needed to produce and disseminate embodiments of a group's creative output. Open source software, for example, may be produced and disseminated entirely by the community. User innovator communities often rely on group members to make their own embodiments based on plans, descriptions, or instructions distributed electronically or by word of mouth. Groups sometimes also collaborate internally to produce infrastructure for the collection, codification, and supply of embodiments to members of the group (or even to outsiders). Examples of such arrangements include some peer-reviewed journals, biological resource centers, databanks, conferences, repositories for open source software, and informal trading regimes.[9]

Even when a group needs to rely on outside expertise, there may be no real cross-boundary collaboration. Outside expertise may sometimes be available through arm's-length market contracting for services or through salaried employment. Services such as editing, website design, and publishing are routinely procured in this way. Advances in custom manufacturing, including most importantly the advent of 3D printing, are rapidly expanding the types of situations in which the production and dissemination of embodiments can be procured as an arm's-length service. Groups might arrange for such services by pooling monetary resources either informally or through an association or nonprofit organization.

In some circumstances, however, contracting for services is not sufficient. True collaboration between a member of a creative group and an outsider is desired. This may be the case, for example, when each side has "sticky" knowledge that resists easy codification or when it will be difficult to value the outsider's contributions ex ante. Facilitating creative collaborations is, by some lights, a primary purpose of intellectual property, which does so by resolving Arrow's paradox, spreading risks, and reducing the costs of contracting for joint creative effort.[10] IP is also a standard means for collecting and allocating rewards for joint projects. However, recent work suggests that, even for commercial firms, the availability of formal IP is neither necessary nor sufficient for overcoming the difficulties of organizing and allocating rewards for joint creative work (Burstein 2012; Gilson et al. 2009).

Cross-boundary collaborations may be especially challenging for members of creative groups governed by alternative innovation regimes. They may, for example, be disadvantaged in bargaining over the terms of a collaboration if some part of the input they contribute to the project already has been placed in the public domain. In addition any intellectual property resulting from cross-boundary collaborations may also raise difficult and potentially contentious questions for a group that does not rely on IP for allocating rewards internally. Should intellectual property obtained from cross-boundary collaborations be enforced against fellow members of a creative group? Should the group as a whole somehow share in any profits from the intellectual property, assuming that the joint work builds on the group's prior output? Will the monetary profits that may flow from the cross-boundary collaboration make the participating group member less responsive to the rewards and punishments dealt out by the alternative innovation governance regime? Confronting these questions may challenge or destabilize a creative group's internal information governance regime.

Aligning a Creative Group's Incentives with Social Value

Even if a creative group's internal governance mechanisms do an excellent job of allocating rewards for creative activity among those within the group, there will still be circumstances in which a creative group's internal incentives to create, disclose, and disseminate its creative output do not align with what would be *socially desirable*. Optimizing the social value of a group's creative output may sometimes demand substantial investment in tasks, such as developing it into a form that is usable by outsiders, maintaining its accessibility to outsiders, and producing and disseminating embodiments, that have little intrinsic appeal to the group.

For example, a community of lead users may not have sufficient incentives to bear the cost of disclosing and disseminating its creative output to less expert users. Academic researchers may have insufficient incentives to bridge the gap between research results that are of interest to them and technology that is useful to society. Similarly members of the community that creates Wikipedia presumably are motivated intrinsically to do the work involved in creating and editing its entries and desire to share the results online with as many people as possible. Nonetheless, community members may not be sufficiently motivated to pay the costs of maintaining the necessary servers and other infrastructure, especially as those costs becomes very large. Indeed Wikipedia has conducted public radio-type fundraising drives, seeking the financial support of outsiders who benefit from the community's activities.[11]

Without some means to force outsiders to invest in such efforts, a creative group may have insufficient motivation to engage in (or pay for) these development, codification, and dissemination tasks. Intellectual property is one potential means to increase a creative group's incentives to invest in disclosing and disseminating its creative output in a form that is valuable to outsiders.

University technology transfer provides an illuminating and, in my view, cautionary example of an attempt to deploy intellectual property in this way. In 1980, the US Congress enacted the Bayh–Dole Act,[12] which encouraged the patenting of academic researchers' inventions. Patenting was intended to provide incentives to invest in bridging a presumed gap between the ivory towers of academic science and the commercial market. Its effectiveness in doing so is a subject of considerable dispute, however.[13]

The most commonly articulated theory behind university patenting is that exclusive licenses to patents on university research output will motivate *companies* to invest in developing applications of the research. It has never been entirely clear, however, why such an incentive is needed, given that a company developing downstream applications of upstream research results ordinarily can obtain patents on the applications that result from its efforts (Strandburg 2005).

An alternative justification might rest on the assumption that closing the gap between academia and application requires that academic scientists codify and translate their research results into terms that industry actors can understand. Even here the need for patents to accomplish this seems debatable in many instances. Because the internal governance regime of academic science demands publication, scientists already are incentivized to codify their work so that other scientists can understand it. Companies that are likely to invest in developing downstream applications of academic research usually employ scientists who are capable of understanding the scientific literature. It seems unlikely that patents are more effective disclosures to industry scientists than journal publications.

Perhaps patents are needed to facilitate the transfer of scientists' tacit knowledge that is missing from journal publications? Here, too, some skepticism is warranted. There is a constant flow of tacit knowledge from academia to commercial enterprises, since most PhD recipients are employed by commercial firms. While university patents might facilitate collaborative research between academia and industry, as discussed in the previous section, the primary facilitator of collaboration is probably industry funding, which one suspects is aimed more at pushing academic research in directions of interest to industry than at searching for applications of existing upstream discoveries.

In any event, whether or not university patents sometimes succeed in incentivizing companies or scientists to engage in efforts to bridge the lab-to-market gap, there are indications that patenting often is employed by universities primarily to obtain exclusive rights over and thereby monetize immediately applicable scientific discoveries (Lemley 2008). Indeed a skeptic might argue that, rather than pushing academics to assist in developing downstream applications of their discoveries, enhanced university patenting has tended to push patent doctrine in the direction of more upstream claims. If this is the case, university patenting may have distracted entrepreneurs on both sides of the academic-commercial divide from the hard work of developing practical applications of upstream university discoveries and focused them instead on monetizing patents on discoveries, such as at least some medical diagnostic methods, for which much of the research is publicly funded and additional development costs are minimal.[14] While university patenting undoubtedly results in a transfer of money to universities in this scenario, it does not lead to greater efforts to bridge the gap between university and marketplace. (Recently the US Supreme Court has cut back on the patentability of upstream research results.[15] It will be interesting to see what effects, if any, these doctrinal changes have on university technology transfer.)

In hindsight, it is not surprising that academic scientists would try to bend the availability of patents to suit the goals of the research community, rather than the social goals of the Bayh–Dole legislation, while at the same time the availability of patents might distort the goals and policies of the research community. Any boundary-spanning activity is a negotiation, in which players on both sides seek to further their own goals. Academic scientists are motivated primarily by and rewarded primarily for the discovery and publication of cutting-edge scientific results. They presumably chose the academic career path because of their preferences for its rewards. Though patents may offer them a way to "earn money on the side," the benefit of that additional income (whether they receive it personally or fold it back into their research budgets) must be balanced against the opportunity costs of time spent away from their primary research activities.

Clearly, if academic researchers can "have their cake and eat it too" by patenting research tools and immediately commercializable scientific discoveries for which the internal governance system *also* rewards them, they will do so, thus avoiding the opportunity costs of investing time and effort in bridging the gap between the market and upstream research results. At the same time, the availability of patents may incline them to shift their research agendas into areas that are both scientifically interesting and relatively easily commercializable (the so-called Pasteur's quadrant) (Stokes 1997). Only very large outside rewards, however, are likely to motivate academic scientists to invest significant effort in technology development that has no substantial scientific payoff.

To step back from this specific example, the general point is that the disclosure and dissemination of creative output from a creative group to the broader public will often require investments that the group is not internally motivated to make. Intellectual property is one means to attempt to incentivize those investments. However, as the academic research example shows, the implications and effectiveness of "tacking on" intellectual property to a group's governance regime may be unpredictable and complex.

A far less risky approach, when possible, would be to shift a group's incentives by decreasing the costs of disclosure and dissemination to outsiders. Clearly the Internet and other digital technologies have vastly decreased these costs overall, permitting creative groups to extend their reach both to fellow creators and to outsiders. However, it is also clear from the internal experience of many creative groups that the mere availability of cheap communication channels may not be sufficient. Developing institutional arrangements to lower these costs is also an important task, which the groups themselves may or may not be motivated to undertake. (Indeed developing infrastructure is challenging for creative groups even when that infrastructure serves their internal goals; see Frischmann et al. 2014.)

It may also be worth exploring the role that trademarks can play at the interface between creative groups and outsiders. Trademarks do not constrain the use of creative output in the way that patents and copyrights do. Perhaps for this reason, they seem to be the intellectual property regime of choice for at least some user innovator entrepreneurs, who do invest in making technologies available to outsiders via the commercial market (O'Mahony 2003), and of open source software projects.

Potential Ramifications of Intellectual Property for the Stability of Alternative Innovation Governance Regimes

Even if intellectual property is a useful tool for navigating the boundaries of a group's alternative innovation governance regime, the acquisition of intellectual property by some members of a group may put that governance regime at risk. The availability of intellectual property as an alternative means to be rewarded for creative work necessarily lowers the costs of defecting from the group. Those who have outside sources of rewards are less bound to the norms of the group. This is particularly so if intellectual property, because of its doctrinal features, provides a reward that is out of line with the internal regime's assessment of the value of a given contribution. If enough members defect, the internal governance regime may simply unravel.

Concerns about the potential for destabilization of a creative group's information governance regime may partly account for several situations in which insiders have lobbied against patents in their fields of technology. In one interesting "defense" of a group's governance regime, physicians reacted strongly when a fellow physician attempted to enforce patent claims on a medical procedure, lobbying for and obtaining a statutory change that abolished patent remedies for infringement of such patents by physicians (Strandburg 2014). Since its enactment, the statute has lain virtually dormant, though it would seem ripe for litigation as to the scope of its operation, perhaps because the push to obtain the statute reinforced a strong social norm among physician innovators that improvements in medical procedures must be, in effect, returned to the common pool.

The general observation that the availability of intellectual property to individual members of a creative group may lower the costs of defecting from the group tells us little, however, about many important empirical questions. Under what circumstances, for example, will groups adopt governance regimes that permit or preclude particular uses of intellectual property? When will the availability of intellectual property rights lower the costs of defecting sufficiently to have a significant impact on a group's internal governance regime, potentially even destroying it? In what situations do the benefits of intellectual property as a means to navigate boundary situations outweigh its risks to a group's innovation governance regime?

Moreover open source software provides an example in which intellectual property is used to define a creative group and enforce its governance regime. Consider the function of the *copyleft* clause found in some open source software licenses (notably the General Public License or "GPL").[16] The *copyleft* clause requires that any modified version of the software be distributed under the same *copyleft* license, which generally requires that the software be distributed along with a copy of the source code and explicitly permits recipients to modify it as they desire.

The purpose of *copyleft* is often loosely described as keeping outsiders (particularly commercial firms) from "propertizing" the open source code (O'Mahony 2003). But this is a puzzling claim. Whatever an outsider does with open source software, it has no power to constrain the open source community's ability to use and distribute the *original software* in open source form. Nor can it prohibit the open source community from continuing to modify and improve the code. Indeed, the outsider's activities have no effect whatsoever on the community's rights to its original software. In other words, there is simply no way that an outsider can "propertize" the community's preexisting code.

The *copyleft* clause prohibits only a very specific kind of free-riding—distributing a modification of the original software without contributing the source code for the modification to the common pool. The effect of this provision is not to protect a particular code embodiment from "propertization," but to protect the *system* for code production from defectors. Thus, according to a study by O'Mahony (O'Mahony and Ferraro 2004; see also von Hippel and von Krogh 2003), the *copyleft* provision plays two distinct roles: setting the norms of the creative group, which are usually enforced informally, and providing copyright "teeth" to be bared when outsiders attempt to profit from violating the provision. The *copyleft* clause helps to preserve the open source system by ensuring reciprocity between members of the loosely knit group involved in improving the code. It is an ingenious mechanism for pooling the individual copyrights of a loosely defined community so that members cannot use those individual rights to defect from and extract value from the community. The *copyleft* example thus begs the question of when and how intellectual property can be deployed to reinforce an alternative innovation governance system.

Finally, even if it were empirically established that the availability of intellectual property poses a threat to a particular creative group's information governance regime, it is not immediately apparent that this is problematic from a societal perspective. A group's information governance regime might be designed, at least in part, to serve the vested (and potentially anticompetitive) interests of current members at the expense of the larger society. The medieval guild system is widely cited as an example of such a regime (Merges 2004). Individuals may be excluded from creative groups for all kinds of reasons, including, potentially, gender or racial bias. Government-administered intellectual property rights are one way for outsiders to force their way into a creative arena, to disrupt overly friendly relations between competitors or to break barriers of bias (this is the flip side of the "patent troll" issue). The availability of legally defined intellectual property rights thus can threaten both fruitful innovation governance systems and cartels.

Where Do We Go from Here?

Recognizing the important role of non–IP-based innovation governance regimes complicates the already difficult task of evaluating and designing intellectual property law. The social value of an IP system depends not only on how well it balances between upstream creators and downstream creators and users, but also on whether it leaves space for and supports socially valuable alternative innovation governance regimes. As a result I see two types of research tasks ahead.

First, it is eminently clear that we need more empirical information about creative groups, how they are governed internally, how they interact with outsiders, and how they relate to the intellectual property system. If it is true, as it appears to be, that creative groups that have opted out of the legally defined intellectual property system play a major role in creative production, understanding these groups cannot be a peripheral part of intellectual property scholarship but must move to the center, as it is beginning to do. At the same time, those who study groups that employ alternative innovation regimes cannot afford to focus only on their internal governance if those groups have important interactions with the IP-based market. Interdisciplinary research involving both intellectual property scholars and innovation researchers is needed.

Second, despite the lack of conclusive empirical information, policy makers and legal scholars must begin to incorporate these institutional considerations into debates about current intellectual property doctrine and the desirability of proposed reforms. For example, patent law's long-standing prohibition on patenting natural phenomena and scientific principles should be recognized explicitly as a means of negotiating the institutional boundary between the open science governance regime and the IP-based market. Debates about intellectual property doctrines should be informed not only (and perhaps not even principally) by the upstream-downstream balance, but also by the interactions between different innovation governance institutions.

Notes

I gratefully acknowledge research support from the Filomen D'Agostino and Max E. Greenberg Research Fund.

1. This volume celebrates the work of Eric von Hippel. While Eric is most well known as a pioneer in the recognition and study of user innovation (e.g., see von Hippel 2005), his path-breaking paper on the "norms-based intellectual property system" that governs copying and reuse of recipes among high-end French chefs (Fauchart and von Hippel 2008) has been equally influential among legal scholars. This article helped to spawn a literature focused on investigating situations in which community norms replace formal intellectual property in governing innovation and considering the potential implications of such private ordering for intellectual property policy (e.g., see Raustiala and Sprigman 2012). This chapter flows from that line of research. It builds on the emerging literature on knowledge commons governance (Frischmann et al. 2014), which in turn grows out of studies of commons governance of natural resources (Ostrom 2005).

2. For discussions of the traditional incentive theories of patenting, see, for example., Blair and Cotter (2001: 78–80), Eisenberg (1989: 1024–28), and Strandburg (2004).

3. For discussions of various ways in which inventors recoup their inventive investments, see generally Cohen et al. (2000), Levin et al. (1987), Arundel (2001), Harabi (1995), and Sattler (2003).

4. Indeed, copyright law explicitly recognizes this issue with its "work for hire" doctrine. See Burk (2004) for a discussion of this and other considerations regarding intellectual property and the theory of the firm.

5. See http://en.wikipedia.org/wiki/Wikipedia:Copyrights.

6. http://www.openinventionnetwork.com.

7. Indeed this is not an uncommon sentiment. For example, users of the Creative Commons copyright licenses, which seek to encourage sharing of copyrighted works, most often choose to license only noncommercial use. See https://wiki.creativecommons.org/Metrics/License_statistics.

8. For open source licenses, see http://www.opensource.org/licenses/category. For Creative Commons licenses, see http://creativecommons.org/licenses/..

9. Here I sweep quite a bit under the rug. As the difficulties associated with attempts within the scientific community to collect and maintain biological materials and data attest, groups often struggle with organizing, managing, and providing appropriate credit for this kind of task (e.g., see Stern 2004; Murray 2010; Uhlir 2011).

10. For an overview of this literature see Barnett (2011).

11. http://article.wn.com/view/2012/01/03/Wikipedia_gets_20M_in_annual_fundraising_drive_5/.

12. 35 USC §§200–212.

13. See, for example, Lemley (2008) for a recent overview of the literature.

14. I am setting aside here the clinical research funded by pharmaceutical and medical device companies that is conducted in many academic hospitals and medical schools. The costs of clinical trials are obviously very high. Such research is very different from the academic-style research that is my focus in this example.

15. *Mayo Collaborative Servs. v. Prometheus Labs., Inc.* 566 US __ (2012); *Ass'n for Molecular Pathology v. Myriad Genetics, Inc.*, 569 US __ (2013).

16. http://www.gnu.org/copyleft/gpl.html.

References

Agarwal, Rajshree, and Sonali K. Shah. 2014. Knowledge sources of entrepreneurship: Firm formation by academic, user and employee innovators. *Research Policy* 43 (7): 1109–33.

Arundel, Anthony. 2001. The relative effectiveness of patents and secrecy for appropriation. *Research Policy* 30 (4): 611–24.

Barnett, Jonathan M. 2011. Intellectual property as a law of organization. *Southern California Law Review* 84 (4): 785–858.

Benkler, Yochai. 2006. *The Wealth of Networks*. New Haven: Yale University Press.

Bessen, James, and Michael J. Meurer. 2008. *Patent Failure: How Judges, Bureaucrats, and Lawyers Put Innovators at Risk*. Princeton: Princeton University Press.

Blair, Roger D., and Thomas F. Cotter. 2001. Rethinking patent damages. *Texas Intellectual Property Law Journal* 10 (1): 1–94.

Burk, Dan L. 2004. Intellectual property and the firm. *University of Chicago Law Review. University of Chicago. Law School* 71 (1): 3–20.

Burstein, Michael J. 2012. Exchanging information without intellectual property. *Texas Law Review* 91 (2): 227–82.

Cohen, Wesley M., Richard R. Nelson, and John P. Walsh. 2000. Protecting their intellectual assets: Appropriability conditions and why U.S. manufacturing firms patent (or not). Working paper 7552. NBER. *http://www.nber.org/papers/w7552*.

Coleman, E. Gabriella. 2013. *Coding Freedom: The Ethics and Aesthetics of Hacking*. Princeton: Princeton University Press.

Dorfman, Avihay, and Assaf Jacob. 2011. Copyright as tort. *Theoretical Inquiries in Law* 12 (1): 59–97.

Fauchart, Emmanuelle, and Eric von Hippel. 2008. Norms-based intellectual property systems: The case of French chefs. *Organization Science* 19 (2): 187–201.

Franke, Nikolaus, and Sonali K. Shah. 2003. How communities support innovative activities: An exploration of assistance and sharing among end-users. *Research Policy* 32 (1): 157–78.

Frischmann, Brett M., Michael J. Madison, and Katherine J. Strandburg. 2014. *Governing Knowledge Commons*. New York: Oxford University Press.

Gilson, Ronald J., Charles F. Sabel, and Robert E. Scott. 2009. Contracting for innovation: Vertical disintegration and interfirm collaboration. *Columbia Law Review* 109 (3): 431–502.

Harabi, Najib. 1995. Appropriability of technical innovations: An empirical analysis. *Research Policy* 24 (6): 981–92.

Harhoff, Dietmar, Joachim Henkel, and Eric von Hippel. 2003. Profiting from voluntary information spillovers: How users benefit by freely revealing their innovations. *Research Policy* 32 (10): 1753–69.

Henkel, Joachim, and Markus G. Reitzig. 2010. Patent trolls, the sustainability of "locking-in-to-extort" strategies, and implications for innovating firms. Working paper. SSRN. *http://ssrn.com/abstract=985602*.

Kuusisto, Jari, Jeroen P.J. de Jong, Fred Gault, Christina Raasch, and Eric von Hippel. 2013. Consumer innovation in Finland: Incidence, diffusion and policy implications. Report 189. Proceedings of the University of Vaasa.

Lemley, Mark A., and Carl Shapiro. 2007. Patent holdup and royalty stacking. *Texas Law Review* 85 (7): 1991–2049.

Lemley, Mark A. 2008. Are universities patent trolls? *Fordham Intellectual Property, Media and Entertainment Law Journal* 18 (3): 611–31.

Levin, Richard C., Alvin K. Klevorick, Richard R. Nelson, Sidney G. Winter, Richard Gilbert, and Zvi Griliches. 1987. Appropriating the returns from industrial research and development. *Brookings Papers on Economic Activity* (3): 783–831.

Madison, Michael J., Brett M. Frischmann, and Katherine J. Strandburg. 2010. Constructing commons in the cultural environment. *Cornell Law Review* 95 (4): 657–710.

Mehra, Salil, and David Hoffman. 2009. Wikitruth through Wikiorder. *Emory Law Journal* 59 (1): 151–210.

Merges, Robert P. 2004. From medieval guilds to open source software: Informal norms, appropriability institutions, and innovation. Working paper. *http://ssrn.com/abstract=661543*.

Murray, Fiona. 2010. The oncomouse that roared: Hybrid exchange strategies as a source of distinction at the boundary of overlapping institutions. *American Journal of Sociology* 116 (2): 341–88.

O'Mahony, Siobhan. 2003. Guarding the commons: How community managed software projects protect their work. *Research Policy* 32 (7): 1179–98.

O'Mahony, Siobhan, and Fabrizio Ferraro. 2004. Managing the boundary of an "open" project. Working paper 03–60. SSRN. *http://ssrn.com/abstract=474782*.

Ostrom, Elinor. 2005. *Understanding Institutional Diversity*. Princeton: Princeton University Press.

Raustiala, Kal, and Christopher Sprigman. 2012. *The Knockoff Economy: How Imitation Sparks Innovation*. New York: Oxford University Press.

Raymond, Eric. 2000. The cathedral and the bazaar. http://www.catb.org/~esr/writings/homesteading/cathedral-bazaar/.

Sattler, Henrik. 2003. Appropriability of product innovations: An empirical analysis for Germany. *International Journal of Technology Management* 26 (5/6): 502–16.

Schultz, Jason, and Jennifer M. Urban. 2012. Protecting open innovation: The defensive patent license as a new approach to patent disarmament. *Harvard Journal of Law & Technology* 26 (1): 1–67.

Stern, Scott. 2004. *Biological Resource Centers: Knowledge Hubs for the Life Sciences*. Washington, DC: Brookings Institution Press.

Stokes, Donald E. 1997. *Pasteur's Quadrant: Basic Science and Technological Innovation*. Washington, DC: Brookings Institution Press.

Strandburg, Katherine J. 2004. What does the public get? Experimental use and the patent bargain. *Wisconsin Law Review* (1): 81–155.

Strandburg, Katherine J. 2005. Curiosity-driven research and university technology transfer. In *University Entrepreneurship and Technology Transfer*, ed. Gary D. Libecap, 93–122. Amsterdam: Elsevier.

Strandburg, Katherine J. 2008. Users as innovators: Implications for patent doctrine. *University of Colorado Law Review* 79 (2): 467–544.

Strandburg, Katherine J. 2009. User innovator community norms at the boundary between academic and industrial research. *Fordham Law Review* 77 (5): 2237–74.

Strandburg, Katherine J. 2010. Norms and the sharing of research Materials and tacit knowledge. In *Working within the Boundaries of Intellectual Property*, ed. Rochelle C. Dreyfuss, Harry First, and Diane L. Zimmerman. Oxford: Oxford University Press.

Strandburg, Katherine J. 2014. Legal but unacceptable: *Pallin v. Singer* and physician patenting norms. In *Intellectual Property at the Edge: The Contested Contours of IP*, ed. Rochelle C. Dreyfuss and Jane Ginsburg. New York: Cambridge University Press.

Uhlir, Paul F., ed. 2011. Designing the microbial research commons: *Proceedings of an International Workshop*. http://www.nap.edu/catalog.php?record_id=13245.

von Hippel, Eric. 1987. Cooperation between rivals: Informal know-how trading. *Research Policy* 16 (6): 291–302.

von Hippel, Eric. 2001. Innovation by user communities: Learning from open-source software. *MIT Sloan Management Review* 42 (4): 82–86.

von Hippel, E., and Georg von Krogh. 2003. Open source software and the "Private-collective" innovation model: Issues for organization science. *Organization Science* 14 (2): 209–23.

von Hippel, Eric. 2005. *Democratizing Innovation*. Cambridge: MIT Press.

13

Will Innovation Thrive without Patents? A Natural Experiment in Biotechnology

Andrew W. Torrance

Innovation occurs within a complex web of law. Of the myriad legal doctrines that affect innovation, the most directly relevant is intellectual property, particularly patent law. The United States Constitution, in Article I, Section 8, states a strong public policy goal for the granting of patents (and copyrights) to inventors: "To promote the Progress of Science and useful Arts, by securing for limited Times to Authors and Inventors the exclusive Right to their respective Writings and Discoveries." Despite the Founding Fathers' apparent faith in the societal benefits afforded by patent protection, a crescendo of recent critics have accused the patent system of complicating, slowing, or even thwarting innovation (von Hippel 2005; Benkler 2006; Bessen and Meurer 2006; Jaffe and Lerner 2006; Boldrin and Levine 2008; Torrance and Tomlinson 2009; Burk and Lemley 2009; Torrance and Tomlinson 2011). Patents certainly present significant hurdles for open and user innovation. Moreover von Hippel (2005) and Strandburg (2008) have demonstrated that user innovators, especially individuals, tend to be poorly served, and often harmed, by the patent system.

Empirical evidence evaluating how well the patent system achieves its stated goals of encouraging innovation is notably scarce (Torrance and Tomlinson 2009, Torrance and Tomlinson 2011). Even the US Congress, in Section 30 of the America Invents Act of 2011 ("AIA"), has voiced its anxiety that patents may sometimes impede innovation, urging the need "[to protect] the rights of small business and inventors from predatory behavior that could result in the cutting off of innovation." Although some have called for the abolition of patent protection (Boldrin and Levine 2008), commitment to the patent system remains strong among US policy makers, as evidenced by the recent passage of the AIA, and has

been a treaty obligation since the US ratified the World Trade Organization Agreement on Trade-Related Aspects of Intellectual Property ("WTO-
TRIPS") in 1995. Thus the United States is likely to maintain a patent
system for the foreseeable future. However, one section in the AIA—
Section 33—may offer a rare and valuable opportunity to explore how
innovation, especially open and user innovation, might perform without
the protections or constraints of patents.

When President Barack Obama signed the AIA into law on September
16, 2011, he formally created, within the field of biotechnology, an exception to patentable subject matter. His predecessor, President George W.
Bush, had called on Congress, in his 2008 State of the Union address, "to
pass legislation that bans unethical practices, such as the . . . patenting . . . of human life." Section 33 of the AIA states that "[n]otwithstand-
ing any other provision of law, no patent may issue on a claim directed to
or encompassing a human organism." Section 33 took full legal effect on
September 16, 2011, but did not retroactively invalidate patents already
in force. Although patents claiming inventions "directed to or encompassing" aspects of human organisms, such as human bodies, organs, tissues,
cells, genes, chemical products of physiological processes, and even
thoughts have often been granted by the United States Patent and Trademark Office ("USPTO"), patents claiming this class of biotechnological
inventions have proved increasingly difficult successfully to assert in
court (Torrance 2008, 2009, 2010a, 2013). It is too early to know
precisely how the USPTO and the courts will interpret Section 33.
Nevertheless, a rich body of judicial decisions on the validity, enforcement, and infringement of patents claiming human genes, human embryonic stem cells ("hESCs"), chemicals produced by human physiology, and
human thought (especially relating to diagnosis and therapy) do provide
valuable insight into how far Section 33 may reach. These decisions
suggest that inventions related to the human body and its functions represent a lacuna in patentable subject matter. If interpreted in a manner
consistent with this body of court decisions, Section 33 may represent
an apotheosis of the marked common law trend against the patenting
of inventions relating to humans, the human body, and human bodily
processes.

Exceptions to patentable subject matter have rarely been formally
incorporated into the Patent Act. With the addition of Section 33 to the

patent law, both statute and judicial precedent have now created a space in which innovation "directed to or encompassing a human organism" may take place substantially unfettered from fears of infringing new patent rights. This safe harbor from patent infringement, though circumscribed by the limits of Section 33, allows a natural experiment to take place in which innovation may operate without interference from new patent rights. Far from a desire to foster user and open innovation in human-related biotechnology, the primary rationale for this amendment to the Patent Act was strong repugnance to biological research leading to, and the possibility of resultant ownership interests in, inventions involving human beings. Rather, it is incidental that this natural experiment may provide valuable insight into how patents affect innovation, especially user and open innovation. Under these rare conditions of freedom from patents, innovation, especially user and open innovation, may flourish.

Strictly controlled access to biological laboratories and the specter of legal liability, especially that related to biosafety and intellectual property rights, have combined to discourage open and user innovation in biotechnology (Torrance 2010b). Nevertheless, even prior to the patent-safe harbor created by Section 33, biotechnology had already begun to migrate out of the professional laboratory, and into the realm of open and user innovation. Detailed protocols for carrying out molecular biological techniques have long been accessible on the Internet. Both prices and availability of machines, apparatus, chemical reagents, and biological materials required in biotechnology have improved markedly, a trend accelerated by the outsourcing of services such as gene sequencing and synthesis and the rise of biotech company bankruptcies during the economic downturn that began in 2008. Furthermore the BioBricks Foundation has assembled, and makes widely available, a vast and growing collection of well-characterized Lego-like genetic building blocks (the eponymous "BioBricks") cataloged in its Registry of Standard Biological Parts. The International Genetically Engineered Machine ("iGEM") Foundation has dramatically increased undergraduate, and even high school, student participation in synthetic biology worldwide through the annual iGEM competition, which is held at the Massachusetts Institute of Technology and involves the construction of genetically-engineered organisms and systems built with BioBricks (Torrance 2010b; Torrance and Kahl 2014). At the grassroots level, do-it-yourself biology ("DIY Bio") organizations, such as BioCurious, have formed to democratize access to biological knowledge and practice by providing common laboratory space and expertise sharing to anyone interested in learning and doing biotechnology.

Formerly, such endeavors were the exclusive domains of large and well-funded university, government, institution, and commercial laboratories accessible almost exclusively to those having formal scientific credentials, such as doctorates. If Section 33 were to lead to even greater amounts of user and open innovation in human-related biotechnology, this patent-safe harbor could provide a model for further patent reform creating additional patent-safe harbors in other fields of technology. A negative effect on innovation would provide evidence supporting the traditional assumption that patents spur relatively more innovation. No significant change in overall innovation rate is yet another possible outcome. Such a result might align with earlier empirical comparison of innovation rates across countries with and without patent systems, in which innovation rates were observed to have remained relatively stable with or without patent protection, while protection by trade secrecy rose markedly in systems without patents (Moser 2005). Regardless of which of these patterns is observed, the legal change heralded by Section 33 provides rare and valuable insight into how to craft patent policy that successfully promotes innovation.

This chapter introduces the broad contours of the US patent system, including some of the major reforms made to patent law by the AIA. It discusses the unease with which the law of property and intellectual property apply to human beings. Next, it explores the reluctances courts have shown toward the patentability of inventions directed to human beings: specifically, human genes, hESCs, chemical products of human physiological processes, and human thought (especially methods of diagnosis and treatment). The chapter concludes by suggesting that Section 33 offers a rare opportunity to observe a natural experiment in which innovation may operate unconstrained by patents, and that the results of this experiment may provide a model for future reform of the patent system to the benefit of innovation, especially open and user innovation.

The Patent System

The US patent system differs in a number of respects from the patent systems that predominate in other countries. The pre-AIA system rewarded the first person to invent with a patent, rather than the first person to file a patent application. In addition, the US patent system is more likely to consider personal, noncommercial, educational, and research uses to be infringing than would many other countries.

Patent Requirements

To qualify for a patent, an invention must meet several legal requirements set out in the Patent Act. An invention must fall within acceptable categories of subject matter and be useful, new (both literally new and nonobvious), and adequately described in a patent application. Furthermore the metes and bounds of any aspects of the invention its inventor wishes to protect must be carefully defined in the stylized form of patent claims. If a patent applicant can demonstrate to the USPTO that her patent application satisfies all of these requirements, in addition to a number of formalities, the USPTO will issue a patent whose claims describe the monopoly rights to exclude others conferred on the patent owner.

Patentable Subject Matter

Section 101 of the Patent Act enumerates several categories of inventions eligible for patent protection. These are "any new and useful process, machine, manufacture, or composition of matter, or any new and useful improvement thereof." In 1980, when the United States Supreme Court decided the patent case *Diamond v. Chakrabarty*, it famously ratified a Congressional Committee Report that had interpreted Section 101 as including "anything under the sun that is made by man." Nonetheless, the Court was careful to highlight the unpatentability of "laws of nature, physical phenomena, and abstract ideas." In interpreting these exceptions to patentable subject matter, the courts have only limited the patent-eligibility of a small number of categories of inventions. One class of technology to which courts have paid particular attention involves inventions that implicate a human organism, human body, or substituent body parts or processes; courts have tended to place these inventions toward the unpatentable end of the patentability spectrum. Section 33 is likely to reinforce the unpatentability of such inventions.

The Right to Exclude Others

Once a patent has been issued by the USPTO, Section 271 of the Patent Act allows a patent owner to exclude others from making, using, selling, offering to sell, or importing any inventions claimed in the patent. This negative monopoly right to exclude others can be powerful because it is based on the legal theory of strict liability. Under strict liability, knowledge and intent tend to be relatively unimportant compared to occurrence of an infringing act. Even independent invention tends not to be a defense to patent infringement. Consequently a patent owner may successfully sue anyone who infringes a patent claim, whether or not such infringement is knowing, unknowing, deliberate, accidental, commercial, noncommercial, or even for educational, research, or personal use. This relatively unforgiving standard of liability contrasts with the more lenient treatment for noncommercial, educational, research, and personal use that tends to prevail under the patent laws of other countries. With rare exceptions (for example, experimentation necessary to achieve regulatory approval for a generic version of a patented pharmaceutical drug), liability for patent infringement hinges solely on proof of infringing acts.

The law of patent infringement applies with full force to open innovation and user innovators, whether individuals or firms. The costs involved in patent lawsuits tend to be prohibitively expensive, with patent litigation costs often exceeding $3 million (Torrance 2007). Because firms usually possess relatively greater financial resources than do individuals to mount the expensive legal efforts necessary to defend themselves against patent infringement lawsuits, it is individuals, such as user innovators, who are most at risk of catastrophic outcomes when sued by patent owners. The mere risk of being sued for patent infringement can chill user and open innovation. Locating patents that one might infringe is challenging. Furthermore patent claims are often devilishly difficult to interpret prior to expensive litigation (Bessen and Meurer 2008), making it challenging for potential infringers to know a priori how to order their behavior to avoid infringement.

Even if it is necessary to practice the claims of a patent in order to improve a claimed invention, practicing the claims even for this socially useful purpose can trigger infringement. Similarly, practicing patent claims for purely personal and noncommercial purposes may still result in liability for infringement. Open and user innovators possess no special privileges that allow them to escape liability for patent infringement. Under such conditions, there is likely to be a substantial chill on open and user innovation, as those involved in such kinds of innovation weigh the benefits of inventing against the potential threat of ruinous infringement litigation. Even though larger commercial entities with greater access to financial resources are much more likely to be sued for patent infringement, smaller parties, such as user innovators, may still fear the unlikely, yet catastrophic, possibility of having to defend themselves against infringement allegations.

The America Invents Act of 2011

For years there have been efforts in Congress to bring comprehensive reform to the patent statutes. Since their last great reformulation, in 1952, numerous piecemeal amendments have been made to the Patent Act. For example, in response to the WTO-TRIPs, the United States amended the Patent Act in 1995 to provide patent owners with 20 years of potential patent protection from first filing date instead of the previous 17 years of patent term from patent issuance. Despite a steady drumbeat of individual amendments to the patent statutes, momentum for major patent reform grew over the past decade, and culminated with passage of the AIA.

The AIA includes many changes to US patent law, some of which will help to harmonize American patent law with practice in the rest of the world. Some of these changes may even benefit user and open innovators. Under amended Section 102 of the patent statutes, there is a new first-inventor-to-file rule to encourage inventors to file patent applications as soon as inventions are completed, as only the first inventor who files a patent application claiming an invention will be eligible for a patent. Section 102 also institutes a new absolute novelty standard under which an inventor risks complete loss of patent rights if any third party discloses the inventor's invention prior to the filing of a patent application. One beneficial implication of this reform may be to place detailed information about new inventions into the possession of the public earlier, which could encourage follow-on innovation.

Another substantial change to current patent law involves the creation of a post-grant review procedure (Sections 321–30), a new and potentially powerful means for challenging the validity of newly-granted patents. Like the patent opposition system already in place in Europe, post-grant review will create a formal administrative proceeding in the USPTO that anyone may use to challenge patents. Post-grant review will be much more rapid and less expensive than litigation in court. In addition, new Section 273 offers a defense to patent infringement for secret commercial use of a patented invention that began prior to the filing of a patent application or public disclosure by the patent owner. As discussed above, the new patent reforms also include a notable subject matter exclusion in biotechnology in the form of Section 33.

Each of these amendments will affect user and open innovators. Although the actual effects of these provisions may not be understood until courts begin to interpret the AIA, user and open innovation should benefit from the early elimination of poor quality patents, acceleration in patent application filings (and concomitant acceleration in patent expirations), availability of a prior commercial use defense, and creation of a patent-safe harbor for certain types of biotechnology.

Patents on Human Beings

The possibility that a patent could claim a human being, either in whole or in part, is repugnant to many people. There exists a widely shared opinion that humans must not be treated as property—even intellectual property—under the law. Patents that claim mere parts of a human, such as genes, may inspire "the visceral fear of corporate interests claiming ownership over our very bodies" (Crease and Schlich 2003). The law is clear that human beings cannot constitute property. The Thirteenth Amendment of the US Constitution prohibits property interests in humans. Nor can human beings be intellectual property. In its 1987 *Policy Statement on Patentability of Animals*, the USPTO announced that "[t]he grant of a limited, but exclusive property right in a human being is prohibited by the Constitution." The issue of patenting humans has even reached the highest levels of political discussion. President George W. Bush used his final *State of the Union* address on January 29, 2008, to exhort "Congress to pass legislation to ban unethical practices such as the . . . patenting . . . of human life." Inventions directed to or encompassing human beings, their bodies, or the parts or processes thereof, do not fit well within either property or intellectual property.

Humans as Property

Anglo-American law forbids the ownership of human beings or their bodies. Just as people cannot constitute property according to the Thirteenth Amendment of the US Constitution, the common law has long prohibited human bodies from constituting property (Madoff 2010). Markets in human body parts have also tended to be illegal, whether those body parts derived from living human beings (Rao 2007) or dead human bodies (Goodwin 2006). Similarly, intellectual property protection for inventions that encompass aspects of humans and their bodies is difficult to obtain, and even more difficult to enforce in court.

Experimentation involving human beings has profound ethical and moral implications for most people. Patent law provides only one set of legal constraints on such activity: the ability to exclude others from practicing a claimed invention. Criminal, health, tort, family, and abortion law all offer more direct and robust regulation of the uses and abuses of humans at various developmental stages. Thus, despite Congress' legislative action on the issue of patentability, other areas of law, morality, and ethics are likely to play more decisive roles in regulating human-related inventions.

Humans as Intellectual Property

Many inventions incorporate human participation, or involve substituent parts of humans, such as genes, proteins, cells, tissues, or organs. Some patents, such as US Patent No. 6,200,806 ("Primate Embryonic Stem Cells"), even claim cells having the potential to develop into entire human beings. The USPTO and the European Patent Office ("EPO") have long granted patents claiming such human subject matter. However, whatever administrative agencies, such as patent offices, may grant, courts and legislatures may take away.

Until the passage of Section 33, patents on human-related inventions were formally constrained by an *ad hoc* assemblage of Congressional riders, judicial opinions, USPTO policies, and presidential statements regarding the patenting of human beings, human body parts, and human bodily

processes. A few examples may serve to illustrate this piecemeal regulation. In the 1972 case, *Gottschalk v. Benson*, the Supreme Court barred
patentability of any process made up of "purely human thought." Section
287 of the patent statute limits liability for patent infringement of methods of surgery by medical personnel and medical facilities. The USPTO
has declared human-nonhuman genetic hybrids, or chimaeras, unpatentable. Since 2004, the "Weldon Amendment" Congressional rider was
repeatedly renewed by each new Congress, ensuring that "[n]one of the
funds appropriated or otherwise made available under this Act may be
used to issue patents on claims directed to or encompassing a human
organism." The USPTO Manual of Patent Examining Procedure ("MPEP")
specifically states at §2105 that, "[i]f the broadest reasonable interpretation of the claimed invention as a whole encompasses a human being,
then a rejection under 35 U.S.C. 101 must be made indicating that the
claimed invention is directed to nonstatutory subject matter." And, in
2000, President Bill Clinton and Prime Minister Tony Blair together
publicly urged the biotechnology industry not to seek patents claiming
human genes.

However, even though the patent statute lacked any definitive prohibition regarding the patenting of human-related inventions prior to Section
33, the courts have successfully limited the patentability of human
genes, hESCs, products of *in vivo* conversion, and human thought. This
judicial regulation of patents claiming human-related inventions possesses considerable value in providing guidance for the interpretation of
Section 33.

Patents Directed to or Encompassing Human Beings

Patents on four categories of human-related biotechnological inventions
have attracted considerable attention in the courts: human genes, hESCs,
chemical products of *in vivo* conversion, and methods involving elements
of human thought. Each of these categories fits comfortably as patent-
eligible within the codified provisions of the pre-AIA patent statute, as
interpreted by the Supreme Court. Nevertheless, lower courts, the federal
executive branch of government, and Congress have all contributed to a
trend whose direction has been the increasing curtailment of patent rights
covering human-related inventions.

Patents Claiming Human Genes

According to Jensen and Murray (2005), approximately 20 percent of the known genes in the human genome have been claimed in patents issued by the United States Patent and Trademark Office. Allowing such a patent gold rush has been challenged on ethical grounds (Hollon 2000). Heller and Eisenberg (1998) have warned that excessive patenting of genes could result in a tragedy of the anticommons for genetic research. Michael Crichton (2007) expressed the more extreme fears of the public when he wrote in the *New York Times*, "YOU, or someone you love, may die because of a gene patent. . . . Gene patents are now used to halt research, prevent medical testing and keep vital information from you and your doctor." In short, the patenting of DNA has captured the attention of the public, politicians, and judges over the last decade. The result has been an increasingly unfavorable climate for patents claiming human genes, with judicial decisions making their contribution by curtailing patent rights in genes.

In 2005, the Court of Appeals for the Federal Circuit ("CAFC") decided the *In re Fisher* appeal. This case concerned whether patent claims to certain partial sequences of genes, called "ESTs" or "expressed sequence tags," possessed the requisite utility and enabling disclosure. The CAFC ruled that these claims to gene fragments were invalid, and thereby cast doubt on the patentability of EST gene fragments. In 2007, two members of the House of Representatives, Xavier Becerra (Democrat of California) and Dave Weldon (Republican of Florida), proposed the *Genomic Research and Accessibility Act*. Section 106 would have required that "[n]otwithstanding any other provision of law, no patent may be obtained for a nucleotide sequence, or its functions or correlations, or the naturally occurring products it specifies." This proposed statutory amendment would have eliminated gene patents—whether derived from humans or other organisms—from US law. Though Congress has never passed this bill, it did hold hearings into the issue of gene patents in late 2007.

In 2009, the American Civil Liberties Union ("ACLU") represented several female patients and supporting organizations in suing to end gene patents and genetic methods of diagnosis. The plaintiffs sued the USPTO on the grounds that issuing gene patents was impermissible. In addition, they sued a Utah-based biotechnology firm, Myriad Genetics, and the Directors of the University of Utah Research Foundation, seeking to invalidate their gene patents, which claimed, among other inventions, the BRCA1 and BRCA2 gene mutations useful in predicting the risk of developing breast and ovarian cancer. As the plaintiff's complaint argued,

Every person's body contains human genes, passed down to each individual from his or her parents. These genes determine, in part, the structure and function of every human body. This case challenges the legality and constitutionality of granting patents over this most basic element of every person's individuality.

To the surprise of many, the district court sided decisively with ACLU, holding that neither human genes nor genetic tests that relied on human genes constituted eligible subject matter for patent protection. Instead, Judge Sweet argued that genes "containing sequences found in nature . . . are deemed unpatentable subject matter." The plaintiffs filed an appeal with the CAFC. In October 2010, the United States, a defendant in the case by way of the USPTO, confused both the plaintiffs and its fellow defendants by filing an *amicus curiae* brief with the CAFC taking the position that "isolated but otherwise unaltered" human genes should be considered unpatentable under the law. In July 2011, a panel of three CAFC judges reversed much of Judge Sweet's decision, in *AMP v. Myriad Genetics*, and reaffirmed the patent-eligibility of human genes. However, the legal pendulum swung back on March 26, 2012, when the Supreme Court vacated *AMP v. Myriad Genetics*, and ordered the lower court to reconsider the patentability of human genes in light of *Mayo v. Prometheus*, a case the Supreme Court had decided a week earlier. In *Mayo v. Prometheus* (discussed further below), the court unanimously held methods of using human metabolites in diagnosis and therapy to constitute unpatentable subject matter. By vacating *AMP v. Myriad Genetics*, and demanding a new decision consistent with *Mayo v. Prometheus*, the Supreme Court cast considerable doubt on the patentability of human genes. This doubt was dispelled on June 13, 2013, when the Supreme Court unanimously decided *AMP v. Myriad*, invalidating Myriad's patent claims covering isolated human genomic DNA, though it also suggested that at least some synthetic DNA remained patent-eligible subject matter.

Human Embryonic Stem Cells

In 1998, the University of Wisconsin Alumni Research Foundation ("WARF") filed the first in a series of patent applications claiming hESCs, methods of producing them, and their various uses in therapeutic and other applications (Rimmer 2008). These patent applications were based on foundational research by Dr. James Thomson and his research group that took place at the University of Wisconsin. Thomson and his colleagues were the first to identify and culture pluripotent hESCs. Then Commissioner of the USPTO, Todd Dickenson, addressed the Congressional Subcommittee on Labor, Health and Human Services, Education and Related Agencies of the Senate Appropriations Committee in 1999 to clarify that hESCs could indeed constitute patentable subject matter under existing patent law. The first patent resulting from the research of the Thomson laboratory issued as US Patent Number 6,200,806 ("Primate Embryonic Stem Cells") in March 2001. It claimed both methods of isolating hESCs and all five hESC cell lines themselves. Several other related hESC patents would later issue based on research carried out by Thomson and his team of researchers.

The WARF patents were licensed to Geron Corporation, a biotechnology firm specializing in the development of regenerative medicine products and therapeutic methods. Opponents of patents claiming hESCs, including the Public Patent Foundation, challenged the WARF patents using a USPTO procedure called a reexamination. In the first round of reexaminations, three major WARF patents were found to be invalid. To salvage these patents, WARF was forced to amend and narrow the coverage of these patents' claims. These amendments marked a retreat away from claiming later stages of embryonic development (e.g., "post-implantation embryonic germ cells") and toward claiming much earlier-stage cells (e.g., derived from a "pre-implantation embryo" or "human blastocyst") and "*in vitro* cell cultures" not derived from human embryos. In effect, these amendments distanced the patent claims from human embryos per se or even later stages of embryonic development. After additional rounds of reexamination, resulting in more amendments that further narrowed the scopes of the claims, the surviving patents emerged from reexamination without claims that could cover totipotent hESCs capable of producing a human being. Given the ethical controversies surrounding hESCs, it is likely that these WARF patents, and other patents claiming hESCs, will continue to face patentability challenges to the extent that their claims implicate human beings or methods of producing them.

European patent law has tended to limit patents on hESCs more explicitly than US patent law. For example, the same WARF patents whose claims have been substantially narrowed in reexamination in the USPTO have been found invalid in Europe. Articles 5 and 6 of the 1998 *European Union Directive on the Legal Protection of Biotechnological Inventions* offer a number of grounds for prohibiting patenting inventions involving hESCs. In its 2002 Opinion on the *Ethical Aspects of Patenting Inventions Involving Human Embryonic Stem Cells*, the European Commission's European Group on Ethics in Science and New Technologies warned that "such isolated cells are so close to the human body, to the foetus or to the embryo they have been isolated from that their patenting may be considered as a form of commercialization of the human body." Furthermore Rule 29(1) of the *Implementing Regulations to the Convention on the Grant of European Patents* warns that "[t]he human body, at the various stages of its formation and development, and the simple discovery of one of its elements . . . cannot constitute patentable inventions." Finally, on October 18, 2011, the Court of Justice of the European Union decided the case of *Oliver Brüstle v. Greenpeace e.V.*, holding unpatentable any inventions that "require the prior destruction of human embryos or their use as base material, whatever the stage at which that takes place." Thus, based on these various legal authorities, many aspects of hESCs are unpatentable in the European Union. Now that Section 33 is law, both the US and European patent systems share considerable similarities in their treatment of patents claiming inventions related to hESCs.

Chemical Products of Human Physiology

The human body routinely converts ingested or injected chemicals into different chemical products through physiological biochemistry. This process is called *in vivo* conversion because the chemical transformation of precursor chemicals, or "prodrugs," into physiological products, or "drugs," takes place within the living human body. Drugs produced from prodrugs through *in vivo* conversion are sometimes therapeutically effective (Silverman 2004). Consequently patent applicants have routinely sought patent protection to cover products of *in vivo* conversion, or the uses thereof, and the USPTO has granted many patents that claim products or processes of *in vivo* conversion. However, patent claims whose elements involve physiological processes that occur within the human body have consistently fared poorly in court. US courts of final appeal overwhelmingly do not find patents claiming products of *in vivo* conversion to be valid, enforceable, and infringed (Torrance 2008).

Courts deciding *in vivo* conversion patent cases have offered a variety of rationales to justify this consensus outcome. These have pointed to the difficulties of securing evidence inside a living human body, invoked inherency, and made distinctions between "natural" and "synthetic" drugs and chemical changes that occur inside versus outside the human body. Despite this diversity of rationales, what links these outcomes together is the apparent discomfort courts have had in enforcing patents that claim products or processes that originate from physiological processes of the human body. Torrance (2008) has ascribed the unanimous result of such patent cases to the existence in the law of a "physiological steps doctrine." In 2012, the Supreme Court finally decided a case, *Mayo v. Prometheus*, involving inventions related to human metabolites, and unanimously held these inventions to constitute unpatentable subject matter.

As in the case of hESCs, European patent law is more explicit in setting limits on the patentability of inventions relating to therapy. The European Patent Convention (EPC) Article 52(4) prohibits patents covering "methods for treatment of the human or animal body by surgery or therapy and diagnostic methods practised on the human or animal body." Although Article 52(4) recognizes an exception for "products," drugs whose therapeutic effects are produced through *in vivo* conversion have fared poorly under European patent law, just as they have under US patent law.

Human Thought

Although lacking the obvious physical embodiment possessed by a human gene, hESC, or metabolite, human thought is still a product of the human body, specifically neurological processes within the brain. Like patents claiming genes, hESCs, and metabolites, patents claiming aspects of human thought have experienced much resistance from US courts. In a 1951 case, *In re Abrams*, the United States Court of Customs and Patent Appeals (the predecessor of the CAFC) declared that "[i]t is self-evident that thought is not patentable." Inventions with methods including elements of human thought are often held unpatentable by courts under the "mental steps doctrine." In its 1972 decision, *Gottschalk v. Benson*, the

Supreme Court declared that an invention must be considered unpatentable if its claimed elements are composed of "purely mental steps." Human thought itself is closely associated with the human body, especially the brain. More precisely, thought results, at least in part, from neural pathways made up of neuronal cells (Purves et al. 2008). This close association with the human body provides a modern scientific rationale for the mental steps doctrine (Torrance 2009), and provides a linkage between thought patents and patents claiming other human-related inventions.

In recent years there have been several influential court decisions regarding the patentability of inventions involving human thought, particularly methods of human diagnosis that include mental steps as claim elements. In 2006 the Supreme Court agreed to hear the appeal of *Laboratory Corporation of America Holdings v. Metabolite Laboratories*, a case involving US Patent 4,940,658, claiming methods for testing homocysteine levels in a patient, and then using the homocysteine levels thus measured to diagnose that patient. Laboratory Corporation first licensed these methods from Metabolite Laboratories, but then discontinued paying royalties to Metabolite Laboratories after switching to an alternate test owned by Abbott Laboratories. When Metabolite Laboratories subsequently sued it for patent infringement, Laboratory Corporation countered by arguing that the patent claim asserted against it—claim 13—was invalid because it impermissibly required a mental step. Claim 13 involved a "method for detecting a deficiency of cobalamin or folate" that included the step of "correlating an elevated level of total homocysteine in [a measured] body fluid with a deficiency of cobalamin or folate." At trial, the inventors of claim 13 agreed that "correlating" referred to recognition of an elevated concentration of homocysteine by a physician, and "would occur automatically in the mind of any competent physician." Both the district court and the CAFC found claim 13 valid. After accepting the appeal, the Supreme Court limited its inquiry to the following narrow question: "[w]hether a method patent . . . directing a party simply to 'correlate' test results can validly claim a monopoly over a basic scientific relationship . . . such that any doctor necessarily infringes the patent merely by thinking about the relationship after looking at a test result." In a surprise to both litigants, the Court finally declined to decide the case, instead deciding that it had granted *certiorari* improvidently.

Although the Court issued no decision on the merits of the case, Justice Stephen Breyer filed a vigorous dissent to the decision to dismiss the appeal, in which he made it clear that he would have found claim 13 invalid for requiring a mental step.

The Supreme Court considered the patentability of claims having mental steps again in 2010, this time issuing a decision in *Bilski v. Kappos*. In this case, the claimed invention at issue involved a method of hedging risk in commodity trading. Both the Board of Patent Appeals and Interferences (an administrative court within the USPTO) and the CAFC held the claims at issue invalid. The Supreme Court found similarly, stating that "[t]he patent application here can be rejected under our precedents on the unpatentability of abstract ideas."

In 2011 the Supreme Court agreed to hear *Mayo v. Prometheus*, an appeal whose central issue concerned the patentability of methods of diagnosis and therapy. The claims at issue involved three principle steps: (1) administration of thiopurine to a patient, (2) measurement of thiopurine in the patient, and (3) calibration of drug dosage to be administered to the patient based on the measured amount of thiopurine. The district court had held these claims to be unpatentable, while the CAFC reversed in 2010, instead finding the claims patentable.

Just one day after deciding *Bilski v. Kappos*, the Supreme Court ordered the CAFC to reconsider its decision in light of the Supreme Court's decision in *Bilski v. Kappos*. Upon reconsideration, the CAFC came to the same decision it had before, this time justifying its result based on the *Bilski v. Kappos* decision. Subsequently, the Supreme Court granted *certiorari* to hear an appeal of *Mayo v. Prometheus*. On March 20, 2012, the Supreme Court unanimously reversed the CAFC, holding that methods of using human metabolites in diagnosis and therapy do not qualify as patentable subject matter. This decision also effectively reversed the CAFC's recent decision in *Classen Immunotherapies v. Biogen IDEC*, a 2011 decision that had upheld the validity of several claims to methods of evaluating and improving the safety of immunization schedules. Justice Breyer's dissent in *Laboratory Corporation of America Holdings v. Metabolite Laboratories* in 2006 turned out to be a harbinger that the Supreme Court was on the verge of establishing a new and unforgiving rule against the patentability of methods of human diagnosis and treatment—a rule that accords with the wider trend against the patentability of human-related inventions. More recently, on June 19, 2014, the Supreme Court's decision in *Alice v. CLS Bank International* placed a capstone on this trend, confirming the principle that methods that, if patented, could constrain "building blocks of human ingenuity" are unpatentable subject matter. Like other human-related inventions, those based on human thought may not be patented.

Discussion and Conclusions

A Patent-Safe Harbor for Human-Related Innovation
It is too early to know precisely what scope of inventions Section 33 will exclude from patentability. Oddly for an issue as controversial as human experimentation, the AIA was not accompanied by any formal legislative history useful in interpreting what sorts of inventions Congress and the President intended Section 33 to cover. The phrase "directed to or encompassing a human organism" is vague on its face, and, although some of the words it contains are suggestive of language sometimes employed among patent attorneys, even this usage usually depends upon specific context to choose between alternative interpretations. Patent attorneys sometimes use the phrase "directed to" to indicate the core of a claimed invention, so "directed to . . . a human organism" could suggest that a claimed invention is essentially a human being per se. On the other hand, "directed to" could be interpreted to refer to an invention having a close connection to a human organism; human genes, hESCs, products of *in vivo* conversion, or thoughts might satisfy this criterion. The word "encompassing" is similar in meaning to "open transition phrases," such as "comprising" or "including," that link the introductory phrase of a claim with the specific elements recited by the claim. In this sense, its meaning implies that an invention would include an element (in this case, "a human organism") without excluding other elements from the invention. Under this interpretation, "encompassing a human organism" could mean any invention that includes, as one of its constituent elements, a human; methods of *in vivo* conversion or inventions including mental steps, such as methods of diagnosis or treatment of a human, might satisfy this interpretation. Without interpretive legislative history, the meaning of Section 33 will have to found elsewhere in the law, such as in the decisions of courts.

Unless Congress decides to amend it, clarification of Section 33 will only arrive in the form of the regulations and rules promulgated by the USPTO and judicial decisions delivered by the federal courts. In the meantime, valuable guidance is available in the form of judicial decisions concerning the patentability of human-related inventions, notably human genes, hESCs, products of *in vivo* conversion, and thought. The 2012 Supreme Court decision, *Mayo v. Prometheus*, and the same court's 2013 decision, *AMP v. Myriad*, exemplify this trend away from patent-eligibility for human-related inventions. Courts have not been indulgent when asked to enforce, find infringement of, or uphold the validity of human-related patents, suggesting that patent protection for such inventions is already generally weak at common law. The effect of Section 33 will probably be to undermine even further patent protection for human-related patents. Consistent with previous judicial decisions concerning patents claiming human-related inventions, such as *Mayo v. Prometheus* and *AMP v. Myriad*, Section 33 will likely prohibit not only those patents that claim human beings per se, but also emanate a wider penumbra of prohibition that excludes that patenting of other human-related inventions. This penumbra will likely include human genes, embryonic stem cells, products of *in vivo* conversion, thoughts, and other types of biotechnological inventions having close connections to "a human organism."

The patent-safe harbor Section 33 creates within biotechnology formalizes a trend in US patent law, but also brings US patent law into closer accord with the treatment of biotechnological inventions in European patent law. As noted above, the European Patent Convention and the European Union have both established formal legal limitations on human-related inventions, notably human genes, hESCs, thought, and methods of medical treatment and diagnosis. As in Europe, US patent law now formally recognizes a lacuna of unpatentable subject matter within biotechnology.

A Natural Experiment on Innovation without Patents

Section 33 now offers a valuable opportunity to observe a natural experiment on how innovation behaves when patent protection is formally removed. Biotechnology has operated within the context of robust patent protection since the Supreme Court decision in *Diamond v. Chakrabarty*. Moreover the biotechnology industry has long depended on the availability of patents to attract the investment necessary to justify large expenditures on research, development, and securing required federal regulatory approvals (Jasanoff 2005). If the successes of open and user innovation reported for fields outside biotechnology also translate into biotechnology, and, if patents hamper such innovation, then a patent-safe harbor could spur increased innovation in human-related biotechnology. The natural experiment in innovation made possible by Section 33 offers the possibility of falsifying the innovation-needs-patents assumption that pervades biotechnology, and identifying a new set of conditions in which patent protection does not drive innovation.

Human-Related Inventions as a Charter Technology

A patent-safe harbor may play a role in innovation analogous to the role that has been proposed for "charter cities." Fuller and Romer (2010) have suggested that special reform zones, called charter cities, might serve salutary purposes, such as fostering good governance practices, ensuring liberty for citizens, and encouraging economic prosperity. His proposal imagines that any country wishing to improve its governance and economy could set aside vacant land large enough for a city, import, establish, and enforce a set of rules already proven to promote good governance elsewhere, and then invite any people who agree to abide by these rules to immigrate to this new jurisdiction voluntarily. By supporting trustworthy laws and prosperity-supporting institutions in one geographically circumscribed region of a country otherwise plagued by untrustworthy laws and failing institutions, a charter city would allow its host country to run an experiment that compared new and old—and, perhaps, good and poor—governance. On the one hand, if the charter city produced desirable results, it could then provide a model for how to reform the laws and institutions of its host country. On the other hand, if the charter city were to underperform, or perform no better than, its host country, this result would also be useful in avoiding undesirable or detrimental reforms.

Section 33 may play a role analogous to a charter city, with human-related biotechnological inventions representing a "charter technology" within the wider field of biotechnology. If innovation thrives disproportionately within this charter technology in the absence of patent protection, Congress could use such results as a model for how to improve innovation outcomes in other fields of technology. Patent-safe harbors could be introduced in other fields of technology, and innovation outcomes similarly monitored. If open and user innovation in human-related biotechnology were to thrive in the absence of patent rights, this would provide a strong argument to policy makers to reconsider the assumption that the patent system is the best policy tool with which to encourage technological innovation.

A New Paradigm for Designing Innovation Policy

Some critics of patent rights suggest that the rate and quality of technological innovation might increase *sans* patent protection (von Hippel 2005; Benkler 2006; Boldrin and Levine 2008). Section 33 may allow this proposition to be tested, at least with respect to a circumscribed field of research within biotechnology. The results of this experiment could influence future public policy by helping to guide the wise choice of legal instruments for promoting innovation. Without patent protection, innovation in human-related biotechnology may thrive, or it may not. Some fields of technological innovation may respond better than others to patent-free conditions. A decrease in the rate or quality of innovation in the absence of patent protection could even reinforce the current orthodoxy that patents best spur innovation. Regardless of the results of the experiment Section 33 has made possible, it is an experiment in technological innovation that is well worth conducting and learning from. It provides a rare opportunity to tip the balance of innovation policy away from patent protection and toward open and user innovation.

References

Benkler, Y. 2006. *The Wealth of Networks: How Social Production Transforms Markets and Freedom*. New Haven: Yale University Press.

Bessen, J., and M. Meurer. 2008. *Patent Failure: How Judges, Bureaucrats, and Lawyers Put Innovators at Risk*. Princeton: Princeton University Press.

Boldrin, M., and D. K. Levine. 2008. *Against Intellectual Monopoly*. New York: Cambridge University Press.

Burk, D. L., and M. A. Lemley. 2009. *The Patent Crisis and How the Courts Can Solve It*. Chicago: The University of Chicago Press.

Crease, D., and G. Schlich. 2003. Is there a future for "speculative" gene patents in Europe? *Nature Reviews. Drug Discovery* 2 (5): 407–10.

Crichton, M. 2007. Patenting life. *New York Times*, February 13: A2.

Fuller, B., and P. Romer. 2010. Cities from scratch: A new path for development. *City Journal* (New York) 20 (4).

Goodwin, M. 2006. *Black markets: The Supply and Demand of Body Parts*. New York: Cambridge University Press.

Heller, M. A., and R. S. Eisenberg. 1998. Can patents deter innovation? The anticommons in biomedical research. *Science* 280 (5364): 698–701.

Hollon, T. 2000. Gene patent revisions to remove some controversies. *Nature Medicine* 6 (4): 362–63.

Jaffe, A. B., and J. Lerner. 2006. *Innovation and Its Discontents: How Our Broken Patent System Is Endangering Innovation and Progress, and What to Do about It*. Princeton: Princeton University Press.

Jasanoff, S. 2005. *Designs on Nature*. Princeton: Princeton University Press.

Jensen, K., and F. Murray. 2005. Intellectual property landscape of the human genome. *Science* 310 (5746): 239–40.

Madoff, R. D. 2010. *Immortality and the Law—The Rising Power of the American Dead*. New Haven: Yale University Press.

Moser, P. 2005. How do patent laws influence innovation? Evidence from nineteenth-century World Fairs. *American Economic Review* 95 (4): 1215–36.

Purves, D., E. M. Brannon, R. Cabeza, S. A. Huettel, K. S. LaBar, M. L. Platt, and M. Woldorff. 2008. *Principles of Cognitive Neuroscience*. Sunderland, MA: Sinauer Associates.

Rao, R. 2007. Genes and spleens: Property, contract, or privacy rights in the human body? *Journal of Law, Medicine and Ethics* 35 (3): 371–382.

Rimmer, M. 2008. *Intellectual Property and Biotechnology—Biological Inventions*. Cheltenham, UK: Edward Elgar.

Silverman, R. B. 2004. *The Organic Chemistry of Drug Design and Drug Action*, 2nd ed. Burlington, MA: Elsevier Academic.

Strandburg, K. J. 2008. Users as innovators: Implications for patent doctrine. *University of Colorado Law Review* 79 (46): 467–544.

Torrance, A. W. 2007. Patents to the rescue: Disasters and patent law. *DePaul Journal of Health Care Law* 10 (3): 309–58.

Torrance, A. W. 2008. Physiological steps doctrine. *Berkeley Technology Law Journal* 23 (4): 1471–1505.

Torrance, A. W. 2009. Neurobiology and patenting thought. *IDEA the Journal of Law and Technology* 50: 27–58.

Torrance, A. W., and W. M. Tomlinson. 2009. Patents and the regress of useful arts. *Columbia Science and Technology Law Review* 10: 130–68.

Torrance, A. W. 2010a. Gene concepts, gene talk, and gene patents. *Minnesota Journal of Law, Science and Technology* 11 (1): 157–91.

Torrance, A. W. 2010b. Synthesizing law for synthetic biology. *Minnesota Journal of Law, Science and Technology* 11 (2): 629–64.

Torrance, A. W. 2013. The unpatentable human being. *Hastings Center Report* 43 (5): 10–11.

Torrance, A. W., and L. J. Kahl. 2014. Bringing standards to life: Synthetic biology standards and intellectual property. *Santa Clara High Technology Law Journal* 30 (2): 199–230.

Torrance, A. W., and W. M. Tomlinson. 2011. Property rules, liability rules, and patents: One experimental view of the cathedral. *Yale Journal of Law and Technology* 14 (1): 138–61.

von Hippel, E. 2005. *Democratizing Innovation.* Cambridge: MIT Press.

IV

User-Innovators in New Roles

14

When Do User-Innovators Start Firms? A Theory of User Entrepreneurship

Sonali K. Shah and Mary Tripsas

The importance of user innovation as a source of novel technologies and products has been well documented in the innovation literature (von Hippel 1988; Kline and Pinch 1996; Oudshoorn and Pinch 2003). Users innovate frequently and create economically significant innovations. Research in this tradition has posited that although users innovate, they do not generally attempt to commercialize their innovations (von Hippel 1988). The established wisdom is that users frequently contribute their innovations to manufacturers for commercialization, capturing limited economic benefit beyond their own use.

Recent studies, however, point to many cases where users found firms to capture economic value from their innovations. Entrepreneurial users have commercialized their own innovations in industries ranging from medical devices to sporting equipment, ice harvesting to juvenile products, and stereo components to new media (Langlois and Robinson 1992; Utterback 1994; Shah 2005; Shah and Tripsas 2007; Haefliger et al. 2010; Winston Smith and Shah 2014). This phenomenon has been labeled *user entrepreneurship* (Shah and Tripsas 2007). The process by which user-innovators become entrepreneurs differs from the typical entrepreneurial journey. Users tend to experience a need in their own lives, develop an innovation to address their need, and sometimes even openly share their solution with others *before* commercializing a product. Many users are "accidental entrepreneurs" in that starting a for-profit company was not the initial motivation for their innovation, but rather the outcome of a journey inspired by their own needs (Shah and Tripsas 2007). Surprisingly, user entrepreneurship occurs frequently and across many industries: 46.6 percent of innovative startups founded in the United States in 2004 that survive to age five are founded by users (Shah et al. 2011).

We make sense of these varied empirical findings by developing a theory of user entrepreneurship that explains when users are likely to commercialize their innovations as opposed to simply benefiting from their use. More specifically, we articulate the conditions under which users, manufacturers, neither, or both are likely to enter the product market. Our model hinges upon the interplay of two factors experienced by both users and manufacturers: their estimates of the financial returns to entering the product market and their profit thresholds. User's and other manufacturers' estimates are likely to differ due to access to complementary assets, information asymmetries, and distinct interpretations of available information. Our model suggests that users are most likely to commercialize their innovations when they have access to complementary assets such as distribution channels (e.g., Teece 1986), when they possess informational advantages enabling them to uniquely identify opportunities that established firms would underestimate, and when the rents from entrepreneurial activity exceed the opportunity costs of their time. These factors help explain why user entrepreneurs are likely to spawn the creation of altogether new product markets and even industries. We illustrate the model with examples from the field of consumer sporting goods.

The User Innovation Phenomenon

A rich and distinguished body of research from a variety of disciplines has documented the importance of user innovations (e.g., von Hippel 1988; Oudshoorn and Pinch 2003). Anecdotal examples of user innovation have been described in the literature for decades, but von Hippel produced the first systematic documentation and theoretical development of the concept in a series of articles leading to the publication of *The Sources of Innovation* in 1988. This detailed and thorough body of work has shown us that users are an important and frequent source of innovation, that they innovate across a wide variety of product domains, and that their innovations may be qualitatively different than those of manufacturers. This research also held that users rarely, if ever, commercialize their own innovations, however this assumption has been challenged and corrected by empirical evidence that has emerged over the past ten years. We review each of these empirical patterns below.

Numerous studies conducted during the last 30 years have documented the importance and magnitude of user innovation in a wide range of industries, offering the following key insights. (1) *Many important innovations are developed by users.* Users are responsible for creating a large fraction—and sometimes even the majority—of key innovations in a wide variety of product domains, including medical devices, scientific instruments, semiconductors, software, and sports equipment (for a review of this literature, see von Hippel 2005). For example, 76 percent of the key innovations in the field of scientific instruments (von Hippel 1976), 67 percent of the key innovations in semiconductor and electronics subassembly manufacturing equipment (von Hippel 1977), and 60 percent of the innovations in consumer sporting equipment (Shah 2005) were developed by users. (2) *A large fraction of users innovate.* Many individuals innovate to solve their own unique needs, resulting in a large number of innovations (Morrison et al. 2000; Franke and Shah 2003; Franke and von Hippel 2003; Lüthje et al. 2005). For example, 26 percent of the users of library information systems (Morrison et al. 2000), 19 percent of the users of Apache security software (Franke and von Hippel 2003), and up to 38 percent of consumer sports enthusiasts (Franke and Shah 2003; Lüthje et al. 2005) report innovating for their own use. Even in the general population, user innovation is common: In a recent survey of 2,019 consumers in the United Kingdom, 6.2 percent of respondents reported engaging in user innovation (von Hippel et al. 2012). (3) *Users innovate over a wide variety of product domains.* Users have created radical and incremental innovations across a range of product classes, industries, and scientific disciplines (Nuvolari 2004; Shah 2005; von Hippel 2005). In additions to the fields mentioned above, these include industries as diverse as automobiles, astronomy equipment (i.e., telescopes), medical devices, and designs for blast furnaces (Allen 1983; Kline and Pinch 1996; Franz 1999; Ferris 2002; Chatterji and Fabrizio 2011).

Existing work also suggests that the *content* of user innovations is distinct from manufacturer innovations: In a study of scientific equipment innovations, user innovations tended to embody more novel functionality—that is, they tended to do altogether new things—whereas manufacturer innovations tended to address needs that are more widely recognized (Riggs and von Hippel 1994). Lead user theory takes this observation a step further and suggests that *some* user innovations will presage the creation of new market niches. Lead users (1) experience needs months or years before the bulk of the marketplace encounters them and (2) are positioned to benefit significantly by obtaining a solution to those needs (von Hippel 1986). Product concepts developed by lead users are often rated more highly—and are often more profitable for manufacturers—than those developed by the manufacturers alone (von Hippel 1986; Urban and von Hippel 1988; von Hippel et al. 1999).

Finally, early theory proposed that innovative users would *not* engage in economic activity through either licensing or commercialization. Instead, it argued that manufacturers of existing or related equipment would find out about user innovations, refine them, and introduce them to the market if they had commercial value (von Hippel 1988).[1] Early empirical studies seemed to support this view. For example, in the field of scientific instruments, user innovations include the electron microscope, well-regulated high voltage power supplies, and the high temperature specimen stage. Innovating users—often academic scientists or technicians—communicated their ideas to others via publication, symposia, and visits with other users (von Hippel 1988). In the case of innovations to the semiconductor and printed circuit board assembly processes, von Hippel (1988) notes that details of the transfer process between users and manufacturers were not well documented, but it appears that innovating users (most often employees of user firms) shared their information freely with the staff of other user and manufacturer firms.

These studies appear to support the assumption that users innovate, but do not engage in commercialization activity; however, we believe that these early results were driven by the contexts studied: many studies conducted in the first 25 years of this literature that focused on innovations made by employees of firms or users who were academic scientists. These users faced significant opportunity costs to starting a firm, and therefore relayed their ideas to manufacturers for integration into future products. Noncompetition agreements might have restricted some innovative users from engaging in entrepreneurial opportunities in fields similar to their employers. In addition many academic scientists *want* to be scientists (e.g., see Stern 2004) or could have felt inhibited from starting a venture due to cultural norms within their professional societies, decreasing the appeal of an entrepreneurial venture. As a result most users could have confined their activities to innovation, and those that did commercialize or license their innovations would have appeared to be outliers (to point, a close reading of the early user innovation literature shows that in a small number of cases, users—although not necessarily the user who created the innovation—became equipment producers; see von Hippel 1988: 24).

Recent theoretical and empirical work indicate that innovative users engage in entrepreneurship (Franke and Shah 2003; Shah 2005; Baldwin et al. 2006; Mody 2006; Shah and Tripsas 2007; Shah and Mody 2014). Next we briefly present data on the prevalence and significance of user entrepreneurship. Then, we present a model that predicts when users will become entrepreneurs. Applying the parameters of this model will help us reconcile why early studies of user innovation found little evidence of user entrepreneurship, despite its pervasiveness as a phenomenon.

The Prevalence and Significance of User Entrepreneurship

Data from several recent studies paint a striking picture of the phenomenon of user entrepreneurship. These studies illustrate both the prevalence of user entrepreneurship and the importance of user entrepreneurship as a mechanism for introducing innovations into industrial systems.

Prevalence

A recent study finds that 10.7 percent of all startups and 46.6 percent of innovative startups founded in the United States in 2004 that survive to age five are founded by users (Shah et al. 2011). User entrepreneurship occurs in vastly different industries. Physicians frequently innovate and commercialize novel devices to treat their patients: 29 percent of US-based medical device startups were founded by physicians (Chatterji 2009). In the juvenile products industry (firms producing products for infants and toddlers, such as strollers, car seats, diaper bags, etc.), 84 percent of the firms present in the market in 2007 were founded by users, namely parents, grandparents, and babysitters.

Technological Significance

Entrepreneurship by users introduces technological change into the industrial system. At a high level, innovative startups founded by users are more likely to possess patents—indicators of the technological knowledge possessed by the venture—than other startups (Shah et al. 2011). While some user entrepreneurs commercialize incremental product improvements, others introduce groundbreaking new products that spark the creation of new industries as diverse as extreme sports (Shah 2005) and atomic force microscopy (Mody 2006). In extreme sports, 43 percent of all key innovations were first commercialized by the users who developed them (Shah 2005). In the atomic force microscopy industry, all (three) early firms were founded by users or individuals closely connected to users (Mody 2006). In the typesetter industry, two out of three major technological revolutions were ignited by products developed and introduced into the marketplace by user entrepreneurs (Tripsas 2008). User entrepreneurs were among the first to commercially produce *Machinima*, a new film genre characterized by shooting film in video games (Haefliger et al. 2010). Similarly Winston Smith and Shah (2014) argued and found evidence supporting the notion that user entrepreneurs introduce *highly novel* insights into the industrial system. These studies highlight the innovative contributions of these firms to society and the commercial marketplace.

Economic Significance

Firms founded by user entrepreneurs differ in meaningful ways from both the average startup and even from other innovative firms (Shah et al. 2011).[2] Firms founded by *professional user entrepreneurs*—users whose innovations were meant for use in a previous job or business—are less likely to be founded at home, less reliant on self-financing, more likely to have revenues, and generate higher revenues than both comparison groups. The data suggest that professional user entrepreneurs may be particularly highly skilled and may also reap significant pecuniary benefits through entrepreneurship.

In contrast, firms founded by *end-user entrepreneurs*—users whose innovations were meant for personal use—may possess fewer resources and come from less privileged populations. Firms founded by end-users employ fewer workers, have lower revenues, are more likely to be founded at home and operate from home five years after founding, are more heavily self-financed five years after founding, and are less likely to receive bank financing. End-user entrepreneurs are more likely to be female and members of minority groups. Specifically, they are more likely to be an

American Indian, Alaskan Native, or Black, and less likely to be Asian. End user entrepreneurship may be one of the few entrepreneurial paths followed by members of these groups—and hence worth investigating further as a path toward meaningful career options and economic self-sufficiency.

Despite these differences, firms whose founders are professional user-entrepreneurs or end-user entrepreneurs each introduce novel or customized products into the marketplace and are more likely than other firms to receive venture capital financing and obtain patents than firms in either comparison groups. Specifically, 5.8 percent of firms founded by professional user-entrepreneurs and 4.0 percent of firms founded by end user-entrepreneurs receive venture capital financing in their first five years of operation, versus 1.1 percent of all startups and 3.7 percent of other innovative firms. This is a striking finding: The venture capital interest in these firms suggests that user-entrepreneurs commercialize innovations with high market potential more frequently than other entrepreneurs.

A Theory of User Entrepreneurship

We next develop a model that predicts when a user will attempt to appropriate financial benefit from his or her innovation by commercializing it—through patent licensing, patent assignment, or by entering the product market—as opposed to simply benefiting through use and letting manufacturers exploit any potential commercial value. Our conceptualization of manufacturers is a broad one: It includes any manufacturer, typically firms that operate in the same or a related industry or that possess relevant complementary assets.[3] At the core of our model is the notion that users and manufacturers differ along two critical dimensions: their estimates of the financial returns to entering the product market and their profit thresholds. Depending on the magnitude of these differences, we propose alternative commercialization outcomes.

Sources of Divergence in User and Manufacturer Estimates of Financial Returns

When deciding whether to commercialize an innovation, potential entrants estimate financial returns based on a number of factors, including projected market size and growth, customer needs, competitive conditions, and the firm's unique ability to add value. Users and manufacturers are likely to have different estimates of the profit potential from commercializing the same innovation for many reasons, including complementary assets, information asymmetries, and differing interpretations of available information.

The commercialization of any technology in the product market requires complementary assets such as access to distribution, brand recognition, or manufacturing capability (Teece 1986). In situations where necessary complementary assets are controlled by established manufacturers and potential new entrants cannot contract for those assets, successful new entry is difficult, even if new entrants possess superior technical solutions (Tripsas 1997; Gans and Stern 2003). Under these conditions user-innovators would be at a disadvantage, and manufacturers' estimated profits would exceed those of users. Manufacturers will also have a higher profit estimate if they can achieve a superior cost position by leveraging existing capital-intensive manufacturing facilities or taking advantage of economies of scope in other activities such as distribution (Teece 1986; Baldwin et al. 2006).

Information asymmetries are another source of the disparity between users' and manufacturers' expected profits. Informational advantages have long been recognized as a source of entrepreneurial opportunity (Shane and Venkataraman 2000). Schumpeter (1934) argued that the constant state of disequilibrium in which economies operate, and the resulting unequal distribution of information, enables actors with informational advantages to earn entrepreneurial profits. Similarly unequal distribution of knowledge creates asymmetries in beliefs about the potential profits associated with entrepreneurial activity, resulting in new entry by parties who have "discovered" an opportunity first (Hayek 1945).

Users are often better positioned than manufacturers to both recognize and commercialize an innovation given their unique, private knowledge of the market. In particular, users have significant informational advantages in emerging markets where the knowledge is rapidly evolving, sticky, and difficult to verify. When a market is new, needs are uncertain and continuously evolving (Clark 1985). Potential consumers—the likely subjects of firm-sponsored market research—have not used the product and therefore have difficulty articulating their preferences, making it difficult for manufacturers to gauge market potential (von Hippel 1986; Nonaka and Takeuchi 1995). Use, however, enables learning about the product's reliability, its durability, what features are valuable, and how the product works in combination with other products. Experimentation, an important element for managing uncertainty in novel ventures (Murray and Tripsas 2004) occurs naturally through usage. Experienced users are thus best positioned to create and understand needs for these novel products. In addition users have an advantage since knowledge of needs might be "sticky," meaning costly to access, transfer, and use in a new location, even when both the sender and receiver are committed to its transfer (Polanyi 1958; von Hippel 1994; Szulanski 1996; Tyre and von Hippel 1997).

Users may also be well positioned to create, refine, diffuse, and value an innovation through participation in innovation communities (Franke and Shah 2003; Shah 2005; Baldwin et al. 2006). Community members are likely to provide assistance with improving and refining the innovation, thereby improving the design and functionality of the product. If the innovation is adopted by many community participants, the user-innovator can observe its value and begin to assess others' willingness to pay. In fact some user-entrepreneurs did not think to produce their innovation for sale to others until after receiving multiple requests to purchase a copy of the innovation (Shah 2005).

In addition to having preferential access to information, user-innovators may also interpret the information related to an innovation through a different lens from manufacturers. Individuals with different backgrounds have been found to perceive different sources of value in the exact same technology, highlighting the importance of prior experience in the conception of opportunity (Shane 2000) and the framing of a new product category (Benner and Tripsas 2012). Since users are not embedded in the existing industry belief systems of manufacturers, their interpretation of the potential value of an innovation will likely differ.

Sources of Divergence in User and Manufacturer Profit Thresholds

We propose that, on average, users will require a lower profit threshold than manufacturers to justify entering the product market. Lower profit thresholds can result from a user's lower opportunity costs or from non-economic factors (e.g., personal preference, legal barriers).

Opportunity costs—what the user would forego to start a firm—will vary by profession. The innovative bicycling enthusiast who is also an orthopedic surgeon will likely require higher financial returns to start a bicycle firm than the innovative bicycling enthusiast who is a "sports fanatic"—taking odd jobs in order to support a sports-centric lifestyle. Amit et al. (1995) provide large-sample empirical support for this phenomenon. A user-innovator may also choose to start a firm in her spare time. Such a decision generally decreases the profit threshold required of the business as returns are viewed as additional—rather than primary—sources of income.

Considerable research indicates that many entrepreneurs are motivated, at least in part, by noneconomic goals, including the satisfaction derived from self-employment or from engaging in work that they enjoy (Smith and John 1983; Lafuente and Salas 1989; Gimeno et al. 1997; Scott-Morton and Podolny 2002). Starting a business may be the user-innovator's vehicle for fulfilling these goals. The utility generated from self-employment or working in an area that she is passionate about may lead the user-innovator to substitute "love" for "money" (Douglas and Shepherd 1999).

In general, one would expect manufacturers to have higher profit thresholds than individual users since nonmonetary personal benefits are not included as part of the upside when evaluating the venture. Instead, investments are viewed relative to a set of possible projects competing for resources. Many firms even have a "hurdle rate" that new projects must exceed in order to receive funding (Bower 1970; Brealey and Myers 1984).

Commercialization Outcomes

In this section we describe commercialization outcomes for the user innovation using examples from the sporting goods industry.[4] The general context of sports equipment is appropriate for two reasons. First, new sports emerge relatively frequently. It is therefore possible to study the economic and social history of new sports via primary data collection methods, including discussions with early innovators and other actors. Second, the fields are relatively free of government regulation compared to some other industries (e.g., pharmaceuticals), a factor that could shift activity toward firms and institutions able to bear legal and financial risk.

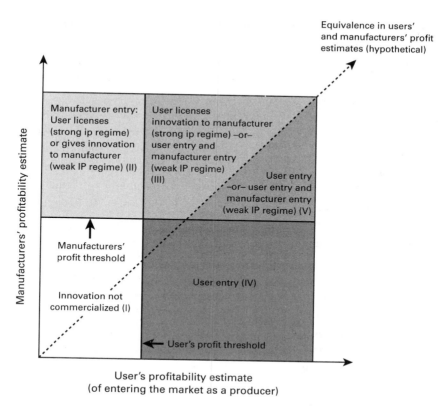

Figure 14.1

Region I: Innovation Not Commercialized

In region I of figure 14.1, we predict that a user innovation will not be commercialized; its projected returns fall below the profit threshold of both users and manufacturers. This situation would prevail when an innovation meets idiosyncratic user needs such that neither the user nor the manufacturer would expect high levels of demand (Franke and von Hippel 2003). Similarly commercializing incremental user innovations that add only a small amount of value relative to the overall value of the product would not likely appeal to either users or manufacturers. Such innovations may still diffuse from user to user, even though they are not commercialized. That said, if the innovation becomes popular enough, manufacturers might incorporate it into their product designs at a later point.

Region II: Manufacturer Entry: User Licenses (Strong IP Regime) or Gives Innovation to Manufacturer (Weak IP Regime)

In region II of figure 14.1, the user's estimated profit from entry falls below his or her threshold level, but the manufacturer's estimated profit exceeds its threshold. Many of the innovations studied in the first two decades of the user innovation literature fall into this category; for example, we see this pattern in the field of scientific instruments, where scientists face high opportunity costs to starting a business, so manufacturers commercialize user innovations (von Hippel 1976). Such conditions might also exist when established firms control essential complementary assets, thereby leading the user to either give the innovation to a manufacturer for commercialization or license it if the intellectual property regime[5] is strong. Since the manufacturer's estimated profit from product market entry exceeds its threshold, the manufacturer should be a willing licensee.

Sherman Poppen is an example of a user-innovator in region II. The "formal" history of the snowboard began with Poppen's *Snurfer* (short for *snow surfer*) (Stevens 1998). Poppen was a full-time chemical gases engineer in Muskegon, Michigan, with several industrial gas patents to his name. His opportunity costs for starting a business were most likely high and his professional training likely made him familiar with the patent and licensing process. Poppen licensed his patented *Snurfer* design to an existing manufacturer of children's toys. The *Snurfer* became commercially quite successful. In fact many subsequent snowboarding innovators first experienced the thrill of the sport as children riding on Poppen's *Snurfers*.

Sherman Poppen's background and actions suggest a potential area for future research: Are user-innovators with prior knowledge of the intellectual property system more likely to protect and then license their innovations out than are other user-innovators? Are such user-innovators equally or less likely to share their innovations with others and hence less likely to benefit from community involvement?

Region III: User Licenses Innovation to Manufacturer (Strong IP Regime) or User and Manufacturer Both Enter Product Market (Weak IP Regime)

In region III both the user's and the manufacturer's profit estimates are above their profit thresholds; however, the manufacturer expects to achieve a higher financial return than the user does. These conditions provide the user an opportunity to either enter the product market or attempt to license the innovation to a manufacturer.

Whether the user enters the product market or licenses in this situation will depend upon three factors: the intellectual property regime for the innovation, the newness of the market, and the licensing fees the user is able to extract given the difference in the user's and manufacturer's expected profits. We discuss each factor below.

If the intellectual property regime in the product area surrounding the innovation is strong—for instance, when patents are effective—then there is a market for ideas (Gans and Stern 2003) and the user can attempt to license. If the intellectual property regime is weak, the user's only commercialization alternative is to enter the product market. It is also possible that the costs of patenting and/or enforcing a patent are high enough that licensing is no longer viable, leaving product market entry as the preferred alternative.

When a market is relatively new, the costs of contracting are likely to be high due to the time and effort required to explain the technology and/ or describe the market, and take into account contingencies arising from the high uncertainty. If the cost of contracting is high, the user is more likely to start a firm than attempt licensing.

Finally, if licensing seems feasible (because the intellectual property regime is strong and the cost of contracting is low), a negotiation between the manufacturer and user will determine whether the user enters the product market or licenses. Because the manufacturer's estimate of the profitability of the market is *higher* than the user's in region III, there is a good chance that a licensing agreement that appeals to the user can be negotiated. We believe that licensing will be a common outcome in this region. However, in some cases, manufacturers will not be interested in licensing the innovation and users seeking to financially benefit from their innovation will need to enter the market as entrepreneurs. Manufacturers may choose to enter the market as well, particularly in industries characterized by weak intellectual property regimes.

In the field of windsurfing, a user-innovator was granted a patent on *camber inducers* in the 1980s—a product used to hold the leading edge of the sail stable and hence generate greater stability and power. At this point windsurfing was a young but established market, manufacturers acknowledged the value of the innovation, and those manufacturers expected to profit by commercializing the innovation and selling it as a component of a full windsurfer. As a result it is likely that the manufacturers might have expected to profit more highly from commercializing the innovation than its inventor might have profited by selling the innovation on its own. So he chose to license the patent to a large firm. Initially he consulted for the firm and received royalty payments. Unfortunately, the royalty payments stopped when the manufacturer's management changed and the consulting relationship ended. The case was brought to court and decided in the innovator's favor; however, the innovator never received the full royalty payment. This example illustrates the difficulty faced by user-innovators when licensing to large, established firms with financial and legal resources. This user may well have been better off entering the product market himself.

Region IV: User-Entrepreneur Enters the Product Market

In region IV of figure 14.1 we predict that the user-innovator would choose to enter the product market. Since the expected profit exceeds his or her profit threshold, but not the manufacturer's, this is the only commercialization option available to the user.

A description of innovation activities among "the Hawaiians" conveys the flavor of innovation, fun, and competition that can result in product market entry. The Hawaiians were a group of 4 to 7 people in their early 20s who lived together in a house in Kailua, Hawaii, in the 1970 through the early 1980s. They windsurfed daily off a beach near their house. As they experienced the very high wind and wave conditions common to the area and experimented with various new windsurfing techniques and tricks, new needs emerged—needs that the existing equipment could not fulfill. They innovated in order to tailor the equipment to the conditions they were experiencing and the techniques they were developing. As people who saw or heard about their advanced sailing techniques and equipment asked to purchase the equipment, the Hawaiians made and sold handmade copies of the products from their house (for the first 3 or 4 years) and then from a small storefront. Eventually their brand became one of the most popular in the windsurfing industry.

Why did the Hawaiians—and not an established manufacturer—commercialize their innovations? The Hawaiians valued the commercial potential of the innovations more highly than manufacturers and possessed a lower profit threshold. In fact we know that the Hawaiians presented their early innovations to an existing manufacturer and asked the manufacturer to consider producing the innovations (they did not request financial remuneration). The manufacturer declined. The Hawaiians then shared their prototypical designs with friends and visitors to the island of Hawaii who witnessed the fun they derived from the sport, and contributed articles describing how to make and use the innovations to early enthusiast newsletters. Eventually they received requests from enthusiasts interested in buying the innovation; these requests signaled the potential profitability of the innovation in the then-emerging commercial marketplace. In addition the Hawaiians possessed a low profit threshold as their opportunity costs for starting a business were low: Most of them worked in the tourism and construction industries in order to live a sports-centered lifestyle in Hawaii.

Region V: User-Entrepreneur Enters the Product Market—and So Do Manufacturers When the IP Regime Is Weak

In region V the value of commercializing the innovation exceeds both the user's and the manufacturer's profitability thresholds, with the user's estimate being higher. The manufacturer's willingness to pay for a license will be based on a lower estimate of the potential opportunity, and therefore, it is unlikely the user would be able to negotiate a licensing deal that is more attractive than product market entry regardless of the strength of the intellectual property regime. However, in this region, manufacturers will also find product market entry attractive and may choose to enter in weak intellectual property regimes where they can either invent around or even copy the innovation freely.

Extensions

The model we present here is a simple and stylized one; however, it can be used to explain changes in commercialization outcomes over time and commercialization outcomes in different intellectual property regimes. Over time, users and manufacturers might adjust their profitability estimates, leading them to enter or exit the product space. In particular, many users who create a new market may exit if the market does not grow, whereas many manufacturers may observe a small market grow and subsequently enter. This issue is more pronounced in the early stages of industry formation where commercial activity may be sparked by users in regions I and IV. As the industry matures, manufacturers will enter the product market, initiating activity in regions III and V. As existing firms begin to dominate an industry, subsequent user innovations may be commercialized in region II. Recent work in the sports equipment and film industries provide preliminary support for these predictions (Shah 2005; Haefliger et al. 2010).

Discussion and Conclusions

The importance, frequency, and pervasiveness of the phenomenon of user entrepreneurship suggests that it is a vital component of the innovation ecosystem worthy of further study, further theoretical and conceptual development, and integration into existing theories of innovation and economic change. In this chapter we developed a theory of user entrepreneurship and articulated the conditions under which user-innovators are likely to commercialize their innovations as opposed to simply using them. We examined differences between users and manufacturers along two dimensions, while also taking into account the strength of the appropriability regime: their assessment of the innovation's profit potential, and their required profit threshold. The model allows us to explain when users will share innovations freely with manufacturers, license innovations to manufacturers, or attempt to commercialize their innovations independently. By parsing out the underlying drivers of commercialization decisions, the model reconciles the existing literature on user innovation, which documents user innovations being commercialized by existing manufacturers, with the phenomenon of user entrepreneurship.

The model also allows us to identify the factors that make a product context particularly *favorable* for user entrepreneurship. These conditions include open product design, modular product architecture, early stages of the industry life cycle, and government regulation that small, early-stage ventures can comprehend and afford to comply with. By making it easier for users to experiment with a product, open product design and modular product architecture enable user innovation and thus user entrepreneurship. In addition modular product architectures have standardized, documented interfaces among components, thereby allowing innovation by more actors and entry by more firms (Langlois and Robinson 1992; Baldwin and Clark 2000). The stage of the industry life cycle can also make it more or less difficult for users to start firms; in general, user-entrepreneurs will have an advantage over established firms during the early, fluid phase of industry development, although conditions may favor their emergence throughout the industry life cycle (e.g., as parts or components suppliers in modular product domains). Finally, significant government regulation may also lead to low levels of user innovation and user entrepreneurship, *if* such regulation significantly increases barriers to entry by new firms. To this end, some government agencies lower the financial costs of regulatory approval for startup firms in order to increase competition, while providing consumer safeguards.

Theoretical Contributions

The model has implications for theories of innovation, entrepreneurship, and industry evolution. Innovations—and their diffusion—are critical to economic progress (Solow 1957). Understanding the ways in which user innovations are commercialized brings us a step closer to understanding how to support the commercial diffusion of innovative ideas. To date, only two studies have documented content differences between knowledge generated by users and other sources (Riggs and von Hippel 1994; Winston Smith and Shah 2014). Our model also suggests—albeit indirectly—that user knowledge contains more novel content than knowledge from other sources.

Entrepreneurship scholars have focused much attention on spin-outs from incumbent firms (also referred to as *employee entrepreneurship*) (Klepper and Sleeper 2005; Franco et al. 2009). A robust line of research examines how these startups differ from their parents. It is likely that a high fraction of employee-founded firms are also user-founded firms, allowing employees to benefit from their knowledge of a particular industry without competing with their parent firm; they may even become a supplier to their parent firm (data in Shah et al. 2011 provide support for this idea). Finally, analyzing the behaviors of user-entrepreneurs enriches our theoretical understanding of the sources of entrepreneurial ideas and drivers of new firm formation. In particular, the user-entrepreneurship phenomenon highlights the importance of social interactions and prior experience in identifying and framing opportunities (Shah 2005; Shah and Tripsas 2007; Shah and Mody 2014). Whereas past work has emphasized the importance of beliefs that originate from prior industry experience (e.g., Shane 2000; Benner and Tripsas 2012), user-entrepreneurship research emphasizes the importance of beliefs that originate from interactions associated with use.

Many firms enter and exit during the early or "fluid" phase of industry development; however, existing research tells us little about where these firms come from (Tushman and Anderson 1986; Utterback and Suarez 1993; Fligstein 2001; McKendrick and Carroll 2001; Agarwal and Gort 2002). This chapter suggests that at least some of these firms are founded by user-innovators, and that user-entrepreneurs have informational advantages over other entrepreneurs due to rapidly developing and evolving user preferences, participation in innovation communities, and knowledge from experimentation and use. User-innovators and user-entrepreneurs may also play a role in creating technological discontinuities or subsequent eras of ferment. These areas are ripe for elaboration.

Policy Implications

Much government policy, firm strategy, and academic research has been guided by the assumption that profit-driven firms, supported by regimes with strong intellectual property rights, drive product innovation and commercialization (Schumpeter 1934; Demsetz 1967; Dosi 1988).[6] As we have seen, user-entrepreneurs also engage in innovation and commercialization activity; however, many user-entrepreneurs are guided by different motives. As a result the impact of these policies on user-innovators and user-entrepreneurs needs to be carefully examined. First, while intellectual property protection methods should ideally protect the rights of users as well as manufacturers who innovate, a better understanding of whether or not the system upholds the rights of user-innovators in practice is needed and system-wide safeguards or additional policies might need to be put into place to prevent inequity. Second, user-innovators may be less likely to patent innovations immediately, instead choosing first to share the innovation with others. Some user-innovators purposely release their work into the public sphere in order to benefit from incremental improvements on the innovation by other users. As a result they may be prevented by law from patenting if they do not file for patent protection within the first year after disclosing details of the innovation. While such sharing is discouraged by the existing system, it is these very behaviors that help generate interest in the product and give rise to new product markets. Policy makers wishing to spur economic growth by crafting programs and policies that encourage and support startup activity should consider the prevalence, technological importance, and distinctive behaviors of user-entrepreneurs. Who will commercialize a user innovation? Note: This illustration sets the user's profit threshold at a lower level the manu-facturer's profit threshold.

Notes

We thank Rajshree Agarwal, Janet Bercovitz, Glenn Hoetker, Andrew Torrance, and Charlie Williams for thoughtful comments on this manuscript.

1. The situation is similar in the history and sociology of technology literature: although users might relay product preferences to designers or perhaps even inno-vate for themselves, it was largely assumed that users do *not* engage in economic or commercial activity (Oudshoorn and Pinch 2003).

2. Conduct of R&D in the first year of operations is the proxy used to identify other innovative firms.

3. The conceptual model can also be used to consider when non-user-founded start-ups might commercialize a user innovation. Such firms would likely fall somewhere between users and manufacturers in terms of the information they possess and their assessments of the innovation's profit potential.

4. Examples of sporting equipment innovations and their commercial histories are based on descriptions and analyses found in Franke and Shah (2003) and Shah (2005).

5. By intellectual property regime, we are primarily referring to the effectiveness of formal IP mechanisms such as patents or copyright, in the industry context in which the user is engaged. See, for instance, Cohen, Nelson, and Walsh (2000) for a discussion of how the strength of the IP regime varies by industry.

6. A number of scholars, policy makers, and practioners have questioned the va-lidity of this assumption, although this assumption is often used to guide policy and practice. Readers interested in learning more about whether or not patents spur innovation might start with a recent report by the National Research Coun-cil of the National Academies (2003), as well as a recent paper by Tomlinson and Torrance (2009) titled "Patents and the Regress of the Useful Arts."

References

Agarwal, R., and M. Gort. 2002. Firm and product life cycles and firm survival. *American Economic Review* 92 (2): 184–90.

Allen, R. C. 1983. Collective invention. *Journal of Economic Behavior and Organization* 4 (1): 1–24.

Amit, R., E. Muller, and I. Cockburn. 1995. Opportunity costs and entrepreneurial activity. *Journal of Business Venturing* 10 (2): 95–106.

Baldwin, C., and K. Clark. 2000. *Design Rules*. Cambridge: Harvard Business School Press.

Baldwin, C., C. Hienerth, and E. von Hippel. 2006. How user innovations become commercial products: A theoretical investigation and case Study. *Research Policy* 35 (9): 1291–1313.

Benner, M., and M. Tripsas. 2012. Prior industry affiliation and framing in ascent industries: The evolution of digital cameras. *Strategic Management Journal* 33 (3): 277–302.

Bower, J. L. 1970. *Managing the Resource Allocation Process*. Boston: Harvard Business School Press.

Brealey, R., and S. Myers. 1984. *Principles of Corporate Finance*. New York: McGraw-Hill.

Chatterji, A. K. 2009. Spawned with a silver spoon? Entrepreneurial performance andinnovation in the medical device industry. *Strategic Management Journal* 30 (2): 185–206.

Chatterji, A., and K. R. Fabrizio. 2012. How do product users influence corporate invention? *Organization Science* 23: 951–970.

Clark, K. B. 1985. The interaction of design hierarchies and market concepts in technological evolution. *Research Policy* 14 (5): 235–51.

Cohen, W. M., R. R. Nelson, and J. Walsh. 2000. Protecting their intellectual assets: Appropriability conditions and why U.S. manufacturing firms patent (or not). Working paper 7552. NBER.

Demsetz, H. 1967. Towards a theory of property rights. *American Economic Review* 57 (2): 347–59.

Dosi, G. 1988. Sources, procedures, and microeconomic effects of innovation. *Journal of Economic Literature* 26 (3): 1120–71.

Douglas, E. J., and D. A. Shepherd. 1999. Entrepreneurship as a utility maximizing response. *Journal of Business Venturing* 15 (3): 231–51.

Ferris, T. 2002. *Seeing in the Dark: How Backyard Stargazers Are Probing Deep Space and Guarding Earth from Interplanetary Peril*. New York: Simon and Schuster.

Finkelstein, S., and E. von Hippel. 1979. Analysis of innovation in automated clinical chemistry analyzers. *Science and Public Policy* 6 (1): 24–37.

Fligstein, N. 2001. *The Architecture of Markets*. Princeton: Princeton University Press.

Franco, A., M. Sarkar, R. Agarwal, and R. Echambadi. 2009. Swift and smart: The moderating effects of technological capabilities on the market pioneering-firm survival relationship. *Management Science* 55 (11): 1842–60.

Franke, N., and S. K. Shah. 2003. How communities support innovative activities: An exploration of assistance and sharing among end-users. *Research Policy* 32 (1): 157–78.

Franke, N., and E. von Hippel. 2003. Satisfying heterogeneous user needs via innovation toolkits: The case of Apache Security software. *Research Policy* 32 (7): 1199–1215.

Franz, K. 1999. Narrating automobility: Travelers, tinkerers, and technological authority in the twentieth century. PhD thesis. Brown University.

Gans, J., and S. Stern. 2003. The product market and the market for ideas. *Research Policy* 32 (2): 333–50.

Gimeno, J., T. B. Folta, A. C. Cooper, and C. Y. Woo. 1997. Survival of the fittest? Entrepreneurial human capital and the persistence of underperforming firms. *Administrative Science Quarterly* 42 (4): 750–83.

Haefliger, S., P. Jaeger, and G. v. Krogh. 2010. Under the radar: Industry entry by user entrepreneurs. *Research Policy* 39 (9): 1198–1213.

Hayek, F. A. 1945. The use of knowledge in society. *American Economic Review* 35 (4): 519–30.

Klepper, S., and S. Sleeper. 2005. Entry by spinoffs. *Management Science* 51 (8): 1291–1306.

Kline, R., and T. Pinch. 1996. Users as agents of technological change: The social construction of the automobile in the rural United States. *Technology and Culture* 37 (4): 763–95.

Lafuente, A., and V. Salas. 1989. Types of entrepreneurs and firms: The case of new Spanish firms. *Strategic Management Journal* 10 (1): 17–30.

Langlois, R. N., and P. L. Robinson. 1992. Networks and innovation in a modular system: Lessons from the microcomputer and stereo component industries. *Research Policy* 21 (4): 297–313.

Lüthje, C., C. Herstatt, and E. von Hippel. 2005. The dominant role of "local" information in user innovation: The case of mountain biking. *Research Policy* 34 (6): 951–65.

McKendrick, D., and G. Carroll. 2001. On the genesis of organizational forms: Evidence from the market for disk arrays. *Organization Science* 12 (6): 661–82.

Mody, C. C. M. 2006. Universities, corporations, and instrumental communities: Commercializing probe microscopy, 1981–1996. *Technology and Culture* 47 (1): 56–80.

Morrison, P. D., J. H. Roberts, and E. von Hippel. 2000. Determinants of user innovation and innovation sharing in a local market. *Management Science* 46 (12): 1513–27.

Murray, F., and M. Tripsas. 2004. "Understanding the Exploratory Processes of Entrepreneurial Firms," in Advances in Strategic Management, Vol. 21, editors Joel Baum and Anita McGahan, JAI-Elsevier, 2004.

National Research Council of The National Academies. 2003. *Patents in the Knowledge-Based Economy*. Washington, DC: National Academies Press.

Nonaka, I., and H. Takeuchi. 1995. *The Knowledge-Creating Company*. New York: Oxford University Press.

Nuvolari, A. 2004. Collective invention during the British Industrial Revolution. *Cambridge Journal of Economics* 28 (3): 347–63.

Oudshoorn, N., and T. Pinch. 2003. How users and non-users matter. In *How Users Matter: The Co-Construction of Users and Technology*, ed. T. Pinch and N. Oudshoorn. Cambridge: MIT Press.

Polanyi, M. 1958. *Personal Knowledge: Towards a Post-Critical Philosophy*. Chicago: University of Chicago Press.

Riggs, W., and E. von Hippel. 1994. Incentives to innovate and the sources of innovation: The case of scientific instruments. *Research Policy* 23 (4): 459–69.

Schumpeter, J. 1934. *The Theory of Economic Development*. Cambridge: Harvard University Press.

Scott-Morton, F. M., and J. M. Podolny. 2002. Love or money? The effects of owner motivation in the California wine industry. *Journal of Industrial Economics* 50 (4): 431–56.

Shah, S. K., and C. C. M. Mody. 2014. *Creating a Context for Entrepreneurship: Examining How Users' Technological and Organizational Innovations Set the Stage for Entrepreneurial Activity*. Oxford: Oxford University Press.

Shah, S. K. 2005. Open beyond software. In *Open Sources 2: The Continuing Evolution*, ed. C. Dibona, D. Cooper, and M. Stone, 339–60. Sebastopol, CA: O'Reilly Media.

Shah, S. K., and M. Tripsas. 2007. The accidental entrepreneur: The emergent and collective process of user entrepreneurship. *Strategic Entrepreneurship Journal* 1 (1–2): 123–40.

Shah, S. K., S. Winston Smith, and E. J. Reedy. 2011. *Who Are User Entrepreneurs? Findings on Innovation, Founder Characteristics and Firm Characteristics*. *Kauffman Foundation Report*. Kansas City, MO: Kauffman.

Shane, S. 2000. Prior knowledge and the discovery of entrepreneurial opportunities. *Organization Science* 11 (4): 448–69.

Shane, S., and S. Venkataraman. 2000. The promise of entrepreneurship as a field of research. *Academy of Management Review* 25 (1): 217–26.

Smith, N. R., and M. R. John. 1983. Type of entrepreneur, type of firm, and managerial motivation: Implications for organizational life cycle theory. *Strategic Management Journal* 4 (4): 325–40.

Solow, R. 1957. Technical change and the aggregate production function. *Review of Economics and Statistics* 39 (3): 312–20.

Stern, S. 2004. Do scientists pay to be scientists? *Management Science* 50 (6): 835–53.

Stevens, B. 1998. *Ultimate Snowboarding*. New York: Contemporary Books.

Szulanski, G. 1996. Exploring internal stickiness: Impediments to the transfer of best practice within the firm. *Strategic Management Journal* 17 (special issue): 27–43.

Teece, D. J. 1986. Profiting from technological innovation: Implications for integration, collaboration, licensing and public policy. *Research Policy* 15 (6): 285–305.

Torrance, A. W., and B. Tomlinson. 2009. Patents and the regress of useful arts. *Columbia Science and Technology Law Review* 10:130–68.

Tripsas, M. 1997. Unraveling the process of creative destruction: Complementary assets and incumbent survival in the typesetter industry. *Strategic Management Journal* 18 (special issue): 119–42.

Tripsas, M. 2008. Customer preference discontinuities: A trigger for radical technological change. *Managerial and Decision Economics* 29 (2–3): 79–97.

Tushman, M. L., and P. Anderson. 1986. Technological discontinuities and organizational environments. *Administrative Science Quarterly* 31 (3): 439–65.

Tyre, M. J., and E. von Hippel. 1997. The situated nature of adaptive learning in organizations. *Organization Science* 8 (1): 71–83.

Urban, G. L., and E. von Hippel. 1988. Lead user analyses for the development of new industrial products. *Management Science* 34 (5): 569–82.

Utterback, J., and F. Suarez. 1993. Patterns of industrial evolution, dominant designs, and firms' survival. In *Research on technological innovation, management and policy*, ed. R. Rosenbloom and R. Burgelman, 47–87. Greenwich, CT: JAI Press.

Utterback, J. M. 1994. *Mastering the Dynamics of Innovation*. Boston: Harvard University Press.

von Hippel, E. 1976. The dominant role of users in the scientific instrument innovation process. *Research Policy* 5 (3): 212–39.

von Hippel, E. 1977. The dominant role of the user in semiconductor and electronic subassembly process innovation. *IEEE Transactions on Engineering Management* 24 (2): 60–71.

von Hippel, E. 1986. Lead users: A source of novel product concepts. *Management Science* 32 (7): 791–805.

von Hippel, E. 1988. *The Sources of Innovation*. New York: Oxford University Press.

von Hippel, E. 1994. "Sticky information" and the locus of problem solving: Implications for innovation. *Management Science* 40 (4): 429–39.

von Hippel, E. 2005. *Democratizing Innovation*. Cambridge: MIT Press.

von Hippel, E., S. Thomke, and M. Sonnack. 1999. Creating breakthroughs at 3M. *Harvard Business Review* 77 (5): 47–57.

von Hippel, E. A., J. de Jong, and S. Flowers. 2012. Comparing business and household sector innovation in consumer products: Findings from a representative study in the UK. *Management Science* 58: 1669–81.

Winston Smith, S., and S. K. Shah. 2014. Do innovative users generate more useful insights? An analysis of CVC investment in the medical device industry. *Strategic Entrepreneurship Journal* 7: 151–67.

15

Users as Service-Innovators: Evidence across Healthcare and Financial Services

Pedro Oliveira and Helena Canhão

Services are usually thought of as something that involves a provider and a consumer. For example, healthcare professionals can provide healthcare services to patients, but it is also true that a patient can help himself/ herself in coping with a disease or overcoming a disability, by self-providing healthcare services. This possibility is well understood in the literature on services. Vargo and Lusch (2004: 2) define services as "the application of specialized competences (knowledge and skills) through deeds, processes, and performances for the benefit of another entity or the entity itself."

Since users *can* "serve themselves" in many cases, it seems reasonable to consider that users can innovate with respect to the services they deliver to themselves. Despite this possibility and despite the economic importance of services, most research on sources of innovation has explored service development only as a process carried out by service providers (e.g., den Hertog 2000; Menor and Roth 2008; Tether et al. 2001; Oliveira and Roth 2012a, b). In fact researchers in the topic of services traditionally conceive new service development as a producer-centered process similar to producer-centered new product development. They prescriptively focus on "how service providers should develop new services" rather than on exploring user roles in service innovation stories. In the multistep processes generally prescribed, firms wishing to provide new services—for example, healthcare institutions and banks—are instructed to study users in order to discern and better understand their articulated and unarticulated service-related needs. Then the firm's service developers are tasked with creating and testing new services intended to be responsive to the identified needs (e.g., Shostack 1981, 1984; Storey and Easingwood 1995; Flikkema et al. 2003). Some authors in the literature already describe processes in which users are viewed as "co-creators" and should be invited in to work jointly with the firm's service development personnel (e.g., Lengnick-Hall 1996; Prahalad and Ramaswamy 2002; Moller et al. 2008; Payne et al. 2008; Skiba and Herstatt 2011; Nambisan and Baron 2009). For example, Moller et al. (2008) provide a recipe for managing service co-creation and propose guidelines on how to succeed through collaborative capabilities and culture. Along the same lines, Prahalad and Ramaswamy (2002) and Payne et al. (2008) propose a framework for on how they can better understand consumers' views, and work with them to co-create solutions. Lüthje (2000), among others, supports the potential utility of this approach and argues that the most effective service users to incorporate in co-creation exercises are those providing new service ideas with high commercial potential, the "lead users." Nonetheless, service users are still not viewed as potential service creators without the active participation of the producer. In this chapter we present evidence on the major role played by patients of chronic diseases in the development of treatments and medical devices, as well as the role of banking users in the development of new financial services, despite an eventual producer participation in the service development process.

In this context, following this introductory section, we begin by first reviewing the role of users in developing new services. Then we discuss the empirical findings on user innovation in services present in the literature and finally their managerial implications.

Role of Users in Developing New Services

Service users are either *firms or individuals* that expect to benefit from using a service. In contrast, service providers are firms or individuals that expect to benefit from selling a service (e.g., von Hippel 1998). A service innovation is therefore user-developed if the developer expects to benefit from use, and provider-developed if the developer expects to benefit from sales (e.g., Oliveira and von Hippel 2011).

The literature on user innovation in services has identified examples of service development by users in a few fields. For example, Voss (1985) explored the role of users in developing software and found the circumstances where users lead the development of new applications. von Hippel and Riggs (1996) reported on user development of novel banking services related to an early form of electronic home banking that utilized a telephone channel between customer and bank. Potential study participants (*lead users*) were recruited by an email directed to a sample of convenience—approximately 1,300 research and development engineers employed by a telecom firm. These individuals were asked whether they had ". . . found novel ways to take care of their personal banking service needs via electronic home banking. For example, . . . written or adapted a home software program to automate a manual procedure, found a novel way to use a service offered by the bank to achieve a purpose other than was originally intended, or devised a novel procedure for paying bills or keeping records" (von Hippel and Riggs 1996: 7) Fifteen individuals responded with return messages, which included a brief description of novel home banking services they had self-developed for their own use. Skiba and Herstatt (2009) explored Internet and newspaper reports and identified three examples of commercially important services that had been developed by users for their own use and then commercialized by these same user-innovator. One of these, the pre-commercial history of the service firm Weight Watchers, is illustrative. To briefly summarize, in 1961 an American housewife named Jean Nidetch was frustrated at her repeated failure to lose weight. As a new approach, she created weekly group meetings with her overweight friends to provide a peer-to-peer support service to augment their previously independent efforts to lose weight. This self-developed and self-provided service proved very effective for the members of her group. In 1963 she incorporated the firm Weight Watchers—now a major service provider—to commercialize the service and diffuse it more widely.

More recently Oliveira and von Hippel (2011) reported on the first study of the role of user-innovators in the development of new financial services, using as a sample all important retail and commercial service innovations commercialized by banks between 1975 and 2010. The authors found that both retail and corporate users often develop and self-provide services before banks begin to offer them. For example, computerized payroll processing was first developed and used in the early 1950s as a self-service by J. Lyons and Co, a major baking and catering firm in the United Kingdom (Ferry 2003). Other user firms followed. Banks first offered that service to commercial customers in the 1980s. The study further shows that individual users of retail bank services had developed and self-provided computerized versions of these services before banks or other types of service providers offered them. For example, computerized aggregation of account information across multiple institutions was first implemented by individual "hackers" for their own use in the 1980s (Hemenway and Calishain 2004). Consider this personal history:

I do my banking online, but I quickly get bored with having to go to my bank's site, log in, navigate around to my accounts, and check the balance on each of them. One quick Perl module (Finance::Bank::HSBC) later, I can loop through each of my accounts and print their balances, all from a shell prompt. With some more code, I can do something the bank's site doesn't ordinarily let me do: I can treat my accounts as a whole instead of as individual accounts, and find out how much money I have, could possibly spend and owe, all in total. (Hemenway and Calishain 2004: 62)

Commercial versions of this service were first offered in 1999 by Yodlee, a nonbank commercial provider (Spiotto 2002), and introduced by a bank as a commercial service to retail customers in 2006 (Bruene 2006). In the case of manual versions of banking services that typically were developed before the development of computerized services, users were almost always the initial developers. As illustration of what Oliveira and von Hippel (2011) call the "manual precursors" of computerized banking services, consider the computerized "keep-the-change" service introduced by the Bank of America in 2005 (Tufano and Schneider 2009). Enrollees in Bank of America's computerized "keep-the-change" service authorize the bank to automatically round up the value of every debit-card purchase to the nearest dollar, and transfer the difference from their checking account to a traditional savings account. According to a senior executive of Bank of America interviewed by the authors, the idea for this service was triggered by a woman attending a focus group, who had developed a manual prototype of their service. She told the interviewers that each time she wrote a check, she rounded up the amount she wrote in her record of the transaction to the nearest dollar. As a result the "change" from this rounding disappeared from her checkbook balance calculations and became a form of savings.

Overview of Empirical Evidence of User Innovation in Services

In this section we summarize empirical evidence of user innovation across different sectors, namely in healthcare services and financial services, more specifically crowdfunding and mobile banking.

Patients as Healthcare-Innovators

Transferring the notion of user innovation to the healthcare domain, we define patient-innovators as those patients, non-professional caregivers or collaborators who come up with novel treatments, strategies, and equipment to help them (or those they care about) cope with a disease or disability. While it may seem impossible that patients can introduce impactful innovations due to the complexity of the underlying mechanisms of their illness, recent studies show this to be possible. Several innovations by patients are documented to have made strong impact on the disease-related practice, and some even represent the state-of-the-art in technology (Habicht et al. 2012; Oliveira et al. 2015). Consider the case of Tal Golesworthy, a process engineer who was diagnosed with the Marfan syndrome in 1992, a rare disease that results in a decreasing functionality and resilience of the aorta. Tal was told that surgery was unavoidable and that after the surgery he would be bound to lifetime anticoagulation therapy. He considered both options (surgery or no surgery) to be troubling. Being an engineer, he decided to create a more suitable solution for himself: "So I said to myself, I'm an engineer, I'm in R&D. This is just a plumbing problem. I can do this. I can change this." He invented the External Aortic Root Support (EARS), which matches the patient's aorta and eliminates the need for anticoagulant drugs. In 2004, Tal became the first patient to have the EARS implanted. In 2014, when he celebrated the 10th anniversary of his innovation, there were already 46 patients with this implant.

Intrigued by this and many other cases, Oliveira et al. (2015) performed the first empirical exploration of disease-related innovations by rare diseases patients and their nonprofessional caregivers. The authors administered a phone survey to a sample of 500 rare disease patients and caregivers, and 53 percent of the respondents reported that they had developed a way to improve the management of their diseases, which they thought to be novel. An initial screening removed 81 solutions, leaving 182 (36 percent of 500) potentially novel solutions. Further evaluation by the expert medical evaluators suggested the solutions reported by 8 percent of our respondents to be truly "new." The remaining claimed innovations that passed the initial filtering were judged by our expert evaluators to be redevelopments—new to the patient developer but not unknown to medicine. As shown in table 15.1, 22 percent of the 182 solutions were evaluated and considered novel by two expert medical evaluators.

Table 15.1
Type and novelty of the reported solutions

	New to the patient (n = 142)	New to the world (n = 40)	Total (n = 182)
Products	4 (3%)	15 (37%)	10%
Services	138 (97%)	25 (63%)	90%
Total	142 (78%)	40 (22%)	100%

Source: Oliveira, Zejnilovic, Canhão and von Hippel (2015)

Also these innovations did significantly improve the quality of life of the patients and nonprofessional caregivers. The remaining 78 percent of the solutions were already known to medicine, though thought novel by the patients who recreated them.

According to this study, the likelihood of a reported patient innovation increased as education level increased and as the patient's perception of the limitations imposed by their disease increased. Moreover the study suggests that patients very rarely show their innovations to medical professionals. In fact patients make little effort to publicize their innovative solutions. Finally, the study suggests a significantly positive impact of own innovation on the respondents' overall quality of life.

Given that there are hundreds of millions of people worldwide estimated to be afflicted by rare diseases, patients and their caregivers may be a tremendous potential source of innovations and information to improve management and care for many who are similarly afflicted. The authors suggest that many patients could be greatly assisted by improved means of diffusion of known best practices to and among patients and their caregivers.

But innovation by patients and their nonprofessional caregivers is not confined to rare diseases. In October 1969, Richard Bernstein, a type 1 diabetes patient, came across an advertisement for the first blood glucose meter that would give a reading in one minute, using a single drop of blood. The device was intended for emergency staff at hospitals to distinguish unconscious diabetics from unconscious drunks. The instrument weighed three pounds, cost $650, and was only available to certified physicians and hospitals. Determined to take control of his situation, Bernstein asked his wife, a doctor, to order the instrument for him. Bernstein began to measure his blood sugar about 5 times each day and soon realized that the levels fluctuated wildly throughout the day. To even out his blood sugars, he adjusted his insulin regimen from one injection per day to two and experimented with his diet, notably by reducing his consumption of carbohydrates. Three years after Bernstein began monitoring his own blood sugar levels, his complications were still progressing and he began researching scientific articles about the disease. Bernstein, a "user," is believed to be the first individual to self-monitor his blood sugar and was an early advocate for such monitoring by diabetics (Bernstein 2007). Bernstein is just one of many users who developed important solutions for their own disease.

In the current study we further explored the role of users in developing their own medical treatments, especially for chronic diseases such as cystic fibrosis (CF), a fatal disease with no cure that causes the body to produce abnormally thick and sticky mucus that can lead to life-threatening lung infections. We analyze a sample of CF treatments for which patients (users) developed a very large number of their own alternative treatments (table 15.2). These treatments (along with pharmacological and surgery measures) are found to have increased the life expectancy of the patients by 5 to 37 years and to have improved their quality of life. For example, (1) the use of trampolines for children, a physiotherapeutic tool for enhancing cardiopulmonary performance and improving general well-being discovered by the parents of a young girl with CF who observed that when she used the trampoline many times a day, she didn't need extra treatment for lung drainage; (2) inhaling hypertonic saline, a treatment discovered by an Australian surfer and CF patient who realized she felt much better during and after practicing surf and inhaling saline water; (3) low-frequency vibrations for bronchial drainage developed by a CF patient who had to leave a concert because of excessive coughing while sitting in proximity to a large speaker; and (4) chest percussion with electrical percussion as in this personal recount by the person who developed the technique:

My daughter, 26 with CF, depended for most of her life on us, her parents to do her chest physiotherapy. So her independence was constantly compromised and she hated it. On other hand, we not always delivered the best physiotherapy; simply because were tired, or didn't have all this time required or were sick. Sure, you know all of this . . . Many times I was thinking about a simple solution, which would deliver a good physiotherapy and wouldn't require a caregiver. And I am

Table 15.2
Sources of chest physical therapy techniques and devices for Cystic Fibrosis

Treatments (sample of devices and techniques)	Innovator U = user P = producer	Who exactly is the innovator?
Use of low-frequency vibrations for bronchial drainage	U (patient)	Louis Plante, CF patient, engineer
Inhaling hypertonic saline	U (patient)	Emily Haager, CF patient, surfer
Use of trampolines in children	U (non-professional caregiver)	Parents of child w/ CF (according to Dr.J. K. Stanghelle)
Use of electric percussor for chest percussion	U (nonprofessional caregiver)	Hanna Boguslawska, (mother of girl w/ CF)
Online games to help during CF treatments	U (nonprofessional caregiver)	David Day (father of girl w/ CF)
Pedi-neb pacifier, nebulizer administration tubing	U (nurse)	Nurse
Use of the flutter for mucus clearance device	P (doctor)	Dr. Patrick Althaus, physiotherapist
Postural drainage	P (doctor)	Dr. William Ewart
Vest therapy/chest compression	P (doctor)	Dr W. Warwick, CF researcher

very happy I could do it. My daughter uses my eper 100 (stands for electrical percussor, and 100 symbolizes all my percussion ideas which were never realized) all the time. According to her it is much better than the human hand and she can do it alone.
(Hanna Boguslawska, mother of Natalia and founder of eper ltd.)

In line with this report, Shcherbatiuk and Oliveira (2012) studied several other chronic diseases besides respiratory diseases (cystic fibrosis, asthma, and sleep apnea): cancer, diabetes, and medical devices and treatment for general purposes. Despite some sampling limitations, they found that the majority (54 percent) of new medical treatment and devices for the diseases were developed by patients or their families and friends. The percentage of patient-developed treatments and devices varied across the diseases studied by these authors: 42 percent for cystic fibrosis, 50 percent for asthma, 50 percent for sleep apnea, 47 percent for cancer, and 79 percent for diabetes. Moreover 53 percent of the patients who were user-innovators became entrepreneurs and created their own firms to produce their inventions. The proportion of user-innovators who developed new firms to commercialize their medical treatments and devices also varied across the diseases. Despite some sampling limitations, the empirical evidence does show that patients have an important role in the development of new treatments and medical devices. Considering that healthcare alone represents roughly 17 percent of US GDP, this is an important finding.

Users as Financial Services-Innovators

Table 15.3 identifies three main services in the computerized corporate banking services sample. The locus of innovation was coded in three ways. If one or more users/firms were already applying the service before (banks or nonbanks) providers of financial services offered it as a commercial service, the innovation is coded as user-developed (U). If banks had already commercialized the innovation prior to any user/firm developing the computerized service for their own in-house use, the service is coded as producer-developed (P). If user and producer jointly developed the innovation, the dates of user introduction and producer introduction in the table are the same, and the service innovation is coded as joint (J).

In table 15.4 we group these services under three headings: (1) account information services, (2) account transaction services, and (3) new channels to access banking services. As can be seen, the proportion of user-developed services is highest in category 1 and lowest in category 3. This seems reasonable to us, given that user access to the information and controls they need to innovate for themselves is likely to be increasingly difficult/costly as one moves from new service development opportunities in category 1 to those in category 3.

In the case of corporate services, 6 of the 20 cases have a common origin—they were first created as part of a pioneering electronic data interchange (EDI) system developed collaboratively by GM and a group of its major suppliers. In the initial stages of development in the early 1980s, banks were not included in this consortium, and information exchange services stopped short of actual financial transfers. In 1985 the

Table 15.3

Sources of innovation of computerized corporate banking services

Corporate banking services ($n = 20$)	Innovator U=user P = producer J = joint
A. Information services and planning solutions	
1. Multiple institution information aggregation	U
2. Online corporate forums and communities	U
3. Corporate taxes preparation and computation services	U
4. Alerts, notifications, or reminders via telephone/email	P
B. Products, transaction services, and security	
1. Payroll processing services	U
2. Payment processing services	J
3. Invoice processing services	U
4. Remote payment/payroll services	U
5. Corporate salary account	J
6. Lockbox	J
7. Sweep services between accounts within the same bank	J
8. Sweep services between different institutions	U
9. Zero balance accounting	U
10. Risk assessment/computerized	U
11. Overdraft protection	P
12. Merchant services and card solutions	U
13. Remote deposit	J
C. Channels to access banking services	
1. Data link with bank	J
2. Telephone banking (via voice response technology)	P
3. Online banking	P

Source: Oliveira and von Hippel (2011)

Table 15.4
Sources of computerized versions of corporate banking services

Service types	% User	% Bank	% Joint
A. Information services and planning solutions	75%	25%	0%
B. Products, transaction services, and security	54%	8%	38%
C. Channels to access banking services	0%	67%	33%
Corporate services total	55% (11)	15% (3)	30% (6)

Source: Oliveira and von Hippel (2011)

consortium was extended to include 8 banks, so that actual payments as well as information regarding transactions could flow through the system via the common, user-developed EDI format. Even though it was clear from the written histories that user firms and not banks were the dominant developers in this consortium, the authors conservatively coded these services as joint innovations, with the single exception of invoice processing. The initial invoice-processing service developed did not involve money transactions, and was implemented without the involvement of banks.

The development histories of the remaining 14 corporate service offerings in the sample were totally independent cases. For example, computerized payroll processing—programmed calculation of taxes and other matters associated with wage payments—was pioneered in the early 1950s as a self-service by J. Lyons and Co. This user firm, a major baking and catering firm in the United Kingdom, innovated independently of others. The software involved was developed by J. Lyons and Co. for its own use only. In the United States, GE was also an early user firm as it developed payroll software for its own use on the UNIVAC computer in early 1950s.

The possibility that individual retail customers might develop computerized bank services for themselves prior to banks commercially providing it might initially seem surprising. But, as tables 15.5 and 15.6 show, this was the case for only 44 percent of present-day retail banking services. As a further illustration, consider the service of "multiple institution account information aggregation," a solution that automatically contacts

Table 15.5
Sources of innovation of computerized *retail* banking services

Retail banking services ($n = 16$)	Innovator U = user P = producer J = joint
A. *Information services and planning solutions*	
1. Multiple institutions account information aggregation	U
2. Relationship statements	U
3. Online consumer forums and communities	U
4. Alerts, notifications, or reminders via telephone/email	P
B. *Products, transaction services, and security*	
1. Electronic person-to-person (P2P) funds transfer	U
2. Personal budget planner	U
3. Manual/automatic bill paying	P
4. Sweep service between accounts in the same bank	P
5. Sweep services across different institutions	U
6. "Keep the change" program	P
7. Overdraft protection	P
8. Frequent password updating	P
C. *Channels to access banking services*	
1. Telephone banking	P
2. Text messaging services	P
3. Online banking	P
4. Mobile banking	U

Source: Oliveira and von Hippel (2011)

Table 15.6
Sources of computerized versions of retail banking services

Service type	% User	% Bank	% Joint
A. Information services and planning solutions	75%	25%	0%
B. Products, transaction services, and security	38%	62%	0%
C. Channels to access banking services	25%	75%	0%
Retail services total	44% (7)	56% (9)	0% (0)

Source: Oliveira and von Hippel (2011)

each financial institution where a retail user has an account, logs on with the user's password, collects information on the account status (balances, etc.), logs off, and then assembles the information from all accounts into a convenient spreadsheet tailored to the user's specifications. Commercial versions of this service were first introduced by start-ups (e.g., Yodlee in the late 1990s) and then eventually by banks. Well before the late 1990s, however, many users were already polling their accounts manually and putting the data into their own multi-account spreadsheets. Some users had even developed fully or partially automated versions of the services very much like the commercial services eventually offered. They generally acquired their data via "screen scraping."

We further grouped the retail banking services under three headings: (1) account information services, (2) account transaction services, and (3) new channels to access banking services (table 15.6). As was the case with corporate banking services, the authors found that in retail banking services, the proportion of user innovations drops from category 1 to category 3. Again, this is because user access to the information and controls they need to innovate for themselves becomes increasingly difficult/costly as one moves from new service development opportunities in category 1 to those in category 3.

Interestingly, however, retail users were able to pioneer mobile banking, a channel-related category 3 innovation. Channels do require both ends of the channel to be set up, so that both sender and receiver are linked together in the system. When a channel is built from scratch, both ends must be constructed simultaneously, and such innovations are for that reason coded as joint. However, sometimes one end of the channel has been set up for an earlier purpose, and in such cases, one actor is free to exploit the preexisting channel to create the new service without the requirement of joint action. Internet banking via cell phone—"mobile banking"—is an example of this, and is coded as a user innovation in table 15.5. As soon as cell phones became Internet enabled, customers had the technology at hand to access preexisting Internet banking channels. Initially users found it difficult to do so, but persevered. One problem was that banks had not expected users to access the channel via cell phone, and so the web pages on bank Internet banking sites had been designed with the screen size of a personal computer in mind. When banks became aware of such a new user application, they created appropriate web pages for cell phone screens.

The Case of Crowdfunding

The term *crowdfunding* derives from *crowdsourcing*, which means outsourcing to the public tasks typically performed by employees. If you want to start a T-shirt business, why not ask the public to submit designs (crowdsourcing) and finance those most liked (crowdfunding). Lambert and Schwienbacher (2010: 6) extend the concept of crowdsourcing provided by Kleemann et al. (2008) and define crowdfunding as "an open call, essentially through the Internet, for the provision of financial resources either in form of donation or in exchange for some form of reward and/or voting rights in order to support initiatives for specific purposes." The term *crowdfunding* has also been applied to raising money for companies or charity (Lawton and Marom 2010). But there are regulatory limits on micro-investing, so the term is most widely used to refer to fundraising for creative work. Crowdfunding has benefited from the rise of social networking, which allows noncelebrities to gather large numbers of fans or followers online to whom they can reach out when a project needs funding.

We studied the origin and development of this new service and again found that users in fact developed it. In 1997, when the British band Marillion scheduled a European tour to promote its new album, keyboardist Mark Kelly posted a message on the Internet saying that the band would not tour the United States because of a lack of support from their record company. Fans of the band worldwide joined forces to raise more than $60,000, which enabled the band to undertake its largest North American tour since 1991. Since then, Marillion has been able to tour and record several more times as a result of direct fan support. This passionate, grassroots support has enabled Marillion to step outside the conventional music industry and find its own path. This saga represents one of the first modern examples of "crowd funding" via the Web, a bottom-up strategy whereby fans and customers drive and direct music markets. Several music services have now emerged to bring this idea into new territories. The key factor in Marillion's story is that the fans who first developed crowdfunding (at the time called *fan-funding*) are users, as they benefited from using it (i.e., bringing the band to the United States) and not from selling or commercializing the service. Meanwhile, this user-led new "industry" has evolved and changed. In 2013 the World Bank commissioned a study on how crowdfunding could be applied internationally and what its potential could be for affecting entrepreneurship in developing countries, which predicts a $93 billion equivalent crowdfunding market by 2025.

The Case of Mobile-Banking

If necessity is the mother of invention, new products and services should naturally occur in contexts where they are most needed. Van der Boor, Oliveira, and Veloso (2014) examine the extent to which users in developing countries innovate and whether these innovations are meaningful on a global stage. An empirical investigation was made into innovations in financial services offered via the mobile phone. The authors used the complete list of mobile financial services as reported by the GSM Association (GSMA), and collected detailed stories of these services' development and innovation process. Their analysis shows that 85 percent of the innovations in this field originated in emerging markets. They also conclude that at least 50 percent of all mobile financial services was pioneered by users. Additionally services developed by users diffused at more than double the rate of producer innovations. Finally, they observed that three-quarters of the innovations that originated in emerging markets had already been diffused to OECD countries, and therefore these (user) innovations are globally meaningful.

Discussion

This chapter illustrates the relevance of the pioneering work on user innovation by von Hippel (e.g., von Hippel 1986, 1988, 1994, 2005) to the service innovation literature, by studying the sources of relevant service innovations across different fields, namely in healthcare and financial services. The extant research on user innovation has demonstrated empirically this phenomenon as occurring in many industries (e.g., von Hippel 2010). Yet so far there has been little systematic exploration of user innovation by patients and their nonprofessional caregivers. We use the term *patient-innovators* to refer to patients or their nonprofessional caregivers (e.g., parents, family members, spouses or partners) who modify or develop a treatment, behavioral strategy, technical aid or a medical device to cope with their ailment (Shcherbatiuk and Oliveira 2012). Given that there are hundreds of millions of people worldwide estimated to be afflicted by chronic diseases (both rare and non-rare), patients and their caregivers may be a tremendous potential source of innovations and information to improve management and care for many who are similarly afflicted.

Regarding financial services, von Hippel and Riggs (1996) reported on user development of novel banking services, and more recently Oliveira and von Hippel (2011) documented that banking services users frequently develop and self-provide what they need before banks or nonbanks financial service providers commercially offer those services. Moreover Oliveira and von Hippel (2011) confirmed their expectation that further empirical research would show users as being the initial developers of many of the services they need (via self-service versions) across a broad range of fields and conditions (see also van der Boor et al. 2014). There are three good explanations for this expectation. First, users generally understand their needs better than producers do. Since the need information originates with the user, there is often a significant cost involved in transferring that information to the producer (von Hippel 1994). Second, emergent needs that will become general are often encountered first by the principal users situated at the leading edge. The nature and extent of demand is both small and uncertain at the leading edge, and so the potential commercial opportunity may not appear attractive for a commercial provider at an early stage of a leading-edge development (von Hippel 2005). Third, only a subgroup of users facing a given leading-edge need will be able to develop a service innovation for themselves at very low cost. It will fall within their personal or corporate "low-cost innovation niche" because of their specific preexisting expertise and tools, and most important, their ability to conduct low-cost trial-and-error experiments within their own user environments (Lüthje et al. 2005).

In this regard individual services are really only modules within larger systems of interconnecting activities—and these modules only have utility in the context of a complete system. At the leading edge, where markets are small and uncertain, lead users will generally be the ones to innovate at the system level (von Hippel 1977).

These findings differ significantly from prevalent producer-centered views of service development. If the patterns observed with respect to the major role of users in service development are indeed quite general, this will be an important matter. On the order of 75 percent of GDP in advanced economies today is derived from services, and an improved understanding of the services innovation process should therefore be quite useful.

Managerial Implications

There are clear practical implications of these findings for service providers seeking to offer new services to their customers. First, it is useful to recognize that lead users are often the first to develop service innovations (e.g., Oliveira and von Hippel 2011; Shcherbatiuk and Oliveira 2012; van der Boor et al. 2014; Oliveira et al. 2015; Zejnilovic et al. 2014; Zejnilovic 2014). Skiba (2010) found that 40 percent of innovative services across various service industries was created by lead users; and that the majority of service companies integrating such innovating solutions greatly value these contributions for their "originality," "producibility," and "user-value." In this regard it may be useful for service providers to actively search for service innovations by actual users. When firms use user innovations as inputs to their product or service development processes, they obtain critical information on leading-edge user needs. They also acquire information on prototype product designs responsive to user needs, and information on the value of use derived from deployment of those user-developed prototypes under real-life conditions.

It will be especially valuable for service providers to seek out the self-service innovations of lead users when these innovations contain functional novelty. Here users have a major advantage over producers with respect to privileged access to sticky need information—they are the generators of that information. In contrast, when the service innovation issues involve less functional novelty—"dimension of merit improvements"—inputs from lead users are less likely to be essential (Riggs and von Hippel 1994).

Many services provided by commercial entities are modules in larger user systems of interlinked products and services. A good way for a particular provider to search for additional commercial services opportunities is therefore to explore these user systems and identify modules that precede and follow the ones that the service/product provider already offers. For example, users know how to access banking-related data for other purposes before and after they utilize bank services. They may, for example, use the data in budgeting or in tax preparation. To bankers, these "adjacent" activities in the larger user system are not automatically visible, and so must be purposefully identified and explored.

An interesting cost effect in the substitution of a self-provided service by a commercial one is that often the service introduced by a firm takes away the user's freedom to make modifications and adjustments. For example, in earlier days, when users aggregated and reconciled their own monthly banking activities in a ledger, they could set up, adapt, and evolve this ledger according to their preferences— the service was user-adjustable. Once banks introduced a commercial multi-account reconciliation statement, users abandoned personal ledgers because of the gain in convenience, despite the loss of user-adjustability.

When service providers offer commercial versions of user-developed services, they should consider the value of offering these in the form of "toolkits" that retain users' ability to modify and update these on their own. If users *can* modify and build improvements upon the service offered by a commercial provider many will do so. Producers can then study these user-developed improvements as a valuable feedstock of potential improvements to their commercially offered service (Franke and von Hippel 2003).

Also, as reported here, patients and their nonprofessional caregivers can improve their quality of life and health outcomes by innovating. One important observation is that while patients and caregivers of rare chronic diseases often develop new medical treatments that significantly improve the quality of their lives, these innovations rarely diffuse and the innovators don't have many incentives to make their solutions better known (Oliveira et al 2015). A way to facilitate diffusion of innovations by patients and caregivers may be to reduce the diffusion costs and develop a centralized online inventory of solutions developed by patients or caregivers. With this in mind, we developed Patient Innovation—https://patient-innovation.com—a nonprofit international, multilingual and open platform, designed to allow patients and caregivers to show and share the innovative solutions they developed to fight their diseases, as well as to foster collaboration among patients, caregivers and others. This experimental platform is aimed at increasing both the rate of patient innovations and its diffusion. Major institutions and leading practitioners, including several Nobel Laureates, distinguished scholars, and patient associations from around the world have endorsed this platform. In the first 16 months of operation (from February 2014 to May 2015) the Patient Innovation platform has collected and curated more than 300 innovative treatments developed by patients and caregivers from 30 countries.

References

Bernstein, R. K. 2007. *Dr. Bernstein's Diabetes Solution.* New York: Little, Brown.

Bruene, J. 2006. Bank of America is first major U.S. bank to integrate personal finance into online banking. *Netbanker,* December 26.

Den Hertog, P. 2000. Knowledge intensive business services as co-producers of innovation. *International Journal of Innovation Management* 4 (4): 491–528.

Ferry, G. 2003. *A Computer Called LEO: Lyons Tea Shops and the World's First Office Computer.* Hammersmith, UK: Harper Perennial.

Flikkema, M. J., A. J. Cozijnsen, and M. Hart. 2003. The innovation climate as a catalyser of innovation in services. [in Dutch] *Holland Management Review* 91 (September/October): 68–82.

Franke, N., and E. von Hippel. 2003. Satisfying heterogeneous user needs via innovation toolkits: The case of Apache Security software. *Research Policy* 32 (7): 1199–1215.

Habicht, H., P. Oliveira, and V. Shcherbatiuk. 2012. User innovators: when patients set out to help themselves and end up helping many. *Die Unternehmung* 66 (3): 277–94.

Hemenway, K., and T. Calishain. 2004. *Spidering Hacks*. Cambridge, MA: O'Reilly Media, Inc.

Kleemann, F., G. G. Voß, and K. Rieder. 2008. Un(der)paid innovators: The commercial utilization of consumer work through crowdsourcing. *Science, Technology and Innovation Studies* 4 (1): 5–26

Lambert, T., and A. Schwienbacher. 2010. An empirical analysis of crowdfunding. SSRN. http://papers.ssrn.com/sol3/papers.cfm?abstract_id=1578175.

Lawton, K., and D. Marom. 2010. *The Crowdfunding Revolution: Social Networking Meets Venture Financing*. Scotts Valley: CreateSpace.

Lengnick-Hall, C. 1996. Customer contributions to quality: A different view of the customer oriented firm. *Academy of Management Review* 21 (3): 791–810.

Lüthje, C. 2000. *Kundenorientierung im Innovationsprozess—Eine Untersuchung der Kunden-Hersteller-Interaktion in Konsumgütermärkten*. Wiesbaden: Deutscher Universitäts-Verlag.

Lüthje, C., C. Herstatt, and E. von Hippel. 2005. User-innovators and "local" information: The case of mountain biking. *Research Policy* 34 (6): 951–65.

Menor, L. J., and A. V. Roth. 2008. New service development competence and performance: An empirical investigation in retail banking. *Production and Operations Management* 17 (3): 267–84.

Moller, K., R. Rajala, and M. Westerlund. 2008. Service innovation myopia? A new recipe for client-provider value creation. *California Management Review* 50 (3): 31–48.

Nambisan, S., and R. A. Baron. 2009. Virtual customer environments: Testing a model of voluntary participation in value co-creation activities. *Journal of Product Innovation Management* 26 (4): 388–406.

Oliveira, P., and E. von Hippel. 2011. Users as service innovators: The case of banking services. *Research Policy* 40 (6): 806–18.

Oliveira, P., and A. V. Roth. 2012a. The influence of service orientation on B2B E-service capabilities. *Production and Operations Management* 21 (3): 423–43.

Oliveira, P., and A. V. Roth. 2012b. Service orientation: The derivation of underlying constructs and measures. *International Journal of Operations and Production Management* 32 (2): 156–90.

Oliveira, P., L. Zejnilovic, H. Canhão, and E. von Hippel. 2015. Innovation by patients with rare diseases and chronic needs. *Orphanet Journal of Rare Diseases* 10: 41.

Payne, A. F., K. Storbacka, and P. Frow. 2008. Managing the co-creation of value. *Journal of the Academy of Marketing Science* 36 (1): 83–96.

Prahalad, C. K., and V. Ramaswamy. 2002. The co-creation connection. *Strategy and Business* 27 (2): 50–61.

Riggs, W., and E. von Hippel. 1994. The impact of scientific and commercial values on the sources of scientific instrument innovation. *Research Policy* 23 (4): 459–69.

Skiba, F. 2010. *Service Users as Sources for Innovation: An Empirical Study in the German Services Industry.* Hamburg: Books on Demand.

Skiba, F., and C. Herstatt. 2009. Users as sources for radical service innovations: Opportunities from collaboration with service lead users. *International Journal of Services Technology and Management* 12 (3): 317–37.

Skiba, F., and Herstatt, C. 2011. Users as sources of radical service innovation: A closer look into opportunities for integrating service lead users in service development. In *Practice-Based Innovation: Insights, Applications and Policy Implications,* ed. H. Melkas and V. Harmaakorpi, 233–53. Heidelberg: Springer.

Shcherbatiuk, V., and P. Oliveira. 2012. Users as developers and entrepreneurs of medical treatments/devices: The case of patients and their families and friends. Working paper. Carnegie Mellon Portugal.

Shostack, G. L. 1981. How to design a service. *European Journal of Marketing* 16 (1): 49–63.

Shostack, G. L. 1984. Service design in the operating environment. In *Developing New Services,* ed. W. R. George and C. E. Marshall, 27–43. Chicago: American Marketing Association.

Spiotto, A. H. 2002. Financial account aggregation: The liability perspective. Emerging Payments Occasional Paper series, Federal Reserve Bank of Chicago.

Storey, C., and C. J. Easingwood. 1995. Determinants of new product performance: A study in the financial services sector. *International Journal of Service Industry Management* 7 (1): 32–55.

Tether, B. S., C. Hipp, and I. Mile. 2001. Standardization and particularization in services; evidence from Germany. *Research Policy* 30 (7): 1115–38.

Tufano, P., and D. Schneider. 2009. Using financial innovation to support savers: From coercion to excitement. In *Insufficient Funds: Savings, Assets, Credit and Banking Among Low-Income Households,* ed. R. Blank and M. Barr, 149–90. New York: Russell Sage.

Van der Boor, P., P. Oliveira, and F. Veloso. 2014. Users as innovators in developing countries: The global sources of innovation and diffusion in mobile banking services. *Research Policy* 43 (9): 1594–1607.

Vargo, S. L., and R. F. Lusch. 2004. The four service marketing myths: Remnants of a goods-based, manufacturing model. *Journal of Service Research* 6 (4): 324–35.

von Hippel, E. 1977. The dominant role of the user in semiconductor and electronic subassembly process innovation. *IEEE Transactions on Engineering Management* EM-24 (2): 60–71.

von Hippel, E. 1986. Lead users: A source of novel product concepts. *Management Science* 32 (7): 791–805.

von Hippel, E. 1988. *The Sources of Innovation.* New York: Oxford University Press.

von Hippel, E. 1994. "Sticky information" and the locus of problem solving: Implications for innovation. *Management Science* 40 (4): 429–39.

von Hippel, E., and W. Riggs. 1996. A lead user study of electronic home banking services: Lessons from the learning curve. *Working paper. Sloan School of Management, MIT.*

von Hippel, E. 1998. Economics of product development by users: The impact of "sticky" local information. *Management Science* 44 (5): 629–44.

von Hippel, E. 2005. *Democratizing Innovation.* Cambridge: MIT Press.

von Hippel, E. 2010. Open user innovation. In *Handbook of the Economics of Innovation.* vol. 1, ed. B. H. Hall and N. Rosenberg, 411–27. Amsterdam: Elsevier-North Holland.

Voss, C. 1985. The role of users in the development of applications software. *Journal of Product Innovation Management* 2 (2): 113–21.

Zejnilovic, L., P. Oliveira, and F. Veloso. 2014. Employees as user innovators: An empirical investigation of an idea management system. Working paper. Carnegie Mellon Portugal.

Zejnilovic, L. 2014. Essays in user innovation. PhD dissertation. Carnegie Mellon University, Pittsburgh/Universidade Católica Portuguesa and Universidade de Lisboa, Lisbon.

16

Technique Innovation

Christoph Hienerth

There has been much concern with the sources of innovation in physical products. But really, the value of a physical product is largely determined by what you can do with it. In the case of tools and equipment that humans manipulate what you can do with an artifact is a function of *technique*. Thus *innovation in technique* can have an influence on the development of artifacts, and vice versa.

Over the last thirty years studies from different fields have shown that users are the sources of innovation in various industries, for new products, processes, services and technologies (Baldwin et al. 2006; Franke and von Hippel 2003; Herstatt and von Hippel 1992; Jeppesen and Frederiksen 2006; Lettl et al. 2008; Lüthje et al. 2005; Morrison et al. 2004; Urban and von Hippel 1988; von Hippel 1988). The examples of user innovation span wide fields and a huge variety of innovations such as in sporting equipment, medical equipment, open source software, pharmaceuticals, chemical processes, musical instruments, and IT solutions. Furthermore studies have shown that users frequently share their ideas and innovations in communities (Baldwin et al. 2006; Franke and Shah 2003; Franke and von Hippel 2003; Jeppesen and Frederiksen 2006). Studies on lead users have shown that individuals with specific characteristics can develop radical innovations that only later on get recognition from the market and from companies (Morrison et al. 2004; Urban and von Hippel 1988; von Hippel 1986, 1988, 2005).

Although we have broad information on different types of user innovations and different characteristics of different types of user innovators, most studies on user innovation focus on artifacts. It seems that *what users actually do* is taken for granted and not given too much attention. Rather, the final outcome, usually a physical object or solution, is given full attention. This is surprising, as prominent narrative episodes and case studies on user innovation processes are often based on what the users have been *doing in a novel way*. Furthermore the actual benefit of a user innovation seems closely linked to that novel way (i.e., *technique*) as users benefit mainly from using an innovation (von Hippel 1988). Applying common sense, use benefit should emerge out of innovative and not repetitive and already existing ways of *doing*. Therefore it seems worth investigating what influence novel techniques have on the development of novel artifacts and on reaching a desired outcome by the user applying it. The chapter is organized in the following sections exploring that specific research interest: in the next section *technique innovation* is defined. Then literature on user innovation regarding novel techniques is analyzed. Subsequently a framework for development scenarios including novel techniques is introduced. Last is the presentation of two illustrative and one main case development scenarios, and the economic impact, and in this regard further research avenues are discussed.

Defining *Technique Innovation*

As the term *technique innovation* has not been used in the field of user innovation before, it seems essential to first discuss how the term *technique* differs from other related terms such as *procedure, process, practice,* or *service*. The Oxford Dictionary and Merriam-Webster provide useful insights: *Service* and *practice* are probably not too closely related to what is analyzed here. While *practice* defines a rather repetitive, habitual activity (missing the innovative element), *service* is something clearly done for a third party, not addressing the individual user's own need and his/her effort to find an innovative solution for exactly that problem. *Procedure* and *process* are quite close in their meaning and definition. However, while *procedure* and *process* both involve various steps in a sequence of activities, *technique* can be an activity that is independent of prior and post steps or activities. Furthermore both *procedure* and *process* involve standardized routines and probably already established ways of doing something while *technique* seems to relate to a more free and individual activity of a person. Also *technique* is the only term that clearly involves a human activity, whereas both, *process* and *procedure* can be activities that are done by a machine or computer only, for instance, within an automated manufacturing process.

Summarizing these different aspects and including the element of newness, *technique innovation* can be defined as follows:

Technique innovation

1. is a new kind of activity/action ("new way of doing");
2. is done by a person, either individually or within a firm;
3. is a skillful, planned activity;
4. either directly involves some physical equipment; or
5. is needed to operate/maneuver within an environment composed of specific artifacts.

Furthermore it is important to highlight that any kind of innovation involves the aspect of diffusion, that is, adoption by other individuals. Diffusion is also true for technique innovation. Thus an individual new technique that is just done to satisfy a very personal need and not communicated to and used by others would not be considered innovation, while a novel technique adopted by others would.

User Innovation Literature Dealing with the Development of Novel Techniques

After having defined *technique innovation*, it is interesting to see whether aspects of it have been addressed in innovation studies, and more specifically in the field of user innovation. The following examples show that what users actually do (in terms of a new technique) is often mentioned or done in parallel to the hardware innovation process but left aside from the actual analysis. For instance, Shah (2000: 11) is reporting on the innovative activities of users developing windsurfing equipment:

As they experimented and created various windsurfing techniques, tricks, and tried to go faster and faster in high wind and wave conditions, new needs emerged—needs that the existing equipment could not fulfill. They created innovations in windsurfing equipment in order to tailor the equipment to the techniques and conditions they were experiencing.

It is evident from Shah's paper and the users quoted here that innovative techniques are an important driver to develop new equipment and that new equipment in turn leads to the opportunity to develop further technique. While innovative users definitely can experience conditions and tailor the equipment accordingly, technique is something that includes active application and development from the user innovator (Shah 2000: 12):

Interview data indicate that they were 12 passionate users of the sporting equipment and were eagerly seeking and developing new techniques that required related innovations in equipment. They are in some ways the sports equivalent of software hackers, always trying to test and push the limits of their sport via innovations in technique and equipment.

Similarly Lüthje et al. (2005: 954f.) wrote about innovative users in the field of mountain biking and how their technique innovations changed existing products and equipment:

Mountain biking enthusiasts did not stop their innovation activities after the introduction of commercially manufactured mountain bikes. They kept pushing mountain biking into more extreme environmental conditions and also continuously developed new sports techniques involving mountain bikes (Mountain Bike Magazine, 1996). Thus, some began jumping with their bikes from house roofs and water towers and developing other forms of acrobatics. As they did so, they steadily discovered needs for improvements to their equipment and, as we shall see in this paper, many responded by developing and building improvements for themselves.

Other studies focus on the equipment innovation only without including detailed information about the relationship between innovative techniques and equipment (Franke and Shah 2003: 158). Similarly Hienerth and Lettl (2011) clearly describe innovative techniques of lead users in various fields such as medical equipment industry and sporting equipment industry but focus on the development of the respective equipment and the commercialization process.

If the authors quoted did not include and analyze novel techniques, how can we judge if they were relevant at all? Basically technique innovations should be relevant if they have a clear influence on the development of artifacts (and vice versa), if their development somehow precedes the development of artifacts and thus can be used to predict further development, and/or if there is clear economic effort on the side of the user innovators that is substantial and comparable to the effort done for other types of innovations. Therefore, and as a first step, we develop a framework of different development scenarios, involving technique and product innovation.

Table 16.1
Development scenarios for novel techniques and artifacts

Satisfying need or solving problem with:		Artifact	
		Existing	New
Technique	New	B	D
	Existing	A	C

A Framework of Technique Innovation and Product Innovation

As outlined above, literature has so far focused on users developing novel artifacts or products. The core reason for such activity is that users want to satisfy unmet needs or solve a problem. Introducing and investigating the concept of technique innovation is adding to our understanding of such user innovation processes: It shows that solving problems or satisfying needs can basically be done by different means, which are summarized in a simple model of development scenarios (table 16.1). First, users can try to use artifacts at hand and do something in a novel way (pure technique innovation first, B). Second, users can try to develop a novel artifact that satisfies the need without having to develop new ways of dealing or operating with it (pure equipment/hardware innovation first, C). Third, a parallel development process is possible, when technique and artifact innovation happens as a stepwise, linked process (D). A case that does not require the development of novel artifacts or techniques is scenario A.

Two simple cases based on secondary data can be used to illustrate that technique innovation may follow product/artifact innovation and vice versa (scenarios B and C):

A Case of Technique Innovation Following Product Innovation: Impressionist Painters

It is widely known that Impressionist painters like Monet, Pissarro, or Renoir were able to create artistic artifacts that had a radical degree of novelty within the art world of the mid to late 19th century. However, what is interesting for this study is that such novel type of paintings could only be achieved by a development of novel products followed by various *novel techniques*. An exhibition and the following publication from the Albertina in Vienna, *Painting Light. The Hidden Techniques of the Impressionists* (Schaefer et al. 2008) provides an excellent overview of the emergence of novel products during the first decades of the 19th century:

One important novel product developed during that time was the paint tube. It was originally developed by the artist (i.e., *user*) John Goffe Rand in 1841 and further improved by adding a screw top by the color manufacturer Alexander Lefranc. Before, artists had been using pig bladders to carry around pigments. Those were leaking and did not guarantee similar quality, hue, and intensity of the colors. The paint tube allowed for an easy, transportable way to store colors that would no longer be affected by oxygen, light, or humidity. The Lefranc company started selling tube paint in 1850. From that time on, painters could paint outside, on the spot, whereas before they were bound to their studios to grind pigments and to mix in chemical additives. Another important development was the introduction of new colors. While only around a dozen of basic colors was available in the early 19th century, innovations in the field of chemistry and mineralogy lead to the enlargement of the palette to a full range of green, blue, red, and especially yellow pigments that were much light faster than the limited colors known before. Further innovations were, for instance, mobile easels, novel shapes of paintbrushes, and pre-primed supports (canvas), again enabling outdoor painting techniques. The diffusion of the innovations developed was enabled by a rapidly growing network of art supplies. The trade directory of Paris in 1850 lists as much as 276 paint dealers. Some of the original manufacturers are still operating today, such as the French Sennelier or the London-based Winsor & Newton.

In the years following (the first Impressionist exhibition was held in 1874), there was an explosion of novel techniques: Painters developed *plein air painting,* in general, and experimented with painting series such as the Haystacks by Monet (1891) in order to explore the effect of light on an object. They achieved new luminosity of the colors applied, suppressed fine details of modeling and coloration for the sake of the overall impression of shapes and started using palette knives for painting. Developing these novel techniques, the Impressionists broke with several traditions in painting that had been established by Old Masters such as Caravaggio and Rembrandt in the 17th century. As a result, in their time, the Impressionists faced full incomprehension by their public. However, their novel techniques built the basis for the further technique developments of the expressionist movement and modern art we know today.

A Case of Equipment Innovation Following Technique Innovation: The Development of Anesthetic Treatment

The history of anesthesia and the related techniques to lower or deaden pain evolved in several steps before the first medical equipment was introduced. The mentioning of first techniques goes back more than 2000 years. A prominent example which is used by several medical history books (Schüttler 2003) comes from the Old Testament saying:

God caused a deep sleep to fall upon the man, and he slept; then he took one of his ribs and closed up its place with flesh.
(First book of Moses, Genesis 2.1)

While this excerpt cannot literally be taken as an actual act of applying anesthesia, medical historians still see it as an indication that people living in the 4th to 5th century BC were aware of techniques to cause unconsciousness. In the centuries following, numerous examples of anesthetic techniques have been reported such as medication with various natural substances (herbs, herbal liquids), alcohol, or hypnosis (Zorab 2003). Main developments in anesthetic treatment and pathbreaking novel techniques happened in the 19th century, when physicians started medication with ether, nitrous oxide (laughing gas), and chloroform. The substances had been developed outside of the medical field and were mainly used for public amusement and intoxication by the well-to-do of society. A first dissertation on the effects of ether gas inhalation was done by Mathew B. Caleb 1824 in Philadelphia. However, applying it as a new medical technique happened in 1844, when the dentist Horace Wells pulled one of his own teeth painlessly, and more widely known when William Morten used ether as an anesthetic at the Massachusetts General Hospital (Bynum 2008; Magner 1992). It is important to stress that the physicians did not invent the substance itself but, rather, developed novel techniques using them: They had to find out what substance to use for what treatment, how to mix substances with oxygen, how to use the right dose of anesthetics or the timing to start and end a treatment. In the following three decades, physicians kept on experimenting and innovating techniques using ether, nitrous oxide, and chloroform. Based on their insights first, simple medical equipment was developed, such as glass or metal masks holding sponges on which the narcotic fluid was poured. First machines to assist in mixing oxygen and nitrous oxide were developed in 1887 by Sir Frederick Hewitt. More sophisticated versions of that machine allowing for dosing and proportioning are reported from 1910 on (Schirmer 1998). A very similar pattern of development is reported for the field of antiseptics, in which physicians experimented and developed novel techniques around the application of various chemical substances (e.g., carbolic acid) to avoid infection of open wounds (Ackerknecht 1982). Together, technique innovations in the field of anesthesia and antiseptics build the basis for breakthrough technique and equipment innovations in modern surgery.

As these first illustrative cases have shown rather subsequent paths of development it is interesting to further investigate more complex developments in which all three different scenarios outlined in the framework (table 16.1: B, C, and D) might be observed.

Main Case Study: Development of Whitewater Kayaking Technique and Equipment

The purpose of this main case is to allow exploring the development of technique innovation and hardware/equipment innovation in a field with rich information. The case needs to satisfy requirements of external validity, namely that findings from the case can be transferred to other cases or settings (Yin 2009; Eisenhardt 1989). The field of whitewater kayaking has a number of characteristics that are advantageous for the study of technique innovation and its interrelationship with hardware and equipment development. There is a long development of both types of innovations so that interrelationships can be studied over more than 50 years. Furthermore techniques and hardware/equipment in the whitewater kayaking industry are rather simple, so they can be studied and understood quite easily and isolated. Dependencies can be analyzed avoiding biases from hidden effects or alternative causes.

In order to identify technique innovations and innovations in hardware and equipment and the expenditures involved in developing both types of innovations, the following data were collected and analyzed:

1. The complete primary and secondary data used in Hienerth (2006), about the rodeo kayaking industry.
2. Innovation history data from "The River Chasers" by Sue Taft (2001) and "The Call of the River," a historic documentary movie of the whitewater sport and industry by Kent Ford.
3. A complete analysis of all *American Whitewater Association Magazine* issues starting in 1955 and the analysis of the annual "gear issue" of the *Canoe and Kayak Magazine*, produced every year since 1975.
4. An online survey (conducted from April to June 2010) of whitewater kayakers to determine innovation types, expenditures, and innovation motivations since 1950 (340 responses).

These data provide a unique overview of different types of innovations over the entire development phase of the whitewater kayak industry since the 1950s. The data allow specific development phases of the industry to be identified and also the most important or main hardware/equipment development steps that influenced the industry and developed the market. Innovations in hardware/equipment identified concern the kayak hull (e.g., length, form, and air volume distribution), the kayak interior (called *fittings*), kayaking gear (apparel, helmets, protection, and floatation vests), and kayak paddles. Innovations in technique identified concern river running techniques and freestyle techniques. River running techniques are about steering and maneuvering the kayak in whitewater, depending on the difficulty and topography of the river. Freestyle techniques are playful moves with kayaks in holes or on waves, often three-dimensional.

A Description of Development Phases in the Whitewater Kayaking Industry

Early Whitewater Kayaking (from 1950s to Introduction of Plastic Kayaks in Late 1970s and Early 1980s)

Fiberglas kayaks for whitewater kayaking were first mainly manufactured in kayak clubs or supplied from very small companies owned by paddlers basically making copies for fellow paddlers and developing material thus needed. In Europe, slalom kayaking emerged, a sport that used the new composite kayaks, heavily relying on long and thin boat designs that could maneuver through gates in the river and could be paddled upstream. In the United States, slalom was not that popular in the beginning (1950s to the 1960s). Instead, kayak clubs arranged the exploration of various rivers with increasing difficulties in whitewater. They continuously developed essential techniques for river running, mainly paddling in and out of eddies, ferrying across the river, bracing with the paddle and rolling. In parallel they needed to reduce the length and adapt the hull design of the slalom boats, to make them more suitable for heavy whitewater paddling and to reduce the repair time after rock contact.

Plastic Revolution (Introduction of Plastic Kayaks by Industry External Companies and Subsequent Developments from Late 1970s to Late 1980s)

Whitewater kayaking was considered the next big outdoor sports after the success of skiing in the 1960s. It became so popular that two manufacturers of plastic, Uniroyal (using thermoforming technology, building canoes) and Hollowform (using rotational molding technology, building kayaks), entered the market and started producing the first plastic canoes and kayaks. Existing kayak companies had been too small to test the new material and to apply the new technology. In 1973 Hollowform produced the first rotomolded plastic kayak, the *river chaser* (13 feet long, at $129.95 plus tax and shipping). However, after a few years of business and changing management, Hollowform moved out of the kayak market and sold its molds to Perception, which became the largest manufacturer of traditional composite kayaks. With the new material, paddlers could run steeper and more dangerous rivers than before and explore waves and holes in the river. Doing so, they discovered and developed new techniques: They found out that by dropping into a hole, one end would be pulled beneath the surface level while the other end would be pushed upside. The first kayak freestyle move was born. In June 1977 Joe Leonard, a raft outfitter, had the idea to make an event for paddlers to show their river running skills in Stanley, Idaho. The result was the first Rodeo ever held, the Stanley Rodeo, attended by 26 paddlers. A year later, another event, the Salmon River Days, took place. More and more paddlers participated in these events.

Counterrevolution in Composite Materials (Emergence and Development of Squirt Boating from 1980s to Early 1990s)

Some of the paddlers at that time (early 1980s) did not like the plastic boats that were available on the market. The design of the plastic kayak hull, which was very big and voluminous, could not be changed by the users and developed for river running. The plastic hulls were good for paddling straight and doing some basic turns, but not for more playful moves in the river, using sub-currents and water drops. Some users wanted to develop exactly those novel techniques. As the material plastic required investments in expensive molding, the users developed their designs in composite materials. They could adapt the hull designs quite easily, depending on the technique they wanted to test. That is how squirt boating came up. The kayak hulls had to be tailored to the body-weight of the paddler. With only 51 percent of buoyancy, paddlers were able to control vertical paddle techniques for the first time in kayak history. Still, squirt boating did not attract a mass market. On the one hand, it was very uncomfortable to be squeezed into a squirt boat and to stay under water most of the time. On the other hand, standard customers were not used to repair their boats and to change material themselves anymore. Consequently squirt boating remained a niche sport for a small number of paddlers. However, nearly all vertical paddling techniques still used today were developed in this phase.

Rodeo and Freestyle Kayaking (Rise of New Design and Growth of Market from Late 1990s until Today)

In the early 1990s the new vertical paddling techniques in squirt boating had been established and new ones were constantly evolving. In plastic and downriver kayaking, techniques for heavy whitewater and waterfall riding had evolved. Some of the users realized that one could probably integrate the benefits of the squirt boats and the plastic kayaks to come up with a design solution that would allow applying all paddling techniques available. That was the birth of the rodeo kayak. It combined at least four important design features that allowed vertical techniques, surfing, river running, and waterfall riding. First, the rodeo kayak was shorter than the traditional plastic kayaks. Second it had low air volume, the same as squirt boats. Third, it concentrated the air volume around the cockpit of the paddler, increasing safety and allowing the user to rotate the ends vertically. Fourth, it had a flat planing hull, a requirement for surfing techniques. As that hull was conceptually new, a number of further design changes were needed to optimize performance of the new rodeo kayaks in waves and holes. Thus the number of designs began a steadily increasing each year, along with size differentiation strategies for the overall kayak designs. Altogether, almost three times the number of plastic kayak designs were introduced in the mid to late 1990s than all the previous years combined since plastic kayaks were first introduced in 1973.

From the analysis of all innovations in equipment and hardware, the major steps of development can be identified:

- Reduction of the kayak to a length of around 3 meters (1960s to mid-1970s)
- Production of the kayak in plastic (mid-1970s)
- Development of the squirt boat design (1980s)
- Development of the rodeo kayak (late 1990s and early 2000s)

The data collected in this case study also allow the major development steps in technique to be identified:

- Turning/steering in the river (1950s to 1980s)
- Rolling (continuous development; but main standards emerged in early phases 1950s to 1970s)
- Riding over waterfalls and drops (1970s and 1980s)
- Submerged moves (putting one or both ends of a kayak below the surface of the river) (mostly in the 1980s and early 1990s)
- Aerial moves (lifting parts of the kayak or the whole kayak out of the water) (late 1990s and 2000s)

These two sets of data as combined with data from the prior two case studies suggest some interesting interrelationships and dependencies between equipment innovations and technique innovations.

Discussion of Development Scenarios and Relevance

The main case and additional illustrative cases described have shown different development paths of novel artifacts and novel techniques. As a common starting point of development, users wanted to satisfy an unmet need or to solve a problem relying on different means available to them as introduced in the development scenarios (table 16.1).

In the main case, the development of whitewater kayak equipment and paddling techniques, we can find examples for parallel development processes (D) as well as for either prior technique development (B) or prior artifact development (C):

An example for the continuous exploration of the design space of both novel techniques and novel artifacts (D) is the very first stage of whitewater kayaking (starting in the 1950s). In that period users continuously developed novel river running techniques in parallel to working on and improving their artifacts, mainly shortening and strengthening the kayak hulls. A further example for parallel development is the phase of squirt boating in the 1980s. A handful of lead users in whitewater kayaking developed completely novel techniques and completely novel shapes of kayak hulls. They revolutionized the way of paddling by introducing vertical moves. Such novel techniques were only possible by a close, parallel development of kayak shapes that would allow the partly or full immersion of the paddler.

The introduction of the plastic kayak is an example of prior artifact development (C). As the material plastic allowed stone contact in the river, kayakers could start developing novel techniques for river running such as sliding over rocks, maneuvering much closer to rocks and paddling waterfalls. It allowed them to explore new parts of the river and lead to a full new range of paddling techniques: creek boating. An example of novel artifacts being developed after the development of novel techniques (B) is the case of the modern rodeo kayak. Its development was dependent on the invention of numerous novel techniques from different fields of paddling during the prior 20 to 30 years. User manufacturers developing the rodeo kayak in the late 1990s wanted to create an artifact that would allow the users to apply all techniques known for river running as well as performing the more recent technique innovations from squirt boating. Thus the artifact had to be stable enough to allow running heavy whitewater and waterfalls, but it also had to be controllable and short enough to perform freestyle moves in waves and holes.

The two illustrative cases have been chosen to document the existence of technique innovations in other fields and to illustrate extreme examples of development. The case of anesthetics development illustrates scenario B, in which novel techniques are developed prior to first artifacts. It is evident from the status quo of anesthetics today that artifacts (medical equipment that assists the patient's breathing, controls the dosing of the narcotic substances, etc.) have a vital role for the anesthetic process. However, the case documents that first artifacts were only developed once the physicians had experimented with various novel techniques. The case of the Impressionist painting techniques is an illustration for the scenario of prior artifact and subsequent technique development (C). More than fifty years of painting technique development heavily depend on the introduction of the paint tube and new types of chemically produced colors.

Regarding the relevance of novel techniques, the cases chosen suggest the existence and significance of technique innovations. The overall set of options (table 16.1) indicates that in two scenarios (B and D), novel techniques are needed to develop novel artifacts. In a case where the artifact is developed first (C), the cases show that the following novel techniques are becoming central part of the value such artifacts can generate and the space of options that is available to users.

Discussion of Economic Importance of Technique Innovation

The cases analyzed have given indicative examples of development scenarios and not demonstrated economic importance quantitatively. However, research is starting to explore the types and amount of expenditures involved in developing technique innovations (Hienerth et al. 2011). Expenditures in the development process can be calculated in different ways. The two illustrative cases used here do only allow a very rough assessment of costs. Both cases show that users have at least invested years and decades of effort in developing novel techniques. In the main case of whitewater kayaking, a recent study (Hienerth et al. 2011) provides first insights on how to calculate expenditures in technique development and how efficient user innovators are, compared to manufacturers. Expenditures of technique innovation in that study have been calculated in two ways: First, by using historic data on the development process of novel techniques and calculating the most likely expenditures by simply adding the different resources put into the process. Second, the authors collected direct information from the users via questionnaires.

Results of that study show that costs involved in developing important technique innovations are comparable to developing important hardware innovations ($209K per important technique innovation; $332K per important equipment innovation) on the side of the users. Furthermore users develop technique innovations about three times more efficient than manufacturers. Overall, users are responsible for over 90 percent of the technique innovations developed over a period of more than 50 years in whitewater kayaking.

Regarding research on user innovation, the development of novel techniques is at the core of what users are actually doing. While we have so far mainly been confronted with the results of innovative activities by users, the concept of technique innovation can contribute to understanding the processes and activities better that lead to novel artifacts or are induced by novel artifacts. Thus in studies of lead user innovation (Lilien et al. 2002) the concept of technique innovation can contribute to a more comprehensive analysis of lead user activities. It can show whether the innovative activities are radically novel or a consequence of related activities (product or equipment development). This knowledge can enable companies to absorb lead user knowledge better. Else, in terms of research dealing with open source software development, the notion of technique innovation can help us recognize the novelty around the behavior and individual innovative activities of specific community members, in addition to analyzing and measuring efficiency and quality of the outcome. While everyone in the field of open source research is familiar with Linus's law ("given enough eyeballs, all bugs are shallow"), little is documented on how and what techniques users develop in order to control for errors and how much time and effort they invested.

Discussion of Implications for Industry Evolution and Design Theory

A potential importance of analyzing novel techniques is anticipating development paths of related products and solutions. Therefore technique innovation should be of relevance within a larger framework of industry evolution and the emergence of dominant designs. The essence of dominant design theory is that with the emergence of a dominant design, efforts in R&D shift from product innovation to process innovation (Abernathy and Utterback 1978). Before the emergence of a dominant design, firms compete around many different variations in products and face small, uncertain market segments. Murmann and Frenken (2006) have analyzed studies on dominant designs and the development of new technologies and industries resulting in a comparison of 24 articles. It is interesting that all studies selected by Murmann and Frenken (2006) do not provide or show indicators of a development prior to the emergence of first products or available technologies. This is not surprising as studies on dominant designs often use historical data on the introduction of new products (hard disk drives, flight simulators, helicopters, walkmen, etc.) or the emergence of new firms. They are bound to historical databases or listings of companies. As a summary of all articles analyzed, the authors come up with a new definition of dominant designs that

> rests fundamentally on the concept of "nested hierarchies of design spaces." Search in these hierarchically organized, modular design spaces gives rise to "technology cycles," that is, episodes of variation, selection and retention in various parts of the complex technological system. (Murmann and Frenken 2006: 931)

The notion of design spaces connects to design theory, which deals with the composition, functionality, quality, and development of novel artifacts (Baldwin and Clark 2000). The definition of Murmann and Frenken indicates that for the development of dominant designs, not only the development of overall technological systems is important but also the contributing parts to that system which ultimately goes back to individual designs and artifacts. What can be done or achieved with such designs or artifacts (i.e., the functionality) represents the smallest unit within hierarchies and technological cycles. Conceptually framing and empirically analyzing technique innovation as in this study can thus provide novel and better understanding of the emergence of new designs via the novel use (i.e., technique innovation) of such designs and probably expected parallel development of both the design and related activity.

What can design theory tell us about such use and functionality of individual designs and the development of new designs within an overall framework of options, the design space? First, design theory can give us an idea of the characteristics of designs and explain when and why individual, new designs emerge. A basic design characteristic is design quality (Baldwin et al. 2006). It represents the value a design has for a user and is a function of the functionality of the design or, in other words, how well it satisfies the user's needs. In early stages of development, designs are rather basic and have low design quality as they represent only first experiments of the users to develop a solution for their needs. Then every new design and every new effort can increase the quality of the next design. Options of what can be done will increase. The development of each individual new design requires some effort (resources as time, money, material, etc.). Users will judge whether the expected quality (functionality) of the new design will justify their effort to develop the new design. Thus, with design quality rising over time, ever more effort will be required to come up with more design quality or functionality and fewer users will make the effort. Regarding innovations in technique, any activity a user does in a novel way with a given design might raise design quality. Any new activity or technique might initiate a novel design. And vice versa, novel designs might suggest a new set of alternatives or options of what can be done.

Second, design theory has introduced the understanding of design spaces, options and variations in designs that individuals can explore and map out. For instance, Baldwin et al. (2006: 1297) have described the process of a design space opening up and connected that event to an innovative activity, which can be considered technique innovation:

The "opening" of a new design space is often a datable event—like the time that Walt Blackader first used a kayak to do tricks in the whitewater of a river. As in this case, user-innovators may trigger the opening by doing something in a new way.

As the authors have outlined, a datable event is followed by a series of innovations, which in the language of design theory are simply called *new designs*. While such an event is seen and understood as a starting point for a series of new designs and design activity by a lot of users, little is analyzed in what is actually done with the artifact or design. Thus the idea of a design space and the process of mining out a design space so far is rather seen as the overall group of different but related designs within one related field and how much or far that field is developed and how many options remain. Innovations in techniques increase the options within any given design space, as it can be assumed that they do not only lead to novel designs but also increase the functionality and options for already existing designs.

Third, technique innovation can be seen as investment in new designs. As design theory explains, users face innovation costs when they develop novel designs. Such costs are basically made up by all resources that flow into the design process, also including time. Thus an individual developing a novel technique, spending time and effort in order to find out how things can be done in a novel way, is clearly investing his or her resources in the overall design development process. That effort might lead to a physical artifact or new technology or it might not. It might also be observed by other individuals who might be able to build upon it and then develop novel designs. The challenge with regards to technique innovation is that unlike to physical artifacts or technologies, it might be harder to see and judge individual steps of development.

Implications for Further Research on Design and Industry Evolution

The potential contribution of novel insights on technique innovation is twofold. First, better understanding of development cycles can extend the usual scope of models of industry evolution. The emergence of novel techniques can be an early indicator of needs connecting to physical artifacts or solutions. Thus the idea of technique innovations can contribute to better insights about when companies will start competing around new products and standards and also what the most likely winning solution or standard will be. Furthermore insights about technique innovation can help to understand the full range of functionality of given artifacts and thus increase the knowledge about design quality. Another aspect is design space, its extension and exploitation. The emergence of novel techniques using existing artifacts can be a signal of open design spaces. Once the techniques as well as the artifacts start to change, new design spaces emerge and displace the existing solutions and designs. The technique innovations can indicate connections between an overall architecture and subsystems of designs: Technique innovations can lead to small changes within the overall architecture as well. A novel technique might function with a subsystem and only need small adjustments. However, once those adjustments become too many or the technique becomes too advanced, there will be an overall change in the system. An increased use of innovative techniques can even be an early indicator for emerging market segments. An increased use of novel techniques can show a need for adaptation in existing artifacts or the development and supply of completely new artifacts. The more individuals apply novel techniques, the higher is the potential of developing a new market segment.

Conclusion

This chapter provides some insights into the existence and development of technique innovations. By analyzing innovation literature, literature on design theory and industry evolution, as well as three different cases of novel technique applications, a model for development scenarios of technique innovation and artifact innovation was introduced. The findings and discussion points suggest that broader and more generalized consideration of the insights and effects of technique innovations is merited. Aspects of technique innovations are present in all settings in which individuals apply some kind of skillful activity in dealing with existing or novel artifacts. Insights may be transferable among fields as different as medical, military, construction, and creative arts industries.

The evidence so far is limited to case studies and initial surveys in the field of whitewater kayaking. The two cases chosen as further illustration (anesthetics and Impressionist painters) are based on secondary data only. Furthermore the models discussed here point to sequences of development paths whereby often one type of innovation leads to the other. It often may even be difficult to judge which type of innovation is the predecessor for the other and when exactly innovations emerge in parallel. In effect it is the tacit nature of technique innovations that imposes challenges for observing development steps. However, these limitations do not question the existence of the phenomenon of technique innovation but rather open up avenues for further research.

Table 16.2

Characteristics of the early stages of whitewater kayaking

Number of innovators and consumers	Growing number of lead users up to 200; growing number of innovators up to 5,000; not yet actual consumers.
Number of companies	First only a handful of household companies; business sector companies rising up to 14.
Number and types of equipment innovations	51 equipment innovations (all by users): mainly reduction of length of the kayak hull, some first apparel innovations, some first safety gear innovations.
Number and types of technique innovations	56 technique innovations (all by users): river running techniques, bracing techniques, rolling techniques, slalom techniques.

Table 16.3
Characteristics of the "plastic" phase in whitewater kayaking

Number of innovators and consumers	100–200 lead users, between 2,000 and 4,000 user innovators and between 60,000 and 100,000 consumers.
Number of companies	Number of composite kayak manufacturers ranging between 5 and 20; number of plastic kayak manufacturers rising from 2 to 10.
Number and types of equipment innovations	26 equipment innovations (20 by users, 6 by companies), mainly concerning the form of the kayak hull and safety features.
Number and types of technique innovations	29 technique innovations (all by users) such as different turning, rolling and bracing techniques. First freestyle and creek boating techniques.

Table 16.4
Characteristics of the "squirt boat" phase

Number of innovators and consumers	2–4 lead users, up to 1,000 user innovators; no real consumer segment.
Number of companies	Between 1 and 2 companies producing lead user designs.
Number and types of hardware innovations	12 equipment innovations (10 by users, 2 by companies): flattening and shortening the kayak designs.
Number and types of technique innovations	21 technique innovations (all by users): Emergence of vertical and submerged paddle techniques.

Table 16.5
Characteristics of the rodeo kayak phase

Number of innovators and consumers	200 to 400 lead users, between 4,000 to 10,000 user innovators and number of consumers for the overall kayak market over one million people.
Number of companies	Between 3–6 composite kayak manufacturers and around 10–15 plastic kayak manufacturers, often started by lead users from the 1990s.
Number and types of hardware innovations	39 equipment innovations (13 by users, 26 by companies), developing the standard rodeo kayak design.
Number and types of technique innovations	42 technique innovations (29 by users, 13 by companies): vertical, aerial techniques and surfing.

References

Abernathy, W. J., and J. M. Utterback. 1978. Patterns of industrial innovation. *Technology Review* 80 (7): 40–47.

Ackerknecht, Erwin Heinz. 1982. *A Short History of Medicine*. Baltimore: Johns Hopkins University Press.

Baldwin, C., C. Hienerth, and E. von Hippel. 2006. How user innovations become commercial products: A theoretical investigation and case study. *Research Policy* 35 (9): 1291–1313.

Baldwin, C., and K. B. Clark. 2000. *Design Rules: The Power of Modularity*. vol. 1. Cambridge: MIT Press.

Bynum, William. 2008. *History of Medicine: A Very Short Introduction*. New York: Oxford University Press.

Eisenhardt, K. M. 1989. Building theories from case study research. *Academy of Management Review* 14 (4): 532–50.

Franke, N., and E. von Hippel. 2003. Satisfying heterogeneous user needs via innovation toolkits: The case of Apache Security software. *Research Policy* 32 (7): 1199–1215.

Franke, N., and S. Shah. 2003. How communities support innovative activities: An exploration of assistance and sharing among end-users. *Research Policy* 32 (1): 157–78.

Herstatt, C., and E. von Hippel. 1992. From experience: Developing new product concepts via the lead user method: A case study in a "low-tech" field. *Journal of Product Innovation Management* 9 (3): 213–21.

Hienerth, C., and C. Lettl. 2011. Exploring how peer communities enable lead user innovations to become standard equipment in the industry: Community pull effects. *Journal of Product Innovation Management* 28 (s1): 175–95.

Jeppesen, L. B., and L. Frederiksen. 2006. Why do users contribute to firm-hosted user communities? The case of computer-controlled music instruments. *Organization Science* 17 (1): 45–63.

Lettl, C., C. Hienerth, and H. G. Gemuenden. 2008. Exploring how Lead users develop radical innovation: Opportunity recognition and exploitation in the field of medical equipment technology. *IEEE Transactions on Engineering Management* 55 (2): 219–33.

Lilien, G. L., P. D. Morrison, K. Searls, M. Sonnack, and E. von Hippel. 2002. Performance assessment of the lead user idea-generation process for new product development. *Management Science* 48 (8): 1042–59.

Lüthje, C., C. Herstatt, and E. von Hippel. 2005. User-innovators and "local" information: The case of mountain biking. *Research Policy* 34 (6): 951–65.

Magner, Lois N. 1992. *A History of Medicine*. New York: Dekker.

Morrison, P. D., J. H. Roberts, and D. F. Midgley. 2004. The nature of lead users and measurement of leading edge status. *Research Policy* 33 (2): 351–62.

Murmann, J. P., and K. Frenken. 2006. Toward a systematic framework for research on dominant designs, technological innovations, and industrial change. *Research Policy* 35 (7): 925–52.

Schaefer, I., C. von Saint-George, and K. Lewerentz. Wallraf-Richartz-Museum Fondation Corboud, and F. P. Strozzi. 2008. *Painting Light: The Hidden Techniques of the Impressionists.* Milano: Skira.

Schirmer, U. 1998. Nitrous oxide. Trends and current importance. *Der Anaesthesist* 47 (3): 245–55.

Schüttler, Jürgen. 2003. *50 Jahre Deutsche Gesellschaft für Anästhesiologie und Intensivmedizin.* Berlin: Springer.

Shah, S. 2000. Sources and patterns of innovation in a consumer products field: Innovations in sporting equipment. h*ttp://flosshub.org/sites/flosshub.org/files/shahsportspaper.pd.f*

Taft, S. L. 2001. *The River Chasers.* Mukilteo, WA: Flowing Water Press/Alpen Books Press.

Urban, G. L., and E. von Hippel. 1988. Lead user analyses for the development of new industrial products. *Management Science* 34 (5): 569–82.

von Hippel, E. 1986. Lead users: A source of novel product concepts. *Management Science* 32 (7): 791–805.

von Hippel, E. 1988. *The Sources of Innovation.* New York: Oxford University Press.

von Hippel, E. 2005. *Democratizing Innovation.* Cambridge: MIT Press.

Yin, R. K. 2009. *Case Study Research: Design and Methods.* Los Angeles: Sage.

Zorab, J. 2003. History of anaesthesia. *Anaesthesia* 58 (9): 935.

17

The Power of Community Brands—How User-Generated Brands Emerge

Johann Füller

Today users and user communities are known as promising sources of innovation. Products such as the mountainbike or rodeo kayak (von Hippel 2005) and services such as computerized commercial banking services (Oliveira and von Hippel 2011) originate from users and not from companies. In the domain of innovation it is widely recognized that users and communities are not only co-creators who support firms and innovate in collaboration with them, but are able to develop their own products and present a real alternative to the company-centered innovation paradigm. The possibility that users and communities not only innovate but may also create attractive brands has been rather neglected so far (Füller et al. 2013). One of the reasons for this is the high media costs associated with marketing and branding activities that users could not afford previously. However, this has significantly changed due to the Internet and the social media revolution. Nowadays, user-generated content becomes as popular and important as content professionally generated by ad agencies (Kozinets et al. 2010). After the tremendous success of Facebook, Twitter, and YouTube, companies are aware of the impact of user-generated content on the marketing sphere and the creation of brands (Hautz et al. 2014). Nevertheless, the predominant thinking is still that users and communities may only co-create (Schau et al. 2009; Mathwick et al. 2008), manipulate (Klein 2000; Lee et al. 2009), or sometimes highjack (Wipperfürth 2005) the meaning of existing brands, but are not able to create their own brands. However, the latter is exactly the case (Füller et al. 2007; Pitt et al. 2006).

In the field of open source software (OSS), Apache, Firefox, and Linux are well-known examples where community members not only developed their own software applications but also created their own strong brands.

All three brands are created and owned by users and their community. Through members' joint development activities, deeds, and intense interactions, the Apache brand arose standing for superior software products created by software geeks who share the common vision to create great software. Community brands can be described as the reverse phenomenon of brand communities (Muniz and O'Guinn 2001). While brand communities such as the Apple I-lounge community or the Niketalk community evolve around existing company-driven brands and consist of fans who share their enthusiasm for Apple or Nike, user-generated brands are generated by community members as a quasi side effect of their joint activities.

This chapter explores the rather new phenomenon of user-generated brands. We term those brands *community brands* as they are created by users in collaboration with other users. We are especially interested in how community brands emerge and what makes them attractive. Further we discuss under which conditions community brands may be successful. Finally, implications for the common brand-creation practices of companies are given. Apache and Outdoorseiten.net (ODS), an outdoor community consisting of enthusiastic hikers and outdoor lovers, serve as research context for this study. In our qualitative study, data collection comprised community observation, participant observation, and interviews on users' brand creation activities. We find that users come up with and create their own community brands quite frequently. Community members create their own brands because they want to build their own identity and demonstrate their belongingness to the community. They enjoy using their self-created logos and community markers. For them, the meaning of the community brand is of high value and presents an alternative to existing company-driven brands. Once users progress in their branding activities, they aim for the basic functions a brand is able to serve: They want to protect and promote their creations; signal quality; attract fans; and create an identity that is meaningful to them and delineates them from others. Becoming known as creator is often the only way to protect one's intellectual property rights and to benefit from reputational gains when freely revealing the innovated good. Initially, user-generated community brands emerge more or less accidentally as a side effect of joint activities in the community. Later on, communities try to manage their brand more professionally, for example by providing guidelines and materials to their members. While community brands are able to fulfill basically the same functions as company-driven brands, they significantly differ from them. Through the distribution of the branding activities among their members, community brands are able to build brands at practically no cost. In most cases community brands do not aim to monetize or exploit their brand, so they are perceived as authentic. Not facing the threat of being overtaken by the next fashion wave makes community brands attractive not only for community members but also for non-community members. The study shows that user-generated community brands, like user innovations, may become a real alternative to the company-generated brands paradigm. They may also offer new co-branding possibilities for company brands. Companies may leverage their branding activities through collaboration with community brand members just like they benefit from collaborating with communities and lead users for innovation.

The chapter is structured as follows: First, relevant literature is reviewed in the area of brands and user-generated content. The problems of traditional views of brands and brand creation are discussed, as well as where theories of co-creation and customer integration fall short in order to explain the dynamics of community brands. Second comes a description of the research setting and methods. Community brands are discussed in the context of existing theory, on how community brands may impact markets currently dominated by company brands and offer directions for further research.

From Proprietary Brands toward Open Brands

Although brands as markers of ownership existed for centuries (Stern 2006), it was not until the second half of the 19th century that brands emerged as a mass phenomenon in the business context. Improvements in production, transportation, and communication processes enabled manufacturers to compete directly with local retailers as they were able to cost-efficiently produce a large number of goods and reach a wider audience (Low and Fullerton 1994). Throughout the 19th century, brands were utilized as markers of ownership. Goods could be traced back to their origins, which forced manufacturers to take over responsibility for their products and helped customers to get a consistent level of quality (Low and Fullerton 1994; Keller 2008). At that time, brands were largely managed by firm owners or top managers. Starting in the first half of the 20th century, brand management was increasingly professionalized. In general, companies began to rely on specialized professionals to carry out functions traditionally performed by the owner or top level managers (Low and Fullerton 1994). Brand management was either outsourced to advertising agencies or companies, such as Procter & Gamble, installed "brand managers." The basic idea behind the "brand manager system" was that each of the company's brands is best managed by a separate brand manager. By the middle of the 20th century, scholars and practitioners realized that a brand could be more than a label put on a product. Gardner and Levy argued that a brand is better described as "a complex symbol that represents a variety of ideas and attributes" (1955: 35). It was the image consumers bought, and some consumers developed powerful mental associations, extending far beyond the functional attributes of specific products, with brands. During that time, advertising agencies played a key role in the proliferation of brands (Ogilvy 1983). Brands might come to represent general, positively valued attributes such as good taste, luxury, or freedom. It was at that time that such iconic characters as the "Marlboro Man" were born. Throughout the second half of the 20th century, brands became not only more central to consumers' lives but also to corporate management. For consumers, brands became important resources to express their lifestyles, social status, and group affiliation. For companies, brands became core financial assets. Brands allowed companies to enhance their profits. The valuation of the brand as a financial asset—the price at which it can be sold or a valuation of achievable licensing fees and royalties—was termed "brand equity." To measure the strength of a brand in a simple and manageable way, Ailawadi et al. (2003), for example, suggested comparing the revenue premium a branded product generates with that of a private label product. From a user perspective, brand equity may be considered as the "differential effect of brand knowledge on consumer/(user) response to the marketing of the brand" (Keller 1993: 2). Based on their associations and knowledge, users decide if they are willing to pay the charged premium price for the brand product or not.

Toward the end of the 20th century and in the early years of the 21st century, a more dynamic and consumer-centered perspective of brands and brand management emerged. Instead of being reduced to static outcomes of marketers' actions, brands were perceived as dynamic entities, actively contributing to the lives of consumers (Aaker 1997; Fournier 1998). Brand value was seen as evolving in-use and Fournier argued that "brands can and do serve as viable relationship partners" (1998: 344). The active role of the consumer in the branding and value creation process was put forward. Instead of being passive recipients of marketers' actions, consumers are increasingly perceived as co-creators of value (Vargo and Lusch 2004; Prahalad and Ramaswamy 2000).

Today, it is widely accepted that consumers can and often do shape, appropriate, and co-create the meaning of commercial brands (Cova and Pace 2006; Kozinets et al. 2004; Muniz and Schau 2005; Thompson and Arsel 2004; Thompson et al. 2006). Producers may develop and introduce a brand on the marketplace, but then consumers and other stakeholders may modify its meaning in unexpected ways. Consumers may openly denunciate brands (Klein 2000), challenge the producer-intended meaning (Kates 2004; Thompson et al. 2006), decide upon legitimate brand ownership (Kirmani et al. 1999), or even hijack a brand (Muniz and Schau 2005; Wipperfürth 2005).

While earlier research on consumer value creation focused on moderate consumer involvement, recent studies draw a more radical picture of the consumer's role in the brand- and-value-creation process. Schau et al., for example, demonstrate not only that value-creating activities go beyond the exchange of knowledge, but also that communities "realize value beyond that which the firm creates or anticipates" (2009: 30). In the case of the Apple Newton brand, the loyal fan community continued the brand's management against the will of Apple, who had abandoned the brand in 1998. Without any support from Apple, the community engaged in the creation of brand-related content such as logos, slogans, and ads (Muniz and Schau 2007). Open source software (OSS) communities demonstrate that users are not only able to create brand-relevant content around existing brands but also to develop entirely user-generated brands. Linux, Apache, and Mozilla Firefox are only three examples out of a number of strong and well-known OSS brands. According to Pitt et al. (2006), an OSS brand is a brand like any other because it fulfills the same functions a corporate brand does. However, OSS brands offer unique value for their users due to their noncommercial interests, strong authenticity, and independence from the profit logic of the corporate world.

Despite the new possibilities for users to generate and disseminate their own brands, little is known about how user-generated brands emerge, what makes them attractive, and how they affect current marketing and brand management practices. This article contributes to a better understanding of the creation and management of community brands and sheds light on the impact of user-generated brands on current marketing practices.

Method

We selected the Apache community in the field of open source software and the outdoorseiten.net (ODS) community in the outdoor sports sector to explore how community brands emerge and what makes them so attractive. We decided to explore community brands for digital goods and physical goods in order to identify if such brands exist in both categories and to detect potential differences. Apache was chosen as the phenomenon of community brands first became important in the field of OSS and Apache is a well-known brand for webservers, with more than 60 percent market share. Outdoorseiten.net seemed to be interesting as physical equipment plays a crucial role and outdoor sports are quite popular and practiced by a great number of people around the world. Further many user innovation studies refer to the sports context.

Outdoorseiten.net is a 15-year old, online community with more than 28,600 German-speaking members dedicated to outdoor sports such as backpacking, multiday hiking, climbing, and ski touring. The forum counts more than 68,000 topics and almost 1.3 million posts where its members share their outdoor experiences with like-minded others. They spend a significant amount of time in activities related to outdoor sports, ranging from actively doing the sport to reading magazines, preparing their equipment, or communicating with people who share the same interests, both on- and offline. Product-creation related discussions play an important role in the interaction among members. The forum even has a separate subsection entirely dedicated to self-made gear and equipment. Their high involvement in outdoor sports is shown, for instance, by their impressive stories of climbing the world's highest mountains. In each community there are a small number of members who contribute the majority of all postings. It is not uncommon for the most enthusiastic members to have hundreds of postings on their community "resume" and—except when they are outdoors—they rarely miss a day of posting messages. At Outdoorseiten, 121 members have posted more than 1,000 messages, 1,000 members have posted more than 100 posts, and 12,900 have at least one post.

Altogether 20 in-depth interviews were conducted. The sample consists of 12 members from the Apache community and 8 from the ODS community (see table 17.1 for interviewee profiles). The respondents from the Apache community were between 29 and 48 years of age and male due to the predominance of male community members. The respondents of the ODS community were between 20 and 45 years old.

For our study we applied qualitative-inductive methodology (Denzin and Lincoln 1994) in order to gain rich insights into the phenomenon studied (Creswell 1998; Maxwell 2005). Data collection comprised community observation and participant observation, and interviews on community brand creation activities and brand perception. The exploration of the community archive of posts allowed us to follow the history of the Apache and ODS brand creation process.

In order to look at the phenomenon from different perspectives, respondents varied among their level of involvement ranging from founders and administrators to infrequent members. The interviews lasted between 35 and 90 minutes. We tape-recorded the interviews and transcribed them verbatim. The interviews were content-analyzed and interpreted until theoretical saturation (Goulding 2002) was achieved. Typical verbatims were selected to demonstrate our main findings.

Findings

Costless Creation and Shaping of Community Brands

Our study shows that the Apache community did not intend to create a strong brand, nor did the community engage in any advertising, marketing, or branding activities. At the beginning there was only a group of people who shared a common interest and a passion for programming.

Table 17.1

Profiles of interview participants

Pseudonym	Community	Community involvement	Role
Adam	Apache	2003	ASF member, BoD
Bill	Apache	1999	ASF member, committer
Bruce	Apache	1997	Committer
Chris	Apache	2000	ASF member, former project chairman
George	Apache	1996 (co-founder of the ASF)	ASF member, VP conference planning
Justin	Apache	2002	ASF member, committer
Mike	Apache	2001	President of the ASF
Peter	Apache	2001	committer
Roland	Apache	1996 (co-founder of the ASF)	Chairman of the ASF
Robert	Apache	2003	Committer
Steven	Apache	1996	ASF member, documentation project contributor
Thomas	Apache	1999	ASF member, director of the BoD
Nichtübertreiben	ODS	2002	Moderator forum tent
Thefly	ODS	2005	Administrator
Boehm22	ODS	2002	ODS treasurer
Bananenquark	ODS	2004	Contributor to ODS label discussion
Traeuma	ODS	2003	ODS board member
Nam	ODS	2003	ODS board member
Jasper	ODS	2003	Moderator travel
Snuffy	ODS	2003	Contributor to ODS label discussion
David0815	ODS	2003	Moderator Own Gear

ASF: Apache Software Foundation; BoD: Board of Directors; CTO: Chief Technology Officer; VP: Vice President; IT: Information Technology; ODS: Outdoorseiten. net Community

The Apache brand emerged as a quasi-costless side effect of activities carried out for other community or usage purposes. Following quotes reflect the "accidental character" of brand creation.

Up until very recently . . . we did not look at it as a brand and as something to market. (Tom)
    We never did any kind of advertising—not even today. We also never did marketing. We only have a Public Relations committee for the conference, but that's not the same. But we do not do marketing in the traditional sense. (Alex)

Basically the Apache brand emerged as an inescapable side effect of the joint activities of the community members. The Apache brand is further spread among community and non-community members who use the (free) product and thereby also create awareness for the Apache brand. Because the product is high quality and has unique attributes, "strong, favorable and unique brand" associations are created in the case of Apache, and positive brand responses, and "intense, active, and loyal relationships" with users result as well. Even non-users can be affected via viral transmission of positive impressions about Apache diffused by community members and non-community users.

Recently the Apache Software Foundation has begun to engage in active, purposeful brand management activities. In 2009 the Foundation appointed a Vice President of Brand Management (Apache 2009). In addition the Public Relations Committee (PRC) has started to issue branding guidelines, giving clear instructions on how to use the brand name as well as the Apache logo (Apache 2010). The Foundation has also begun to engage in activities directed at extracting value from the brand, notably with a sponsorship program. Sponsors include companies such as Google, Microsoft, and Hewlett-Packard. However, the brand name is emphatically not for sale to anyone. Whether a sponsor fits Apache is discussed openly in the community. If the fit is perceived as being too low or the community feels exploited, sponsorship is denied. Sponsors in the IT sector, for example, have to be known for their high-quality goods in order to become a potential partner. Besides offering money, sponsors have to fit the Apache quality principle and associated high-expertise level.

It's not for sale. We do not do it to get money. (Tom)

ODS

The ODS brand was created and strengthened in a similar manner. The community spent essentially nothing on developing its brand, on shaping

First draft

Final logo design

Figure 17.1

Excerpt of ODS logo designs

its meaning, or on strengthening the affiliation of their membership to the brand. Members voluntarily engaged in all those activities for free. The brand emerged as a costless side effect of participation in community activities that members valued and enjoyed for their own sake.

In essence, the brand development process began with a community member saying: "*Hey, let's design a logo!*" The idea of developing an out-doorseiten.net logo came up in the discussion of two core members in July 2005: *David0815* who had just developed and showcased his own personal logo and *Traeuma* who was so attracted by the idea that he proposed a community logo:

I want something like this from our forum, for my backpack! (Traeuma)

An astonishing number of other members immediately expressed their enthusiasm for such a project and the creation process of an Out-doorseiten.net logo began. As part of the development process, which spanned 5 weeks, more than 10 different design versions (see figure 17.1) of the logo were discussed extensively within the inner circle as well as the entire community. Most of the designs were done by Nam, one of the ODS board members and one of the most senior community members. After several changes and modifications of the design, the name and the final design of the new forum badge was chosen. At the same time the community consulted with different emblem shops about the kind of pro-duction and price, and organized the method of sale. Core as well as peripheral community members engaged in the branding process. However, most of the actual work and overall moderation of the process was performed by the core members.

Once the logos were distributed, community members began to attach the ODS logo on their self-made gear and their purchased outdoor equipment. Immediately products modified this way were referred to as belonging to the outdoorseiten.net brand:

Now I have to think where to place the badges on my backpacks. Watch out: "outdoorseiten.net" as a new backpack brand. (Silvia)

Contact with a maker of identity products like simple clothes and cheap personal items such as coffee cups then followed. In 2008 the ODS community launched its first self-developed product. Within a timeframe of approximately two years and with an active engagement of more than 200 members, ODS developed its own community tent, which then was produced and distributed in collaboration with a tent manufacturer called Wechsel. As the tent was developed, every active member had a say. In the ODS community, the preferences of the actively engaging community members are more important than any individual opinion even if it stems from the initiator or one of the board members.

Value of Community Brands

This section explores the value of community brands and demonstrates that the community itself embodies a great part of the brand value.

Apache

An important aspect of Apache's brand value is its ability to connect like-minded people, create a sense of community, and provide a platform for exchange, as the following statements demonstrate:

It's an immediate connection that we have . . . So when I meet someone now there is little chance that we actually have commonality on the project we are involved with. But we are part of that larger community and there is an immediate connection.

The "community over code" principle present in the community demonstrates that it is the community and the social relations between members that are valued above everything else, as shown by the following quote:

[T]here is this slogan that the community is more important than the code. And that's more than a slogan. If there are technical decisions there is a real effort to resolve the community issues before solving the code issues. (Steven)

The importance of the community and the social relations among the individual members fits well to Cova's notion that the link is more important than the thing (1997), and further corroborates Schau et al.'s notion of value creation through community practices (2009). Individuals are increasingly looking for brands that enable them to connect with others and enable them to engage in meaningful activities.

[T]here is also a community of experts within the Microsoft community. But I definitely think that we have the upper hand in terms of giving something back to society . . . Our software can make a difference in life and I believe that is more Apache than it is Microsoft.

The Apache brand derives much of its meaning from the motivation to give something back to society and thus find meaning in life. Being a member of the Apache community is not just a personal expression of preferences and social belongingness. The Apache brand can be seen as a lifetime partner, a valuable companion for one's identity construction and something that is worth living for. This idealistic and ethical notion is hardly found in traditional, commercial brands.

The Apache brand also signals high levels of quality and expertise. The only way to become a core member in the Apache community is by contributing excellent code and earning the respect and acceptance of the existing members. Thereby, not only is someone's work under constant review but also is their behavior to determine whether they fit the community and the so called "Apache Way."

But I think what is difficult is to teach the new committers the "Apache Way," the way you have to behave when you are in a project. (Chris)

The "Apache Way" not only guarantees that projects are executed in a specific way but also safeguards the special community culture by teaching new members how to behave. As the brand cannot be separated from the individual community member it is essential for the brand that the right people are chosen to represent the brand. The brand is the community, and the individual members are the brand.

Being associated with the Apache community does carry a lot of value in the IT area. The prestige and status associated with membership in the Apache community manifests itself in various situations, for instance during job interviews.

[T]here are stories, like people going to job interviews and mentioning that they are a community member . . . It makes the people listen, because it does carry some value. (Roland)

Value of ODS Brand

The value users derive from the ODS brand varies a bit. Members seem to derive value from using their unique solutions that better fit their needs. Besides the utility gained from their self-created solutions and the fun derived from the creative act, pride, recognition, and community identity present further important aspects. Members are keen on belonging to a group that is skilled to create their unique gear. Following quotes reflect the underlying value of the ODS brand.

[B]ut who besides us can claim to wear a jacket of one's own brand? (Felö)

ODS community members like to identify each other as community members even when they do not know each other and have never met before.

Wouldn't it be cool if we meet and get to know each other at any place and at any time with an outdoorseiten.net logo? (Bananenquark)

The pride of belonging to the community and creating their own label is so strong that some of the less skilled community members buy, for example, pants and jackets from established manufacturers, remove the original labels, and replace them with their outdoorseiten .net logo.

Place them right on the Haglöfs Logo. I'm wondering if the size fits. Yes. Directly on the firm logo. There, the logo is spotted best. (Erny)

In addition to that, community members think that their self-created stuff is much cooler than offers from more costly known brands.

I get a lot of satisfaction (creative and otherwise) from knowing that I saved forty bucks by making my own silnylon tarp. I get satisfaction from knowing I can construct better than the gear companies. They don't make nice wide, genuine French fell seams, with five rows of stitching. My four ounce homemade cooking set that cost me under a dollar gives me satisfaction too. (Stupe)

For many community members using ODS labeled products is a way to escape the logic of commercial brands and demonstrate their independence. This kind of "David against Goliath" logic resembles Cova and White's (2011) description of counter and alter brand communities, which create value by generating their own concepts and services. Similarly to the Apache community, for the core community members, ODS is not just a hobby but a philosophy and a way of life that is reflected in the logo.

Discussion

This chapter explores how community-driven brands emerge and what makes them valuable. Community brands are created by people who share common interests—not by firms. They represent meanings, ideologies, and modes of self-organization that suit the majority needs of the active members. Community brands are inspired by the independence, creativity, knowledge, and distinction of their members. The ability to commonly design products that suit particular functional and symbolic needs at lower expenses enchants the users and fans of community brands. The research shows that community brands are not limited to open source software; brands are ubiquitous in the material world. While community brands are fulfilling the same functions as commercial brands, they differ along various dimensions (see table 17.2).

Community brands are created as a quasi-costless side effect of community members' voluntary engagement in certain activities and interactions. While almost every online community engages in some branding activities such as finding a name for their community or designing a logo, only about 25 percent come up with logo-imprinted products such as T-shirts that may serve as identity markers signaling community membership (Füller and von Hippel 2008). Only a small minority of communities is further able to develop high-quality products such as software or tents that can be used by community and non-community members. However, those community brands are highly authentic, as they strive for excellent products, are represented by the deeds and interactions of their members and are not running after each fashion wave in order to maximize economic profit (Holt 2002). Although they are noncommercial they do not try to escape the logic of the market (Kozinets 2002). Rather, they evade

Table 17.2

Comparison of corporate brands with community brands

Dimension	Corporate brand	Community brand
Initiation	Created by commercial companies	Created by community members, often members of interest groups
Community type	Brand community: centered around existing commercial brands	Interest groups who create their own branded products and become a community brand
Meaning	Suggested by a company, interpreted and appropriated by different interest groups	Results from and is constantly shaped by community discourse
Products	Products are designed, produced and marketed by companies	Products are designed and marketed by the community. Production and logistics are outsourced and managed by companies
Narrative/ archetype	Centered around the offering provided by company and centered on attractive stories—artificial.	Centered on the community. The community is the brand. All interactions and discourses of the community are part of the story and manifested through all members (texts, discussions, products, artifacts)
Customers	Members of various communities and interest groups; including commercial consumers only, symbolic free rider	Predominantly members of the online community self-supporters: producer = customer
Relationship	Typically professional rather than social bonds between "creators" of brands	Strong emotional bonds of the community members especially of those who actively engage in the creation process who form the core
Control	By company and community	Community
Communication	Through mass media, community discourse, social media campaigns	Word-of mouth through community ambassadors
Aim	To maximize earnings and make customers happy; ensure survival of the company	To satisfy own needs! To ensure survival of the community and provide best products

the dependence on corporate innovation and brands by creating their own products as well as brands. They jointly create and manage the meaning as well as usage of the brand. In contrast, enthusiasts of commercial brands are constantly threatened by corporate decisions, as they have no voice in the innovation process but only an exit option (Hirschman 1970). Apple introduced the Intel processor and abandoned the Newton handheld; Harley Davidson launched bikes for yuppies; and Hummer introduced a small mass-market sport utility vehicle. Traditional users and admirers of these brands have struggled with these decisions for various reasons, but predominantly because they resented the destruction of a brand element that was important to the respective owner. Whereas firms can dictate the objects and strongly influence the meanings and experiences of brands, community brands create their own ideologies, define their own qualities, advance at their own pace, and define the prices they want to pay or charge democratically.

In the Internet age, there are many user communities that are actually creating their own brand as shown by the analysis of the outdoor sector. However, the strength and appeal of the brand created in any specific case varies and depends on a number of factors such as the intensity and breadth of interest in the community product outside of the community. While the Apache brand with its web-server enjoys great popularity within and outside the community, the ODS brand and its products are mainly interesting for its community members but not so much for outsiders.

Implications

For many firms, especially in consumer goods fields, proprietary brands have become core financial assets. For example, the value of the McDonalds brand has been calculated to be 71 percent of that firm's total value on the stock market, and the value of the Coca Cola brand has been calculated as 64 percent of the total market value of that firm (Keller 2008). Proprietary brands can enable their owners to command high brand premiums, which are a major source of profits for companies. Thus, for grocery products across 20 product categories (e.g., coffee, cereals, and soft drinks), national brands on average achieve a price premium of 35 percent compared to private label brands (Sethuraman and Cole 1999). In the luxury segment, top brands achieve price premiums between 20 and 200 percent over normal brands in the segment (Colyer 2005).

User-generated brands are a potentially serious challenge to at least some commercial brands' premiums for economic reasons. When users generate brands entirely on their own, and then couple them with a product or service and release them onto the marketplace for free, they can disrupt existing markets for similar paid content—because it is "difficult to compete with free." This disruptive effect can occur without communities actually managing their brands or attempting to profit from them. Apache offers free web server software labeled with a trusted and authentic user-generated brand. How can this not be a serious challenge both to Microsoft web server software products, and to the brand premium that the Microsoft brand customarily commands? Wikipedia is a further good example of a brand that consists of a product that is generated by a large user community and has ruined the market for commercial brands such as Encyclopedia Britannica. As such communities create their products and build their brands essentially without expenses, and in addition are often not interested in making profit, they may become serious competitors to commercial brands that have to generate revenue and make profit in order to satisfy their stakeholders such as employees and shareholders. Meanwhile community members may benefit from their community brand engagements, even if they receive no money. Similar to the private collective model of innovation (von Hippel and von Krogh 2003), the brand development process and the meaning of the brand may be considered as a private good that arises in the process of developing a collectively shared good—a community brand in our case. Community members engaging in community branding activities may enjoy their participation, increase their personal reputation and career chances, and develop a sense of belongingness and collective identity, all of which non-participants may not be able to benefit from. In addition both contributing community members and non-community members stand to gain from collectively shared community brands with respect to two major matters. First, they may benefit from the just-mentioned lower cost of user-generated brands compared to the price premiums charged by the owners of competing commercial brands. Second, they may benefit from the presence of brands that are more precisely tailored to their needs.

With respect to the second matter, consider that when users create a brand for themselves, those users and user communities can create brands that precisely suit their needs for identity and community. Passion for an activity (e.g., programming in the case of Apache) is at the core of community activities. Brand associations derived from these activities should inherently have high authenticity (Füller and von Hippel 2008).

Producers, in contrast, seek to link products they wish to sell to users' identity and community. Often the fit is not perfect. If that is the case, the perceived authenticity of the brand, and also its utility to consumers, must suffer. Holt (2002) argues that consumers will always know that there is a profit interest behind every claim the company makes.

However, user-generated brands and commercial brands may also offer opportunities for co-branding when their brand meanings are synergistic. For example, the ODS community collaborated with Wechsel, a tent manufacturer, in order to manufacture and distribute their own community tent. The community collaborated with Wechsel because they were looking for a partner with excellent manufacturing and distribution skills. In cases like this, synergistic co-branding can add value relative to each brand taken independently (Füller and von Hippel 2008).

Outlook on Brand Management and Future Research

Brands as user-generated content is a topic with close links to other important work being done on user-generated content and on brands. Thus this topic contributes to the ongoing debate on value co-creation by users and producers (Grönroos 2006; Jaworski and Kohli 2006; Vargo and Lusch 2004). Consumers are not dependent on, nor are they waiting for, companies to offer them co-creation opportunities. Consumers create value (e.g., brands) independently. This research also relates closely to research on brand communities (Muniz and O'Guinn 2001; Muniz and Schau 2007). In the case of a brand community, the brand preexists the community: Individuals gather around a brand, and a community forms. In the case of user-generated brands the community pre-exists the brand, and the brand evolves out of community members' interactions. However, the creative processes occurring during brand shaping in brand communities will probably be found to be very similar to user-generated brand creation processes.

While in this chapter the definition proposed for a user-generated brand was as a brand created out of user-generated content by a group of users acting collaboratively, future researchers may want to revisit and refine this definition as research progresses. For example, can a user-generated brand also be created by an individual user? Perhaps not, considering that an individual can intentionally or unintentionally create critical content for what will become a strong brand—but cannot costlessly strengthen it via user-generated content on his or her own. And a brand is not a brand unless it has created "a certain amount of awareness, reputation, and prominence in the marketplace." For example, consider the powerful brand "Oprah" that was seeded by the individual performer "Oprah." This seed could never have become a powerful brand without the costless activities of Oprah's fan clubs, and/or the activities induced by commercially motivated investments from her sponsors.

Furthermore it may be interesting to explore where and under which conditions community brands will be most powerful, and what the effects will be in detail. Candidate markets for strong community brands seem to be markets where one or a few community brands have large market shares and where the community creates goods which can be easily used and distributed outside of the community. This is the case today in markets of digital goods where community brands like Wikipedia or Linux are quite prominent. Of course, powerful examples may also exist beyond digital goods. With respect to theory, brands have generally been viewed as a scarce resource—costly to develop and sometimes very profitable once developed. In the fields of innovation and design, similar scarcity-based views have been replaced with a view based on abundance. It is now understood that many users develop innovations for their own purposes and at low cost, and that innovations are not scarce—they are abundant (von Hippel 2005). In the light of low-cost creation of brands by user communities, it is reasonable that a similar transition in thinking will be appropriate with respect to brands. Further it could well be that the effects of costless communications now accessible to all via the Internet will have the effect of making user-generated brands progressively still cheaper to create and diffuse, and so progressively more powerful relative to commercial brands. Today, broad exposure can increasingly be obtained at low cost through user-generated content (Hautz et al. 2014).

It would also be important to explore what the phenomenon of user-generated brands means for corporate brand management. As noted by Cova and Cova (2002), the role of brand managers is changing, from creating finished entities to facilitating consumer interactions. Instead of creating and diffusing content via advertising, marketing may shift emphasis to offering platforms where brand fans organized in communities as well as ordinary consumers can contribute and diffuse content. Marketing may increasingly serve as a network integrator (Achrol and Kotler 1999), facilitator and "structurer" (Payne et al. 2008), which has the duty to establish and manage co-creation networks that provide compelling experiences and high value to their participants. As in the case of the network co-production model for word of mouth (WOM) introduced by Kozinets et al. (2010), brand managers may be able to capitalize on the power of user-generated brands. Yet, though community brands present a threat to existing firms, they do entail new business opportunities (Thompson et al. 2006). Companies such as "Threadless," "Quirky," "Spreadshirt," and "Local Motors," for instance, already profitably provide services for creative community brands. They offer professional fulfillment services for products created and branded by the community. For community brands it may be interesting to partner with such fulfillment companies in order to get access to complementary know-how and skills as well as access to production facilities and distribution channels. For a producer brand it may be interesting to leverage the resources of a community brand: their knowledge, creativity, brand meaning, and purchasing power. Complimentary commercial services around the community brand offerings may be another growing business opportunity. Red Hat and IBM, for example, create substantial business around the Linux open source software. It will be interesting to see how community brands evolve over time and what kind of businesses emerge around community brands.

References

Ailawadi, K. L., D. R. Lehmann, and S. A. Neslin. 2003. Revenue premium as an outcome measure of brand equity. *Journal of Marketing* 67 (4): 1–17.

Aaker, J. 1997. Dimensions of brand personality. *JMR, Journal of Marketing Research* 34 (3): 347–56.

Achrol, R. S., and P. Kotler. 1999. Marketing in the network economy. *Journal of Marketing* 63 (Special Issue): 146–63.

Apache. 2009. *The Apache Software Foundation Board of Directors Meeting Minutes.* Forest Hill, MD: Apache Software Foundation.

Apache. 2010. *Incubator Branding Guide.* Forest Hill, MD: Apache Software Foundation.

Arsel, Z., and C. Thompson. 2004. The Starbucks brandscape and consumers' (anticorporate) experiences of globalization. *Journal of Consumer Research* 31.

Cova, B., and V. Cova. 2002. Tribal marketing. *European Journal of Marketing* 36 (5/6): 595–620.

Cova, B., and S. Pace. 2006. Brand community of convenience products: New forms of customer empowerment—The case "my Nutella the Community." *European Journal of Marketing* 40 (9/10): 1087–1105.

Cova, B., and T. White. 2011. Counter-brand and alter-brand communities: The impact of web 2.0 on tribal marketing approaches. *Journal of Marketing Management* 26 (3/4): 256–70.

Colyer, E. 2005. That's rich: Redefining luxury brands. *brandchannel.com*, June 13.

Cresswell, J. W. 1998. *Qualitative Inquiry and Research Design: Choosing among Five Traditions.* Thousand Oaks, CA: Sage.

Denzin, N., and Y. Lincoln. 1994. Introduction: Entering the field of qualitative research. In *Handbook of Qualitative Research*, ed. Y. Lincoln and N. Denzin. Thousand Oaks, CA: Sage.

Fournier, S. 1998. Consumers and their brands: Developing relationship theory in consumer research. *Journal of Consumer Research* 24 (4): 343–53.

Füller, J., M. K. Lüdicke, and G. Jawecki. 2007. How brands enchant: Insights from observing community driven brand ceation. In *Annual North American Conference*, ed. Association for Consumer Research. Memphis: ACR.

Füller, J., and E. von Hippel. 2008. Costless creation of strong brands by user communities: Implications for producer-owned brands. Research paper 4718–08. Sloan School of Management, MIT. *http://ssrn.com/abstract=1756941*.

Füller, J., R. Schroll, and E. von Hippel. 2013. User generated brands and their contribution to the diffusion of user innovations. *Research Policy* 42 (6–7): 1197–1209.

Goulding, Christina. 2002. *Grounded Theory: A Practical Guide for Management, Business and Market Researchers.* London: Sage.

Grönroos, C. 2006. Adopting a service logic for marketing. *Marketing Theory* 6 (3): 317–33.

Hautz, J., J. Füller, K. Hutter, and C. Thürridl. 2014. Let users generate your video ads? The impact of video source and quality on consumers' perceptions and intended behaviors. *Journal of Interactive Marketing* 28 (1): 1–15.

Hirschman, A. O. 1970. *Exit, Voice, and Loyalty: Responses to Decline in Firms, Organizations, and States.* Cambridge: Harvard University Press.

Holt, D. 2002. Why do brands cause trouble? A dialectical theory of consumer culture and branding. *Journal of Consumer Research* 29 (1): 70–90.

Jaworski, B., and A. K. Kohli. 2006. Co-creating the voice of the customer. In *The Service-Dominant Logic of Marketing: Dialog, Debate, and Directions*, ed. R. F. Lusch and S. L. Vargo, 109–17. Armonk, NY: Sharpe.

Kates, Steven. 2004. The dynamics of brand legitimacy: An interpretive study of gay men's community. *Journal of Consumer Research* 31 (2): 455–464.

Keller, K. L. 1993. Conceptualizing, measuring, and managing customer-based brand equity. *Journal of Marketing* 57 (1): 1–22.

Keller, K. L. 2008. *Strategic Brand Management: Building, Measuring, and Managing Brand Equity*, 3rd ed. Upper Saddle River, NJ: Pearson Education.

Kirmani, A., S. Sood, and S. Bridges. 1999. The ownership effect in consumer responses to brand line stretches. *Journal of Marketing* 63 (1): 88–101.

Klein, N. 2000. *No Logo: Taking Aim at the Brand Bullies.* Toronto: Vintage Canada.

Kozinets, Robert V. 2002. Can consumers escape from the market? Emancipatory illuminations from *Burning Man. Journal of Consumer Research* 29 (1): 20–38.

Kozinets, R., J. F. Sherry, Jr., D. Storm, A. Duhachek, K. Nuttavuthisit, and B. DeBerry-Spence. 2004. Ludic Agency and retail spectacle. *Journal of Consumer Research* 31 (3): 658–72.

Kozinets, R. V., K. De Valck, A. C. Wojnicki, and S. J. S. Wilner. 2010. Networked narratives: Understanding word-of-mouth marketing in online communities. *Journal of Marketing* 74 (2): 71–89.

Lee, M. S. W., J. Motion, and D. Conroy. 2009. Anti-consumption and brand avoidance. *Journal of Business Research* 62 (2): 169–80.

Low, G., and R. Fullerton. 1994. Brands, brand management, and the brand manager system: A critical-historical evaluation. *Journal of Marketing Research* 31 (2, special issue): 173–90.

Mathwick, C., C. Wiertz, and K. de Ruyter. 2008. Social capital production in a virtual P3 community. *Journal of Consumer Research* 34 (6): 832–49.

Maxwell, Joseph A. 2005. *Qualitative Research Design: An Interactive Approach.* Thousand Oaks, CA: Sage.

Muniz, A., and T. O'Guinn. 2001. Brand community. *Journal of Consumer Research* 27 (4): 412–32.

Muniz, A. M. J., and H. J. Schau. 2005. Religiosity in the abandoned Apple Newton brand community. *Journal of Consumer Research* 31 (4): 737–47.

Muniz, A. M., and H. J. Schau. 2007. Vigilante marketing and consumer-created communications. *Journal of Advertising* 36 (3): 35–50.

Ogilvy, D. 1983. *Ogilvy on Advertising.* New York: Crown Publishers.

Oliveira, P., and E. von Hippel. 2011. Users as service innovators: The case of banking services. *Research Policy* 40 (6): 806–18.

Payne, A. F., K. Storbacka, and P. Frow. 2008. Managing the co-creation of value. *Journal of the Academy of Marketing Science* 36 (1): 83–96.

Pitt, L., R. Watson, P. Berthon, D. Wynn, and G. Zinkhan. 2006. The penguin's window: Corporate brands from an open-source perspective. *Journal of the Academy of Marketing Science* 34 (2): 115–27.

Prahalad, C., and V. Ramaswamy. 2000. Co-opting customer competence. *Harvard Business Review* 78 (1): 79–90.

Schau, H. J., A. M. Muniz, and E. J. Arnould. 2009. How brand community practices creates value. *Journal of Marketing* 73 (5): 30–51.

Sethuraman, R., and C. Cole. 1999. Factors influencing the price premiums that consumers pay for national brands over store brands. *Journal of Product and Brand Management* 8 (4): 340–51.

Stern, B. 2006. What does *brand* mean? Historical-analysis method and construct definition. *Journal of the Academy of Marketing Science* 34 (2): 216–23.

Thompson, C. J., A. Rindfleisch, and Z. Arsel. 2006. Emotional branding and the strategic value of the doppelgänger brand image. *Journal of Marketing* 70 (1): 50–64.

Vargo, S., and R. Lusch. 2004. Evolving to a new dominant logic for marketing. *Journal of Marketing* 68 (1): 1–17.

von Hippel, E. 2005. *Democratizing Innovation*. Cambridge: MIT Press.

von Hippel, E., and G. von Krogh. 2003. Open source software and the "private-collective" innovation model: Issues for organization science. *Organization Science* 14 (2): 209–23.

Wipperfürth, A. 2005. *Brand Hijack: Marketing without Marketing*. New York: Portfolio.

V

User Interactions with Firms

18

Selling to Competitors? Competitive Implications of User-Manufacturer Integration

Joachim Henkel, Annika Stiegler, and Jörn H. Block

A successful user-innovator could, in principle, benefit from its innovation by manufacturing and selling it. However, in his path-breaking work on the sources of innovation, Eric von Hippel (1988) noted that user-innovators face various difficulties in changing their functional role from user to manufacturer. Being a manufacturer requires rather different skills and resources than being a user. The significant switching costs that exist between the two functional roles often keep user-innovators from becoming manufacturers. Rather, a user-innovator may find it in its best interest to freely reveal its innovation to an established manufacturer that then turns it into a commercial product (Harhoff et al. 2003). Yet von Hippel and coauthors also showed that user innovations are ubiquitous and occur in huge numbers (De Jong and von Hippel 2009; von Hippel et al. 2010). Thus, while it may be highly unlikely that a specific user-innovator becomes a manufacturer, the resulting overall number of users-turned-manufacturers is significant.

A recent stream in the literature describes the circumstances under which user-innovators accomplish this change in their functional role toward the innovation (Baldwin et al. 2006; Haefliger et al. 2010; Hienerth 2006; Shah and Tripsas 2007). Shah and Tripsas (2007) refer to this phenomenon as *user entrepreneurship*. Drawing on case study evidence from (end) user-innovators active in juvenile products (Shah and Tripsas 2007) and the rodeo kayak industry (Baldwin et al. 2006), it is suggested that user entrepreneurship is favored when the user-innovator enjoys the initial production and use of its innovation and its opportunity costs are low. Furthermore industry structure and market turbulence also play a crucial role: User entrepreneurship is most likely to happen in industries characterized by small-scale, niche markets as well as markets that are characterized by high levels of turbulence. Building on several cases of user entrepreneurship from the video game industry, Haefliger et al. (2010) describe user entrepreneurship as a two-phase process, where, in the first phase, user-innovators develop the user innovation "under the radar" of incumbent firms—thereby gaining industry experience and attracting first customers—and, in the second phase, start the commercialization process.

Not only end users but also commercial users may become manufacturers and sellers of internally developed user innovations. Of particular interest is the case in which the user-innovator adopts the new role of manufacturer while it maintains the role of a user, since in this situation—as a *user-manufacturer innovator*—it may gain from sustained innovation-related benefits between the two business units (Block et al. 2010). Building on several in-depth case studies from the construction, tea-packaging, and mining industries, Block et al. (2010) describe the antecedents, the process, the environmental conditions, and the organizational challenges and consequences when a user-innovator turns into a vertically integrated user-manufacturer innovator. By vertically diversifying (rather than just building machines for in-house use), user-manufacturer innovators tap a second source of revenues, stabilize their business against cyclicality (if the user and the manufacturer industry have asynchronous business cycles), and become less dependent on single customers and industry-specific market movements. In addition the firm's user unit can benefit from feedback from external customers, thereby improving the quality and market attractiveness of the user innovation.

A user manufacturer is a rather specific instance of vertical diversification, since the upstream unit supplies tools rather than inputs (as in most other cases of vertical differentiation) to the downstream unit. As a result the upstream unit can potentially benefit from a continuous flow of downstream user innovations, which in turn affects the nature of the integrated firm's product innovations. In particular, these should have a stronger focus on new functionality than innovations brought forth by pure manufacturers. Thus the linkage to the user innovation literature is indispensable in order to understand this specific instance of vertical differentiation.

Becoming a user-manufacturer innovator, however, is a challenging managerial task (Block et al. 2010). Different roles toward the innovation need to be combined in one firm. User-manufacturer innovators thus have to manage potential conflicts that can arise between the user and the manufacturing units. In particular, selling the focal user innovation to competitors may imply increased competition and a loss in competitive advantage for the user-manufacturer innovator's user unit. This outcome can lead to internal rivalries and, in the worst case scenario, to a situation of standstill, even if turning user-manufacturer would benefit the firm as a whole. But—and this is the crucial question for a user-innovator considering to manufacture and sell its innovation—when is this the case? Under what conditions are losses in the user business caused by selling improved tools to competitors more than outweighed by profits of the newly created manufacturing unit?

This chapter addresses these challenges. For the firms we study, the question of whom to sell to, and if to sell a specific user innovation at all, becomes critical for exploiting the competitive advantage that the firm created by innovating in the first place. Commercializing a user innovation by selling the innovation on the market will create additional revenues for the firm's manufacturing unit, but it may also imply increased competition for the firm's user unit. However, such competition may arise anyway, since by withholding the innovation from the market, the firm may invite imitation or independent reinvention by other manufacturers. It is this trade-off on which we focus.

We do so by first analyzing two case studies from the construction and tea-packaging industries. As expected, all firms benefited from revenues created by selling their user innovations, and from other, indirect advantages such as broader user feedback (Block et al. 2010). For one firm, the downside of increased competition for their user units was mitigated through selling selectively and avoiding sales to direct competitors. Interestingly, we find a long-term effect of the innovator's commercialization decision on the market structure of the manufacturer unit, with a strong indirect effect on both units of the focal firm.

Building on the insights gained from the case studies, we develop a game-theoretical model describing the competitive conditions under which a user-manufacturer innovator benefits from commercialization of its user innovations. It turns out that depending on the intensity of competition in the downstream (user) industry, the additional profits that using the innovation would create for competing users, and the cost of imitation of the focal innovation, the user-innovator may find itself in one of four situations. In the most interesting case, the competition is intense and the cost of imitation is low compared to the potential value created for other users. Thus the user-innovator may be better off commercializing the innovation, even though doing so reduces overall profits compared to a situation of exclusive use. The logic behind this counterintuitive finding is that commercialization preempts imitation and market entry by competing manufacturers, which would imply a loss of competitive advantage for the innovator's user business without any revenues from sales to outweigh this loss.

The rest of the chapter is organized as follows. The next section introduces the two case studies on the commercialization of user innovations by manufacturing firms. The insights from the case studies are then developed as a game-theoretical model to capture the decision of a user-innovator to turn user-manufacturer innovator or not. We conclude with a discussion of the implications of our findings for practice and further research.

Case Studies

To gain a thorough understanding of the main factors influencing the decision of user innovating firms to turn to manufacturing and selling their user innovations to competitors of the user unit, we conducted two qualitative case studies from two rather different industries, the tea-packing and the tunnel construction industries. The process to select our two case firms was an iterative one. After several in-depth interviews with experts in the specialist foundation construction industry, where we first discovered the phenomenon of user-manufacturer innovators (see Block et al. 2010), we created an extensive list of various industries in which user-manufacturer innovation could potentially play a role. These industries were very different in nature and included, among others, the construction, energy, mining, and consumer product packaging industries. After searching industry registers, member lists of industry associations and contacting several industry experts, we ended up with a list of case firms. From this list we picked Teekanne Group and Wüwa Bau GmbH & Co. KG for the present study.

Table 18.1

Overview of interviews conducted

Case	Interviewee	Position	Date	Duration
Wüwa	Hans Loser	Member of the management board of WÜWA Bau GmbH & Co. KG	Nov 2010	1:30 h
Teekanne	Dr. Stefan Lambertz	Member of the management board of Teepack Spezialmaschinen GmbH & Co. KG	Feb 2011	0:55 h
	Wilhelm Lohrey	Technical director of Teepack Spezialmaschinen GmbH & Co. KG (retired)	Feb 2011	0:50 h
			Mar 2011	0:30 h

A case study approach, using various data sources, has the advantage that it allows us to triangulate the findings and to gain a deep understanding of the commercialization decision at hand (Yin 2003). Table 18.1 summarizes the interviews we conducted, which were recorded and completely transcribed. Based on the transcription of these interviews, we developed a coding scheme that was used in further analysis. In addition to the interviews, we had access to several types of archival data such as annual reports, company magazines (e.g., Max Bögl Bauservice GmbH 2001), patent data, and books about the company's respective histories (e.g., Teekanne GmbH 2007). The use of archival data in conjunction with interview data allowed us to proceed by means of data triangulation (Yin 2003). This way we could verify and extend the findings from the interviews through archival data. For example, using patent data, we were able to verify and put into perspective the invention activity of the company's user and manufacturing units. As another example, using information from annual reports, we were able to evaluate the economic importance of the commercialization of user innovations.

Teekanne Group

Our first case concerns Teekanne Group (hereafter Teekanne), a family firm founded in 1882 in Dresden, Germany. While the firm's roots lie in the packaged tea business (i.e., selling tea in bags), Teekanne started to develop and construct its own tea-packing machines in the early 1920s (Teekanne GmbH 2007). Today Teekanne consists of several subsidiaries of which the packaged tea business (the user unit) and the tea-packing machines business (the manufacturing unit, named *Teepack*) are the most important. Today the firm generates annual sales of about €400 million with more than 200 employees.

Through effective patents, Teekanne was able to protect its two main user innovations, the double chamber tea bag and the *Constanta* machine, from imitation by competitors. Until 1968 Teekanne was the dominant player in the business of tea-packing machines. Its machines were sold to firms all over the world, with the only restriction that Teekanne's direct competitors in the packaged tea business were not to be supplied.[1] This restriction outlasted the end of the patent protection and still exists in a slightly modified form. Today Teekanne also sells its machines to tea-packing firms in Germany. However, these firms are only allowed to use the machines at those production sites where merchandise destined for countries other than Germany are produced. No machine has ever been sold to Ostfriesische Teegesellschaft, Teekanne's main competitor in Germany.

While Teekanne has maintained these restrictions for decades, Wilhelm Lohrey, the former technical director of the manufacturing unit, wonders if it has always been in the firm's best interest:

> The patent on the double chamber tea bag machine lasted till 1968, and in this time [Teepack] has not supplied machines to [tea-packaging firms in] Germany. Thus competitors [of the manufacturing unit] could position themselves. After expiry of the patent, many firms jumped at the tea bag and built machines. Two of these [firms] have remained.[2] (Wilhelm Lohrey)

After the patent protection of the user innovations expired, other machinery firms started to imitate the tea-packing machines of Teekanne. Mr. Lohrey notes in this regard:

> Thus, they copied the machine. The constructor himself admitted this to me. . . . Some parts of their machine you could have integrated into our Constanta [because they were so similar].[3]

Today, Teekanne's largest competitors in the machines business are two machine manufacturing firms located in Italy. Both firms come from the packing machines business and at least one of them positioned itself prior to the patent expiry in 1968. This firm benefited from Teepack's policy of selling selectively, as after the patent expiry, Teekanne's direct competitors in Germany that were not supplied with tea-packing machines from Teepack were the first customers of this firm.

WÜWA Bau

Our second case deals with Wüwa Bau GmbH & Co. KG (hereafter Wüwa), which was founded as a family firm in 1984 by former employees of a specialist foundation engineering firm. Today Wüwa is active in the fields of infrastructure tunnel construction,[4] pipe-jacking machines,[5] and equipment manufacturing.[6] Since the year 2000, Wüwa has been a 100 percent subsidiary of Max Bögl, the largest family-run construction firm in Germany (Max Bögl Bauservice GmbH 2001). In 2008 Wüwa generated revenues of €15.3 million with approximately 67 employees.

In the 1980s, the construction of infrastructure tunnels through tunnel drilling—instead of open construction—was still in its infancy and no dedicated machine manufacturer existed at that time. Thus, during its early years as a tunnel construction firm, Wüwa perceived the urgent need to develop and manufacture its own machines (Max Bögl Bauservice GmbH 2001). In the following years, Herrenknecht,[7] a newly founded firm in the manufacturing industry entered the market and offered pipe-jacking machines as well as drilling equipment. However, since Wüwa found those machines too expensive to stay competitive in its construction business, it continued to develop and use its own machines.

The decision to use the construction machines not only internally but also to sell them to other firms was made around the year 2000, mainly for economic reasons. First, at this time only one manufacturer was active in this market, and so Wüwa's management determined there would be sufficient demand to sustain a second player. Second, the construction machines business seemed to be an attractive market as the profit margins were high compared to the extremely low profit margins in the construction business. Additionally Wüwa already sold construction machines and drilling tools to other firms at that time, although not in a systematic way and not based on a strategic decision. The decision to sell the machines triggered the development of a dedicated manufacturing business unit at Wüwa as the firm then began to hire its own construction and sales personnel for the machines business.

The commercialization decision at Wüwa was accompanied by concerns that the machines sales would enable competitors of Wüwa's construction business to bid for the same projects as Wüwa. However, at that time, other machines manufacturers already sold similar machines as Wüwa. Hans Loser, member of the management board of Wüwa, noted in this regard:

Of course, we had the worry that we strengthen our competitors [by selling our machines to them]. On the other hand, I have to realize that if [a competitor] doesn't buy the machine from me, it will buy it from Herrenknecht. (Hans Loser)

Wüwa has never been the only company on the market that offered specific construction machines. Thus, it was more the positive aspects of the commercialization of the construction machines instead of the potential conflicts due to a potential cannibalization of the construction business by the activities of the manufacturing business on which management focused. Selling or renting the machines to other construction firms offered a unique way to benefit from a construction project even if Wüwa's construction business did not win the contract itself.

[I]f I don't win the construction job, maybe I can at least participate by selling machines. (Hans Loser)

Summary of Findings from the Two Case Studies

The case studies illustrate the main parameters and mechanisms to be considered in the decision for or against commercializing a user innovation, and thus for or against vertically diversifying to become a user-manufacturer innovator. While Teekanne decided on a selective selling strategy, selling only to those firms that were not in direct competition to its user unit, Wüwa decided to sell its user innovations without any restriction to all firms in the market. As a consequence, Teekanne's selective selling strategy lowered entry barriers for existing and potential competitors of its manufacturing unit since these could find unserved customers more easily. Ironically, when patent protection expired, the firm's tea-packaging unit faced similarly strong competition, according to our interviews, as it would have if Teepack had sold its machines unrestrictedly. However, no additional revenues of the manufacturing unit made up for the negative competitive effect. By contrast, Wüwa was always aware of the fact that similar products to the user innovation can be bought from specialized machine manufacturers and therefore decided not to employ a selective selling strategy.

We thus identify three main parameters that determine the decision to sell the user innovation on the market: (1) the cost that existing and potential competitors of the manufacturing business would have to bear in order to imitate the user innovation, relative to (2) the value that this innovation would create for other users, and (3) the intensity and nature of competition on the market in which the user unit is active. These three parameters are at the core of the model developed below.

Modeling the User-Innovator's Commercialization Decision

Model Setup

Building on the insights from the two above case studies, we develop a simple game-theoretical model to capture the essence of the user-manufacturer's decision for or against market commercialization of its innovation. Consider two industries. Firms in the manufacturing industry develop and build capital goods that are used by firms in the user industry. Without loss of generality, we set the variable and fixed cost of manufacturing to zero. One firm in the user industry is a successful user-innovator: It has developed a machine that is superior to those used by its competitors, and manufactures this machine for its own use. This machine allows the user to perform a job with higher profitability than its competitors, due either to lower cost or to higher quality. We refer to this firm as the user-manufacturer (UM); there is additionally one dedicated manufacturing firm (M). We assume full information in the game, that is, all players know all payoffs as well as earlier moves by others.

In stage 1 of the game, the user manufacturer decides whether or not to sell its improved machine to the other firms in the user industry. We assume that the innovator sells it either to all competitors or to none. The payoffs in the user industry are denoted by π, where the superscript distinguishes between the user manufacturer's user unit (UMU) and the competing users (CU), and the subscript (excl/all) indicates if the user manufacturer is in exclusive possession of the focal innovation or if all firms in the user industry have it. These payoffs do not reflect investments in improved machines (if such investments are made), so these costs will have to be subtracted to arrive at the user firms' final payoffs. In stage 2,

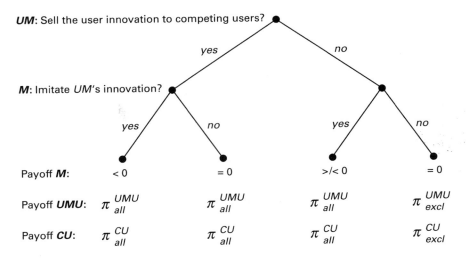

Figure 18.1

Game tree

the nonintegrated manufacturer M decides whether it will imitate the focal innovation at cost F. Figure 18.1 shows the game tree.

If the focal innovation is available to all competing users, competition for the user manufacturer's user unit is stronger and its profits are lower. Only in the extreme case of entirely separate markets will its profits remain unaffected (since the "competing users" are then in fact not competing anymore). In turn the combined profits of the competing users will be higher if all have the innovation due to reduced cost, higher revenue, or a combination of both. Thus

$$\pi_{all}^{UMU} \leq \pi_{excl}^{UMU}, \quad \pi_{all}^{CU} > \pi_{excl}^{CU}. \tag{1}$$

In terms of the user industry's overall profits, both an increase and a decrease are possible. To see that both outcomes may occur, consider the extreme cases. If the markets served by the user manufacturer's user unit and by the competing users are entirely separate, combined profits are higher if all firms use the innovation. In the other extreme, if the user manufacturer's user unit enjoys monopoly profits as an exclusive user but would see its prices driven down to marginal cost if all firms use the focal innovation, then combined profits are higher in the case of exclusive use by the user manufacturer. The outcome in any concrete situation will lie between these extremes and will depend on industry characteristics such as the degree of differentiation and the existence of various market segments. Finally, we assume that if both the user manufacturer and the non-integrated manufacturer M enter the market as sellers, then M cannot recoup the cost F of imitating the focal innovation (due to reduced market share and reduced margins), and so entry becomes unattractive (leftmost node in the bottom level of the game tree). This assumption is made in order to keep the model simple.[8]

Analysis

If the user manufacturer has decided to sell its innovation to the competing users, it will remain the only seller. In contrast, if it has decided against market commercialization, entering the market may be attractive for the other manufacturer, M. This will be the case if M can at least realize the revenue F, which is possible if the competing users' combined profits are higher by at least F in the case that they use the improved machines compared to the situation that they do not:[9]

$$\pi_{all}^{CU} - \pi_{excl}^{CU} \geq F. \tag{2}$$

Depicting the two conditions above in figure 18.2 allows us to identify areas in parameter space that give rise to different outcomes. The inequality $\pi_{all}^{UMU} \leq \pi_{excl}^{UMU}$ (1) implies that only parameter combinations below the horizontal broken line are possible, while the fact that the horizontal axis starts at $\pi_{all}^{CU} - \pi_{excl}^{CU} = 0$ reflects the inequality $\pi_{all}^{CU} > \pi_{excl}^{CU}$ (2); this means that it is pointless to depict areas where $\pi_{all}^{CU} - \pi_{excl}^{CU} < 0$. The downward-sloping, broken line separates areas in which the user industry's combined profits are higher in the case that all firms use the focal innovation (northeast of the line) from those in which they are lower (southwest of the line). Finally, the vertical broken line reflects inequality (2), that is, only to the right of this line can M profitably enter the market.

Results

Area a in figure 18.2 corresponds to settings in which neither the prospect of increased profits through selling nor the threat of entry by M makes market commercialization attractive for the user manufacturer. Also, in area b, the user manufacturer is protected from entry due to the fact that

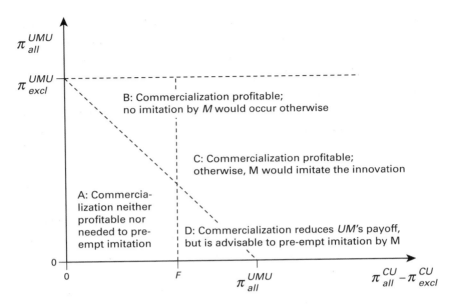

Figure 18.2
Areas in parameter space with distinct rationales for UM's market commercialization decision.

the cost F that M would have to bear in order to imitate the focal innovation is high relative to the value that the availability of this machine would create for the other firms in the user industry. However, combined profits of the competing users increase through the improved machines to such an extent that this increase can more than offset the user manufacturer's profit decrease in its user unit. Since the user manufacturer's reservation price for selling the machines (considering the sale to all competing users as a single transaction) is its profit decrease in its user unit, and the competing users' reservation price their profit increase, the user manufacturer can negotiate a price that increases its overall payoff compared to the situation in which it does not sell the innovation. In area c both the prospect of increased profits through selling the innovation and the threat of imitation speak for market commercialization. Finally, in area d the user manufacturer will enter the market as a seller even though doing so implies lower profits than in a situation of exclusive use of the innovation. It does so because if it decides against commercialization, then M

will enter and the user manufacturer will accordingly forgo both its premium profits in the user industry and its profits as a manufacturer. The firm thus has to accept lower profits compared to the situation in which it is the only user of the focal innovation. Note that, while areas a, b, and c always exist, area d only exists if $F < \pi_{excl}^{UMU}$.

Discussion and Conclusions

We have presented two case studies of user-innovating firms that became manufacturers of their own innovations, and then faced the question of whether or not to supply their innovative products to competitors of their user units. Teekanne settled for a selective approach, selling to most other firms in the packaged tea industry but not to direct competitors. Wüwa, in contrast, sold its tunnel drilling machines without restrictions, realizing that its competitors in the construction business could have obtained similar machines from other suppliers. Ironically this is what happened to Teekanne; in fact by restricting its sales, Teekanne actually seems to have invited entry by other manufacturers.

Our game-theoretical analysis shows how these cases hinge on three central parameters. The first parameter is the reduction in profits that the user manufacturer's user unit faces when its innovation becomes available to all its competitors. This reduction depends on the intensity of competition in the user industry and on the extent of competitive advantage that the innovation creates for the user manufacturer if used in exclusivity. The second parameter is the additional value that availability of this innovation creates for the other firms in the user industry; and the third, the cost that other manufacturers have to bear in order to imitate the focal user innovation. The user manufacturer can make up for losses in its user unit by profits in its manufacturing unit only if the value that the innovation creates for competing users is high and/or the intensity of competition is low. This condition is fulfilled in the area northeast of the downward-sloping line in figure 18.2, where by commercializing the innovation the user manufacturer earns a payoff above that which is attainable by using it exclusively. Interestingly, the payoff that results from not commercializing the innovation is either that of exclusive use (area a) or, in area c, the even lower payoff in the case of general availability of the innovation.

In area c the competing manufacturer M would enter the market, and thus commercializing the innovation would not only increase the user manufacturer's profits but also serve to prevent market entry by M. A similar situation is found in area d, with the difference that the user manufacturer's overall profits in the case of commercialization are lower than those from exclusive use. Yet it needs to enter the market in order to preempt entry by M. Finally, if competition is intense and the innovation creates little value for the competing users compared to its development cost F (area a), then commercialization is neither profitable nor needed to preempt competition from M.

Our study complements earlier work on user entrepreneurship (Baldwin et al. 2006; Haefliger et al. 2010; Hienerth 2006; Shah and Tripsas 2007) in two respects. First, as Block et al. (2010), we studied user entrepreneurship by an established firm rather than by end users. Second, in our case the commercialization does not entail a switch of functional roles, but rather the adoption of the additional role of a manufacturer followed by the ongoing coexistence of both functional roles.

The questions addressed in this chapter have interesting parallels to "transactional hierarchies" studied by Luo et al. (2011). Firms constitute a transactional hierarchy if they can be ordered by the direction of the flow of goods between them. Comparing transactions within the Japanese auto parts and electronics industries, the authors found that the former exhibits a much higher degree of transactional hierarchy, while the latter is characterized by frequent "transaction cycles"—that is, situations in which firm A supplies firm B and B supplies A. Such transaction cycles will often imply that a firm supplies a unit of its counterpart that is in competition with one of its own units, a situation analogous to the one we study. The finding by Luo et al. (2011) of pronounced industry differences raises the question if, and how, industry characteristics also matter for a user-innovator's commercialization decision.

More generally, our study is related to the broad literature on vertical diversification, or integration. We comment on two contributions. Hill et al. (1992) show that related and unrelated diversification strategies yield different sets of economic benefits and require different internal organizational arrangements. Since the integration of user and manufacturer is a rather specific case of related diversification, a more detailed analysis may help inform and extend the theory of related diversification.

Markides and Williamson (1996) link related diversification to the resource-based view of the firm, and emphasize the role of competences that enable the diversified firm to build new strategic assets. Precisely such competences are created by an integration of user and manufacturer unit if the upstream unit benefits from downstream user innovations.

By manufacturing and selling its innovation, the user-innovator does not practice "free revealing" in the sense of Harhoff et al. (2003). However, by commercializing the innovation, the user-innovator makes it available to competing users. In doing so, it may choose to be selective by making only some of its user innovations available to competitors or by keeping others exclusive for a certain while, following quite the same logic as in the selective revealing of commercial contributions to open source software (Henkel 2006).

Our analysis has several limitations, which point to opportunities for further research. The case of Teekanne showed that the user-manufacturer innovator may decide to sell selectively (even if this approach did not work out for Teekanne in the long run), a possibility not captured in our model. Similarly competition in the upstream industry could be modeled in a more general way by allowing more than one firm to enter and by considering imitative market entry even if the user manufacturer commercialized its innovation. Next our model only addresses the decision to commercialize one specific user innovation, and leaves out what characterizes an integrated user-manufacturer innovator in the long run—not only the possibility of ongoing user innovations from the downstream unit and positive marketing externalities between the two units but also the frictions that come along with such integration. Finally, future research should link the emergence of user manufacturers more explicitly to transaction cost economics.

Implications for managers are that selling the firm's user innovations to competitors may be a profitable course of action under a variety of circumstances. Practitioners should, thus, avoid a categorical attitude against this type of diversification in the sense of "we never sell our superior tools" and should rather adopt a nonemotional view of it. And even if selling to competitors is not profitable compared to maintaining exclusivity, it may still be preferable to imitation by other manufacturers.

As Eric von Hippel and many coauthors and colleagues have shown, the phenomenon of user innovation is broad and variegated, occurring in industries as diverse as clinical chemistry analyzers (von Hippel and Finkelstein 1979), sailplaning (Franke and Shah 2003), and software (Lakhani and von Hippel 2003; von Krogh et al. 2012), to name but a few. By studying user-manufacturer diversification as a way to exploit user innovations, and showing that users and manufacturers as functional sources of innovation need not be organizationally separate, this chapter aims to add a piece to the colorful mosaic of user innovation research that we owe to Eric von Hippel.

Notes

We thank Hans Loser, Dr. Stefan Lambertz, and Wilhelm Lohrey for being very open interview partners and providing us with detailed information about their respective companies. Comments by Carliss Baldwin, participants at the 2011 Open and User Innovation Workshop, and two anonymous reviewers are gratefully acknowledged.

1. Such selling restrictions may prompt scrutiny by competition authorities as it could constitute anticompetitive behavior. The legal details are beyond the scope of this chapter.

2. All direct quotes were translated from German to English by the authors.

3. *Constanta* is the brand name of Teekanne's tea-packing machine.

4. Infrastructure tunnels are tunnels with a smaller profile than traffic tunnels, and are used for infrastructure such as water supply and electricity.

5. Pipe-jacking machines are machines that drill the infrastructure tunnels.

6. Equipment manufacturing refers to drilling tools such as drilling heads.

7. Today Herrenknecht AG is one of the leading companies in mechanized tunnel drilling machines and equipment. With approximately 3,200 employees, the firm generated sales of €935 million in 2010. The firm's headquarters is located in Schwanau in southwest Germany.

8. In reality it may be, for instance, that the market does support two competing sellers but not three. The user manufacturer's consideration in this case is analogous to that in the present, simplified model, namely that its own entering the market preempts entry by the second competitor.

9. We simplify here by assuming that M negotiates the sales contracts for its improved machine before investing in the development. Without this assumption, once the development cost F is sunk, it depends on M's and the CU's relative negotiation power if M can appropriate a share of the surplus shown on the left-hand side of equation (2) that is larger than F. Alternatively, one could drop this assumption and interpret inequality (2) as a necessary, but not sufficient, condition for profitable imitation by M.

References

Baldwin, C., C. Hienerth, and E. von Hippel. 2006. How user innovations become commercial products: A theoretical investigation and case study. *Research Policy* 35 (9): 1291–1313.

Block, J., A. Bock, and J. Henkel. 2010. Commercializing user innovations by vertical diversification: The user-manufacturer innovator. Working paper. Munich University of Technology. http://ssrn.com/abstract=1674903.

De Jong, J. P. J., and E. von Hippel. 2009. Transfers of user process innovations to process equipment producers: A study of Dutch high-tech firms. *Research Policy* 38 (7): 1181–91.

Franke, N., and S. Shah. 2003. How communities support innovative activities: An exploration of assistance and sharing among end-users. *Research Policy* 32 (1): 157–78.

Haefliger, S., P. Jäger, and G. von Krogh. 2010. Under the radar: Industry entry by user entrepreneurs. *Research Policy* 39 (9): 1198–1213.

Harhoff, D., J. Henkel, and E. von Hippel. 2003. Profiting from voluntary information spillovers: How users benefit by freely revealing their innovations. *Research Policy* 32 (10): 1753–69.

Henkel, J. 2006. Selective revealing in open innovation processes: The case of embedded Linux. *Research Policy* 35 (7): 953–69.

Hienerth, C. 2006. The commercialization of user innovations: The development of the rodeo kajaking industry. *R&D Management* 36 (3): 273–94.

Hill, C. W. L., M. A. Hitt, and R. E. Hoskisson. 1992. Cooperative versus competitive structures in related and unrelated diversified firms. *Organization Science* 3 (4): 501–21.

Lakhani, K. R., and E. von Hippel. 2003. How open source software works: "Free" user-to-user assistance. *Research Policy* 32 (6): 923–43.

Luo, J., D. E. Whitney, C. Y. Baldwin, and C. L. Magee. 2012. The architecture of transaction networks: A comparative analysis of hierarchy in two sectors. *Industrial and Corporate Change* 21 (6): 1307–35.

Markides, C. C., and P. J. Williamson. 1996. Corporate diversification and organizational structure: A resource-based view. *Academy of Management Journal* 39 (2): 340–67.

Max Bögl Bauservice GmbH und Co. KG. 2001. Neue Tochter im Firmenverbund: Die WÜWA Bau GmbH. *Kundenmagazin Max Bögl*: 30–31.

Shah, S., and M. Tripsas. 2007. The accidential entrepreneur: The emergent and collective process of user entrepreneurship. *Strategic Entrepreneurship Journal* 1 (1/2): 123–40.

Teekanne GmbH & Co. KG. 2007. *125 Jahre Teekanne*. Düsseldorf: Teekanne.

von Hippel, E. 1988. *The Sources of Innovation*. New York: Oxford University Press.

von Hippel, E., J. De Jong, and S. Flowers. 2010. Comparing business and household sector innovation in consumer products: Findings from a representative survey in the UK. Working paper. Sloan School of MIT. SSRN. *http://ssrn.com/abstract=1683503* or *http://dx.doi.org/10.2139/ssrn.1683503.*

von Hippel, E., and S. N. Finkelstein. 1979. Analysis of innovation in automated clinical chemistry analyzers. *Science & Public Policy* 6 (1): 24–37.

von Krogh, G., S. Haefliger, S. Spaeth, and M. W. Wallin. 2012. Forthcoming. Carrots and rainbows: Motivation and social practice in open source software development. *Management Information Systems Quarterly.*

Yin, R. K. 2003. *Case Study Research: Design and Methods.* Thousand Oaks, CA: Sage.

19

When Passion Meets Profession: How Embedded Lead Users Contribute to Corporate Innovation

Cornelius Herstatt, Tim Schweisfurth, and Christina Raasch

This study enriches the dialectic view of producer versus user innovation by exploring the innovation-related behavior of embedded lead users (ELUs). ELUs are employees who have lead user characteristics in relation to one or more of their employing firm's products or services. They are located inside the firm boundaries and therefore operate within firm hierarchies and routines. At the same time they are embedded in use contexts, for example, in user communities that typically operate based on different goals, norms, and resource constraints.

It is well known that firms innovate with respect to processes that they themselves *use* to operate (Harhoff et al. 2003; von Hippel and Tyre 1995). The literature shows *process innovation* by user firms to be quite prevalent (de Jong and von Hippel 2009; Harhoff et al. 2003; von Hippel and Tyre 1995). Our research, by contrast, focuses on the *product innovation*-related behavior of individual users inside producer organizations. (Recall that a producer is defined by its functional role in relation to the innovation: Producers innovate in order to profit from selling, not from using a product; von Hippel 2005).

To our knowledge, beyond some anecdotal mention (Chouinard 2005; Levitt 2009; Hyysalo 2009) and one other study (Schweisfurth and Raasch 2015), this is the first study devoted to ELUs. We therefore take a phenomenon-based research approach to explore how ELUs contribute to corporate product innovation. We draw on interviews with 35 informants from 23 firms in the sports, leisure, and healthcare industries.

We find that ELUs are a special source of need knowledge and solution knowledge to their employing firm. As boundary spanners between the firm and the user community, they acquire user information and filter and translate it for easier absorption by other firm employees. They also provide access to user networks to accelerate innovation diffusion. Compared to external lead users, ELUs tend to contribute ideas that are better aligned with their firm's technological capabilities, less radically novel, and more implementable. ELUs' personal involvement in product use and the user community enhances their motivation to innovate, but can also engender opportunistic behavior and information bias.

Our findings suggest that ELU's multiple roles and hybrid identities lead to differences in behavior compared to other employees; they create trade-offs that raise questions relating to the boundaries of the firm and to organizational design. We hope that this chapter will encourage research on what we believe to be an empirically significant as well as under-researched phenomenon.

The remainder of the chapter is structured as follows: After explaining the theoretical context and methods of this study, we lay out our main findings on innovation activities by ELUs. We subsequently discuss our results in the light of extant theory and offer some final observations.

Theoretical Background and Definitions

The Dichotomy of User and Producer Innovation

A fundamental question in the study of innovation is what motivates innovation. As explained elsewhere in this volume, producer innovators are defined by the profit motive that drives them to innovate. User innovators, by contrast, are firms or individuals for whom the principal motivation to develop a new product or service is their own need to use it (von Hippel 1982).

The user-producer dichotomy has become core to a thriving research stream (Baldwin and von Hippel 2011). Theory has been developed to explain how the two functional sources of innovation differ (e.g., in terms of their knowledge, see Lüthje et al. 2005 and von Hippel 1998) and how this impacts on their innovation (Baldwin et al. 2006; Hienerth et al. 2011) and knowledge-sharing behavior (von Hippel 1982; von Krogh et al. 2003).

User innovation and producer innovation are operationally different modes (Jensen et al. 2007): Users are located in user environments and draw on local resources and knowledge to innovate (Lüthje et al. 2005; von Hippel and Tyre 1995), such as in communities. Users tend to have high intrinsic motivation (Franke and Shah, 2003; Janzik 2010) and to share their ideas and solutions freely with other members of the user community as well as producers (Raasch et al. 2008; von Hippel and von Krogh 2006). Producer innovation, in contrast, draws on a broad range of internal and external resources and sources of knowledge (Cohen and Levinthal 1990), is primarily extrinsically motivated (Rynes et al. 2004), is subject to corporate rules and rigidities (Leonard-Barton 1992), and follows a logic of intellectual property protection for the purpose of rent extraction (Demsetz 1967).

Importantly, the user-producer dichotomy has promoted a view whereby users and producers are organizationally distinct. Almost by definition, users (often taken to be the "the customers") are located outside the producer firm's boundaries (Bogers et al. 2010). Even when users are firms themselves (von Hippel and Tyre 1995), the user and the producer, for example, of an instrument or machine tool, are separate firms (de Jong and von Hippel 2009) or business units (see chapter18 of this volume by Henkel, Stiegler, and Block Henkel).

Two Innovation Modes Interacting

Many studies confirm that designs created by users are often commercially attractive to producers (Lilien et al. 2002). From a producer perspective therefore, user knowledge and ideas are valuable inputs in new product development. As firm-accessible external resources, they remain outside the producer firm's boundaries and thus outside hierarchical control, but can be integrated into the innovation process.

In order to identify, access, and assimilate user knowledge and to isolate the value co-created by users (Cohen and Levinthal 1990), producers have different options. Previous research mentions, for example, lead user workshops (Lüthje and Herstatt 2004), user toolkits (von Hippel and Katz 2002), and sponsored user communities (Jeppesen and Frederiksen 2006).

In this chapter we take a different approach. We focus on *users inside the boundaries of the producer firm*. Analyses of innovation by product users inside the producer firm are scarce and often anecdotal in nature. Still, in some industries—such as sports—product use by employees is the rule rather than the exception (Chouinard 2005; Levitt 2009). Moreover producer firms have been known to hire members of the user community for their expertise and social capital (Hertel et al. 2003).

With respect to the user-producer dichotomy, it is important to point out that user-employees, to the extent that they are involved in product innovation in the firm, are involved in *producer innovation*. The organizational unit paying for their work is the producer firm. (This is the principal classification criterion, as applied in the literature to date.) Additionally they may be involved in innovation motivated by their own needs in their leisure time. Although clear in theory, this distinction may be harder to make in practice: amalgamations of both types of activities and motives, cross-fertilization, and multiple other interdependencies likely abound.

ELUs and Other Actors in the Innovation Process

Individual actors are known to add to the competitive advantage of firms. Previous research has analyzed boundary roles, in particular, that affect the innovation process and outcome, for example, gatekeepers (e.g., Allen and Cohen 1969) and boundary spanners (e.g., Aldrich and Herker 1977). These past analyses focused on how individuals' standing at the interface of the firm and its environment, as well as at interfaces internal to the firm, can affect innovation processes and outcomes.

Likewise, we argue that ELUs are special due to their cognition, competence, and enthusiasm (Salvato and Rerup 2011). We define ELUs as firm employees who exhibit lead user characteristics in relation to one or more of their employing firm's products or services. In contrast to the aforementioned roles, embedded lead userness is a *characteristic* that is, at least by its definition, not necessarily tied to any specific activity or behavior. It combines two elements: lead userness and employment in the producer firm.

Lead users are defined by two principal characteristics that set them apart from ordinary users: They are at the leading edge of trends in a marketplace and thus experience needs ahead of other users; and they stand to gain in particular ways from obtaining solutions to their needs. (von Hippel 1986)

ELUs are *employed* by the producer firm, embedded in corporate routines and structures. Their behavior is thus influenced by personal factors such as job satisfaction (e.g., Yuan and Woodman 2010) and contextual factors such as job autonomy (e.g., Spreitzer 1995). Corporate culture and collective corporate beliefs influence their mental processes, cognitive states, and sense of identity. These and other influences set ELUs apart from external lead users, and are likely to stimulate innovation-related activity.

Other such individuals (e.g., former employees or family members of staff) may also exhibit some degree of dual embeddedness in a firm and in a user environment. However, they are likely to differ from ELUs, as narrowly defined here, as to their motivations, their formal and informal roles in the organization, and their involvement in the corporate innovation culture.

It is important to distinguish ELUs from other employee users. Prior research in the field of biking finds that almost all employees of producer firms are bikers themselves; but only some of them exhibit have user characteristics toward bikes, and only some of them innovate (Lüthje et al. 2005). Similarly we may expect that among the employees of Ford, many own a car, but the number of ELUs will be very few.

Methods

Due to the dearth of research on ELUs to date, we take a phenomenon-based approach (Edmondson and McManus 2007). We seek to "capture, describe, document, and conceptualize [the] phenomenon" (von Krogh and Rossi Lamastra 2010) and prepare inductive theory building (Eisenhardt 1989).

To increase the external validity of our findings (Yin 2003), the study relies on data from three different industries: sports products, leisure products, and healthcare/medical devices. This sampling choice is advantageous, as these industries have been analyzed in depth in prior research (e.g., Baldwin et al. 2006; Franke et al. 2006; Hienerth 2006; Lüthje et al. 2005; Raasch et al. 2008). This body of research shows that user innovation is prevalent in these industries, an indication that the phenomenon under investigation, ELUs, may also be observable there (Eisenhardt 1989).

We use "theoretical sampling" (Glaser and Strauss 1967); that is, we follow a replication logic such that each new case either supports or extends our findings until saturation is reached (Eisenhardt 1989). As we have variation due to differences in industrial context, we include 6 to 9

Table 19.1
Overview of the dataset

Industry	product categories	Firms	Dyads	Senior managers only	ELUs only
Sports	Sailmaking, bicycles, skiing, goggles, helmets, raquets, rowing equipment	8	4	0	4
Health	Prosthetics, wheelchairs, hearing devices	6	2	3	3
Leisure	Gaming gear, record players, music software, online games, household appliances	9	4	4	1

firms per industry (23 altogether), a number within the optimal range for cross-case analysis according to Eisenhardt (1989). This approach adds to the accuracy of our claims, eliminates coincidental findings, and captures the different facets of the observed phenomenon (Eisenhardt 1989; Eisenhardt 1991; Yin 2003).

We use two main data sources: interviews with higher level managers and interviews with ELUs, both conducted in 2010 and 2011. Altogether, we interviewed 35 individuals. Whenever possible (10 out of 23 firms), we conducted paired interviews with both a higher level manager and an ELU in the same firm. Table 19.1 describes the composition of our group of interviewees.

We began by contacting firm headquarters to find out if they were aware of employees that used the products of the company extensively. All but two companies immediately confirmed the existence of ELUs inside their walls. This suggests that, at least in some industries, ELUs may be quite prevalent. We then asked if they were willing to participate in our study and if they could refer us to the higher level manager responsible for innovation. 23 out of approximately 50 firms agreed. In most cases, the higher level manager responsible for innovation was the head of R&D; in the other cases (particularly smaller firms) we were directed to marketing or product management. We then conducted interviews with 18 managers from 18 firms to capture the corporate and managerial perspective pertaining to the phenomenon. During these initial interviews we presented and discussed our definition of ELUs and asked whether the interviewee could identify members of the organization who fit the definition of an ELU. We also asked a series of questions relating to how ELUs contribute to corporate innovation. These interviews lasted approximately 30 minutes.

Next we contacted the putative, manager-identified ELUs and arranged a second set of interviews. We began by validating the lead-userness of each interviewee using items suggested in prior research on the lead user construct (Franke et al. 2006). We also asked our respondents whether they had ever innovated, and whether their innovations originated from their own needs and use experience. Innovation is an important indicator of lead-userness (Hienerth et al. 2011). With the ELUs thus identified, we conducted semi-structured interviews that lasted 30 to 60 minutes. We asked them about their roles within the firm, use experience, involvement in a user community, innovation-related activities, and knowledge sources (table 19.2).

We coded all transcripts of the interviews. For data reduction we started with a generic coding scheme that reflected our research objective. These initial codes were rather broad and included themes like ELUs' characteristics, their structural roles, their contributions to corporate innovation, their behaviors and ties to other users. During the analysis we developed new codes and sub-codes to reflect the emerging findings. The final coding scheme included 19 codes and 39 sub-codes. We built meta-matrices and other depictions for codes and cases in order to find patterns and emerging themes (Eisenhardt 1989; Miles and Huberman 1994).

In order to establish reliability and validity of our findings, we sent our draft chapter to our informants and asked them for their opinion on our results (Kozinets 2002). We also discussed our findings with industry experts we had met during fieldwork (Lincoln and Guba 1985).

Findings

ELUs—Who Are They?
ELUs are dually embedded, as users among other users and as employees in producer firms.

ELUs are typically highly reputed members of the user community who stand out as advanced users and strong innovators. They are often

Table 19.2
Characteristics of interviewees (ELUs)

ID	Product category	Function	Tenure (years)	Use experience (years)	Ahead of trend	High benefit	ELU innovated
Sport 1	Sailmaking	Product management	3	30	Professional racer	Yes	Yes
Sport 2	Bicycles	Product management	3	7	Amateur racer	Yes	Yes
Sport 3	Bicycles	Marketing	4	17	Amateur racer	Yes	Yes
Sport 4	Skiing	Product management	3	-	Skiing instructor	Yes	Yes
Sport 5	Goggles, Helmets	Product design	5	-	Amateur racer	Yes	Yes
Sport 6	Raquets	Public relations	11	20	-	Yes	Yes
Sport 7	Raquets	Product management	10	29	-	Yes	Yes
Sport 8	Rowing equipment	Marketing	15	20	Competitive rower	Yes	Yes
Health 1	Prosthetics	Product management	3	n.a.	Test runner	Yes	Yes
Health 1	Prosthetics	Product management	1	n.a.	Test runner	Yes	Yes
Health 2	Prosthetics	Product management	12	n.a.	Biker, runner	Yes	Yes

Table 19.2 (continued)

ID	Product category	Function	Tenure (years)	Use experience (years)	Ahead of trend	High benefit	ELU innovated
Health 6	Hearing devices	R&D	37	n.a.	-	Yes	Yes
Leisure 1	Gaming gear	Marketing	3	10	Advisor national team	Yes	Yes
Leisure 4	Record players	Production	6	-	-	Yes	Yes
Leisure 5	Music software	Product management	11	20	Music producer	Yes	Yes
Leisure 6	Gaming gear	Marketing	6	7	Advisor factory team	Yes	Yes

opinion leaders who are "ahead of the trend" (Sport1–6; Health1; Leisure5). Their status and credibility are earned primarily by superior expertise, rather than firm affiliation.

> Of course I am an opinion leader, especially since I am the strongest rider in our group, just because of that. I have biked since I was 13, have worked in biking stores . . . . So when people ask me, or if I tell them something, they'll get a competent answer, and that is why I am an opinion leader. (Sport3, ELU)

In most cases in our sample, use experience predates employment in the producer company, although the converse can also be observed. Advanced users often select into producer firms to be able to follow their interests in a professional environment (Sport5). Following this logic, most of the ELUs we interviewed were in functions close to the product: The majority worked in product management (8/16) and marketing (4/16); the remainder worked in R&D/product design (2/16), public relations and production (1 each) (see table 19.2). Average tenure was 8 years.

ELUs in the Innovation Process

In this section we show that ELUs provide need- and solution information to their employing firms, ideate and co-develop new products, and are early testers of prototypes. They leverage their own use experience for all these activities.

Two archetypal processes can be distinguished, depending on whether the original idea for the innovation was generated during use, or as part of a corporate process.

In the first case—we may call it *user-first*—ideas originate from shortcomings ELUs experience during use; they are then actively brought into the producer firm, either as ideas or as prototypes (e.g., Sport5, 8; Health4):

> [My ideas] come from my gaming, because by playing games you realize what is missing and what could be improved. (Leisure1, ELU)

One ELU in the gaming industry, for example, invented a cable conduit for a computer mouse. The cable outlet was fixed at the top of the mouse, but while playing, the ELU found that maximum freedom and speed of movement requires matching the position to the game situation. He developed a solution whereby the cable could be bent inside the mouse, and then left the mouse at adjustable angles and positions (Leisure2). Another

ELU found it difficult to grasp and maintain hold of the throttle grip of his electric wheelchair, as designed by the producer firm. He therefore created a new, more ergonomic design (Health4). In both examples the ELUs drew on knowledge they acquired during product use. Their designs were taken up by the firm and turned into new product features.

In the second example—we call it *producer-first*—ELUs interact with other employees who seek to involve them in one or several phases of the innovation process.

Even before a new product being developed, they [R&D employees] ask me for my opinion, 'Does a racer need x, or maybe y, or are those things not needed at all?' and . . . they turn to me and ask, 'Hey, what do you think?' (Sport3, ELU)

ELUs then contribute to ideating new functionalities or solutions to current functional limitations (e.g., Sport5; Health4, 6; Leisure2, 5). In the development phase, ELUs help formulate specifications for new or improved functionalities (e.g., Sport1–4, 6, 7; Health2; Leisure2, 5). ELUs also build prototypes of new or improved products (Sport2, 3; Health2).

In *every* firm that we sampled, both in user-first and producer-first processes, embedded (lead) users are involved in testing prototypes. Most of this testing does not follow formal procedures of secrecy, documentation and evaluation: R&D departments supply ELUs with prototypes and ELUs provide personal, direct feedback (e.g., Sport1–5; Health1–4, 6; Leisure1, 2, 5, 6, 8).

When we develop biking goggles, we have certain people at work we know . . . this person is a mountain biker, that one is a racer . . . . So we just go to these guys and ask them: 'Can you try this out for a weekend? Would you give us some feedback? How do you like this? Does that fit? What would you improve?' (Sport5, Manager)

In two out of 23 companies, both of them in the prosthetics industry, we find more formal arrangements: Physically impaired persons are employed specifically to do test runs of new products (Health1, 2).

Interactions between Firm Affiliation and Use Experience in Innovation
Next we consider how the combination of use experience employment affects innovation behavior and outcomes. We show that as lead users become embedded in producer firms, their innovation focus increases, and also shifts to become more aligned with firm objectives and capabilities.

Several of our interviewees suggest that their use experience is changed by corporate affiliation. During product use, even in their leisure time, they experience, observe and analyze their own activities as well as those of other users, searching for opportunities for improvement (Health2; Sport1, 3, 6). They are simultaneously experiencing the use situation and analyzing it. This suggests that becoming embedded in a producer firm increases lead users' innovation focus, even during their leisure time.

My relationship [to biking] has changed, but not in a negative way. . . . Before, I was riding just for fun and to get better. Now I listen to the material when I ride, try to feel it and to become more competent, also in order to assess other products. So biking now always has to do with improvement of the product, becoming a better tester, and being able to compare. (Sport3, ELU)

We also find qualitative evidence that embedded lead userness (re-)directs users' innovation focus. They take a corporate perspective on use and innovation. They keep corporate objectives and constraints in mind and turn their attention to issues that have priority for the firm.

Our internal [users] care for things that are important to us as a company, things like quality . . . , e.g., things like gap clearances, which is something very technical . . . . Those of my colleagues who regularly test our products recognize a product that does not meet our internal quality standards. (Leisure 9, Manager)

We also asked our interviewees to compare the innovative ideas provided by ELUs to those of internal R&D staff on the one hand and external users on the other hand. As compared to R&D staff, our evidence suggests, ELUs tend to contribute ideas and product solutions that are less novel technically, and mostly involve modifications of existing product platforms, but are better aligned with market needs (Health3; Leisure2, 4; Sport3, 7).

[Radical innovations] more often come from R&D and are more difficult to realize in terms of technology. (Health3, Manager)

[ELUs] have more practical ideas because they know how the customer will use the product. [The ideas of internal engineers tend to] have lower usability in everyday life. (Health3, Manager)

On the floor of your well-heated, cozy workshop it is all very easy. . . . But when you want to do the same thing on the foredeck with waves three meters high and temperatures below zero and your fingers icy-cold, this is very, very different. That's why I think that we [ELUs] have a much deeper understanding than the guys who spend all of their time in the office. (Sport1, ELU)

As compared to external lead users, involving ELUs offer several advantages to firms. There is a lower risk of unintended leakage of design information, since employees are usually under nondisclosure agreements (Sport5; Leisure1; Health1, 2). Moreover getting feedback from ELUs can be much quicker: External lead users need to be identified, established to be well-informed and trustworthy, conditioned by formal agreements, and the like, all of which takes time (Health3).

ELUs are more likely to contribute ideas and solutions that are implementable and immediately useful for the firm (Sport1, 2, 7; Leisure2, 5).

Concrete, detailed, implementable solutions are mostly developed by our internal user employees [rather than external lead users]. (Sport2, Manager)

The ideas of external users are perceived to be very valuable but sometimes "radical" and even "fantastical."

I got to know guys and tennis players who are totally crazy about tennis, who have the wildest ideas. . . . We just wouldn't have such ideas, and it is important to talk to them and listen, and sometimes be open to their ideas. Still, you know what is realizable and what isn't. (Sport7, Manager)

ELUs, by contrast, are embedded in the constraints of corporate innovation processes, which narrows their thinking, for better or worse:

[I]f you are inside the product development process and if you know how much of an effort it is, and you know how many units of the products you can sell later on, then it's different [from what external users would do], because you are somehow limited internally, because you know all that is involved. (Leisure1, Manager)

Overall, this evidence suggests ELUs can make a distinct contribution to corporate innovation that fits both corporate technological capabilities and market needs. However, companies need to be aware that the answers they get will differ in nature depending on who they ask—corporate R&D, external users, or ELUs.

ELUs as Boundary Spanners between Firms and Markets

ELUs act as boundary spanners between the firm and the user community, facilitating inbound and outbound information transfer. They leverage their position in the user network to prospect for new ideas and concrete solutions for their employing firm. As a member of the user community, they attend events such as competitions and patient meetings (e.g., Leisure1, 4, 7). Increasingly, ELUs also tap knowledge shared in online user communities:

Many [of our user employees] follow online communities and gather all the feedback from other users, simply because they themselves are interested in the topic. And if they find good ideas, they knock on my door. (Leisure1, Manager)

ELUs observe other users in natural use environments to recognize and discuss use-related problems and solutions (Sport1, 6; Health2; Leisure1, 5). Occasionally they also show prototypes developed by the firm to other users for spontaneous comments and feedback (Leisure5). Conversely, as external users regard ELUs as links to their companies, they seek contact with ELUs to share their ideas with the producer (e.g., Sport4; Health1; Leisure2).

ELUs forward these comments, ideas and solutions within the organization, mostly to the R&D department (Sport1, 2; Health2, 4; Leisure1):

Due to the fact that I hang around a lot with other gamers, I get a lot of input about what these people wish for. So I would be stupid if I did not pass on the information I get. (Leisure1, ELU)

ELUs have higher status and credibility than other employees as sources of product knowledge and ideas. Therefore they tend to get better and more direct access to R&D (Sport1–3, 6–7; Health2; Leisure1).

Importantly, ELUs filter, translate, consolidate, and extend the information they obtain (e.g., Health2; Sport6; Sport4). They apply criteria that originate from their personal use and market experience as well as their knowledge of the firm. For example, ELUs identify and exclude user feedback that seems unwarranted. First-hand observation of product use often helps them to do so, as one ELU from a sail-making company explains:

Since you have direct access, all the time, you can see the sails and the material, the products directly in action . . . . You can decide if there is a problem with the sail itself or if the customers are just too, let's say, clumsy. (Sport1, ELU)

If some valid user needs are not met by the present product, ELUs leverage their own experience and technical know-how to identify potential solutions that either the user or the producer can implement. Thus, they go beyond reporting functional errors and imperfections. Being exposed to similar user experiences, or at least seeing them first-hand, ELUs can diagnose the problem and devise possible solutions much more effectively.

In addition to their experience of what is technically possible and viable in use, ELUs rely on their knowledge of the producer firm's strategic objectives, processes, routines, competencies, and economic requirements (e.g., Leisure1; Sport2, 3). From the socialization process they have undergone in the producer firm, they have an understanding of the "rules of the game" and also of the language used in the firm (e.g., Health2; Sport4, 6). The ELU's endorsement of customer input, and its translation into the right "language," gives it additional credibility and therefore increases the chances that the issue will be addressed by the producer firm (Sport1, Leisure5).

ELUs also leverage their user network for marketing purposes. Even if they are not front-line employees and their formal role is not in sales, they are frequently in contact with users in their leisure time. In some cases, external users notice ELUs testing new devices and then directly place orders with the ELU, even before the market launch (Sport1, 2, 6).

This week I took part in a race and had a new frame with me. I think I was asked about ten times if that was a new frame by Sport2. (Sport2, ELU)

Since ELUs are advanced users themselves, their advocacy and/or adoption of a new product carries weight in the user community (Sport1–3; Leisure5).

I'm a very active sailor in this class of boats. Two years ago, we had a market share in this class of 40 or 50%. Then we started actively participating in regattas ourselves. We introduced the new sails. Now, two years later, we have won the championship, and our market share is 90%. . . . It is good for the company to have employees who are good sailors; it's also really good promotion. (Sport1, ELU)

In summary, we find that ELUs span firm boundaries, facilitating inbound and outbound information transfer. They acquire user information and filter and translate it for easier absorption by other firm employees. They also provide access to user networks to accelerate diffusion.

Costs to Firms

In this section we show that firms benefit as ELUs derive personal benefits from innovation, other than pay, that motivate them to undertake extra effort in their leisure time; their hybrid incentives and resource base also raise risks of opportunistic behavior and information bias.

We find that ELUs pursue activities that benefit their employing firm in their leisure time, without pay. They are aware of the benefits to the firms and seem to consider how much private effort seems "fair," and at what point the idea should be turned into a firm project.

I just cannot stop it. If I have an idea at home, I will do a sketch. . . . But I will not work for hours at home, if it's for the firm. I would try to integrate my idea into my work, as a project or whatever. And if they really don't like it, but I am convinced of it, I may do it after work, for myself. (Sport5, ELU)

This quote illustrates the amalgamation of private and firm interests, and the combination of private and firm resources, in the innovation process. Private benefits such as personal use or the "scratching of an itch" reinforce ELUs' motivation to innovate.

While such private benefits are recognized as beneficial to firms, they also raise the possibility of opportunistic behavior. We found some limited evidence of two flavors of such behavior: using firm resources and neglecting job duties in favor of more personally rewarding use-related activities, and influencing R&D trajectories to suit their own use-related agenda.

Many ELUs are granted slack resources (especially discretionary time) to carry out their informal innovation-related tasks (Sport4, 7). For example, ELUs in some firms can use and test products during their work time. Managers are aware of the fact that some ELUs might exploit this freedom in pursuit of more rewarding work experiences. Some informants reported that they request some formal feedback from their employees after testing sessions, specifically to contain opportunistic behavior:

[Out of 35 tennis-playing ELUs testing products for their firm,] there will be one or two who are on the court and are not testing, but just playing and having fun. Then, in my opinion, you have to tell them . . . : "If you play here, I want a report afterwards." . . . The wrong thing to do would be to impose more stringent rules on the other 33, just because of these two guys, such as "no product testing during work time." (Sport7, Manager)

Overall, however, the firms we studied mostly maintain an approach of low control, informal procedures, and no incentive contracts that target user innovation.

We found more concern among R&D managers that ELUs might champion advanced, even radical solutions over products that are palatable to a larger market. In at least one case, the R&D manager believed this propensity to have negatively impacted on commercial success (Sport7).

At the same time, we can't get carried away in this. If you keep listening to them they will propose something so specific to their needs, but not relevant to others, that it will just never leave development. (Health1, Manager)

This behavior may be opportunistic, but in many cases seems due simply to ELUs' perceptions being those of advanced users. Several interviewees reported that this was a source of unintentional information bias (Health1–2, 5; Sport 5, 7; Leisure1).

The more own, personal experience you have, the harder it is to listen to the problems out there. . . . Someone who is really talented, a person for whom tennis has always been really easy, can't imagine why you would need an oversize racket for beginners who always miss the ball. (Sport7, Manager)

Some managers therefore reported that they are careful not to rely on ELUs exclusively. One manager intentionally involves non–lead user employees in testing, to counteract potential bias.

Let's give an e-bike [electric bicycle] to the girl from the bill-of-materials department, who does not really have a clue, to see how she perceives it, and try to persuade the extreme racing biker, who would never choose to come near e-bike to try it, in order to get many opinions, as much diversity as possible. (Sport2, Manager)

Discussion in the Light of Extant Theory

In this section we discuss our findings in the light of existing theory and point out interesting questions for future research. In particular, we consider cognitive and structural aspects of dual sources of knowledge and dual embeddedness; the interplay of ELU's intrinsic and extrinsic motivation; and avenues for research on ELUs and the boundaries of the firm.

Cognition and Position in the Innovation Network

ELUs are embedded in two environments—they get stimuli both from the corporate and from the user environment. Prior research has shown that need knowledge mostly resides with users, while solution knowledge often resides with producer firms. Both types of knowledge are often sticky—that is, costly to transfer (von Hippel 1998). ELUs have direct access to both types of knowledge. Speaking the same language and sharing a mindset as external (lead) users, they can easily interact with them, empathize with them, and absorb information from them (Nooteboom 2000). At the same time ELUs communicate with firm employees, with whom they share a common knowledge base and a corporate perspective toward product innovation. From the perspective of knowledge transfer and learning, the employment of ELUs may therefore offer a solution to the trade-off firms face between absorptive capacity for external information and absorptive capacity in intra-firm knowledge transfers (Cohen and Levinthal 1990). Their low cognitive distance to both worlds can allow ELUs to play a special boundary-spanning role (Nooteboom 2000).

It can be expected that this ability is mirrored in ELU's special structural and relational characteristics in the innovation network (see Dahlander and Wallin, 2006 on "men on the inside"). To the extent that they share the norms and culture of both environments, ELUs may have high social capital in both environments. On the other hand, their credibility may suffer from dual embeddedness; it may also germinate dual loyalties and goal conflicts (Chan and Husted 2010).

Motivation and Incentives

ELUs are likely to be unique in terms of their motivations. Benefits from using superior products, payment, enjoyment of and passion for their work and also the product, and several other aspects are intertwined in their motivational configuration. These aspects may be mutually reinforcing, but the literature also points to the potential for motivation crowding (Deci 1971).

Related to the question of motivation, issues of incentives and control seem to invite future study, such as in the field of organization design. ELUs use the company's product and interact informally with other users in their leisure time, usually outside the control of the firm. This creates a high degree of overlap between firm goals and personal goals, but also opportunities for moral hazard and opportunistic behavior, such as in the leakage of company information, the influencing of corporate innovation processes to suit their own use agenda, or the neglect of their job duties in favor of more personally rewarding use-related activities. This suggests that ELUs' personal and professional interests are intertwined in particular and interesting ways that future research should analyze further.

Firm Strategy and the Boundaries of the Firm

At the firm level, future research should understand the strategic value of ELUs and its contingencies, with obvious implications for boundary decisions. It needs to investigate when and how users should be brought inside the boundaries of the firm, and to what extent this can complement and/ or substitute the involvement of external users in new product development. Internal and external lead users, as well as internal and external ordinary users, operate under different motivations and constraints that are likely to impact their innovative behavior. Thus it seems likely that the optimal location of users within and/or outside firm boundaries is contingent on many factors associated with innovation objectives as well as firm and technology characteristics, among other aspects. It can be expected that a transaction cost lens (Williamson 1973) and the knowledge-based view of the firm (Grant 1996) can help us understand how users' specific knowledge can best be accessed and turned into competitive advantage.

Conclusion

In this chapter we analyzed a phenomenon that is novel to research and appears to be significant in practice. Our empirical findings suggest that there are employees in many producer firms who are lead users with respect to the firm's own range of products or services. We called these employees embedded lead users (ELUs). Their role in the innovation process is a special one, we argued, that deserves attention in future research as well as practice. Among other things, ELUs contribute novel ideas and solutions that differ in nature from both those of internal R&D staff and external lead users and act as boundary spanners between the firm and the market; their hybrid motivational setup and access to discretionary resources also raise the possibility of opportunistic behavior and information bias. Our findings are qualitative and in need of extension and quantitative validation.

Research on user innovation to date has focused on user innovation external to the firm, or on firms reaching out to involve external lead users in corporate innovation processes. Thus the most common theoretical perspective on user and producer innovation is a dichotomic one.

Our findings break up this dichotomy and suggest that users are more important drivers of innovation in an economy than is generally thought. Within the realm of producer innovation, there are the users who play a central role. It may turn out that in certain industries a large fraction of what we have hitherto considered as producer innovation is in fact the work of users.

References

Aldrich, H., and D. Herker. 1977. Boundary spanning roles and organization structure. *Academy of Management Review* 2 (2): 217–30.

Allen, T. J., and S. I. Cohen. 1969. Information flow in research and development laboratories. *Administrative Science Quarterly* 14 (1): 12–19.

Baldwin, C. Y., C. Hienerth, and E. von Hippel. 2006. How user innovations become commercial products: A theoretical investigation and case study. *Research Policy* 35 (9): 1291–1313.

Baldwin, C. Y., and E. von Hippel. 2011. Modeling a paradigm shift: From producer innovation to user and open collaborative innovation. *Organization Science* 22 (6): 1399–1417.

Bogers, M., A. Afuah, and B. Bastian. 2010. Users as innovators: A review, critique, and future research directions. *Journal of Management* 36 (4): 857–75.

Chan, J., and K. Husted. 2010. Dual allegiance and knowledge sharing in open source software firms. *Creativity and Innovation Management* 19 (3): 314–26.

Chouinard, Y. 2005. *Let My People Go Surfing: The Education of a Reluctant Businessman.* New York: Penguin.

Cohen, W. M., and D. A. Levinthal. 1990. Absorptive capacity: A new perspective on learning and innovation. *Administrative Science Quarterly* 35 (1): 128–52.

Dahlander, L., and M. W. Wallin. 2006. A aan on the inside: Unlocking communities as complementary assets. *Research Policy* 35 (8): 1243–59.

De Jong, J. P. J., and E. von Hippel. 2009. Transfers of user process innovations to process equipment producers: A study of Dutch high-tech firms. *Research Policy* 38 (7): 1181–91.

Deci, E. L. 1971. Effects of externally mediated rewards on intrinsic motivation. *Journal of Personality and Social Psychology* 18 (1): 105–15.

Demsetz, H. 1967. Toward a theory of property rights. *American Economic Review* 57 (2): 347–59.

Edmondson, A. C., and S. E. McManus. 2007. Methodological fit in management field research. *Academy of Management Review* 32 (4): 1155–79.

Eisenhardt, K. M. 1989. Building theories from case study research. *Academy of Management Review* 14 (4): 532–50.

Eisenhardt, K. M. 1991. Better stories and better constructs: The case for rigor and comparative logic. *Academy of Management Review* 16 (3): 620–27.

Franke, N., and S. Shah. 2003. How communities support innovative activities: An exploration of assistance and sharing among end-users. *Research Policy* 32 (1): 157–78.

Franke, N., E. von Hippel, and M. Schreier. 2006. Finding commercially attractive user innovations: A test of lead-user theory. *Journal of Product Innovation Management* 23 (4): 301–15.

Glaser, B. G., and A. L. Strauss. 1967. *The Discovery of Grounded Theory: Strategies for Qualitative Research*. New York: DeGruyter.

Grant, R. M. 1996. Toward a knowledge-based theory of the firm. *Strategic Management Journal* 17 (1): 109–22.

Harhoff, D., J. Henkel, and E. von Hippel. 2003. Profiting from voluntary information spillovers: How users benefit by freely revealing their innovations. *Research Policy* 32 (10): 1753–69.

Hertel, G., S. Niedner, and S. Herrmann. 2003. Motivation of software developers in open-source projects: An Internet-based survey of contributors of the Linux kernel. *Research Policy* 32 (7): 1159–78.

Hienerth, C. 2006. The commercialization of user innovations: The developement of the rodeo kayak industry. *R&D Management* 36 (3): 273–94.

Hienerth, C., E. von Hippel, and M. B. Jensen. 2011. User community vs. producer innovation development efficiency: A first empirical study. *Research Policy* 43 (1): 190–201.

Hyysalo, S. 2009. User innovation and everyday practices: Micro-innovation in sports industry development. *R&D Management* 39 (3): 247–58.

Janzik, L. 2010. Contribution and participation in innovation communities: A classification of incentives and motives. *International Journal of Innovation and Technology Management* 7 (3): 247–62.

Jensen, M. B., B. Johnson, E. Lorenz, and B. Lundvall. 2007. Forms of knowledge and modes of innovation. *Research Policy* 36 (5): 680–93.

Jeppesen, L. B., and L. Frederiksen. 2006. Why do users contribute to firm-hosted user communities? The case of computer-controlled music instruments. *Organization Science* 17 (1): 45–63.

Kozinets, R. V. 2002. The field behind the screen: Using netnography for marketing research in online communities. *JMR, Journal of Marketing Research* 39 (1): 61–72.

Leonard-Barton, D. 1992. Core capabilities and core rigidities: A paradox in managing new product development. *Strategic Management Journal* 13 (1): 111–25.

Levitt, M. 2009. *Herding Tigers: The North Sails Story*. North Sails Group LLC.

Lilien, G. L., P. D. Morrison, K. Searls, M. Sonnack, and E. von Hippel. 2002. Performance assessment of the lead user idea-generation process for new product development. *Management Science* 48 (8): 1042–59.

Lincoln, Y. S., and E. G. Guba. 1985. *Naturalistic inquiry*. Beverly Hills: Sage.

Lüthje, C., and C. Herstatt. 2004. The lead user method: An outline of empirical findings and issues for future research. *R&D Management* 34 (5): 553–68.

Lüthje, C., C. Herstatt, and E. von Hippel. 2005. User-innovators and "local" information: The case of mountain biking. *Research Policy* 34 (5): 951–65.

Miles, M. B., and A. M. Huberman. 1994. *Qualitative Data Analysis: An Expanded Sourcebook*. Thousand Oaks, CA: Sage.

Nooteboom, B. 2000. Learning by interaction: Absorptive capacity, cognitive distance and governance. *Journal of Management and Governance* 4 (1): 69–92.

Raasch, C., C. Herstatt, and P. Lock. 2008. The dynamics of user innovation: Drivers and impediment of innovation activities. *International Journal of Innovation Management* 12 (3): 377–98.

Rynes, S. L., B. Gerhart, and K. A. Minette. 2004. The importance of pay in employee motivation: Discrepancies between what people say and what they do. *Human Resource Management* 43 (4): 381–94.

Salvato, C., and C. Rerup. 2011. Beyond collective entities: Multilevel research on organizational routines and capabilities. *Journal of Management* 37 (2): 468–90.

Schweisfurth, T. G., and C. Raasch. 2015. Embedded lead users: The benefits of employing users for corporate innovation. *Research Policy* 44 (1): 168–80.

Spreitzer, G. M. 1995. Psychological empowerment in the workplace: Dimensions, measurement, and validation. *Academy of Management Journal* 38 (5): 1442–65.

von Hippel, E. 1982. Appropriability of innovation benefit as a predictor of the source of innovation. *Research Policy* 11 (2): 95–115.

von Hippel, E. 1986. Lead users: A source of novel product concepts. *Management Science* 32 (7): 791–805.

von Hippel, E. 1998. Economics of product development by users: The impact of "sticky" local information. *Management Science* 44 (5): 629–44.

von Hippel, E. 2005. *Democratizing Innovation*. Cambridge: MIT Press.

von Hippel, E., and R. Katz. 2002. Shifting innovation to users via toolkits. *Management Science* 48 (7): 821–33.

von Hippel, E., and M. J. Tyre. 1995. How learning by doing is done: Problem identification in novel process equipment. *Research Policy* 24 (1): 1–12.

von Hippel, E., and G. von Krogh. 2006. Free revealing and the private-collective model for innovation incentives. *R&D Management* 36 (3): 295–306.

von Krogh, G., and C. Rossi Lamastra. and S. Haefliger S. 2010. Phenomenon-based research in management and organization science: Towards a research strategy. Working paper. ETH Zürich.

von Krogh, G., S. Spaeth, and K. R. Lakhani. 2003. Community, joining, and specialization in open source software innovation: A case study. *Research Policy* 32 (7): 1217–41.

Williamson, O. E. 1973. Markets and hierarchies: Some elementary considerations. *American Economic Review* 63 (2): 316–25.

Yin, R. K. 2003. *Case Study Research: Design and Methods.* Thousand Oaks, CA: Sage.

Yuan, F., and R. W. Woodman. 2010. Innovative behavior in the workplace: The role of performance and image outcome expectations. *Academy of Management Journal* 53 (2): 323–42.

20

Exploring Why and to What Extent Lead Users Share Knowledge with Producer Firms

Christopher Lettl, Stefan Perkmann Berger, and Susanne Roiser

The concept of lead users as well as the lead user method—both pioneered by Eric von Hippel—have gained high attention and popularity among academic researchers and practitioners alike. With respect to academic research, the lead user concept has been introduced and elaborated in leading academic journals such as *Management Science* (von Hippel 1986; Morrison et al. 2000; Lilien et al. 2002), *Journal of Consumer Research* (Kratzer and Lettl 2009), *Research Policy* (Jeppesen and Laursen 2009; Ozer 2009) or *The Journal of Product Innovation Management* (Herstatt and von Hippel 1992; Olson and Bakke 2001; Franke et al. 2006; Schreier and Prügl 2008; Hienerth and Lettl 2011). From a practitioner point of view, pioneering firms such as 3M, HILTI, Johnson & Johnson and Nortel have successfully applied the lead user method (Herstatt and von Hippel 1992; von Hippel et al. 1999; Lilien et al. 2002) which increasingly becomes a standard practice in new product development endeavors of producer firms.

The lead user method is a heuristic to identify lead users, i.e., individuals or organizations that are on the leading edge with respect to important market or technological trends and that derive a high benefit from a solution to their needs, and to involve them into the new product development process of a producer firm (Lüthje and Herstatt 2004). The benefits for producer firms of involving lead users into their new product development activities are evident and significant: They receive access to highly valuable tacit knowledge and sometimes even ready-made solutions for the development of breakthrough new products. Lilien et al. (2002) report an eight times higher sales potential of new products generated by lead users compared to new products generated with traditional market research techniques. Involving lead users in new product development activities also helps to overcome negative effects of local search biases (Katila and Ahuja 2002). Furthermore Herstatt and von Hippel (1992) find that the lead user method significantly reduces both development costs and development time.

While the benefits for producer firms are well established and documented, less insights are available to date on the benefits or motives of lead users to share their proprietary knowledge with producer firms. This question becomes even more relevant as the common practice at lead user workshops is that lead users need to sign nondisclosure agreements (NDA) stating that any intellectual property that is produced during the lead user workshop will be owned by the focal producer firm. At least at first glance one could seriously question that this is a *fair deal* and thus that lead users may tend to become exploited at lead user workshops. Our article therefore addresses the following research question: Why and to what extent do lead users reveal their knowledge to producer firms? Providing insights with respect to those questions is important to better understand the motive structure of lead users and to further enhance the collaboration between lead users and focal producer firms.

The article proceeds as follows: Next the relevant literature is reviewed and an initial research framework is developed. The section that follows provides a description of the applied research design and method. Then the findings of the study are presented. Last, these results are discussed and their implications for research and practice are outlined.

Literature Review and Theoretical Aspects

Lead Users

The lead user concept as invented by Eric von Hippel has challenged traditional market research techniques for innovation and suggested a fundamental different approach. While traditional methods focus on representative users for a particular market (segment), lead users are defined as users who are at the leading edge of important trends in a marketplace under study, obtaining relatively high benefits from obtaining a solution to their needs and do often originate from distant fields of experience (von Hippel 1986; Urban and von Hippel 1988). While in traditional methods users have a rather passive role in the NPD process, the lead user approach acknowledges that some users are capable to develop breakthrough solutions which foreshadow general demand.

Lead users can be found within the target market as well as from so called analogous markets, that is, in fields in which the respective trend and need has been prevalent in an even more extreme form. To make systematic use of the lead user concept, a multi stage-method has been developed by which lead users are being identified and involved in the fuzzy front end of innovation (Lüthje and Herstatt 2004; von Hippel 2005). This method has been refined over the last years and basically consists of four major steps: (1) definition of the search field and setting up an internal team including key stakeholders, (2) identification of most relevant needs and trends, (3) identification of the lead users following pre-defined criteria via search methods such as screening, broadcast search and pyramiding, and (4) developing new product concepts by involving the identified lead users (Lüthje and Herstatt 2004). The development of new products is often done in a workshop setting where the identified lead users and experts work together in small groups over two or three days.

The application of the lead user method by different companies in the fuzzy front end has led to promising results. Some published cases involving the PCCAD (Urban and von Hippel 1988), pipe-hanger (Herstatt and von Hippel 1992), and medical supplies (von Hippel et al. 1999) product categories showed that the method improved teamwork and was significantly faster and cheaper at developing new product concepts than more conventional marketing research methods (Olson and Bakke 2001). A first empirical comparison reveals that ideas generated with the involvement of lead user versus ideas generated without the involvement of lead users score significantly higher in terms of innovativeness, strategic importance and sales potential (Lilien et al. 2002). Subsequent work has extended the lead user-approach to different settings and phases of the innovation process. Lead users have been shown to increase the accuracy of product evaluations (Ozer 2009), to enhance the adoption and diffusion process of new products (Schreier et al. 2007), to have a positive influence on knowledge sharing within a community (Jeppesen and Laursen 2009) or to create communities around their inventions (Hienerth and Lettl 2011).

With regard to their knowledge sharing behavior two contrasting arguments can be put forward: On the one hand, lead users may seek to keep their innovation secret to prevent the transfer of their inventions to other (rival) users without an adequate compensation. On the other hand, lead users may be more inclined toward co-operation with producer firms if they expect to set their solution as a standard in the market or if they hope to get valuable help in return (Harhoff et al. 2003). They can also expect to benefit via rewards like the access to exclusive information or the chance to obtain the ready developed product earlier than others (Brockhoff 2003).

Knowledge Sharing of Users

Recently there have been a number of studies focusing on free-revealing by individuals or organizations. This trend can partly be explained by the increasing popularity of OSS communities, where knowledge is—at least to a large extent—openly shared between users and companies without insisting on property rights and direct monetary returns (von Hippel and von Krogh 2003; Harhoff et al. 2003). The free and voluntarily exchange of knowledge between actors in specific open source communities has been conceptualized as "the private-collective model" (von Hippel and von Krogh 2003) as contributing users obtain private benefits in the process of developing the public good.

Free revealing activities by users have been found to take place in different fields such as chemistry analyzers (Urban and von Hippel 1988), iron production (Allen 1983), library information systems (Morrison et al. 2000), and sporting goods (Franke and Shah 2003). Research has shown that the underlying motives of users to contribute to the communities' collective innovation process are similar and robust across different settings. Such motives include factors based on self-interest, that is, a mix of intrinsic rewards, such as fun and the intellectual challenge, and extrinsic rewards, such as gaining reputation, signaling to relevant stakeholders, benefits from faster diffusion, learning effects or perceived obligations toward reciprocity (e.g., Raymond 1999; Kogut and Metiu 2001; Lerner and Tirole 2002; Franke and Shah 2003; Lakhani and von Hippel 2003; Harhoff et al. 2003; von Hippel and von Krogh 2003; Lakhani and Wolf 2005; Shah 2005; Jeppesen and Frederiksen 2006), personal identity (David and Shapiro 2008; Füller 2010), and social capital (Nambisan and Baron 2010). From a case study in the field of computer-controlled music instruments, Jeppesen and Frederiksen (2006) conclude that users are likely to be hobbyists and are responsive to recognition by the hosting firm.

In the context of crowdsourcing activities, it has been shown that above all interest in the task (Füller 2006; Füller, 2010) and fairness considerations (Franke et al. 2011) are important motives that influence users' willingness to participate. While the focus has been on contributions in virtual settings such as online communities and crowdsourcing activities, knowledge sharing and induced fairness considerations when actors that reside outside a producer firms' boundaries—such as lead users—significantly contribute to a focal producer firm's new product development endeavors have received less attention (Harhoff and Mayrhofer 2008).

Synopsis: Knowledge-Sharing Behavior of Lead Users in Lead User Workshops

The private-collective model and its related insights may not be fully applicable in the context of lead user workshops for two reasons. First, lead user workshops do not resemble a collaborative community of users. Second, workshop participants are not granted access to solutions generated as the IP rights belong exclusively to the company and NDAs have to be signed (common practice at lead user workshops). This is in contrast to the setting of OSS communities where there is open access to the source code which thus becomes a public good (see the corresponding discussion in Lerner and Tirole 2002; O'Mahony 2003; Osterloh and Rota 2007). Following the definition of Wellman et al. (2002: 153), communities resemble "networks of interpersonal ties that provide sociability, support, information, a sense of belonging and social identity." Lead user workshops do not resemble such a community setting. Therefore a number of motivational factors such as building reputation among peers (Raymond 1999), reciprocity (Harhoff et al. 2003), identification with a specific community (Hertel et al. 2003), and development support (Franke and Shah 2003) may not be addressed or may not be as strong in the lead user workshop setting.

Additionally, the individuals involved in a lead user workshop do not necessarily share a common interest in a product and its tools. Gächter et al. (2011) show that especially in the absence of a strong community knowledge sharing is fragile due to strong conflicts of interest. Henkel

(2006) reports that even in an OSS community setting a combination of free revealing and various means of protecting one's intellectual property do coexist.

Conceptually, lead users can follow three major strategies: share all their knowledge, share part of it, or share nothing. It has been argued that there might be a number of conditions influencing the economic benefit and hence the decision to follow a certain knowledge sharing strategy such as the strength of the appropriability regime (Teece 1986), the value of the patent, licensing costs, the ability to keep intellectual property secret (Harhoff et al. 2003), and, as needed, complementary assets to commercialize one's idea (Teece 1986). A recent study by Franke et al. (2011) finds that in addition to factors related to self-interest perceived fairness and trust seem to have a large impact on the individuals' propensity to contribute to an open innovation setting.

To summarize, there is lack of insight with respect to the motives and kind of knowledge sharing of lead users when interacting with producer firms. We therefore conducted an explorative empirical study to generate more insights into this.

Research Design and Methodology

To examine the addressed research questions, we studied knowledge sharing behavior of lead users in an empirical context, namely in lead user workshops. Our sample consists of an array of five lead user workshops of the same setting that took place between 2008 and 2011 across several industries: consumer goods, food processing, aircraft construction, manufacturing, and telecommunications. This diverse collection of workshops was chosen in order to facilitate the identification of common elements (Yin 2003; Miles and Huberman 1994).

We chose an inductive case study research design, being particularly apt for examining phenomena that are emergent or poorly understood, allowing room for the unanticipated and to arrive at an encompassing view of the personal attributes of knowledge sharing behavior within lead user workshops (Eisenhardt 1989; Yin 1993; Edmondson and McManus 2006). The case study method has been used in innovative, new technology fields to question existing theory and develop further theory (O'Connor 1998; Perry 1998; Song and Montoya-Weiss 1998; de Weerd-Nederhof 2001; McDermott and O'Connor 2002; Rowley 2002).

Our data include 19 semi-structured interviews with lead user workshop participants and corporate project managers, focusing on expectations and perceptions concerning knowledge sharing, fairness issues, and reward systems. The interviews were carried out ex post. The semi-structured set of interview guidelines focused on references derived from existing literature to ensure consistency with the current state of research. Prior to the narrative interviews, a starting list of codes was compiled on the basis of the study's conceptual framework and research questions. We analyzed our data using NVivo software, an open coding application for qualitative data, having two independent coders.

Findings

This section is organized according to the two addressed research questions and illustrates the identified patterns with exemplary quotes from our interviews with lead users.

Motives of Lead Users to Reveal Their Knowledge to Focal Producer Firms

Our interviews reveal a mix of intrinsic and extrinsic motives. We present our findings in table 20.1 where we outline the identified motives and the corresponding quotes.

With respect to fairness perceptions, lead users reported that a high degree of autonomy provided by the focal producer firm in the ideation process is significantly influencing their perception of fairness:

"If the company was sitting there taking lots of notes, asking a few pointed questions here and there, asking us to do a lot of stuff for free, then I would say, yeah, that would be unfair."

"If I wouldn't have the freedom to pursue my ideas and to discuss and examine them with the other experts here, then that would be a problem for me."

In addition participants perceived the setting as fair due to the nature of the output generated: The company would still have to invest a lot of effort to profit commercially from the generated ideas.

"The information that we provided still requires the company to do a lot of work before they could get true patent protection, and so forth, so I don't think there was any problem, I think it was fair in that sense."

With respect to future perspectives, the large majority of the interviewees agreed that they would be willing to enter some kind of long-term

Table 20.1
Identified intrinsic and extrinsic motives and corresponding quotes

Extrinsic motives	*Quotes*
Fun, enjoyment, and intellectual challenge	- "I see it as a benefit for me to disengage for a few days, let my brain roam freely for a bit, and really get those gears cranking again."
	"On the other hand it is very pleasant to be able to become detached from all other daily occurrences and spend two days together with experts developing and discussing ideas. This is simply a very welcome experience and actually almost a luxury that perhaps we don't get to enjoy too often."
	"I personally had a lot of fun, and if it's not fun, then I don't think you really generate any results. So yes, it worked very well!"
Extrinsic motives	*Quotes*
Learning effects	- "From the bigger breakout sections and the packaging people I actually learned quite a lot, they had wonderful ideas, they shared their process of taking boxes and folding them into new concepts, so that I found very fascinating."
	"I think just the design contacts and the people who have done some interesting things in other industries were valuable and I think those aspects have proven very useful in other work that I'd been involved in since."
Getting connected with other lead users	- "Monetary wise as an agency you would have expected a little bit of compensation of some form that would have been very helpful, but at the very beginning I agreed that it was OK for me to come with no expectations other than meeting people and having a nice conversation with other colleagues."
	"For me certainly the highlight was to meet so many people and work with them in a very focused way on the project and both the people in my group and the people from your school, so you know the participants . . . you know I really enjoyed the collaboration."

Table 20.1 (continued)

Extrinsic motives	Quotes
Establish an ongoing collaboration with peers	- "I will have a more serious meeting with one of the other participants in the summer to look if we can do projects together, in the field of bionic and packaging. It's a really interesting topic and a major outcome from my participation in the workshop." "I think a lot of people expect to make connections with other workshop participants to have some projects together in the future."
Getting in contact with the focal producer firm that may create monetary rewards in the future	- "I'm beginning to think that it is still possible in some way to keep a close tie, or to work with the project, or somehow still find a way to collaborate on the project." "I actually did hope that there is the chance to further work together with the company, that I might be invited to participate in follow-up meetings or other workshops from the firm. I am still highly interested in working together or for the company." "It's a marketing tool. When you get the chance to participate in a workshop like this you should bring your good ideas and if people really think you have good ideas and they like working with you, then they'll follow up."
Being acknowledged as someone special by the focal producer firm	- "I am pretty sure that the company invited me, because I developed a niche product that was in demand lately, based on a very good idea mainly. That was in a way my motivation to participate." "I mean I was definitely flattered to receive the invitation."
Being strongly dependent on the focal producer firm with respect to turning a solution into a commercial product (producer firm has the complementary assets)	- "I had and still have a lot of ideas for increasing the status-quo; I simply don't have access to the technical infrastructure needed to really implement them in reality. I can think of physical products as well as web-based solutions that both require a certain network or implementation assistance or even access to producers." "I'm not very big on protecting ideas, because if I don't have the capability to actually execute it, then someone else should . . . and so, I felt like it was good to see that my ideas were valued."

relationship provided that the focal producer firm would grant monetary rewards:

"Well, if this becomes a regular occurrence, then I would have to look at my position as a consultant and look at my benefit."

"I'm not asking them to gold plate my living space, but I would like an adequate compensation for my performance."

From the interviews it also turned out that the participants are keen to know what happens with the ideas generated after the workshop. It seems that participants develop a feeling of ownership toward the ideas as they do not receive any monetary compensation from the company.

"I've heard no feedback from the company or of where they have gone with the ideas, so I don't know about the usefulness and I cannot judge that. I'd like to think it was useful, and I also would be more than happy if the opportunity enrolls to follow up with the company to carry the ideas further just because it is sort of frustrating, but I like to not leave things in the air, so it is a great desire of mine to see ideas forward through."

"But if the motivation is to come up with something truly new, then there definitely should be a follow-up. I believe that immediately after the workshop, me and my colleagues were convinced of the concepts we came up with and would really like to know what became of our baby. Instead, we went back to routine. We would have been happy if we could have somehow continued, maybe get together for a post-session and then take a look at this and that, or collaborate with certain lead users."

Extent of Knowledge Sharing by Lead Users

Our interviews reveal that at the beginning of the lead user workshop lead users observe the knowledge sharing behavior of other lead users and adapt their behavior accordingly. Apparently, there unfolds a *swift norm of knowledge sharing* right at the outset of each workshop:

". . . the most important thing in my experience, and I would say this was backed up what I saw when you have people who are open, and especially when the industry is open, then the other people tend to open up and share more also. There are also a few people who think that their knowledge is somehow special and so they are going to keep that, but once you have a group together that has several people sharing, at that point a lot of these barriers just drop, and that is what I saw, most of the people were quite willing to share."

Interestingly, we find that lead users even though they accepted the IP approach ex ante, are still very much considering costs and benefits of knowledge sharing at the workshop:

"Yes, the benefits are clear; otherwise, I would not do it, but costs are there, that is clear, even if it just cost in terms of time and knowledge. I have to consider that as a consultant, the disclosure of my knowledge would have generated a fee."

This rationale leads to a range of uncommon and unexplored revealing patterns in the lead user workshop context. In fact, several lead users told us that they held back critical knowledge during the workshop:

"I would say of the people that I have talked to there, maybe 90 percent were sharing and maybe 10 percent of the people were holding back information because they thought it had special value."

Participants held back critical knowledge when they felt that holding back knowledge could lead to higher private returns:

"Well, I mean, there were a few participants were you could tell they were holding back quite a bit, but I think the kind of business they're in, at least some of them, they make products or they manufacture something and its very critical to their business that they have that, I guess, strategic advantage."

"I felt that some of the attendees or experts were not as willing to offer ideas or to participate, they were more maybe holding back ideas, so not in a very positive or proactive sort of state."

"They contributed special knowledge but I think it was extremely shallow, they are supposedly experts in the field and so they told you their opinion, they didn't really share."

A number of lead users noted that they have been fine with openly sharing knowledge as they had the feeling that a certain level of depth had not been achieved. As long as the ideas generated remained on a broad concept level and they did not have to give detailed information, they openly contributed.

"It was more of an atmosphere for discussing and clarifying ideas. 50 percent of the time was actually defining the problem. So, I actually don't have a problem with conveying my knowledge, especially since this was only a workshop and it did not really go in-depth regarding implementation aspects."

"In fact . . . primarily we were not asked to provide any detailed data around, like engineering specifications or costs estimations or anything that they could directly use to manufacture something. Because we were not asked to provide any of that kind of information I think it was fair."

"But I bet you if you go further and if you want to discuss more details about the process or approaches than maybe more sensitive information has to come up and maybe people will withhold information. But as far as this workshop is concerned I did not see any people hiding or withholding information."

Another interesting finding is that lead users from analogous domains seem to be more open in terms of knowledge sharing as the generated results at the workshop are less applicable in their field, whereas lead users from target domains are more conscious of what they reveal but do have more benefits in terms of learning.

Quote from a lead user from an analogous market:

"I think I had a decided advantage concerning open knowledge sharing, as I participated in my role as director of a research institute that is acting in another context, and therefore I am not seeking after the generation of like, for example, trade mark rights or intellectual property rights anyway."

Quote from a lead user from the target market:

"There are certain areas I am not allowed to talk about, there are certain areas where the university gets the rights, and so I went in knowing pretty much what the ground rules were, but I was working far enough outside my expertise that I don't think there was any issue with proprietary exchange there."

Discussion and Conclusion

Our study reveals that lead users derive private benefits by participating in a lead user workshop. Those benefits comprise a mix of intrinsic and extrinsic rewards similar to those identified in open source community settings. Due to the lack of a community in a lead user workshop setting, motives like obligations toward the community or a feeling of solidarity and community citizenship are less prevalent. An important aspect for lead users at workshops—according to our study—is the need for transparency and autonomy to create. As they do not derive any monetary reward from participating, it is important to the lead users that they have at least contributed to something useful and meaningful. Furthermore a feeling of freedom to follow up on their or others' ideas allows them to enjoy their task and thus reduces the risk that lead users feel exploited by the focal producer firm. Our study indicates that the more lead user workshops provide the different private benefits as identified in this study, the more lead users perceive the exchange relationship with the producer firm as fair.

It is important to note that this study is only a very first step in better understanding motive structures, fairness perceptions and knowledge sharing behaviors of lead users in lead user-workshop settings. Further research is needed to better understand whether different types of lead users have different motive profiles (different combinations of intrinsic and/or extrinsic motives and weight different motives differently). For example, we would expect that for a lead user coming from the target domain the urgent need to receive a commercial product that fits her needs is an important driver for participation. In contrast, a lead user from an analogous market may be more driven by motives such as fun, networking, learning effects, access to the company, simply because in her domain the problem may already be solved or the insights gained might not be transferable back in the analogous market. Furthermore, motives may differ with respect to the specific sector in which a lead user project is carried out. For example, in highly regulated sectors where producer firms possess most of the complementary assets (e.g., medical device industry, pharmaceutical industry) lead users are more dependent on a cooperation with a producer firm than in lifestyle sectors (e.g., extreme sporting equipment). Different sectors may also induce different opportunity costs for participating lead users (e.g., a professor for neurosurgery versus a professional kite surfer).

If different types of lead users have different motive profiles, then focal producer firms may need to design tailored reward systems for each user type. Whether this tailored approach is feasible in practice, however, remains to be seen: Different reward systems may optimize the knowledge sharing behavior of lead users but they may—at the same time—distort collaboration and fairness perceptions among participants. Also the costs of such a tailored approach need to be taken into account.

Our study also shows that lead users act far more strategically with respect to knowledge sharing than so far assumed. First, lead users make their knowledge sharing behavior dependent on the behavior of other participating lead users. Interestingly, there seems to emerge a kind of swift norm right at the beginning of the workshop on which level of knowledge sharing is appropriate. Second, lead users do not unconditionally freely reveal but do make benefit–cost considerations. As an outcome of such considerations, we could observe selective revealing behavior of lead users: some knowledge is freely revealed while knowledge that is crucial for the lead user in terms of IP and potential private return is deliberately held back. This implies that the concepts that are developed during lead user workshops could potentially have more depth and thus quality than the ones that are being developed under the currently practiced reward system.

It also became apparent, that the more the lead users have the feeling that the content being discussed and shared was of a rather broad and unspecific nature, the more they were willing to openly share their knowledge. The identified selective revealing behavior of lead users raises the question whether different reward systems at a lead user-workshop may yield a more open knowledge sharing behavior. Further research should investigate this aspect. In addition it can be assumed that the strong cost–benefit considerations by participants lead to inherent self-selection biases in the application of the lead user method. This may imply that there is a crowd of lead users deliberately not participating due to unfavorable cost–benefit ratios.

From a managerial point of view, our study provides insights on how to design lead user workshops so that (1) lead users derive private benefits from participating, and (2) lead users are more inclined to openly share their knowledge. In this respect firms need to manage the balance of freedom for lead users and alignment of the development efforts with corporate goals and strategy very carefully. With respect to the perceived fairness of lead users in terms of the exchange relationship with the focal producer firm, firms need to be aware that there is "word of mouth" among lead users on how fair the firm dealt with them during and after the workshop. This effect can be used for positive branding and public relation if managed well. If managed badly, the company may not be able to apply the lead user method on a sustainable basis.

Furthermore, as lead users expressed a need to establish a long-term relationship, producer firms that host lead user workshops need to think about models how such long-term relationships may be designed. Building up such relationships with lead users would entail many benefits for the company. First, a continuous collaboration enables to build up trust and hence allows the transfer of tacit knowledge which is a crucial ingredient for truly innovative solutions. Second, a continuous collaboration enables the company to leverage the creative potential, knowledge, and status of lead users in all stages of the innovation process (including development, market testing, market launch and diffusion). Third, a sustainable relationship with lead users enables a company to benefit from their contributions in subsequent projects.

We hope that this article spurs a discussion on fairness and knowledge sharing aspects in lead user settings and greatly look forward to seeing corresponding future research endeavors.

References

Allen, Robert C. 1983. Collective invention. *Journal of Economic Behavior and Organization* 4 (1): 1–24.

Brockhoff, Klaus. 2003. Customers' perspectives of involvement in new product development. *International Journal of Technology Management* 26 (5–6): 464–81.

David, Paul A., and Joseph S. Shapiro. 2008. Community-based production of open-source software: What do we know about the developers who participate? *Information Economics and Policy* 20 (4): 364–98.

De Weerd-Nederhof, Petra C. 2001. Qualitative case study research. The case of a PhD research project on organising and managing new product development systems. *Management Decision* 39 (7): 513–38.

Eisenhardt, Kathleen M. 1989. Building theories from case study research. *Academy of Management Review* 14 (4): 532–50.

Franke, Nikolaus, and Sonali Shah. 2003. How communities support innovative activities: An exploration of assistance and sharing among end-users. *Research Policy* 32 (1): 157–78.

Franke, Nikolaus, Eric von Hippel, and Martin Schreier. 2006. Finding commercially attractive user innovations: A test of lead user theory. *Journal of Product Innovation Management* 23 (4): 301–15.

Franke, Nikolaus, Katharina Klausberger, and Peter Keinz. 2011. Does this sound like a fair deal? The role of fairness perceptions in the individual's decision to participate in firm innovation. Working paper. Vienna University of Economics and Business.

Füller, Johann. 2006. Why consumers engage in virtual new product developments initiated by producers. *Advances in Consumer Research. Association for Consumer Research (U. S.)* 33 (1): 639–46.

Füller, Johann. 2010. Refining virtual co-creation from a consumer perspective. *California Management Review* 52 (2): 98–122.

Harhoff, Dietmar, Joachim Henkel, and Eric von Hippel. 2003. Profiting from voluntary information spillovers: How users benefit by freely revealing their innovations. *Research Policy* 32 (10): 1753–69.

Harhoff, Dietmar, and Philip Mayrhofer. 2008. User communities and hybrid innovation processes: Theoretical foundations and implications for policy and research. DIME/DRUID.

Henkel, Joachim. 2006. Selective revealing in open innovation processes: The case of embedded Linux. *Research Policy* 35 (7): 953–69.

Herstatt, Cornelius, Christian Lüthje, and Christopher Lettl. 2002. Wie fortschrittliche Kunden zu Innovationen stimulieren. *Harvard Business Manager* 24 (1): 60–68.

Herstatt, Cornelius, and Eric von Hippel. 1992. From experience: Developing new product concepts via the lead user method. A case study in a "low-tech" field. *Journal of Product Innovation Management* 9 (3): 213–21.

Hertel, Guido, Sven Niedner, and Stefanie Herrmann. 2003. Motivation of software developers in open source projects: An Internet-based survey of contributors to the Linux kernel. *Research Policy* 32 (7): 1159–77.

Hienerth, Christoph, and Christopher Lettl. 2011. Exploring how peer communities enable lead user innovations to become the industry standard: Community pull effects. *Journal of Product Innovation Management* (28) 175–95.

Jeppesen, Lars B., and Keld Laursen. 2009. The role of lead users in knowledge sharing. *Research Policy* 38 (10): 1582–89.

Jeppesen, Lars B., and Lars Frederiksen. 2006. Why do users contribute to firm-hosted user communities? The case of computer controlled music instruments. *Organization Science* 17 (1): 45–63.

Katila, Riitta, and Gautam Ahuja. 2002. Something old, something new: A longitudinal study of search behavior and new product introduction. *Academy of Management Journal* 45 (6): 1183–94.

Kratzer, Jan, and Christopher Lettl. 2009. Distinctive roles of lead users and opinion leaders in the social networks of schoolchildren. *Journal of Consumer Research* 36 (4): 646–59.

Kogut, Bruce, and Anca Metiu. 2001. Open-source software development and distributedinnovation. *Oxford Review of Economic Policy* 17 (2): 248–64.

Lakhani, Karim R., and Robert G. Wolf. 2005. Why hackers do what they do: Understanding motivation and effort in free/open source software projects. In *Perspectives on Free and Open Source Software*, ed. Joseph Feller, Brian Fitzgerald, Scott Hissam, and Karim Lakhani, 3–22. Cambridge: MIT Press.

Lerner, Josh, and Jean Tirole. 2002. Some simple economics of open source. *Journal of Industrial Economics* 50 (2): 197–234.

Lilien, Gary L., Pamela D. Morrison, Kathleen Searls, Mary Sonnack, and Eric von Hippel. 2002. Performance assessment of the lead user idea-generation process for new product development. *Management Science* 48 (8): 1042–59.

Lüthje, Christian, and Cornelius Herstatt. 2004. The lead user method: An outline of empirical findings and issues for future research. *R&D Management* 34 (5): 553–68.

McDermott, Christopher M., and Gina C. O'Connor. 2002. Managing radical innovation: An overview of emergent strategy issues. *Journal of Product Innovation Management* 19 (6): 424–38.

Morrison, Pamela D., John H. Roberts, and Eric von Hippel. 2000. Determinants of user innovation and innovation sharing in a local market. *Management Science* 46 (12): 1513–27.

Nambisan, Satish, and Robert A. Baron. 2010. Different roles, different strokes: Organizing virtual customer environments to promote two types of customer contributions. *Organization Science* 21 (2): 554–72.

O'Connor, Gina C. 1998. Market learning and radical innovation: A cross case comparison of eight radical innovation projects. *Journal of Product Innovation Management* 15 (2): 151–66.

Olson, Erik L., and Geir Bakke. 2001. Implementing the lead user method in a high technology firm: A longitudinal study of intentions versus actions. *Journal of Product Innovation Management* 18 (6): 388–95.

O'Mahony, Siobhan. 2003. Guarding the commons: How community managed software projects protect their work. *Research Policy* 32 (7): 1179–98.

Osterloh, Margit, and Sandra Rota. 2007. Open source development: Just another case of collective invention? *Research Policy* 36 (2): 157–71.

Ozer, Muammer. 2009. The roles of product lead-users and product experts in new product evaluation. *Research Policy* 38 (8): 1340–49.

Perry, Chad. 1998. Processes of a case study methodology for postgraduate research in marketing. *European Journal of Marketing* 32 (9–10): 785–802.

Raymond, Eric. 1999. The cathedral and the bazaar. *Knowledge, Technology and Policy* 12 (3): 23–49.

Rowley, Jennifer. 2002. Using case studies in research. *Management Research News* 25 (1): 16–27.

Schreier, Martin, Stefan Oberhauser, and Reinhard Prügl. 2007. Lead users and the adoption and diffusion of new products: Insights from two extreme sports communities. *Marketing Letters* 18 (1–2): 15–30.

Schreier, Martin, and Reinhard Prügl. 2008. Extending lead user theory: Antecedents and consequences of consumers' lead userness. *Journal of Product Innovation Management* 25 (4): 331–46.

Song, X. Michael, and Mitzi M. Montoya-Weiss. 1998. Critical development activities for really new versus incremental products. *Journal of Product Innovation Management* 15 (2): 124–35.

Teece, David J. 1986. Profiting from technological innovation: Implications for integration, collaboration, licensing and public policy. *Research Policy* 15 (6): 285–305.

Urban, Glen L., and Eric von Hippel. 1988. Lead user analyses for the development of new industrial products. *Management Science* 34 (5): 569–82.

von Hippel, Eric. 1986. Lead users: A source of novel product concepts. *Management Science* 32 (7): 791–805.

von Hippel, Eric, Stefan Thomke, and Mary Sonnack. 1999. Creating breakthroughs at 3M. *Harvard Business Review* 77 (5): 47–57.

von Hippel, Eric. 2005. *Democratizing Innovation*. Boston: MIT Press.

von Hippel, Eric, and Georg von Krogh. 2003. Open Source Software Development and the "Private-Collective" Innovation Model: Issues for Organization Science. *Organization Science* 14 (2): 209–23.

Wellman, Barry, Jeffrey Boase, and Wenhong Chen. 2002. The Networked Nature of Community: Online and Offline. *IT & Society* 1 (1): 151–165.

Yin, Robert K. 1993. *Applications of Case Study Research*. Beverly Hills, CA: Sage.

21

Crowdsourcing at MUJI

Susumu Ogawa and Hidehiko Nishikawa

This chapter aims to identify how crowdsourcing has been put into practice by Ryohin Keikaku, one of the pioneering enterprises in the field, why it was successful, and what results have been achieved, by describing a case study of the changes crowdsourcing has undergone and undertaking a comparative analysis with traditional methods.

Recent advances in Internet technology have made it possible for enterprises to incorporate large and indeterminate "crowds" into the ideation stage of product development (von Hippel 2005). This practice of leaving the creation of product ideas up to a large and indeterminate number of users is called *crowdsourcing* (Agerfalk and Fitzgerald 2008; Howe 2006, 2008; Pisano and Verganti 2008). Some examples of crowdsourcing have already been reported, including Dell's Idea Storm and Threadless.com (Howe 2008; Ogawa and Piller 2006). These cases indicate that crowdsourcing provides a means of utilizing a wider range of perspectives and resources in product development than would be available through in-house professionals only (Piller and Walcher 2006; Poetz and Schreier 2012; von Hippel et al. 2011).

While many different enterprises engage in crowdsourcing, this chapter focuses on Ryohin Keikaku Co., Ltd. Ryohin Keikaku is an enterprise that develops products and stores under the MUJI brand name. Ryohin Keikaku operates on a global scale; as of the time of writing (the end of FY 2010), it had 493 stores in 22 countries including Japan, United States, United Kingdom, France, Italy, Germany, Sweden, Norway, China, Taiwan, and South Korea. It has a wide range of products: 1,915 items in the apparel and sundries category, 4,893 in the interior/household goods category, and 652 in the foods category, giving a total of 7,460 items. It is a vertically integrated enterprise that handles the entire process from planning through manufacturing, wholesaling, and retailing. In FY 2010, the company reported sales of 47 billion yen in apparel and sundries, 80.7 billion yen in interior/household goods, and 14.4 billion yen in foods. Overall, it reported consolidated sales of 170 billion yen for a net profit of 7.9 billion yen.

Ryohin Keikaku began to utilize crowdsourcing—though it was not initially called that—in its product development activities in 2000, and as of the time of writing (2011), had already completed more than 40 such projects. There are very few enterprises that can claim to have successfully practiced crowdsourcing for more than 10 years. This chapter describes the approaches taken by Ryohin Keikaku as a pioneer in crowdsourcing and how it was able to be successful.[1]

Initial Crowdsourcing at Ryohin Keikaku

Ryohin Keikaku began to search for ways to use the Internet, which became widely used in product development during the 1990s. One such attempt was called "Product Development for Furniture and Appliances." The key concept underlying the project was to develop products based on ideas provided by consumers. It took advantage of one idea each month, for a total of 12 ideas over the course of a year, at the end of which the project was concluded.

In the fall of 1999, Ryohin Keikaku was looking to the Internet as a new channel for the development and marketing of its MUJI brand products. There were several reasons for this. The first was that the Internet was beginning to come into widespread use. The second was that there was strong demand for Internet sales both from customers living in areas without MUJI stores and from customers who, because they had children or for other reasons, were unable to visit stores very frequently. The third was a desire to enable customers to purchase all of the products handled by Ryohin Keikaku without the physical constraints associated with brick and mortar stores. To that point in time Ryohin Keikaku outlets carried different numbers of products depending upon the size of their sales space, so one was not necessarily able to purchase every MUJI product at every MUJI store. The Internet overcame these constraints and enabled the customer to purchase any product they desired.

At the end of 1999, there was discussion within Ryohin Keikaku about beginning Internet sales, and by 2000 the plan had been fleshed out. Rather than merely using the Internet as a new channel for selling products developed for brick and mortar stores, it would be used as a tool for developing new products and businesses Ryohin Keikaku had never touched to that point in time. The Product Development for Furniture and Appliances project was one of the experiments to emerge from this. The intention behind the project was to use unconventional methods to develop products with high degrees of novelty.

One of the directions given for this project was to employ product concepts broader than those traditionally seen in MUJI products. More specifically, those involved in the project were instructed to focus on development that "explores new functions" rather than development that "focuses on a narrow range of core functions."

Until then, MUJI product development had emphasized a narrow range of core functions, the ideal being a product that "can be explained in a few lines on the tag." In short, the traditional MUJI development concept was to strip out all of the unnecessary functions of existing products. When customers came to the store, all they needed do was read the tag to be able to understand how the product worked and decide whether they wished to purchase it, with no explanations from salespeople being necessary. These were the kinds of products the company developed.

The new project sought to develop products with new functions. The Internet would serve as a vehicle for explaining these new functions to the consumer and how they were to be used. This would, it was hoped, produce a new Internet-driven style of product development. The Product Development for Furniture and Appliances project was conducted from September 2002 to December 2003 to explore this.

Under the project, the company sought to develop products and businesses that had been impossible to develop with its traditional approach. It was therefore decided that ideas already in development or under study would not be included. It was also decided not to work on ideas related to the basic modules of existing products. MUJI practice was to create basic modules of sizes, materials, and colors so that products within specific groupings could be easily combined and configured. Standalone products are much simpler to develop. It was therefore decided to eliminate from the scope of the project any product that would need to take account of basic modules in its development.

Use of Outside Resources

The Product Development for Furniture and Appliances project was an experiment in developing a different range of products and services, and it innovated in aspects other than the product conditions described above. One of the key innovations was the use of outside resources. There were two ways it did this. The first was consumer-driven development (i.e., crowdsourcing); the other was partnering with outside companies.

In consumer-driven development, Ryohin Keikaku had traditionally engaged in exchanges of opinions with consumers, which it referred to as "opinion catch-ball." At the time the company had already collected approximately 90,000 comments from its customers in the form of postcards, email, telephone calls, and in-store discussions. These comments were put to use in product development.

However, the only way to inform consumers that developers had listened to what they said was, for example, to put up product announcement posters. One of the aims of this project was to directly involve customers in the development process, creating closer, more frequent interactions that, it was hoped, would produce something different.

The other use of outside resources was in the form of partner companies. Here too, Ryohin Keikaku had specific goals. Bringing in automotive companies, site operators, and other outside specialists for joint development projects would enable the company to tackle ideas and techniques that it could not have tackled on its own. The hope was that this too would lead to the creation of new products and businesses.

Use of Parent Company Resources

As described above, the Product Development for Furniture and Appliances project was expected to produce innovative ideas, techniques, products, and businesses, and accomplishing this required different development focuses and the active recruitment of outside resources.

While the project was tasked with new functions and roles, it also made as much use as possible of internal resources. One of its emphases was utilizing the business resources MUJI had accumulated to that point in time.

To begin with, the project's design rules were based on those traditionally employed by the MUJI brand. While it sought to move in new directions in terms of ideas, content, and product and service approaches, the basic design rules were those traditionally employed by the MUJI brand.

The company's website describes MUJI design rules thus:

1. Manufacturing should wherever possible exploit the properties of materials without excessive decoration, additives, or processing.
2. Manufacturing should take care of all aspects of the global environment, including materials, processing, packaging, and disposal.
3. Products should suit the atmosphere of the times, and should embody and express them.
4. Products should be simple, easy for anyone to use, beautiful, of high quality, and functional.
5. Products should be priced appropriately, and it should be easy to understand what makes them different.

The Product Development for Furniture and Appliances project aimed to maximize the use of MUJI's design rules, and to do so, it gave Ryohin Keikaku product development managers final authority over the adoption of ideas. This was because development managers were well versed in MUJI product concepts and purchaser behavior in brick and mortar stores. It was therefore decided to develop only products consistent with MUJI concepts. There were in fact a number of ideas that were not commercialized by the project because they were not considered a good fit for MUJI.

The second MUJI resource used by the project was the customer interface in brick and mortar stores. The intention from the beginning was to utilize Ryohin Keikaku's brick and mortar store network—in November 2002, the company had a domestic Japanese network totaling 269 outlets—and the catalogs, shopping bags, and other items available there to promote Internet sales. The goal was to use existing resources in brick and mortar stores wherever possible to highlight Internet-developed products to as many consumers as possible.

Development of the MUJI Car

Ryohin Keikaku had actually already experimented with the incorporation of consumers into the ideation stage of product development even before the launch of the Product Development for Furniture and Appliances project. In September 2000 the company began collaborating with Nissan Motor on the development of a car, and started to receive orders for the car from customers in April 2001. The product, known as the "MUJI Car," was a special version of Nissan Motor's "March." It had a 1,000 cc, 4-speed automatic transmission, came in ivory only, and cost 930,000 yen, which was 25,000 yen less than an ordinary March. It was a limited edition of something over 1,000 vehicles and could only be purchased through the MUJI website.

The idea for the product came from comments provided by approximately 500 customers on the MUJI website. Some functions were eliminated from the car in order to reduce the price. Ultimately the company sold 164 of the vehicles. At the time that was considered a very good result for Internet automobile sales, but even so, it was not a resounding success.

Lessons from the MUJI Car

Ryohin Keikaku learned several things from this development process. The first was that it needed a means of contacting idea providers and identifying their customer profiles during development. In developing the MUJI Car, it was not known what kinds of consumers were providing ideas, which made it impossible to account for their characteristics and profiles, and therefore rendered it impossible to forecast demand with any precision.

Second, when it comes to actual purchases, people who read comments on the Internet play a much more important role in sales than those who actively write them. Only a few of the roughly 500 consumers who provided ideas actually purchased MUJI Cars. The people who bought the product were, for the most part, consumers who read the opinions and not those who wrote them.

Third, the development process requires a higher degree of openness. The restrictions of the automotive industry meant that the company was unable to disclose the name of the base car or details about the design even six months after the MUJI Car development project commenced. This created gaps between the real product and the images consumers had in their minds. There was no effective and efficient means of exchanging opinions between consumers and developers.

Fourth, it is important to retain brick and mortar store sales, and not just Internet sales, as a possibility during development and testing. Without this, it is difficult to obtain the cooperation of manufacturers and dealers. The plan was to sell the MUJI Car on the Internet only, and this made it impossible to obtain satisfactory levels of cooperation from outlets and the manufacturer, where the priority was on existing channels. In addition the relatively low MUJI Car sales were partially attributable to the nature of Internet-based ideas and evaluations; there were some comments that the car was only being sold on the net because no one could buy it in ordinary stores and dealerships.

The MUJI Car experience identified four issues in consumer-driven product development: (1) increasing the traceability of consumers providing ideas, (2) developing mechanisms to more actively involve read-only consumers in the development process, (3) increasing the transparency of development, and (4) linking real-store and net sales.

The Product Development for the Furniture and Appliances project attempted to address these issues. First, to better trace the people proposing ideas, it introduced a membership registration system. Second, it asked people to vote on development ideas and used the results to drive product development, which enabled read-only members (ROMs or lurkers) to more actively express their opinions on the net. Third, to improve the transparency of the development process, it partnered with a venture company called "Elephant Design" that had similar development experiences, which enabled it to make use of insights from past projects. Finally, to better link real-store and net sales, development work proceeded from the very beginning under the assumption that products would also be sold in brick and mortar stores.

The "Product Development for Furniture and Appliances" Project

After the initial preparations were completed, the Product Development for Furniture and Appliances project commenced on September 25, 2001. The initial plan was to take up one development theme each month, for a total of 12 themes during the year, and in all cases it was to be consumers who drove the development process.

Figure 21.1
Body Fit Cushion
Source: Ryohin Keikaku

The "Product Development for Furniture and Appliances" Development Flow

Individual Product Development for Furniture and Appliances projects proceeded according to the following steps. The steps are explained with examples from the development theme and final product that earned the highest sales, "Suwaru Seikatsu" and "Body Fit Cushion," respectively (see figure 21.1).

Step 1. Consumers register (free of charge) to participate in the project. Registered consumers write comments on an Internet bulletin board, which trigger the following process.[2]

Step 2. Product development themes identified from consumer posts are announced.

(Ex.) Suwaru Seikatsu ("Sit down Life")

Step 3. Consumers post product ideas for the themes indicated.

(Ex.) The "Suwaru Seikatsu" theme

(Ex.) A large cushion that supports your entire body, a floor sofa with a good backrest

(Ex.) A cushion mat that lets you relax while lying down, a "relax" tatami chair

Step 4. MUJI organizes and consolidates the ideas provided by consumers and asks consumers to vote on which of the many ideas they like the best. At the same time MUJI invites consumers to post more input for the idea they have chosen.

(Ex.)	A large cushion that supports your entire body	90 votes
	A floor sofa with a good backrest	47 votes
	A cushion mat that lets you relax while lying down	34 votes
	A "relax" tatami chair	31 votes
	A tatami chair with legs, a tatami chair for sitting cross-legged	25 votes

Step 5. MUJI creates design proposals for the idea with the most votes in step 4 and asks consumers to vote on the one they like the best. At the same time MUJI invites consumers to post more input for the design they have chosen.

(Ex.)	For the "large cushion that supports your entire body"	
	Fabric type	177 votes
	Unit type	97 votes
	Relax support type	57 votes
	Mid-air type	19 votes

Step 6. The proposal with the most votes in step 5 is studied for potential commercialization, with decisions made on detailed specifications, manufacturers, minimum commercialization lots, and expected sales prices.

(Ex.)	Product name:	Body Fit Cushion
	Product specs:	
	Cover materials	Stretch material (74% nylon, 26% polyurethane
		Canvas (100% cotton)
	Internal materials	Approximately 6 kg of 0.5 mm beads
	Size	65 (W) × 65 (D) × 43 (H) cm
	Minimum lot	50
	Sales price	19,000 yen

Step 7. After the product proposal is finalized, pre-orders are solicited, and if the number of pre-orders exceeds the minimum commercialization

lot, the product is commercialized. However, if the number of pre-orders fails to reach the minimum lot within 3 months, commercialization is abandoned.

Step 8. After sales to pre-ordering customers are complete, sales begin at brick and mortar stores in addition to on the net.

Step 9. Comments are received from consumers after they make their purchases, and that information is used in new product development and ongoing improvements.

Development Process Innovations

Ryohin Keikaku made several innovations to facilitate this project. It used pre-order pricing to give consumers an incentive to pre-order, and included in the product manual the names of consumers who had placed pre-orders by the time a decision had been made on commercialization of the product.

Second, it brought greater systematization to the development process, besides greater transparency. For example, it used explicit schedule management: focusing on one product development theme each month; setting the voting period at approximately two weeks after the announcement; and curtailing the project if the minimum pre-order lot had not been reached within three months of the start of pre-ordering.

Third, it took sales in brick and mortar stores into account in development; development therefore focused on functions, pricing, and minimum commercialization lots that would lead to mass sales in stores. For example, the criterion for deciding whether to commercialize the product was that pre-orders were at least 10 percent of the initial production lot. The figure of 10 percent came from internal sales data that suggested that even if the ideas and evaluations provided on the Internet were a bit eccentric, the company could conservatively hope to sell more than 10 times the Internet volume in real stores. As discussed by Ogawa and Piller (2006), taking pre-orders as part of the crowdsourcing process reduces the risks associated with product development. Novelty and originality are meaningless if there is no market for the product developed. Companies can, however, launch new products on the market with a certain degree of confidence if they have at least a set level of pre-orders from the crowd. This is one of the reasons Ryohin Keikaku adopted

Table 21.1
Product Development for Furniture and Appliances sales results

Product name	Minimum commercialization lot	Sales in first year in yen	Unit sales in first year
Portable Light	300	102 million	17,939
Body Fit Cushion	50	492 million	48,542
Wall Shelves	300	71 million	84,975

pre-ordering for the Product Development for Furniture and Appliances project.

Development Results

This initiative lasted from September 2002 to December 2003. It ultimately involved the study of eight themes that led to the commercialization of three products. The number of themes studied was lower than originally planned for several reasons: (1) development required longer than expected; (2) as development ideas were studied and considered, it became apparent that they did not fit in with MUJI brand concepts; (3) as development ideas were studied and considered, it was found that similar products were already being sold; and (4) as development ideas were studied and considered, it was found that similar products existed in development proposals under consideration by other units.

The number of themes studied and the number of products commercialized did not go according to plan. Nonetheless, those that were commercialized produced more than adequate sales.

There are approximately 5,000 conventionally developed MUJI items, and they produce average annual turnover of approximately 30 million yen each. By contrast, the "Portable Light" produced turnover of 102 million yen in its first year; "Body Fit Cushion" 492 million yen; and "Wall Shelves" 71 million yen (see table 21.1). All of these figures were well above the average, and "Body Fit Cushion" was a particularly big hit, ranking fifth on sales within the entire interior and household goods segment. In addition, they all produced sales volumes well above their initial production lots (10 times the minimum commercialization lot), which eliminated concerns that Internet consumers would produce eccentric ideas and evaluations that would not lead to products that could be sold in brick and mortar stores.

Comparison against Traditional Methods

Products developed using crowdsourcing in the Product Development for Furniture and Appliances project achieved higher sales results than products developed in the same categories using conventional approaches— traditional marketing approaches—and also scored higher on novelty and originality.

With the cooperation of Ryohin Keikaku, we compared the novelty, originality (as assessed by the product development manager's supervisors[3]), and sales results (actual sales data) of the three crowdsourcing products against those of products developed using traditional methods by the same product development managers in the same product categories during roughly the same periods of time. The results are shown in table 21.2. As the table indicates, crowdsourcing produces greater degrees of novelty and originality than traditional methods, and achieves high sales results.[4]

Crowdsourcing without Pre-Orders

The success of the three crowdsourcing products gave Ryohin Keikaku an understanding of how crowdsourcing could be used to supplement traditional methods. It therefore decided to simplify the process by eliminating pre-ordering and continuing to engage in crowdsourcing in parallel with traditional methods. This occurred in July 2003.

There were several reasons for eliminating pre-ordering. (1) The sales results for the three products confirmed that the ideas and evaluations (votes) provided by Internet consumers were not eccentric, and the commercialization of final product proposals given high marks by net consumers was therefore likely to boost sales results. (2) Consumers were dissatisfied with the pre-ordering system because they were unable to view the actual products in stores and were asked to pre-order between six months and a year prior to the scheduled launch (manufacturing period). (3) There was no mechanism to shift from pre-ordering to purchasing, which resulted in consumers being asked to go through cumbersome procedures. Some pre-ordering consumers could not be contacted, and some simply failed to purchase.

Table 21.2

Crowdsourcing method versus traditional marketing approach (Mann–Whitney U test)

	Crowdsourcing method ($n = 3$)		Traditional marketing method ($n = 27$)		Z-value
	Rank	Mean (SD)	Rank	Mean (SD)	(*p*-value)
Novelty compared with competition[a]	28.17	9.00 (1.73)	14.09	4.30 (1.56)	-2.817 (0.005)
Originality/ newness of customer needs addressed[a]	29.00	10.00(0.00)	14.00	3.96 (1.16)	-3.081 (0.002)
Sales in first year in yen	25.00	222million (235million)	14.44	59million (47million)	-1.970 (0.049)
Unit sales in first year	27.33	50,485 (33,560)	14.19	11,168 (10,738)	-2.454 (0.014)

a. These items were measured using a 10-point rating scale where 10 = high, 1 = low.

What, then, were the results of crowdsourcing without pre-orders? We performed a comparative analysis of products developed in no–pre-ordering crowdsourcing against products developed by the same product development team in the same categories at the same periods of time using traditional methods. Table 21.3 reports the results. As can be seen, products developed using crowdsourcing scored higher on novelty, originality, and sales results than those developed using traditional methods.[5]

Conclusion and Implications

This chapter examines a case study in crowdsourcing by describing how one of the pioneering enterprises in the field, Ryohin Keikaku, put the method into practice and why it was successful.

Ryohin Keikaku first experimented with the method in the development of an automobile and, through a process of trial and error, identified and resolved issues and simplified mechanisms. Ryohin Keikaku started by conducting "crowdsourcing with pre-orders," but its approach was later transformed into "crowdsourcing without pre-orders." The results

Table 21.3

No–pre-ordering crowdsourcing method vs. traditional marketing approach (Mann–Whitney U test)

	No–pre-ordering crowdsourcing method ($n = 6$)		Traditional marketing method ($n = 37$)		Z-value (p-value)
	Rank	Mean (SD)	Rank	Mean (SD)	
Novelty compared with competition[a]	34.67	6.83 (1.84)	19.95	4.57 (1.26)	-2.939 (0.003)
Originality/ newness of customer needs addressed[a]	35.67	6.33 (1.03)	19.78	4.46 (1.02)	-3.354 (0.001)
Sales in first year in yen	36.67	501million (339million)	19.62	141million (139million)	-3.084 (0.002)
Unit sales in first year	31.83	30,182 (23,230)	20.41	14,192 (19,383)	-2.068 (0.039)

a. These items were measured using a 10-point rating scale where 10 = high, 1 = low.

indicate that Ryohin Keikaku was able to use both types of crowdsourcing to develop products with greater degrees of novelty and originality, as well as higher sales results, than those of products developed using traditional methods.

Even without pre-ordering, crowdsourcing products scored higher than traditionally developed products on novelty, originality, and sales results. Existing literature on crowdsourcing indicates that this probably involved the following factors:

First, crowdsourcing differs from traditional methods in that it uses a broadcast search to collect information from a large and indeterminate number of people. Traditional methods narrow down targets and use them as their primary sources of information. In crowdsourcing, by contrast, information is collected from users without filtering by profile. Crowdsourcing also differs from traditional methods in that it involves the collection of information from large numbers of consumers. In crowdsourcing, anyone can participate in product development at any point in time. This brings a greater degree of user diversity than traditional methods, and also involves larger numbers of participants. These factors, in turn, can be expected to increase the novelty and originality of product development proposals. Groups that have a high degree of diversity among the people participating in problem solving tend to create more novel solutions than groups of experts in particular fields (Page 2007; Jeppesen and Lakhani 2010).

Second, crowdsourcing differs from traditional methods in that the evaluation of a large and indeterminate number of consumers is given the highest priority in selecting potential products and making decisions on final candidates. Although traditional methods involve collecting information from users to create product ideas, internal professionals determine which of several potential products are ultimately marketed according to their own criteria. By contrast, in crowdsourcing, a large and indeterminate number of users are asked to make choices from among several potential products, and decisions on final product proposals are made according to how they are ranked. Users, in other words, make the final decision. By relying on the "wisdom of crowds" instead of the assessments of a small group of specific professionals, organizations are able to forecast market reception more accurately (Surowiecki 2004). Because this allows them to avoid launching new products that will achieve only low sales results on the market, all other factors being equal, sales will be higher than for products developed using traditional methods.

If one refers to previous research, it may be concluded that these two reasons explain the tendency of products developed using crowdsourcing to generate greater sales than those developed using traditional methods. The results of the case analysis presented in this chapter, however, suggest that the following third reason may be added to the two mentioned above.

Third, crowdsourcing differs from traditional methods in that the product development process is open. Under traditional methods, information is collected from users, but the subsequent process to market launch is closed to outsiders. By contrast, crowdsourcing allows outsiders to see the entire process from the collection of user information through the evaluation, selection, and commercialization of potential products.

An open development process means that observers of the development process will have a greater degree of awareness of the product under development. This enables the creation, during the development stage, of a more positive attitude toward purchasing the product, and encourages user purchases later on. Opening up the development process can be expected to have a positive effect on sales results by playing a promotional role, even for observers who do not provide comments or votes (Fuchs and Schreier 2011).

These would seem to be the primary factors enabling crowdsourcing, even without pre-ordering, to achieve better novelty, originality, and sales results at MUJI than those for products developed using traditional methods. The success of the company's crowdsourcing strategy can be attributed to (1) a broadcast search to ensure diversity, (2) development processes that create promotional effects, and (3) crowd-based product evaluations.

This chapter has made several theoretical contributions to the literature by identifying how crowdsourcing—an approach that had been rarely utilized continuously with any success and that had yet to be fully studied—has been put into practice, why it was successful, and what results have been achieved, by describing a case study of the changes crowdsourcing has undergone and undertaking a comparative analysis with traditional methods. Particular mention must be made of the finding that crowdsourcing achieves results better than those realized through traditional methods even without pre-ordering, a factor to which its success had been attributed by previous research, and that its open development process plays a role in promotion.

These findings also represent the practical contributions of this chapter. The insights made herein should be of great use not only to enterprises that have already introduced crowdsourcing but also to those considering its introduction. The authors expect that the research outcomes of this chapter will help such enterprises further improve their crowdsourcing techniques, thereby ensuring their continued success.

Notes

1. One of the authors (Hidehiko Nishikawa) was responsible for the Ryohin Keikaku crowdsourcing project through 2005. He subsequently entered academe but continues to report on Ryohin Keikaku's crowdsourcing as an outside observer. The other author (Susumu Ogawa) has observed the company's crowdsourcing project as a researcher since its inception. This chapter therefore contains a case analysis from the perspectives of both insiders and outsiders.

2. At that time Ryohin Keikaku's online members numbered approximately 40,000.

3. A supervisor was asked to make the assessment based on the assumption that he/she would be able to perform the job more objectively than the product development manager.

4. See Lilien et al. (2002) for the survey design and observed metrics.

5. See Nishikawa et al. (2013) for more details on the comparative analysis of MUJI.

References

Agerfalk, Par J., and Brian Fitzgerald. 2008. Outsourcing to an unknown workforce: Exploring opensourcing as a global sourcing strategy. *Management Information Systems Quarterly* 32 (2): 385–409.

Fuchs, Christoph, and Martin Schreier. 2011. Customer empowerment in new product development. *Journal of Product Innovation Management* 28 (1): 17–32.

Howe, Jeff. 2006. The Rise of Crowdsourcing. *Wired* 14 (6). http://archive.wired.com/wired/archive/14.06/crowds.html.

Howe, Jeff. 2008. *Crowdsourcing: Why the Power of the Crowd Is Driving the Future of Business.* New York: Crown Business.

Jeppesen, Lars Bo, and Karim R. Lakhani. 2010. Marginality and problem-solving effectiveness in broadcast search. *Organization Science* 21 (5): 1016–33.

Lilien, Gary L., Pamela D. Morrison, Kathleen K. Searls, Mary Sonnack, and Eric von Hippel. 2002. Performance assessment of the lead user idea-generation process. *Management Science* 48 (8): 1042–59.

MUJI website at http://www.muji.com/.

Nishikawa, Hidehiko, Martin Schreier, and Susumu Ogawa. 2013. User-generated versus designer-generated products: A performance assessment at Muji. *International Journal of Research in Marketing* 30 (2): 160–67.

Ogawa, Susumu, and Frank T. Piller. 2006. Reducing the risks of new product development. *MIT Sloan Management Review* 47 (2): 65–71.

Page, Scott E. 2007. *The Difference: How the Power of Diversity Creates Better Groups, Firms, Schools, and Societies.* Princeton: Princeton University Press.

Piller, Frank T., and Dominik Walcher. 2006. Toolkits for idea competitions: A novel method to integrate users in new product development. *R&D Management* 36 (3): 307–18.

Pisano, Gary P., and Roberto Verganti. 2008. Which kind of collaboration is right for you? *Harvard Business Review* 86 (12): 78–86.

Poetz, Marion K., and Martin Schreier. 2012. The value of crowdsourcing: Can users really compete with professionals in generating new product ideas? *Journal of Product Innovation Management* 29 (2): 245–56.

Surowiecki, James. 2004. *The Wisdom of Crowds: Why the Many Are Smarter Than the Few and How Collective Wisdom Shapes Business, Economies, Societies, and Nations.* New York: Doubleday.

von Hippel, Eric. 2005. *Democratizing Innovation.* Cambridge: MIT Press.

von Hippel, Eric, Susumu Ogawa, and Jeroen P. J. De Jong. 2011. The age of the consumer-innovator. *MIT Sloan Management Review* 53 (1): 27–35.

VI

From Theory to Practice: Experiments, Toolkits, and Crowdfunding for Innovation

22

The Innovators' Tools[1]

Stefan Thomke

When Intel announces yet another breakthrough in chip technology, the triumph is as much a testimony to the rapid advances of modern development tools as it is to the proficient skills of the R&D team. Indeed the exponential performance gains of integrated circuits have fueled dramatic advances in computer modeling and simulation and tools for today's design teams. This progress has now come full circle: today's complex chips would be impossible to design and manufacture without the tools that they helped create. Not surprisingly, companies in many fields have invested extensively in innovation tools, expecting that they will lead to huge leaps in performance, reduce costs, and somehow foster innovation.

Research has found that new tools can significantly increase developers' problem-solving capacity as well as their productivity, enabling them to address categories of problems that would otherwise be impossible to tackle. This is particularly true in the pharmaceutical, aerospace, semiconductor and automotive industries, among others. Furthermore state-of-the-art tools can enhance the communication and interaction among communities of developers, even those who are "distributed" in time and space. In short, new tools *do* hold the promise of faster, better, cheaper, and will continue to change how innovation work is being done.

Yet, despite some early work by Eric von Hippel and his collaborators, research on the role of tools in innovation can best be described as "emerging" (von Hippel and Katz 2002; Thomke and von Hippel 2002). Most mainstream research on innovation focuses on economic incentives, organization, resource allocation, sources of new ideas, cognition, design structure, and the like. If one were to use the quantity and citations of scholarly publications as an indicator of the importance of tools in innovation, it could mistakenly be concluded that they play a small role.[2] Indeed a field visit to a modern engineering center or laboratory would result in the opposite conclusion: design tools are everywhere and play an integral role in the discovery and development of new products and technologies. Entire companies (e.g., Dassault Systemes) and industry sectors (e.g., electronic design automation) focus on the creation of tools that are used in the engineering profession. Moreover software design tools are at the heart of large commercial platforms such as Apple's App Store (iOS software development tools) and have been instrumental in the advancement of scientific discovery itself. Thus the historian Peter Galison showed that the creation of scientific knowledge is as much about the scientist's gadgets and instruments as it is about the battle of ideas (Galison 1997). Astronomy would be at a very different place today if it weren't for advances in telescopes and the discovery of the double-helix structure in biology can be directly attributed to X-ray crystallography (Watson 1968).[3]

Experimentation Tools

At the heart of every company's ability to innovate lies a process of experimentation that enables the organization to create and refine its products and technologies. In fact no product can *be* a product without its first having been an idea subsequently shaped through experimentation. Today a major development project involves literally thousands of experiments, all with the same objective: to *learn*, through rounds of organized testing, whether the product concept or proposed technical solution holds promise for addressing a need or problem. The information derived from each round is then incorporated into the next set of experiments, until the final product ultimately results. In short, innovations do not arrive full-fledged but are nurtured—through an experimentation process that takes place in laboratories and development organizations.[4]

Despite the critical role that experimentation plays in innovation, complex experiments have traditionally been costly and time-consuming to run, and companies have been parsimonious in expenditures to provide for them. Two interrelated consequences followed. Experimentation capacity has been constrained and the number of experimental iterations limited. More subtly, the notion of "experimentation" has often been confined to verification of known outcomes; testing at the end of development programs are managed to find late-stage problems. And when the test itself becomes a high-profile event, such as the preliminary evaluation of a new and expensive weapon system, companies regard a successful outcome as one that results in no new information or surprises and, hence, in no learning at all.

To make more capacity available, we have essentially two choices available: Either we change the fundamental economics of experimentation through new tools and related process innovations or we must try to get more out of each experiment itself—make experiments more efficient. Statistical methods for designing experiments have focused primarily on the latter and have had a big impact on industrial R&D (e.g., see Box et al. 1978; Fisher 1921; Montgomery 1991; Phadke 1989). By manipulating multiple variables in a single experiment, while maintaining integrity in its statistical analysis, scientists and engineers have been able to get more learning out of their experiments than their professional peers one hundred years earlier. However, even more structured methods cannot overcome all the limitations that scarce experimentation capacity poses.

Alternatively, new tools that slash experimentation cost and time would not only bring much needed capacity but could also make possible "what-if" experiments that, up to now, have been either prohibitively expensive or nearly impossible to run: What if an airplane, a car, a drug or a business were designed in a particular way? Such tools could potentially provide not only new knowledge about how nature works but they could also fundamentally change how the fruits of that effort are harvested in innovations, process improvements, and ultimately the new technologies themselves. Moreover, by putting these tools into the hands of innovators, wherever they may be, we can truly "democratize innovation" (von Hippel 2005).

The Promise of New Tools

Traditionally production tools can be characterized as devices that participate in and perform mechanical work and are neither consumed in the process, nor are they the intended output of the work itself—unless, of course, tool making is the work. Thus a hammer is a tool that makes the insertion of nails more economical, and a nail gun raises a carpenter's productivity quite dramatically. Similarly modern problem-solving tools such as simulation enable more learning to be created more rapidly, and the results can be incorporated in even more experiments at less expense. In other words, new tools drive down the marginal costs of experimentation just as they have decreased the marginal costs in many production and distribution systems. Moreover an experimental system that integrates new information-based tools *effectively* does more than lower costs; it also increases the opportunities for problem-solving and learning. Thus some technologies can make existing experimental activities more efficient, while others introduce entirely new ways of discovering novel concepts and/or solutions.

Businesses positioned to benefit most significantly from these tools have high product development costs, such as in the pharmaceutical, automotive, and software industries. Examining how tools influence experimentation in these industries lets us draw lessons that are applicable to other industries. As the cost of computing keeps falling thereby making all sorts of complex calculations faster and cheaper, and as new technologies emerge, virtually all companies will discover that they have a greater capacity for rapid experimentation to investigate diverse product concepts. At the same time deeper knowledge of the underlying phenomena has led to much better experimentation models, thus providing us with results that are closer to reality. Financial institutions, for example, now use computer simulations to test new financial instruments. In fact, the development of spreadsheet software itself has forever changed financial modeling; even novices can perform many sophisticated what-if experiments that were once prohibitively expensive.[5]

Examples of Advances in Tools[6]

Without the knowledge that came from computer-based modeling and simulation tools, many scientific breakthroughs, products, and even services that we take for granted today simply would not exist.[7] Once the first prototype computer became operable around 1945 and Monte Carlo methods for numerical simulation had been introduced, computer-generated artificial worlds and experiments were essential to the development of the first hydrogen bomb[8] and many scientific discoveries ever since (e.g., see Brenner 1996). The rapid emergence of the semiconductor industry then accelerated the trend toward low cost "digital" experiments and the advancement of tools and methodologies. The steady decrease in

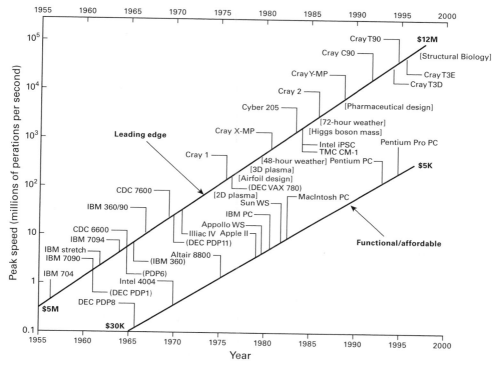

Figure 22.1

Advances in problems being solved by computer simulation. Growth of computer technology since 1955, showing advances in average commercial performance and milestone events (redrawn with modifications from Brenner, 1996). Problems that are solvable in reasonable times at the indicated level of computer performance are shown in brackets. Approximate system prices are shown in dollars at the time.

computational cost, following Moore's law, and the associated knowledge in modeling complex phenomena allowed for rapid increases in simulation capacity whereas the design of integrated circuits themselves demanded tools and models for complex experiments which, in turn, benefited many fields of science and engineering (see Figure 22.1).

At the same time, research organizations supported by the Department of Defense continued to advance their capacity for running computer-based simulation for applications such as missile design and warfare. Today the ability to run massive experiments via simulation has become critical in many fields, ranging from the sequencing and analysis of the human genome, to the design of modern airplanes and automobiles, to understanding the flow of fluids in the development of baby diapers. The potential impact that simulation and other experimentation technologies have had and will have in the future is only limited by imagination. Scientists and engineers are already joining forces to model regulatory mechanisms of genes and, eventually, entire cells, tissues and organs in the human body. These simulation models will allow researchers to run experiments *in silico* not only faster and cheaper but also make possible experiments that cannot be done today because of practical or ethical limitations (see Taubes 2002). Building the complex computer models necessary to run simulations will continue to advance our knowledge itself, perhaps in ways that we cannot anticipate today. Indeed one area that has already benefited from simulation is crash safety, one of the most difficult problems in the development of new cars.

Crash Simulation Tools in Automotive Development

Cars that are better designed to protect their human occupants in crashes are a major reason the rate of fatalities is lower today than it was in the mid-1980s. Unfortunately, competitive pressures in the automobile industry are forcing most companies to spend less money and time developing new automobiles. As a result, while customers and governments alike are demanding safer cars, the budgets to design them are shrinking. An increased use of computer simulation tools helps auto manufacturers deal with this dilemma. Traditional crash tests—characterized by running heavily instrumented prototype cars into concrete barriers—and being replaced by "virtual" crashes, that is, with high-performance computers simulating a collision. Over the past 10 years, tremendous increases in computer speed and improved software models have advanced crash simulation to the point where results are trusted with a high degree of confidence. The resulting surge in the use of design tools is revolutionizing the way vehicles are designed.

Consider how much time and money such simulation tools can save. Traditional ("real") crash testing begins with building a prototype vehicle, which usually takes anywhere from four to six months and costs hundreds of thousands of dollars. The prototype is then outfitted with costly crash-test dummies that contain electronic sensors to record

Table 22.1

Potential impact of simulation tools

Traditional prototype crashes	Modeling and simulation tools
• Safety design verification because of late and slow feedback	• Learning and experimentation through early and fast feedback
• Costly and time-consuming construction of each crash prototypes	• Cheap, fast generation of virtual prototypes after initial model is "built"
• Destructive testing difficult to analyze	• Simulation testing allows for careful and deep analysis
• Minimize experiments because of high cost	• Maximize experiments with diverse concepts
• Experimental conditions limited to standard laboratory setup	• Experimental conditions can be changed easily
• Prototypes are closer to reality for some crashes	• Models are approximations of reality and maybe too complex for some tests
• Allows for a more natural interaction with humans because it is physical	• Requires better human–machine interfaces to maximize acceptance and learning

Note: Actual differences between technologies vary and are intended for illustrative purposes only.

acceleration. Various instruments, including high-speed cameras, record the crash. However, glass and other debris from the crash itself frequently obstruct the view—and the dummies may accelerate through interior regions of the vehicle that are not covered by the cameras. As such, the post-crash films usually offer little to engineers hoping to improve the car's design.

By contrast, a simulated test can be conceived, programmed on a computer, then carried out in days or weeks; the main expense is for the simulation engineers' salaries. Yes, the computers are typically either top-of-the-line workstations costing tens of thousands of dollars. But unlike the crash-test prototype vehicles, the computers and their software and models are used over and over and sometimes have other applications within the company apart from verifying "crashworthiness." Perhaps most important, computer simulation tools let design engineers work in ways that would be otherwise impossible. In a relatively short period, for example, they can carry out a barrage of tests aimed at improving a structural piece—like one of the "pillars" connecting the car's roof to the chassis below the window—that affects the crashworthiness of the entire vehicle. They can "replay" a simulation as slowly as they like and zoom in on any structural element or even on a small piece of it to see how it reacts. Such capabilities not only generate a wealth of useful detail, they also enable engineers to learn and make the most of the expensive proto-type collision tests. And some of their learning flows back into improved computer models, which are essential to making simulation experiments useful to designers. With a good set of simulated crashes, the development team can reduce the chances that an actual prototype crash test will go poorly and trigger another round of costly redesign and re-testing.

The questions that simulation can answer today are limited by the range of phenomena that can be modeled. So, it is difficult to simulate and predict the outcome of rollover accidents, for instance. A rollover can take a full three seconds, as opposed to 100 to 150 milliseconds for a more typical smashup, and simulating that much time requires prodigious computer power. The behavior of a car in a rollover can also be difficult to predict, because it depends on road friction and other factors. It is also essentially impossible to use computers to discover whether any parts of the car will present a fire hazard in an accident: for example, whether a fuel tank is prone to explode.

The power of simulation tools—beyond overall reduction of costs and increases in speed—comes from introducing a new capability for running experiments. A project at the German car company BMW illustrates this well. The project included a "simulation specialist," a test engineer and several design engineers from different functional areas who were attempt-ing to develop technical concepts that would improve the side-impact safety for all BMW vehicles. The team set out to explore the potential of simulation tools, and decided to limit prototype testing to only two crashes at the end to verify final design concepts. An existing production model served as the project's starting point. After each simulation, the team met, analyzed results, and designed another experiment. As expected, the team enjoyed quick feedback, enabling the members to try out an idea and accept or reject it within days. The surprise was that as the trials began to accrue, the whole was more than the sum of the iterations; the group was increasing its *fundamental* understanding of the underlying mechanics.

A fruitful example involved the "B pillar," one of six structural elements connecting the roof to the chassis below the windows (there are three pillars on each side of the car, labeled A, B, C from front to back). By analyzing the records of prototype side-impact crashes from earlier development projects, team engineers on the team had learned that in crash after crash, a small section of the B pillar folded. And, when a pillar so buckled, its use as a barrier was compromised and the probability of injury to passengers thereby rose.

Although the engineers assumed that adding metal would strengthen the bottom of the pillar, making the car more resistant to penetration from the side, no one felt it was necessary to test that assumption. One development team member, however, insisted on verification, pointing out that it would be neither difficult nor expensive to do this via computer simulation. When the program was run, the group was shocked to discover that strengthening the folded area actually *decreased* crashworthiness. But what caused that phenomenon? After more iterations and careful analysis, they found out. Reinforcing the lower part of the B pillar made the part higher up—above the reinforced part—prone to buckling. So, the passenger compartment would be more vulnerable to being penetrated higher up—closer to passengers' midsection, chest, and head. As such, the solution to the folding-B pillar problem turned out to be completely counterintuitive: *weaken* it rather than reinforce it.

When the team finished its work, it had carried out 91 virtual accidents and two prototype crashes in about a year. For the developmental vehicles that were redesigned, side-impact crashworthiness advanced an average of 30 percent over the initial design, measured in various ways, e.g., calculating and comparing simulated and "dummy" acceleration in both virtual and "real" crashes. Significantly, the two prototype crashes at the end of the project strongly confirmed the simulation results and also the economics of testing: At a total of about $300,000, the two prototypes cost more to build, prepare, and test than did the entire series of the 91 virtual crashes.

Combinatorial Methods and Rapid Prototyping Tools

While computer modeling and simulation tools have the potential to fundamentally change innovation, there have been parallel advances in the physical world that will complement the power of simulation. According to Dr. Peter Schultz, head of the Genomics Institute for the Novartis Research foundation:

The [other] revolution that has occurred during the last 10 years in the biological and physical sciences is the way in which we carry out experimental science. There has been a tremendous increase in our ability to design, implement and analyze experiments – to carry them out not one at a time but thousands or millions at a time. That has made been made possible by combinatorial technologies, computational tools and advances in engineering and miniaturization—the kind of tools and processes that revolutionized the semiconductor industry are being moved over into the biological and physical science. (Schultz 2002: 96)

All these combinatorial technologies have dramatically reduced the cost and time of generating physical artifacts of an idea or concept ("prototypes"), thus allowing for many combinations to be generated over a short period of time. Developers use these rapid prototyping technologies to quickly generate an inexpensive, easy to modify prototype that can be tested against the actual use environment; this allows for experimentation under real—as opposed to virtual—conditions. Such technologies can be found in areas ranging from mechanical designs to the design of integrated circuits. Rapid prototyping, therefore, is usually an inexpensive and fast way to build models that preserve the advantages of working in the physical world and thus overcomes any limitations that simulation may have. Thus a high-quality prototype of a connector that links computers to external devices like scanners or printers can be "plugged" into a real system, generating immediate feedback from customers. Technical as well as customer need uncertainty can be resolved quickly via a process of iterative trial and error experiments.

Impact of Tools on the Locus of Innovation[9]

A number of companies have adopted an intriguing approach that takes advantage of tools discussed so far. These companies have essentially abandoned their efforts to understand exactly what products their customers want and have instead equipped them with tools to design and develop their own new products, ranging from minor modifications to major new innovations. The user-friendly tools, often integrated into a "toolkit" package, deploy tools (e.g., computer simulation and rapid prototyping) to make innovation faster, less expensive, and, most important, better as customers run what-if experiments themselves.

A variety of industries have started to use this approach. Bush Boake Allen (BBA), a global supplier of specialty flavors to companies like Nestlé and now part of International Flavors & Fragrances, created a toolkit that enabled its customers to develop their own flavors, which BBA then manufactures. In the materials field, companies provide customers with Web-based tools for designing better plastic products. In software, a number of companies allow people to add custom-designed modules to their standard products and then commercialize the best of those components. Open-source software allows users to design, build, distribute, and support their own programs—no manufacturer required. Shifting experimentation and innovation to customers has indeed the power to completely transform industries. In the semiconductor business, it has led to a multi-billion dollar custom-chip market.

Tapping into the innovativeness and imagination of customers and users—not just R&D departments—can indeed generate tremendous value, but capturing that value is hardly a simple or straightforward process. Not only must companies develop the right design tools, they must also revamp their business models as well as their management mind-sets. When companies relinquish a fundamental task—such as designing a new product—to outsiders, the two parties must redefine their relationship, and this change can be risky. With custom computer chips, for instance, companies traditionally captured value by both designing and manufacturing innovative products. Now, with customers taking over more of the design task, companies must focus more intently on providing the best custom manufacturing. In other words, the location where value is created and captured changes, and companies must reconfigure their business models accordingly.

Matching Need with Solution Information

Product development is often difficult because the "need" information (what the customer wants) resides with the customer, and the "solution" information (how to satisfy those needs) lies with the manufacturer. Traditionally the onus has been on manufacturers to collect the customer need information through various means, including market research and information gathered from the field. The process can be costly and time-consuming because customer needs are often complex, subtle, and fast changing.[10] Frequently customers don't fully understand their needs until they try out prototypes to explore exactly what does—and doesn't—work. Many companies are familiar with customers' reactions when they see and use a finished product for the first time: "This is exactly what I asked you to develop, but it is not what I want." In other words, customers learn about their needs through informal experimentation while using new products or services. Not surprisingly, traditional product development is a drawn-out process of trial and error, often ping-ponging between manufacturer and customer.[11] First, the manufacturer develops a prototype based on information from customers that is incomplete and only partially correct. The customer then tries out the product, finds flaws, and requests corrections. This "learning-by-experimentation" cycle repeats until a satisfactory solution is reached, frequently requiring many costly and time-consuming iterations.[12] When companies have to work with hundreds of customers with different needs, each requiring market research and a well-managed iteration process, one can see how those firms become overwhelmed and thus focus only on the largest and most profitable customers.

The reason why firms may want customers to experiment with alternative design solutions has to do with the fact that it can be a win-win proposition for both. Instead of moving "need" information from customers to a supplier, "solution" information is moved from a supplier to customers via innovation toolkits (figure 22.2). This puts experimentation power into the hands of users who become an integral part of a company's innovation process.

The manufacturer can focus on developing better solution platforms that are customized through user-friendly tools in the hands of customers. The customer can experiment and get feedback more rapidly, control intellectual property on the application-specific part of a design, and, most important, find a solution that closely matches her needs. To be sure, shifting product development activities to customers does not eliminate learning by experimentation—nor should it. What it does is make traditional product development better and faster—for several reasons. First, a company can bypass the expensive and error-prone effort to understand customer needs in detail. Second, the trial-and-error cycles that inevitably occur during product development can progress much more quickly because the iterations will be performed solely by the customer (figure 22.3).

Need information comes *from* customer

Solution information flows *to* customers

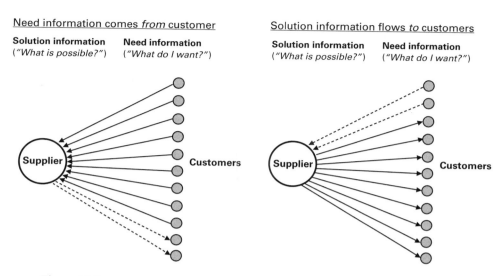

Figure 22.2

Moving information between supplier and customers. Traditionally "need" information is primarily collected and moved from customers to suppliers via market research methods (left side). This process can be costly and time-consuming when needs are unique, complex and fast-changing. In the new model the supplier's "solution" information is embodied in tools that are moved to customers so that they can experiment and design their own products (right side).

Leveraging User Innovation

Shifting experimentation to customers and users leverages what scholars already know about the sources of innovation. Research has shown that many commercially important products are initially thought of and even prototyped by users rather than manufacturers.[13] It was also discovered that such products tend to be developed by "lead users"—companies, organizations, or individuals that are well ahead of market trends and have needs that go far beyond those of the average user.[14] Most people are already familiar with standard products that were originally developed by such lead users. The prototype for protein-based hair conditioners, for instance, came from daring women in the 1950s who experimented with home-made concoctions containing beer or eggs to impart more body and shine. Similarly antilock braking systems (ABS) that are standard on most cars today were first developed in aerospace: Military aircraft commands have a very high incentive to design ways to stop their

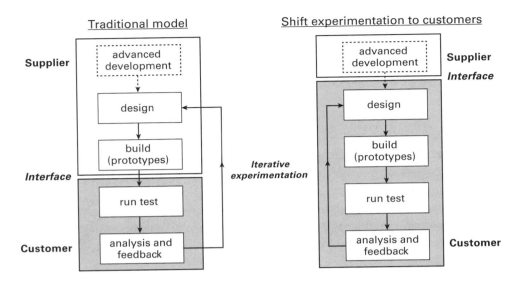

Figure 22.3

Shifting experimentation to customers. Traditionally suppliers have taken on most
of the work—and responsibility—of product development. The result has been
costly and time-consuming iterations between supplier and customer to reach a
satisfactory solution. When the locus of experimentation is shifted to customers, a
supplier provides the design tools so they can develop the application-specific part
of a product on their own. This also shifts the location of the supplier-customer
interface, and the iterative experimentation necessary for product development is
now carried out by the customer.

expensive vehicles before they run out of runway. Like other lead users,
they opted for designing custom solutions instead of waiting for markets
to become large enough before manufacturers would consider developing
and selling standard products. Lead users also expect to benefit significantly from their custom solutions, as they often have to overcome considerable barriers to innovating. In other words, research has already
shown that a small group of customers—lead users—is developing their
own products, in spite of the difficulties of doing so. Now consider the
fact that "do-it-yourself" tools can lower the cost of experimenting and
designing custom solutions quite dramatically. By lowering the barriers to
innovation, it is thus not surprising that the number of users willing to
participate in developing new products can be expected to rise substantially (figure 22.4).

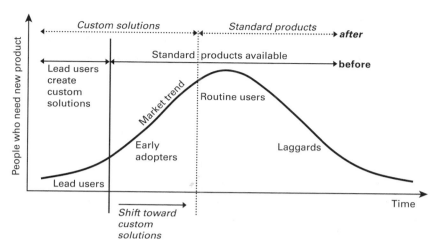

Figure 22.4

Potential shift toward custom products. Lead users have needs that are well ahead of a market trend and create custom solutions for themselves. Development tool-kits lower the cost of designing such custom solutions and thus can significantly shift innovation activity towards customers.

By lowering the barriers to innovation, it is thus not surprising that the number of users willing to participate in developing new products can be expected to rise substantially (figure 22.4).

Building Tools for User Innovation

Developing the right tools for customers is hardly a simple matter. Specifically, such tools must provide four important capabilities. First and most important, they must enable people to iterate through the series of experimentation steps: design, build, run [tests] and analyze. Computer simulation, for example, allows users to quickly try out ideas and design alternatives without having to manufacture the actual products. When the simulation technology lacks the desired accuracy, it can be supplemented with rapid prototyping methods. As users carry out experimentation cycles with the help of user-friendly tools, learning and improvement can take place locally, without having to involve the manufacturer.

Second, toolkits must be user-friendly. Customers should be able to operate them using their existing skills, and it should not be necessary to learn an entirely new design language (e.g., flavorists think in terms of formulations and chemical compounds, whereas customers think of tastes as smoky, sweet, fresh, etc.). Third, they must contain libraries of useful components and modules that have been pretested and debugged. These save users from having to reinvent the wheel. Instead, people can focus their efforts on the truly novel elements of their design. Fourth, toolkits must contain information about the capabilities and limitations of the production process that will be used to manufacture the product. This will ensure that a user's design will in fact be producible.

Companies will continue to develop many great products using a deep understanding of customer needs and well-managed development processes. The new model of development described here makes most sense when products require a high degree of design customization and the "need" information is costly to transfer. When companies intend to develop standard products with little customization, other approaches will continue to work very well as long as markets are sufficiently large. For example, some sophisticated methods such as emphatic design or the Zaltman Metaphor Elicitation Technique (ZMET) can explore basic and potentially common need areas at a deep level, which in turn can be used to minimize unnecessary product features. [15]

To see how other approaches relate to innovation toolkits, one needs to consider two important need dimensions (figure 22.5). The first dimension—need distribution—characterizes the degree to which a set of needs is common within a market segment. At one extreme, all needs are shared and can be satisfied with a standard product. At the other extreme, all needs are unique and require full custom products ("markets of one"). The second dimension characterizes the need itself and the ease or difficulty of getting to the information. Again, at one extreme, the needs are unarticulated and perhaps unknown to customers themselves (in short, *tacit*), which require very sophisticated and often costly market research techniques. [16] At the other extreme, customers can easily express what they want if one simply asks them. Depending where a supplier ends up in these dimensions, different techniques turn out to be most useful. However, many business-to-business setting involve high degree of customization and difficulty in getting the "right" customer requirements in place as they often change over the course of a development project.

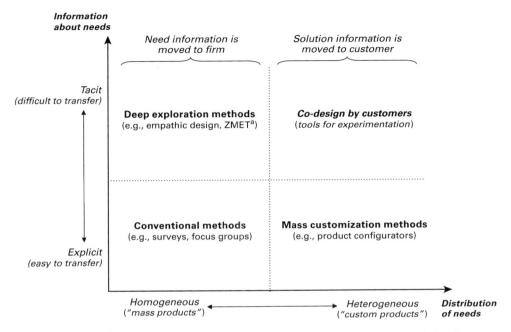

a ZMET (Zaltman Metaphor Elicitation Technique) identifies common deep-level needs that often drive observable secondary needs in products

Figure 22.5

Complementary approaches to addressing customer needs. Different approaches are appropriate to addressing customer needs. When needs are relatively homogeneous, it usually makes sense for firms to learn about these needs via market research techniques that vary in sophistication and cost. In contrast, when needs become heterogeneous and are difficult to transfer, making solution information available to customers and allowing them to design themselves can be more effective.

Lessons from Integrated Circuits

To understand the major impact that shifting design and experimentation to users can have, consider the integrated circuit industry. Its history holds several profound lessons about how the right toolkit can turn a market on its ear. During the late 1970s a typical customer of specialized semiconductors, such as a toy manufacturer that needed circuitry to operate its new robotic dog, might have hired a chip supplier to develop a custom design. Because that process was complicated and costly, the chip company could only afford to undertake projects for high-volume customers.

Smaller customers were turned away and had no choice but to use standard circuit components. That in turn limited the extent to which they could develop products that were smaller, better in performance, lower in cost or simply more innovative. In other words, there was a very large unfilled demand for custom chips because the dominant suppliers couldn't economically serve smaller customers.

Then a handful of start-ups turned everything upside down. New firms like LSI Logic and VLSI Technology provided both large and small customers with do-it-yourself tools that enabled them to design their own specialized chips. As Wilf Corrigan, LSI's CEO and principal founder, recalled:

> Having decided to start a semiconductor company, I spent quite a few months visiting people I knew in the computer industry, both in the United States and in Europe. A pattern started to emerge: most of these companies needed custom circuits. I had flashbacks of when I was at Fairchild and good customers would ask me, "Would you do a custom program for us?" At Fairchild, I always said no, but in retrospect, I should have recognized that over the previous few years there was an opportunity bubbling up in custom circuits . . . . Custom circuits —the big guys don't want to mess with them, the customers seem to need them, yet there don't seem to be any viable sources in spite of increasing demand. (Walker 1992: 47)

Corrigan's inability to respond while working at Fairchild, a leading semiconductor firm in the 1960s and 1970s, was certainly not because he lacked influence: He was its CEO from 1974 to 1980. In fact many members of LSI's founding team, and its design tool expertise came from Fairchild Semiconductor, which had abandoned its custom IC efforts because it was losing money for the firm. With LSI's new development system, customers could benefit by getting what they wanted through their own experimentation, and the fledgling chip firms could profit by manufacturing those customer designs. The win-win solution was right on the money. Between the 1980s and 2000, the market for such custom integrated circuits has soared from virtually nothing to more than $15 billion, with the number of customers growing from a handful of high-volume buyers to hundreds of thousands of firms with very diverse end-user applications.

One of the keys to that market is the tools. In principle, outsourcing custom design to customers can help slash development times and costs, but customers are not experts in a supplier's R&D or production process.

So how could customers possibly be expected to create custom designs that are producible on a manufacturer's sophisticated process equipment? The answer to that was found in a major shift that had been taking place in the semiconductor industry.

Traditionally specialized information used by a manufacturer to design and build custom products has been locked in the minds of the company's development engineers. This knowledge accumulates over decades of experience. In recent years companies have been able to incorporate a considerable amount of this human expertise into computer-based tools. These computer-aided design, engineering, and manufacturing programs (CAD/CAE/CAM) have grown increasingly sophisticated, and many now contain libraries of tested and debugged modules that people can simply plug into a new design. The best tools also enable rapid testing through computer simulation and provide links to automated equipment that can build prototypes quickly. This leading-edge technology, which manufacturers had been using internally to increase R&D productivity and innovation, has become the basic building block for tools geared to customers.

When LSI was founded in 1981, R&D engineers at large semiconductor companies were already using many elements of the customer tools, but there was no integrated system that less-skilled customers would be comfortable with. So LSI bought some of the pieces, made them customer-friendly by adding graphical user interfaces, and integrated them into a package called the LSI Development System (LDS). The result was a packaged toolkit that enabled customers to design their own chips with little support from LSI.

The insight that made possible a toolkit for less-skilled customers was that the design of the chip's fundamental elements, such as its transistors, could be standardized and could incorporate the manufacturer's solution information of how semiconductors are fabricated. Then all the information the customer needed about how the chip would function could be concentrated within the electrical wiring that connects those fundamental elements. In other words, this new type of chip, called a "gate array," had a novel architecture created specifically to separate the manufacturer's solution information from the customer's need information. As a result all customers had to do was use a toolkit that could interconnect a gate array based on their specific needs. For its part, LSI had to rethink how to make its production processes more flexible so that it could manufacture the custom chips at low cost.

Customer toolkits based on gate-array technology offer the four major capabilities described earlier. They contain a range of tools, including those to test a design, that enable users to create their own prototypes via trial and error. They are customer-friendly in that they use Boolean algebra, which is the design language commonly taught to electrical engineers. They contain extensive libraries of pretested circuit modules. And they also contain information about production processes so that users can test their designs to ensure that they can be manufactured.

Research Questions

New tools such as computer simulation and modeling are lifting the cost constraint by changing the economics of experimentation. These technologies are not only slashing cost and time to free up testing capacity but also make possible what-if experiments that have been either prohibitively expensive or nearly impossible to carry out. They amplify the impact of learning, thus creating the potential for higher R&D performance and breakthrough products. More important, these tools are expanding the number of people involved in innovation, whether it is through customers developing their own products, or communities of app developers that solve problems we aren't even aware of today.

Without question, there are many new research opportunities and what we pursue is limited by our understanding of the phenomena and the research tools we employ. First, more work needs to be done documenting the use of tools in innovation. What is the role of tools, how are they created, and what is their impact on innovation outcomes? Second, we still have limited evidence on their impact on performance (cost, time, and quality). Companies are investing heavily in tools and field observations suggest that the impact can be quite dramatic. Yet more systematic work is needed to show how these improvements are being achieved. Third, case evidence suggests that tools and problem-solving spaces are closely linked. As tools are advancing rapidly, is there evidence that the problems being solved are changing as well? How? Fourth, design tools are important to setting industry standards (e.g., semiconductors, software) and are instrumental in coordination (e.g., CAD tools in manufacturing supply chains). Again, empirical research could shed some light on the role that tools play.

Notes

1. Most of the material in this chapter is derived from Thomke (2003).

2. In January 2012, I ran an informal search on Google Scholar. I looked for specific words in the titles of Google's article database. The word "innovation" yielded about 190,000 hits, "innovation" and "organization" yielded about 1,400 hits, and *"innovation"* and "process" were used in about 4,700 article titles. Many articles had more than 1,000 citations. In contrast, the words "innovation" and "tools" yielded less than 500 hits, with low citation counts, and most articles were about the description of specific management tools (e.g., creativity tools, financial tools). A small number of papers explored the role of problem-solving and experimentation tools in the innovation process.

3. A recent example: The 2014 Nobel Prize in chemistry was awarded to three scientists for their work on optical microscopy. Because their tool overcame the limit of what could be seen with conventional microscopes, scientists can now see how the human body works at a cellular level.

4. See Thomke (2003) for a deeper discussion of experimentation in product and technological innovation.

5. A more complete description of how the financial spreadsheet has slashed the cost of financial modeling and changed the way business professionals experiment can be found in Schrage (1999).

6. The following section draws extensively from Thomke (1998) and Thomke et al. (1999). Both of these publications contain more detailed discussions of the ideas and issues described here.

7. While the word "simulation" is used in many contexts, I will adhere to the following definition: *Simulation* is the representation of selected characteristics of the behavior of one physical or abstract system by another system. In a digital computer system simulation is done by software, which uses mathematical equations and/or approximations that represent the behavior of such a system.

8. The history of Monte Carlo methods and its role in the development of nuclear weapons, particularly the hydrogen bomb in the late 1940s and early 1950s, also provides us with an account of the importance of simulation in physics more than fifty years ago. An excellent description and analysis of this history can be found in Galison (1997).

9. This section draws extensively from Thomke and von Hippel (2002).

10. Recent research has aimed at making market research and testing more rapid and cheaper through the use of "virtual" techniques that leverage the Internet (e.g., see Dahan and Srinivasan 2000).

11. In part, this is caused by information transfer costs, which can be high when such information is "sticky" or difficult to encode. For a discussion of interaction patterns between user and manufacturer as a result of information stickiness, see von Hippel (1994).

12. "Learning by doing" often has iterative experimentation as part of the doing (e.g., see von Hippel and Tyre 1995).

13. Research on users as an important source of innovations can be found in von Hippel (1988) whose pioneering work has changed how we view the way innovation happens.

14. Lead users can be an important source of new product concepts and were identified as part of von Hippel's research on user innovation. Many firms, such as 3M, have tapped into the expertise of lead users and their prototype solutions. For an explanation of how this can be done, see von Hippel et al. (1999).

15. For more information on empathic design techniques, see Leonard-Barton (1995). Alternatively, ZMET was developed by Gerald Zaltman and more information can be found in Zaltman (2003). For a comprehensive summary of market research in product development, see Urban and Hauser (1993).

16. The notion of "tacit" information has been used extensively in innovation and knowledge management research (e.g., see Polanyi 1958).

References

Box, G., W. Hunter, and S. Hunter. 1978. *Statistics for Experimenters: An Introduction to Design, Data Analysis, and Model Building.* New York: Wiley.

Brenner, A. 1996. The computer revolution and the physics community. *Physics Today* 49 (10): 24–39.

Dahan, E., and V. Srinivasan. 2000. The predictive power of Internet-based product concept testing using visual depiction and animation. *Journal of Product Innovation Management* 17 (2): 99–109.

Fisher, R. 1921. Studies in crop variation: I. An examination of the yield of dressed grain from Broadbalk. *Journal of Agricultural Science* 11:107–35.

Galison, P. 1997. *Image and Logic: A Material Culture of Microphysics.* Chicago: University of Chicago Press.

Leonard-Barton, D. 1995. *Wellsprings of Knowledge.* Boston: Harvard Business School Press.

Montgomery, D. 1991. *Design and Analysis of Experiments.* New York: Wiley.

Phadke, M. 1989. *Quality Engineering Using Robust Design.* Englewood Cliffs, NJ: Prentice Hall.

Polanyi, M. 1958. *Personal Knowledge: Towards a Post-critical Philosophy.* Chicago: University of Chicago Press.

Schrage, M. 1999. *Serious Play: How the World's Best Companies Simulate to Innovate.* Boston: Harvard Business School Press.

Schultz, P. 2000. The Bell Labs of biology. *Technology Review* 103 (2): 94–98.

Taubes, G. 2002. The virtual cell. *Technology Review* 105 (3): 63–70.

Thomke, S. 1998. Simulation, learning and R&D performance: Evidence from automotive development. *Research Policy* 27 (1): 55–74.

Thomke, S. 2003. *Experimentation Matters: Unlocking the Potential of New Technologies for Innovation*. Boston: Harvard Business School Press.

Thomke, S., M. Holzner, and T. Gholami. 1999. The crash in the machine. *Scientific American* 280 (3): 92–97.

Thomke, S., and E. von Hippel. 2002. Customers as innovators: A new way to create value. *Harvard Business Review* 80 (4): 74–81.

Urban, G., and J. Hauser. 1993. *Design and Marketing of New Products*, 2nd ed. Upper Saddle River, NJ: Prentice Hall.

von Hippel, E. 1988. *The Sources of Innovation*. New York: Oxford University Press.

von Hippel, E. 1994. "Sticky information" and the locus of problem solving: Implications for innovation. *Management Science* 40 (4): 429–39.

von Hippel, Eric. 2005. *Democratizing Innovation*. Cambridge: MIT Press.

von Hippel, E., and R. Katz. 2002. Shifting innovation to users via toolkits. *Management Science* 48 (7): 821–33.

von Hippel, E., S. Thomke, and M. Sonnack. 1999. Creating breakthroughs at 3M. *Harvard Business Review* 77 (5): 47–57.

von Hippel, E., and M. J. Tyre. 1995. How "learning by doing" is done: Problem identification in novel process equipment. *Research Policy* 24 (1): 1–12.

Walker, R. 1992. *Silicon Destiny: The History of Application Specific Integrated Circuits and LSI Logic Corporation*. Milpitas, CA: CMC Publications.

Watson, James D. 1968. *The Double Helix: A Personal Account of the Discovery of the Structure of DNA*. New York: Atheneum.

Zaltman, G. 2003. *How Customers Think: Essential Insights into the Mind of the Market*. Boston: Harvard Business School Press.

23

Design Toolkits, Organizational Capabilities, and Firm Performance

Frank Piller and Fabrizio Salvador

Eric von Hippel's research has shown that user-driven innovation is a pervasive phenomenon (von Hippel et al. 2011). Much of his original research focused on lead users who autonomously engaged into innovation activities, without the support or involvement of any manufacturer. The success of lead user innovation led von Hippel and other scholars to question the role and relevance of traditional manufacturers in a changing economic environment (von Hippel 2005). We observe, however, that manufacturers are just not passively witnessing the emergence of user-driven innovation. They are adapting to tap the potential of user innovation by devising co-creation processes wherein the customer and the manufacturer can synergistically create novel solutions to satisfy unmet needs. Some manufacturers are extending co-creation processes to even include masses of customers that will not all develop highly innovative solutions but nevertheless have creative needs that can be nurtured. To this end, manufacturers have to learn to operate as enablers and partners of user innovation, integrating innovation toolkits into their business models. In this chapter we argue that "democratizing innovation" (i.e., making it available to the masses) takes more than creating innovation toolkits: it requires the creation of specific capabilities that allow organizations to create value by engaging in co-creation activities with large pools of users.

The contribution of our chapter is twofold. We first offer a theoretical overview of the requisite capabilities that manufacturers have to develop in order to engage in customer co-creation activities, creating value for both their customers and for themselves. Building on our earlier research (Salvador et al. 2009) we introduce three capabilities that are essential within any toolkit-based business model, namely (1) *solution space definition* (i.e., the ability of an organization to identify the product or service attributes along which customer needs diverge), (2) *robust process design* (i.e., the ability to reuse or recombine existing organizational and supply chain resources), and (3) *choice navigation* (i.e., the ability to help customers identify or build solutions to their own needs). With this framework we complement the literature on user toolkits moving beyond the dominant research focus on the link between toolkit design, user decision-making, and user utility.

In addition we provide an overview of the state-of-the-practice in design toolkits and empirically examine the validity of our theoretical arguments by means of a recently completed multi-method study of manufacturing companies engaging in customer co-creation activities. Our database includes the *Customization500*, a large-scale empirical analysis of 500 toolkits that is, to the best of our knowledge, the largest and broadest empirical study of mass toolkits. Additionally we were able to collect survey information on internal processes and operational performance for 120 of the companies included in the Customization500 database. In discussing our empirical results we also rely on information collected through qualitative interviews with managers operating within the surveyed companies, as well as on a smaller explorative survey of 68 entrepreneurs and consultants active in the MC business conducted by the authors in 2009.

The remainder of the chapter is organized as follows. We first contrast the concept of expert toolkits with that of "mass toolkits," which we link with the pursuit of mass customization (MC). We next provide an overview of the state of toolkit implementation in industry based on our large-scale empirical study, highlighting their broad relevance as well as the challenges associated to making toolkit-based business models work. We then describe the requisite organizational capabilities and their impact on value creation for the customer-manufacturer dyad, briefly reporting empirical insights we draw from our database. We conclude by revisiting the contribution of this chapter and outlining a number opportunities for future research.

Expert Toolkits, Mass Toolkits, and Mass Customization

In this section we contrast the original concept of innovation toolkits by von Hippel with that of "mass toolkits," which we later link to the pursuit of mass customization (MC) strategies. These two types of toolkits also correspond to two related, but different concepts of integrating user input in the innovation process: user innovation versus customer co-creation. While the term *user innovation* focuses on the role of the innovating user, often without any interaction with a manufacturer, the term *customer co-creation* today is frequently used to denote an act of company–customer interaction where customers are actively involved and take part in the design or development of an offering in a process facilitated by the manufacturer (Wikstroem 1996; Ramirez 1999; Prahalad and Ramaswamy 2004). More specifically, customer co-creation has been defined as an active, creative, and social process, based on collaboration between producers (retailers) and customers (users) (Roser et al. 2009; for extended reviews refer to O'Hern and Rindfleisch 2009; Piller and Ihl 2010). Customer co-creation is not new. Already in 1991 Udwadia and Kumar (1991) were envisioning that customers and manufacturers would become "co-constructors" (i.e., co-designers) of those products intended for each customer's individual use. In their view, co-construction would occur when customers only had a nebulous sense of what they wanted. Without the customers' deep involvement, the manufacturer would be unable to cater to each individualized product demand adequately. Eric von Hippel's seminal publications (von Hippel 1994, 1998) brought this thinking into the management domain, establishing the notion that user-need information is hard to transfer to the manufacturer (i.e., "sticky"), and so it is more proficiently utilized by the users themselves.

One of the pivotal ideas of von Hippel's research is that users' innovation capabilities can be fostered via design toolkits (Thomke and von Hippel 2002, von Hippel 2001; von Hippel and Katz 2002). Toolkits are software tools similar to a CAD system, but with an easy-to-use interface and a library of basic modules and functionalities. They provide an environment that enables customers to transfer their preferences iteratively into a concrete solution or product design. Following Franke and Schreier (2002), we distinguish two types of toolkits according to the degrees of freedom that the underlying solution space provides to customers: (1) expert toolkits for user innovation and (2) mass toolkits for user customer co-creation and customization.

Expert toolkits for user innovation resemble, in principle, a chemistry set, in the sense that the set of possible solutions open to the user is boundless—at least relative to certain product design parameters. Users of expert toolkits not only combine standard modules and components, they also engage in iterative trial-and-error processes that possibly lead to the discovery of totally novel solutions. The toolkit provides the necessary solution information in the form of, for example, programming languages or drawing software. A good example comes from the semiconductor industry where firms equipped customers with toolkits for custom development of integrated circuits and computer chips (von Hippel and Katz 2002). Or consider BAA, an international developer of flavors for food (Thomke and von Hippel 2002). The company provided toolkits to product developers of commercial food processors to generate new flavors and ingredients for seasoning. The Apache toolkit, described in various previous chapters of this book, is another example of this category. Despite these famous cases, however, we still do not find many expert toolkits for real user innovation in practice today.

However, *mass toolkits for user co-design* (shortly, mass toolkits) offer a set of possible solutions that is bounded by predefined constraints that reflect the manufacturer's economic and technological capabilities. Mass toolkits are meant to enable nonexpert users to create unique designs that express their needs and preferences, without any uncertainty relative to manufacturability, price and delivery conditions. Mass toolkits deliver a pre-engineered solution, rather that developing a new one. They promise to empower large pools of "average" customers without lead user characteristics to create innovative solutions for their own use. The developments in computer technology, particularly the capacities to simulate potential product designs before a purchase and to interact with large numbers of users with low transaction cost, have strongly enabled this collaborative effort. Mass toolkits are typically found in the context of consumer products where customers are characterized by significant heterogeneity. Well-known examples of this type of toolkits are the ubiquitous product configurators, used within product categories as different as computers (e.g., dell.com), motor vehicles (mini.com), toys (ego.com), bicycles (koga-signature.com), or snacks (mandm.com).

Mass toolkits are logically associated to the pursuit of mass customization (MC) strategies. Since they do not require significant user expertise, mass toolkits hold the potential for enabling manufacturers to engage in co-creation with large masses of customers. This precisely is the goal of

MC, which aims to develop, produce, market, and deliver affordable goods and services with enough customization that nearly everyone finds exactly what they want (Pine 1993). Consequently understanding how manufacturers can extract rents from mass toolkits calls for understanding how they integrate these toolkits within their broader MC business models. Before exploring this question in greater detail, we provide descriptive insights relative to the current state of the practice of mass toolkits in different industries and about the structural characteristics of the companies relying on these toolkits.

Mass Toolkit-Based Businesses: State of Practice and Challenges

What are the application fields and features of mass toolkits used by mass customizers? In this section, we address this question by reporting selected results from a recent study we conducted with our colleagues Dominik Walcher and Thorsten Harzer (Walcher and Piller 2012; Harzer et al. 2012). Based on information collected from several web portals specialized on MC (e.g., configurator-database.com, egoo.de), we identified a population of more than 900 companies selling mass customized consumer goods on the net via either English or German language websites. After a first screening of the associated websites, we narrowed down our sample to 500 companies that had active mass toolkits, as defined in the previous section. We created a data collection tool to codify the characteristics of these toolkits (e.g., 3D visualization, use of peer input in the design process) and instructed a group of evaluators to use such tool to rate the characteristics of each toolkit. In order to assess and improve measurement reliability, we had three different raters evaluate each toolkit.[1]

The Customization 500 study offers, in the first place, an overview of the present application fields of mass toolkits (table 23.1). A quick scan of the composition of our sample reveals that the option to personalize items by applying a user design on a basic product by different forms of digital printing is leading the field (categories 1, 2, and 4). This option offers new degrees of freedom to the user without requiring deep expertise, and makes low cost customization possible for the manufacturer by applying the principle of delayed product differentiation (Lee and Tang 1997). Interestingly the food and nutrition industry is an important application domain for mass toolkits as well. This suggests that toolkit applications in the food industry are not limited to von Hippel's well-known examples of expert toolkits (e.g., Nestle Food Service and BAA). We only found few notable toolkits in the field of consumer electronics and computers—a finding that can be explained by today's pre-dominance of smart products with embedded configuration capabilities (Piller et al. 2010). Overall, applications of mass toolkits span very different product categories within the domain of consumer products. Notably, customers engage in personalization not only of durable goods (e.g., furniture, computers) but also of nondurable goods (e.g., food), suggesting that customer co-creation strategies are pervasive, and that toolkit-based business models are of general interest for high-volume manufacturers. Mass toolkits have become a widespread phenomenon.

Mass toolkits can deliver significant value to the customer, as Nik Franke has shown in the previous chapter. Furthermore, as illustrated by the Customization500 study, they have broad applications in consumer markets. However, from the manufacturer's standpoint, the toolkit is just the "tip of the iceberg." Incorporating mass toolkits into a business model underscores profound changes in the value creating processes of the organization, including product planning and development as well as order acquisition and fulfillment processes (Salvador et al. 2009). Silent witnesses to the scope of these changes are the difficulties companies encounter when attempting to build a profitable toolkit-based business (Piller 2005; Franke et al. 2010), and the risk of disruption associated with a firm's transition toward MC (Rungtusanatham and Salvador 2008).

To gain insights relative to the companies that implemented these toolkits, we complemented our study of the 500 toolkits with a survey of the same sample of companies (Harzer 2012) that yielded a total of 120 usable answers (response rate = 24 percent). When looking into the characteristics of the companies participating in the survey, we find that the current dynamism in MC is driven primarily by SMEs that have focused their business entirely on the promise of MC (see table 23.2 for descriptive statistics). About 83 percent of the firms were founded exclusively with the purpose of MC, only 16 percent of the MC offerings are older than five years, their majority has sales for less than $1 million (83.5 percent), and has less than five employees (54 percent).

Table 23.1

Categories of application for mass toolkits ($n = 500$)

	Category	Description	Exemplary products	Frequency
1	Personalized media	Flat prints on paper or "near paper" objects, such as canvas	Book, calendar, canvas, wallpaper	96 (19.2%)
2	Personalized fashion and textiles	Mostly printed T-shirts plus other fabrics	T-shirt, blanket, underwear	78 (15.6%)
3	Food and nutrition	All you can eat or drink	Chocolate, cereals, tea	57 (11.4%)
4	Personalized look	Prints on nonpaper materials	Bag, mug, skin	49 (9.8%)
5	Made-to-measure Apparel	Women's and men's formal apparel	Suit, shirt, jacket, skirt	48 (9.6%)
6	Jewelry, bags, and accessories	All the things that improve your personal appearance	Ring, sun (glasses), watch, bag, belt	41 (8.2%)
7	Miscellaneous	All the things that do not fit into the other categories	Toys, instruments, stuff	38 (7.6%)
8	Household and furniture	Big and small things you use at home	Garden shed, bed, table, pet equipment	31 (6.2%)
9	Sports	Sports equipment	Bike, skateboard, golf ball	30 (6.0%)
10	Footwear	All that covers your feet	Shoes, boots, flip flops	23 (4.6%)
11	Computer and electronics	Different electronic products	PC, notebook, accumulator	9 (1.8%)

Table 23.2
Descriptive data from the company survey of responding firms ($n = 120$)

Metric	Frequency	Percentage	Cumulative percentage
Company type			
Company founded with the purpose of MC	95	82.6%	82.6%
MC business unit of an established company with standard product range	20	17.4%	100.0%
MC offering online			
< 1 year	32	27.8%	27.8%
1 to 5 years	65	56.5%	84.3%
> 5 years	18	15.7%	100.0%
Sales in fiscal year 2010 (in USD)			
< 100.000	57	49.6%	49.6%
< 500.000	23	20.0%	69.6%
< 1 million	16	13.9%	83.5%
< 5 million	10	8.7%	92.2%
> 5 million	9	7.8%	100.0%
Number of employees (FTEs)			
< 5	62	53.9%	53.9%
5 to 24	38	33.1%	87.0%
25 to 100	10	8.7%	95.1%
> 100	5	4,3%	100,0%
Location			
Germany	68	59.1%	59.1%
United States	31	27.0%	86.1%
Western Europe (excl. Germany)	13	11.3%	97.4%
Rest of world	3	2.6%	100.0%

The dynamism companies building their business models around mass toolkits is somehow surprising, given that the idea has been described extensively in the literature. Also the underlying web technologies have been available for at least ten years. But additional interviews with some of the entrepreneurs participating in the survey revealed that entry barriers to start a MC company have been significantly lowered in the last few years. One reason is the decreasing cost for launching a toolkit-based start-up. Providers like Cyledge in Europe, Treehouse Logic in the United States, and No-Refresh in India have developed standard software for mass toolkits, offering good solutions far beyond the $0.5 million price tag of traditional toolkit development in the consumer market (indeed, these companies promise a fully operating toolkit for 1/100th of this cost). At the same time, a specialized supply chain infrastructure is emerging. Dedicated MC suppliers allow start-ups to outsource their complete fulfillment solutions in some categories, hence turning capital investment for manufacturing and shipping equipment into variable cost. Finally, MC has become a topic in the general business press, attracting the attention of venture capitalists that have been exposed to the success stories of entrepreneurs like Lukas Gadowski (Spreadshirt), Jeff and Bobby Beaver (Zazzle), Ben Kaufman (Quirky), and Matt Lauzon (Gemvara). All these factors drive the current dynamism of companies with a business models based on mass toolkits.

Failure among these companies is quite frequent, however. Over a one-year time span, our population of companies in the Customization500 revealed a quite high mortality rate of 20 percent, an indicator of the difficulty of making mass toolkit-based business models work. Also the relatively small percentage of incumbents (17 percent) in our sample suggests that these models imply nontrivial changes to core organizational processes and, therefore, are not easily embraced. We have two preliminary explanations for these failures.

First, difficulties encountered by the studied MC companies may be ascertained to possible inadequacies of their toolkits. As shown in table 23.3, the 500 toolkits that we studied do not follow many design principles suggested as success factors by the experimental literature (e.g., Randall et al. 2005; Dellaert and Dabholkar 2009; Franke et al. 2009): Only 55 percent instantly visualize consumer input, less than 20 percent of vendors make use of peer input in the design process, 61 percent do not

Table 23.3
State of mass toolkit features in practice vs. recommendations in research
(*n* = 500)

Design parameters suggested for successful toolkits by Randall et al. (2005)	Percentage of toolkits showing this feature in the customization 500 population
Provide "help buttons" leading to meaningful information	59
Provide rich illustrations of the product	55
Provide short-cuts through attribute space	39
Provide multiple access points for customization	30
Allow consumers to save their designs	27
Explain the product attributes and how they map to design parameters e product	20
Show the distribution of design parameters and product attributes across the consumer population	11
Provide novice consumers with needs-based interface, and expert users with parameter-based interface	3
Allow for side-by-side comparison	2

provide information on progress of purchasing process. Only 22 percent allow customers to share their creations with others, just to mention a few shortcomings. The reality of toolkits clearly falls behind the academic research on toolkit design, suggesting a large shortcoming in transferring research into practice.

Second, problems in making mass toolkit-based business models work may also lie elsewhere. In an exploratory survey of 68 entrepreneurs and consultants active in the MC business (conducted by the authors in October 2009), for instance, we discovered that detecting customer idiosyncratic needs and creating flexible fulfillment processes are considered as more serious concerns (average score=4.0/5 and 3.9/5) than creating toolkits that support the sales process (average score=3.5/5). This research, the preliminary results of the Customization500 study, and many interactions with managers during our interviews lend support to our claim that profiting from mass toolkits demands a larger and more comprehensive set of capabilities.

Requisite Organizational Capabilities

How can manufacturers serving their customers via mass toolkits prosper? To answer this question it is essential to engage in an analysis of how value is created in the context of a MC strategy. In this section we first will build a simple theoretical framework to distinguish three strategic capabilities companies need to offer MC successfully. We will then discuss the three capabilities in larger detail. At the end of this section, we will discuss the relationships between the three MC capabilities and their synergistic effects on firm performance, drawing on the survey data from our database.

MC Capabilities: A Theoretical Framework

Our theoretical framework to distinguish MC capabilities starts with the perspective of the customer and drivers of customer value. Following Day and Wensley (1988), we differentiate between sources of customer value and performance outcomes that result from delivering superior customer value. If different vendors offer a requested product, customers will buy from the firm that they believe offers the highest value. To determine the net value (NV) from an offering, customers compare the gross utility (GU) they receive from it to its associated acquisition costs (AC) and search-and-evaluation costs (SEC):

$$NV = GU - (AV + SEC).$$

Customers only purchase a product if they can expect a positive surplus (Villas-Boas 2009). Consumer theory builds on the behavioral assumption that all customers are rational decision makers who seek to maximize their gross utility (GU), given their disposable income (Silberberg and Suen 2001). Acquisitions costs (AC) include the quoted price for a product, less any discounts allowed, plus shipping charges, and the opportunity cost of the time waited for delivery of the product or to have the product repaired or substituted in case of nonconformance.

Customers' main motivation to search for products is to find a lower price or a product that better fits their needs, but they naturally incur a search and evaluation cost (Anderson and Renault 1999). Search-and-evaluation costs (*SEC*) include any monetary costs of acquiring the information, the opportunity cost of the time devoted to searching, and the cognitive costs that are determined by the consumers' ability to undertake the search, depending on their prior knowledge, education, and training (Smith et al. 1999).

From a customer perspective, the appeal of MC via toolkits for user co-design depends on a simple economic equation: If the perceived benefits exceed the expected sacrifices, customers are more likely to adopt MC. MC can increase perceived benefits; customers can expect to receive better fitting products and a more enjoyable shopping experience. But it also may increase their sacrifices in terms of a price premium, time and effort spent, and uncertainty (Broekhuizen and Alsem 2002; Squire et al. 2004). Applying the previously outlined logic, MC potentially creates value by increasing the gross utility (ΔGU) to the customer but also raises both acquisition costs (ΔAC) and search-and-evaluation costs (ΔSEC) (figure 23.1a).

We can argue that MC can create greater value for the customer to the extent that (1) customization increases gross utility (ΔGU), more than it does increase (2) acquisition costs (ΔAC) and (3) search costs (ΔSEC). Evidently mass toolkits have an effect on these quantities, but many other practices and principles come into play, such as form postponement, product modularization (Duray et al. 2000; Salvador et al. 2002), cellular manufacturing, dynamic teaming (Tu et al. 2001), and sociotechnical system design (Liu et al. 2006), to mention a few.

We contend that MC needs to be conceptualized at a more abstract level than best practices, in the sense that MC can be best understood as a set of requisite organizational capabilities that are generally needed by any firm wishing to create value by engaging customers in co-creation activities. By "organizational capability" we refer to a value adding mechanism meant to hone a set of assets and routines to some user need. Building on our previous work on capabilities for MC (e.g., Salvador et al. 2002, 2004; Salvador and Forza 2007; Franke and Piller 2004; Piller 2008), we have progressively developed such a framework. Its first empirical validation has been conducted with a sample of 238 plants in

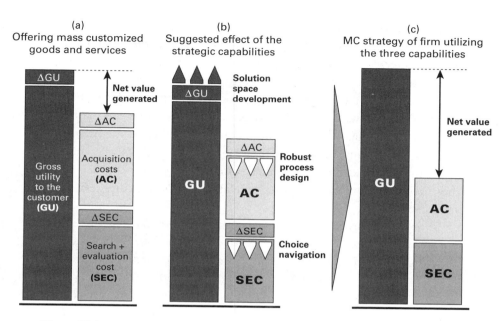

Figure 23.1

Implications of the strategic capabilities on customer value

eight European countries by Salvador et al. (2008). This study laid the foundation for the seminal framework proposed in Salvador et al. (2009), on which we elaborate on the remainder of this section.

Following our reasoning relative to how MC creates value for the customer, we propose that three capabilities are necessary and sufficient for a MC business model to thrive (figures 23.1b and 23.1c), namely:

- *Solution space development* The capability of the manufacturer to identify customers' idiosyncratic needs that are not addressed by competitors and target them with appropriate offerings, thus increasing gross utility (ΔGU).

- *Robust process design* The capability of the manufacturer to reuse or recombine existing resources to efficiently deliver a stream of differentiated solutions, resulting in lower manufacturing cost that allow got lower acquisition costs (ΔAC).

- *Choice navigation capability* The capability of the manufacturer to support customers in creating their own solutions while minimizing choice complexity, thus reducing search costs (ΔSEC).

Solution Space Development

A basic assumption for the creation of any toolkit is the definition of a *solution space*, i.e., a statement of all the possible permutations of design parameters that are offered to prospective customers (von Hippel 2001; Pine et al. 1993). This space determines what universe of benefits the manufacturer is willing to offer to its customers. For expert toolkits, such space has blurred borders and manufacturability of admitted solutions is not certain. Instead, in the case of mass toolkits, the solution space is precisely delimited and delivery conditions can be associated to any option without any uncertainty relative to price, quality levels and manufacturability.

Setting an appropriate solution space is a major challenge for a MC company as it directly affects the customers' perception of the utility of the customized product and determines the efficiency of downstream processes in the fulfillment system (Tseng and Piller 2003). To set its solution space, a mass customizer must first identify the idiosyncratic needs of its customers, specifically the product attributes along which customer needs diverge the most. This is in stark contrast to a mass producer which must focus on serving universal needs, ideally shared by all the target customers. Once that information is known and understood, the business can define its solution space, clearly delineating what it will offer—and what it will not.

Despite the importance of solution space development, there is surprisingly little research in the MC literature on how to develop a solution space (Piller 2005). Also the traditional literature on user toolkits (Franke and Schreier 2002; Franke and Piller 2003, 2004; Thomke and von Hippel 2002; von Hippel 2001; von Hippel and Katz 2002) does not cover this topic. Hence, we want to comment briefly on some of the potential methods. The first option for solution space development is to engage in conventional market research techniques (e.g., Griffin and Hauser 1993). The manufacturer selects and surveys a group of representative customers to obtain information on needs for new products, analyses the data, develops a responsive product idea, and screens this idea against customer preferences (needs) and purchasing decisions. This model is dominating in the world of consumer goods, where market research methodology such as focus groups, conjoint analysis, customer surveys, and analyses of customer complaints is used regularly to identify and evaluate customer needs and desires. However, there is no dedicated market research methods developed especially for the development of a solution space. What is needed is a method that decomposes the customer heterogeneities that allows a firm to understand for which components of an offering people want choice, and how much and along which spectrum. From our experience of working with companies, most existing methods do not provide answers in appropriate detail on these questions.

A second approach for solution space development for mass toolkits could be to provide (advanced) customers with an expert toolkit for user innovation. When Fiat was developing its retro Fiat 500, for example, the automaker created Concept Lab, an innovation toolkit that enabled customers to freely express their preferences regarding the interior of the car long before the first vehicle had been built. The company received more than 160,000 designs from customers—a product-development effort that no automaker could replicate internally. And Fiat allowed people to comment on others' submissions, providing a first evaluation of those ideas. Of course, mass producers can also benefit from innovation toolkits, but the technology is particularly useful for MC, because it can be deployed at low-cost for large pools of heterogeneous customers.

Third, in developing their solution space, companies can employ some form of "customer experience intelligence," that is, to apply methods for continuously collecting data on customer transactions, behaviors, or experiences, and analyzing that information to determine preferences. This also includes incorporating data not just from customers, but also from people who might have taken their business elsewhere. Consider, for example, information about products that someone has evaluated, but did not order. Such data can be obtained from log files generated by the browsing behavior of people using online configurators (Rangaswamy and Pal 2003). By systematically analyzing that information, managers can learn much about customer preferences, ultimately leading to a refined solution space. A company could, for instance, eliminate options that are rarely explored or selected, and it could add more choices for the popular components. Hence, it is important to note that solution space development is not a one-off activity but rather a continual, iterative improvement process. What customers want today may be different tomorrow (Simonson 2005). Companies would thus be well advised to implement a formal process to revise, trim, or extend their solution space at regular intervals.

The Customization500 study has shown that the practice of mass toolkits is dominated by start-up companies. Research on entrepreneurship has investigated the nature of opportunity recognition—the process through which ideas for potentially profitable new business ventures are identified (Kirzner 1979). Our study has shown that opportunity recognition also plays an important role in developing the initial solution space (Harzer 2012). Many entrepreneurs in fact started their businesses simply by translating their own unsatisfied needs into a custom product offering—MC meets lead users. In the era of mass production, customers implicitly agreed to trade off less customization for lower prices (Addis and Holbrook 2001). If customers take a mass produced product and adjust it to their own needs, it indicates the potential that other customers out there would prefer a similarly customized item. For example, indicustom.com and smart-jeans.com built their business model on the realization that many customers take their jeans to a tailor after purchasing them. Also the first customized chocolate bar by Chocri was an attempt to create an original, last-minute birthday gift. The tricky task in determining what should be customized, or not, is to detect what sacrifices most customers make, not just one. But as lead user theory has shown, lead user entrepreneurs know this much better than the traditional manufacturer.

Robust Process Design

The opportunities of toolkits to create value for customers only realize when the individual user design can be "translated into production" (von Hippel and Katz 2002: 828) that is, it can be manufactured without excessive price, quality and delivery penalties to the customer. This is a crucial problem, because variability in customers' requirements tends to generate costs in the operating system of the manufacturer. These costs arise for the need to reconfigure or dynamically recombine different manufacturing and supply chain resources in response to differentiated customer orders (Salvador et al. 2008; Pine et al. 1993). This demands a robust process design—defined as the capability to reuse or re-combine existing organizational and supply chain resources to fulfill a stream of differentiated customers' needs. With robust process design, customized solutions can be delivered with near mass production efficiency and reliability. Hence a successful MC system is characterized by stable, but still flexible, responsive processes that provide a dynamic flow of products (Pine 1993; Tu et al. 2001; Salvador et al. 2004).

A number of different methods can be employed to reduce these additional costs, or even to prevent their occurrence at all. Given the focus of this book, we will keep the discussion of these methods rather short. A primary mechanism to create robust processes in MC is *flexible automation* (Tu et al. 2001; Zhang et al. 2003). Although the words "flexible" and "automation" might have been contradictory in the past, this is no longer the case. In the automotive industry, robots and automation are compatible with high levels of versatility and customization. Even process industries (pharmaceuticals and food for example), once synonymous with rigid automation and large batches, nowadays enjoy levels of flexibility once considered unattainable. Similarly many intangible goods and services also lend themselves to flexible automated solutions, often based on the Internet. In the case of the entertainment industry, increasing digitalization is turning the entire product system over from the real to the virtual world.

A complementary approach to flexible automation is *process modularity*, which can be achieved by thinking of operational and supply chain processes as segments, each one linked to a specific source of variability in the customers' needs (Pine et al. 1993). As such, the company can serve different customer requirements by appropriately recombining the process segments, without the need to create costly ad hoc modules (Zhang et al. 2003). BMW's Mini factory, for instance, relies on individual mobile production cells with standardized robotic units. BMW can integrate the cells into an existing system in the plant within a few days, thus enabling the company to quickly adapt to unexpected swings in customer preferences without extensive modifications of its production areas. Process modularity can also be applied to service industries. IBM, for example, has been redesigning its consulting unit around configurable processes (called "engagement models"). The objective is to fix the overall architecture of even complex projects while retaining enough adaptability to respond to the specific needs of a client. Another widespread application of the principle of process modularity is delayed product differentiation or postponement (Yang and Burns 2003; Yang et al. 2004): A standardized portion of the product is produced during the first stage, while the 'differentiated' portion of the product is produced in the second stage, based on customer preferences which have been expressed in an order. The key advantage of postponement is to reduce inventory cost associated to serving heterogeneous customers and to ensure economies of scale in the first segment of the supply chain where standard operations prevail (Yang et al. 2004).

To ensure the success of robust process designs, companies also need to invest in adaptive human capital (Bhattacharya et al. 2005). Specifically, employees and managers have to be capable of dealing with novel and ambiguous tasks in order to offset any potential rigidness that is embedded in process structures and technologies. After all, machines aren't capable of determining what a future solution space will look like. That task clearly requires managerial decision making, not software algorithms. Individuals need a broad knowledge base that stretches beyond their immediate functional specialization, in order to be able to proficiently interact with other functions in the process of identifying and delivering tailored solutions to the customer. Such a broad knowledge base has to be complemented with relational attitudes that allow the individual to easily connect with other employees on an ad hoc basis.

The capability of robust process design denotes that turning a toolkit design into a custom solution for an individual user is not for free. Manufacturing firms embarking on toolkits for user co-design must ensure that the increased variability in customers' demand does not significantly impair their operations or supply chains. We believe that a larger exchange between the community of operations scholars and those in (user) innovation management could result in fruitful interactions and very interesting research.

Choice Navigation

Last, a mass customizer must support customers in identifying their own needs and creating solutions while minimizing complexity and the burden of choice. To enable this task is the original function of a toolkit. In consequence toolkits have to be user-friendly in the endeavor to enable trial-and-error learning of users (von Hippel and Katz 2002). When a customer is exposed to myriad choices, the cost of evaluating those options can easily outweigh the additional benefit from having so many alternatives. The resulting syndrome has been called the "paradox of choice" (Schwartz 2004), in which too many options can actually reduce customer value instead of increasing it (Huffman and Kahn 1998). In such situations customers might postpone their buying decisions and, worse, classify the vendor as difficult and undesirable. Recent research in marketing has addressed this issue in more detail and found that the perceived cognitive cost is one of the highest hurdles toward a larger adoption of MC (Dellaert and Stremersch 2005). To avoid this, companies have to provide choice navigation to simplify the ways in which people explore their offerings. This capability also relates to the design parameters of toolkits themselves, another rather open field of research in MC and user innovation alike. Design parameters of toolkits that provide choice navigation are, for example, help functionality, process orientation, recommendation systems, or visualization features (Randall et al. 2005; Dellaert and Dabholkar 2009; Franke et al. 2009), but also community functionality or design libraries by other users (Ihl 2009). However, the state of the practice of mass toolkits, as shown before by data from our Customization500 study, clearly falls behind research on toolkit design. Choice navigation, however, does not just refer to preventing "complexity of choice" and the negative effects of variety from the customers' perspective. Offering choice to customers in a meaningful way, on the contrary, can become a way for new profit opportunities. Recent research has shown that up to 50 percent of the additional willingness to pay for customized (consumer) products can be explained by the positive perception of the co-design process itself (Franke and Piller 2004; Schreier 2006; Franke and Schreier 2010; Merle et al. 2010). Product co-designs by customers may also provide symbolic (intrinsic and social) benefits, resulting from the actual process of co-design rather than its outcome. Schreier (2006) quotes, for example, a pride-of-authorship effect. Customers may co-create something by themselves, which may add value due to the sheer enthusiasm about the result. In addition to enjoyment, participating in a co-design process may be considered a highly creative problem-solving process by the individuals engaged in this task, thus becoming a motivator to purchase a MC product.

While one can argue that the process value delivered by a MC offering is a result of good solution space development, it is the design of the choice navigation process that delivers and realizes this opportunity. The rather preliminary state of implementation of mass toolkits in practice, as described before, indicates that there still is plenty of room for improvement—and strategic differentiation—in developing systems for choice navigation that do both guide the users to their "perfect" solution and provide a feeling of fun, pride, and achievement.

Relating the Capabilities with Each Other

Before, we described three strategic capabilities that companies need to build and utilize to make a mass toolkit-based business model work. But how do the three capabilities relate to each other? Data from our company survey ($n = 120$), a subset of the Customization500, further allowed us to test several alternative models for the relationships between the three capabilities (and their antecedents). First, we find that the three capability dimensions are empirically distinguishable, emphasizing the multidimensional nature of MC (for detailed data and statistical proofs of these findings, refer to Harzer et al. 2012). Second, and more interestingly in the context of this chapter, we find that the three strategic capabilities do not (significantly) improve performance of the companies in our sample on their own but show strong complementarities with each other. Complementarity theory implies that the magnitude of the effect of overall MC capability is greater than the sum of marginal effects from developing each capability individually (Milgrom and Roberts 1990). Following Peng et al. (2008), we modeled the MC capability of a manufacturer as a reflective second-order construct to capture complementarities arising from the three capabilities (Harzer et al. 2012). This second-order construct accounts for multilateral interactions between the three capabilities and can be shown to be statistically superior compared to a conceptualization of MC as three distinct yet correlated capabilities (Whittington et al. 1999). It is the complementary and synergistic effects of the three distinct but highly interrelated capabilities that enable firms to achieve multiple performance goals, such as (in our sample) market success and financial success.

Unfortunately, transforming a business along all the three dimensions subsumed by the three capabilities is difficult, both for start-ups and for incumbents, although for different reasons. In the case of start-ups, the major challenge for the entrepreneur is to develop a vision that does not overlook key capabilities. Consider the case of myMuesli (not a failure, by any means). This provider of customized cereal had a well-designed toolkit that enabled users to overcome the challenge of simulating taste online. MyMuesli also was rather proficient in solution space development, predominantly building on lead user characteristics of their founders and continuously learning from past interactions. However, myMuesli neglected robust processes, especially with regard to flexible automation. Whenever a press report in their favor was published, their manufacturing capacity (plenty of human labor mixing muesli from about 65 different categories of options by hand using precision scales) was overwhelmed by demand, and the company had to turn down prospective customers by setting a daily order limit. Only after investing into a fully automated, scalable mixing system, the complementarities of the business model could be exploited, and the company began to generate profits. In many other examples we investigated, it was especially the capability to develop the solution space that was lacking, leading to failure when the toolkit options did not represent the heterogeneities of demand that mattered for users in the particular market, hence offering to little additional GU in lieu of high AC and SEC.

In the case of incumbents, the core problem associated with the implementation of sustainable business models leveraging mass toolkits is that the changes associated to the development of the three abovementioned capabilities are pervasive and are opposed by powerful inertial forces. Take, for instance, John Deere, one of the world's largest manufacturers of garden equipment. To keep up with its market for premium lawn tractors, which had been evolving toward greater fragmentation and customization for more than a decade, the company began to offer more products, but that then resulted in a proliferation of parts and processes. Divisional managers were aware of this and they knew that they could save millions of dollars every year by simplifying their product platforms. Yet it took years to the division to implement the needed changes, and this required overhauling accounting and performance measurement systems, product development as well as manufacturing and supply chain processes. John Deere realized that these changes had to be done simultaneously, because MC capabilities relate to all the major areas of the value chain.

Conclusions

We started this chapter from the simple observation that innovativeness is not a dichotomous feature of a customer, splitting the world between innovative lead users and non-innovative consumers. To some extent, also ordinary users have innovation capabilities, although they may perhaps be limited. Engaging each customer into innovative activities presents a tremendous opportunity to manufacturers, and seizing this opportunity calls for devising a well-functioning mass customization (MC) strategy. Mass toolkits (or toolkits for user innovation and co-design) are one key instrument toward this end, but they have to be implemented in the context of a profound revision of the manufacturer's core capabilities.

To substantiate our claims we examined a sample of 500 mass customizers who enable their customers to create individualized products via web-based mass toolkits. We found that these companies rely on toolkits that lag behind the standards recommended by experimental research, thus undermining their ability to profitably engage in customer co-creation. We further find that these companies need to develop three specific capabilities to create successful toolkit-based business models, capabilities that link to the definition of an appropriate solutions space, to the creation of robust operational processes, and to the matching of customers' needs with the manufacturer's offerings.

The pervasive changes associated to the creation of successful toolkit-based business models resonate with a long-held assumption of von Hippel (2005) who observed that

[t]he ongoing shift of product development activities from manufacturers to users is painful and difficult for many manufacturers. . . . Many firms and industries must make fundamental changes to long-held business models in order to adapt. (von Hippel 2005: 2)

We believe that the path toward executing these changes has to rest on a profound understanding of the organizational mechanism and capabilities associated to MC and customer co-creation.

Despite all these difficulties, our data suggest that MC strategies based on mass toolkits are viable and can sustain financial and market success of an organization. Looking forward, we suggest that future research should look more in depth into the relation between mass toolkits, MC business models and firm performance, expanding the traditional consumer behavior focus of most toolkit research. There also are ample opportunities for further research on the three capabilities. With regard to choice navigation, we found that toolkits in practice clearly do not utilize the broad body of academic research on design parameters of a successful toolkit. What are the reasons why MC entrepreneurs do not build better toolkits? And what are contingency factors that determine the effectiveness of specific design parameters of a toolkit? We also found a lack of research on solution space development. For instance, we do not know how heterogeneities in the customer domain can be understood and translated into meaningful product attributes. Finally, we see the need for more research on the simultaneous design of toolkits and fulfillment systems, a topic that has been largely ignored so far. Eric von Hippel's idea of toolkits for user innovation and his underlying research and frameworks will, without any doubt, continue to inspire many future generations of students and scholars.

Notes

This chapter builds on our earlier research on capabilities as presented in Salvador, de Holan, and Piller (2009) and recent research conducted with Thorsten Harzer, Christoph Ihl, and Dominik Walcher (Walcher and Piller 2012; Harzer 2012; Harzer et al. 2012). Their input for this chapter is greatly acknowledged.

1. Refer to Walcher and Piller (2012) for more details on our sampling and data codification strategy. Note that our sample population does not cover the entire range of MC offerings, as not all mass customizers rely on a toolkit. Customized products or services can be offered automatically by making inferences from past customers' transactions, as in the case of Amazon.com (customized book recommendations) or Pandora.com (customized radio channels). In other cases, MC is achieved by offering products that adapt themselves to the user's needs, as in the case of voice-recognition software (e.g., Dragon Dictate) or smart automatic transmissions that configure themselves based on the driving style of the driver (e.g., Porsche's Tiptronic system). Also we excluded from our population all providers of customized products that do not provide their customers with an online toolkit because of the difficulty to identify relevant companies. Finally, to ensure sufficient homogeneity among the sampled manufacturers, we excluded firms with toolkits meant to personalize only service-related aspects of their products (insurance terms, delivery options, after-sales services, etc.).

References

Addis, M., and M. B. Holbrook. 2001. On the conceptual link between mass customisation and experiential consumption. *Journal of Consumer Behaviour* 1 (1): 50–66.

Anderson, S. P., and R. Renault. 1999. Pricing, product diversity, and search costs: A Bertrand–Chamberlin–Diamond model. *Rand Journal of Economics* 30 (4): 719–35.

Bhattacharya, M., D. E. Gibson, and D. Doty. 2005. The effects of flexibility in employee skills, employee behaviors, and human resource practices on firm performance. *Journal of Management* 31 (4): 622–40.

Broekhuizen, T., and K. J. Alsem. 2002. Success factors for mass customization: A conceptual model. *Journal of Market-Focused Management* 5 (2): 309–30.

Day, G. S., and R. Wensley. 1988. Assessing advantage: A framework for diagnosing competitive superiority. *Journal of Marketing* 52 (2): 1–20.

Dellaert, B. G. C., and P. A. Dabholkar. 2009. Increasing the attractiveness of mass customization. *International Journal of Electronic Commerce* 13 (3): 43–70.

Dellaert, B. G. C., and S. Stremersch. 2005. Marketing mass-customized products: Striking a balance between utility and complexity. *JMR, Journal of Marketing Research* 42 (2): 219–27.

Duray, R., P. T. Ward, G. W. Milligan, and W. L. Berry. 2000. Approaches to mass customization: Configurations and empirical validation. *Journal of Operations Management* 18 (11): 605–625.

Franke, N., and F. Piller. 2003. Key research issues in user interaction with configuration toolkits. *International Journal of Technology Management* 26 (5–6): 578–99.

Franke, N., and F. Piller. 2004. Value creation by toolkits for user innovation and design: The case of the watch market. *Journal of Product Innovation Management* 21 (6): 401–15.

Franke, N., and M. Schreier. 2002. Entrepreneurial opportunities with toolkits for user innovation and design. *International Journal on Media Management* 4 (4): 225–34.

Franke, N., and M. Schreier. 2010. Why customers value mass-customized products: The importance of process effort and enjoyment. *Journal of Product Innovation Management* 27 (7): 1020–31.

Franke, N., P. Keinz, and C. J. Steger. 2009. Testing the value of customization: When do customers really prefer products tailored to their preferences? *Journal of Marketing* 73 (5): 103–21.

Franke, N., M. Schreier, and U. Kaiser. 2010. The "I designed it myself" effect in mass customization. *Management Science* 65 (1): 125–40.

Griffin, A., and J. R. Hauser. 1993. The voice of the customer. *Marketing Science* 12 (1): 1–27.

Harzer, T. 2012. Value creation through mass customization: An empirical analysis of the requisite strategic capabilities. PhD thesis. RWTH Aachen University.

Harzer, T., F. Piller, and F. Salvador. 2012. Complementarities in mass customization. Working paper. MIT Smart Customization Group.

Huffman, C., and B. E. Kahn. 1998. Variety for sale: Mass customization or mass confusion? *Journal of Retailing* 74 (4): 491–513.

Ihl, J. C. 2009. Marketing for mass customization: Consumer behavior and marketing policies in the context of customizable products. PhD thesis. TUM Business School, TU Munich.

Kirzner, I. 1979. *Perception, Opportunity, and Profit.* Chicago: University of Chicago Press.

Lee, H. L., and C. Tang. 1997. Modelling the costs and benefits of delayed product differentiation. *Management Science* 43 (1): 40–53.

Liu, G., R. Shah, and R. Schroeder. 2006. Linking work design to mass customization: A sociotechnical systems perspective. *Decision Sciences* 37 (4): 519–45.

Merle, A., J.-L. Chandon, E. Roux, and F. Alizon. 2010. Perceived value of the mass-customized product and experience for individual consumers. *Production and Operations Management* 19 (5): 503–14.

Milgrom, P., and J. Roberts. 1990. The economics of modern manufacturing: Technology, strategy and organization. *American Economic Review* 80 (3): 511–28.

O'Hern, M. S., and A. Rindfleisch. 2009. Customer co-creation: A typology and research agenda. In *Review of Marketing Research*, vol. 6, ed. K. M. Naresh, 84–106. Armonk, NY: Sharpe.

Peng, D. X., R. Schroeder, and R. Shah. 2008. Linking routines to operations capabilities: A new perspective. *Journal of Operations Management* 26 (6): 730–48.

Piller, F. 2005. Mass customization: Reflections on the state of the concept. *Journal of Flexible Manufacturing Systems* 16 (4): 313–34.

Piller, F. 2008. Mass customization. In *The Handbook of 21st Century Management*, ed. C. Wankel, 420–30. Thousand Oaks, CA: Sage.

Piller, F., and C. Ihl. 2010. *Open Innovation with Customers—Foundations, Competences and International Trends. Expert study commissioned by the European Union.* Aachen: RWTH ZLW-IMA.

Piller, F., C. Ihl, and F. Steiner. 2010. Embedded toolkits for user co-design: A technology acceptance study of product adaptability in the usage stage. *Proceedings of the 43th Hawaii International Conference on Systems Science* (HICSS). IEEE.

Pine, J. B. 1993. *Mass Customization.* Boston: Harvard Business School Press.

Pine, J. B., J. H. Gilmore, and A. C. Boynton. 1993. Making mass customization work. *Harvard Business Review* 71 (5): 108–18.

Prahalad, C. K., and V. Ramaswamy. 2004. *The Future of Competition: Co-creating Unique Value with Customers.* Boston: Harvard Business School Press.

Ramirez, R. 1999. Value co-production: Intellectual origins and implications for practice and research. *Strategic Management Journal* 20 (1): 49–65.

Randall, T., C. Terwiesch, and K. T. Ulrich. 2005. Principles for user design of customized products. *California Management Review* 47 (4): 68–85.

Rangaswamy, A., and N. Pal. 2003. Gaining business value from personalization technologies. In *The Power of One*, ed. N. Pal and A. Rangaswamy, 1–9. Victoria, BC: Trafford.

Roser, T., A. Samson, P. Humphreys, and E. Cruz-Valdivieso. 2009. New pathways to value: Co-creating products by collaborating with customers. Working paper. LSE.

Rungtusanatham, M., and F. Salvador. 2008. From mass production to mass customization: Hindrance factors, structural inertia, and transition hazard. *Production and Operations Management* 17 (3): 385–96.

Salvador, F., and C. Forza. 2007. Principles for efficient and effective sales configuration design. *International Journal of Mass Customisation* 2 (1–2): 114–27.

Salvador, F., M. Rungtusanatham, and C. Forza. 2002. Modularity, product variety, production volume, and component sourcing: Theorizing beyond generic prescriptions. *Journal of Operations Management* 20 (5): 549–75.

Salvador, F., M. Rungtusanatham, and C. Forza. 2004. Supply chain configurations for mass customization. *Production Planning and Control* 15 (4): 381–97.

Salvador, F., M. Rungtusanatham, A. Akpinar, and C. Forza. 2008. Strategic capabilities for mass customization: Theoretical synthesis and empirical evidence. *Academy of Management Proceedings*: 1–6.

Salvador, F., P. M. de Holan, and F. Piller. 2009. Cracking the code of mass customization. *MIT Sloan Managment Review* 50 (3): 71–78.

Schreier, M. 2006. The value increment of mass-customized products. *Journal of Consumer Behaviour* 5 (4): 317–27.

Schwartz, B. 2004. *The Paradox of Choice: Why More Is Less.* New York: Harper.

Silberberg, E., and W. Suen. 2001. *The Structure of Economics: A Mathematical Analysis.* New York: McGraw-Hill/Irwin.

Simonson, I. 2005. Determinants of customers' responses to Customized offers: Conceptual framework and research propositions. *Journal of Marketing* 69 (1): 32–45.

Smith, G. E., M. P. Venkatraman, and R. R. Dholakia. 1999. Diagnosing the search cost effect: Waiting time and the moderating impact of prior category knowledge. *Journal of Economic Psychology* 20 (3): 285–314.

Squire, B., J. Readman, S. Brown, and J. Bessant. 2004. Mass customization: The key to customer value? *Production Planning and Control* 15 (4): 459–71.

Thomke, S., and E. von Hippel. 2002. Customers as innovators: A new way to create value. *Harvard Business Review* 80 (4): 74–81.

Tseng, M., and F. Piller. 2003. *The Customer Centric Enterprise: Advances in Mass Customization and Personalization.* New York: Springer.

Tu, Q., M. A. Vonderembse, and T. S. Ragu-Nathan. 2001. The impact of time-based manufacturing practices on mass customization and value to customer. *Journal of Operations Management* 19 (2): 201–17.

Udwadia, F. E., and R. Kumar. 1991. Impact of customer co-construction in product/service markets. *International Journal of Technological Forecasting and Social Change* 40 (2): 261–72.

Villas-Boas, J. M. 2009. Product variety and endogenous pricing with evaluation cost. *Management Science* 55 (8): 1338–46.

von Hippel, E. 1994. "Sticky information" and the locus of problem solving: Implications for innovation. *Management Science* 40 (4): 429–39.

von Hippel, E. 1998. Economics of product development by users: The impact of "sticky" local information. *Management Science* 44 (5): 629–44.

von Hippel, E. 2001. User toolkits for innovation. *Journal of Product Innovation Management* 18 (4): 247–57.

von Hippel, E. 2005. *Democratizing innovation.* Cambridge: MIT Press.

von Hippel, E., and R. Katz. 2002. Shifting innovation to users via toolkits. *Management Science* 48 (7): 821–33.

von Hippel, E., S. Ogawa, and J. De Jong. 2011. The age of the consumer innovator. *MIT Sloan Management Review* 53 (1): 21–35.

Walcher, D., and F. Piller. 2012. *The Customization500: An International Benchmark Study.* Raleigh, NC: Lulu.

Whittington, R., A. Pettigrew, S. Peck, E. Fenton, and M. Conyon. 1999. Change and complementarities in the new competitive landscape: A European panel study. *Organization Science* 10 (5): 583–600.

Wikstroem, S. 1996. Value creation by company–consumer interaction. *Journal of Marketing Management* 12 (5): 359–74.

Yang, B., and N. D. Burns. 2003. Implications of postponement for the supply chain. *International Journal of Production Research* 41 (9): 2075–90.

Yang, B., N. D. Burns, and C. J. Backhouse. 2004. Postponement: A review and an integrated framework. *International Journal of Operations and Production Management* 24 (5): 468–87.

Zhang, Q., M. A. Vonderembse, and J.-S. Lim. 2003. Manufacturing flexibility: Defining and analyzing relationships among competence, capability, and customer satisfaction. *Journal of Operations Management* 21 (2): 173–91.

24

The Value of Toolkits for User Innovation and Design

Nikolaus Franke

Eric von Hippel conceptualized a *Toolkit for User Innovation and Design* as a coordinated set of design tools that allow individual users to self-design their own individual product according to their individual preferences and give visual and informational feedback on (virtual) interim solutions (von Hippel 1998; von Hippel 2001; von Hippel and Katz 2002). If the customers like what they designed, they can order their products. The toolkit provider in turn will produce the products according to their individual design specifications.

Many companies have started offering toolkits that enable users to create online their own individual computer chips, machines, flavors, custom food, software, plastic polymers, industrial refrigerators, security systems, climate control and air-conditioning systems, windows, electronic equipment, T-shirts, watches, breakfast cereals, cars, kitchens, sofas, skis, jewelry, laptops, pens, sneakers, and so forth, which the manufacturer then can produce to order. Toolkits can, of course, be applied in service industries too. There are examples of websites that allow the individual user to customize events like wedding feasts, trips, electronic newspapers, financial investments and insurances, music, ring tones, mobile phone contracts, and so on, and there are many other services where toolkits not yet exist but would make a lot of sense. Also in service industries, toolkits provide design tools that allow the user to determine the design of the service, and give some sort of feedback. Very often toolkits are incorporated in PC games and allow to extending, modifying, and newly creating game characters, maps, surroundings, and so forth.[1] An interesting feature of software is that here, the design simulation and the product often go together: The simulation is the product. A new map designed for a game needs not to be produced anymore by a producer—the outcome of the self-design process is already the product, and the user is also the producer.

Albeit their differences with regard to the product arena, toolkits share two common principles: First, they all contain some form of design tools that enable the user to create and modify a design. Some come in a quite restricted form of lists to choose from. Others are in the drag-and-drop style, for example, when users can choose graphic symbols, place them on skis, define their size, and shift them around in order to find the position where the design looks best. There are also toolkits that allow using product components modular-wise, similar to building an artifact with Lego bricks. Still others allow free design like a graphic computer program. They comprise functional aspects of the product (e.g., material, size, shape, and functions included), the product's aesthetics (e.g., color, incorporated graphics, and other forms of style), and the possibility of personalization (e.g., by adding one's name or other symbols).

The second principle these heterogeneous toolkits have in common is that they give some sort of feedback information during the design process. In consumer goods settings the most common form of feedback is a virtual, simulated visual representation of the current product design that is updated in real time with every design change users make. If the toolkit allows for functional product manipulation, feedback of course should also be functional. For example, a gardening toolkit that allows creating one's own garden gave me some sort of alarm when I positioned a garden pond too close to a broadleaf tree: "In fall leaves might fall on the pond— they might quickly silt up your pond, in summer the tree might provide too much shade and so stopping aquatic plants from growing." Others inform about weight, price, or technical performance. In sum, a good toolkit provides the user with information about the anticipated consequences of design decisions, like a capable salesperson would do. This enables the user to conduct what is called trial-and-error learning (von Hippel 1998, 2001; von Hippel and Katz 2002). Few of us have the imagination to come up with a precise, detailed, and definitive product specification. Most cannot design a product just in their mind—they need to play around, try different things, and iteratively find out what they like best. The toolkit supports this way of problem solving.

In a way, toolkits allow what von Hippel (2005) terms "democratizing innovation"—potentially innovative,[2] new products that allow individual users to satisfy their very needs and preferences are no longer a privilege for the small subgroup of particularly capable or resourceful individuals. For producers, it is no longer necessary to try to understand what the customer wants—costly and error-prone market research can be saved. Instead, the users will design their products themselves. Many scholars and practitioners herald the new possibilities as the indicators of a new paradigm (Sharma and Sheth 2004; Cook 2008; Prahalad and Ramaswamy 2008; O'Hern and Rindfleisch 2010). The promise of toolkits is that they generate welfare by freeing users from standard product restrictions and generate superior value for the individual and welfare for society. As a personal note, I would like to emphasize what important moment it was for me when I read the working paper that later became von Hippel (2001) and von Hippel and Katz (2002). In 2000 I had just begun a one year research scholarship at MIT and enjoyed the intellectually stimulating atmosphere and the warm hospitality of my host Eric von Hippel who had invited me. With him I had wonderful discussions in which we considered numerous ideas, concepts, and potential research projects in the area of user innovation. At that time, user innovation was still underestimated as a "niche phenomenon" by the majority of innovation management scholars. However, at least for those who were so lucky to be in contact with Eric, it was clear that something important was going on and that the Internet, connectedness, open source software, and user communities would change the general appreciation of the importance of innovating users forever. Such fascinating developments! So many possibilities! And so much fun! But even against this background, when I read Eric's conceptualization of toolkits, I had this rare and overwhelming sensation that this idea is something *really* big. What a revolutionary, powerful vision! And it was instantly clear to me that I wanted to research toolkits more in-depth and the way they work and can potentially work.

Therefore Eric and I set up a research project in which we measured the value created by toolkits. Obviously it is not enough to simply "assume" this potential—there was (and is) skepticism. The failures of some pioneers in the field, Levi Strauss (with its "Original Spin" jeans) and Mattel's "MyDesign Barbie" (see Franke and Piller 2004), that have discontinued their mass customization operations are often cited. And based on theoretical considerations also a number of scholars have expressed doubts that empowering users with toolkits will actually generate value for them because the complexity and difficulty of the self-designing task might overstrain them (e.g., Zipkin 2001; Simonson 2005; Fang 2008; Huffman and Kahn 1998). Indeed it has been found that customers sometimes prefer the default configurations provided by the producer and fail to recognize the self-designing opportunities offered (Dellaert and Stremersch 2003; Hill 2003).

Therefore we launched an initially large-scale survey of 138 *Apache* web server software users (for details, see Franke and von Hippel 2003).

A Study of Apaches

Apache is a very successful open source server software product that is today used to run more than 60 percent of all Internet websites. Web server software is used on computer servers connected to the Internet. A server's function is to "service" requests from Internet browsers for particular documents or content. Initial versions of web server software were developed in the early to mid-1990s and offered relatively simple functionality. Over time, however, Apache and other web server software programs have evolved into the complicated front end for many of the technically demanding applications that now run on the Internet. For example, web server software is now used to handle security and authentication of users, provide e-commerce shopping carts and gateways to databases. Apache is "open source" software that is explicitly designed to enable modification and individualization by users. Tools for software design and test ranging from software languages such as C to compilers and debuggers are also available in open source form on the web. Taken together with the possibility of testing newly-written server functionality on one's own website, these elements comprise a complete toolkit for user innovation for Apache users: It allows users to self-design and get immediate feedback on the outcome.

One specific aspect made this product particularly eligible for our research: Users *may*, but do *not have to* customize the software. Given that users have the technical capability, they can freely decide if they only use the standard version of the software or if they change or adapt the existing modules or even create totally new solutions that better match their specific needs. This allows for a comparison of the two groups of technically capable Apache users who *customized* and equally capable users who did *not*. Had we surveyed customers of, for example, a toolkit company, we would lack information on the latter and could therefore not interpret findings in a meaningful way. The focus of the study was the important security function of the software, and we surveyed 138 webmasters using Apache.

The first interesting finding is that among those users who are capable of modifying Apache by writing new code, 28 percent actually did so in the area of security functions (we have no information on this, but it is reasonable to assume that a much larger proportion modified Apache at all, i.e., beyond the security function). This means that although the standard version of Apache already covers this aspect quite extensively, a considerable number of users had needs that were not addressed—and they expected to obtain concrete value from customization. In order to explore whether their expectations were met, we analyzed the satisfaction of both groups. The pattern was clear: Users who had customized the software were more satisfied with the security of the software than those who used the standard version only. This pattern holds for the overall satisfaction as well as for most of the different security aspects (basic web server functionality, authentication of client, e-commerce related functions, within-site user access control), and in most cases the difference was significant. In sum, findings suggest that self-customizing a product indeed creates value for the individual users (table 24.1).

The obvious next question is how valid findings from satisfaction measures in surveys are. One can at least question them. Simply checking a box saying "I am very satisfied with function X" in a questionnaire can be criticized as being only "cheap talk"—because it does not bear any economic consequences for the subject. Therefore our interpretation that customization actually yields benefits to the subject is not the only interpretation of our findings. For example, it might be that those who invested effort by programming actually were not more satisfied but felt obliged *reporting* higher satisfaction because this "justifies" their behavior ex post. Such effects are termed *social desirability* and is known to be a problem in questionnaire research for a long time (Edwards 1957). Also surveys and the validity of the results they yield depend on factors difficult to control for the researcher, such as the subjects' motivation, honesty, and ability to respond. Frank Piller from RWTH Aachen University and I

Table 24.1
Satisfaction of Apache customizers versus noncustomizers

User satisfaction with the following web server security functions	Users that customized[a]	Users that did not customize[a]	*P*
Satisfaction with basic web server Functionality	5.5	4.3	0.100
Satisfaction with authentication of client	3.0	1.0	0.001
Satisfaction with e-commerce Related functions	1.3	0.0	0.023
Satisfaction with within-site user Access control	8.5	6.9	0.170
Satisfaction with other	3.9	3.9	0.699
Overall satisfaction	4.3	2.6	0.010

a. Based on adequacy-importance model of satisfaction and importance scale (each ranging from [1; 7]) of constituting functions divided by the number of functions; for details, see Franke and von Hippel (2003).

therefore decided to study the value created by self-designing a product with a toolkit in a more sophisticated way, namely by an experiment (for details see Franke and Piller 2004).

Value of Experiments for Investigating the Value Generation by Toolkits

In experiments, the researcher sets a stimulus and observes the effects under controlled conditions. Compared to surveys and other forms of observational data, experiments allow much better to test causal relationships, isolate effects, and rule out alternative explanations. Their high "internal validity" is the reason why they are the standard procedure in (natural) sciences and psychology and why in the past years they have been used increasingly also in the areas of business, management, and marketing research. Yet experiments require high effort. Samples must be recruited, laboratories need to be prepared, experimentation processes must be supervised, and results and side effects documented precisely. Therefore they are relatively expensive. An important downside is also their sometimes problematic external validity: Particularly when being conducted as laboratory experiments (with purposefully created settings in order to control the effects) experiments are often criticized because it is not clear in how far their results can be generalized to real-life conditions. Problems may result both from investigating very special populations (e.g., studying the behavior of students for testing hypotheses about top management behavior) as from the realism of tasks, stimuli, and settings (e.g., drawing circles or counting dots and in order to derive conclusions about real-life behavior). Winer (1999) for the field of marketing and Loewenstein (1999) for the area of experimental economics provide interesting examples for such problems. The "distance" between the actual behavior in the experiment and the universal conclusions drawn may be substantial. Loewenstein (1999: F33) therefore concludes that researchers often "have not, in my opinion, been able to avoid the problem of low external validity that is the Achilles heel of all laboratory experimentation."

Of course, methods are not good or bad as such. Rather, their choice should follow from the research question, and they must fit to the research context. For the research questions in the area of toolkits, laboratory experiments have great advantages. Most important, the experimental conditions can be made very realistic with quite little effort—their external validity is relatively high. Toolkits are available on the web and can be directly used as stimuli. For participants, designing a product sitting in front of a PC in a laboratory (which helps controlling situation specific factors and thus ensures a high internal validity) is quite similar to the usual conditions at home or at work or wherever people self-design— there is hardly anything artificial in this situation that limits the generalization of the findings. Also it is quite easy to introduce incentives that make it likely that participants reveal their real motives and show unbiased "real" behavior. In many of our experiments, we let participants bid for their self-designed products in auctions. The possibility to buy one's self-designed product prevented participants from interpreting the experiment just as amusement. Our experience is that they took their job as self-designers as serious as they would in real life. Second, student samples constitute a smaller problem for generalization in this area than in many other settings. After all, young, adept, and Internet-experienced users are the prime target group of many toolkit providers in B2C businesses. Third, it is possible to achieve a relatively high number of cases with relatively low costs. After all, the unit of analysis is the individual users' interaction with the toolkit, thus the number of cases equals the number of participants. Getting a sufficient number of cases becomes much more costly, when the behavior of groups or the behavior of organizations is the unit of analysis.

An Experiment on the Additional Value of Self-Design

Frank and I came up with an experimental design that has been replicated thereafter several times (figure 24.1 and table 24.1). We recruited a sample of $n = 304$ business students. Then we gave one group of students the opportunity to design their own individual ideal wristwatch. We equipped them with a real toolkit provided by a Hong Kong company called *IdTown* that allows customers to configure their own mid-market Swatch-type timepiece by choosing a case, band, face, and hour/minute/second hands.[3] Although the design tools of this toolkit only comprised a few dimensions and being really creative was not possible, the range of possible designs runs into the hundreds of millions. The solution space was not overly great for a toolkit, but still large enough for our purposes. Having finished, subjects had the opportunity to bid for "their own" self-designed watch. Their willingness to pay (WTP) or reservation price is a good measure of the subjective value created. It denotes the maximum amount of money a subject is willing to sacrifice for an object and thus constitutes a hard proxy to measure the benefit consumers (expect to) derive from it.

As mechanism, we employed a Vickrey auction. A *Vickrey auction* is an auction in which participants' bids are sealed and no bidder knows what other staked. The item is sold to the highest bidder at a price equal to the second-highest bid, thus the winner pays less than the highest bid (Vickrey 1961). There is a huge body of literature both empirical as theoretical that shows that in this procedure it is the best strategy to bid the same as the actual maximum willingness to pay (e.g., Cox et al. 1982; Hoffman et al. 1993). We made clear that the bids were binding and participants had to confirm their bid with a signature. Eventually we "sold" a number of watches, and the fact that winners readily paid indicates that they well understood that the values indicated was by no means "cheap talk."

In order to interpret the willingness to pay for their self-designed watches, we needed a reference object we can compare the sums with. Because students did not participate at the experiment with the intention to buy watches, we expected that their bids were below actual market prices—but how much?

We therefore had decided to put up a second group of students who would indicate their willingness to pay for already existing watches we took from the market. Of course, the assignment to the two groups was strictly random in order to avoid any kind of bias, and for the same reason the setting was similar for both groups. To make the comparison even more challenging, we did not use an arbitrarily chosen professional watch design, but the four *most successful professional watch designs in the Austrian market*. If we believe in evolutionary economics, then the strong competition should have delivered us the best standard designs in the eyes of the customers.

To identify these bestsellers, we had thoroughly interviewed a huge number of retailers, manufacturers, and industry experts. Bestsellers all came from the Swiss brand *Swatch* (we concealed the brand label in order to isolate the design aspect). In the experiment the standard watches were displayed showing the products in real size on computer screens, similar to the self-designed products in the other experimental group. Both groups had received identical information regarding the technical quality of the watches, and the experimental setting was similar. Differences found thus can be attributed to the customization of the watch.

We were curious about the results. Would the amateur self-designs really stand a chance against their professional competitors? When I asked a group of marketing practitioners what outcome they would expect from the experiment, they were undecided. Some thought it might be possible that user designs are somewhat more valuable to their originators, but most doubted that average self-designs by students could equal professional designers. After all, as professionals, they had acquired specific skills and considerable experience, and being well paid, they also have a high incentive to provide really good design solutions. During the experiment the facial expression of the subjects who self-designed did not give us much indication of the outcome. Some seemed quite pleased, others looked reserved.

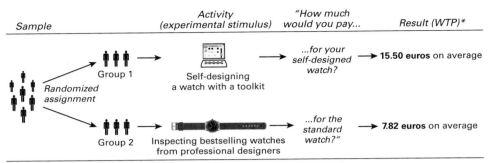

Figure 24.1

Measuring the value of self-design

Therefore, when we obtained the results, we were *greatly* surprised. Self-designs were valued significantly more than standard products and effect sizes were considerable: Bids for self-designed watches were 15.50 euros on average while the willingness to pay for standard best-seller watches was only 7.82 euros (figure 24.1). This means that self-designing a product with a toolkit results in an impressive value increment of 100 percent—despite their technical and functional identity! In sports, one would call this a walkover against the favorites. Recall that subjects in the experiment were business students without any training in product design and their bids were no "cheap talk." The self-designing processes took students only 13 minutes on average which is almost nothing compared to the time a professional designer usually spends on the same task (I asked a designer, and she estimated this time would be at least 2 to 5 weeks for such a watch design). The standard watches on the other hand were actually the designs that have proved to be the most appealing of the many hundred watch designs in the Austrian market, designed by highly paid professional designers of the leading watch manufacturer *Swatch*. Obviously the toolkit empowered customers *considerably*.

The findings prompted questions. Albeit the realistic measurement of willingness to pay—is 8 euros respectively 15 euros not quite a low sum for a watch of the Swatch class? After all, these watches are sold at a much higher market price of around 30 to 40 euros. Might it be that for any reason the measurement method we employed constituted an unfair disadvantage only for the standard watches? Buying a watch on a university campus is uncommon. Theoretically this might have affected the bids regarding the standard watch more.

Although we saw no particular reason why this should have been the case, we wanted to rule out this possibility. Therefore we conducted another experiment with 413 students (independent from the other sample), again randomly split in two groups, one being self-designers and bidding for their "own" watches, the other being buyers of standard watch bestsellers. The difference to the experiment reported above is that we measured their willingness to pay for the respective watches in a different way, using the *Contingent Valuation Method* (CVM) (for details of the study, see Franke and Piller 2004). In this method, subjects are asked how much they would pay if they *needed* a watch. This method does not preclude "cheap talk" but bears the advantage of adjusting for situational factors like the lack of a present need for the product at question or the locus of the purchase. Findings comforted doubts regarding the level of willingness to pay. Subjects in the first group indicated that they would be willing to pay 48.50 euros for their self-designed watches, subjects in the second group again showed a much lower willingness to pay of 24.50 euros on average. This is more in line with market prices and suggests that the findings of the experiments are realistic (it should not come as a surprise that willingness to pay for standard watches is still somewhat below market prices as indeed not everybody likes plastic watches). It is striking, however, that the value increment (98 percent) is almost identical with the value increment found by means of the Vickrey auction. We can conclude that the findings with regard to the value increment are independent of the method of measuring willingness to pay.

In this experiment, we also asked the group of self-designers for their willingness to pay (measured by the contingent valuation method) for standard watches. Technically, this experiment is a within-subject design: Every participant is subjected to both treatments. Our motivation was again a validation of the findings because in reality, people would also compare. Thus, if the pattern generated from independent groups (which is called a between-subject design) would remain stable in this within-group setting, this would give us greater confidence in the effect found. As reference we used two *well-selling* standard watches (not best-selling), thus slightly less attractive objects. The reason for this was that we wanted

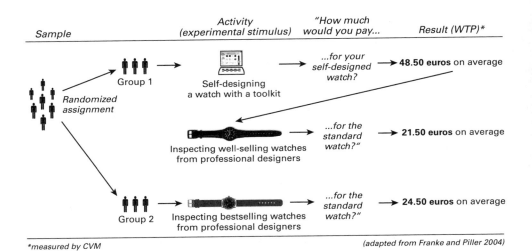

Figure 24.2

Validating the value of self-designed products with different methods

to validate our assumption that the watches identified as bestseller watches are more attractive than normal standard watches.

Findings showed the same pattern again: When we compared the self-designers' willingness to pay for "their own" watches (48.50 euros, as indicated above) with their willingness to pay for standard watches, the familiar patterns again became visible: for these standard watches, the user-designers were willing pay only 21.50 euros (figure 24.2). Again, the value difference is over 100 percent. Also our identification of best-sellers was supported as the value of the well-selling watches was signifi-cantly below the value of the bestselling watches.

Summarizing these experiments, we can say that the ability to self-design a watch with a relatively simple toolkit in a relatively short time period of only a few minutes generates an impressive subjective value for the user-designers.

A Closer Look at Individual Differences

Note that willingness to pay values reported are *average* values for the population studied. The standard deviations were relatively high: When we used the Vickrey auction, the mean of 15.50 euros had a standard

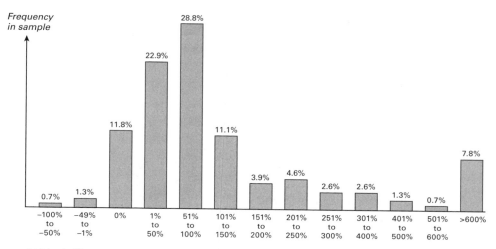

Additional willingness to pay in % for the self-designed product relative to willingness to pay for the standard product (intra-individual)

Figure 24.3

Individual differences in value generation by toolkits

deviation of 18.90 euros. In the experiment with the contingent valuation method of measuring willingness to pay (where the mean was 48.50 euros), we obtained a standard deviation of 50.00 euros. Technically this means that data are spread out over a large range of values—meaning there are huge differences among users. Some users really cared a lot for their self-designed products, whereas others did not derive much benefit.

Figure 24.3 displays these individual differences. We calculated the increment in willingness to pay for a self-designed product and the standard product on the individual level. The x-axis denotes the interval in which in this individual increment falls. A negative value means that the user preferred the standard product over the self-designed watch, a positive value that the opposite was the case. On the y-axis we computed the percentage of study participants who fall into this category.

We see that the distribution is fairly normal distributed. Only 2 percent of the users favored the standard watches over their own designs and 12 percent saw no difference in subjective value—for them the self-designed watch and the standard watch were of equal meaning. For the overwhelming majority (86 percent), however, self-designing resulted in a positive value increment. Most users reported an increase in value in the area of 50 to 100 percent. It is interesting, however, that the distribution has such a long tail. Obviously there is also a considerable number of users who prefer their self-designed watch several hundred percent over the bestselling standard watch in the market. The most extreme relationship was 4,800 percent—in this case the user's willingness to pay for a standard watch was only 1 euro while the willingness to pay for his self-designed individualized watch was 48 euros. The user explained: "Normally, I would not buy watches in this category. I would rather like a watch for my lifetime than buy a cheap watch every year."

Obviously 49 euros sounds less grandiose than 4,800 percent. But this particular person would be someone who might start to consider buying a watch in this quality segment, which he had not beforehand. 49 euros indicates that he is indeed interested in such a watch, whereas a willingness of 1 euro can be translated in "I have no interest in standard plastic watches unless they are essentially free." From such examples we can conclude that letting users self-design their products would not only increases their willingness to pay, but could turn people not interested in a product category into potential buyers.

However, does the picture change if we take the general market price for watches of this quality (35 euros) as reference point and not the individual willingness to pay for the standard model? This value increment is not sensitive to unrealistically low sums users are willing to pay for standard products—it informs about the additional value compared to the market price for standard watches as it is now. For a producer this might even be more interesting than the increment we calculated before because it tells what *premium* users are willing to pay for their self-designed products. Again, we find that only a minority of 8.5 percent reports that their willingness to pay for "their own" watch is lower than or similar to the market price in this quality segment. Over 90 percent of the subjects in the sample reported to be willing to pay a price premium, and over 50 percent declared they would pay more than twice the price for standard watches of the same technical quality. Interpreting these figures, we must not forget that usually firms are content with market shares far below 100 percent. So if we only consider the 10 percent top segment of users in the sample who proved to be really keen on getting a self-designed product (recall that our sample was not recruited upon the a priori interest in self-design), the average willingness to pay again jumps notably. For the

10 percent segment of hardcore self-design aficionados among students we found an average additional willingness to pay of 750 percent! For managers who usually struggle hard to realize an advance in prices of a handful of percent these figures must sound like a fairytale.

Just Watches or Just Everything?

The obvious next question is if these findings are contingent on the specific product category—plastic watches—or if they point to a general phenomenon. In order to address this question, a number of colleagues and I launched a series of studies that replicated the findings in different product categories and accordingly also using different toolkits. Products ranged from low-price goods such as T-shirts to high-price products involving extensive decision processes such as kitchens, and they ranged from hedonic products used in public such as scarves or skis to utilitarian products consumed in private such as breakfast cereals or newspapers. Also the samples varied. Beyond student samples, we also used a large sample representative for Austrian citizens (Franke et al. 2009). Finally, we also varied the measurement of willingness to pay and included the use of Vickrey auctions, the contingent valuation method (Voelckner 2006), and so called *BDM auctions* (Becker, DeGroot, and Marschak 1964; Wertenbroch and Skiera 2002). Like the Vickrey auction, the BDM auction method is a nonhypothetical measurement often used in economic and marketing research. The difference between the two methods is that BDM forces subjects to buy the product directly on spot if their bid is higher than a price randomly drawn from an urn (for the price drawn). If the bid is lower, the individual cannot buy the product. Also this method makes the individuals reveal their real maximum willingness to pay. Finally, we also altered the reference objects. Not always was it possible to determine the bestselling or even just particularly successful standard products, and therefore we used average products or products recommended by market experts.

The general pattern of the 15 experiments with a total of over 5,000 participants is impressively stable: Despite the identical technical quality and thus a similar "objective" value of the products, self-designing with a toolkit results in a considerable increase of the subjective value of the resulting self-designed product when compared to standard products (table 24.2). In 15 out of 15 studies, a highly significant and positive increase in willingness to pay became visible. On average, the increase in willingness to pay is 89 percent. The lowest premium is 19 percent, measured in a study of individualized newspapers, where the solution space of the toolkit was unusually small. The highest premium is 208 percent, obtained from users who self-designed scarves. Also note that in virtually every study the standard deviations are quite high, pointing to huge differences among individuals.

Further Value-Generating Effects by Toolkits

So far we focused on the direct value-creating effect of toolkits—the value users obtained from getting their own self-designed and individual products. The price premium user-designers were willing to pay for such products is certainly the most important effect. However, there are also indirect effects of toolkit-use. If users perceive the self-designing experience and the resulting product outcome as something positive, it is plausible that they carry these positive emotions over to the brand or the company and potentially also to other products of the company. Thus leading thinkers, as among them Peppers and Rogers (1997), Wind and Rangaswamy (2001), and Reichheld and Schefter (2000), argue that self-design with toolkits might strengthen the customer–company relationship.

My colleague Martin Schreier from WU (then my habilitation student), his habilitation student Ulrike Kaiser (then my doctoral student), and Chezy Ofir (Hebrew University and Bocconi University) studied these indirect effects empirically. In a series of sophisticated experiments they confirmed that self-designing a product indeed leads to an increased valuation for a standard product that comes under the same brand name (though not self-designed). They formed two groups. The self-design group was asked to design their own muesli mix, using a real toolkit. The second group had the task of choosing one of 10 ready-made mixes made by the same company and an identical brand name. The products then were manufactured according to the order of the individual users and shipped to them. After a time long enough to allow participants trying and experiencing the mueslis, they measured the willingness to pay for a brand extension, namely a muesli bar under the same brand umbrella using the realistic BDM measurement method. The willingness to pay in the first group was 2.51 euros, and in the second only 1.86 euros. In other words, having self-designed an *individual* product with a toolkit increases the willingness to pay for a *standard* product with the same brand but in a different product category and obviously independent from any self-designing activities by an astonishing rate of 35 percent! In the course of the experiments, they found that the reason for this effect was the increased attachment to the brand, resulting from self-designing (Kaiser et al. 2011). This means that toolkits have important further value-generating effects.

What Follows from All This?

The empirical evidence presented in this chapter should demonstrate that in many seemingly saturated markets there still is pretty much "money on the table." It can be skimmed if companies provide their users with tool-kits that allow them to self-design products. Despite the time and effort involved, customers were willing to pay considerable price premiums for their individual products. Recall again that the data we used is unusually "hard." Participants in many of the studies not only *reported* to be willing to pay, they actually *paid* the sums. Also we did *not* sample subjects with a particular a priori interest in self-design or self-designed products (which would have created a bias favoring self-designing and high premiums). Participants in the some experiments were normal students who participated in the experiments for a small compensation—thus it is fair to assume that they were not particularly wealthy or lavish. In other experiments, we have used nationally representative samples. Also consider that the toolkits we used were not "optimized" for maximizing the benefits from self-designing. We took what was available on the web, and in most cases our impression was that toolkits could easily be improved so that they even might generate more value for their users. Finally, the high number of 15 separate studies with a total of over 5,000 participants reduces the risk that the patterns found are just a coincidence to practically nil.

For producing firms this means that outsourcing product design to the users by employing the toolkit business model can be a way to increase prices for their products. Consider how often managers complain about stiff competition and seemingly inevitably eroding market prices—particularly also in such consumer markets as we have analyzed. Think of how rare it is that companies actually manage to raise prices, and if so, how high the raises are. At the same time, one should not forget that an effective increase in prices of a few percent multiply to a much, much greater increase in EBIT margins. Of course, firms could use the increased value also for attracting new customers instead of charging price premiums—those customers who had bought products from competitors or in other product categories beforehand. The case of the user who was willing to pay only 1 euro for a standard plastic watch (thereby stating that he simply had no interest in this product) but 48 euros for his or her self-designed plastic watch is not a single case. In sum, offering customers the possibility of self-designing the product appears as an unusually promising market strategy and business model that allows to increasing turnovers.

Naturally, managers deciding whether to exploit this opportunity or not of course must make an estimation if the increased benefits exceeds increased cost which include setting up and maintaining the toolkit interface, costs of producing lot sizes of one, and strategic costs and risks. However, in the past years we have seen huge advances in production technologies such as flexible manufacturing systems and modular product structures, coupled with constant costs for smaller lot sizes (e.g., Duray et al. 2000). The Internet has decreased the cost of direct and individualized communication with customers and facilitated inexpensive new forms of interaction (Ansari and Mela 2003; Sheth et al. 2000). The monetary costs of individualized offerings are likely to continue declining, allowing the conclusion that empowering users with toolkits that allow effective self-design will be a mega-trend in very many industries.

Which Factors Are Responsible for the High Value Generated?

From a research perspective, the obvious next question is *why exactly* users are willing to pay such high price premiums for their self-designed products. If we know more about the reasons for their behavior, we should also be able to give more precise advice for managers how toolkits should be designed in order to allow to skimming the customers' willingness to pay most effectively.

If we have a better understanding of the factors driving the value generation by self-design, we can also better generalize into other markets. Although we analyzed a fair number of product areas already, and even if we would continue this with increased resources in more and more markets in the future, there will always be more markets missing than markets being examined. If instead we discover which underlying factors cause the value increment, we can infer that in markets characterized by similar structures and for users with similar motives there might be a high probability that self-design with toolkits generates great value.

So why exactly are users willing to pay such high price premiums? In this overview, we can only briefly touch the ensuing studies on this issue. Basically one can model the value users attribute to self-designed products as the result of an economic equation of costs and benefits. The first factor delivering value is the increased preference fit of the self-designed products. A product tailored to my very wants and needs should deliver more value to me than a product where I have to compromise. This *preference fit hypothesis* is a core assumption of the mass customization literature and recently received clear empirical support (Franke et al. 2009). Second, an individual, self-designed product often satisfies the psychological motive of need for uniqueness. In a world of digitalization and unlimited reproduction possibilities, the desire for owning authentic, exclusive, one-of-its-kind objects might increase. Toolkits with their almost infinite solution spaces offer the possibility to get unique and personal products. Thus the perceived uniqueness of the self-designed product often contributes to the value attribution, independent from the preference fit achieved (Franke and Schreier 2008). Third, we must not forget that a self-designed product has also a totally different genesis than a ready-made, off-the-shelf standard product. Its design was made by the individual users themselves! This increased involvement in the process and factors such as pride, feelings of accomplishment and control, lead to a higher identification with the product—which in turn fosters the subjective value attribution by the user. This "I designed it myself effect" also was clearly confirmed in a series of experiments (Franke et al. 2010). Finally, as "there is no such thing as a free lunch," self-designing a product also involves costs for the user. The main cost components are the time and the cognitive effort of handling the toolkit, and the subjective risk (Dellaert and Stremersch 2005).

Table 24.2
Value increment achieved by self-designing the product relative to standard products of similar technical quality

Product category	Experimental design	Reference object	Sample	Measurement of WTP	WTP for self-designed product (std. dev.)	WTP for standard product (std. dev.)	Value increment	P
Breakfast cereals (Franke, Keinz, Steger 2009)	Within-subject	Popular standard products	n = 209 representative Austrian citizens	CVM	3.16 euros (1.08)	2.11 euros (0.84)	+ 50%	< 0.001
Carving skis (Franke, Keinz, Steger 2009)	Within-subject	Popular standard products	n = 201 representative Austrian citizens	CVM	282.85 euros (147.67)	211.82 euros (107.51)	+ 34%	< 0.001
Cell phone cover (Franke and Schreier 2008)	Within-subject	Average standard products	n = 127 students	Vickrey	9.43 euros (9.61)	3.07 euros (4.43)	+ 207%	< 0.001
Cell phone cover (Schreier 2006)	Within-subject	Realistic and appealing standard products	n = 60 students	Vickrey	11.40 euros (9.50)	3.70 euros (4.50)	+ 208%	< 0.001

Table 24.2 (continued)

Product category	Experimental design	Reference object	Sample	Measurement of WTP	WTP for self-designed product (std. dev.)	WTP for standard product (std. dev.)	Value increment	P
Fountain pens (Franke, Keinz, Steger 2009)	Within-subject	Popular standard products	$n = 200$ representative Austrian citizens	CVM	59.12 euros (39.57)	42.21 euros (27.54)	+ 40%	< 0.001
Kitchens (Franke, Keinz, Steger 2009)	Within-subject	Popular standard products	$n = 198$ representative Austrian citizens	CVM	3406.76 euros (1369.04)	2481.80 euros (954.22)	+ 37%	< 0.001
Newspapers (Franke, Keinz, Steger 2009)	Within-subject	Popular standard products	$n = 231$ representative Austrian citizens	CVM	1.02 euros (0.66)	0.75 euros (0.52)	+ 36%	< 0.001
Newspapers (Franke, Keinz, Steger 2009)	Within-subject	product expert solution	$n = 2522$ representative Austrian citizens	CVM	1.00 euros (0.57)	0.84 euros (0.56)	+ 19%	< 0.001

Table 24.2 (continued)

Product category	Experimental design	Reference object	Sample	Measurement of WTP	WTP for self-designed product (std. dev.)	WTP for standard product (std. dev.)	Value increment	P
Scarves (Franke and Schreier 2010)	Within-subject	Average standard products	$n = 186$ students	Vickrey	10.21 Euros (9.23)	5.35 euros (5.93)	+ 91%	< 0.001
Scarves (Schreier 2006)	Within-subject	realistic and appealing standard products	$n = 62$ students	Vickrey	10.10 euros (9.40)	4.90 euros (4.70)	+ 106%	< 0.001
Skis (Franke, Schreier, and Kaiser 2010)	Within-subject	Average standard products	$n = 116$ students	BDM	74.42 euros (56.85)	45.89 euros (43.58)	+ 62%	< 0.001

Fulfilling the Promise of Toolkits

Concluding, we can say that Eric von Hippel's vision of toolkits as a means of democratizing innovation is manifested by hard empirical data. If users are given the possibility for defining their products themselves, this indeed results in much greater value. It remains to managers to fulfill the promise of toolkits by offering more and better toolkits to users—a task where the current state in most industries cannot be termed satisfactory. Many of the toolkits have quite restricted solution spaces, many are not really user-friendly, many focus on the low-price segment only. Particularly larger firms are often reluctant to introduce toolkits (Thomke and von Hippel 2002; Franke and Schreier 2002). One reason may be that incumbents generally are relatively slow adopters of radical new technology. Christensen (1997) specifies several reasons this problem, ranging from cultural and psychological factors (arrogance, bureaucracy, short-term thinking, etc.) to economic aspects (high fixed costs forcing companies to focus on large markets only, reluctance to turn past investments into sunk costs, etc.). Firms may also be worried because they fear that outsourcing a valuable capability might constitute a major competitive disadvantage (Thomke and von Hippel 2002). However, given the huge potential benefits probably a new entrant will introduce a toolkit. Or, as Eric von Hippel in his radical mind might welcome even more, *users* take over the task of designing toolkits, further reducing the economic justification for the existence of producers.

Notes

1. In a broader sense, many business software programs like Word, Excel, and Powerpoint can be considered toolkits—they involve tools that allow the user to self-design an entity (a text, a calculation, or a presentation) and give instant feedback on the outcome.

2. There has been much discussion in how far toolkits allow for innovations or "just" for new combinations within a limited solution space. It is true that toolkits restrict solutions possible—a T-shirt toolkit cannot be used to invent a better steam engine. Also the emphasis of many toolkits today is rather on personalization and individualization than on innovation. But claiming that toolkits do generally not allow for innovation misses Schumpeter's (1911) argument that often innovations are nothing but new combinations.

3. *IdTown* is not existing any longer, but readers can go to www.factory121.com to get an impression of a similar toolkit in the watch market.

References

Ansari, A., and C. F. Mela. 2003. E-Customization. *JMR, Journal of Marketing Research* 40 (2): 131–45.

Becker, G. M., M. H. Degroot, and J. Marschak. 1964. Measuring utility by a single-response sequential method. *Behavioral Science* 9 (3): 226–32.

Christensen, C. M. 1997. *The Innovator's Dilemma: When New Technologies Cause Great Firms to Fall.* Boston: Harvard Business School Press.

Cook, S. 2008. The contribution revolution. *Harvard Business Review* 86 (10): 60–69.

Cox, J. C., B. Roberson, and V. L. Smith. 1982. Theory and behavior of single object auctions. In *Research in Experimental Economics*, vol. 2, ed. Vernon L. Smith, 375–88. Greenwich, CT: JAI Press.

Dellaert, B. G. C., and S. Stremersch. 2005. Marketing mass-Customized products: Striking a balance between utility and complexity. *JMR, Journal of Marketing Research* 42 (2): 219–27.

Duray, R., P. T. Ward, G. W. Milligan, and W. L. Berry. 2000. Approaches to mass customization: Configurations and empirical validation. *Journal of Operations Management* 18 (6): 605–25.

Edwards, A. L. 1957. *The Social Desirability Variable in Personality Assessments and Research.* New York: Dryden.

Fang, E. 2008. Customer participation and the trade-off between new product innovativeness and speed to market. *Journal of Marketing* 72 (4): 90–104.

Franke, N., and F. Piller. 2004. Value creation by toolkits for user innovation and design: The case of the watch market. *Journal of Product Innovation Management* 21 (6): 401–15.

Franke, N., and M. Schreier. 2002. Entrepreneurial opportunities with toolkits for user innovation and design. *International Journal on Media Management* 4 (4): 225–34.

Franke, N., and M. Schreier. 2008. Product uniqueness as a driver of customer utility in mass customization. *Marketing Letters* 19 (2): 93–107.

Franke, N., and M. Schreier. 2010. Why customers value mass-customized products: The importance of process effort and enjoyment. *Journal of Product Innovation Management* 27 (7): 1020–31.

Franke, N., and E. von Hippel. 2003. Satisfying heterogeneous user needs via innovation toolkits: The case of Apache Security software. *Research Policy* 32 (7): 1199–1215.

Franke, N., P. Keinz, and C. J. Steger. 2009. Testing the value of customization: When do customers really prefer products tailored to their preferences? *Journal of Marketing* 73 (5): 103–21.

Franke, N., M. Schreier, and U. Kaiser. 2010. The "I designed it myself" effect in mass customization. *Management Science* 65 (1): 125–40.

Hill, K. 2003. Customers love/hate customization. *CRM-Daily.com* (online e-zine).

Hoffman, E., D. J. Menkhaus, D. Chakravarti, R. F. Field, and G. D. Whipple. 1993. Using laboratory experimental auctions in marketing research: A case study of packaging for fresh beef. *Marketing Science* 12 (3): 318–38.

Huffman, C., and B. E. Kahn. 1998. Variety for sale: Mass customization or mass confusion? *Journal of Retailing* 74 (4): 491–513.

Kahn, B. E. 1998. Dynamic relationships with customers: High-variety strategies. *Journal of the Academy of Marketing Science* 26 (1): 45–53.

Kaiser, U., C. Ofir, and M. Schreier. 2011. Self-customization effects on brand extension. Working paper.

Loewenstein, G. 1999. Experimental economics from the vantage-point of behavioural economics. *Economic Journal* 109 (453): F25–F34.

O'Hern, M., and A. Rindfleisch. 2010. Customer co-creation: A typology and research agenda. In *Review of Marketing Research*, vol. 6, ed. Naresh K. Malhotra, 84–106. Howard House: Emerald Group Publishing Limited.

Peppers, D., and M. Rogers. 1997. *Enterprise One to One*. New York: Currency-Doubleday.

Pine, J. B. 1993. *Mass Customization—The New Frontier in Business Competition*. Boston: Harvard Business School Press.

Prahalad, C. K., and V. Ramaswamy. 2004. *The Future of Competition: Co-Creating Unique Value with Customers*. Boston: Harvard Business School Press.

Reichheld, F. F., and P. Schefter. 2000. E-Loyalty. Your secret weapon on the web. *Harvard Business Review* 78 (4): 105–13.

Schreier, M. 2006. The value increment of mass-customized products: An empirical assessment. *Journal of Consumer Behaviour* 5 (4): 317–27.

Schumpeter, J. 1911. *Theorie der wirtschaftlichen Entwicklung*. Berlin: Duncker Humblot.

Sharma, A., and J. N. Sheth. 2004. Web-based marketing. The coming revolution in marketing thought and strategy. *Journal of Business Research* 57 (7): 696–702.

Sheth, J. N., R. S. Sisodia, and A. Sharma. 2000. The antecedents and consequences of customer-centric marketing. *Journal of the Academy of Marketing Science* 28 (1): 55–66.

Simonson, I. 2005. Determinants of customers' responses to customized offers: Conceptual framework and research propositions. *Journal of Marketing* 69 (1): 32–45.

Thomke, S., and E. von Hippel. 2002. Customers as innovators: A new way to create value. *Harvard Business Review* 80 (4): 74–81.

Vickrey, W. S. 1961. Counter speculation: Auctions and competitive sealed tenders. *Journal of Finance* 16 (1): 8–37.

Voelckner, F. 2006. An empirical comparison of methods for measuring consumers' willingness to pay. *Marketing Letters* 17 (2): 137–49.

von Hippel, E. 2005. *Democratizing Innovation.* Cambridge: MIT Press.

von Hippel, E. 2001. User toolkits for innovation. *Journal of Product Innovation Management* 18 (4): 247–57.

von Hippel, E. 1998. Economics of product development by users: The impact of "sticky" local information. *Management Science* 44 (5): 629–44.

von Hippel, E., and R. Katz. 2002. Shifting innovation to users via toolkits. *Management Science* 48 (7): 821–33.

Wertenbroch, K., and B. Skiera. 2002. Measuring consumer willingness to pay at the point of purchase. *JMR, Journal of Marketing Research* 39 (2): 228–41.

Wind, J., and V. Mahajan. 2001. *Digital Marketing: Global Strategies from the World's Leading Experts.* New York: Wiley.

Wind, J., and A. Rangaswamy. 2001. Customerization: The next revolution in mass customization. *Journal of Interactive Marketing* 15 (1): 13–32.

Winer, R. S. 1999. Experimentation in the 21st century: The importance of external validity. *Journal of the Academy of Marketing Science* 27 (3): 349–58.

Zipkin, P. 2001. The limits of mass customization. *Sloan Management Review* 42 (3): 81–87.

25

Crowdfunding: Evidence on the Democratization of Start-up Funding

Ethan Mollick and Venkat Kuppuswamy

As the process of innovation has become democratized (von Hippel 2005), so too has the commercialization of innovation—the process of creating new goods and services, usually through entrepreneurship. This has been driven by a range of changes that make starting and running new ventures cheaper and easier including advances in production technology ranging from 3D printing to software tools; outsourcing that has reduced the human capital required to launch companies; and communities that increasingly support the start-up process. Though much has been democratized, there has historically been a gap around one critical aspect of the start-up process: the funding of start-ups. In this chapter we use survey data to argue that crowdfunding—the provision of financial resources online through many small contributions by large numbers of individuals (Agrawal et al. 2013; Mollick 2014)—is allowing the funding of start-ups, too, to become democratized.

To examine this potential, we conducted a survey of design, technology, and video games projects that attempted to raise money using the largest crowdfunding site, Kickstarter, before mid-2012. We found that non-equity crowdfunding can indeed support more traditional entrepreneurship. A very high percentage (over 90 percent) of successful projects remained ongoing ventures, 32 percent of which reported yearly revenues of over $100,000 a year after the Kickstarter campaign[1] and added an average of 2.2 employees per successful project. The survey also suggested that crowdfunding provided many potential benefits beyond the immediate funds sourced from the crowd, including better access to customers, press, employees, and outside funders. While the 270 successful companies in our sample raised relatively modest and highly variable amounts from crowdfunding individually (mean = $111,469, s.d. = $641,026), this money was raised from 355,135 people—a far cry from the oligarchic few who traditionally control the funding process associated with developing and commercializing innovation.

Oligarchic Funding: Venture Capital and Angel Investors

For at least a quarter of a century, the funding of innovative organizations has largely been defined by the Silicon Valley model (Kenney and Burg 1999, Saxenian 1996). In that model, venture capital firms (VC) and, to a lesser extent, angel investors serve as key actors, and are often considered to be the most important entities in the system outside of the entrepreneurs themselves (Ferrary and Granovetter 2009; Kenney and Burg 1999). VC has held this critical position in the institutional environment of technology entrepreneurship since at least the 1970s, and, though the industry has expanded and contracted several times since then, the nature of venture capital itself has been fairly stable (Gompers and Lerner 2001, 2004).

The traditional *venture capital cycle* (Gompers and Lerner 2004) begins when venture capitalists locate firms of interest, primarily through network connections and direct contact with entrepreneurs. Out of this population, venture capitalists select firms for financial investment based on expected return and fit with an existing portfolio (Amit et al. 1998; Baum and Silverman 2004; Gompers and Lerner 2004; Shane and Venkataraman 2003). After this initial investment, the venture capital firm then plays an active role in shaping the portfolio firms, granting them reputational effects from VC endorsement (Hsu 2004; Stuart et al. 1999), providing them monitoring and governance (Gompers and Lerner 2004, Lerner 2012), and facilitating access to additional resources for the firm (Baum and Silverman 2004; Ferrary and Granovetter 2009). Since VC firms sit at the center of so many networks of influence, they fulfill a critical role in the innovation process of high-technology ventures (Ferrary and Granovetter 2009).

Venture capitalists, by choosing which firms to provide resources to, help determine which entrepreneurs (and ultimately which innovations) will succeed. Evidence suggests that venture capitalists are quite efficient at the selection of promising technological opportunities relative to other sorts of corporate entities (Kortum and Lerner 2000; Lerner 2002; Ueda 2004). However, the venture capital process depends on just a few thousand experts worldwide concentrated in just a few regions. Furthermore venture capital decisions are often made on relatively little data, and are subject to cognitive biases and limitations on knowledge (Baum and Silverman 2004; Ferrary and Granovetter 2009).

One particularly well-studied bias is geographic. Venture capital investments are highly concentrated in just a few areas, where both entrepreneurs and venture capital firms are located (Chen et al. 2009, Kenney and Burg 1999; Owen-Smith and Powell 2004; Shane and Cable 2002; Stuart and Sorenson 2003, 2008). There are many reasons for this clustering, including spillover benefits and talented pools of successful entrepreneurs (Feldman 2001; Kenney and Burg 1999; Owen-Smith and Powell 2004). However, part of the reasons why VC selection is limited in this regard is the limited breadth of VC networks and the necessity of face-to-face interaction. Specifically, VCs prefer to have direct access to and oversight of portfolio firms, and such monitoring is significantly easier when firms are within a driving distance of the office of the VC (Chen et al. 2009). Along these lines, Sorenson and Stuart (2005) find that the average distance between a lead VC and their investment is 70 miles.

A second set of biases is related to the gender of entrepreneurs: though women make up over 40 percent of all business owners in the United States, less than 6 percent of venture capital funding has historically gone to companies with female CEOs, and only 1.3 percent of VC-backed companies have female founders (Canning et al. 2012; Greene et al. 2003; Harrison and Mason 2007, Stuart and Sorenson 2008). Furthermore only 14 percent of all venture capitalists are women, and many female entrepreneurs believe that there are strong gender biases in VC funding (Miller 2010). These biases may be due to gender prejudices. However, scholars have also suggested that an alternate cause of these biases is homophily—male entrepreneurs are more likely to be selected by male venture capitalists based on shared networks and social preferences (Ruef et al. 2003; Stuart and Sorenson 2008).

Consequently, to successfully receive VC funding and the resources that follow, entrepreneurs have been required to possess the right background, network ties, and signals of preparation. It has also pushed founders toward male-dominated teams, and helped increase agglomeration. However, a new alternative approach to funding has emerged in the form of crowdfunding.

Democratized Funding: Crowdfunding[2]

Crowdfunding refers to the efforts by entrepreneurial individuals and groups—cultural, social, and for-profit—to fund their ventures by drawing on relatively small contributions from a relatively large number of individuals using the Internet, without standard financial intermediaries (Mollick 2014; Schwienbacher and Larralde 2010). Crowdfunding draws inspiration from concepts like microfinance (Morduch 1999) and crowdsourcing (Poetz and Schreier 2012) but represents its own unique category of fundraising, facilitated by a growing number of Internet platforms dedicated to the cause.

There are at least four main types of crowdfunding: The first type is donation-based crowdfunding, a patronage model where funders represent philanthropists who expect no direct return for their donations. As a result this model is common in the context of charitable giving as well as the humanities. A second model, lending-based crowdfunding, is one where funds are offered as a loan, with the expectation of some rate of return on the capital invested. This can range from microloans made to individuals from the developing world, to more traditional peer-to-peer lending.

A third approach, commonly called reward-based crowdfunding, has been the dominant form of crowdfunding through 2014. In this approach funders are given a tangible but nonfinancial reward in return for their financial support. This can include being credited in a movie, having creative input into a product under development, or being given an opportunity to meet the creators of a project. Alternately, for many reward-based crowdfunding projects, funders represent early customers who contribute in order to gain early access to the product being pitched, or to obtain a lower price for it. The "pre-selling" of products to early customers is a common feature of those crowdfunding projects that more traditionally resemble entrepreneurial ventures, such as projects producing novel software, hardware, or consumer products.

The final category is equity crowdfunding, made legal in the United States by the Jumpstart Our Business Start-ups Act, passed in April 2012, and previously introduced in other countries. This form of funding treats funders as investors, giving them equity stakes or similar consideration in return for their funding. Regulation has generally slowed the development of equity crowdfunding, making it a very small part of crowdfunding in 2014, accounting for less than 5 percent of all crowdfunding investment (Massolution 2013). Equity crowdfunding is subject to high levels of regulation (Heminway and Hoffman 2010), and the eventual adoption of the approach relative to other forms of crowdfunding is uncertain. Even in the absence of equity crowdfunding, the investor model of crowdfunding can take other forms. For example, funders may receive a share of the venture's future profits or royalties; a portion of returns from a future planned public offering or acquisition; or a share of a real estate investment, among other options.

Adding to this heterogeneity is the fact that crowdfunding encompasses a variety of goals, both for potential backers and for project creators. Many crowdfunded projects seek to raise small amounts of capital, often under $1,000, to pursue a specific one-time project (e.g., an event). In these cases capital is often provided by friends and family. Other projects seek to raise hundreds of thousands, or even millions, of dollars in order to launch ongoing businesses. Furthermore funding may not represent the only goal of project creators. As an example of other goals, crowdfunding has been used by founders to demonstrate demand for a proposed product, which can lead to funding from more traditional sources. This objective is well illustrated by the Pebble *smart watch*, which was initially rejected for venture capital funding but was able to secure a large amount of VC funding after its Kickstarter campaign (Dingman 2013). Conversely, a lack of demand makes it easy for founders to "fail quickly" if they see little interest in a project, without the need to invest additional capital or effort.

Essentially crowdfunding offers a method of funding entrepreneurial ventures that differs in almost all aspects from venture capital funding. First, rather than being oligopolistic, it is democratic—over six million people have funded projects on Kickstarter alone. Second, as opposed to the tightly knit VC community, crowdfunding backers are loosely organized, if at all. Third, compared to the closed networks of Silicon Valley, in crowdfunding almost all communication between those seeking funding and potential backers occurs in open, online communities. Fourth, crowdfunding in its current form involves no equity or monitoring rights;[3] backers have little to no further influence over organizations they backed, and gain no return other than the potential of a future product.

The process of crowdfunding is also very different from fundraising through venture capital. Individuals seeking funding publicaly list their projects, along with a fundraising window, and their desired capital raise (called a "goal" in crowdfunding). This public information also includes a description of what they hope to accomplish with the money, rewards they offer in return for funding, and any other material they hope will make the case for their efforts, including videos and pictures of prototypes. The project initiator then tries to promote the project, using social networks, media, influential individuals, and other means. The goal is to attract individual backers, or funders, that will pledge to support the project if the fundraising goal is met. There is often a substantial dialogue that develops between project proposers and potential backers, as comments, questions, and discussions take place on both the crowdfunding website, as well as external venues such as Twitter and Facebook. If the project achieves its goal, the money is transferred to the proposer, who has no legal obligation to the backers to complete the project, though, in practice, almost all projects make a serious effort at achieving their goals (Mollick 2014).

Due to its novelty, there are relatively few academic studies of crowdfunding as of the time of this writing. A first description of crowdfunding was offered by Schweinbacher and Larralde (2010) and there have been attempts to build a theoretical model of when individuals would chose to crowdfund (Agrawal et al. 2013; Belleflamme et al. 2014). Other studies have examined how project characteristics, timing, geography, and other characteristics affect backer contributions (Agrawal et al. 2010; Ahlers et al. 2012; Burtch et al. 2013; Kuppuswamy and Bayus 2013; Mollick 2014). The field is still nascent, however, and more work is needed.

Given its novelty, then, why do we care about crowdfunding? This question is especially relevant, as a relatively small proportion of individuals seeking crowdfunding are traditional entrepreneurs, with crowdfunding being increasingly popular in the arts and other fields (in 2012, 10 percent of Sundance films were crowdfunded; see Dvorkin 2013). However, even in its nascent state, crowdfunded entrepreneurs have proved to be extremely innovative, and have tapped into the same communities that seem so important in user innovation (Lakhani and von

Hippel 2003; West and Lakhani 2008). According to industry experts, many of the most important projects in consumer electronics in recent years have been funded through crowdfunding, including novel 3D printers, electronic watches, video game consoles, and computer hardware (Jeffries 2013). Some of the most successful crowdfunded projects were even turned down by venture capitalists before successfully raising funding from sites such as Kickstarter (Jeffries 2013).

Even more important, crowdfunding democratizes the process of funding, allowing communities of users to band together to fund their projects. It offers a potential way to avoid the biases of venture capital. For example, Greenberg and Mollick (2014) found that women actually outperform men in crowdfunding, while women are disadvantaged in almost all other forms of raising capital. Similarly there is wider geographic dispersion in crowdfunding than in venture capital (Agrawal et al. 2010; Mollick 2014). Together, these factors suggest that crowdfunding, as a way of working around more oligarchic methods of funding, has the potential to allow innovators to more easily commercialize a wider range of projects.

In this chapter we are particularly interested in exactly these kinds of projects, where crowdfunding serves as a potential source of funding for new ventures. To that end, we conducted a survey of projects that raised funding on Kickstarter to examine the long-term implications of crowdfunding.

Study Methods

Our idea was to sample both successful and unsuccessful projects. In order to examine projects that most closely approximated more conventional start-up companies that might be funded by VC or angel investors, we limited our sample to three categories: technology, product design, and video games. We also examined only larger projects, seeking over $5,000 in funding, and those that completed funding between 2009 and July, 2012. This resulted in a sample of 596 successful and 1,509 failed projects. Of the failed projects, we randomly selected 550 for follow-up (for more information on this dataset, including how it was constructed and the factors that led to successful funding, see Mollick 2014).

We used Kickstarter's internal messaging feature to request project creators to complete on online survey. We followed up these initial messages with emails to creators, when their email addresses were publicaly available. For successful projects, we received responses from 230 subjects (response rate of 39 percent) and after accounting for duplicate and incomplete entries, we had complete response data from 158 projects (26.5 percent of the original sampling frame), although many other responses were substantially complete. Our response rate is in line with similar studies in the literature that have used web-based surveys (see Kriauciunas et al. 2011 for a comprehensive review of response rates). Statistical testing showed the successful respondents to be representative in terms of goals, funding, and other factors. Response rates for unsuccessful projects was lower, with 128 total responses (23.3 percent) of which 83 (15.1 percent) were complete. This subsample was on the lower bound of response rates published in the literature. We report results for the full sample, and separately report data for both successful and unsuccessful projects. See table 25.1 for a summary of this data we collected, and the appendix for an explanation of the variables.

Who Is Crowdfunding?

In the categories we examined, project creators were generally well educated, with 95 percent having at least some college experience. At the time they started their project, 42 percent were employed full time, and nearly 50 percent reported some form of self-employment (either founders of a company, independent contractors, or something else), and 46 percent reported incomes of below $50,000 a year in the year before their project (15 percent reported over $125,000). The average age of respondents was 35, and over 40 percent had children.

Consistent with other research, 84 percent of respondents from successful projects were male, as were 90 percent of respondents from failed projects (the video games, technology, and product design categories have higher percentages of males than other categories on Kickstarter, which were not featured in this study). Though the group was overwhelmingly male, other research has shown that females starting projects in technology, while rare, significantly outperform their male peers (Greenberg and Mollick 2014). Women are better represented in other categories that were not part of the study.

Why Are Innovators Crowdfunding?

Many creators saw their project as a first step to launching a business (59 percent). One theme running through our results is that crowdfunding is not just about the money received from backers—successful projects also receive other benefits. We asked our sample about why they chose to seek crowdfunding. Among successful projects, the most agreed-upon reason was "To see if there was demand for the project," followed by "As a way of marketing my project," and "To connect directly with a community of my fans or supporters." The answer "The project could not have been funded without raising the goal" was actually the fourth most popular answer, at 54 percent of respondents agreeing.

Additionally crowdfunding clearly goes beyond a convenient platform for asking for money from existing contacts. In the survey, 70 percent of creators either disagreed or strongly disagreed that their backers were "mostly family and friends." Only 3.5 percent of people strongly agreed with that statement.

What Happens after a Crowdfunding Campaign?

We collected a variety of outcome measures to help us judge the long-term success of crowdfunding.

First, we asked whether the organization was continuing to operate as of the end of December, 2013. Over 90 percent of projects were active at the time of the survey. A total of 38.5 percent of entities who successfully raised funds reported yearly revenues of $0 to $25,000, 24.5 percent reported $25,000 to $100,000, and 32 percent reported over $100,000. For the same group prior to the campaign, 44 percent of entities did not exist and 31 percent reported yearly revenues of 0 to $25,000, 13 percent reported $25,000 to $100,000, and 11 percent reported over $100,000. This suggests that crowdfunded ventures can turn into ongoing revenue-generating businesses.

We also asked whether projects raised additional money from venture capitalists, angel investors, or banks after the campaign concluded. While it was far from universal, crowdfunding did help a number of firms achieve further funding. Most common was additional self-funding (in over 20 percent of successful projects) or friends and family funding (in over 15 percent of successful projects), but outside risk capital in the forms of loans, venture capital, or angel investing occurred as well—15

Table 25.1
Summary statistics

	Variable	All projects			Unsuccessful projects			Successful projects		
		Obs	Mean	Std. dev.	Obs	Mean	Std. dev.	Obs	Mean	Std. dev.
Outcomes	Active entity	253	0.79	0.41	90	0.60	0.49	163	0.90	0.31
	Outside funding (VC, angels, banks, other companies)	223	0.18	0.38	86	0.09	0.29	137	0.23	0.42
	On-time delivery	167	0.31	0.46				167	0.31	0.46
	Benefit: additional funding	264	1.81	1.07	98	1.42	0.84	166	2.04	1.12
	Benefit: employees	264	1.49	0.85	98	1.33	0.67	166	1.58	0.93
	Benefit: publicity	265	2.78	1.16	98	1.92	1.04	167	3.28	0.90
	Benefit: customer base	264	2.58	1.17	98	1.62	0.87	166	3.15	0.94
Original project characteristics	Goal	341	31207	65676	128	36543	73427	213	28001	60500
	Featured project	341	0.10	0.30	128	0.00	0.00	213	0.16	0.37
	Duration	336	38.83	13.25	123	39.17	14.61	213	38.64	12.44
	Design	341	0.43	0.50	128	0.35	0.48	213	0.47	0.50

Table 25.1 (continued)

		All projects			Unsuccessful projects			Successful projects		
	Variable	Obs	Mean	Std. dev.	Obs	Mean	Std. dev.	Obs	Mean	Std. dev.
	Technology	341	0.29	0.46	128	0.34	0.48	213	0.26	0.44
	Proof of concept	341	0.96	0.19	128	0.95	0.23	213	0.97	0.17
	By name	341	0.43	0.50	128	0.35	0.48	213	0.48	0.50
	Endorsements	341	0.32	0.47	128	0.16	0.37	213	0.41	0.49
	Facebook friends	341	241.71	443.81	128	164.95	332.99	213	287.84	493.73
	Year 2010	341	0.06	0.25	128	0.08	0.27	213	0.06	0.23
	Year 2011	341	0.41	0.49	128	0.37	0.48	213	0.44	0.50
Entity variables	Project funded	341	0.62	0.48	128	0.00	0.00	213	1.00	0.00
	Entity objective: start of ongoing business	258	0.59	0.49	93	0.56	0.50	165	0.60	0.49
	Entity objective: new product from existing business	258	0.17	0.38	93	0.16	0.37	165	0.18	0.38
Completeness	Number of founders	258	1.58	1.22	93	1.31	0.71	165	1.73	1.41
	Degree of completeness: design	265	4.17	0.96	98	4.09	1.00	167	4.22	0.94

Table 25.1 (continued)

Variable	All projects			Unsuccessful projects			Successful projects		
	Obs	Mean	Std. dev.	Obs	Mean	Std. dev.	Obs	Mean	Std. dev.
Degree of completeness: financial plan	264	4.16	0.89	97	4.25	0.90	167	4.10	0.89
Degree of completeness: schedule	264	3.92	0.92	97	4.11	0.83	167	3.80	0.96
Degree of completeness: business plan	264	3.28	1.29	97	3.45	1.35	167	3.17	1.25
Degree of completeness: team	264	3.92	1.13	97	3.86	1.09	167	3.96	1.16

percent of successful projects raised angel funds, and around 3 percent raised venture capital. As reported in table 25.2, we found several factors that were positively correlated with the likelihood of outside funding at a statistically significant level (5 percent or below). Specifically, we found that projects with larger goals were most likely to achieve outside funding. Having a substantially complete business plan before fundraising also seemed to predict outside funding. In addition, projects where the creators had specific industry experience were three times as likely to get outside funding as those that did not have similar backgrounds. Finally, projects that succeed in their campaigns are more likely to gain outside funding than those that don't.

Crowdfunding was not just a way of attracting funding, it also provided other potential benefits to those seeking funding. We tracked four types of ex post benefits, all of which were measured using a 7-point Likert scale ranging from 1 ("not at all") to 7 ("very much"): *additional funding*, the extent to which a project "Raise[d] additional funds from outside sources after the campaign"; *employees*, the degree to which the campaign helped organizations "find and/or hire employees"; *publicity*, whether the campaign helped "bring press attention to my project"; and *customer base*, where we examined whether success helped "develop a customer base from those who contributed." Receiving press attention and building a customer base were both widely reported outcomes of crowdfunding campaigns. Figure 25.1 shows these benefits.

When we model the ex post benefits using an ordinal logit, as can be seen in table 25.2, we found several variables to have a positive association with the level of ex post benefits realized (at the 5 percent significance level or below). Projects that received these ex post benefits generally had higher goals, more funding, and more developed business plans. Outside endorsements and appropriate backgrounds were helpful in gaining benefits from the campaign beyond money. Successful campaigns also had more benefits.

While there were many positive impacts for the firms raising crowdfunding, those benefits did not always translate into delivering promised goods on schedule. The same as Mollick (2014), we found that delivery delays were common, and a few products had failed to deliver entirely to

Table 25.2
Impact of project characteristics on project outcomes, exponentiated form

	Active entity		Outside funding (VC, angels, bank, companies)		Ex post campaign benefits (Likert scale)			
Variables					Additional funding	Employee	Publicity	Customer base
Original project characteristics								
Log (goal)	1.6 (-0.962)	1.61 (-1.055)	6.688*** (-3.62)	8.667** (-6.058)	3.379** (-1.534)	4.783*** (-2.269)	4.607* (-3.153)	1.581 (-0.805)
Featured project	1.789 (-1.466)	2.651 (-2.921)	1.159 (-0.752)	0.961 (-0.648)	0.705 (-0.371)	5.942*** (-3.059)	1.016 (-0.0186)	1.367 (-1.487)
Duration	0.966* (-0.0147)	0.964* (—0.0138)	0.981 (-0.0157)	0.978 (-0.0172)	1.003 (-0.0119)	1.001 (-0.0117)	2.141 (-1.089)	1.009 (-0.0155)
Design	0.543 (-0.232)	0.371 (-0.199)	0.673 (-0.336)	0.914 (-0.56)	1.293 (-0.537)	0.417* (-0.173)	1.523 (-0.796)	0.989 (-0.567)
Technology	2.619 (-1.699)	2.111 (-1.45)	0.838 (-0.439)	1.163 (-0.71)	1.706 (-0.763)	0.406* (-0.186)	0.431 (-0.555)	1.133 (-0.631)
Proof of concept	3.534 (-3.198)	3.438 (-3.379)	0.479 (-0.453)	0.456 (-0.387)	0.625 (-0.429)	0.596 (-0.549)	0.883 (-0.354)	0.67 (-0.586)
By name	0.985 (-0.394)	0.756 (-0.311)	1.596 (-0.67)	3.076* (-1.574)	1.009 (-0.323)	0.987 (-0.354)	6.026* (-4.274)	1.774 (-0.806)
Endorsements	1.085 (-0.464)	1.088 (-0.473)	1.614 (-0.655)	1.646 (-0.795)	2.075* (-0.661)	1.514 (-0.543)	0.938 (-0.068)	2.682* (-1.283)

Table 25.2 (continued)

	Outside funding (VC, angels, bank, companies)				Ex post campaign benefits (Likert scale)			
Variables	Active entity				Additional funding	Employee	Publicity	Customer base
Log (Facebook friends)	1.038 (-0.0625)	1.007 (-0.063)	1.056 (-0.0699)	1.005 (-0.0754)	0.972 (-0.0518)	0.993 (-0.0572)	2.556 (-2.005)	1.098 (-0.0849)
Year 2010	0.184* (-0.126)	0.139** (-0.1)	1.06 (-1.39)	1.855 (-1.677)	2.407 (-1.591)	1.317 (-1.023)	1.482 (-0.685)	1.434 (-1.037)
Year 2011	2.328 (-1.046)	1.978 (-0.888)	2.647* (-1.216)	2.743 (-1.507)	1.645 (-0.549)	2.015 (-0.737)	17.20*** (-8.567)	1.194 (-0.537)
Project funded	7.050*** (-3.057)	6.328*** (-2.878)	2.762 (-1.493)	3.626* (-2.056)	4.716*** (-1.832)	1.644 (-0.696)	1.036 (-0.497)	27.32*** (-13.72)
Entity objective: start of ongoing business		1.703 (-0.778)		2.424 (-1.484)	1.614 (-0.594)	1.723 (-0.738)	1.19 (-0.705)	1.5 (-0.698)
Entity objective: new product from existing business		2.098 (-1.231)		0.403 (-0.296)	1.802 (-0.823)	1.739 (-0.948)	1.108 (-0.251)	1.088 (-0.619)

Entity variables

Table 25.2 (continued)

	Active entity		Outside funding (VC, angels, bank, companies)		Ex post campaign benefits (Likert scale)			
Variables					Additional funding	Employee	Publicity	Customer base
Number of founders	1.48 (−0.398)		1.024 (−0.23)		1.14 (−0.138)	0.99 (−0.12)	1.208 (−0.284)	0.841 (−0.116)
Completeness Degree of completeness: design	1.38 (−0.278)		0.65 (−0.145)		0.802 (−0.135)	0.813 (−0.148)	0.934 (−0.266)	1.016 (−0.236)
Degree of completeness: financial plan	1.25 (−0.316)		1.403 (−0.396)		1.281 (−0.25)	1.128 (−0.264)	0.713 (−0.275)	1.189 (−0.316)
Degree of completeness: schedule	0.787 (−0.245)		0.491 (−0.182)		1.058 (−0.236)	0.759 (−0.167)	1.338 (−0.233)	0.529* (−0.157)
Degree of completeness: business plan	1.004 (−0.177)		1.649* (−0.366)		1.125 (−0.132)	1.749*** (−0.271)	1.006 (−0.206)	1.446* (−0.239)
Degree of completeness: team	1.188 (−0.227)		1.465 (−0.387)		1.046 (−0.175)	0.968 (−0.161)		1.207 (−0.224)
Constant	0.182 (−0.429)	0.0185 (−0.0549)	6.40e-05*** (−0.00017)	6.33e-06*** (−2.25E-05)	0.000271*** (−0.00063)	0.000321** (−0.0008)	0.000675* (−0.00222)	0.0328 (−0.0817)
Observations	250	248	220	213	252	252	228	252

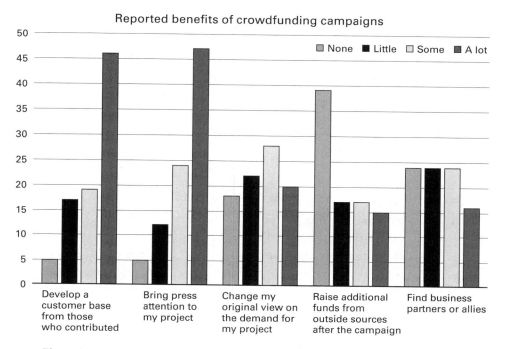

Figure 25.1

Reported benefits of crowdfunding campaigns

date, despite the fact that all project delivery deadlines were in 2013 or earlier.

Why Do People Believe They Failed?

Though Mollick (2014) identifies a number of reasons why campaigns succeed or fail, the survey also offered the opportunity to ask creators of unsuccessful projects to explain their concerns. While this is a relatively small sample, the qualitative data is illuminating. For those campaigns did not succeed, generally people felt that a badly defined market (51 percent agreed) and bad marketing (70 percent agreed) were the largest causes of failure. They were less likely to agree that either their team was to blame (7 percent), or that their idea was not appealing (30 percent). It may be for this reason that few people gave up on their ideas in the face of failure and 60 percent of respondents agreed or strongly agreed that they would continue to work on their idea.

Crowdfunding as a Force for Innovation

Our survey, combined with other research on crowdfunding, suggests that reward-based crowdfunding is a viable path for commercializing innovation. The amounts raised were relatively small by venture capital scales, but they resulted in many successful companies. The vast majority of projects in our sample turned into ongoing business efforts. Successfully funded projects added, on average, 2.2 employees (std. dev. 9.6) since their campaigns ended, with some growing much more quickly. Additionally, though successful campaigns raised over $28M in capital, that was not the only benefit that crowdfunding provided. Many firms reported that their campaigns provided benefits in building customer communities, learning about markets, and publicity.

The data suggest that crowdfunding may play three roles in democratizing funding for innovation. First, highly innovative users often do not choose to develop products themselves; they instead give them away or else fail to recognize their value (Bogers et al. 2010; von Hippel 1986). One of the main purposes in crowdfunding, as expressed by our respondents, is as a way of understanding market demand for a product. With an easy tool available to gauge interest in an innovation, and a fast path to commercialization, users may be more likely to follow the path of "accidental entrepreneurship" described by Shah and Tripsas (2007), increasing the rate at which user innovators turn their ideas into start-ups.

Second, crowdfunding changes the economics of user production, even when innovators are not looking to profit from their products (Baldwin et al. 2006; Baldwin and von Hippel 2011; Hienerth 2006). By providing a relatively ready source of funds to support development of products and services, even at a small scale, crowdfunding allows communities to more efficiently support the production of innovations without the need for a manufacturer. Communities including video game enthusiasts, home automation developers, and even open source programmers have successfully used crowdfunding to advance their own innovations, without the need to go outside the community structure itself.

Finally, crowdfunding can act as a precursor to more traditional investment. Our survey found that crowdfunding success can translate into more conventional VC or angel funding. Examples like Facebook's acquisition of virtual reality company Oculus Rift for $2B suggests the viability of this approach.

Crowdfunding has recently emerged as a new source of seed capital for entrepreneurs. However, the benefits of crowdfunding extend beyond the immediate funds raised from a successful campaign. As a result crowdfunding represents a potentially powerful way to create and nurture new businesses, as well as creative projects. It creates a new approach by which communities and users can innovate and fund products or services that they find important or valuable.

Appendix: Project Characteristics in Survey

Project goal   Amount founders seek to raise using crowdfunding. Kickstarter follows an "all or nothing" model, so funders' pledge money is only collected if the goal is reached. While other crowdfunding efforts do not always follow this model, it is currently the dominant approach to crowdfunding, and parallels the way that other funding efforts for new ventures work.

Project funded   An indicator for whether the project was successful in its fundraising effort. Projects that raise at least their goal are considered successful or funded projects, and they are paid the total pledged to them by the crowdfunding site. Projects can raise more than their goal.

Facebook friends of founders   Role of social networks in funding new ventures has long been noted as important (Hsu 2007; Shane and Cable 2002). Since many accounts in Kickstarter are linked to Facebook, it is possible to determine how many Facebook connections each founder has. This provides a control for the size of a founder's social network. Nonzero Facebook friends are available for slightly under half of all observations.

Reward levels   Most projects offer rewards to funders, depending on the level of funds they pledge. These can range from credits in film or art projects to large-scale rewards, such as the ability to direct or influence projects. A common category of rewards are the products being developed by the founders, in which case crowdfunding acts as a "pre-order" system. Rewards levels are the number of reward tiers offered to funders, typically these would start relatively small, with an acknowledgment or formal thanks, and escalate to larger rewards, including on-site visits or special versions of products.

Category   Projects are categorized by Kickstarter into one of a number of categories, including film, dance, art, design, and technology.

Design and technology projects are treated somewhat differently by Kickstarter, since they usually deliver concrete products as rewards. These projects need to produce a manufacturing plan when starting a Kickstarter project.

Duration   Number of days for which a project accepts funding. Although Kickstarter initially allowed projects to raise funds for as many as 90 days, it now limits this time to 60 days, but encourages 30-day funding windows.

By name, proof of concept, background   Code for the degree to which projects demonstrated outside endorsements (e.g., media quotes), providing evidence of prototypes or early versions of projects, and invoking past successful projects or employers by name. Our two research assistants were used as raters. They agreed in the vast majority of cases (88 percent agreement on endorsement, 91 percent on prototypes, and 81 percent on the use of past project names). Kappa was substantial with regards to project names ($\varkappa = 0.57$) and endorsements ($\varkappa = 0.52$), and moderate on prototypes ($\varkappa = 0.45$) (Munoz and Bangdiwala 1997). Though the models proved robust regardless of which RA ratings were used, for the tables herein we used the union of the two ratings. That is, if one RA felt there was an endorsement, and another RA did not, we coded that as an endorsement. This is because the signals of quality in crowdfunding result from the perception of an untrained group of investors—if at least part of the group of investors saw a signal as present, they would be expected to act as if the signal was identified.

Degree of completeness   Degree to which founders have completed product design, a financial plan (budget), schedule, business plan, or assembled a team prior to the campaign.

Objective   Goal of the campaign involved starting a new business or creating a new product from an existing business.

Notes

1. In 10 percent of the projects, the reported revenues were over $100,000 before the launching of the campaign. This may be due to the fact that many campaigns were being launched by existing organizations.

2. Some material in this section comes directly from Mollick (2014).

3. The data collected are from a period of crowdfunding during which no equity investment was permitted, though the US Congress had authorized equity crowdfunding (JOBS Act, 112th Congress).

References

Agrawal, A., C. Catalini, and A. Goldfarb. 2010. The geography of crowdfunding. Working paper 10–08. NET Institute. SSRN. http://ssrn.com/abstract=1692661.

Agrawal, A., C. Catalini, and A. Goldfarb. 2013. The simple economics of crowdfunding. In *NBER Book Series Innovation Policy and the Economy*, vol. 14, ed. Josh Lerner and Scott Stern, 63–79. Chicago: Chicago University Press.

Ahlers, G. K. C., D. Cumming, C. Günther, and D. Schweizer. 2012. Signaling in equity crowdfunding. SSRN. http://ssrn.com/abstract=2161587.

Amit, R., J. Brander, and C. Zott, C. 1998. Why do venture capital firms exist? Theory and Canadian evidence. *Journal of Business Venturing* 13 (6): 441–66.

Baldwin, C., C. Hienerth, and E. von Hippel. 2006. How user innovations become commercial products: A theoretical investigation and case study. *Research Policy* 35 (9): 1291–1313.

Baldwin, C., and E. von Hippel. 2011. Modeling a paradigm shift: From producer innovation to user and open collaborative innovation. *Organization Science* 22 (6): 1399–1417.

Baum, J., and B. Silverman. 2004. Picking winners or building them? Alliance, intellectual, and human capital as selection criteria in venture financing and performance of biotechnology startups. *Journal of Business Venturing* 19 (3): 411–36.

Belleflamme, P., T. Lambert, and A. Schwienbacher. 2014. Crowdfunding: Tapping the right crowd. *Journal of Business Venturing* 29 (5): 585–609.

Bogers, M., A. Afuah, and B. Bastian. 2010. Users as innovators: A review, critique, and future research directions. *Journal of Management* 36 (4): 857–75.

Burtch, G., A. Ghose, and S. Wattal. 2013. An empirical examination of the antecedents and consequences of contribution patterns in crowd-funded markets. *Information Systems Research* 24 (3): 499–519.

Canning, J., M. Haque, and Y. Wang. 2012. *Women at the Wheel. Do Female Executives Drive Start-Up Success?* New York: Dow Jones. http://www.dowjones.com/collateral/files/WomenPE_report_final.pdf.

Chen, H., P. Gompers, A. Kovner, and J. Lerner. 2009. Buy local? The geography of successful and unsuccessful venture capital expansion. Working paper 15102. NBER. http://www.nber.org/papers/w15102.

Congress, US, 112th. 2012. Jumpstart our business startups (JOBS) Act. Pub. L. No. 112–106, 126 Stat. 313 (2012). Washington, DC: GPO.

Dingman, S. 2013. Canadian's smartwatch startup matches record $15-million in VC funding. *Globe and Mail*, May 16.

Dvorkin, E. 2013. Kickstarter-funded films headline "Sundance." *Kickstarter Blog*. Retrieved February 05, 2013, from http://www.kickstarter.com/blog/kickstarter-funded-films-headline-sundance.

Feldman, M. 2001. The entrepreneurial event revisited: Firm formation in a regional context. *Industrial and Corporate Change* 10 (4): 861–91.

Ferrary, M., and M. Granovetter. 2009. The role of venture capital firms in Silicon Valley's complex innovation network. *Economy and Society* 38 (2): 326–59.

Gompers, P., and J. Lerner. 2001. The venture capital revolution. *Journal of Economic Perspectives* 15 (2): 145–68.

Gompers, P., and J. Lerner. 2004. *The Venture Capital Cycle*. Cambridge: MIT Press.

Greenberg, J., and E. Mollick. E. 2014. Leaning in or leaning on? Representation, homophily, and activism in crowdfunding. SSRN. *http://ssrn.com/abstract=2462254*.

Greene, P. G., M. Hart, E. J. Gatewood, C. G. Brush, and N. M. Carter. 2003. Women entrepreneurs: Moving front and center: An overview of research and theory." *Coleman White Paper Series* 3: 1–47.

Harrison, R., and C. Mason. 2007. Does gender matter? Women business angels and the supply of entrepreneurial finance. *Entrepreneurship Theory and Practice* 31 (3): 445–72.

Heminway, J., and S. Hoffman. 2010. Proceed at your peril: Crowdfunding and the Securities Act of 1933. *Tennessee Law Review* 78 (4): 879–972.

Hienerth, C. 2006. The commercialization of user innovations: The development of the rodeo kayak industry. *R&D Management* 36 (3): 273–94.

Hsu, D. H. 2004. What do entrepreneurs pay for venture capital affiliation? *Journal of Finance* 59 (4): 1805–44.

Hsu, D. H. 2007. Experienced entrepreneurial founders, organizational capital, and venture capital funding. *Research Policy* 36 (5): 722–41.

Jeffries, A. 2013. How Kickstarter stole CES: The rise of the Indie hardware developer. *The Verge*. Retrieved January 12, 2013. http://www.theverge.com/2013/1/10/3861406/kickstarter-at-ces.

Kenney, M., and U. von Burg. 1999. Technology, entrepreneurship and path dependence: Industrial clustering in Silicon Valley and route 128. *Industrial and Corporate Change* 8 (1): 67–103.

Kuppuswamy, V., and B. L. Bayus. 2013. *Crowdfunding creative ideas: The dynamics of project backers in Kickstarter*. SSRN Electronic Journal. .10.2139/ssrn.2234765

Lakhani, K. R., and E. von Hippel. 2003. How open source software works. *Research Policy* 32 (6): 923–43.

Lerner, J. 2012. Venture capitalists and the oversight of private firms. *Journal of Finance* 50 (1): 301–18.

Massolution. 2013. The Crowdfunding Industry report.

Miller, C. C. 2010. Why so few women in Silicon Valley? Out of the loop in Silicon Valley. *New York Times*, April 17.

Mollick, E. 2014. The dynamics of crowdfunding: An exploratory study. *Journal of Business Venturing* 29 (1): 1–16.

Morduch, J. 1999. The microfinance promise. *Journal of Economic Literature* 37 (4): 1569–1614.

Munoz, S., and S. Bangdiwal. 1997. Interpretation of kappa and B statistics measures of agreement. *Journal of Applied Statistics* 24 (1): 105–12.

Owen-Smith, J., and W. W. Powell. 2004. Knowledge networks as channels and conduits: The effects of spillovers in the Boston biotechnology community. *Organization Science* 15 (1): 5–21.

Poetz, M. K., and M. Schreier. 2012. The value of crowdsourcing: Can users really compete with professionals in generating new product ideas? *Journal of Product Innovation Management* 29 (2): 245–56.

Ruef, M., H. E. Aldrich, and N. M. Carter. 2003. The structure of founding teams: Homophily, strong ties, and isolation among US entrepreneurs. *American Sociological Review* 68 (2): 195–222.

Saxenian, A. 1996. *Regional Advantage: Culture and Competition in Silicon Valley and Route 128*. Cambridge: Harvard University Press.

Schwienbacher, A., and B. Larralde. 2010. *Crowdfunding of small entrepreneurial ventures*. SSRN. .10.2139/ssrn.1699183

Shah, S. K., and M. Tripsas. 2007. The accidental entrepreneur: The emergent and collective process of user entrepreneurship. *Strategic Entrepreneurship Journal* 1 (1–2): 123–40.

Shane, S., and D. Cable. 2002. Network ties, reputation, and the financing of new ventures. *Management Science* 48 (3): 364–81.

Shane, S., and S. Venkataraman. 2003. Guest editors' introduction to the special issue on technology entrepreneurship. *Research Policy* 32 (2): 181–84.

Sorenson, O., and T. Stuart. 2005. *The Evolution of Venture Capital Investment Networks*. Atlanta: Federal Reserve Bank of Atlanta.

Stuart, T., H. Hoang, and R. C. Hybels. 1999. Interorganizational endorsements and the performance of entrepreneurial ventures. *Administrative Science Quarterly* 44 (2): 315–49.

Stuart, T., and O. Sorenson. 2003. The geography of opportunity: Spatial heterogeneity in founding rates and the performance of biotechnology firms. *Research Policy* 32 (2): 229–53.

Stuart, T., and O. Sorenson. 2008. Strategic networks and entrepreneurial ventures. *Strategic Entrepreneurship Journal* 1 (3–4): 211–27.

von Hippel, E. 1986. Lead users: A source of novel product concepts. *Management Science* 32 (7): 791–805.

von Hippel, E. 2005. *Democratizing Innovation*. Cambridge: MIT Press.

West, J., and K. R. Lakhani. 2008. Getting clear about communities in open innovation. *Industry and Innovation* 15 (2): 223–31.

Index

Technique innovation (cont.)
user innovation literature dealing
with development of, 333–34
whitewater kayaking equipment and,
338–42, 349, *350*
Technology
communities as drivers of innovation
in, 111
human-related inventions as charter,
278–79
Oslo Manual on, 91
social construction of technology
(SCOT), 303n1
use and planned use of, 92–95
ways of adopting, 93
Teekanne Group, 383–85, 386, 393
Terra prohibita, 50
Testing and refining solutions, 57–60
Thomson, James, 271
Tinari, Robert, 92
Tinkering, 217, 228–29
with computer programs, 222–23
contractual restrictions on,
224–25
IP rules that allow, 218–21
limits placed on, 221–28
technical limitations on, 225–28
through add-on and filtering
programs, 223–24
Toolkits, innovation, 483–84,
503–505, 533
additional value of self-design and,
518–22
Apache, 514–16
choice navigation, 484, 495,
500–502
common principles, 512
expert and mass, 484–87
mass customization capabilities and,
493–95
mass toolkit-based businesses and,
487–93
requisite organizational capabilities
and, 493–503
robust process design, 484, 495,
498–500
self-design, 518–29

solution space development, 483–84,
495, 496–98
value of, 511–14
value of experiments for
investigating value generation by,
516–18
Tools, 459–60
advances in, 462–64
built for user innovation, 472–75
combinatorial methods and rapid
prototyping, 467–68
crash simulation, 464–67
experimentation, 460–68
impact on locus of innovation,
468–77
integrated circuits and, 475–77
leveraging user innovation, 471–72
matching need with solution
information, 469–71
promise of new, 461–62
research questions for, 477–79
TopCoder platform, 116, 118, 123,
124, 125
Torvalds, Linus, 165
TPMs. *See* Technical protection
measures (TPMs)
Trade knowledge, collective ownership
of, 140
Trademark law, 220
Trade secrecy law, 219
Transactional hierarchies, 392
Transaction-cost theory, 157
Treehouse Logic, 491
Twitter, 353, 542

Ubiquitous experimentation,
199–200
United Kingdom, the
collective invention in, 111
consumers as user-innovators in, 74
firms as user-innovators in, *71, 72*
knowledge sharing in, 138, 141–43,
145
openness of user innovation in, *77,
78*
Oslo Manual and, 100
public sector, 101